MICROSOFT®

OFFICE 2016

MICROSOFT OFFICE 365™

D0146953

Fundamentals

For Microsoft® Office updates, go to sam.cengage.com

HUNT + CLEMENS

CENGAGE
Learning®

Australia • Brazil • Mexico • Singapore • United Kingdom • United States

**Illustrated Microsoft® Office 365™ &
Office 2016 Fundamentals**
Marjorie Hunt and Barbara Clemens

SVP, GM Skills & Global Product Management:
    Dawn Gerrain

Product Director: Kathleen McMahon

Senior Product Team Manager: Lauren Murphy

Product Team Manager: Andrea Topping

Associate Product Manager: Melissa Stehler

Senior Director, Development: Marah Bellegarde

Product Development Manager: Leigh Hefferon

Senior Content Developer: Alyssa Pratt

Contributing Author: Dave Belden

Developmental Editor: MT Cozzola

Product Assistant: Erica Chapman

Marketing Director: Michele McTighe

Marketing Manager: Stephanie Albracht

Marketing Coordinator: Cassie Cloutier

Senior Production Director: Wendy Troeger

Production Director: Patty Stephan

Content Project Manager: GEX Publishing Services

Art Director: Diana Graham

Text Designer: Joseph Lee, Black Fish Design

Cover Template Designer: Lisa Kuhn, Curio Press, LLC
    www.curiopress.com

Composition: GEX Publishing Services

Mac users: If you're working through this product using a Mac, some of the
steps may vary. Additional information for Mac users is included with the
Data Files for this product.

Some of the product names and company names used in this book have
been used for identification purposes only and may be trademarks or
registered trademarks of their respective manufacturers and sellers.

Windows® is a registered trademark of Microsoft Corporation. © 2012
Microsoft. Microsoft and the Office logo are either registered trademarks
or trademarks of Microsoft Corporation in the United States and/or other
countries. Cengage Learning is an independent entity from Microsoft
Corporation and not affiliated with Microsoft in any manner. Microsoft
product screenshots used with permission from Microsoft Corporation.
Unless otherwise noted, all clip art is courtesy of openclipart.org.

Disclaimer: Any fictional data related to persons or companies or URLs used
throughout this text is intended for instructional purposes only. At the time
this text was published, any such data was fictional and not belonging to
any real persons or companies.

Disclaimer: The material in this text was written using Microsoft Office 365
ProPlus and Microsoft Office 2016 running on Microsoft Windows 10
Professional, and was Quality Assurance tested prior to the publication date.
As Microsoft continually updates the Microsoft Office suite and the
Windows 10 operating system, your software experience may vary slightly
from what is presented in the printed text.

Library of Congress Control Number: 2016934770
Soft-cover Edition ISBN: 978-1-305-87894-5
Looseleaf Edition ISBN: 978-1-337-25077-1

Cengage Learning
20 Channel Center Street
Boston, MA 02210
USA

Cengage Learning is a leading provider of customized learning solutions
with employees residing in nearly 40 different countries and sales in more
than 125 countries around the world. Find your local representative at
www.cengage.com

Cengage Learning products are represented in Canada by
Nelson Education, Ltd.

For your course and learning solutions, visit **www.cengage.com**

Purchase any of our products at your local college store or at our
preferred online store **www.cengagebrain.com**

Printed in the United States of America
Print Number: 05   Print Year: 2019

Contents

Concepts

Module 0: Understanding Essential Computer Concepts .... Concepts 1

Recognize You Live and Work in the Digital World .... Concepts 2
    How to be a good online citizen

Distinguish Types of Computers .... Concepts 4
    Touchscreens

Identify Computer System Components .... Concepts 6
    About microprocessor speeds

Compare Types of Memory .... Concepts 8
    Upgrading RAM

Summarize Types of Storage Media .... Concepts 10
    Storage in the Cloud

Differentiate Between Input Devices .... Concepts 12
    Understanding assistive devices

Explain Output Devices .... Concepts 14
    About 3D printers

Describe Data Communications .... Concepts 16
    Understanding USB types and connectors
    How computers represent and interpret data

Define Types of Networks .... Concepts 18
    Understanding telecommunications

Assess Security Threats .... Concepts 20
    Understanding two-factor authentication

Understand System Software .... Concepts 22
    Protecting information with passwords
    Examining Windows 10 hardware requirements

Describe Types of Application Software .... Concepts 24

Practice .... Concepts 26

Windows 10

Module 1: Getting Started with Windows 10 .... Windows 33

Start Windows 10 .... Windows 34
    Using a touch screen with Windows

Navigate the Desktop and Start Menu .... Windows 36

Point, Click, and Drag .... Windows 38
    Selecting and moving items using touch-screen devices

Start an App .... Windows 40
    Using the Windows Store

Work with a Window .... Windows 42
    Using the Quick Access toolbar

Manage Multiple Windows .... Windows 44

Use Buttons, Menus, and Dialog Boxes .... Windows 46
Get Help .... Windows 48
    Using Cortana
Exit Windows 10 .... Windows 50
    Installing updates when you exit Windows
Practice .... Windows 52

Module 2: Understanding File Management .... Windows 57

Understand Files and Folders .... Windows 58
    Plan your file organization
Create and Save a File .... Windows 60
Explore the Files and Folders on Your Computer .... Windows 62
    Using and disabling Quick Access view
Change File and Folder Views .... Windows 64
    Using the Windows Action Center
    Customizing Details view
Open, Edit, and Save Files .... Windows 66
    Comparing Save and Save As
    Using Microsoft OneDrive
Copy Files .... Windows 68
    Copying files using Send to
Move and Rename Files .... Windows 70
    Using Task View to create multiple desktops
Search for Files and Folders .... Windows 72
    Using the Search Tools tab in File Explorer
    Using Microsoft Edge
Delete and Restore Files .... Windows 74
    More techniques for selecting and moving files
Practice .... Windows 76

Office 2016

Module 3: Getting Started with Microsoft Office 2016 .... Office 81

Understand Office 2016 .... Office 82
    Using Office Online apps
Start an Office App .... Office 84
    The many editions of Microsoft Office
Identify Common Elements in an Office App .... Office 86
Use the Ribbon and Zoom Controls .... Office 88
Use the Quick Access Toolbar .... Office 90
    Customizing the Quick Access Toolbar
Save a File .... Office 92
    Using OneDrive and Office Online
Get Help .... Office 94
Exit an Office App .... Office 96
    Using Office on a touch screen device
    Sharing your saved documents
Practice .... Office 98

Module 4: Creating a Document ....**Word 99**

Create a New Document from an Existing File .... Word 100
  Creating a new document from a template
Enter Text in a Document... Word 102
  Using AutoCorrect
Select and Edit Text.. Word 104
Copy Text .... Word 106
Move Text .... Word 108
  Activating the Office Clipboard
Find and Replace Text .... Word 110
  Using Insights for Office
Format Text Using the Mini Toolbar... Word 112
Check Spelling and Grammar... Word 114
  Translating documents into other languages
Preview and Print a Document... Word 116
  Using research and writing tools
Practice .... Word 118

Module 5: Enhancing a Document ....**Word 127**

Change Font and Font Size... Word 128
Change Font Color, Style, and Effects .... Word 130
Change Alignment and Line Spacing .... Word 132
Change Margin Settings .... Word 134
Set Tabs .... Word 136
Set Indents .... Word 138
Add Bulleted and Numbered Lists .... Word 140
  Creating a custom bullet
Apply Styles .... Word 142
Practice .... Word 144

Module 6: Adding Special Elements to a Document ....**Word 151**

Create a Table.. Word 152
Insert and Delete Table Columns and Rows .... Word 154
  Other ways to create tables
Format a Table... Word 156
Insert and Format a Picture.. Word 158
Add Footnotes and Citations .... Word 160
Insert a Header or Footer.. Word 162
Add Borders and Shading.. Word 164
Work with Themes .... Word 166
Format a Research Paper .... Word 168
Practice .... Word 170

Module 7: Creating a Worksheet...**Excel 179**

Navigate a Workbook...Excel 180

Enter Labels and Values...Excel 182

Work with Columns and Rows..Excel 184

Use Formulas...Excel 186

Use AutoSum...Excel 188

Viewing sum data on the status bar

Change Alignment and Number Format..Excel 190

Enhance a Worksheet..Excel 192

Preview and Print a Worksheet...Excel 194

Practice..Excel 196

Module 8: Using Complex Formulas, Functions, and Tables ....**Excel 205**

Create Complex Formulas...Excel 206

Using the Clear button

Use Absolute Cell References...Excel 208

Understand Functions..Excel 210

Use Date and Time Functions...Excel 212

Understanding how dates are calculated using serial values

Use Statistical Functions..Excel 214

Apply Conditional Formatting...Excel 216

Sort Rows in a Table...Excel 218

Filter Table Data...Excel 220

Practice..Excel 222

Module 9: Working with Charts ....**Excel 229**

Understand and Plan a Chart..Excel 230

Interpreting charts

Create a Chart..Excel 232

Move and Resize Charts and Chart Elements.....................................Excel 234

Creating a chart using the Quick Analysis tool

Apply Chart Layouts and Styles..Excel 236

Customize Chart Elements...Excel 238

Enhance a Chart..Excel 240

Printing charts with or without worksheet data

Create a Pie Chart...Excel 242

Create Sparklines..Excel 244

Practice..Excel 246

Module 10: Creating a Database...**Access 253**

Understand Databases..Access 254

Create a Database..Access 256

Creating databases and Access apps from templates

Create a Table in Datasheet View..Access 258

Create a Table in Design View..Access 260

Modify a Table and Set Properties...Access 262

Enter Data in a Table...Access 264

Edit Data in Datasheet View ....Access 266
  Printing objects in Access

Create and Use a Form ....Access 268

Practice ....Access 270

Module 11: Working with Data ....Access 279

Open an Existing Database ....Access 280

Sort Records in a Table...Access 282
  Capturing a screenshot of your sorted table
  Sorting on multiple fields

Filter Records in a Table ....Access 284

Create a Query..Access 286

Modify a Query in Design View..Access 288

Relate Two Tables ....Access 290
  Understanding good database design

Create a Query Using Two Tables ....Access 292

Add a Calculated Field to a Table...Access 294

Practice ....Access 296

Module 12: Creating Database Reports ....Access 305

Create a Report Using the Report Wizard..Access 306

View a Report ....Access 308

Modify a Report...Access 310

Add a Field to a Report..Access 312

Apply Conditional Formatting to a Report ....Access 314

Add Summary Information to a Report...Access 316

Create Mailing Labels..Access 318

Practice ....Access 320

PowerPoint 2016

Module 13: Creating a Presentation ....PowerPoint 327

Open and View a Presentation...PowerPoint 328

Create a New Presentation ....PowerPoint 330

Enter and Format Slide Text..PowerPoint 332
  Indenting and unindenting text

Apply a Theme ....PowerPoint 334
  Using templates

Add and Modify an Online Image...PowerPoint 336
  Using online images legally
  Understanding picture effects

Add and Modify Shapes..PowerPoint 338
  Resizing graphics and images

Create SmartArt .... PowerPoint 340
Insert a Table .... PowerPoint 342
    Adding slide footers
Practice .... PowerPoint 344

Module 14: Polishing and Running a Presentation .... PowerPoint 351

Add Pictures.. PowerPoint 352
Add Sound .... PowerPoint 354
    Adjusting sound playback during a slide show
Add Video.. PowerPoint 356
    Formatting sound and video objects
Set Slide Transitions and Timing .... PowerPoint 358
    Using slide masters
Animate Slide Objects .... PowerPoint 360
    Working with motion paths
    Adding animations using the Animation pane
Use Speaker Notes and Notes Page View .... PowerPoint 362
    Using Presenter view
Print Handouts and Notes Pages... PowerPoint 364
    Printing presentation slides
Design Effective Presentations .... PowerPoint 366
    Creating interactive content with Office Mix
Practice .... PowerPoint 368

Integration 2016

Module 15: Integrating Office 2016 Programs .... Integration 375

Insert an Excel Chart into a PowerPoint Slide........................ Integration 376
Create PowerPoint Slides from a Word Document.................... Integration 378
    Using outlines in Word and PowerPoint
Insert Screen Clips into a Word Document .... Integration 380
Insert Text from a Word File into an Open Document .... Integration 382
    Placing an Access table in a Word document
Link Excel Data to a Word Document .... Integration 384
Update a Linked Excel Chart in a Word Document .... Integration 386
Insert Merge Fields into a Word Document.............................. Integration 388
Perform a Mail Merge.. Integration 390
    Using mail merge to send personalized email messages
Practice .... Integration 392

Glossary .... Online

Index .... Index 1

Productivity Apps for School and Work

Corinne Hoisington

Lochlan keeps track of his class notes, football plays, and internship meetings with OneNote.

Zoe is using the annotation features of Microsoft Edge to take and save web notes for her research paper.

Nori is creating a Sway site to highlight this year's activities for the Student Government Association.

Hunter is adding interactive videos and screen recordings to his PowerPoint resume.

© Rawpixel/Shutterstock.com

Being computer literate no longer means mastery of only Word, Excel, PowerPoint, Outlook, and Access. To become technology power users, Hunter, Nori, Zoe, and Lochlan are exploring Microsoft OneNote, Sway, Mix, and Edge in Office 2016 and Windows 10.

In this Module

Introduction to OneNote 2016 2
Introduction to Sway 6
Introduction to Office Mix 10
Introduction to Microsoft Edge............. 14

Learn to use productivity apps!
Links to companion **Sways**, featuring **videos** with hands-on instructions, are located on www.cengage.com.

Introduction to OneNote 2016

notebook | section tab | To Do tag | screen clipping | note | template | Microsoft OneNote Mobile app | sync | drawing canvas | inked handwriting | Ink to Text

As you glance around any classroom, you invariably see paper notebooks and notepads on each desk. Because deciphering and sharing handwritten notes can be a challenge, Microsoft OneNote 2016 replaces physical notebooks, binders, and paper notes with a searchable, digital notebook. OneNote captures your ideas and schoolwork on any device so you can stay organized, share notes, and work with others on projects. Whether you are a student taking class notes as shown in **Figure 1** or an employee taking notes in company meetings, OneNote is the one place to keep notes for all of your projects.

Figure 1: OneNote 2016 notebook

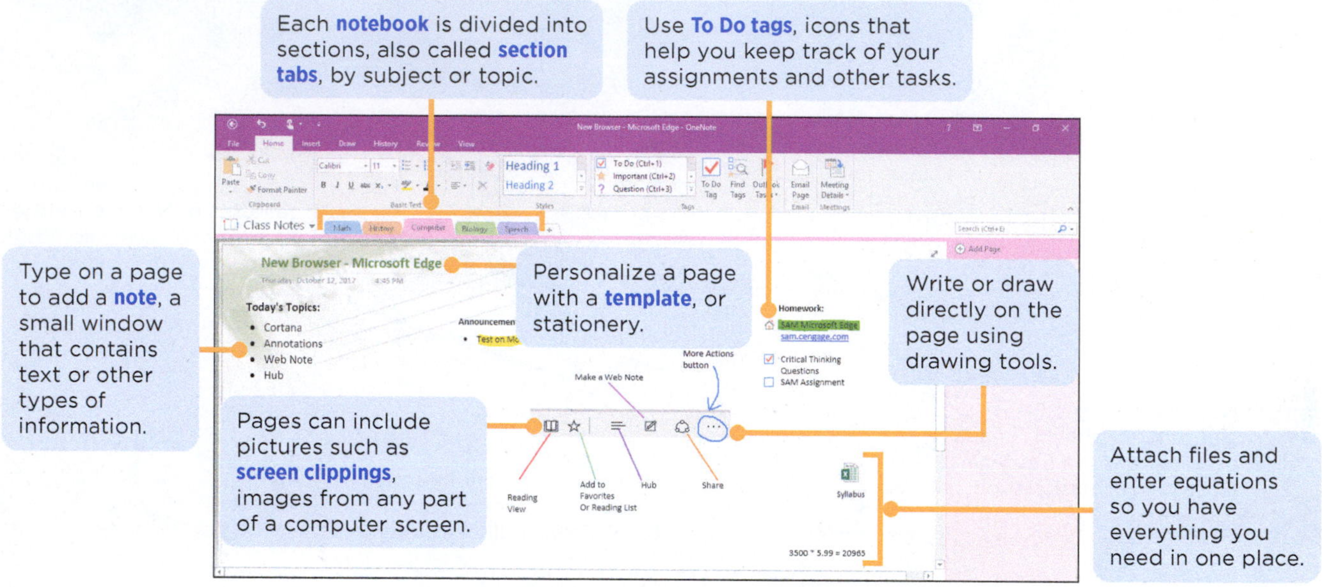

Each **notebook** is divided into sections, also called **section tabs**, by subject or topic.

Use **To Do tags**, icons that help you keep track of your assignments and other tasks.

Type on a page to add a **note**, a small window that contains text or other types of information.

Personalize a page with a **template**, or stationery.

Write or draw directly on the page using drawing tools.

Pages can include pictures such as **screen clippings**, images from any part of a computer screen.

Attach files and enter equations so you have everything you need in one place.

Creating a OneNote Notebook

OneNote is divided into sections similar to those in a spiral-bound notebook. Each OneNote notebook contains sections, pages, and other notebooks. You can use One-Note for school, business, and personal projects. Store information for each type of project in different notebooks to keep your tasks separate, or use any other organization that suits you. OneNote is flexible enough to adapt to the way you want to work.

When you create a notebook, it contains a blank page with a plain white background by default, though you can use templates, or stationery, to apply designs in categories such as Academic, Business, Decorative, and Planners. Start typing or use the buttons on the Insert tab to insert notes, which are small resizable windows that can contain text, equations, tables, on-screen writing, images, audio and video recordings, to-do lists, file attachments, and file printouts. Add as many notes as you need to each page.

Syncing a Notebook to the Cloud

OneNote saves your notes every time you make a change in a notebook. To make sure you can access your notebooks with a laptop, tablet, or smartphone wherever you are, OneNote uses cloud-based storage, such as OneDrive or SharePoint. **Microsoft OneNote Mobile app**, a lightweight version of OneNote 2016 shown in **Figure 2**, is available for free in the Windows Store, Google Play for Android devices, and the AppStore for iOS devices.

If you have a Microsoft account, OneNote saves your notes on OneDrive automatically for all your mobile devices and computers, which is called **syncing**. For example, you can use OneNote to take notes on your laptop during class, and then open OneNote on your phone to study later. To use a notebook stored on your computer with your OneNote Mobile app, move the notebook to OneDrive. You can quickly share notebook content with other people using OneDrive.

Figure 2: Microsoft OneNote Mobile app

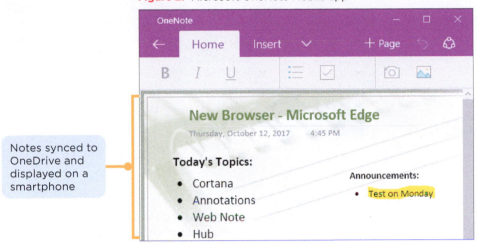

Notes synced to OneDrive and displayed on a smartphone

Taking Notes

Use OneNote pages to organize your notes by class and topic or lecture. Beyond simple typed notes, OneNote stores drawings, converts handwriting to searchable text and mathematical sketches to equations, and records audio and video.

OneNote includes drawing tools that let you sketch freehand drawings such as biological cell diagrams and financial supply-and-demand charts. As shown in **Figure 3**, the Draw tab on the ribbon provides these drawing tools along with shapes so you can insert diagrams and other illustrations to represent your ideas. When you draw on a page, OneNote creates a **drawing canvas**, which is a container for shapes and lines.

On the Job Now

OneNote is ideal for taking notes during meetings, whether you are recording minutes, documenting a discussion, sketching product diagrams, or listing follow-up items. Use a meeting template to add pages with content appropriate for meetings.

Figure 3: Tools on the Draw tab

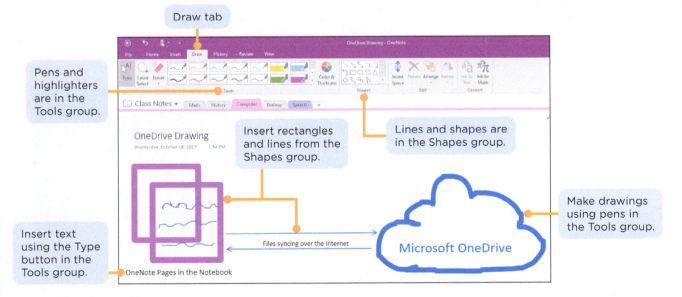

Draw tab

Pens and highlighters are in the Tools group.

Insert rectangles and lines from the Shapes group.

Lines and shapes are in the Shapes group.

Make drawings using pens in the Tools group.

Insert text using the Type button in the Tools group.

Converting Handwriting to Text

When you use a pen tool to write on a notebook page, the text you enter is called **inked handwriting**. OneNote can convert inked handwriting to typed text when you use the **Ink to Text** button in the Convert group on the Draw tab, as shown in **Figure 4**. After OneNote converts the handwriting to text, you can use the Search box to find terms in the converted text or any other note in your notebooks.

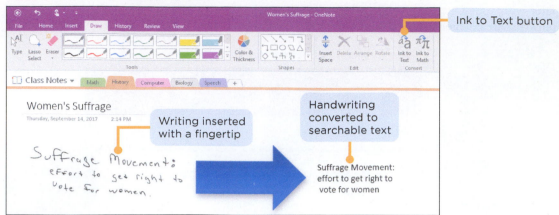

Ink to Text button

Women's Suffrage

Thursday, September 14, 2017   2:14 PM

Suffrage Movements
effort to get right to
vote for women.

Writing inserted
with a fingertip

Handwriting
converted to
searchable text

Suffrage Movement:
effort to get right to
vote for women

On the Job Now

Use OneNote as a place to brainstorm ongoing work projects. If a notebook contains sensitive material, you can password-protect some or all of the notebook so that only certain people can open it.

Recording a Lecture

If your computer or mobile device has a microphone or camera, OneNote can record the audio or video from a lecture or business meeting as shown in **Figure 5**. When you record a lecture (with your instructor's permission), you can follow along, take regular notes at your own pace, and review the video recording later. You can control the start, pause, and stop motions of the recording when you play back the recording of your notes.

Figure 5: Video inserted in a notebook

Record Video
button

Audio & Video
Recording tab

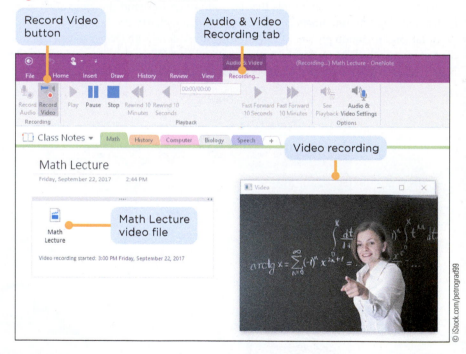

Video recording

Math Lecture

Friday, September 22, 2017   2:44 PM

Math
Lecture

Math Lecture
video file

Video recording started: 3:00 PM Friday, September 22, 2017

Try This Now

1: Taking Notes for a Week

As a student, you can get organized by using OneNote to take detailed notes in your classes. Perform the following tasks:

    a. Create a new OneNote notebook on your Microsoft OneDrive account (the default location for new notebooks). Name the notebook with your first name followed by "Notes," as in **Caleb Notes**.

    b. Create four section tabs, each with a different class name.

    c. Take detailed notes in those classes for one week. Be sure to include notes, drawings, and other types of content.

    d. Sync your notes with your OneDrive. Submit your assignment in the format specified by your instructor.

2: Using OneNote to Organize a Research Paper

You have a research paper due on the topic of three habits of successful students. Use OneNote to organize your research. Perform the following tasks:

    a. Create a new OneNote notebook on your Microsoft OneDrive account. Name the notebook **Success Research**.

    b. Create three section tabs with the following names:

- **Take Detailed Notes**
- **Be Respectful in Class**
- **Come to Class Prepared**

    c. On the web, research the topics and find three sources for each section. Copy a sentence from each source and paste the sentence into the appropriate section. When you paste the sentence, OneNote inserts it in a note with a link to the source.

    d. Sync your notes with your OneDrive. Submit your assignment in the format specified by your instructor.

3: Planning Your Career

Note: This activity requires a webcam or built-in video camera on any type of device.

Consider an occupation that interests you. Using OneNote, examine the responsibilities, education requirements, potential salary, and employment outlook of a specific career. Perform the following tasks:

    a. Create a new OneNote notebook on your Microsoft OneDrive account. Name the notebook with your first name followed by a career title, such as **Kara - App Developer**.

    b. Create four section tabs with the names **Responsibilities, Education Requirements, Median Salary**, and **Employment Outlook**.

    c. Research the responsibilities of your career path. Using OneNote, record a short video (approximately 30 seconds) of yourself explaining the responsibilities of your career path. Place the video in the Responsibilities section.

    d. On the web, research the educational requirements for your career path and find two appropriate sources. Copy a paragraph from each source and paste them into the appropriate section. When you paste a paragraph, OneNote inserts it in a note with a link to the source.

    e. Research the median salary for a single year for this career. Create a mathematical equation in the Median Salary section that multiplies the amount of the median salary times 20 years to calculate how much you will possibly earn.

    f. For the Employment Outlook section, research the outlook for your career path. Take at least four notes about what you find when researching the topic.

    g. Sync your notes with your OneDrive. Submit your assignment in the format specified by your instructor.

Introduction to Sway

Sway site | responsive design | Storyline | card | Creative Commons license | animation emphasis effects | Docs.com

Expressing your ideas in a presentation typically means creating PowerPoint slides or a Word document. Microsoft Sway gives you another way to engage an audience. Sway is a free Microsoft tool available at Sway.com or as an app in Office 365. Using Sway, you can combine text, images, videos, and social media in a website called a **Sway site** that you can share and display on any device. To get started, you create a digital story on a web-based canvas without borders, slides, cells, or page breaks. A Sway site organizes the text, images, and video into a **responsive design**, which means your content adapts perfectly to any screen size as shown in **Figure 6**. You store a Sway site in the cloud on OneDrive using a free Microsoft account.

Figure 6: Sway site with responsive design

You can display a Sway presentation in a web browser.

Sway uses responsive design to make sure pages fit perfectly on any device.

© iStock.com/marinello, © iStock.com/marekuliasz

Creating a Sway Presentation

You can use Sway to build a digital flyer, a club newsletter, a vacation blog, an informational site, a digital art portfolio, or a new product rollout. After you select your topic and sign into Sway with your Microsoft account, a **Storyline** opens, providing tools and a work area for composing your digital story. See **Figure 7**. Each story can include text, images, and videos. You create a Sway by adding text and media content into a Storyline section, or **card**. To add pictures, videos, or documents, select a card in the left pane and then select the Insert Content button. The first card in a Sway presentation contains a title and background image.

Figure 7: Creating a Sway site

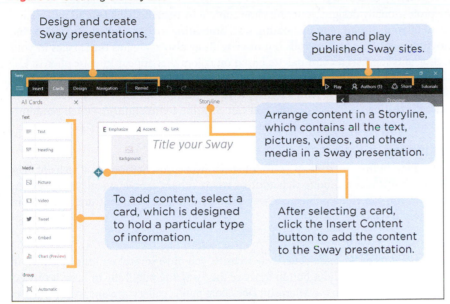

Design and create
Sway presentations.

Share and play
published Sway sites.

Arrange content in a Storyline,
which contains all the text,
pictures, videos, and other
media in a Sway presentation.

To add content, select a
card, which is designed
to hold a particular type
of information.

After selecting a card,
click the Insert Content
button to add the content
to the Sway presentation.

Adding Content to Build a Story

As you work, Sway searches the Internet to help you find relevant images, videos, tweets, and other content from online sources such as Bing, YouTube, Twitter, and Facebook. You can drag content from the search results right into the Storyline. In addition, you can upload your own images and videos directly in the presentation. For example, if you are creating a Sway presentation about the market for commercial drones, Sway suggests content to incorporate into the presentation by displaying it in the left pane as search results. The search results include drone images tagged with a **Creative Commons license** at online sources as shown in **Figure 8**. A Creative Commons license is a public copyright license that allows the free distribution of an otherwise copyrighted work. In addition, you can specify the source of the media. For example, you can add your own Facebook or OneNote pictures and videos in Sway without leaving the app.

On the Job Now

If you have a Microsoft Word document containing an outline of your business content, drag the outline into Sway to create a card for each topic.

Figure 8: Images in Sway search results

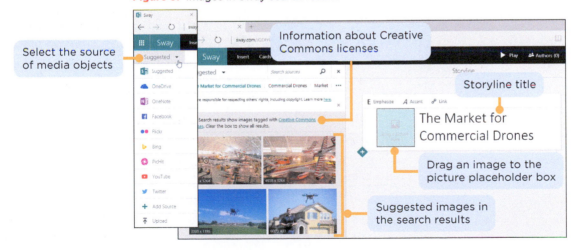

Select the source
of media objects

Information about Creative
Commons licenses

Storyline title

The Market for
Commercial Drones

Drag an image to the
picture placeholder box

Suggested images in
the search results

Designing a Sway

Sway professionally designs your Storyline content by resizing background images and fonts to fit your display, and by floating text, animating media, embedding video, and removing images as a page scrolls out of view. Sway also evaluates the images in your Storyline and suggests a color palette based on colors that appear in your photos. Use the Design button to display tools including color palettes, font choices, **animation emphasis effects**, and style templates to provide a personality for a Sway presentation. Instead of creating your own design, you can click the Remix button, which randomly selects unique designs for your Sway site.

Publishing a Sway

Use the Play button to display your finished Sway presentation as a website. The Address bar includes a unique web address where others can view your Sway site. As the author, you can edit a published Sway site by clicking the Edit button (pencil icon) on the Sway toolbar.

Sharing a Sway

When you are ready to share your Sway website, you have several options as shown in **Figure 9**. Use the Share slider button to share the Sway site publically or keep it private. If you add the Sway site to the Microsoft **Docs.com** public gallery, anyone worldwide can use Bing, Google, or other search engines to find, view, and share your Sway site. You can also share your Sway site using Facebook, Twitter, Google+, Yammer, and other social media sites. Link your presentation to any webpage or email the link to your audience. Sway can also generate a code for embedding the link within another webpage.

Figure 9: Sharing a Sway site

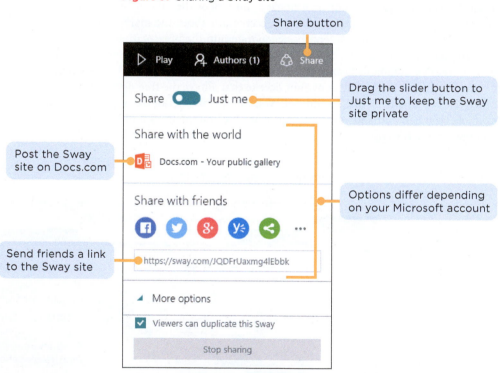

Try This Now

1: Creating a Sway Resume

Learn to use Sway!
Links to companion **Sways**, featuring **videos** with hands-on instructions, are located on www.cengage.com.

Sway is a digital storytelling app. Create a Sway resume to share the skills, job experiences, and achievements you have that match the requirements of a future job interest. Perform the following tasks:

- a. Create a new presentation in Sway to use as a digital resume. Title the Sway Storyline with your full name and then select a background image.
- b. Create three separate sections titled **Academic Background, Work Experience**, and **Skills**, and insert text, a picture, and a paragraph or bulleted points in each section. Be sure to include your own picture.
- c. Add a fourth section that includes a video about your school that you find online.
- d. Customize the design of your presentation.
- e. Submit your assignment link in the format specified by your instructor.

2: Creating an Online Sway Newsletter

Newsletters are designed to capture the attention of their target audience. Using Sway, create a newsletter for a club, organization, or your favorite music group. Perform the following tasks:

- a. Create a new presentation in Sway to use as a digital newsletter for a club, organization, or your favorite music group. Provide a title for the Sway Storyline and select an appropriate background image.
- b. Select three separate sections with appropriate titles, such as Upcoming Events. In each section, insert text, a picture, and a paragraph or bulleted points.
- c. Add a fourth section that includes a video about your selected topic.
- d. Customize the design of your presentation.
- e. Submit your assignment link in the format specified by your instructor.

3: Creating and Sharing a Technology Presentation

To place a Sway presentation in the hands of your entire audience, you can share a link to the Sway presentation. Create a Sway presentation on a new technology and share it with your class. Perform the following tasks:

- a. Create a new presentation in Sway about a cutting-edge technology topic. Provide a title for the Sway Storyline and select a background image.
- b. Create four separate sections about your topic, and include text, a picture, and a paragraph in each section.
- c. Add a fifth section that includes a video about your topic.
- d. Customize the design of your presentation.
- e. Share the link to your Sway with your classmates and submit your assignment link in the format specified by your instructor.

Introduction to Office Mix

add-in | clip | slide recording | Slide Notes | screen recording | free-response quiz

To enliven business meetings and lectures, Microsoft adds a new dimension to presentations with a powerful toolset called Office Mix, a free add-in for PowerPoint. (An **add-in** is software that works with an installed app to extend its features.) Using Office Mix, you can record yourself on video, capture still and moving images on your desktop, and insert interactive elements such as quizzes and live webpages directly into PowerPoint slides. When you post the finished presentation to OneDrive, Office Mix provides a link you can share with friends and colleagues. Anyone with an Internet connection and a web browser can watch a published Office Mix presentation, such as the one in **Figure 10**, on a computer or mobile device.

Figure 10: Office Mix presentation

Adding Office Mix to PowerPoint

To get started, you create an Office Mix account at the website mix.office.com using an email address or a Facebook or Google account. Next, you download and install the Office Mix add-in (see **Figure 11**). Office Mix appears as a new tab named Mix on the PowerPoint ribbon in versions of Office 2013 and Office 2016 running on personal computers (PCs).

Figure 11: Getting started with Office Mix

Capturing Video Clips

A **clip** is a short segment of audio, such as music, or video. After finishing the content on a PowerPoint slide, you can use Office Mix to add a video clip to animate or illustrate the content. Office Mix creates video clips in two ways: by recording live action on a webcam and by capturing screen images and movements. If your computer has a webcam, you can record yourself and annotate the slide to create a **slide recording** as shown in **Figure 12**.

Figure 12: Making a slide recording

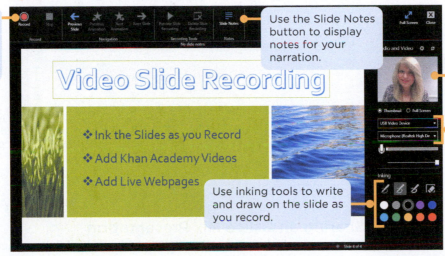

When you are making a slide recording, you can record your spoken narration at the same time. The **Slide Notes** feature works like a teleprompter to help you focus on your presentation content instead of memorizing your narration. Use the Inking tools to make annotations or add highlighting using different pen types and colors. After finishing a recording, edit the video in PowerPoint to trim the length or set playback options.

The second way to create a video is to capture on-screen images and actions with or without a voiceover. This method is ideal if you want to show how to use your favorite website or demonstrate an app such as OneNote. To share your screen with an audience, select the part of the screen you want to show in the video. Office Mix captures everything that happens in that area to create a **screen recording**, as shown in **Figure 13**. Office Mix inserts the screen recording as a video in the slide.

Figure 13: Making a screen recording

Inserting Quizzes, Live Webpages, and Apps

To enhance and assess audience understanding, make your slides interactive by adding quizzes, live webpages, and apps. Quizzes give immediate feedback to the user as shown in **Figure 14**. Office Mix supports several quiz formats, including a **free-response quiz** similar to a short answer quiz, and true/false, multiple-choice, and multiple-response formats.

Figure 14: Creating an interactive quiz

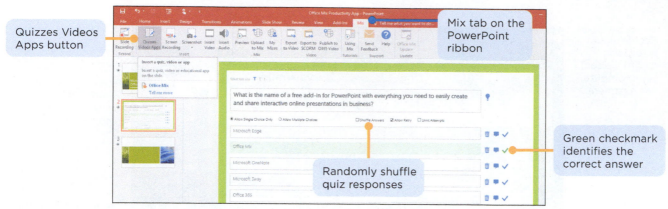

Sharing an Office Mix Presentation

When you complete your work with Office Mix, upload the presentation to your personal Office Mix dashboard as shown in **Figure 15**. Users of PCs, Macs, iOS devices, and Android devices can access and play Office Mix presentations. The Office Mix dashboard displays built-in analytics that include the quiz results and how much time viewers spent on each slide. You can play completed Office Mix presentations online or download them as movies.

Figure 15: Sharing an Office Mix presentation

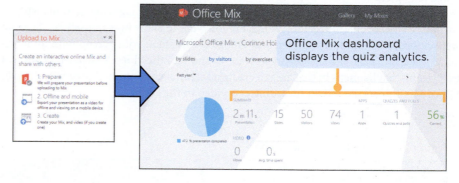

Try This Now

Learn to use Office Mix!

Links to companion **Sways**, featuring **videos** with hands-on instructions, are located on www.cengage.com.

1: Creating an Office Mix Tutorial for OneNote

Note: This activity requires a microphone on your computer.

Office Mix makes it easy to record screens and their contents. Create PowerPoint slides with an Office Mix screen recording to show OneNote 2016 features. Perform the following tasks:

    a. Create a PowerPoint presentation with the Ion Boardroom template. Create an opening slide with the title **My Favorite OneNote Features** and enter your name in the subtitle.

    b. Create three additional slides, each titled with a new feature of OneNote. Open OneNote and use the Mix tab in PowerPoint to capture three separate screen recordings that teach your favorite features.

    c. Add a fifth slide that quizzes the user with a multiple-choice question about OneNote and includes four responses. Be sure to insert a checkmark indicating the correct response.

    d. Upload the completed presentation to your Office Mix dashboard and share the link with your instructor.

    e. Submit your assignment link in the format specified by your instructor.

2: Teaching Augmented Reality with Office Mix

Note: This activity requires a webcam or built-in video camera on your computer.

A local elementary school has asked you to teach augmented reality to its students using Office Mix. Perform the following tasks:

    a. Research augmented reality using your favorite online search tools.

    b. Create a PowerPoint presentation with the Frame template. Create an opening slide with the title **Augmented Reality** and enter your name in the subtitle.

    c. Create a slide with four bullets summarizing your research of augmented reality. Create a 20-second slide recording of yourself providing a quick overview of augmented reality.

    d. Create another slide with a 30-second screen recording of a video about augmented reality from a site such as YouTube or another video-sharing site.

    e. Add a final slide that quizzes the user with a true/false question about augmented reality. Be sure to insert a checkmark indicating the correct response.

    f. Upload the completed presentation to your Office Mix dashboard and share the link with your instructor.

    g. Submit your assignment link in the format specified by your instructor.

3: Marketing a Travel Destination with Office Mix

Note: This activity requires a webcam or built-in video camera on your computer.

To convince your audience to travel to a particular city, create a slide presentation marketing any city in the world using a slide recording, screen recording, and a quiz. Perform the following tasks:

    a. Create a PowerPoint presentation with any template. Create an opening slide with the title of the city you are marketing as a travel destination and your name in the subtitle.

    b. Create a slide with four bullets about the featured city. Create a 30-second slide recording of yourself explaining why this city is the perfect vacation destination.

    c. Create another slide with a 20-second screen recording of a travel video about the city from a site such as YouTube or another video-sharing site.

    d. Add a final slide that quizzes the user with a multiple-choice question about the featured city with five responses. Be sure to include a checkmark indicating the correct response.

    e. Upload the completed presentation to your Office Mix dashboard and share your link with your instructor.

    f. Submit your assignment link in the format specified by your instructor.

Introduction to Microsoft Edge

Reading view | Hub | Cortana | Web Note | Inking | sandbox

Microsoft Edge is the default web browser developed for the Windows 10 operating system as a replacement for Internet Explorer. Unlike its predecessor, Edge lets you write on webpages, read webpages without advertisements and other distractions, and search for information using a virtual personal assistant. The Edge interface is clean and basic, as shown in **Figure 16**, meaning you can pay more attention to the webpage content.

Figure 16: Microsoft Edge tools

Forward button · New tab button · Web address in the Address bar · Add to favorites or reading list button · Back button · Reading view button · More button · Refresh (F5) button · Hub (Favorites, reading list, history, and downloads) button · Share Web Note button · Make a Web Note button

Browsing the Web with Microsoft Edge

One of the fastest browsers available, Edge allows you to type search text directly in the Address bar. As you view the resulting webpage, you can switch to **Reading view**, which is available for most news and research sites, to eliminate distracting advertisements. For example, if you are catching up on technology news online, the webpage might be difficult to read due to a busy layout cluttered with ads. Switch to Reading view to refresh the page and remove the original page formatting, ads, and menu sidebars to read the article distraction-free.

Consider the **Hub** in Microsoft Edge as providing one-stop access to all the things you collect on the web, such as your favorite websites, reading list, surfing history, and downloaded files.

Locating Information with Cortana

Cortana, the Windows 10 virtual assistant, plays an important role in Microsoft Edge. After you turn on Cortana, it appears as an animated circle in the Address bar when you might need assistance, as shown in the restaurant website in **Figure 17**. When you click the Cortana icon, a pane slides in from the right of the browser window to display detailed information about the restaurant, including maps and reviews. Cortana can also assist you in defining words, finding the weather, suggesting coupons for shopping, updating stock market information, and calculating math.

Figure 17: Cortana providing restaurant information

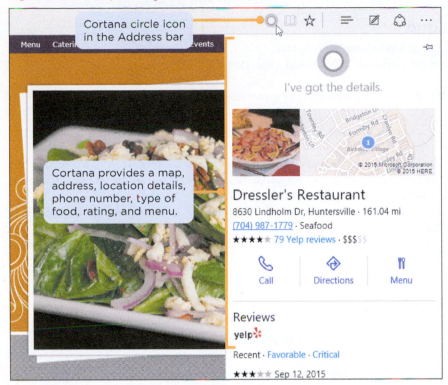

Figure 17: Cortana providing restaurant information

Cortana circle icon in the Address bar

Cortana provides a map, address, location details, phone number, type of food, rating, and menu.

Annotating Webpages

One of the most impressive Microsoft Edge features are the **Web Note** tools, which you use to write on a webpage or to highlight text. When you click the Make a Web Note button, an **Inking** toolbar appears, as shown in **Figure 18**, that provides writing and drawing tools. These tools include an eraser, a pen, and a highlighter with different colors. You can also insert a typed note and copy a screen image (called a screen clipping). You can draw with a pointing device, fingertip, or stylus using different pen colors. Whether you add notes to a recipe, annotate sources for a research paper, or select a product while shopping online, the Web Note tools can enhance your productivity. After you complete your notes, click the Save button to save the annotations to OneNote, your Favorites list, or your Reading list. You can share the inked page with others using the Share Web Note button.

On the Job Now

To enhance security, Microsoft Edge runs in a partial sandbox, an arrangement that prevents attackers from gaining control of your computer. Browsing within the **sandbox** protects computer resources and information from hackers.

Figure 18: Web Note tools in Microsoft Edge

Inking toolbar with Web Note tools for making annotations

Writing and drawing created with the Pen tool

Highlighted text

Save a copy of the webpage with annotations

Typed note

Try This Now

1: Using Cortana in Microsoft Edge

Learn to use Edge!
Links to companion **Sways**, featuring **videos** with hands-on instructions, are located on www.cengage.com.

Note: This activity requires using Microsoft Edge on a Windows 10 computer.

Cortana can assist you in finding information on a webpage in Microsoft Edge. Perform the following tasks:

a. Create a Word document using the Word Screen Clipping tool to capture the following screenshots.

- Screenshot A—Using Microsoft Edge, open a webpage with a technology news article. Right-click a term in the article and ask Cortana to define it.
- Screenshot B—Using Microsoft Edge, open the website of a fancy restaurant in a city near you. Make sure the Cortana circle icon is displayed in the Address bar. (If it's not displayed, find a different restaurant website.) Click the Cortana circle icon to display a pane with information about the restaurant.
- Screenshot C—Using Microsoft Edge, type **10 USD to Euros** in the Address bar without pressing the Enter key. Cortana converts the U.S. dollars to Euros.
- Screenshot D—Using Microsoft Edge, type **Apple stock** in the Address bar without pressing the Enter key. Cortana displays the current stock quote.

b. Submit your assignment in the format specified by your instructor.

2: Viewing Online News with Reading View

Note: This activity requires using Microsoft Edge on a Windows 10 computer.

Reading view in Microsoft Edge can make a webpage less cluttered with ads and other distractions. Perform the following tasks:

a. Create a Word document using the Word Screen Clipping tool to capture the following screenshots.

- Screenshot A—Using Microsoft Edge, open the website **mashable.com**. Open a technology article. Click the Reading view button to display an ad-free page that uses only basic text formatting.
- Screenshot B—Using Microsoft Edge, open the website **bbc.com**. Open any news article. Click the Reading view button to display an ad-free page that uses only basic text formatting.
- Screenshot C—Make three types of annotations (Pen, Highlighter, and Add a typed note) on the BBC article page displayed in Reading view.

b. Submit your assignment in the format specified by your instructor.

3: Inking with Microsoft Edge

Note: This activity requires using Microsoft Edge on a Windows 10 computer.

Microsoft Edge provides many annotation options to record your ideas. Perform the following tasks:

a. Open the website **wolframalpha.com** in the Microsoft Edge browser. Wolfram Alpha is a well-respected academic search engine. Type **US$100 1965 dollars in 2015** in the Wolfram Alpha search text box and press the Enter key.

b. Click the Make a Web Note button to display the Web Note tools. Using the Pen tool, draw a circle around the result on the webpage. Save the page to OneNote.

c. In the Wolfram Alpha search text box, type the name of the city closest to where you live and press the Enter key. Using the Highlighter tool, highlight at least three interesting results. Add a note and then type a sentence about what you learned about this city. Save the page to OneNote. Share your OneNote notebook with your instructor.

d. Submit your assignment link in the format specified by your instructor.

Understanding Essential Computer Concepts

CASE Computers are essential tools for all kinds of activity in virtually every type of business. In this module, you learn about computers, their components, and the software they run. You learn about input and output, how a computer processes data and stores information, how information is transmitted, and ways to secure that information.

Module Objectives

After completing this module, you will be able to:

- Recognize you live and work in the digital world
- Distinguish types of computers
- Identify computer system components
- Compare types of memory
- Summarize types of storage media
- Differentiate between input devices

- Explain output devices
- Describe data communications
- Define types of networks
- Assess security threats
- Understand system software
- Describe types of application software

Files You Will Need

No files needed.

Recognize You Live and Work in the Digital World

The Internet, computers, and mobile devices such as smartphones and tablets provide us with a world of information, literally at our fingertips. **CASE** ▸ *You'll look at some ways in which this "always-on" society is transforming your life.*

DETAILS

Over the last 25 years, the Internet has become an indispensable tool for businesses and for people's everyday needs. Just think of all the ways this time-saving technology serves us:

- Instantly communicate with friends and coworkers across town or on the other side of the planet.
- Store music and movies, and access them anywhere.
- Search and apply for jobs without leaving home.
- Quickly access information, instructions, and advice on almost anything.
- Shop for anything from clothing to food to cars to vacation deals.
- Manage your finances, deposit checks, and pay at the cash register using a mobile device.
- Get directions, view maps, and find nearby restaurants and theaters.

Here are several important ways you can use the Web to get your work done:

• Search for information

Modern search engines are so powerful that you can type in anything from a person's name to a desired flight to a question like, "what time does the game start?" and see hundreds or even thousands of results. A **search engine** is an online tool that allows you to enter keywords or terms; the engine then presents a list of sites that match those terms, organized so the most relevant ones appear first. You've probably used search engines such as Google, Yahoo!, or Bing.

• Communicate with others

Email, an electronic message sent from one person to another, is one of the oldest and most basic forms of Internet communication. Your company may provide email service, or you might use a service such as Microsoft's Outlook.com or Google's Gmail. You can share documents or images with coworkers and friends by sending them as attachments to email messages. **FIGURE 0-1** shows an email being composed in Mail.

Videoconferencing allows simultaneous two-way transmission of audio and video over the Internet. With a service such as Skype, users can talk to one another directly, as well as send and receive files. For example, the couple in **FIGURE 0-2** is using videoconferencing to stay in touch.

QUICK TIP

Many devices come with a built-in camera and microphone for use in videoconferencing.

QUICK TIP

Some companies use a virtual private network (VPN) that allows users to log in from a remote location and easily access documents or communicate with coworkers.

• Telecommuting

One of the biggest changes brought about by the Internet is the ability for a company's employees to work remotely, as shown in **FIGURE 0-3**. If you work out of your home office your company doesn't have to spend as much money on office space—and you can get right to work instead of sitting through rush hour.

• Cloud computing

This is a friendly term for the way in which data, applications, and resources can be accessed over the Internet (in "the cloud") rather than on your individual computer. Put simply, cloud computing is Internet-based computing. The push toward the cloud has been fueled by reliable high-speed Internet connections combined with less expensive Web-based computing power and online storage. Cloud services such as Microsoft OneDrive, Apple iCloud, and Dropbox give you access to your documents from any device that has an Internet connection, including your phone.

FIGURE 0-1: Email being composed in Mail for Windows 10

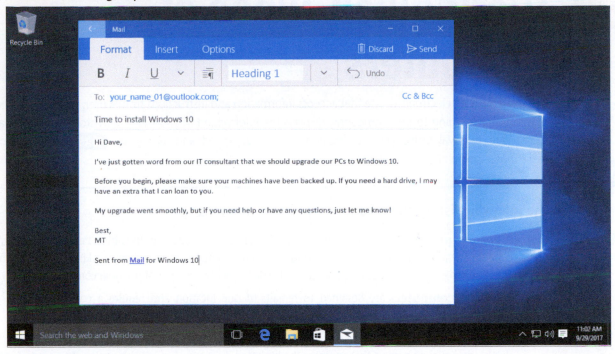

FIGURE 0-2: Couple using videoconferencing to communicate

PressureUA/iStock/Getty Images Plus/Getty Images

FIGURE 0-3: Employee telecommuting from home

Comstock Images/Photos.com

How to be a good online citizen

It's important to understand that your Internet activities can have lasting repercussions on your work and life. For instance, while social networks such as Facebook and Instagram let you hang out with your friends online, some employers are known to keep an eye on employee accounts.

Because the Web is an easy source of photos, illustrations, and text, many people assume this content is free to copy for use in their own work. However, if you plan to use an item that you didn't personally create, it's important to know that copyright laws may protect it. For help with understanding copyright issues, and for sources of "public domain" content, visit Creative Commons at creativecommons.org.

Distinguish Types of Computers

Learning Outcomes
• Define a computer
• Distinguish types of computers

A **computer** is an electronic device that accepts information and instructions from a user, manipulates the information according to the instructions, displays the information in some way, and stores the information for later retrieval. Computers are classified by their size, speed, and capabilities. **CASE** ▶ *You'll look at the most common types of computers.*

DETAILS

The following list describes various types of computers:

QUICK TIP

In common usage, the term "PC" refers to personal computers running the Microsoft Windows operating system. Computers sold by Apple run the Mac (short for "Macintosh") operating system, and are referred to as Macs.

- **Personal computers (PCs)** are typically used by a single user at home or in the office. Personal computers are used for general computing tasks such as word processing, manipulating numbers, working with images or video, exchanging email, and accessing the Internet. The following are types of personal computers:

  - **Desktop computers** are designed to remain in one location and require a constant source of electricity. **FIGURE 0-4** shows a desktop computer's monitor, CPU, keyboard, and mouse.

  - **Laptop computers** like the one shown in **FIGURE 0-5** have a hinged lid that contains the computer's display and a lower portion that contains the keyboard. Laptops, also called **Notebook computers**, are powered by rechargeable batteries, and they easily slip into a bag or briefcase. (**Ultraportable computers** are smaller and generally less powerful than laptops.)

  - **Tablets** are thin computers that do not require a keyboard or a mouse. To interact with a tablet, the user touches the screen or uses a stylus (most tablets also allow you to connect an external keyboard, or other input device). Tablets are ideal for surfing the Web, checking email, delivering presentations, reading electronic books, watching video, and creating artwork. See **FIGURE 0-5**.

  - **Smartphones**, like the one shown in **FIGURE 0-5**, are used to make phone calls, maintain an address book and calendar, send email and text messages, connect to the Internet, play music, and take photos or video. They've become so powerful that for most common computing tasks some users find they don't need a traditional desktop or laptop. Like tablets, most modern smartphones are controlled by touching the screen.

  - The most personal of computers, **wearables** are devices that may be worn on a person's wrist or incorporated into clothing. Smartwatches, fitness and health monitors, and virtual reality headsets are all examples of this emerging category.

- **Mainframe computers** and **supercomputers** like the one shown in **FIGURE 0-6** are used by large businesses, government agencies, and in science and education. They provide centralized storage and processing, and can manipulate tremendous amounts of data.

Touchscreens

In addition to traditional PCs, Microsoft Windows 10 was developed to work with touchscreen monitors, tablets, and smartphones. So, if you have a touchscreen device, you'll find that many tasks are easier to accomplish because they are designed for use with gestures instead of a mouse. A **gesture** is an action you take with your finger (or fingers) directly on the screen, such as tapping or swiping. For example, to switch between different apps in Windows, you can swipe in from the left edge of the touchscreen.

FIGURE 0-4: Desktop computer

Mmaxer/Shutterstock.com

FIGURE 0-5: Laptop computer, smartphone, and tablet

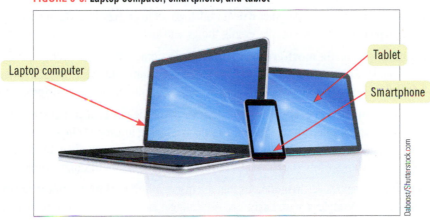

Laptop computer

Tablet

Smartphone

Daboost/Shutterstock.com

FIGURE 0-6: Supercomputer

iStockphoto.com/Senticus

Understanding Essential Computer Concepts

Identify Computer System Components

**Learning
Outcomes**
- Define hardware
  and software
- Define mother-
  board and
  processor
- Define input and
  output

A **computer system** includes computer hardware and software. **Hardware** refers to the physical components of a computer. **Software** refers to the intangible components of a computer system, particularly the **programs**, or data routines, that the computer uses to perform a specific task. **CASE** ▶ *You'll look at how computers work and describe the main components of a computer system.*

DETAILS

The following list provides an overview of computer system components and how they work:

The design and construction of a computer is referred to as its **architecture** or **configuration**. The technical details about each hardware component are called **specifications**. For example, a computer system might be configured to include a printer; a specification for that printer might be a print speed of eight pages per minute or the ability to print in color.

The hardware and software of a computer system work together to process data. **Data** refers to the numbers, words, sounds, and graphics that describe people, events, things, and ideas. Modifying data is referred to as **processing**.

Processing tasks occur on the **motherboard**, the main electronic component inside the computer. See **FIGURE 0-7**. The motherboard is a **circuit board**, which is a rigid piece of non-conducting material with **circuits**—electrical paths—that control specific functions. Motherboards typically contain the following processing hardware:

- The **microprocessor**, also called the **processor** or the **central processing unit (CPU)**, consists of transistors and electronic circuits on a silicon chip (an integrated circuit embedded in semiconductor material). The processor is responsible for executing instructions. It is the "brain" of the computer. **FIGURE 0-8** shows where the CPU sits in the flow of information through a computer.

- **Cards** are removable circuit boards that are inserted into slots in the motherboard to expand its capabilities. For example, a sound card translates digital audio information into analog sounds the human ear can hear.

A **System on a Chip (SoC)** consolidates the functions of the CPU, graphics and sound cards, memory, and more onto a single silicon chip. This miniaturization allows devices to become increasingly compact.

Input is the data or set of instructions you give to a computer. You use an **input device**, such as a keyboard or a mouse, to enter data and issue commands. **Commands** are input instructions that tell the computer how to process data. For example, if you want to enhance the color of a photo in a graphics program, you input the appropriate commands that instruct the computer to modify the data in the image.

Output is the result of the computer processing the input you provide. Output can take many different forms, including printed documents, pictures, audio, and video. Computers produce output using **output devices**, such as a monitor or printer. The output you create may be stored inside the computer itself or on an external storage device, such as a USB flash drive.

The computer itself takes care of the processing functions, but it needs additional components, called **peripheral devices**, to accomplish the input, output, and storage functions. You'll learn more about these devices later in this module.

FIGURE 0-7: Motherboard

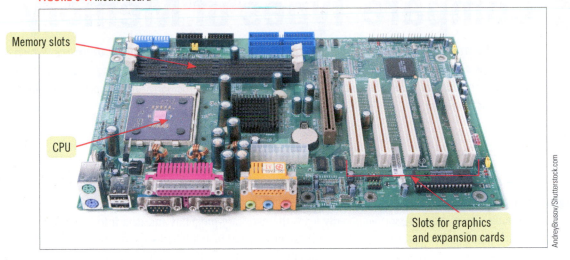

Memory slots

CPU

Slots for graphics
and expansion cards

AndreyBrusov/Shutterstock.com

FIGURE 0-8: Flow of information through a computer system

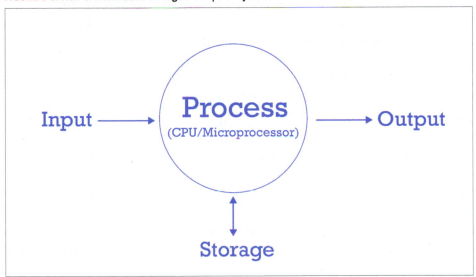

Input → **Process** (CPU/Microprocessor) → Output

Storage

About microprocessor speeds

How fast a computer can process instructions depends partially on the speed of the microprocessor. Among other factors, the speed of the microprocessor is determined by its clock speed, word size, and whether it is single or multicore. **Clock speed** is measured in **megahertz (MHz)**, millions of cycles per second, or in **gigahertz (GHz)**, billions of cycles per second. **Word size** refers to the number of bits—the smallest unit of information in a computer—that are processed at one time; for example, a 32-bit processor processes 32 bits at a time. A computer with a large word size can process faster than a computer with a small word size. Most PCs sold today come with 64-bit processors. Finally, a **dual-core processor**, which has two processors on a single chip, can process information up to twice as fast as a **single-core processor**. Likewise, a **quad-core processor**, with four processors on a chip, processes information up to four times as fast as a single-core processor. Other multicore processors, such as hexacore and octacore, are also available.

Compare Types of Memory

One of the most important components of personal computer hardware is the **memory**, which stores instructions and data. **CASE** *You'll explore the different types of memory found in a typical computer: random access memory, cache memory, virtual memory, read-only memory, and complementary metal oxide semiconductor memory.*

DETAILS

Types of memory include the following:

> **QUICK TIP**
> When the computer is off, RAM is empty.

Random access memory (RAM) holds information only while the computer is on. Whenever you're using a computer, the microprocessor temporarily loads the necessary programs and data into RAM so it can quickly access them. The information present in RAM can be accessed in a different sequence from which it was stored, hence its name. RAM typically consists of chips mounted on cards that are plugged into the motherboard.

- RAM is considered **volatile memory** or **temporary memory** because it's constantly changing or being refreshed. RAM is cleared when the computer is turned off.

- Most personal computers use **synchronous dynamic random access memory (SDRAM)**, which allows faster access to data by synchronizing with the clock speed of the computer's system bus.

> **QUICK TIP**
> You can often add more RAM to a computer by installing additional memory cards on the motherboard. You cannot add ROM; it is permanently installed on the motherboard.

- **Memory capacity** is the amount of data the computer can handle at any given time and is usually measured in gigabytes. For example, a computer that has 4 GB of RAM has the capacity to temporarily use more than four billion bits of data at one time.

Cache memory, sometimes called **RAM cache** or **CPU cache**, is special, high-speed memory located on or near the microprocessor itself. Cache memory sits between the CPU and relatively slow RAM and stores frequently accessed and recently accessed data and commands. See **FIGURE 0-9**.

Virtual memory is space on the computer's storage devices (usually the hard disk drive) that simulates additional RAM. It enables programs to run as if your computer had more RAM by moving data and commands from RAM to the computer's permanent storage device and swapping in the new data and commands. Virtual memory, however, is much slower than RAM.

Read-only memory (ROM), also known as **firmware**, is a chip on the motherboard that permanently stores the **BIOS (basic input/output system)**. The BIOS is activated when you turn on the computer; it initializes the motherboard, recognizes any devices connected to the computer, and starts the boot process. The **boot process**, or **booting up**, includes loading the operating system software and preparing the computer so you can begin working.

- ROM never changes, and it remains intact when the computer is turned off; it is therefore called **nonvolatile memory** or **permanent memory**.

- Some computers allow ROM to be reprogrammed via a **firmware update**, which allows a manufacturer to fix bugs and add features.

Complementary metal oxide semiconductor (**CMOS**, pronounced "SEE-moss") **memory** is a chip on the motherboard that stores the date, time, and system parameters. Often referred to as **semipermanent memory**, a small rechargeable battery powers CMOS so its contents are saved when the computer is turned off.

FIGURE 0-10 shows the basic relationships between the different types of computer memory.

FIGURE 0-9: Microprocessor with CPU cache

Cache memory

Microprocessor (CPU)

rawcaptured/Shutterstock.com

FIGURE 0-10: Relationships between types of computer memory

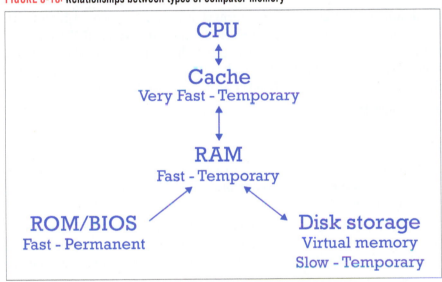

CPU

Cache
Very Fast - Temporary

RAM
Fast - Temporary

ROM/BIOS
Fast - Permanent

Disk storage
Virtual memory
Slow - Temporary

Upgrading RAM

One of the easiest ways to make your computer run faster is to add more RAM. The more RAM a computer has, the more instructions and data can be stored there. You can often add more RAM to a computer by installing additional memory cards on the motherboard, as shown in **FIGURE 0-11**. Currently, you can buy 128 MB to 32 GB RAM cards, and usually, you can add more than one card. Check your computer's specifications to see what size RAM cards the slots on your motherboard will accept. Note that if your computer has a 32-bit processor, it can't use more than 4 GB of RAM, even if the computer has places to plug in more cards.

FIGURE 0-11: Installing RAM on a motherboard

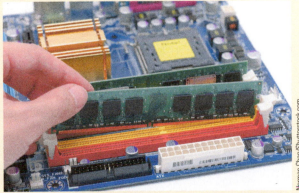

Norman Chan/Shutterstock.com

Understanding Essential Computer Concepts

Summarize Types of Storage Media

Since RAM retains data only while the power is on, your computer must have a more permanent storage option. As **FIGURE 0-12** shows, a storage device receives data from RAM and places it on a storage medium, some of which are described below. The data can later be read back to RAM to use again. All data and programs are stored as files. A computer **file** is a named collection of stored data. An **executable file** is a type of computer file that contains the instructions that tell a computer how to perform a specific task; for instance, the files that are used when the computer starts are executable. Another type of computer file is a **data file**. This is the kind of file you create when you use software. For instance, a report that you write with a word-processing program is data, and it must be saved as a data file if you want to access it later. **CASE** *You'll explore some common types of storage media.*

DETAILS

The types of storage media are discussed below:

Magnetic storage devices use various patterns of magnetization to store data on a magnetized surface. The most common type of magnetic storage device is the **hard disk drive (HDD)**, also called a **hard disk** or a **hard drive**. It contains several spinning platters on which a magnetic head writes and reads data. Most personal computers come with an internal hard drive on which the operating system, programs, and files are all stored. You can also purchase external hard drives for additional storage and for backing up your computer.

Optical storage devices use laser technology to store data in the form of tiny pits or bumps on the reflective surface of a spinning polycarbonate disc. To access the data, a laser illuminates the data path while a read head interprets the reflection.

- Originally developed to store audio recordings, the **CD (compact disc)** was later adapted for data storage; the **CD-ROM** then became the first standard optical storage device available for personal computers. One CD can store 700 MB of data.

- A **DVD** is the same physical size as a CD, but it can store between 4.7 and 15.9 GB of data, depending on whether the data is stored on one or two sides of the disc, and how many layers of data each side contains. **Blu-ray** discs store 25 GB of data per layer. They are used for storing high-definition video.

Flash memory (also called **solid-state storage**) is similar to ROM except that it can be written to more than once. Small **flash memory cards** are used in digital cameras, handheld computers, video game consoles, and many other devices.

- A popular type of flash memory is a **USB flash drive**, also called a **USB drive** or a **flash drive**. See **FIGURE 0-13**. USB drives are available in a wide range of capacities, from one to 512 GB. They are popular for use as a secondary or backup storage device.

- USB drives plug directly into the USB port of a computer where it is recognized as another disk drive. USB ports are usually found on the front, back, or side of a computer.

A **solid-state drive (SSD)** is based on flash memory, but is intended as a replacement for a traditional hard disk drive. Per gigabyte, SSDs are still more expensive than hard drives, but use less power and offer much faster data access and increased reliability.

A **solid-state hybrid drive (SSHD)** economically combines the speed of an SSD with the high capacity and lower cost of a traditional HDD.

Understanding Essential Computer Concepts

FIGURE 0-12: Storage devices and RAM

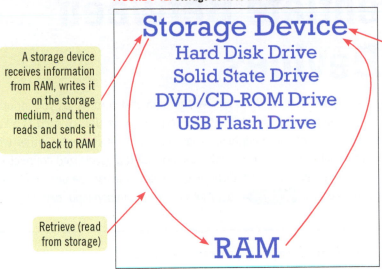

A storage device receives information from RAM, writes it on the storage medium, and then reads and sends it back to RAM

Store (write to storage)

Retrieve (read from storage)

Storage Device
Hard Disk Drive
Solid State Drive
DVD/CD-ROM Drive
USB Flash Drive

RAM

FIGURE 0-13: USB flash drive being inserted into a laptop

Brian A Jackson/Shutterstock.com

Storage in the Cloud

With Internet connections ever more available, Cloud storage can give you easy access to all your documents and photos from any device. Services such as Microsoft OneDrive, Apple iCloud, Dropbox, Google Drive, and Box offer both free and paid storage of your data. Typically, these services copy data stored on your computer and automatically sync it with the data on their remote servers, which are spread around the globe. For instance, when you edit a note in Microsoft OneNote on your PC, the changes are immediately sent to the version in the Cloud (via OneDrive), and then propagate to other devices such as your phone. You can also share a file or folder with colleagues so that everyone has access to the most current version, and most services offer the ability to restore a file to an earlier version. Cloud storage can also serve as an effective **off-site backup**, where your data is backed up to a remote location other than your home or office, protecting it from events like theft or fire. If you decide to use a Cloud service, remember to protect your data by creating a secure password that is difficult for others to guess.

Differentiate Between Input Devices

Learning Outcomes
- Define input device
- Identify various input devices

To accomplish a task, a computer first needs to receive the data and commands you input. In a typical personal computer system, you provide this information using an **input device** such as a keyboard or a mouse. Most input devices are hardware peripherals that connect to a computer either with cables or wirelessly. Wired devices typically connect with a USB cable, or using a specialized connector. Most wireless input devices connect using radio frequency technology, while some use the same infrared technology found in a television remote control. **CASE** ▶ *You'll look at some common input devices.*

DETAILS

There are many types of input devices, as described below:

QUICK TIP

You may be able to avoid repetitive motion injuries by taking frequent breaks from computer work and by carefully stretching your hands, wrists, and arms.

The most frequently used input device is a **keyboard**, which allows you to input text and issue commands by typing. The keyboard on the right in **FIGURE 0-14** is a standard keyboard, but the keyboard on the left is **ergonomic**, meaning that it has been designed to fit the natural placement of your hands and may reduce the risk of repetitive-motion injuries. Many keyboards have additional shortcut keys that are programmed to issue frequently used commands.

Another common input device is a **pointing device**, which controls the **pointer**—a small arrow or other symbol—on the screen. Pointing devices are used to select commands and manipulate text or graphics on the screen.

- The most popular pointing device for a desktop computer is a **mouse**, such as the one shown on the left in **FIGURE 0-15**. You control the pointer by sliding the mouse across a flat surface; this motion is tracked by either a roller ball or by infrared or laser light. A mouse usually has two or more buttons used for clicking objects on the screen. A mouse might also have a **scroll wheel** that you roll to scroll through the page or pages on your screen.

- A **trackball**, shown in the middle of **FIGURE 0-15**, is similar to a mouse except that it remains stationary while you control the motion of the pointer by moving a rolling ball on the top of the device.

- Laptop computers are usually equipped with a touchpad like the one shown on the right in **FIGURE 0-15**. A **touchpad**, also called a **trackpad**, detects the motion of your fingers. Buttons are usually located at the bottom of the touchpad, but many also allow you to click by simply tapping or pressing the pad.

QUICK TIP

Tablets and smartphones typically feature a "virtual keyboard" for inputting text.

A **touchscreen** like the one in **FIGURE 0-16** accepts commands from your fingers (or a stylus), while it simultaneously displays the output. Touchscreens are found on ATMs, smartphones, and tablets. Many newer desktop and laptop computers also have hardware that supports touchscreen technology.

A **microphone** can be used to record sound or communicate with others using audio or video conferencing software. Many devices also have **voice-recognition software** that allows you to input text and commands via the microphone.

A **scanner** is a device that captures the image on a photograph or piece of paper and stores it digitally. If you scan a text document, you can use **optical character recognition (OCR)** software to translate it into text that can be edited in a word-processing program. If you scan a photo, it can be saved as an image file.

FIGURE 0-14: Ergonomic keyboard and standard keyboard

FIGURE 0-15: Personal computer pointing devices: mouse, trackball, and touchpad

Scroll wheels

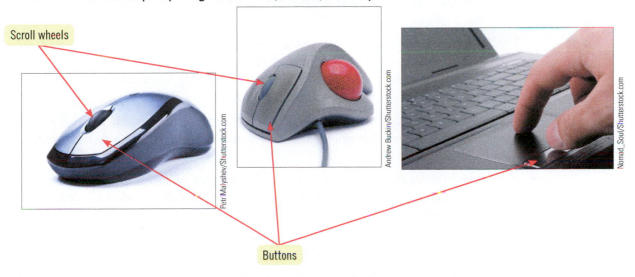

Buttons

FIGURE 0-16: Touchscreen

Understanding assistive devices

Advances in **computer accessibility** mean that people with physical impairments or disabilities can use computers. For example, people who cannot use their arms or hands to operate a mouse may be able to use foot, head, or eye movements to control a specialized assistive device.

Those with poor vision can use keyboards with large keys, screen enlargers that increase the size of objects on a monitor, or screen readers that speak on-screen content aloud. Experiments involving neural implants are already allowing people with disabilities to control robotic limbs.

Explain Output Devices

Learning Outcomes
• Define output device
• Identify different output devices

An **output device** is any hardware peripheral that communicates the results of data processing. As with input devices, output devices may connect to a computer using a cable, or wirelessly via Wi-Fi or Bluetooth. **Bluetooth** is a type of wireless technology that uses short range radio waves. A Bluetooth device must first be "paired" with a computer so that it knows to trust that particular device. **CASE** ▶ *You'll explore the most commonly used output devices: monitors, printers, and speakers.*

DETAILS

Output devices are described below:

The **monitor**, sometimes called the **display** or simply the **screen**, uses video technology to display the output from a computer.

- The **flat panel monitor** shown in **FIGURE 0-17** uses **LCD (liquid crystal display)** technology to create an image by modulating light within a layer of liquid crystal. LCD monitors require a backlight for illumination. Older monitors typically use a fluorescent backlight, while newer ones use **LED (light emitting diode)** technology, which is more energy efficient.

- Monitor **screen size** is the diagonal measurement from one corner of the screen to the other. In general, monitors on desktop computers range in size from 15" to 30", whereas monitors on laptop computers range in size from 10" to 20".

- A monitor's screen is divided into a matrix of small dots called **pixels. Display resolution** is the number of pixels the monitor displays in each dimension, typically expressed as width × height. Common standard resolutions range from 640 × 480 to 5120 × 2880.

- To display graphics, a computer must have a **graphics card**, also called a **video display adapter** or **video card**, or a built-in **graphics processor** (sometimes called a **built-in graphics card**). The graphics card or processor controls the signals the computer sends to the monitor.

A **printer** produces a paper copy, often called a **hard copy**, of the text and graphics processed by a computer. Print quality, or resolution, is measured by the number of **dots per inch (dpi)** that a printer can produce. The speed of a printer is determined by how many **pages per minute (ppm)** it can output.

- **LED printers** and **laser printers**, like the one shown on the left in **FIGURE 0-18**, are popular for business use because they produce high-quality output quickly and reliably. Each type uses its light source to temporarily transfer an image onto a rotating drum, which attracts a powdery substance called **toner**. The toner is then transferred from the drum onto paper. Laser and LED printers typically feature print resolutions of 600 to 2400 DPI and can print in black and white or color. However, they're generally better at producing sharp text and simple graphics than they are at printing clear photographs.

- **Inkjet printers**, such as the one shown on the right in **FIGURE 0-18**, are popular for home and small business use. These printers spray ink onto paper, producing quality comparable to that of a laser printer, though at much slower speeds. Inkjets can also print on a wide variety of paper types, though use of plain paper may result in fuzzy text. Most inkjets sold today print in color, and they excel at producing photos with smooth color, especially when using special glossy photo paper.

Speakers (and **headphones**) allow you to hear sounds generated by your computer. Speakers can be separate peripheral devices, or they can be built into the computer case or monitor. For speakers to work, a sound card must be present on the motherboard. The sound card converts the digital data in an audio file into analog sound that can be played through the speakers.

FIGURE 0-17: LCD monitor

robert_s/Shutterstock.com

FIGURE 0-18: Laser printer and inkjet printer

Maksym Dykha/Shutterstock.com

StockPhotosArt/Shutterstock.com

About 3D printers

A **3D printer** is essentially a robot that deposits multiple layers of material (typically heated plastic) onto a surface. To achieve the desired shape, the tool head may travel in a different direction as each layer is applied. A designer may use a 3D printer to create prototypes of new products, or a doctor could print prosthetic limbs. 3D "bio" printers could someday be used to create living tissue or replacement organs.

Understanding Essential Computer Concepts

Describe Data Communications

Data communications is the transmission of data from one computer to another or to a peripheral device. The computer that originates the message is the **sender**. The message is sent over some type of **channel**, such as a telephone or coaxial cable, or wirelessly. The computer or device at the message's destination is the **receiver**. The rules that establish an orderly transfer of data between the sender and the receiver are called **protocols**. A **device driver**, or simply **driver**, handles the transmission protocols between a computer and its peripheral devices. A driver is a computer program that can establish communication because it understands the characteristics of your computer and of the device. **CASE** ▶ *You'll look at some common ways that computers communicate.*

DETAILS

The following describes some of the ways that computers communicate:

The path along which data travels between the microprocessor, RAM, and peripherals is called the **data bus**.

An external peripheral device must have a corresponding **expansion port** and **cable** that connect it to the computer. Inside the computer, each port connects to a **controller card**, sometimes called an **expansion card** or **interface card**. These cards plug into connectors on the motherboard called **expansion slots** or **slots**. Personal computers can have several types of ports, including parallel, serial, USB, MIDI, Ethernet, and Thunderbolt. **FIGURE 0-19** shows the ports on one desktop computer.

USB (Universal Serial Bus) is a data communications standard which has simplified and largely replaced the need for earlier interfaces such as parallel and serial ports. Many devices have a USB connector, a small rectangular plug that you insert into a USB port on a computer. Printers, keyboards, mice, cameras, smartphones, disk drives, and network adapters all commonly connect using USB. For many USB devices, power is supplied via the port, so there's no need for an extra power supply or cables.

An **Ethernet port**, which resembles a telephone jack, allows data to be transmitted at high speeds over a **local area network (LAN)**. You can use Ethernet to connect to another computer, to a LAN, or to a modem. A **modem** (short for modulator-demodulator) is a device that connects your computer to the Internet via a standard telephone jack or cable connection.

Monitors are connected to computers through HDMI, DVI, or VGA ports. Both **HDMI (high-definition multimedia interface)** and **DVI (digital video interface)** digitally transmit both video and audio. The older **VGA (video graphics array)** only allows analog transmission of video.

Understanding USB types and connectors

When you purchase USB cables, pay special attention to the type of USB your device requires. The USB specification has evolved over the years, resulting in a wide array of speeds and capabilities. USB 1.1 (introduced in 1998) supports a data rate (speed) of 12 megabits per second (Mbit/s). In 2000, USB 2.0 increased that to 480 Mbit/s. The release of USB 3.1, in 2013, further increased it to 10 gigabits per second (Gbit/s), allowing full-quality transmission of audio and video data. Also make sure you purchase the right connector for your device. Common connectors include Type A, Type B, Micro-A, Micro-B, and older Mini-A and Mini-B. There are even USB 3.0 Type-A, Type-B, and Micro-B connectors. The most recent, Type C, features a plug that can be inserted both ways.

FIGURE 0-19: Computer expansion ports

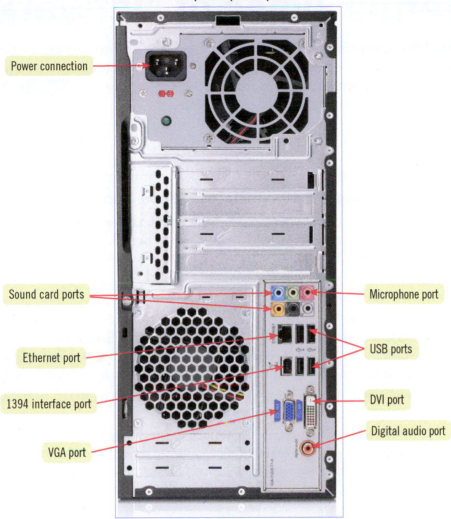

Power connection

Sound card ports

Microphone port

USB ports

Ethernet port

1394 interface port

DVI port

Digital audio port

VGA port

How computers represent and interpret data

A computer sees the world as a series of **binary digits or bits**. A bit can hold one of two numerical values: 1 for "on" or 0 for "off." You might think of bits as miniature light switches. Of course, a single bit doesn't hold much information, so eight of them are combined to form a **byte**, which can be used to represent 256 values. Integer value 1 equals 00000001 (only 1 bit is "flipped" on), while the byte that represents 255 is 11111111 (all the bits are flipped on). A kilobyte (KB or **K**) is 1024 bytes, or about a thousand bytes. A **megabyte (MB)** is 1,048,576 bytes (about a million bytes). A **gigabyte (GB)** is about a billion bytes, and a **terabyte (TB)** is about a trillion bytes.

Define Types of Networks

Learning Outcomes
- Define networking terms
- Identify network types

A **network** connects one computer to other computers and peripheral devices, enabling you to share data and resources with others. There is a wide a variety of network types; however, any type of network has some basic characteristics and requirements that you should know. **CASE** *You'll look at the components that make up some different types of networks.*

DETAILS

Components of networks and the types of networks are described below:

To connect with a network via Ethernet, a computer must have a **network interface card (NIC)** which creates a communications channel between the computer and the network. Many desktop PCs and laptops come with a NIC built-in, and an Ethernet cable is used to make the connection to a router or modem. A **router** is a device that controls traffic between network components.

Network software is also essential, establishing the communications protocols that will be observed on the network and controlling the data "traffic flow."

Some networks have one or more computers, called **servers**, that act as the central storage location for programs and provide mass storage for most of the data used on the network. A network with a server and computers dependent on the server is called a **client/server network**. The dependent computers are the clients.

When a network does not have a server, all the computers are essentially equal, with programs and data distributed among them. This is called a **peer-to-peer network**.

A personal computer that is not connected to a network is called a **stand-alone computer**. When it is connected to the network, it becomes a **workstation**. Any device connected to the network, from computers to printers to routers, is called a **node**. **FIGURE 0-20** illustrates a typical network configuration.

In a **local area network (LAN)**, the nodes are located relatively close to one another, usually in the same building.

A **wide area network (WAN)** is more than one LAN connected together. The **Internet** is the largest example of a WAN.

In a **wireless local area network (WLAN)**, devices communicate using radio waves instead of wires. **Wi-Fi** (short for **wireless fidelity**) is the term created by the nonprofit Wi-Fi Alliance to describe networks connected using a standard radio frequency established by the Institute of Electrical and Electronics Engineers (IEEE). Most Wi-Fi routers can transmit over distances of up to about 200 feet; a technique called **bridging** can be used to increase this range by using multiple routers.

A **personal area network (PAN)** allows two or more devices located close to each other to communicate directly via cables or wirelessly. A PAN can also be used to share one device's Internet connection with another.

Infrared technology uses infrared light waves to "beam" data from one device to another. The devices must be compatible, and they must have their infrared ports pointed at each other to communicate. This is also the technology used in TV remote controls.

Bluetooth uses short range radio waves (up to about 30 feet) to connect devices wirelessly to one another or to the Internet. Bluetooth is often used to connect wireless headsets to cell phones or computers, and for connecting some wireless pointing devices and keyboards.

FIGURE 0-20: Typical network configuration

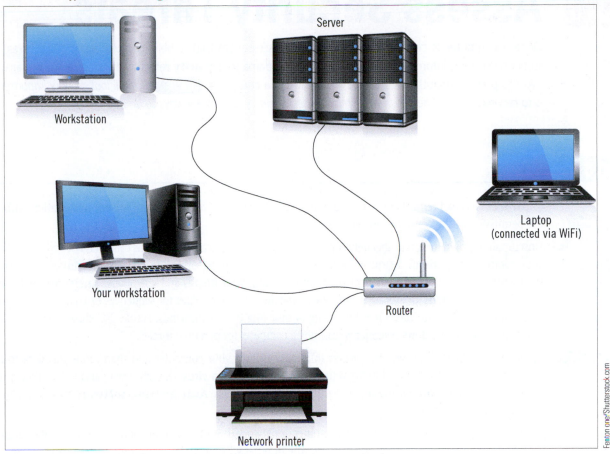

Workstation

Server

Your workstation

Router

Laptop
(connected via WiFi)

Network printer

Fenton one©Shutterstock.com

Understanding telecommunications

Telecommunications means communicating over a relatively long distance using a phone line or other data conduit. To make this connection, you must use a modem, a device that converts the digital signals that your computer understands into analog signals that can travel over ordinary phone lines or cable lines. Though less common today, some PCs still come with a built-in 56K modem that can send and receive about 56,000 **bits per second (bps)** over a phone line. This is slow, so many people opt for a high-speed connection using **DSL (digital subscriber line)**, which also operates over a phone line, or using a cable connection. If you go this route, you may need to purchase or rent an external DSL or cable modem. DSL and cable modems typically connect to a computer's **NIC (network interface card)** via an Ethernet cable or using Wi-Fi. High-speed connections are often called **broadband connections**.

Understanding Essential Computer Concepts

Assess Security Threats

Learning Outcomes
- Define types of security threats
- Establish importance of good security

Once a computer is connected to a network, it is essential that it be protected against the threat of someone stealing information or causing malicious damage. **Security** refers to the steps a computer user takes to prevent unauthorized use of or damage to a computer. **CASE** *You'll look at how important it is to be vigilant about keeping your computers secure and you'll review ways to do this.*

DETAILS

QUICK TIP

Some specific types of viruses are called worms; another type is a Trojan horse. Antivirus software usually protects against both types.

Malware is a broad term that describes any program designed to cause harm or transmit information without the permission of the computer owner.

Unscrupulous programmers deliberately construct harmful, self-replicating programs called **viruses** which instruct your computer to perform destructive activities, such as corrupting or erasing data. Some viruses may spread themselves by hijacking your email program and emailing your friends and coworkers. **Antivirus software**, sometimes called **virus protection software**, searches executable files for sequences of characters that may cause harm, and then disinfects files by erasing or disabling those commands. **FIGURE 0-21** shows the dialog box that appears when Windows Defender is scanning a computer for potential threats.

QUICK TIP

Adware is software installed with another program, often with the user's permission, that generates advertising revenue for the program's creator by displaying ads.

Spyware is software that secretly gathers information from your computer and then sends this data to the company or person that created it. Spyware may be installed by a virus, though it may also be installed along with other software without the user's permission or knowledge. **Anti-spyware software** can detect these programs and delete them.

A **firewall** is like a locked door on your computer or network. It prevents other computers on the Internet from accessing your computer and prevents access to the Internet without your permission.

- A hardware firewall provides strong protection against incoming threats. Many routers come with built-in firewalls.

- Software firewalls, installed directly on your computer, track all incoming and outgoing traffic. If a program that never previously accessed the Internet attempts to do so, the user is notified and can choose to forbid access. There are several free software firewall packages available, including Microsoft Firewall.

Criminals are relentlessly searching for new and aggressive ways of accessing computer users' personal information and passwords.

- A **spoofed** site is a website that's been set up to look exactly like another website, with the intention of convincing customers to enter their personal information. For example, a criminal site developer might create a **URL** (address on the Web) that looks similar to the URL of a legitimate site such as a bank's. If a customer isn't paying attention, he or she may inadvertently enter information such as credit card numbers, Social Security numbers, or passwords. Once a thief has this information, it can be used to steal the customer's money or identity. **FIGURE 0-22** shows the alert displayed in the Microsoft Edge browser when a known spoofed site is visited.

QUICK TIP

If you suspect you've received a phishing message, don't click any links in the email. Instead, open your browser and type the correct URL into the address bar.

- **Phishing** refers to the practice of sending email to customers or potential customers of a legitimate website encouraging them to click a link in the email. When clicked, the user's **browser** (the software program used to access websites) displays a spoofed site where the user is asked to provide personal information.

- A **DNS server** is one of the many computers distributed around the world that's responsible for directing Internet traffic. Using a practice called **pharming**, a criminal can sometimes break into a DNS server and redirect any attempts to access a particular website to the criminal's spoofed site.

FIGURE 0-21: Windows Defender scan in progress

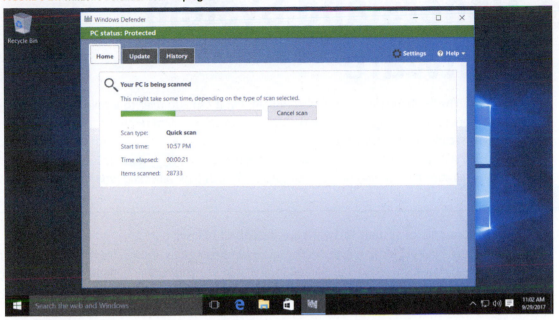

FIGURE 0-22: Microsoft Edge browser when visiting a known spoofed site

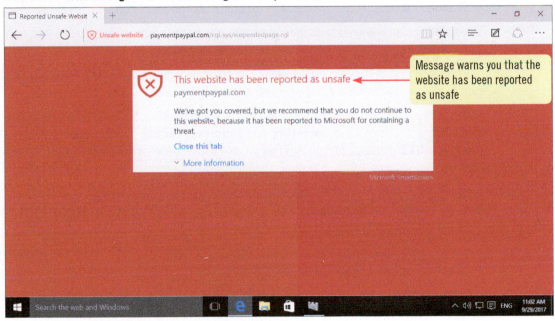

Understanding two-factor authentication

You've probably gotten used to logging in to a website by entering a username and password; this is called **single-factor authentication** because you're entering a single credential, your password. **Two-factor authentication (2FA)** adds another step to the process by requiring an additional credential. For example, when you log in to your bank's website, it may send a text message to your mobile phone that consists of a randomly-generated code. The code is unique to you and to this moment in time. You then enter the code along with your username and password to gain access to the site. 2FA is considered more secure because it's likely that you're the only person in possession of your phone. Biometric devices, such as the fingerprint ID sensors on some smartphones, can also function as a second level of authentication.

Understand System Software

**Learning
Outcomes**
- Define system
  software
- Identify types of
  system software

The term *software* often refers to a single program, but it can also refer to a collection of programs and data that are packaged together. **System software** allocates system resources, manages storage space, maintains security, and detects equipment failure. It provides the basic platform for running specialized application software, which you'll learn about in the next lesson. **CASE** ▸ *You'll look at the components of system software and how they help the computer perform its basic operating tasks.*

DETAILS

The components of system software are described below:

System software (see **FIGURE 0-23**) manages the fundamental operations of your computer, such as loading programs and data into memory, executing programs, saving data to storage devices, displaying information on the monitor, and transmitting data through a port to a peripheral device. There are four basic types of system software: operating systems, utility software, device drivers, and programming languages.

QUICK TIP

As part of its security responsibilities, your computer's operating system may require you to enter a username and password, or it may scan the computer to protect against viruses.

- The **operating system** manages the system resources of a computer so programs run properly. A **system resource** is any part of the computer system, including memory, storage devices, and the microprocessor. The operating system controls basic data **input and output**, or **I/O**, which is the flow of data from the microprocessor to memory to peripherals and back again.

- The operating system also manages the files on your storage devices. It opens and saves files, tracks every part of every file, and lets you know if any part of a file is missing.

- The operating system is always on the lookout for equipment failure. Each electronic circuit is checked periodically, and the user is notified whenever a problem is detected.

- Microsoft Windows, used on many personal computers, and OS X, used exclusively on Apple's Macintosh computers, are referred to as **operating environments** because they provide a **graphical user interface** (**GUI**, pronounced "goo-ey") that acts as a liaison between the user and all of the computer's hardware and software. **FIGURE 0-24** shows the Start menu on a computer using Microsoft Windows 10.

Utility software helps analyze, optimize, configure, and maintain a computer. Examples of utilities include antivirus software, backup tools, and disk tools that allow you to analyze a hard drive or compress data to save space.

As you learned in the discussion of hardware ports, device drivers handle the transmission protocol between a computer and its peripherals. When you add a new device to a computer, the installation process typically involves loading a driver that updates the computer's configuration.

While most of us have no contact with them, it's important to know that computer **programming languages** allow a programmer to write instructions, or code, that a computer can understand. Programmers typically write software in a particular language and then compile the code to create a program that the computer then executes. Popular programming languages include C, C++, Objective-C, Swift, Java, Ruby, and Python.

Protecting information with passwords

You can protect data on your computer by using passwords. You can set up multiple user accounts on your computer and require that users sign in with a username and password before they can use it. This is known as **logging in** or **logging on**. You can also protect individual files on your computer so anyone who tries to access a file must type a password. Many websites, especially e-commerce and banking sites, require a username and password to access the information stored there. To prevent anyone from guessing your passwords, always create and use strong passwords. A **strong password** consists of at least eight characters of upper- and lowercase letters and numbers. Avoid using easy to obtain personal information in your passwords, such as birthdays and addresses, and always create different passwords that are unique to each website you use.

FIGURE 0-23: Relationships between system software and other system components

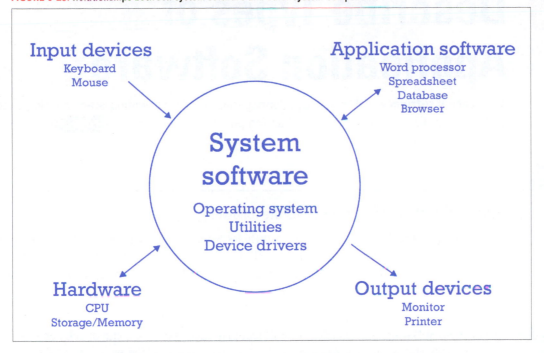

FIGURE 0-24: Windows 10 desktop with Start menu open

Examining Windows 10 hardware requirements

Windows 10, the newest version of the Windows operating system, requires a computer with at least a 1 GHz processor, 1 GB of RAM for the 32-bit version or 2 GB of RAM for the 64-bit version, a DirectX 9 graphics processor, and 16 GB of hard disk space for the 32-bit version or 20 GB for the 64-bit version. Keep in mind that these are the minimum recommendations. To prevent your computer from slowing to a crawl, you should consider upgrading the amount of RAM and the processor speed.

Describe Types of Application Software

Learning Outcomes
- Define application software
- Identify types of application software

Application software enables you to perform specific tasks such as writing letters, creating presentations, analyzing statistics, creating graphics, enhancing photos, and much more. **CASE** ▷ *You'll look at some of the most common application software.*

DETAILS

Typical application software includes the following:

Document production software, which includes word-processing software (such as Microsoft Word) and desktop publishing software (Microsoft Publisher), allows you to write and format text documents. As shown in **FIGURE 0-25**, these tools offer automatic spell checking. You can also customize the look of a document by changing its **font** (the design of the typeface in which text is set) or by adding color and images.

QUICK TIP

In Excel, a workbook is a file made up of multiple worksheets. The terms spreadsheet and worksheet are often used interchangeably.

Spreadsheet software is a numerical analysis tool that displays data in a grid of **cells** arranged in columns and rows. This grid is called a **worksheet**. You can type data into the worksheet's cells, and then enter mathematical formulas that reference that data. **FIGURE 0-26** shows a typical worksheet in Microsoft Excel that includes a simple calculation along with a graph that represents the data in the spreadsheet.

Database management software, such as Microsoft Access, lets you collect and manage data. A **database** is a collection of information organized in a uniform format of fields and records. A **field** contains one piece of information, such as a person's first name. A **record** contains multiple fields and can therefore store a person's full name and address. The online catalog of books at a library is a database that contains one record for each book; each record contains fields that identify the title, the author, and the subjects under which the book is classified.

Presentation software allows you to create a visual slide show to accompany a lecture, demonstration, or training session. In Microsoft PowerPoint, each presentation slide can contain text, illustrations, diagrams, charts, audio, and video. Slide shows can be projected in front of an audience, delivered over the Web, or transmitted to remote computers.

Multimedia authoring software allows you to record and manipulate image files, audio files, and video files. **Graphics software**, such as Microsoft Paint, lets you create illustrations, diagrams, graphs, and charts. **Photo-editing software** allows you to manipulate digital photos; you can make images brighter, add special effects, or crop photos to include only important parts of the image. Examples include Microsoft Photos and Adobe Photoshop. **Video-editing software**, such as Windows Movie Maker or Adobe Premiere, allows you to edit video by clipping it, adding captions and a soundtrack, or rearranging clips.

Information and task management software helps you schedule appointments, manage your address book, and manage projects. Microsoft Outlook is email software that also helps you maintain a contact list and calendar, and allows you to synchronize information between a smartphone and your computer. Microsoft OneNote lets you capture ideas, create To Do lists, and share notes with others.

Website creation and management software allows you to build websites and mobile apps using technologies that include **HTML (Hypertext Markup Language)** and **CSS (Cascading Style Sheets)**, the primary languages of Web design. Adobe Dreamweaver allows you to see how the site will appear as you create it.

FIGURE 0-25: Automatic spell checking in Microsoft Word

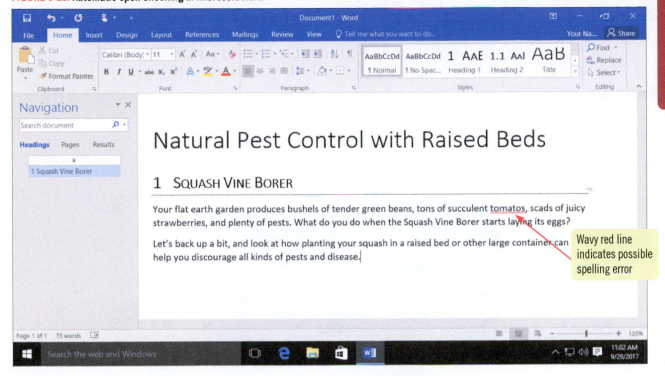

Wavy red line indicates possible spelling error

FIGURE 0-26: Editing a worksheet in Microsoft Excel

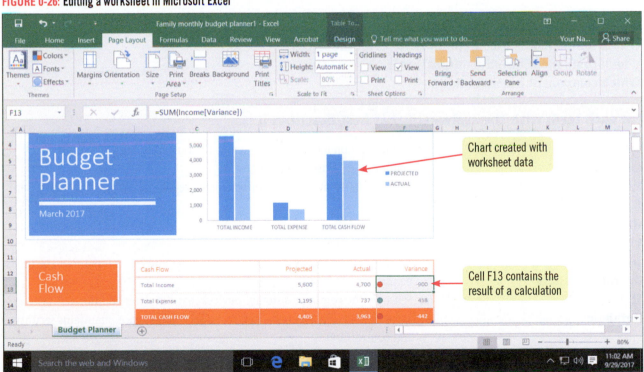

Chart created with worksheet data

Cell F13 contains the result of a calculation

Practice

Concepts Review

Answer the following questions based on the elements labeled in FIGURE 0-27**.**

FIGURE 0-27

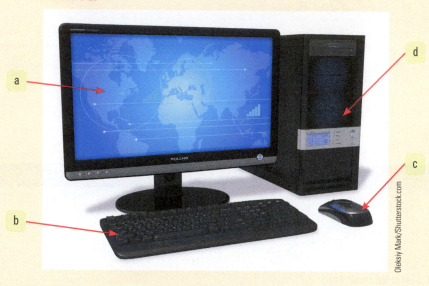

Oleksiy Mark/Shutterstock.com

1. Which component is used to enter text?
2. Which component is used to point to items on the screen?
3. Which component displays output?
4. Which component processes data?

Match each term with the statement that best describes it.

5. Spyware
6. Commands
7. Expansion slot
8. RAM
9. Hard disk
10. Virtual memory
11. Server
12. Operating system
13. SSD
14. Database

a. A computer on a network that acts as the central storage location for programs and data used on the network

b. Based on flash memory and intended as a replacement for a traditional hard disk drive

c. Location on the motherboard into which a controller card for a peripheral device is inserted

d. Secretly gathers information from a computer and sends it without the user's permission

e. Space on the computer's storage devices that simulates additional RAM

f. Software that allocates resources, manages storage space, maintains security, and controls I/O

g. Magnetic storage media that is usually sealed in a case inside the computer

h. A collection of information stored on one or more computers organized in a uniform format of records and fields

i. Temporarily holds data and programs while the computer is on

j. Input instructions that tell the computer how to process data

Understanding Essential Computer Concepts

Select the best answer from the list of choices.

15. **Which of the following is considered volatile or temporary memory?**
    a. RAM
    b. SSD
    c. HDD
    d. ROM

16. **To display graphics, a computer needs a monitor and a:**
    a. Network card (NIC).
    b. Sound card.
    c. Graphics card or graphics processor.
    d. USB cable.

17. **What part of the computer is responsible for executing instructions to process information?**
    a. ROM
    b. Card
    c. Motherboard
    d. CPU

18. **What are the technical details about each hardware component called?**
    a. Configuration
    b. Specifications
    c. Circuits
    d. Architecture

19. **What do you call each 1 or 0 used in the representation of computer data?**
    a. A bit
    b. A quark
    c. A kilobyte
    d. A byte

20. **Which of the following is a pointing device that allows you to control the pointer by moving the entire device around on a desk?**
    a. Scroll wheel
    b. Trackpad
    c. Mouse
    d. Trackball

21. **The programs and data routines that a computer uses to perform tasks are called:**
    a. Specifications.
    b. Peripherals.
    c. Hardware.
    d. Software.

22. **What is a megabyte?**
    a. About a million bytes
    b. About a million bits
    c. About half of a gigabyte
    d. 100 kilobytes

23. **Keyboards, monitors, and printers are all examples of which of the following?**
    a. Peripheral devices
    b. Input devices
    c. Output devices
    d. Data communications

24. **Which of the following permanently stores the set of instructions that the computer uses to activate the software that controls the processing function when you turn the computer on?**
    a. CPU cache
    b. RAM
    c. The hard disk
    d. ROM

25. **Which of the following acts as a locked door on a computer?**
    a. DNS server
    b. Firewall
    c. Antivirus software
    d. Browser

26. **Which one of the following would not be considered a personal computer?**
    a. Mainframe
    b. Desktop
    c. Laptop
    d. Tablet

27. **Which of the following is not a permanent storage medium?**
    a. DVD
    b. CD-ROM
    c. Hard disk
    d. RAM

28. **Which of the following is the data path between the microprocessor, RAM, and the peripherals?**
    a. Data channel
    b. Motherboard
    c. Data bus
    d. Cable

29. **The transmission protocol between a computer and a peripheral device is handled by a:**
   a. Data bus
   b. Channel
   c. Controller card
   d. Driver

30. **The computer that originates a message to send to another computer is called the:**
   a. Sender
   b. Receiver
   c. Firewall
   d. Server

31. **Any device connected to a network is called a:**
   a. Node
   b. Router
   c. Workstation
   d. Modem

32. **Which of the following is space on the computer's storage devices that simulates additional RAM?**
   a. Solid-state memory
   b. Cache memory
   c. Volatile memory
   d. Virtual memory

33. **A _____ consists of connected computers and peripheral devices that are located relatively close to each other.**
   a. WLAN
   b. WAN
   c. LAN
   d. PAN

34. **When data, applications, and resources are stored on servers rather than on users' computers, it is referred to as:**
   a. Shared computing
   b. Cloud computing
   c. Leased computing
   d. Cluster computing

35. **A website that's been set up to look exactly like another website, with the intention of convincing customers to enter their personal information, is a _____ site.**
   a. Phished
   b. Malware
   c. Spoofed
   d. Pharmed

Independent Challenge 1

To run the newest software, many people need to upgrade their existing computer system or purchase a brand new one. But what do you do with your old computer if you buy a new one? Most municipalities have enacted laws regulating the disposal of electronics. Research these laws in your city and state, and write a brief report describing them.
Note: To complete the Independent Challenge, your computer must be connected to the Internet.

a. Start your browser, go to your favorite search engine, and then search for information about laws regarding the disposal of electronics in your city and state. Try searching your city's official Web site for the information, or use **electronics disposal laws** followed by your city name as a search term and then repeat that search using your state's name.

b. Open each website that you find in a separate browser tab or window.

c. Read the information on each website. Can some components be thrown away? Are there laws that apply only to display monitors? Are the laws different for individuals and businesses? Does the size of the business matter? Are manufacturers or resellers required to accept used components they manufactured or sold?

d. Search for organizations you can donate your computer to. How do these organizations promise to protect your privacy? Can you take a deduction on your federal income tax for your donation?

e. Write a short report describing your findings. Include the URLs for all relevant websites. (*Hint*: If you are using a word processor to write your report, you can copy the URLs from your browser and paste them into the document. Drag to select the entire URL in the Address or Location bar in your browser. Right-click the selected text, then click Copy on the shortcut menu. Position the insertion point in the document where you want the URL to appear, then press [Ctrl][V] to paste it.)

Independent Challenge 2

New instances of malware and hacks are reported on an almost daily basis. If you surf the Internet or exchange e-mail, it's important to use antivirus software and to keep it updated. Research the most current malware threats, and create a table that lists them along with details about each threat. *Note: To complete the Independent Challenge, your computer must be connected to the Internet.*

a. Start your browser, go to **www.microsoft.com**, then in the Search text box, type "Malware Protection Center" and press Enter. In the list of search results, select "Microsoft Malware Protection Center Home Page" and then read about the MMPC and its mission.

b. Click the Malware encyclopedia menu, click the "Top threats" link, and then read about some prevalent threats, including the Summary and Technical information provided for each threat.

c. Open a new word-processing document, and create a table that lists five different threats (may include ransomware, families, rogues, exploits, etc.). Include a description of what each threat does, and how damaging it is considered to be (the alert level). Also note any steps you can take to prevent the threat, along with ways to recover an infected computer.

d. Use your search engine to find three different antivirus programs that can be installed on your computer. In your word-processing document, create a new section that lists the programs you found. Include the benefits and costs of using each program.

Independent Challenge 3

You've decided to buy a new desktop or laptop computer to run Windows 10 and Microsoft Office. *Note: To complete the Independent Challenge, your computer must be connected to the Internet.*

a. To help you organize your search, create the table shown below.

	Your Requirements	Computer Retailer 1	Computer Retailer 2	Computer Retailer 3
Windows 10 (Edition)				
Office 2016 (Edition)				
Brand of computer				
Model number				
Processor speed				
RAM (amount)				
Video RAM/Graphics specifications				
Hard disk/SSD (capacity and speed)				
Display (type and size)				
Printer (type and speed)				
Antivirus software				
Firewall (software or router with built-in firewall)				
System price				
Additional costs				
Total price				

b. Decide which edition of Windows 10 you want, and enter it in the Your Requirements column of the table. To read a description of the available editions, go to **www.microsoft.com** and search the site for information about the different editions (Windows 10 Home or Pro).

c. Research the hardware requirements for running the edition of Windows 10 you selected. Search the Microsoft Web site again for features that may require specific hardware (such as a fingerprint reader).

d. Decide which edition of Office you want, and enter it in the first column of the table. Search the Microsoft Web site to find a description of the software titles included with each edition of Office, and then search for the hardware requirements for running the edition of Office that you chose. If necessary, change the hardware requirements in the table.

Independent Challenge 3 (continued)

e. Research the cost of your new computer. To begin, visit local stores, look at advertisements, or search the Web for computer retailers. Most retailers sell complete systems that come with all the necessary hardware, an operating system, and additional software already installed. In the Computer Retailer 1 column of the table, fill in the specifications for the system you chose. If any item listed as a minimum requirement is not included with the system you chose, determine the cost of adding that item and enter the price in the table. Repeat this process with systems from two other retailers, entering the specifications in the Computer Retailer 2 and Computer Retailer 3 columns.

f. If the system you chose does not come with a printer, search the Web for a color inkjet printer.

g. Research the capabilities of the antivirus software that comes with Windows 10. If the system you chose does not come with additional antivirus software, search the Web for the cost, if any, of an antivirus software package. Make sure you look up reviews of the package you choose. Decide whether to purchase this software or use a free one, and enter this cost in the table.

h. Decide whether you need a separate router with a built-in firewall, or if you can use your computer's firewall. Search the Web for the price of routers with firewalls. Enter this information in the table.

i. Determine the total cost for each of the three systems in your table. If the costs exceed your budget, think about items you can downgrade. Can you get a less expensive printer or share someone else's printer? Would a less expensive display still provide the room you need to work? On the other hand, if the total costs come in under your budget, you may be able to upgrade your system; perhaps you can afford a larger display with better resolution or a better mouse or keyboard.

Independent Challenge 4: Explore

As you have learned, Cloud storage allows you to store documents and images on remote servers. You then have access to these items from any compatible device that is connected to the Internet. You need to decide which cloud service is best for you. *Note: To complete this Independent Challenge, your computer must be connected to the Internet.*

a. Use your favorite search engine to locate the sites for Microsoft OneDrive, Apple iCloud, Google Drive, and Dropbox. If there is another service you'd like to investigate, include it as well (e.g., Amazon Cloud Drive).

b. To help you compare the different services, create the table shown below.

	OneDrive	iCloud	Google Drive	Dropbox
Free storage capacity				
Paid storage capacity				
Paid storage cost				
Maximum file size				
Syncs to all your devices? (PC/Mac, mobile)				
Supports version tracking?				
Mobile apps provided*				
Additional features/notes				

*List all known mobile operating systems for which the service provides an app, such as Android, iOS, or Windows Phone.

c. Enter details in the table using the information available on each service's website.

d. Search for online reviews and comparisons of each cloud service, and note any additional information that you feel is important. For example, if you have a large music collection on your computer, is it compatible with each service?

e. Based on your research, explain which service would best serve your needs and why.

Getting Started with Windows 10

CASE You are about to start a new job, and your employer has asked you to get familiar with Windows 10 to help boost your productivity. You'll need to start Windows 10 and Windows apps, work with on-screen windows and commands, get help, and exit Windows. *Note: With the release of Windows 10, Microsoft now provides ongoing updates to Windows instead of releasing new versions periodically. This means that Windows features might change over time, including how they look and how you interact with them. The information provided in this text was accurate at the time this book was published.*

Module Objectives

After completing this module, you will be able to:

- Start Windows 10
- Navigate the desktop and Start menu
- Point, click, and drag
- Start an app
- Work with a window

- Manage multiple windows
- Use buttons, menus, and dialog boxes
- Get help
- Exit Windows 10

Files You Will Need

No files needed.

Start Windows 10

**Learning
Outcomes**
• Power on a
computer
• Log into
Windows 10

Windows 10 is an **operating system**, a type of program that runs your computer and lets you interact with it. A **program** is a set of instructions written for a computer. If your computer did not have an operating system, you wouldn't see anything on the screen after you turned it on. Windows 10 reserves a special area called a **Microsoft account** where each user can keep his or her files. In addition, a Microsoft account lets you use various devices and services such as a Windows Phone or Outlook.com. You may have more than one Microsoft account. When the computer and Windows 10 start, you need to **sign in**, or select your Microsoft account name and enter a password, also called **logging in**. If your computer has only one Microsoft account, you won't need to select an account name. But all users need to enter a **password**, a special sequence of numbers and letters. Users cannot see each other's account areas or services without the other person's password, so passwords help keep your computer information secure. After you sign in, you see the Windows 10 desktop, which you learn about in the next lesson. **CASE** ▶ *You're about to start a new job, so you decide to learn more about Windows 10, the operating system used at your new company.*

STEPS

1. **Press your computer's power button, which might look like ⊙ or ▭▯, then if the monitor is not turned on, press its power button**

   On a desktop computer, the power button is probably on the front panel. On a laptop computer it's likely at the top of the keys on your keyboard. After a few moments, a **lock screen**, showing the date, time, and an image, appears. See **FIGURE 1-1**. The lock screen appears when you first start your computer and also if you leave it unattended for a period of time.

2. **Press [Spacebar], or click once to display the sign-in screen**

   The **sign-in screen** shows your Windows account picture, name, and e-mail address, as well as a space to enter your Microsoft account password. The account may have your name assigned to it, or it might have a general name like "Student" or "Lab User."

3. **Type your password, as shown in FIGURE 1-2, using uppercase and lowercase letters as necessary**

   If necessary, ask your instructor or technical support person what password you should use. Passwords are **case sensitive**, which means that if you type any letter using capital letters when lowercase letters are needed, or vice versa, Windows will not let you use your account. For example, if your password is "booklet43+", typing "Booklet43+" or "BOOKLET43+" will not let you enter your account. For security, Windows substitutes bullets for the password characters you type.

4. **Click or tap the Submit button →**

   The Windows 10 desktop appears. See **FIGURE 1-3**.

Using a touch screen with Windows

Windows 10 was developed to work with touch-screen computers, including tablets and smartphones. See **FIGURE 1-4**. So if you have a touch-screen device, you'll find that you can accomplish many tasks with gestures instead of a mouse. A **gesture** is an action you take with your fingertip directly on the screen, such as tapping or swiping. For example, when you sign into Windows 10, you can tap the Submit button on the screen, instead of clicking it.

FIGURE 1-4: Touch-screen device

© vovan/Shutterstock.com

FIGURE 1-1: Lock screen with time and date

Your lock screen contents may differ

10:49
Friday, July 31

FIGURE 1-2: Typing your password

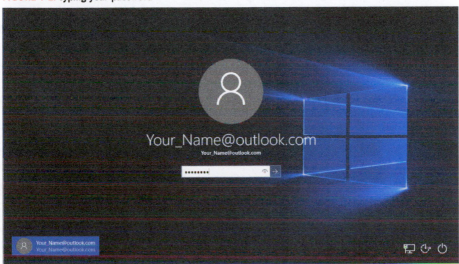

Your_Name@outlook.com
Your_Name@outlook.com

Your_Name@outlook.com
Your_Name@outlook.com

FIGURE 1-3: Windows 10 desktop

Recycle Bin

Ask me anything

Navigate the Desktop and Start Menu

Learning Outcomes
• Examine the desktop
• Open the Start menu
• View Start menu apps
• Close the Start menu

Every time you start your computer and sign in, the Windows 10 desktop appears. The **Windows 10 desktop** is an electronic work area that lets you organize and manage your information, much like your own physical desktop. The desktop contains controls that let you interact with the Windows 10 operating system. These controls are called its **user interface (UI)**. The Windows 10 user interface is called the **Windows 10 UI**. **CASE** *To become better acquainted with Windows 10, you decide to explore the desktop and Start menu.*

STEPS

TROUBLE

If you don't see the taskbar at the bottom of the screen, it may be set to automatically hide. Move the mouse pointer to the bottom edge of the screen to display it; on a touch screen, swipe up from the bottom of the screen.

1. **Examine the Windows 10 desktop**

   As shown in **FIGURE 1-5**, the desktop currently contains one item, an icon representing the **Recycle Bin**, an electronic wastepaper basket. You might see other icons, files, and folders placed there by previous users or by your school lab. The desktop lets you manage the files and folders on your computer. A **file** is a collection of stored information, such as a letter, video, or program. A **folder** is a container that helps you organize your files. A file, folder, or program opens in a window. You can open multiple windows on the desktop at once, and you can move them around so you can easily go back and forth between them. You work with windows later in this module. At the bottom of the screen is a bar called the **taskbar**, with buttons representing commonly used programs and tools. In a default Windows installation, the taskbar contains four buttons, described in **TABLE 1-1**. Also on the taskbar is the search box, which you can use to find an item on your computer or the Internet. On the right side of the status bar you see the **Notification area**, containing the time and date as well as icons that tell you the status of your computer. At the left side of the taskbar, you see the Start button. You click the **Start button** to display the **Start menu**, which lets you start the programs on your computer.

QUICK TIP

To add a button to the taskbar, right-click or tap and hold a Start menu item, then click or tap Pin to taskbar.

2. **Move the pointer to the left side of the taskbar, then click or tap the Start button** ⊞

   The Start menu appears, as shown in **FIGURE 1-6**. Your user account name and an optional picture appear at the top. The menu shows a list of often-used programs and other controls on the left, and variously-sized shaded rectangles called **tiles** on the right. Each tile represents an **app**, short for **application program**. Some tiles show updated content using a feature called **live tile**; for example, the Weather app can show the current weather for any city you choose. (Your screen color and tiles may differ from the figures shown here. Note that the screens in this book do not show live tiles.)

QUICK TIP

You can also click or tap any category letter to display a grid of clickable or tappable letters. Or just begin typing any program name, and it appears at the top of a list of choices.

3. **Move the pointer near the bottom of the Start menu, then click or tap the All apps button**

   You see an alphabetical listing of all the apps on your computer. Only some of the apps are visible.

4. **Move the pointer into the list, until the gray scroll bar appears on the right side of the list, place the pointer over the scroll box, press and hold down the mouse button, then drag to display the remaining programs; on a touch screen, swipe the list to scroll**

5. **Click or tap the Back button at the bottom of the Start menu**

   The previous listing reappears.

QUICK TIP

You can quickly open and close the Start menu by pressing ⊞ on your keyboard.

6. **Move the pointer back up over the desktop, then click or tap once to close the Start menu**

Getting Started with Windows 10

FIGURE 1-5: Windows 10 desktop

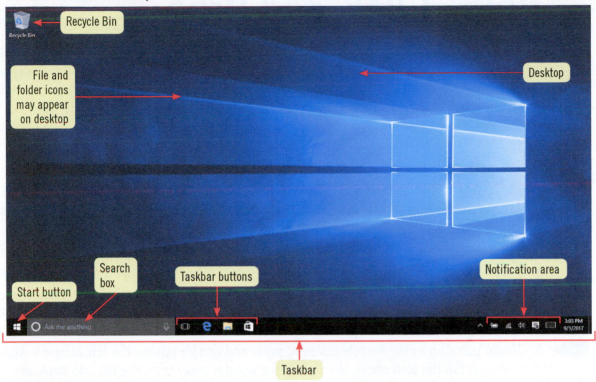

Recycle Bin

File and folder icons may appear on desktop

Desktop

Search box

Start button

Taskbar buttons

Notification area

Taskbar

FIGURE 1-6: Start menu

Tiles representing Windows apps

List of programs you use the most

Start menu

All apps button

Search box

Photos app

TABLE 1-1: Windows taskbar buttons

button	looks like	what it does
Task View		Shows miniatures of all open windows and lets you create multiple desktops, so you can switch from one to another
Microsoft Edge		Opens the Microsoft Edge web browser
File Explorer		Lets you explore the files in your storage locations
Store		Opens the Windows Store featuring downloadable apps, games, music, movies, and TV

Point, Click, and Drag

You communicate with Windows 10 using a variety of pointing devices (or, with a touch-screen device, your finger). A **pointing device** controls the movement of the **pointer**, a small arrow or other symbol that moves on the screen. Your pointing device could be a mouse, trackball, graphics tablet, or touchpad. There are five basic **pointing device actions** you use to communicate with your computer; see **TABLE 1-2**. Touch-screen users can tap, press, and tap and hold. **CASE** *You practice the basic pointing device actions.*

STEPS

1. **Locate the pointer ⤹ on the desktop, then move your pointing device left, right, up, and down (or move your finger across a touch pad or screen)**

   The pointer shape ⤹ is the **Select pointer**. The pointer moves in the same direction as your device.

2. **Move your pointing device so the Select pointer is over the Recycle Bin (if you are using a touch screen, skip this step)**

   You are **pointing to** the Recycle Bin icon. The icon becomes **highlighted**, looking as though it is framed in a box with a lighter color background. (Note that touch-screen users cannot point to items.)

3. **While pointing to the Recycle Bin icon, press and quickly release the left mouse button once (or tap the icon once), then move the pointer away from the Recycle Bin icon**

   You click or tap a desktop icon once to **select** it, which signals that you intend to perform an action. When an icon is selected, its background changes color and maintains the new color even when you point away from it.

4. **With a pointing device, point to (don't click) the Microsoft Edge button e on the taskbar**

   The button becomes highlighted and an informational message called a **ScreenTip** identifies the program the button represents. ScreenTips are useful because they help you to learn about the tools available to you. **Microsoft Edge** is the new Microsoft web browser that lets you display and interact with webpages.

5. **If you are using a pointing device, move the pointer over the time and date in the notification area on the right side of the taskbar, read the ScreenTip, then click or tap once**

   A pop-up window appears, containing the current time and date and a calendar.

6. **Click or tap on the desktop, point to the Recycle Bin icon, then quickly click or tap twice**

   You **double-clicked** (or double-tapped) the icon. You need to double-click or double-tap quickly, without moving the pointer. A window opens, showing the contents of the Recycle Bin, as shown in **FIGURE 1-7**. The area at the top of the window is the title bar, which displays the name of the window. The area below the title bar is the **Ribbon**, which contains tabs, commands, and the Address bar. **Tabs** are groupings of **buttons** and other controls you use to interact with an object or a program.

7. **Click or tap the View tab**

   The buttons on that tab appear. Buttons act as **commands**, which instruct Windows to perform tasks. The **Address bar** shows the name and location of the item you have opened.

8. **Point to the Close button ☒ on the title bar, read the ScreenTip, then click or tap once**

9. **Point to the Recycle Bin icon, hold down the left mouse button, or press and hold the Recycle Bin image with your finger, move the mouse or drag so the object moves right as shown in FIGURE 1-8, release the mouse button or lift your finger, then drag the Recycle Bin back to its original location**

Getting Started with Windows 10

FIGURE 1-7: Recycle Bin window

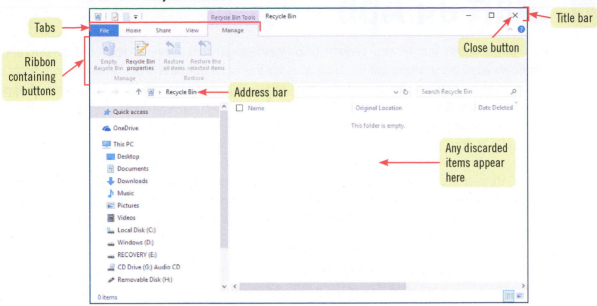

Tabs

Ribbon containing buttons

Address bar

Any discarded items appear here

Title bar

Close button

FIGURE 1-8: Dragging the Recycle Bin icon

Releasing mouse button moves object to this location

TABLE 1-2: Basic pointing device actions

action	with a mouse	with a touch pad	use to
Point	Move mouse to position tip of pointer over an item	Move your finger over touch pad to position tip of pointer over an item	Highlight items or display small informational boxes called ScreenTips
Click	Press and release left mouse button once	Tap touch pad once	Select objects or commands, open menus or items on the taskbar
Double-click	Quickly press and release left mouse button twice	Tap touch pad twice in quick succession	Open programs, folders, or files represented by desktop icons
Drag	Point to an object, press and hold down left mouse button, move object to a new location, then release mouse button	Slide finger across touch pad to point to an object, press and hold left touch pad button, drag across touch pad to move object to new location, then release button	Move objects, such as icons, on the desktop
Right-click	Point to an object, then press and release right mouse button	Point to an object, then press and release right touchpad button	Display a shortcut menu containing options specific to the object

Selecting and moving items using touch-screen devices

If you use a touch-screen computer, a tablet, or a smartphone, you click desktop items by tapping them once on the screen. Tap an icon twice quickly to double-click and open its window. Press and hold an icon, then drag to move it. A touch-screen device does not let you point to an object without selecting it, however, as mice and touchpads do.

Getting Started with Windows 10

Start an App

Apps are programs that let you perform tasks. Windows 10 runs Windows apps and desktop apps. **Windows apps** are small programs that are available free or for purchase in the Windows Store, and can run on Windows desktops, laptops, tablets, and phones. Windows apps are also called **universal apps**. They are specially designed so they can stay open as you work without slowing down your computer, and often have a single purpose. Examples include the Photos app, which lets you view your photographs, and the OneDrive app, which lets you connect to files and programs you have stored on the Microsoft OneDrive website. **Desktop apps** are fully-featured programs; they may be available at an online store or on disk. For example, Microsoft Word allows you to create and edit letters, reports, and other text-based documents. Some smaller desktop apps called **Windows accessories**, such as Paint and Notepad, come already installed in Windows 10. **CASE** ▶ *To prepare for your new job, you start three apps.*

STEPS

1. **Click or tap the Start button ⊞, then click or tap the Weather tile, shown in FIGURE 1-9**
   The Weather app opens, letting you find the current weather in various locations.

2. **If you are asked to choose a location, begin typing your city or town, then click the full name if it appears in the drop-down list**
   The current weather for your selected city appears in Summary view. **FIGURE 1-10** shows a forecast for Boston, MA.

3. **Click or tap the Weather app window's Close button ⊠**

4. **Click or tap ⊞, then type onenote**
   Typing an app name is another way to locate an app. At the top of the Start menu, you see the OneNote Trusted Windows Store app listed, as shown in **FIGURE 1-11**. OneNote is a popular app that lets you create tabbed notebooks where you can store text, images, files, and media such as audio and video.

5. **Click or tap the OneNote Trusted Windows Store app name**
   The OneNote app opens, showing a blank notebook (or a notebook you have previously created).

6. **Click or tap the Close button ⊠ in the upper right corner of the OneNote app window**
   You have opened two Windows apps, Weather and OneNote.

7. **Click or tap ⊞, then type paint**
   The top of the Start menu lists the Paint Desktop app, shown in **FIGURE 1-12**. Paint is a simple accessory that comes installed with Windows and lets you create simple illustrations.

8. **Click or tap the Paint Desktop app name at the top of the Start menu**
   Other accessories besides Paint and Notepad include the Snipping Tool, which lets you capture an image of any screen area, and Sticky Notes, that let you create short notes.

Using the Windows Store

The Windows Store is an app that lets you find all kinds of apps for use on Windows personal computers, tablets, and phones. You can open it by clicking or tapping its tile on the Start menu or by clicking or tapping the Store button on the taskbar. To use the Windows Store, you need to be signed in to your Microsoft account. You can browse lists of popular apps, games, music, movies, and TV including new releases; you can browse the top paid or free apps. Browse app categories to find a specific type of app, such as Business or Entertainment. To locate a specific app, type its name in the Search box. If an app is free, you can go to its page and click the Free button to install it on your computer. If it's a paid app, you can click or tap the Free trial button to try it out, or click or tap its price button to purchase it. Any apps you've added recently appear in the Recently added category of the Start menu.

FIGURE 1-9: Weather tile on the Start menu

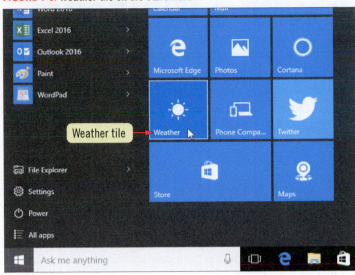

FIGURE 1-10: Weather app

FIGURE 1-11: OneNote Windows app name on Start menu

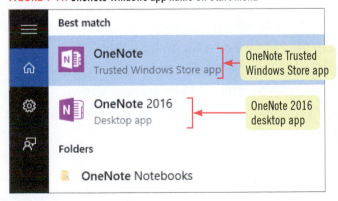

FIGURE 1-12: Paint Desktop app name on Start menu

Work with a Window

Learning Outcomes
- Minimize, restore, and maximize a window
- Scroll a window
- Move a window

When you start an app, its **window**, a frame displaying the app's tools, opens. In many apps, a blank file also opens so you can start creating a new document. For example, in Paint, a blank document opens so you can start drawing right away. All windows in the Windows 10 operating system have similar window elements. Once you can use a window in one app, you will know how to work with windows in many other apps. **CASE** ▶ *To become more familiar with the Windows 10 user interface, you explore elements in the Paint window.*

DETAILS

Many windows have the following common elements. Refer to FIGURE 1-13:

- At the top of the window, you see a **title bar**, a strip that contains the name of the document and app. This document has not been saved, so it has the temporary name "Untitled" and the app name is "Paint."

- On the right side of the title bar, the **Window control buttons** let you control the app window. The **Minimize button** ⊟ temporarily hides the window, making it a button on the taskbar. The app is still running, but its window is temporarily hidden until you click its taskbar button or its miniature window in Task view to reopen it. The **Maximize button** ☐ enlarges the window to fill the entire screen. If a window is already maximized, the Maximize button changes to the **Restore Down button** ❐, which reduces it to the last non-maximized size. Clicking or tapping the **Close button** ✕ closes the app.

- Many windows have a **scroll bar** on the right side and/or the bottom of the window. You click (or press) and drag scroll bar elements to show additional parts of your document. See **TABLE 1-3**.

- Just below the title bar is the Ribbon, a bar containing tabs as well as a Help icon. The Paint window has three tabs: File, Home, and View. Tabs are divided into **groups** of buttons and tool palettes. The Home tab has five groups: Clipboard, Image, Tools, Shapes, and Colors. Many apps also include **menus** you click to show lists of commands, as well as **toolbars** containing buttons.

- The **Quick Access toolbar** lets you quickly perform common actions such as saving a file.

STEPS

1. **Click or tap the Paint window Minimize button** ⊟
   The app is reduced to a taskbar button, as shown in **FIGURE 1-14**. The contrasting line indicates the app is still open.

2. **Click or tap the taskbar button representing the Paint app** 🎨 **to redisplay the app**

3. **Drag the gray scroll box down, notice the lower edge of the work area that appears, then click or tap the Up scroll arrow** ⌃ **until you see the top edge of the work area**

4. **Point to the View tab, then click or tap the View tab once**
   Clicking or tapping the View tab moved it in front of the Home tab. This tab has three groups containing buttons that let you change your view of the document window.

5. **Click the Home tab, then click or tap the Paint window Maximize button** ☐
   The window fills the screen, and the Maximize button becomes the Restore Down button ❐.

6. **Click the window's Restore Down button** ❐ **to return it to its previous size**

7. **Point to the Paint window title bar (if you are using a pointing device), then drag about an inch to the right to move it so it's centered on the screen**

FIGURE 1-13: Typical app window elements

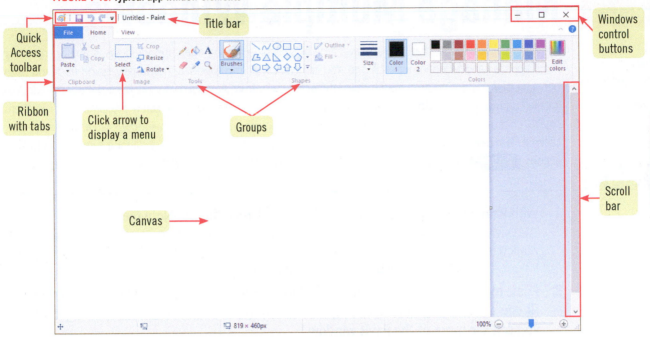

Quick Access toolbar

Ribbon with tabs

Click arrow to display a menu

Groups

Title bar

Windows control buttons

Scroll bar

Canvas

Windows 10

FIGURE 1-14: Taskbar with minimized Paint program button

Buttons without contrasting lines represent programs that are not open

Paint program button with contrasting line indicating program is open

Your buttons may differ

TABLE 1-3: Parts of a scroll bar

name	looks like	to use
Scroll box	☐ (Size may vary)	Drag to scroll quickly through a long document
Scroll arrows	⌃ ⌄	Click or tap to scroll up, down, left, or right in small amounts
Shaded area	(Above, below, or to either side of scroll box)	Click or tap to move up or down by one screen

Using the Quick Access toolbar

On the left side of the title bar, the Quick Access toolbar lets you perform common tasks with just one click. The Save button 💾 saves the changes you have made to a document. The Undo button ↩ lets you reverse (undo) the last action you performed.

The Redo button ↪ reinstates the change you just undid. Use the Customize Quick Access Toolbar button ▼ to add other frequently used buttons to the toolbar, move the toolbar below the Ribbon, or minimize the Ribbon to show only tabs.

Manage Multiple Windows

You can work with more than one app at a time by switching among open app windows. If you open two or more apps, a window opens for each one. You can work with app windows individually, going back and forth between them. The window in front is called the **active window**. Any open window behind the active window is called an **inactive window**. For ease in working with multiple windows, you can move, arrange, make them smaller or larger, minimize, or restore them so they're not in the way. To resize a window, drag a window's edge, called its **border**. You can use the taskbar to switch between windows. See **TABLE 1-4** for a summary of taskbar actions. **CASE** *Keeping the Paint app open, you open the OneNote app and then work with both app windows.*

STEPS

1. **With Paint open, click or tap the Start button 🪟, then the OneNote tile**

   The OneNote window appears as a second window on the desktop, as shown in **FIGURE 1-15**. The OneNote window is in front, indicating that it is the active window. The Paint window is the inactive window. On the taskbar, the contrasting line under the OneNote and Paint app buttons tell you both apps are open.

2. **Point to a blank part of the OneNote window title bar on either side of the app name (if you are using a pointing device), then drag the OneNote window down slightly so you can see more of the Paint window**

3. **Click or tap once on the Paint window's title bar**

   The Paint window is now the active window and appears in front of the OneNote window. You can make any window active by clicking or tapping it, or by clicking or tapping an app's icon in the taskbar.

4. **Point to the taskbar if you are using a pointing device, then click or tap the OneNote window button**

   The OneNote window becomes active. When you open multiple windows on the desktop, you may need to resize windows so they don't get in the way of other open windows.

5. **Point to the lower-right corner of the OneNote window until the pointer changes to ⬂, if you are using a pointing device, or tap and press the corner, then drag down and to the right about an inch to make the window larger**

   You can also point to any edge of a window until you see the ↔ or ↕ pointer, or tap and press any edge, then drag to make it larger or smaller in one direction only.

6. **Click or tap the Task View button ▭ on the taskbar, click or tap the Paint window, click or tap ▭ again, then click or tap the OneNote window**

   The **Task View button** is another convenient way to switch among open windows.

7. **Point to the OneNote window title bar if you are using a pointing device, drag the window to the left side of the screen until the pointer or your finger reaches the screen edge and you see a vertical line down the middle of the screen, then release the mouse button or lift your finger from the screen**

   The OneNote window instantly fills the left side of the screen, and any inactive windows appear on the right side of the screen. This is called the **Snap Assist** feature. You can also drag to any screen corner to snap open app windows to quarter-screen windows.

8. **Click or tap anywhere on the reduced-size version of the Paint window**

   The Paint window fills the right side of the screen. Snapping makes it easy to view the contents of two windows at the same time. See **FIGURE 1-16**.

9. **Click or tap the OneNote window Close button ✕, then click or tap the Maximize button ▢ in the Paint window's title bar**

   The OneNote app closes. The Paint app window remains open.

FIGURE 1-15: Working with multiple windows

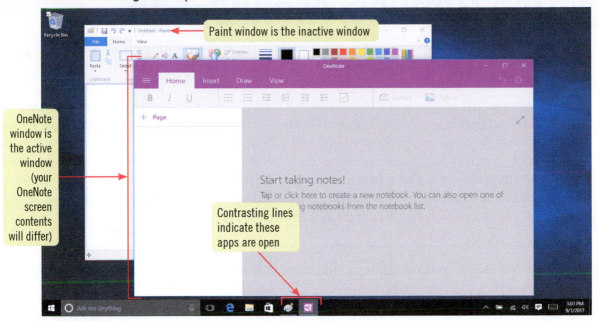

Paint window is the inactive window

OneNote window is the active window (your OneNote screen contents will differ)

Contrasting lines indicate these apps are open

FIGURE 1-16: OneNote and Paint windows snapped to each side of the screen

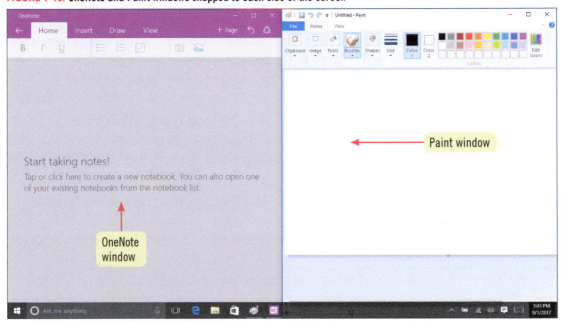

Paint window

OneNote window

TABLE 1-4: Using the taskbar

to	do this
Add buttons to taskbar	Open an app, right-click or press its icon on the taskbar, then click or tap Pin this program to taskbar
Change order of taskbar buttons	Drag any icon to a new taskbar location
See a list of recent documents opened	Right-click or press taskbar app button
Close a document using the taskbar	Point to taskbar button, point to document image, then click its Close button
Minimize/Redisplay all open windows	Click or press Show desktop button (the thin bar) to the right of taskbar date and time
See preview of documents in taskbar	With a pointing device, point to taskbar button for open app
Bring a minimized window to the front	Click or press the Task View button, then click or tap the window or desktop you want in front
Rearrange windows on the desktop	Right-click taskbar, click Cascade Windows, Show windows stacked, or Show windows side by side

Getting Started with Windows 10

Use Buttons, Menus, and Dialog Boxes

When you work in an app, you communicate with it using buttons, menus, and dialog boxes. **Buttons** let you issue instructions to modify app objects. Buttons are often organized on a Ribbon into tabs, and then into groups like those in the Paint window. Some buttons have text on them, and others show only an icon that represents what they do. Other buttons reveal **menus**, lists of commands you can choose. And some buttons open up a **dialog box**, a window with controls that lets you tell Windows what you want. **TABLE 1-5** lists the common types of controls you find in dialog boxes. **CASE** *You practice using buttons, menus, and dialog boxes to create some simple graphics in the Paint app.*

STEPS

1. In the Shapes group, click or tap the More button ⤓ just to the right of the shapes, then click the Triangle button △

2. Click or tap the Turquoise button ◼ in the Colors group, move the pointer or your finger over the white drawing area, then drag down and to the right, to draw a triangle similar to the one in **FIGURE 1-17**

   The white drawing area is called the **canvas**.

3. In the Shapes group, click or tap ⤓, click the down scroll arrow if necessary, click or tap the Five-point star button, click or tap the Indigo color button ◼ in the Colors group, then drag a star shape near the triangle, using **FIGURE 1-17** as a guide

   Don't be concerned if your object isn't exactly like the one in the figure, or in exactly the same place.

4. Click or tap the Fill with color button 🪣 in the Tools group, click or tap the Light turquoise color button ◻ in the Colors group, click or tap inside the triangle, click or tap the Purple color button ◼, click or tap inside the star, then compare your drawing to **FIGURE 1-17**

5. Click or tap the Select list arrow in the Image group, then click or tap Select all, as shown in **FIGURE 1-18**

   The Select all command selects the entire drawing, as indicated by the dotted line surrounding the white drawing area. Other commands on this menu let you select individual elements or change your selection.

6. Click or tap the Rotate button in the Image group, then click or tap Rotate 180°

   You often need to use multiple commands to perform an action—in this case, you used one command to select the items you wanted to work with, and another command to rotate them.

7. Click or tap the File tab, then click or tap Print

   The Print dialog box opens, as shown in **FIGURE 1-19**. This dialog box lets you choose a printer, specify which part of your document or drawing you want to print, and choose how many copies you want to print. The **default**, or automatically selected, number of copies is 1, which is what you want.

8. Click or tap Print, or if you prefer not to print, click or tap Cancel

   The drawing prints on your printer. You decide to close the app without saving your drawing.

9. Click or tap the File tab, click or tap Exit, then click or tap Don't Save

   You closed the file without saving your changes, then exited the app. Most apps include a command for closing a document without exiting the program. However, Paint allows you to open only one document at a time, so it does not include a Close command.

FIGURE 1-17: Triangle and star shapes filled with color

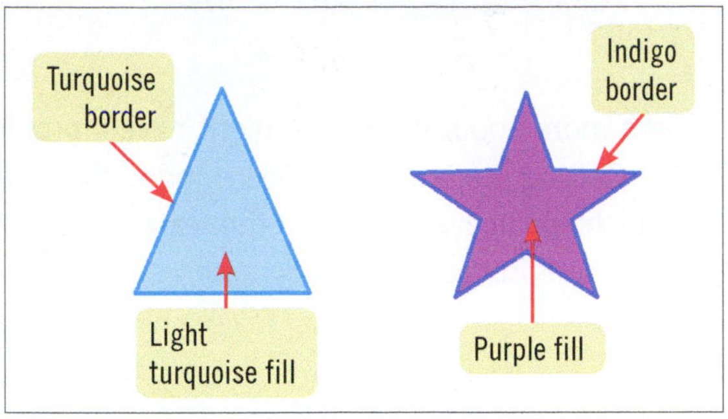

Turquoise border

Indigo border

Light turquoise fill

Purple fill

FIGURE 1-18: Select menu options

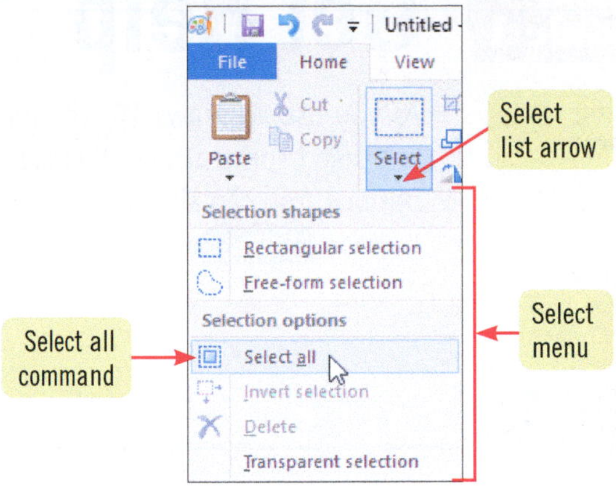

Select list arrow

Select all command

Select menu

FIGURE 1-19: Print dialog box

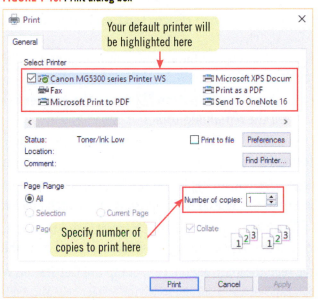

Your default printer will be highlighted here

Specify number of copies to print here

TABLE 1-5: Common dialog box controls

element	example	description
Text box	1 - 27	A box in which you type text or numbers
Spin box	1	A box with up and down arrows; you can click or tap arrows or type to increase or decrease value
Option button	●	A small circle you click or tap to select the option; only one in a set can be selected at once
Check box	☑	A small box that turns an option on when checked or off when unchecked; more than one in a set can be selected at once
List box		A box that lets you select from a list of options
Button	Save	A button you click or tap to issue a command

Get Help

As you use Windows 10, you might feel ready to learn more about it, or you might have a problem and need some advice. You can use the Windows 10 Getting Started app to learn more about help options. You can also search for help using Cortana, which you activate by using the search box on the taskbar. **CASE** ▸ *You explore Windows 10 help using the Get Started app and Cortana.*

STEPS

Note: Because Help in an online resource, topics and information are liable to change over time. If your screen choices do not match the steps below exactly, be flexible by exploring the options that are available to you and searching for the information you need.

1. Click or tap the Start button ⊞, then in the Explore Windows section click or tap the Get Started tile; if the Explore Windows section does not appear on your Start menu, begin typing Get Started, then click or tap Get Started Trusted Windows Store app in the list

   The Get Started app window opens. The window contains a menu expand button ☰ in the upper left and a bar containing buttons on the left side.

2. Click or tap the Menu Expand button ☰, move the pointer over the list of topics, then scroll down to see the remaining topics

3. Click or tap the Search and help topic, click the Search for anything, anywhere tile, then read the information, as shown in FIGURE 1-20, scrolling as necessary

4. Click or tap the Back button ← in the top-left corner of the window, click the Search for help tile, then read the Search for help topic and watch any available videos

5. Click or tap ☰, click or tap a topic that interests you, then read the information or click or tap one of the tiles representing a subtopic if one is available

6. After you have read the information, click or tap the Get started window's Close button ☒

   As the Help topic explained, you can also search the web for help with Windows using Cortana.

7. Click in the search box on the taskbar, then type windows help

   As you type, Cortana begins a search, and shows results on the Start menu. See FIGURE 1-21. Your results may also include topics from the Microsoft Store, the web, Store apps, and OneDrive, your online storage location.

8. Click any web option that interests you

9. When you are finished, click or tap the window's Close button ☒ to return to the desktop

FIGURE 1-20: Get Started Search and Help topic

Menu Expand button →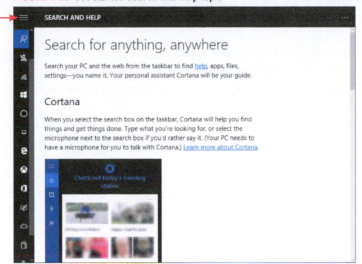

FIGURE 1-21: Search results information

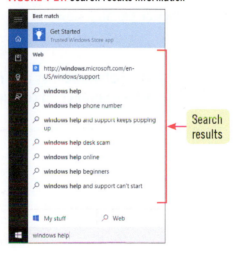

Search results

Using Cortana

Cortana is the digital personal assistant that comes with Windows 10 and Windows phones. You can interact with Cortana typing or using your voice. Use Cortana to search the web, remind you of events or appointments, set alarms, change computer settings, get directions, get current news and weather, track airline flights, play, and even identify music. **FIGURE 1-22** shows Cortana's response to "What's the weather in New York?" which may also give a voice response. You call Cortana by saying, "Hey Cortana," or by clicking or tapping the microphone icon on the right side of the taskbar search box, and then asking a question or saying a command. Depending on your request, Cortana may reply out loud, display results in the Start menu, or display results in a Microsoft Edge web browser window. You may need to set up Cortana on your computer and answer security questions before you use it. The first time you use Cortana, you may be asked to answer questions to help the assistant recognize your voice or solve issues with your computer's microphone.

FIGURE 1-22: Using Cortana to check the weather

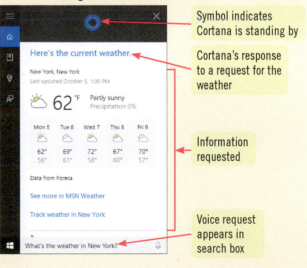

Symbol indicates Cortana is standing by

Cortana's response to a request for the weather

Information requested

Voice request appears in search box

Windows 10

Exit Windows 10

When you finish working on your computer, you should close any open files, exit any open apps, close any open windows, and exit (or **shut down**) Windows 10. **TABLE 1-6** shows options for ending your Windows 10 sessions. Whichever option you choose, it's important to shut down your computer in an orderly way. If you turn off or unplug the computer while Windows 10 is running, you could lose data or damage Windows 10 and your computer. If you are working in a computer lab, follow your instructor's directions and your lab's policies for ending your Windows 10 session. **CASE** *You have examined the basic ways you can use Windows 10, so you are ready to end your Windows 10 session.*

STEPS

QUICK TIP

Instead of shutting down, you may be instructed to sign out, or log out, of your Microsoft account. Click or tap Start, click or tap your account name, then click or tap Sign out.

1. **Click or tap the Start button ⊞, then click or tap Power**

   The Power button menu lists shut down options, as shown in **FIGURE 1-23**.

2. **If you are working in a computer lab, follow the instructions provided by your instructor or technical support person for ending your Windows 10 session; if you are working on your own computer, click or tap Shut down or the option you prefer for ending your Windows 10 session**

QUICK TIP

If you are using a Windows 10 tablet, press the lock button on your tablet to bring up the lock screen, swipe the lock screen, then click or tap the Shut down button to power off your computer.

3. **After you shut down your computer, you may also need to turn off your monitor and other hardware devices, such as a printer, to conserve energy**

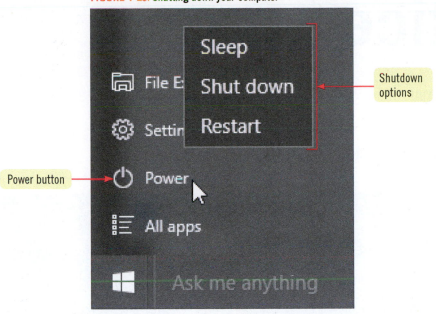

FIGURE 1-23: Shutting down your computer

Shutdown options

Power button

TABLE 1-6: Power options

option	description
Sleep	Puts computer in a low-power state while keeping any open apps open so you can return immediately to where you left off
Shut down	Closes any open apps and completely turns off the computer
Restart	Closes any open apps, shuts down the computer, then restarts it

Installing updates when you exit Windows

Sometimes, after you shut down your machine, you might find that your machine does not shut down immediately. Instead, Windows might install software updates. If you see an option on your Power menu that lets you update, you can click or tap it to update your software. If you see a window indicating that updates are being installed, do not unplug or press the power switch to turn off your machine. Let the updates install completely. After the updates are installed, your computer will shut down, as you originally requested.

Practice

Concepts Review

Label the elements of the Windows 10 window shown in FIGURE 1-24.

FIGURE 1-24

Match each term with the statement that best describes it.

  9. **Cortana**

10. **Snap Assist**

11. **Desktop app**

12. **Microsoft account**

13. **User interface**

14. **Operating system**

15. **Windows app**

a. A special area of the operating system where your files and settings are stored

b. Controls that let you interact with an operating system

c. The personal digital assistant in Windows 10

d. Full-featured program that is installed on a personal computer

e. Feature that displays windows at full height next to each other on the screen

f. Available from the Windows store, it runs on Windows laptops, tablets, and phones

g. A program necessary to run your computer

Select the best answer from the list of choices.

16. **The bar containing buttons and other elements at the bottom of the Windows 10 desktop is called the _____.**

    a. title bar

    b. address bar

    c. scroll bar

    d. taskbar

17. **Paint is an example of a(n) _____.**

    a. group

    b. accessory

    c. active window

    d. operating system

18. **Which of the following is in the upper-left corner of a program window, and lets you perform common actions?**
    a. Application program
    b. Quick Access toolbar
    c. Operating system
    d. Accessory program
19. **The new Microsoft web browser is called Microsoft _____.**
    a. Paint
    b. WordPad
    c. Edge
    d. File Explorer

Skills Review

1. **Start Windows 10.**
    a. If your computer and monitor are not running, press your computer's and (if necessary) your monitor's power buttons.
    b. If necessary, select the user name that represents your user account.
    c. Enter your password, using correct uppercase and lowercase letters.
2. **Navigate the desktop and Start menu.**
    a. Examine the Windows 10 desktop.
    b. Open the Start menu.
    c. Display all the apps using a command on the Start menu, and scroll the list.
    d. Return to the Start menu.
    e. Close the Start menu.
3. **Point, click, and drag.**
    a. On the Windows 10 desktop, click or tap to select the Recycle Bin.
    b. Point to display the ScreenTip for Microsoft Edge in the taskbar, and then display the ScreenTip for each of the other icons on the taskbar.
    c. Double-click or double-tap to open the Recycle Bin window, then close it.
    d. Drag the Recycle Bin to a different corner of the screen, then drag it back to its original location.
    e. Click or tap the Date and Time area to display the calendar and clock, then click or tap it again to close it.
4. **Start an app.**
    a. Open the Start menu, then start the Maps app. (If asked to allow Windows to access your location, do so if you like.)
    b. Click or tap the icons on the left side of the Maps app window and observe the effect of each one.
    c. Close the Maps app.
    d. Reopen the Start menu, then type and click or tap to locate and open the Sticky Notes accessory.
    e. Click or tap the Sticky Notes Close button, clicking or tapping Yes to delete the note.
    f. Open the Weather Windows app.
5. **Work with a window.**
    a. Minimize the Weather window, then use its taskbar button to redisplay the window.
    b. Use the Weather app window's scroll bar or swiping to view the information in the lower part of the window, and then scroll or swipe up to display the top of it. (*Hint*: You need to move the pointer over the Weather app window, or swipe it, in order to display the scroll bar.)
    c. Click or tap the menu expand button, then click Historical Weather.
    d. Read the contents of the window, then click or tap two other menu buttons and read the contents.
    e. Maximize the Weather window, then restore it down.
6. **Manage multiple windows.**
    a. Leaving the Weather app open, go to the Start menu and type to locate the Paint app, open Paint, then restore down the Paint window if necessary.
    b. Click or tap to make the Weather app window the active window.
    c. Click or tap to make the Paint window the active window.
    d. Minimize the Paint window.

Skills Review (continued)

   e. Drag the Weather app window so it's in the middle of the screen.

   f. Redisplay the Paint window.

   g. Drag the Paint window so it automatically fills the right side of the screen.

FIGURE 1-25

   h. Click or tap the Weather app window image so it snaps to the left side of the screen.

   i. Close the Weather app window, maximize the Paint window, then restore down the Paint window.

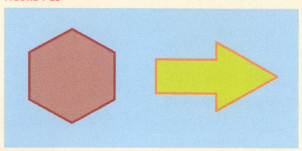

7. Use buttons, menus, and dialog boxes.

   a. In the Paint window, draw a Dark red Hexagon shape, similar to the one shown in **FIGURE 1-25**.

   b. Use the Fill with color button to fill the hexagon with a brown color.

   c. Draw an Orange right arrow to the right of the hexagon shape, using the figure as a guide.

   d. Use the Fill with color button to fill the orange arrow with a lime color.

   e. Fill the drawing background with Light turquoise color, as shown in the figure.

   f. Use the Select list arrow and menu to select the entire drawing, then use the Rotate command to rotate the drawing 180°.

   g. Open the Print dialog box, print a copy of the picture if you wish, then close the Paint app without saving the drawing.

8. Get help.

   a. Open the Get Started app, then use the menu expand button to display the available help topics.

   b. Use the Menu button to display help for Cortana.

   c. Click or tap a tile representing a Cortana help topic that interests you, read the help text, scrolling or swiping as necessary.

   d. Display the Search and Help topic, then close the Get Started window.

   e. In the search box on the taskbar, type Help Microsoft Account, then click the help Microsoft account result to search the web.

   f. In the Microsoft Edge browser window, select a help topic that interests you, read the information (ignore any commercial offers), then click or tap the Microsoft Edge window's Close button.

9. Exit Windows 10.

   a. Sign out of your account, or shut down your computer using the Shut down command in the Start menu's Power command or the preferred command for your work or school setting.

   b. Turn off your monitor if necessary.

Independent Challenge 1

You work for Chicago Instruments, a manufacturer of brass instruments. The company ships instruments and supplies to music stores and musicians in the United States and Canada. The owner, Emerson, wants to know an easy way for his employees to learn about the new features of Windows 10, and he has asked you to help.

   a. Start your computer if necessary, sign in to Windows 10, then use the search text box to search for **what's new in Windows 10**.

   b. Click or tap the Search the web link in the Best match section at the top of the Help menu, then in the Microsoft Edge browser window, click or tap a search result that interests you.

   c. Open the Getting Started app and review the new features listed there.

   d. Using pencil and paper, or the Notepad accessory if you wish, write a short memo to Emerson summarizing, in your own words, three important new features in Windows 10. If you use Notepad to write the memo, use the Print button to print the document, then use the Exit command on the File tab to close Notepad without saving your changes to the document.

Independent Challenge 1 (continued)

e. Close the browser window, then sign out of your account, or shut down your computer using the preferred command for your work or school setting. Turn off your monitor if necessary.

Independent Challenge 2

You are the new manager of Katharine Anne's Garden Supplies, a business that supplies garden tools to San Diego businesses. Some of their tools are from Europe and show metric sizes. For her American customers, Katharine Anne wants to do a simple calculation and then convert the result to inches.

a. Start your computer and log on to Windows 10 if necessary, then type to locate the Windows app called Calculator, and start it.

b. Click or tap to enter the number 96 on the Calculator.

c. Click or tap the division sign (÷) button.

d. Click or tap the number 4.

e. Click or tap the equals sign button (=), and write down the result shown in the Calculator window. (*Hint*: The result should be 24.)

f. Select the menu expand button in the Calculator window, then under CONVERTER, select Length.

g. Enter 24 centimeters, and observe the equivalent length in inches.

h. Start Notepad, write a short memo about how Calculator can help you convert metric measurements to inches and feet, print the document using the Print command on the File tab, then exit Notepad without saving.

i. Close the Calculator, then sign out of your account, or shut down your computer using the preferred command for your work or school setting. Turn off your monitor if necessary.

Independent Challenge 3

You are the office manager for Erica's Pet Shipping, a service business in Dallas, Texas, that specializes in air shipping of cats and dogs across the United States and Canada. It's important to know the temperature in the destination city, so the animals won't be in danger from extreme temperatures when they are unloaded from the aircraft. Erica has asked you to find a way to easily monitor temperatures in destination cities. You decide to use a Windows app so you can see current temperatures in Celsius on your desktop. (Note: To complete the steps below, your computer must be connected to the Internet.)

a. Start your computer and sign in to Windows 10 if necessary, then on the Start menu, click or tap the Weather tile.

b. Click or tap the Search icon in the location text box, then type **Toronto**.

c. Select Toronto, Ontario, Canada, in the drop-down list to view the weather for Toronto.

d. Search on and select another location that interests you.

e. Close the app.

f. Open Notepad, write Erica a memo outlining how you can use the Windows Weather app to help keep pets safe, print the memo if you wish, close Notepad, then sign out, or shut down your computer.

Independent Challenge 4: Explore

Cortana, the Windows 10 personal digital assistant, can help you with everyday tasks. In this Independent Challenge, you explore one of the ways you can use Cortana.

a. Click or tap the microphone icon, to the right of the search box in the Windows 10 taskbar, to activate Cortana and display its menu. (*Note*: If you have not used Cortana before, you will not see the microphone icon until you answer some preliminary questions and verify your user account; you may also need to first help Cortana to understand your speaking voice.) Cortana displays a pulsating circle, indicating that she is listening for speech, and then shows you a greeting and some general information.

Independent Challenge 4: Explore (continued)

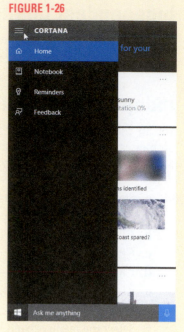

FIGURE 1-26

b. In the list of icons on the left side of the menu, click the menu expand button to show the names of each one, as shown in **FIGURE 1-26**.

c. Click or tap the Reminders button, then click the plus sign at the bottom of the menu. Click or tap Remember to…, then enter information for a to-do item, such as "Walk the dog." Click or tap the time box and use the spin boxes to set the time for one or two minutes from now. Click or tap the check mark, then click Remind to set the reminder. Click or tap the Reminders icon again to see your reminder listed, then click the desktop. When the reminder appears, click Complete.

d. Click or tap the microphone icon again, and when you see the pulsating circle, speak into your computer microphone and tell Cortana to remind you to do something in one minute. Click or tap Remind, then close the Cortana window. When the reminder appears, click or tap Complete.

e. Click or tap the Close button on the Cortana menu, then sign out of your account, or shut down your computer.

Visual Workshop

Using the skills you've learned in this module, open and arrange elements on your screen so it looks similar to **FIGURE 1-27**. Note the position of the Recycle Bin, and the size and location of the Notepad and Weather app windows, as well as the city shown. In Notepad, write a paragraph summarizing how you used pointing, clicking (or tapping), and dragging to make your screen look like the figure. Print your work if you wish, close Notepad and the Weather app without saving changes, then sign out or shut down your computer.

FIGURE 1-27

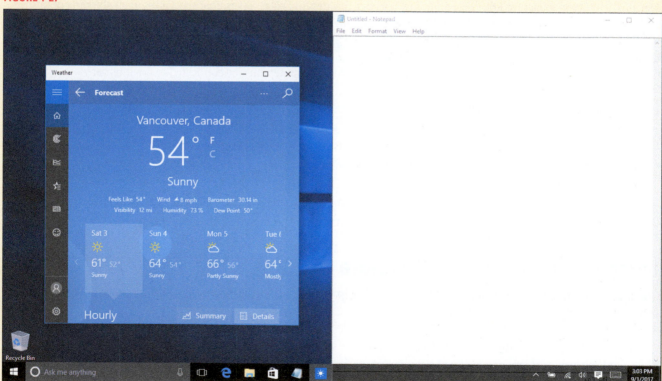

Understanding File Management

CASE Now that you are familiar with the Windows 10 operating system, your new employer has asked you to become familiar with **file management**, or how to create, save, locate and delete the files you create with Windows apps. You begin by reviewing how files are organized on your computer, and then begin working with files you create in the WordPad app. *Note: With the release of Windows 10, Microsoft now provides ongoing updates to Windows instead of releasing new versions periodically. This means that Windows features might change over time, including how they look and how you interact with them. The information provided in this text was accurate at the time this book was published.*

Module Objectives

After completing this module, you will be able to:

- Understand files and folders
- Create and save a file
- Explore the files and folders on your computer
- Change file and folder views

- Open, edit, and save files
- Copy files
- Move and rename files
- Search for files and folders
- Delete and restore files

Files You Will Need

No files needed.

Understand Files and Folders

Learning Outcomes
• Analyze a file hierarchy
• Examine files and folders

As you work with apps, you create and save files, such as letters, drawings, or budgets. When you save files, you usually save them inside folders to help keep them organized. The files and folders on your computer are organized in a **file hierarchy**, a system that arranges files and folders in different levels, like the branches of a tree. **FIGURE 2-1** shows a sample file hierarchy. **CASE** ▶ *You decide to use folders and files to organize the information on your computer.*

DETAILS

Use the following guidelines as you organize files using your computer's file hierarchy:

• **Use folders and subfolders to organize files**

As you work with your computer, you can add folders to your hierarchy and name them to help you organize your work. As you've learned, folders are storage areas in which you can group related files. You should give folders unique names that help you easily identify them. You can also create **subfolders**, which are folders that are inside other folders. Windows 10 comes with several existing folders, such as Documents, Music, Pictures, and Videos, that you can use as a starting point.

QUICK TIP
When you open File Explorer, you see a list of recently opened files and frequently used folders in the Quick Access area that helps you go directly to files and locations.

• **View and manage files in File Explorer**

You can view and manage your computer contents using a built-in program called **File Explorer**, shown in **FIGURE 2-2**. A File Explorer window is divided into **panes**, or sections. The **Navigation pane** on the left side of the window shows the folder structure on your computer. When you click a folder in the Navigation pane, you see its contents in the **File list** on the right side of the window. To open File Explorer from the desktop, click the File Explorer button 🗂 on the taskbar. To open it from the Start menu, click the File Explorer shortcut.

QUICK TIP
The name "File Explorer" only appears in the title bar when you first open it. As you navigate, you'll see the current folder name instead.

• **Understand file addresses**

A window also contains an **Address bar**, an area just below the Ribbon that shows the address, or location, of the files that appear in the File list. An **address** is a sequence of folder names, separated by the ⟩ symbol, which describes a file's location in the file hierarchy. An address shows the folder with the highest hierarchy level on the left and steps through each hierarchy level toward the right; this is sometimes called a **path**. For example, the Documents folder might contain subfolders named Work and Personal. If you clicked the Personal folder in the File list, the Address bar would show Documents ⟩ Personal. Each location between the ⟩ symbols represents a level in the file hierarchy. If you see a file path written out, you'll most likely see it with backslashes. For example, in **FIGURE 2-1**, if you wanted to write the path to the Brochure file, you would write "Documents\Reason2Go\Marketing\Brochure.xlsx. File addresses might look complicated if they may have many levels, but they are helpful because they always describe the exact location of a file or folder in a file hierarchy.

QUICK TIP
Remember that in the Address bar and Navigation pane you single-click a folder or subfolder to show its contents, but in the File list you double-click it.

• **Navigate up and down using the Address bar and File list**

You can use the Address bar and the File list to move up or down in the hierarchy one or more levels at a time. To **navigate up** in your computer's hierarchy, you can click a folder or subfolder name to the left of the current folder name in the Address bar. For example, in **FIGURE 2-2**, you can move up in the hierarchy three levels by clicking once on This PC in the Address bar. Then the File list would show the subfolders and files inside the This PC folder. To **navigate down** in the hierarchy, double-click a subfolder in the File list. The path in the Address bar then shows the path to that subfolder.

• **Navigate up and down using the Navigation pane**

You can also use the Navigation pane to navigate among folders. Move the mouse pointer over the Navigation pane, then click the small arrows to the left of a folder name to show ⟩ or hide ⌄ the folder's contents under the folder name. Subfolders appear indented under the folders that contain them, showing that they are inside that folder.

FIGURE 2-1: Sample folder and file hierarchy

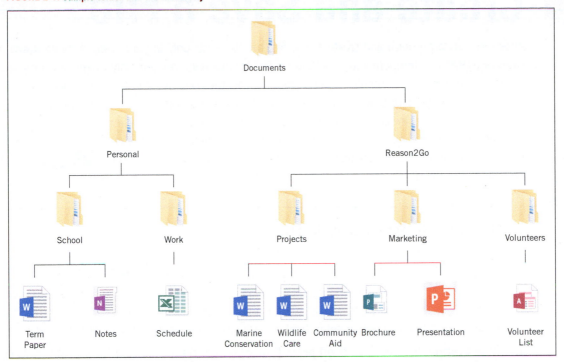

FIGURE 2-2: File Explorer window

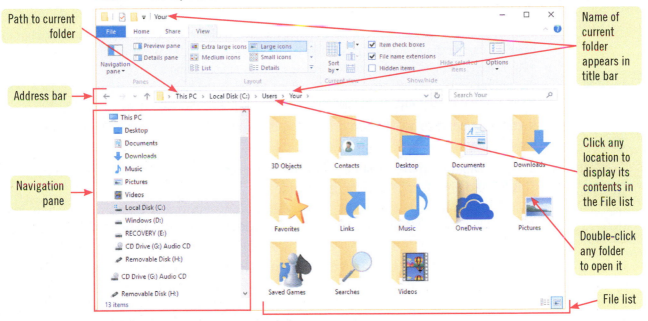

Plan your file organization

As you manage your files, you should plan how you want to organize them. First, identify the types of files you work with, such as images, music, and documents. Think about the content, such as personal, business, clients, or projects. Then think of a folder organization that will help you find them later. For example, you can use subfolders in the Pictures folder to separate family photos from business photos or to group them by location or by month. In the Documents folder, you might group personal files in one subfolder and business files in another subfolder. Then create additional subfolders to further separate sets of files. You can always move files among folders and rename folders. You should periodically reevaluate your folder structure to make sure it continues to meet your needs.

Create and Save a File

Learning Outcomes
• Start WordPad
• Create a file
• Save a file

After you start a program and create a new file, the file exists only in your computer's **random access memory (RAM)**, a temporary storage location. RAM contains information only when your computer is on. When you turn off your computer, it automatically clears the contents of RAM. So you need to save a new file onto a storage device that permanently stores the file so you can open, change, and use it later. One important storage device is your computer's hard drive built into your computer. You might want to store your files online in an online storage location like Microsoft OneDrive. Or you might use a **USB flash drive**, a small, portable storage device that you plug into a USB port on your computer. **CASE** ▶ *You create a document, then save it.*

STEPS

1. **Click or tap the Start button, then type** word
    Available apps with "word" in their names are listed. See **FIGURE 2-3**.

2. **Click the WordPad Desktop app listing, then maximize the WordPad window if necessary**
    Near the top of the WordPad window you see the Ribbon containing buttons, similar to those you used in Paint in Module 1. The Home tab appears in front. A new, blank document appears in the document window. The blinking insertion point shows you where the next character you type will appear.

3. **Type Company Overview, then press [Enter] twice, type Conservation, press [Enter], type Community Work, press [Enter], type Research, press [Enter] twice, then type your name**
    See **FIGURE 2-4**.

4. **Click the File tab, then click Save**
    The first time you save a file using the Save button, the Save As dialog box opens. You use this dialog box to name the file and choose a storage location for it. The Save As dialog box has many of the same elements as a File Explorer window, including an Address bar, a Navigation pane, and a File list. Below the Address bar, the **toolbar** contains buttons you can click to perform actions. In the Address bar, you can see the Documents folder, which is the **default**, or automatically selected, storage location. But you can easily change it.

    QUICK TIP
    On a laptop computer, the USB port is on the left or right side of your computer.

5. **If you are saving to a USB flash drive, plug the drive into a USB port on your computer, if necessary**

    TROUBLE
    If you don't have a USB flash drive, you can save the document in the Documents folder on OneDrive, or you can ask your instructor which storage location is best.

6. **In the Navigation pane scroll bar, click the down scroll arrow ▾ as needed to see This PC and any storage devices listed under it**
    Under This PC, you see the storage locations available on your computer, such as Local Disk (C:) (your hard drive) and Removable Disk (H:) (your USB drive name and letter might differ). Above This PC, you might see your OneDrive listed. These locations are like folders in that you can open them and store files in them.

7. **Click the name of your USB flash drive, or the folder where you store your Data Files**
    The files and folders in the location you chose, if any, appear in the File list. The Address bar shows the location where the file will be saved, which is now Removable Disk (H:) or the name of the location you clicked. You need to give your document a meaningful name so you can find it later.

    TROUBLE
    If your Save As dialog box does not show the .rtf file extension, click Cancel, open File Explorer, click the View tab, then in the Show/hide group, click the File name extensions check box to select it.

8. **Click in the File name text box to select the default name Document.rtf, type Company Overview, compare your screen to FIGURE 2-5, then click Save**
    The document is saved as a file on your USB flash drive. The filename Company Overview.rtf appears in the title bar. The ".rtf" at the end of the filename is the file extension that Windows added automatically. A **file extension** is a three- or four-letter sequence, preceded by a period, which identifies a file to your computer, in this case **Rich Text Format**. The WordPad program creates files in RTF format.

9. **Click the Close button ✕ on the WordPad window**
    The WordPad program closes. Your Company Overview document is now saved in the location you specified.

FIGURE 2-3: Results at top of Start menu

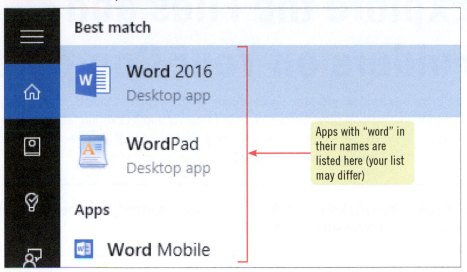

Apps with "word" in their names are listed here (your list may differ)

FIGURE 2-4: WordPad document

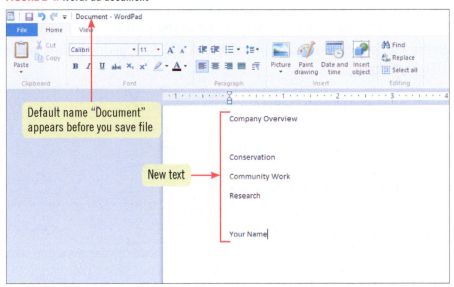

Default name "Document" appears before you save file

New text

Company Overview

Conservation

Community Work

Research

Your Name

FIGURE 2-5: Save As dialog box

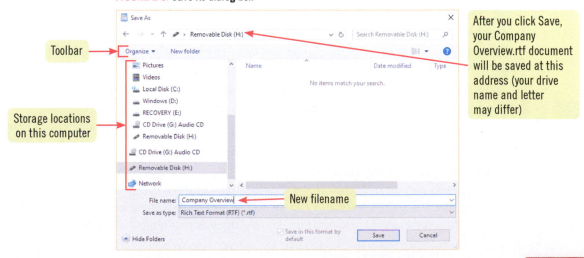

Toolbar

Storage locations on this computer

New filename

After you click Save, your Company Overview.rtf document will be saved at this address (your drive name and letter may differ)

Explore the Files and Folders on Your Computer

In a File Explorer window, you can navigate through your computer contents using the File list, the Address bar, and the Navigation pane. Examining your computer and its existing folder and file structure helps you decide where to save files as you work with Windows 10 apps. **CASE** ▶ *In preparation for organizing documents at your new job, you look at the files and folders on your computer.*

STEPS

1. **At the Windows desktop, click the File Explorer button 📁 on the taskbar, then in the File Explorer Navigation pane, click This PC**

TROUBLE
If you don't see the colored bars, click the View tab, click Tiles in the Layout group.

2. **If you do not see a band of buttons near the top of the window, double-click the View tab**

The band containing buttons is called the **Ribbon**. Your computer's storage devices appear in a window, as shown in **FIGURE 2-6**. These include hard drives; devices with removable storage, such as CD and DVD drives or USB flash drives; portable devices such as smartphones or tablets; and any network storage locations. Colored bars shows you how much space has been taken up on your drives. You decide to move down a level in your computer's hierarchy and see what is on your USB flash drive.

3. **In the File list, double-click Removable Disk (H:) (or the drive name and letter for your USB flash drive)**

You see the contents of your USB flash drive, including the Company Overview.rtf file you saved in the last lesson. You decide to navigate one level up in the file hierarchy.

TROUBLE
If you do not have a USB flash drive, click the Documents folder instead.

4. **In the Address bar, click This PC, or if This PC does not appear, click the far-left address bar arrow ▶ in the Address bar, then click This PC**

You return to the This PC window showing your storage locations.

5. **In the File list, double-click Local Disk (C:)**

The contents of your hard drive appear in the File list.

6. **In the File list, double-click the Users folder**

The Users folder contains a subfolder for each user account on this computer. You might see a folder with your user account name on it. Each user's folder contains that person's documents. User folder names are the names that were used to log in when your computer was set up. When a user logs in, the computer allows that user access to the folder with the same user name. If you are using a computer with more than one user, you might not have permission to view other users' folders. There is also a Public folder that any user can open.

7. **Double-click the folder with your user name on it**

Depending on how your computer is set up, this folder might be labeled with your name; however, if you are using a computer in a lab or a public location, your folder might be called Student or Computer User or something similar. You see a list of folders, such as Documents, Music, and OneDrive. See **FIGURE 2-7**.

QUICK TIP
In the Address bar, you can click ▶ to the right of a folder name to see a list of its subfolders; if the folder is open, its name appears in bold in the list.

8. **Double-click Documents in the File list**

In the Address bar, the path to the Documents folder is This PC ▶ Local Disk (C:) ▶ Users ▶ *Your User Name* ▶ Documents.

9. **In the Navigation pane, click This PC**

You once again see your computer's storage locations. You can also move up one level at a time in your file hierarchy by clicking the Up arrow ⬆ on the toolbar, or by pressing [Backspace] on your keyboard. See **TABLE 2-1** for a summary of techniques for navigating through your computer's file hierarchy.

Understanding File Management

FIGURE 2-6: File Explorer window showing storage locations

Click this arrow if necessary to navigate to a different location

Storage locations on this PC

Colored bars show how full drives are

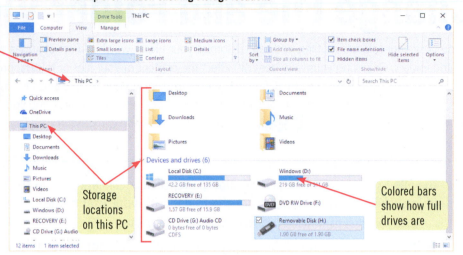

FIGURE 2-7: Your user name folder

Path to your user name folder contents

OneDrive

Your user name folder contents and view may differ

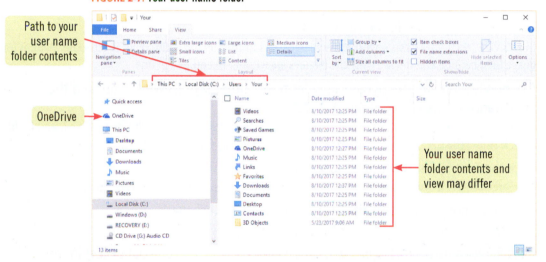

TABLE 2-1: Navigating your computer's file hierarchy

to do this	Navigation pane	Address bar	File list	keyboard
Move up in hierarchy	Click a drive or folder name	Click an item to the left of ▶ or Click the **Up to** button ⬆		Press [**Backspace**]
Move down in hierarchy	Click a drive or folder name that is indented from the left	Click an item to the right of ▶	Double-click a folder	Press ⬆ or ⬇ to select a folder, then press [**Enter**] to open the selected folder
Return to previously viewed location		Click the **Back to** button ⬅ or **Forward** button ➡		

Using and disabling Quick Access view

When you first open File Explorer, you see a list of frequently-used folders and recently used files, called Quick access view. Quick Access view can save you time by giving you one-click access to files and folders you use a lot. If you want File Explorer to open instead to This PC, you can disable Quick Access View. To do this, open a File Explorer window, click the View tab, click the Options button on the right side of the Ribbon, then click Change folder and search options. On the General tab of the Folder Options dialog box, click the Open File Explorer to list arrow, click This PC, then click OK.

Change File and Folder Views

Learning Outcomes
• View files as large icons
• Sort files
• Preview files

As you view your folders and files, you can customize your **view**, which is a set of appearance choices for files and folders. Changing your view does not affect the content of your files or folders, only the way they appear. You can choose from eight different **layouts** to display your folders and files as different sized icons, or as a list. You can change the order in which the folders and files appear, and you can also show a preview of a file in the window. **CASE** ▶ *You experiment with different views of your folders and files.*

STEPS

QUICK TIP

To expand your view of a location in the Navigation pane, click the Expand button ⟩ next to that location.

1. **In the File Explorer window's Navigation pane, click Local Disk (C:); in the File list double-click Users, then double-click the folder with your user name**
   You opened your user name folder, which is inside the Users folder.

2. **Click the View tab on the Ribbon if necessary, then if you don't see eight icons in the Layout list, click the More button ⤓ in the Layout group**
   The list of available layouts appears, as shown in **FIGURE 2-8**.

3. **Click Extra large icons in the Layout list**
   In this view, the folder items appear as very large icons in the File list. This layout is especially helpful for image files, because you can see what the pictures are without opening each one.

QUICK TIP

You can scroll up and down in the Layout group to see views that are not currently visible.

4. **On the View tab, in the Layout list, point to the other layouts while watching the appearance of the File list, then click Details**
   In Details view, shown in **FIGURE 2-9**, you can see each item's name, the date it was modified, and its file type. It shows the size of any files in the current folder, but it does not show sizes for folders.

5. **Click the Sort by button in the Current view group**
   The Sort by menu lets you **sort**, or reorder, your files and folders according to several criteria.

6. **Click Descending if it is not already selected with a check mark**
   Now the folders are sorted in reverse alphabetical order.

QUICK TIP

Clicking Quick Access in the Navigation pane displays folders you use frequently; to add a folder or location to Quick Access, display it in the File list, then drag it to the Quick Access list.

7. **Click Removable Disk (H:) (or the location where you store your Data Files) in the Navigation pane, then click Company Overview.rtf in the File list**

8. **Click the Preview pane button in the Panes group on the View tab if necessary**
   A preview of the selected Company Overview.rtf file you created earlier appears in the Preview pane on the right side of the screen. The WordPad file is not open, but you can still see the file's contents. See **FIGURE 2-10**.

9. **Click the Preview pane button again to close the pane, then click the window's Close button ☒**

Using the Windows Action Center

The Windows Action Center lets you quickly view system notifications and selected computer settings. To open the Action Center, click the All Notifications button on the right side of the taskbar. The Action Center pane opens on the right side of the screen. Any new notifications appear in the upper part of the pane, including messages about apps, Windows tips, and any reminders you may have set. In the lower part of the pane, you see Quick Action buttons, shown in **FIGURE 2-11**, for some commonly-used Windows settings. For example, click Note to open the OneNote app; click the Brightness button repeatedly to cycle though four brightness settings; click the Airplane mode button to place your computer in airplane mode,

which turns off your computer's wireless transmission; click Quiet hours to silence your computer's notification sounds. Clicking the All settings button opens the Settings windows, where you can access all Windows settings categories. Note that the buttons available will vary depending on your hardware and software configuration.

FIGURE 2-11: Quick Action buttons

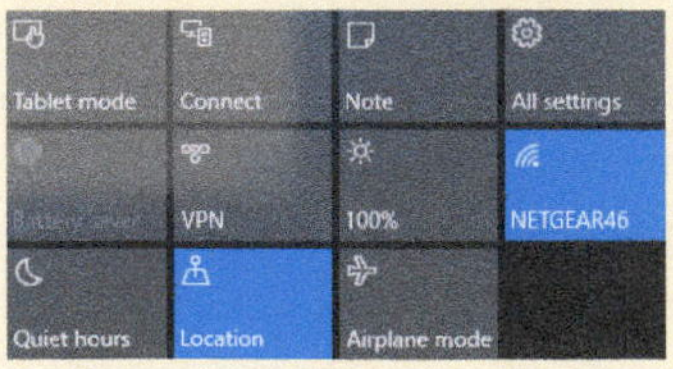

FIGURE 2-8: Layout options for viewing folders and files

FIGURE 2-9: Your user name folder contents in Details view

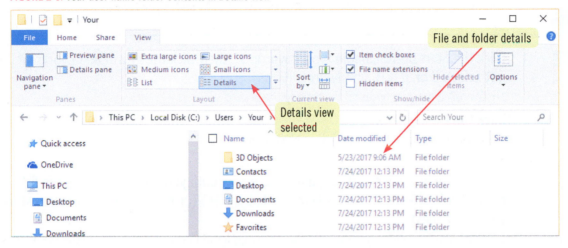

FIGURE 2-10: Preview of selected Company Overview.rtf file

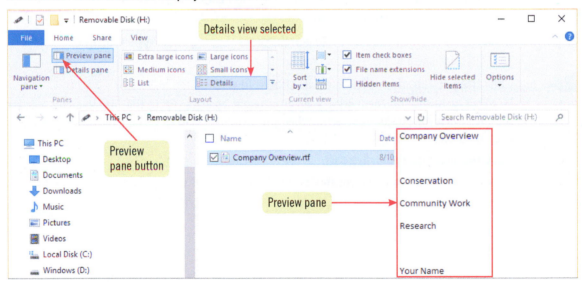

Customizing Details view

When you use File Explorer to view your computer contents in Details view, you see a list of the files and folders in that location. At the top of the list you see each item's Name, Size, Type, and Date Modified. If the list of file and folder details doesn't show what you need, you can customize it. To change a column's location, drag a column heading to move it quickly to a new position. To change the order of, or **sort**, your files and folders, click any column header to sort the list by that detail; click it a second time to reverse the order. To show only a selected group of, or **filter**, files, click the ▼ icon to the right of the Name, Size, Type, or Date Modified, column headers, and select the check boxes for the type of items you want to include. To change the kind of details you see, right-click or tap-hold a column heading in Details view, then click or tap the detail you want to show or hide. To see more details or to change the list order, right-click or tap-hold a column title, then click or tap More.

Open, Edit, and Save Files

Learning Outcomes
- Open a file
- Edit a file
- Save a file

Once you have created a file and saved it with a name to a storage location, you can easily open it and **edit** (make changes to) it. For example, you might want to add or delete text or add a picture. Then you save the file again so the file contains your latest changes. Usually you save a file with the same filename and in the same location as the original, which replaces the existing file with the most up-to-date version. To save a file you have changed, you use the Save command. **CASE** *You need to complete the company overview list, so you need to open the new Company Overview file you created earlier.*

STEPS

QUICK TIP

When you double-click a file in a File Explorer window, the program currently associated with that file type opens the file; to change the program, right-click a file, click Open with, click Choose another app, click the program name, select the Always use this app to open [file type] files check box, then click OK.

1. **Click the** Start button, **begin typing** wordpad, **then click the** WordPad program **if it is not selected or, if it is, simply press** [Enter]
   The WordPad program opens on the desktop.

2. **Click the** File tab, **then click** Open
   The Open dialog box opens. It contains a Navigation pane and a File list like the Save As dialog box and the File Explorer window.

3. **Scroll down in the Navigation pane if necessary until you see This PC and the list of computer locations, then click** Removable Disk (H:) **(or the location where you store your Data Files)**
   The contents of your USB flash drive (or the file storage location you chose) appear in the File list, as shown in **FIGURE 2-12**.

4. **Click** Company Overview.rtf **in the File list, then click** Open
   The document you created earlier opens.

QUICK TIP

You can also double-click a file in the File list to open it.

5. **Click to the right of the "h" in Research, press** [Enter], **then type** Outreach
   The edited document includes the text you just typed. See **FIGURE 2-13**.

QUICK TIP

To save changes to a file, you can also click the Save button 🖫 on the Quick Access toolbar (on the left side of the title bar).

6. **Click the** File tab, **then click** Save, **as shown in** **FIGURE 2-14**
   WordPad saves the document with your most recent changes, using the filename and location you specified when you previously saved it. When you save changes to an existing file, the Save As dialog box does not open.

7. **Click the** File tab, **then click** Exit
   The Company Overview document and the WordPad program close.

Comparing Save and Save As

Many apps, including Wordpad, include two save command options—Save and Save As. The first time you save a file, the Save As dialog box opens (whether you choose Save or Save As). Here you can select the drive and folder where you want to save the file and enter its filename. If you edit a previously saved file, you can save the file to the same location with the same filename using the Save command. The Save command updates the stored file using the same location and filename without opening the Save As dialog box. In some situations, you might want to save a copy of the existing document using a different filename or in a different storage location. To do this, open the document, click the Save As command on the File tab, navigate to the location where you want to save the copy if necessary, and/or edit the name of the file.

FIGURE 2-12: Navigating in the Open dialog box

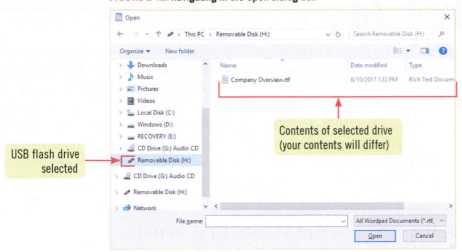

USB flash drive selected

Contents of selected drive (your contents will differ)

FIGURE 2-13: Edited document

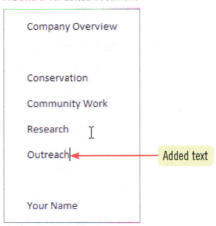

Added text

FIGURE 2-14: Saving the updated document

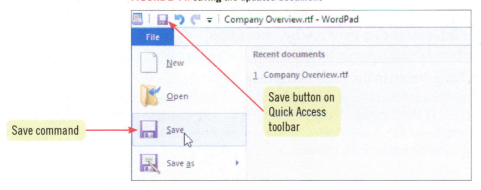

Save command

Save button on Quick Access toolbar

Using Microsoft OneDrive

Microsoft OneDrive is a location on the World Wide Web where you can store your files. Because OneDrive is an online location instead of a disk or USB device, it's often called a **cloud storage location**. When you store your files on OneDrive, you can access them from different devices, including laptops, tablets, and smartphones. Any changes you make to a file stored "in the cloud" are automatically made on OneDrive; this is known as **file syncing**. For example, if you make changes to a file from your laptop, and then open it on your tablet, you will see the changes. You can share OneDrive folders with others so they can view or edit files using a web browser such as Microsoft Edge or Internet Explorer. You can even have multiple users edit a document simultaneously. In Windows 10, OneDrive appears as a storage location in the navigation bar in File Explorer, and in the Open and Save As dialog boxes in Windows apps, so you can easily open, modify, and save files stored there. You can also download the free OneDrive Windows app from the Windows Store to help manage your OneDrive files from all your devices.

Understanding File Management

Copy Files

Sometimes you need to make a copy of an existing file. For example, you might want to put a copy on a USB flash drive so you can open the file on another machine or share it with a friend or colleague. Or you might want to create a copy as a **backup**, or replacement, in case something happens to your original file. You can copy files and folders using the Copy command and then place the copy in another location using the Paste command. You cannot have two copies of a file with the same name in the same folder. If you try to do this, Windows asks you if you want to replace the first one, and then gives you a chance to give the second copy a different name. **CASE** *You want to create a backup copy of the Company Overview document that you can store in a folder for company publicity items. First you need to create the folder, then you can copy the file.*

STEPS

1. On the desktop, click the File Explorer button [icon] on the taskbar

2. In the Navigation pane, click Removable Disk (H:) (or the location where you store your Data Files)

   First you create the new folder you plan to use for storing publicity-related files.

3. In the New group on the Home tab, click the New folder button

   A new folder appears in the File list, with its default name, New folder, selected.

4. Type Publicity Items, then press [Enter]

   Because the folder name was selected, the text you typed, Publicity Items, replaced it. Pressing [Enter] confirmed your entry, and the folder is now named Publicity Items.

5. In the File list, click the Company Overview.rtf document you saved earlier, then click the Copy button in the Clipboard group, as shown in FIGURE 2-15

   After you select the file, its check box becomes selected (the check box appears only if the Item check boxes option in the Show/Hide group on the View tab is selected). When you use the Copy command, Windows places a duplicate copy of the file in an area of your computer's random access memory called the **clipboard**, ready to paste, or place, in a new location. Copying and pasting a file leaves the file in its original location.

6. In the File list, double-click the Publicity Items folder

   The folder opens. Nothing appears in the File list because the folder currently is empty.

7. Click the Paste button in the Clipboard group

   A copy of the Company Overview.rtf file is pasted into the Publicity Items folder. See FIGURE 2-16. You now have two copies of the Company Overview.rtf file: one on your USB flash drive in the main folder, and another in your new Publicity Items folder. The file remains on the clipboard until you end your Windows session or place another item on the clipboard.

Copying files using Send to

You can also copy and paste a file using the Send to command. In File Explorer, right-click the file you want to copy, point to Send to, then in the shortcut menu, click the name of the device you want to send a copy of the file to. This leaves the original file on your hard drive and creates a copy in that location. You can send a file to a compressed file, the desktop, your Documents folder, a mail recipient, or a drive on your computer. See TABLE 2-2.

FIGURE 2-15: Copying a file

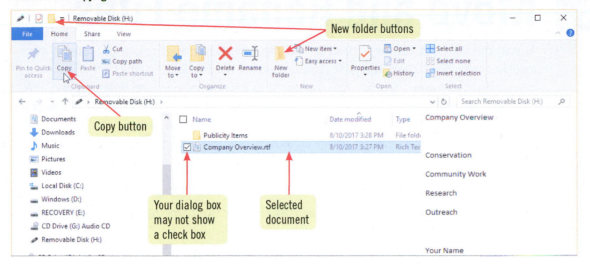

New folder buttons

Copy button

Your dialog box may not show a check box

Selected document

FIGURE 2-16: Duplicate file pasted into Publicity items folder

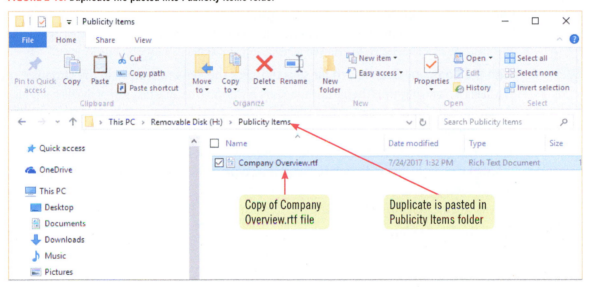

Copy of Company Overview.rtf file

Duplicate is pasted in Publicity Items folder

TABLE 2-2: Selected Send to menu commands

menu option	use to
Compressed (zipped) folder	Create a new, compressed (smaller) file with a .zip file extension
Desktop (create shortcut)	Create a shortcut (link) for the file on the desktop
Documents	Copy the file to the Documents library
Fax recipient	Send a file to a fax recipient
Mail recipient	Create an e-mail with the file attached to it (only if you have an e-mail program on your computer)
DVD RW Drive (D:)	Copy the file to your computer's DVD drive (your drive letter may differ)
CD Drive (G:) audio CD	Copy the file to your computer's CD drive (your drive letter may differ)
Removable Disk (H:)	Copy the file to a removable disk drive (your drive letter may differ)

Understanding File Management

Move and Rename Files

As you work with files, you might need to move files or folders to another location. You can move one or
more files or folders at a time, and you can move them to a different folder on the same drive or to a different
drive. When you **move** a file, the file is transferred to the new location, and unlike copying, it no longer
exists in its original location. You can move a file using the Cut and Paste commands. Before or after you
move a file, you might find that you want to change its name. You can easily rename it to make the name
more descriptive or accurate. **CASE** ▸ *You decide to move your original Company Overview.rtf document to
your Documents folder. After you move it, you edit the filename so it better describes the file contents.*

STEPS

1. **In the Address bar, click** Removable Disk (H:) **(or the name of the location where you
store your Data Files) if necessary**

2. **Click the** Company Overview.rtf **document to select it**

3. **Click the** Cut button **in the Clipboard group on the Ribbon, as shown in** FIGURE 2-17

4. **In the Navigation Pane, under This PC, click** Documents

    You navigated to your Documents folder.

5. **Click the** Paste button **in the Clipboard group**

    The Company Overview.rtf document appears in your Documents folder and remains selected. See **FIGURE 2-18**.
    The filename could be clearer, to help you remember that it contains a list of company goals.

6. **With the Company Overview.rtf file selected, click the** Rename button **in the Organize group**

    The filename is highlighted. The file extension isn't highlighted because that part of the filename identifies
    the file to WordPad and should not be changed. If you deleted or changed the file extension, WordPad
    would be unable to open the file. You decide to change the word "Overview" to "Goals."

7. **Move the** I **pointer after the "w" in "Overview", click to place the insertion point, press
[Backspace] eight times to delete** Overview, **type** Goals **as shown in** FIGURE 2-19, **then
press [Enter]**

    You changed the name of the pasted file in the Documents folder. The filename now reads Company Goals.rtf.

8. **Close the File Explorer window**

Using Task View to create multiple desktops

As you have learned in Module 1, you can have multiple app
windows open on your desktop, such as WordPad, Paint, and
OneNote. But you might need to have a different set of apps
available for a different project. Instead of closing all the apps
and opening different ones, you can use Task View to work with
multiple desktops, each containing its own set of apps. Then,
when you need to work on another project, you can switch to
another desktop to quickly access those apps. To open Task
View, click the **Task View** button 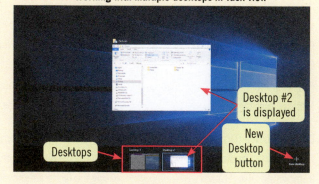 on the taskbar. The
current desktop becomes smaller and a New desktop button
appears in the lower-right corner of the screen. Click the New
desktop button. A new desktop appears in a bar at the bottom
of the screen, which you can click to activate and work with its

apps. See **FIGURE 2-20**. To switch to another desktop, click the
Task View button and click its icon.

FIGURE 2-20: Working with multiple desktops in Task view

Desktop #2
is displayed

New
Desktop
button

Desktops

Understanding File Management

FIGURE 2-17: Cutting a file

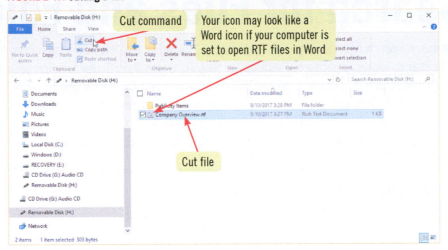

Cut command

Your icon may look like a
Word icon if your computer is
set to open RTF files in Word

Cut file

FIGURE 2-18: Pasted file in Documents folder

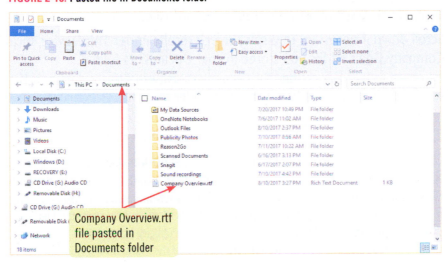

Company Overview.rtf
file pasted in
Documents folder

FIGURE 2-19: Renaming a file

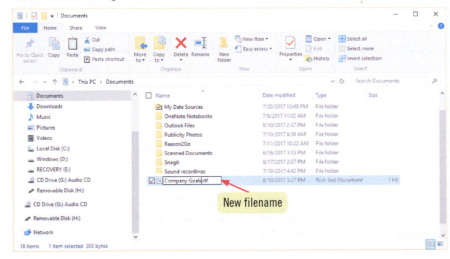

New filename

Understanding File Management

Search for Files and Folders

Windows Search helps you quickly find any app, folder, or file. You can search from the Search box on the taskbar to locate applications, settings, or files. To search a particular location on your computer, you can use the Search box in File Explorer. You enter search text by typing one or more letter sequences or words that help Windows identify the item you want. The search text you type is called your **search criteria**. Your search criteria can be a folder name, a filename, or part of a filename. **CASE** *You want to locate the Company Overview.rtf document so you can print it for a colleague.*

STEPS

1. **Click in the search box on the taskbar**
   The Cortana menu opens.

2. **Type company**
   The Search menu opens with a possible match for your search at the top, and some other possible matches below it. You may see results from The Windows Store, the Internet, or your computer settings.

3. **Click My stuff, near the bottom of the menu**
   This limits your search to the files and folders in your storage locations on this device. It includes documents with the text "company" in the title or in the document text.

4. **Scroll down if necessary to display search results under This Device, including the Company Goals.rtf file you stored in your Documents folder**
   See **FIGURE 2-21**. It does not find the Company Overview.rtf file stored on your Flash drive because it's searching only the items on this device. To open the found file, you could click its listing. You can also search using File Explorer.

   > **QUICK TIP**
   > If you navigate to a specific folder in your file hierarchy, Windows searches that folder and any subfolders below it.

5. **Click the File Explorer button 📁 on the taskbar, then click This PC in the Navigation pane**

6. **Click in the Search This PC box to the right of the Address bar, type company, then press [Enter]**
   Windows searches your computer for files that contain the word "company" in their title. A green bar in the Address bar indicates the progress of your search. After a few moments, the search results, shown in **FIGURE 2-22**, appear. Windows found the renamed file, Company Goals.rtf, in your Documents folder, and the original Company Overview.rtf document on your removable drive, in the Publicity Items folder. It may also locate shortcuts to the file in your Recent folder. It's good to verify the location of the found files, so you can select the right one.

   > **QUICK TIP**
   > Windows search is not case-sensitive, so you can type upper- or lowercase letters, and obtain the same results.

7. **Click the View tab, click Details in the Layout group then look in the Folder column to view the path to each file, dragging the edge of the Folder column header with the ↔ pointer to widen it if necessary**

8. **Double-click the Company Overview.rtf document in your file storage location**
   The file opens in WordPad or in another word-processing program on your computer that reads RTF files.

   > **TROUBLE**
   > If you see a message asking how you want to open the file, click WordPad.

9. **Click the Close button ✕ on the WordPad (or other word-processor) window**

Using the Search Tools tab in File Explorer

The **Search Tools tab** appears in the Ribbon as soon as you click the Search text box, and it lets you narrow your search criteria. Use the commands in the Location group to specify a particular search location. The Refine group lets you limit the search to files modified after a certain date, or to files of a particular kind, size, type, or other property. The Options group lets you repeat previous searches, save searches, and open the folder containing a found file.

FIGURE 2-21: Found file

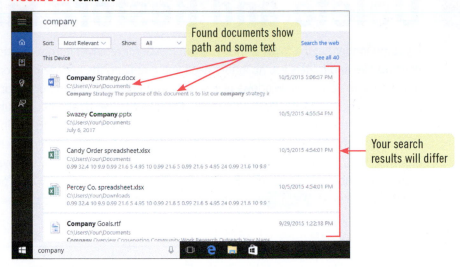

Found documents show path and some text

Your search results will differ

FIGURE 2-22: Apps screen and Search pane

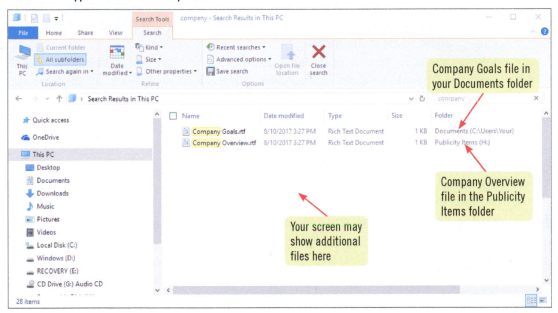

Company Goals file in your Documents folder

Company Overview file in the Publicity Items folder

Your screen may show additional files here

Using Microsoft Edge

When you search for files using the search box on the Windows taskbar and click Web, the new web browser called **Microsoft Edge** opens. You can also open Edge by clicking its icon  on the taskbar. Created to replace the older Internet Explorer browser, Edge is a Windows app that runs on personal computers, tablets, and smartphones. Edge features a reading mode that lets you read a webpage without ads. It also lets you annotate pages with markup tools such as a pen or highlighter, and add typed notes, as shown in **FIGURE 2-23**. You can also add pages to a Reading list or share them with OneNote or a social networking site.

FIGURE 2-23: Web page annotated in Microsoft Edge

Understanding File Management

Delete and Restore Files

Learning Outcomes
• Delete a file
• Restore a file
• Empty the Recycle Bin

If you no longer need a folder or file, you can delete (or remove) it from the storage device. By regularly deleting files and folders you no longer need and emptying the Recycle Bin, you free up valuable storage space on your computer. Windows places folders and files you delete from your hard drive in the Recycle Bin. If you delete a folder, Windows removes the folder as well as all files and subfolders stored in it. If you later discover that you need a deleted file or folder, you can restore it to its original location, as long as you have not yet emptied the Recycle Bin. Emptying the Recycle Bin permanently removes deleted folders and files from your computer. However, files and folders you delete from a removable drive, such as a USB flash drive, do not go to the Recycle Bin. They are immediately and permanently deleted and cannot be restored. **CASE** ▶ *You decide to delete the Company Goals document that you stored in your Documents folder.*

STEPS

1. **Click the Documents folder in the File Explorer Navigation pane**

   Your Documents folder opens.

2. **Click Company Goals.rtf to select it, click the Home tab, then click the Delete list arrow ⊠ in the Organize group; if the Show recycle confirmation command does not have a check mark next to it, click Show recycle confirmation (or if it does have a check mark, click ⊠ again to close the menu)**

   Selecting the Show recycle confirmation command tells Windows that whenever you click the Delete button, you want to see a confirmation dialog box before Windows deletes the file. That way you can change your mind if you want, before deleting the file.

3. **Click the Delete button ☒ in the Organize group**

   The Delete File dialog box opens so you can confirm the deletion, as shown in **FIGURE 2-24**.

4. **Click Yes**

   You deleted the file. Because the file was stored on your computer and not on a removable drive, it was moved to the Recycle Bin.

5. **Click the Minimize button — on the window's title bar, examine the Recycle Bin icon, then double-click the Recycle Bin icon on the desktop**

   The Recycle Bin icon appears to contain crumpled paper, indicating that it contains deleted folders and/or files. The Recycle Bin window displays any previously deleted folders and files, including the Company Goals.rtf file.

6. **Click the Company Goals.rtf file to select it, then click the Restore the selected items button in the Restore group on the Recycle Bin Tools Manage tab, as shown in FIGURE 2-25**

   The file returns to its original location and no longer appears in the Recycle Bin window.

7. **In the Navigation pane, click the Documents folder**

   The Documents folder window contains the restored file. You decide to permanently delete this file after all.

8. **Click the file Company Goals.rtf, click ⊠ in the Organize group on the Home tab, click Permanently delete, then click Yes in the Delete File dialog box**

9. **Minimize the window, double-click the Recycle Bin, notice that the Company Goals.rtf file is no longer there, then close all open windows**

FIGURE 2-24: Delete File dialog box

FIGURE 2-25: Restoring a file from the Recycle Bin

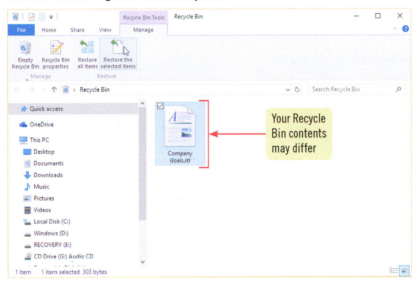

Your Recycle Bin contents may differ

More techniques for selecting and moving files

To select a group of items that are next to each other in a window, click the first item in the group, press and hold [Shift], then click the last item in the group. Both items you click and all the items between them become selected. To select files that are not next to each other, click the first file, press and hold [Ctrl], then click the other items you want to select as a group. Then you can copy, cut, or delete the group of files or folders you selected. **Drag and drop** is a technique in which you use your pointing device to drag a file or folder into a different folder and then drop it, or let go of the mouse button, to place it in that folder. Using drag and drop does not copy your file to the clipboard. If you drag and drop a file to a folder on a different drive, Windows *copies* the file. However, if you drag and drop a file to a folder on the same drive, Windows *moves* the file into that folder

instead. See **FIGURE 2-26**. If you want to move a file to another drive, hold down [Shift] while you drag and drop. If you want to copy a file to another folder on the same drive, hold down [Ctrl] while you drag and drop.

FIGURE 2-26: Moving a file using drag and drop

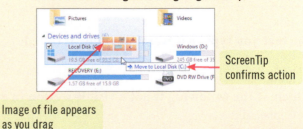

ScreenTip confirms action

Image of file appears as you drag

Practice

Concepts Review

Label the elements of the Windows 10 window shown in FIGURE 2-27.

FIGURE 2-27

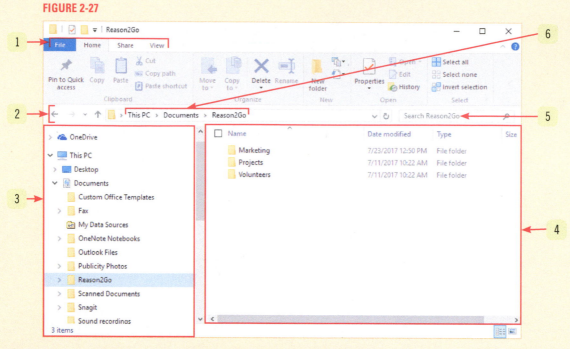

Match each term with the statement that best describes it.

7. **View**
8. **File extension**
9. **Address bar**
10. **Path**
11. **Clipboard**
12. **Snap Assist**

a. A series of locations separated by small triangles or backslashes that describes a file's location in the file hierarchy

b. A feature that helps you arrange windows on the screen

c. An area above the Files list that contains a path

d. A three- or four-letter sequence, preceded by a period, that identifies the type of file

e. A set of appearance choices for files and folders

f. An area of a computer's RAM used for temporary storage

Select the best answer from the list of choices.

13. **Which part of a window lets you see a file's contents without opening the file?**
   a. File list
   b. Address bar
   c. Navigation pane
   d. Preview pane

14. **The new Microsoft web browser is called Microsoft _____.**
   a. View
   b. Task
   c. Edge
   d. Desktop

15. **The text you type in a Search text box is called:**
   a. Sorting.
   b. RAM.
   c. Search criteria.
   d. Clipboard.

16. **Which of the following is not a visible section in a File Explorer window?**
   a. Clipboard
   b. Navigation pane
   c. File list
   d. Address bar

Skills Review

1. **Understand files and folders.**
   a. Create a file hierarchy for an ice cream manufacturing business, using a name that you create. The business has departments for Product Development, Manufacturing, and Personnel. Product development activities include research and testing; manufacturing has facilities for ice cream and frozen yogurt; and Personnel handles hiring and payroll. How would you organize your folders and files using a file hierarchy of three levels? How would you use folders and subfolders to keep the documents related to these activities distinct and easy to navigate? Draw a diagram and write a short paragraph explaining your answer.
   b. Use tools in the File Explorer window to create the folder hierarchy in the Documents folder on your computer.
   c. Open NotePad and write the path of the Hiring folder, using backslashes to indicate levels in the hierarchy. Do the same for the Testing folder.

2. **Create and save a file.**
   a. Connect your USB flash drive to a USB port on your computer, then open WordPad from the Start menu.
   b. Type **Advertising Campaign** as the title, then start a new line.
   c. Type your name, press [Enter] twice, then create the following list:
      Menu ads
      Email customers
      Web page specials
      Local TV spots
   d. Save the WordPad file with the filename **Advertising Campaign.rtf** in the location where you store your Data Files, view the filename in the WordPad title bar, then close WordPad.

3. **Explore the files and folders on your computer.**
   a. Open a File Explorer window.
   b. Use the Navigation pane to navigate to your USB flash drive or the location where you store your Data Files.
   c. Use the Address bar to navigate to This PC.
   d. Use the File list to navigate to your local hard drive (C:).
   e. Use the File list to open the Users folder, and then open the folder that represents your user name.
   f. Open the Documents folder. (*Hint*: The path is This PC\Local Disk (C:) \Users\Your User Name\Documents.)
   g. Use the Navigation pane to navigate back to This PC.

4. **Change file and folder views.**
   a. Navigate to your Documents folder or the location of your Data Files using the method of your choice.
   b. Use the View tab to view its contents as large icons.
   c. View the folder's contents in the seven other views.
   d. Sort the items in this location by date modified in ascending order.
   e. Open the Preview pane, view a selected item's preview, then close the Preview pane.

5. **Open, edit, and save files.**
   a. Start WordPad, then use the Open dialog box to open the Advertising Campaign.rtf document you created.
   b. After the text "Local TV spots," add a line with the text **Social media**.
   c. Save the document and close WordPad.

6. **Copy files.**
   a. In the File Explorer window, navigate to the location where you store your Data Files if necessary.
   b. Copy the Advertising Campaign.rtf document.
   c. Create a new folder named **Advertising** on your USB flash drive or the location where you store your Data Files (*Hint*: Use the Home tab), then open the folder.
   d. Paste the document copy in the new folder.

7. **Move and rename files.**
   a. Navigate to your USB flash drive or the location where you store your Data Files.
   b. Select the Advertising Campaign.rtf document located there, then cut it.

Skills Review (continued)

    c. Navigate to your Documents folder, then paste the file there.

    d. Rename the file **Advertising Campaign - Backup.rtf**.

8. Search for files and folders.

    a. Use the search box on the taskbar to search for a file using the search text **backup**. (*Hint*: Remember to select My stuff.)

    b. If necessary, scroll to the found file, and notice its path.

    c. Open the Advertising Campaign - Backup document from the search results, then close WordPad. (*Hint*: Closing the program automatically closes any open documents.)

    d. Open a File Explorer window, click in the search box, search your USB flash drive using the search text **overview**.

    e. Open the found document from the File list, then close WordPad.

9. Delete and restore files.

    a. Navigate to your Documents folder.

    b. Verify that your Delete preference is Show recycle confirmation, then delete the Advertising Campaign - Backup.rtf file.

    c. Open the Recycle Bin, and restore the document to its original location.

    d. Navigate to your Documents folder, then move the Advertising Campaign - Backup.rtf file to the Advertising folder on your USB flash drive (or the location where you store your Data Files).

Independent Challenge 1

To meet the needs of gardeners in your town, you have opened a vacation garden care business named GreenerInc. Customers hire you to care for their gardens when they go on vacation. To promote your new business, your website designer asks you to give her selling points to include in a web ad.

    a. Connect your USB flash drive to your computer, if necessary.

    b. Create a new folder named **GreenerInc** on your USB flash drive or the location where you store your Data Files.

    c. In the GreenerInc folder, create two subfolders named **Handouts** and **Website**.

    d. Use WordPad to create a short paragraph or list that describes three advantages of your business. Use **GreenerInc Selling Points** as the first line, followed by the paragraph or list. Include your name and email address after the text.

    e. Save the WordPad document with the filename **Selling Points.rtf** in the Website folder, then close the document and exit WordPad.

    f. Open a File Explorer window, then navigate to the Website folder.

    g. View the contents in at least three different views, then choose the view option that you prefer.

    h. Copy the Selling Points.rtf file, then paste a copy in the Documents folder.

    i. Rename the copied file **Selling Points Backup.rtf**.

    j. Cut the Selling Points Backup.rtf file from the Documents folder, and paste it in the GreenerInc\Website folder in the location where you store your Data Files, then close the File Explorer window.

Independent Challenge 2

As a freelance webpage designer for nonprofit businesses, you depend on your computer to meet critical deadlines. Whenever you encounter a computer problem, you contact a computer consultant who helps you resolve the problem. This consultant has asked you to document, or keep records of, your computer's available drives.

    a. Connect your USB flash drive to your computer, if necessary.

    b. Open File Explorer and go to This PC so you can view information on your drives and other installed hardware.

    c. View the window contents using three different views, then choose the one you prefer.

    d. Open WordPad and create a document with the text **My Drives** and your name on separate lines. Save the document as **My Drives.rtf**.

Independent Challenge 2 (continued)

e. Use Snap Assist to view the WordPad and File Explorer windows next to each other on the screen. (*Hint*: Drag the title bar of one of the windows to the left side of the screen.)

f. In WordPad, list the names of the hard drive (or drives), devices with removable storage, and any other hardware devices installed on the computer as shown in the Devices and Drives section of the window.

g. Switch to a view that displays the total size and amount of free space on your hard drive(s) and removable storage drive(s), and edit each WordPad list item to include the amount of free space for each one (for example, 22.1 GB free of 95.5 GB).

h. Save the WordPad document with the filename **My Drives** on your USB flash drive or the location where you store your Data Files.

i. Close WordPad, then maximize the File Explorer window. Navigate to your file storage location, then preview your document in the Preview pane, and close the window.

Independent Challenge 3

You are an attorney at Garcia and Chu, a large accounting firm. You participate in the company's community outreach program by speaking at career days in area schools. You teach students about career opportunities available in the field of accounting. You want to create a folder structure to store the files for each session.

a. Connect your USB flash drive to your computer (if necessary), then open the window for your USB flash drive or the location where you store your Data Files.

b. Create a folder named **Career Days**.

c. In the Career Days folder, create a subfolder named **Valley Intermediate**. Open this folder, then close it.

d. Use WordPad to create a document with the title **Accounting Jobs** at the top of the page and your name on separate lines, and the following list of items:
Current Opportunities:
Bookkeeper
Accounting Clerk
Accountant
Certified Public Accountant (CPA)

e. Save the WordPad document with the filename **Accounting Jobs.rtf** in the Valley Intermediate folder. (*Hint*: After you switch to your USB flash drive in the Save As dialog box, open the Career Days folder, then open the Valley Intermediate folder before saving the file.) Close WordPad.

f. Open WordPad and the Accounting Jobs document again, add **Senior Accountant** after Accountant, then save the file and close WordPad.

g. Store a copy of the file using the Save As command to your Documents folder, renaming it **Accounting Jobs - Copy.rtf**, then close WordPad.

h. In File Explorer, delete the document copy in your Documents folder so it is placed in the Recycle Bin, then restore it.

i. Open the Recycle Bin window, snap the File Explorer to the left side of the screen and the Recycle in to the right side, then verify that the file has been restored to the correct location.

j. Cut the file from the Documents folder and paste it in the Career Days\Valley Intermediate folder in your Data File storage location, then close all windows.

Independent Challenge 4: Explore

Think of a hobby or volunteer activity that you do now, or one that you would like to start. You will use your computer to help you manage your plans or ideas for this activity.

a. Using paper and pencil, sketch a folder structure with at least two subfolders to contain your documents for this activity.

b. Connect your USB flash drive to your computer, then open the window for your USB flash drive.

Independent Challenge 4: Explore (continued)

c. In File Explorer, create the folder structure for your activity, using your sketch as a reference.

d. Think of at least three tasks that you can do to further your work in your chosen activity.

e. Start a new WordPad document. Add the title **Next Steps** at the top of the page and your name on the next line.

f. Below your name, list the three tasks. Save the file in one of the folders created on your USB flash drive, with the title **To Do.rtf**.

g. Close WordPad, then open a File Explorer window and navigate to the folder where you stored the document.

h. Create a copy of the file, place the copied file in your Documents folder, then rename this file with a name you choose.

i. Delete the copied file from your Documents folder, restore it, then cut and paste the file into the folder that contains your To Do.rtf file, ensuring that the filename of the copy is different so it doesn't overwirte the To Do.rtf file.

j. Open Microsoft Edge using its button on the taskbar, click in the search text box, then search for information about others doing your desired hobby or volunteer activity.

k. Click the Make a Web Note button at the top of the window, click the Highlighter tool, then highlight an item that interests you.

l. Click the Share button, click Mail, choose your desired email account, then send the annotated page to yourself. You will receive an email with an attachment showing the annotated page.

m. Close Edge, your email program, and any open windows.

Visual Workshop

Create the folder structure shown in **FIGURE 2-28** on your USB flash drive (or in the location where you store your Data Files). Create a WordPad document containing your name and today's date, type the path to the Midsize folder, and save it with the filename **Midsize.rtf** in a Midsize folder on your USB Flash drive or the location where you store your Data Files.

FIGURE 2-28

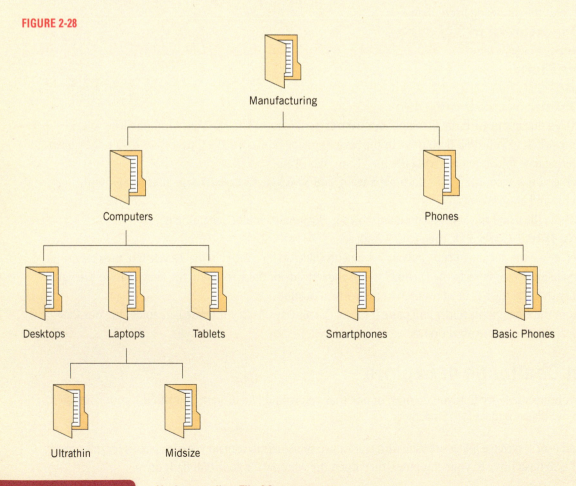

Getting Started with Microsoft Office 2016

CASE You have just joined the marketing team at Pepper's Green Basket, a grocery chain with stores in urban centers that offer wholesome food at reasonable prices. To familiarize yourself with Microsoft Office 2016, you decide to create a shopping list for an in-store healthy breakfast promotion.

Module Objectives

After completing this module, you will be able to:

- Understand Office 2016
- Start an Office app
- Identify common elements in an Office app
- Use the Ribbon and zoom controls
- Use the Quick Access Toolbar
- Save a file
- Get Help
- Exit an Office app

Files You Will Need

No files needed.

Understand Office 2016

Learning Outcomes
• Identify and explain the uses for Office 2016 apps
• Explain benefits of Office 2016

Microsoft Office 2016 is a collection (or **suite**) of programs or **apps** you can use to create documents, analyze data, and complete almost any business task. In this book you will learn how to use the four main productivity apps in the Office suite: Word, Excel, Access, and PowerPoint. Office 2016 is optimized for **the cloud**. In other words, you can work on Office files from a variety of devices including computers, tablets, and smartphones—as long as they are connected to the Internet. Office 2016 also includes **OneDrive**, a cloud-based storage repository you can access from any connected device. A OneDrive storage plan comes included with a Microsoft account (you can purchase more storage if you need it). Using OneDrive, you can create a document on your computer, open it on another computer and make edits to it, and open it on your smartphone to view the edits. Using Office 2016 and OneDrive, you can also share your files with coworkers and work collaboratively in real time on a single document from different devices. This means that if you are making edits to a shared document in Word, your friend viewing the shared document in another location can see the edits happening live as you make them, and vice versa. In addition to the four apps you learn about in this book, Office also includes the apps described in **TABLE 3-1**. **CASE** *Jessica Ramos, marketing director at Pepper's Green Basket, asks you to familiarize yourself with the apps in Office 2016.*

DETAILS

Microsoft Office 2016 contains the following apps:

- **Microsoft Word** is a word processing program you can use to create text documents, such as letters, memos, newsletters, and reports. You can also use Word to add photos, drawings, tables, and other graphical elements to your documents. **FIGURE 3-1** shows an annual report created using Word.

- **Microsoft Excel** is a **spreadsheet app** you can use to manipulate, analyze, and chart quantitative data. Excel is often used to calculate financial information. **FIGURE 3-2** shows a sales report created using Excel.

- **Microsoft Access** is a **database management program** you can use to store, organize, and keep track of information, such as customer names and addresses, product inventories, and employee information. **FIGURE 3-3** shows a form created in Access.

- **Microsoft PowerPoint** is a **presentation graphics program** you can use to develop materials for presentations, including slide shows, computer-based presentations, speaker's notes, and audience handouts. **FIGURE 3-4** shows a slide from a PowerPoint presentation.

TABLE 3-1: Other Office apps

Office app	what it is	what you use it for
Microsoft Outlook	Information manager	Sending and receiving email; scheduling appointments; maintaining to-do lists; storing names, addresses, and other contact information
Microsoft OneNote	Information collection tool and organizer	Organizing captured information like Web addresses, graphics, notes, and research
Microsoft Publisher	Desktop publishing program	Creating printed documents that combine text and graphics such as newsletters, brochures, and business cards
Microsoft Sway	Multimedia presentation tool	Combining text, graphics, and video, to tell a story across devices

Getting Started with Microsoft Office 2016

FIGURE 3-1: Report created in Word

FIGURE 3-2: Worksheet and chart created in Microsoft Excel

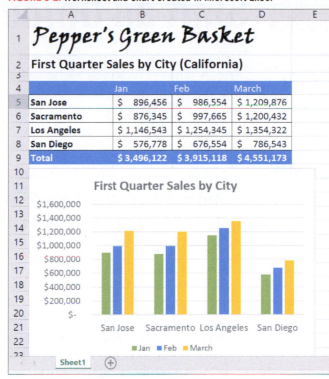

FIGURES 3-3 & 3-4: Database form created in Access and presentation slide created in PowerPoint

Using Office Online apps

Most Office 365 plans include **Office Online apps**, which are scaled-down versions of Word, Excel, OneNote, and PowerPoint that you can use with any browser to edit files, create new ones, and collaborate with others. Using the Office Online apps, you can also collaborate in real time; meaning that if you make edits to a document, your friend in another location can see the edits happening live as you make them and vice versa.

Start an Office App

Learning Outcomes
- Start an Office app
- Explain the purpose of a template

To get started using Office, you need to start, or **launch**, the Office app you want to use. If you are running Office on Windows 10, an easy way to start an app is to go to the Windows 10 Start screen, type the app name for which you want to search, then click the app name in the results list. You can also use the Start menu. **CASE** ▶ *You decide to familiarize yourself with Office by starting Word.*

STEPS

1. **Start your computer to display the Windows 10 desktop**

2. **On the Windows taskbar, click the Start button** ⊞

   The Start menu opens, as shown in **FIGURE 3-5**.

3. **Click All apps on the Start menu, scroll the list, and then click Word 2016**

   Word 2016 launches, and the Word start screen appears, as shown in **FIGURE 3-6**. The **start screen** is a landing page that appears when you first start an Office app. The left side of this screen displays recent files you have opened. (If you have never opened any files, then there will be no files listed under Recent.) The right side displays images depicting different templates you can use to create different types of documents. A **template** is a file containing professionally designed content that you can easily replace with your own. Using a template to create a document can save time and ensure your document looks great. You can also start from scratch using the Blank document option.

The many editions of Microsoft Office

Office 2016 comes in many different editions, each of which includes a different set of apps and services appropriate for different customers including business users, home users, or students. You can buy Office by paying a one-time fee, which allows you to install the software on one computer; purchase an annual or monthly subscription (called Office 365), which lets you install Office on one or more computers or devices; or you can use a free version, Office Online, which includes a smaller set of tools. See **TABLE 3-2** for a sampling of popular Office 2016 editions that are currently available for consumers.

TABLE 3-2: Popular Office product offerings for consumers

version	description	what it includes
Office 365 Home	Installed apps plus online storage and services for up to 5 users; includes version updates	Word, Excel, PowerPoint, Access, OneNote, Outlook, Publisher, Skype
Office 365 Personal	Installed apps plus online storage and services for one user; includes version updates	Word, Excel, PowerPoint, Access, OneNote, Outlook, Publisher
Office Home & Student 2016	One-time purchase; lets you install apps on one computer; does not include version updates	Word, Excel, PowerPoint, OneNote
Office Online	Free online versions of the Office apps, designed for collaborating with others in real time and using across devices	Word, Excel, PowerPoint, OneNote, Sway, Outlook, OneDrive, and more

FIGURE 3-5: Windows 10 desktop with Start menu open

FIGURE 3-6: Word start screen

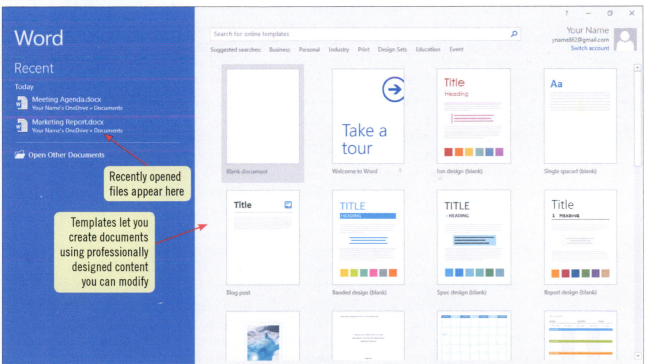

Office 2016

Identify Common Elements in an Office App

No matter what edition of Office 2016 you are using, you will notice that all Office apps share a common user interface. A **user interface** is the collection of buttons and tools you use to interact with a software program or app. Once you are familiar with the user interface of one app, you will be able to recognize and use them in all of the Office apps. **CASE** ▶ *You decide to start a new document and familiarize yourself with the Word app user interface.*

STEPS

1. **Click Blank document in the Start screen**

   The Start screen closes, and a new blank document appears in the Word app window.

2. **Read the information below, then refer to FIGURE 3-7 to learn the different user interface elements of the Word app, most of which are common to all Office apps**

   • The **title bar**, at the top of the window, contains the name of the document (currently the temporary name Document1) and the name of the app (currently Word). The **Ribbon Display Options button** provides commands for hiding or displaying the Ribbon.

   • On the left end of the title bar is the **Quick Access Toolbar**, containing buttons for favorite commands. By default, these include saving a file, undoing an action, and redoing or repeating an action. On touchscreen devices, the toolbar also includes a Touch/Mouse Mode button, to provide more spacing between ribbon buttons. The Quick Access Toolbar is always available no matter what tab is active, making it easy to access favorite commands whenever you need them.

   • The **Ribbon** is the band directly below the title bar. It contains commands in the form of buttons, icons, lists, galleries, and text boxes. A **command** is an instruction you give to a computer to complete a task, such as printing a document or saving your changes. You might see a name at the right end of the Ribbon. Your name and picture appear if you have signed into your Microsoft account. The **Share button** opens a pane where you can share a file saved on your OneDrive with others, and then view who is editing the shared document in real time.

   • Across the top of the Ribbon are several **tabs**, each of which contains a different set of commands for completing a particular type of task. At the moment, the **Home tab** is active, so it appears in front of the other tabs. The Home tab contains commands for performing the most frequently used commands for creating a document. Clicking a different tab displays a different group of commands related to performing a different type of task.

   • The **File tab** contains commands that let you work with the whole document. You use the File tab to open, save, print, and close documents. The File tab is present in all Office programs.

   • Each tab is organized into **groups** of related commands, such as the Clipboard group, Font group, and Paragraph group. You can see these group names at the bottom of each tab. To the right of many group names is a small arrow called a **dialog box launcher**, or **launcher**. Clicking a launcher opens a **dialog box**—a floating window where you can enter additional information to complete a task.

   • The **document window** is the work area within the app window. This is where you type text into your document and format it to look the way you want. The work area looks different in each Office app based on the type of file you are creating. The **insertion point** is a flashing vertical line in the document window that indicates where text will be inserted when you type.

   • The **status bar** at the bottom of the screen displays key information, such as the current page. At the far right of the status bar are the **View buttons**, which you use to change your view of the document. You can use the **Zoom slider**, located to the right of the View buttons, to set the magnification level of your document view.

FIGURE 3-7: Word app window

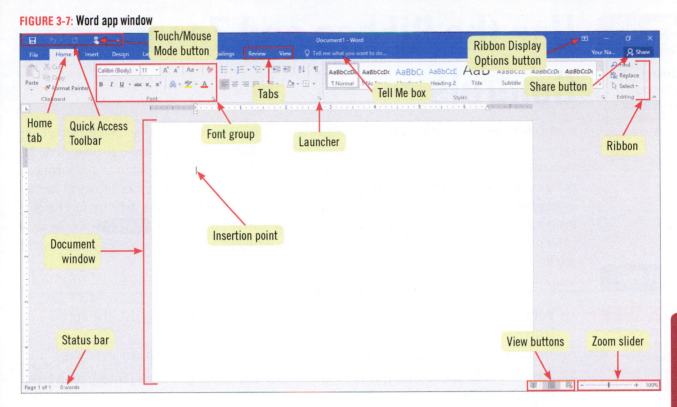

Touch/Mouse Mode button

Ribbon Display Options button

Tabs

Tell Me box

Share button

Home tab

Quick Access Toolbar

Font group

Launcher

Ribbon

Insertion point

Document window

Status bar

View buttons

Zoom slider

Use the Ribbon and Zoom Controls

In all Office apps, you use the Ribbon to initiate commands. Some commands on the Ribbon are the same—or very similar—across all Office apps. For instance, all Office apps have similar commands on the View tab for changing the document view. You can use the View commands to switch to a different pre-defined view, such as Draft or Web Layout, or to adjust the magnification level so your document appears larger or smaller on the screen. Many Office apps also contain a Zoom slider on the status bar for changing the magnification level and View shortcut buttons for switching among views. **CASE** *You decide to create a shopping list for an in-store promotion, then view it in different ways using the buttons on the View tab and the Zoom slider.*

STEPS

1. **With the insertion point at the top of the document, type Shopping List, then press [Enter]**

   The text you typed appears in the first line of the document, and the insertion point moves down.

2. **Type Soy milk, press [Enter], type Pepper's Fiber Crunch Cereal, press [Enter], then type Organic blueberries**

3. **Click the View tab on the Ribbon**

   The View tab is now active. This tab contains commands for changing your view of the document window. Changing your view does not change the document itself; it just lets you see it differently in order to focus on different stages of the project, such as entering text, formatting, or reading. You are currently working in Print Layout view, which shows you exactly how a document will look when it is printed.

4. **Click the Read Mode button 📖 in the Views group**

   Your shopping list now appears in a view better for reading on a computer screen, as shown in **FIGURE 3-8**. The Ribbon is no longer visible, leaving more room for viewing the document. The commands along the top left of the screen let you open the File tab, search for information, or change the view.

5. **Click View, then click Edit Document**

   Your Shopping List now appears in the default view—Print Layout—and the View tab on the Ribbon is visible again.

6. **Scroll up, if necessary, so that the top of the page is in view**

7. **On the Zoom slider in the lower-right corner of the screen, click the Zoom In button ➕ 10 times until 200% appears to the right of the slider**

   Now the text in your Shopping List document appears double its actual size, as shown in **FIGURE 3-9**. Each time you clicked the ➕ button, the zoom increased by 10%. Clicking the Zoom Out button ➖ decreases the zoom by 10%. Note the Zoom commands do not change the actual text size in your document, only the magnification level you see onscreen.

8. **Click the 100% button in the Zoom group on the Ribbon**

   Your Shopping List appears again at 100%, the actual size of the document as it would look printed. Compare your screen to **FIGURE 3-10**.

FIGURE 3-8: Viewing a document in Read Mode view

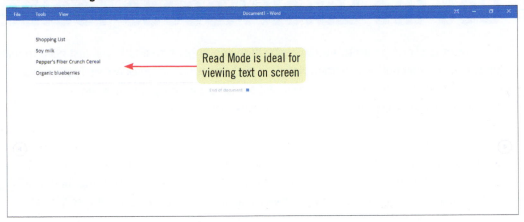

FIGURE 3-9: Document with zoom set to 200%

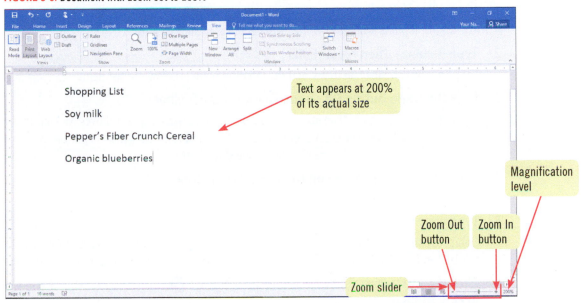

FIGURE 3-10: Document with zoom set to 100%

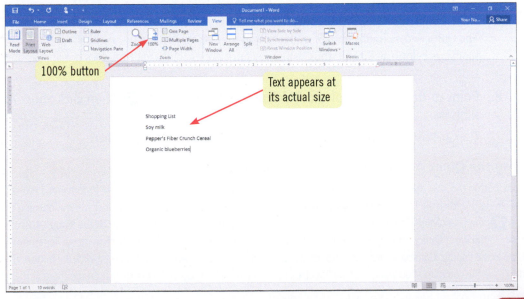

Use the Quick Access Toolbar

If you want to click a particular button in an Office app to perform a task, you first need to make sure the tab containing that button is in front. However, the buttons on the Quick Access Toolbar, located just above the Ribbon on the left side of the screen, are available any time, except when the File tab is active. By default, the Quick Access Toolbar contains buttons that let you save a file, undo your last action, redo or repeat the last action you undid, and adjust the spacing between buttons on the Ribbon. These buttons are also available on other tabs in the Ribbon; having them available on the Quick Access Toolbar lets you work faster. You can add buttons you frequently use to the Quick Access Toolbar using the Customize Quick Access Toolbar menu. You can also move the Quick Access Toolbar below the Ribbon. **CASE** *You continue working on your shopping list while exploring the buttons on the Quick Access Toolbar.*

STEPS

1. **Press [Ctrl][End] to place the insertion point at the end of the document if necessary, then press [Enter]**

   The insertion point is now below the third item in your shopping list.

2. **Type Bananas, then press [Enter]**

   Your list now contains four items, and the insertion point is below the last item.

3. **Click the Undo button ↺ on the Quick Access Toolbar**

   The last word you typed, "Bananas," is deleted, and the insertion point moves back up to the end of the fourth line. The Undo button reverses your last action. You can click the Redo button to restore your document to the state it was in before you clicked the Undo button.

4. **Click the Redo button ↻ on the Quick Access Toolbar**

   The text "Bananas" is now back as the fourth item in your shopping list.

5. **Type your name**

   Compare your screen to **FIGURE 3-11**. The Repeat button ↻ now appears in place of the Redo button; when this button is available, you can click it to repeat the previous action, such as typing your name.

6. **Click the Customize Quick Access Toolbar button ⩢ on the right side of the Quick Access Toolbar**

   A menu opens and displays a list of common commands, as shown in **FIGURE 3-12**. Save, Undo, and Redo all have check marks next to them, indicating these commands are already on the Quick Access Toolbar.

7. **Click Show Below the Ribbon**

   The Quick Access Toolbar moves, and is now located below the Ribbon, as shown in **FIGURE 3-13**. When the toolbar is below the Ribbon, the Customize Quick Access toolbar button does not appear until you point to it.

8. **Point to the right side of the Quick Access Toolbar, click ⩢, then click Show Above the Ribbon**

   The Quick Access Toolbar moves back to its default location above the Ribbon.

Customizing the Quick Access Toolbar

You can add any button that you use frequently to the Quick Access Toolbar. To do this, click the Customize Quick Access Toolbar button ⩢, then click More Commands; the Quick Access Toolbar category in the Word Options dialog box opens. Click any command listed in the Popular Commands list, click Add, then click OK. (If you don't see the command you want, click the Popular Commands list arrow, then click All Commands.) You can also add a button to the Quick Access Toolbar without opening this dialog box: simply right-click the button on the Ribbon, then click Add to Quick Access Toolbar on the shortcut menu. To remove any button from the Quick Access Toolbar, right-click the button, then click Remove from Quick Access Toolbar on the shortcut menu.

FIGURE 3-11: Completed shopping list

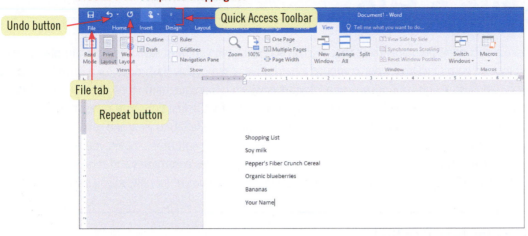

Undo button

Quick Access Toolbar

File tab

Repeat button

Shopping List

Soy milk

Pepper's Fiber Crunch Cereal

Organic blueberries

Bananas

Your Name

FIGURE 3-12: Customize Quick Access Toolbar menu

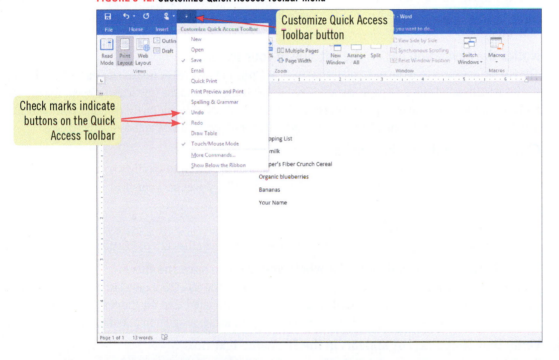

Customize Quick Access Toolbar button

Check marks indicate buttons on the Quick Access Toolbar

FIGURE 3-13: Moving the Quick Access Toolbar

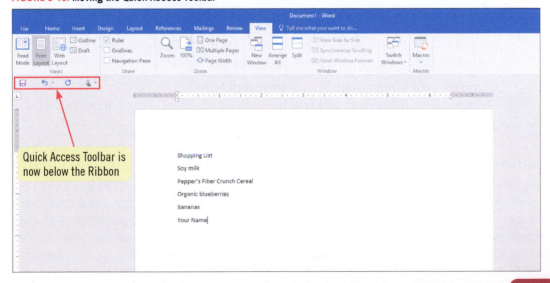

Quick Access Toolbar is now below the Ribbon

Shopping List

Soy milk

Pepper's Fiber Crunch Cereal

Organic blueberries

Bananas

Your Name

Save a File

Learning Outcomes
• Save a file to a specific location

To store a document permanently so that you can access it later, you must save it to a specific place, such as in a folder on your OneDrive, your computer's hard drive, a removable flash drive, or a drive located on a network. You also assign your document a **filename**, which is a unique name for a file, so you can identify and access it later. You use the Save As command to save a file for the first time. You access the Save As command on the File tab. In addition to saving files, you can click the File tab to view and set properties for your document, open and print files, quickly access recent documents, and more. When you open the File tab, you are working in **Backstage view**, which is a view that provides commands and tools to help you work with your files. **CASE** ▸ *You have finished your Shopping List document for now, so you decide to save it.*

STEPS

1. **Click the File tab on the Ribbon**

   A large window opens with "Info" at the top. Your document is no longer visible onscreen, though you can see its filename in the title bar. You are now in Backstage view, which provides commands for working with files.

2. **Notice the navigation bar on the left side of your screen**

   The File tab navigation bar contains commands (such as Open and Save As) as well as tabs that, when clicked, display related commands for a particular task. The Info tab is selected and the Info screen is open. You use the tools here to specify various settings for the open document. The Properties pane on the right shows information about the Shopping List document, including its size, number of pages, author, and last-modified date.

3. **Click Save As on the navigation bar**

   The Save As screen opens, as shown in **FIGURE 3-14**. You use this screen to specify where to save your file. You can specify to save the file on your OneDrive, on a USB drive, on your hard drive, or anywhere you specify.

4. **Click Browse; or click OneDrive to save to the cloud**

   The Save As dialog box opens, showing the list of folders and files in the current location.

5. **Navigate to the drive and/or folder where you want to save the file**

   Now you need to name the file. The File name text box displays the text "Shopping List" because this is the first line of text in the document; Word always suggests a filename based on the first few words in the unsaved open document. "Shopping List" is a good name for the file, so you don't need to type a new name.

QUICK TIP
If you click the Save command before you save a file for the first time, the Save As dialog box opens, so you can assign the file a name and folder location.

6. **Verify that Shopping List appears in the File name text box**

   You might see ".docx" at the end of the filename; .docx is the default file extension for this document. When you save a file, a **file extension** is added automatically to identify the app that created it. Documents created in Word 2016 have the file extension ".docx". Your computer might not be set to display file extensions, in which case you will not see this information in the File name text box or in the title bar of the app; this is not a problem, as the information is still saved with the file.

7. **Compare your screen to FIGURE 3-15, then click Save**

   The Save As dialog box closes, and your Shopping List document is saved in the location you specified. Notice the title bar now displays the new filename.

Using OneDrive and Office Online

If you are signed into your Microsoft account, you can easily save your files to OneDrive and have access to them on other devices—such as a tablet or smartphone. OneDrive is available as an app on smartphones, which makes access very easy. If you have the OneDrive app installed on your phone, you can open files to view and edit them using Office Online. Using OneDrive, you and your colleagues can create, edit, and store documents in the cloud and make the documents available to whomever you grant access. To use OneDrive, you need a free Microsoft account, which you obtain at http://OneDrive.live.com.

FIGURE 3-14: Save As screen

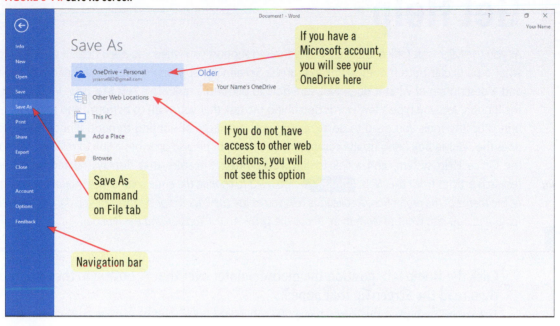

If you have a Microsoft account, you will see your OneDrive here

If you do not have access to other web locations, you will not see this option

Save As command on File tab

Navigation bar

FIGURE 3-15: Save As dialog box

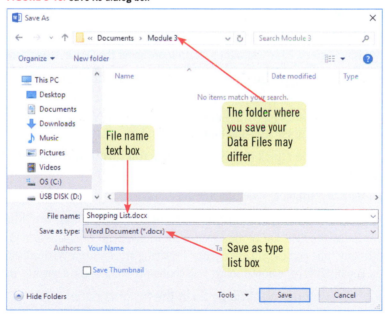

The folder where you save your Data Files may differ

File name text box

Save as type list box

Get Help

Learning Outcomes
- Use ScreenTips to learn about buttons on the Ribbon
- Use the Tell Me box to get instant access to commands
- Use the Tell Me box to access articles

As you use Microsoft Office, there are many tools to support you when you need help. If you need to know what a particular button does, point to it and a **ScreenTip** appears, displaying the name of the button and a description of what it does. Not sure how to perform a task? The **Tell Me box**, located just above the Ribbon, lets you type a few words describing the task that you want to perform, and then immediately brings up the tools you need to do so, saving you the hassle of hunting through Ribbon tabs. Not only does the Tell Me box bring up the commands you need, but it also provides a link to related Help topics in the Office Help system, and a link to **Smart Lookup**, a feature that displays related definitions and research articles from the Web. **CASE** ▶ *You need to change the page color of the shopping list to green to fit the theme of the promotion. A colleague tells you to use the Page Color button, but you don't know where the feature is. You also want to learn more about the Quick Access Toolbar and the Ribbon.*

STEPS

1. **Click the Home tab, position the mouse pointer over the ⬛ button in the Font group, then read the ScreenTip that appears**

   The ScreenTip displays the button name "Text Highlight Color" and its purpose, as shown in **FIGURE 3-16**. This is not the button you want. To save time, you can use the Tell Me box.

QUICK TIP
You can also open the Help window in any Office application by pressing [F1].

2. **Click in the Tell Me box, then type page color**

   A list of commands containing the words "page color" as well as "page" and "color" appears below the Tell Me box. The Page Color command is at the top of the list.

3. **Click Page Color to open a color palette, then move the mouse pointer over each color**

   Notice how the page color changes as the mouse moves over each color. Pointing to a color lets you preview that color before committing to it; this feature is called **Live Preview** and it is active in many formatting features in most Office apps.

4. **Click the lightest shade of green as shown in FIGURE 3-17**

   Your page is now green. Now you want to learn more about the Quick Access Toolbar.

TROUBLE
If this is the first time you are using the Insights pane, click Got It to accept the terms of use and continue.

5. **In the Tell Me box, type Quick Access Toolbar, then click "Get Help on Quick Access Too…"**

   The Word 2016 Help window opens, as shown in **FIGURE 3-18** and displays a list of Help articles on the Quick Access Toolbar. You can type other **keywords**, which are words used to search for information, in the Search box at the top of the screen to find information on any topic you want.

6. **Click Customize the Quick Access Toolbar, scroll through the article to read it, then click the Close button ☒**

   Now you want to learn more about the Ribbon.

7. **Click the Tell Me box, type Ribbon, then click Smart Lookup on "Ribbon"**

   A pane opens on the right side of the screen as shown in **FIGURE 3-19**. This is the **Insights pane**, a window that opens any time you use Smart Lookup, displaying articles from Wikipedia and content from top web searches. The Insights pane now displays web content relating to the keyword "ribbon."

TROUBLE
If you don't see the Wikipedia article in the Insights pane, click another relevant item.

8. **Click Ribbon (Computing)-Wikipedia in the Insights pane**

   Your default browser opens and displays the Wikipedia article. The Word window is no longer visible.

9. **Scroll through the article to scan it, click your browser's close button ☒, click the Word icon ⬛ on the Windows taskbar if necessary to return to Word, then click the Insights pane close button ☒**

   The Insights pane closes.

FIGURE 3-16: ScreenTip showing name and purpose of Text Highlight Color button

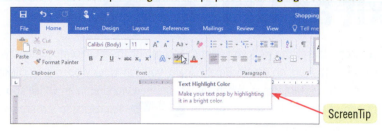

Text Highlight Color
Make your text pop by highlighting it in a bright color.

ScreenTip

FIGURE 3-17: Changing page color using the Tell Me box

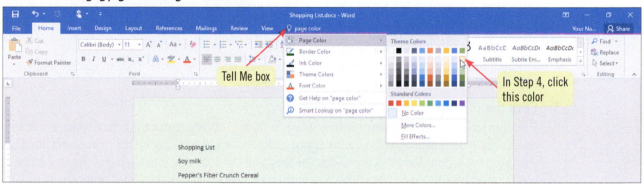

Tell Me box

In Step 4, click this color

Shopping List
Soy milk
Pepper's Fiber Crunch Cereal

FIGURE 3-18: Word Help search results

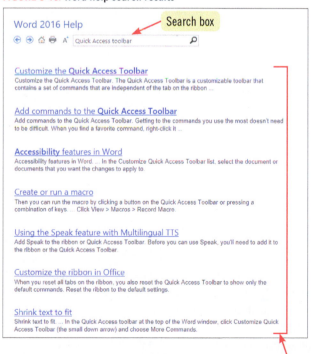

Search box

Word 2016 Help

Quick Access toolbar

Customize the Quick Access Toolbar
Customize the Quick Access Toolbar. The Quick Access Toolbar is a customizable toolbar that contains a set of commands that are independent of the tab on the ribbon ...

Add commands to the Quick Access Toolbar
Add commands to the Quick Access Toolbar. Getting to the commands you use the most doesn't need to be difficult. When you find a favorite command, right-click it ...

Accessibility features in Word
Accessibility features in Word. ... In the Customize Quick Access Toolbar list, select the document or documents that you want the changes to apply to.

Create or run a macro
Then you can run the macro by clicking a button on the Quick Access Toolbar or pressing a combination of keys. ... Click View > Macros > Record Macro.

Using the Speak feature with Multilingual TTS
Add Speak to the ribbon or Quick Access Toolbar. Before you can use Speak, you'll need to add it to the ribbon or the Quick Access Toolbar.

Customize the ribbon in Office
When you reset all tabs on the ribbon, you also reset the Quick Access Toolbar to show only the default commands. Reset the ribbon to the default settings.

Shrink text to fit
Shrink text to fit. ... In the Quick Access toolbar at the top of the Word window, click Customize Quick Access Toolbar (the small down arrow) and choose More Commands.

Links to articles containing "Quick Access Toolbar"

FIGURE 3-19: Insights pane displaying search results for "Ribbon"

Insights pane

Insights

Explore   Define

Explore Wikipedia

Ribbon (computing) - Wikipedia, the free encyclope
Such ribbons use tabs to expose different sets of controls, eliminating the need for many parallel toolbars. ... The ribbon consolidates the functionality previously found in ...

Ribbon - Wikipedia, the free encyclopedia
A ribbon or riband is a thin band of material, typically cloth but also plastic or sometimes metal, used primarily as decorative binding and tying. Cloth ribbons are made of ...

Bing image search

Links to Web articles containing "Ribbon"

Exit an Office App

Learning Outcomes
• Open a file from the Recent list
• Close a file and exit an app

When you complete all the work you want to accomplish in an Office document, you can save and close it. Later, when you want to work on the document again, you can quickly open it by clicking the filename in the Recent section of the app's start screen. When you are finished working in an Office app, you click the close button on the right end of the title bar to exit the app. **CASE** ▶ *You decide to practice opening and closing the Shopping List file. Then, you will exit Word.*

STEPS

1. **Click Save button 🖫 on the Quick Access Toolbar**

   Clicking the Save button on the Quick Access Toolbar is a fast way to save any recent changes you have made to your document. It is a good idea to click the Save button frequently as you work to make sure you do not lose any data if you lose power or your computer crashes.

2. **Click the File tab, then click Close**

   The document closes, but Word remains open. The Home tab is now active. You can quickly locate and open the Shopping List document by using the File tab.

3. **Click the File tab**

   The Open screen opens in Backstage view, as shown in **FIGURE 3-20**. Notice that the Recent option is selected, and names of documents opened recently appear under Today and Yesterday on the right. Other headings you might see include Last Week and Older. The Shopping List document is at the top of the list because it was the most recently opened document. You might see other document names listed below Shopping List.

4. **Click Shopping List below Today**

   The Shopping List document opens. You are now ready to close the document and end your Word session.

5. **Click the Close button ✕ at the far right end of the title bar, as shown in FIGURE 3-21**

   Both the Shopping List document and the Word app close.

Using Office on a touch screen device

If you are running Office 2016 on a Windows device with a touch screen, you can use gestures instead of mouse clicks to do various tasks including choosing commands. The basic gestures are **tap** (touch screen quickly with one finger), **pinch** (bring two fingers together), **stretch** (move two fingers apart), **slide** (drag an object using your finger), and **swipe** (move your finger from left to right). To choose a command on the Ribbon or in a dialog box, tap the button. You can use the Touch/Mouse Mode button 👆▾ on the Quick Access Toolbar to increase spacing between commands. To scroll, swipe the screen up, down, left, or right. To zoom in, stretch two fingers apart. To zoom out, pinch your fingers together. To hide the Ribbon, tap the Ribbon Display Options button 🔲 on the title bar, then tap Auto-hide Ribbon.

FIGURE 3-20: Open screen in Backstage view

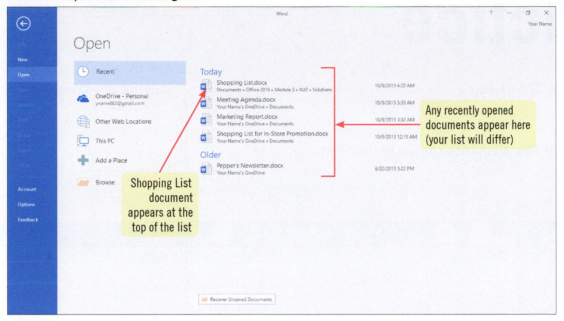

FIGURE 3-21: Exiting an app using the Close button

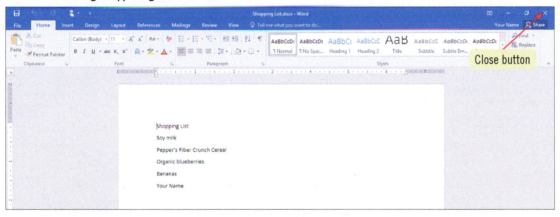

Sharing your saved documents

As you work through this book, you will create documents that you will need to submit to your instructor. You can email your saved documents using the Share screen in Backstage view. To do this, click the File tab, click Share to open the Share screen, click Email, then click Send as Attachment.

In other situations, you might want to share a document with a co-worker and edit it together in real time. To do this, you first must save the open document to your OneDrive. Once it is saved there, you can click the Share button above the Ribbon to open the Share pane, where you can enter the email addresses of people with whom you want to share the document, and then click Share to email the invitations. Once your collaborators receive the email, they can click the link to open the document and begin editing. You will see where in the document each person is working. Each time you click the Save button, any changes made by others will be reflected on your screen and vice versa, and new changes will be highlighted in green.

Office 2016

Practice

Concepts Review

Label each of the elements shown in FIGURE 3-22.

FIGURE 3-22

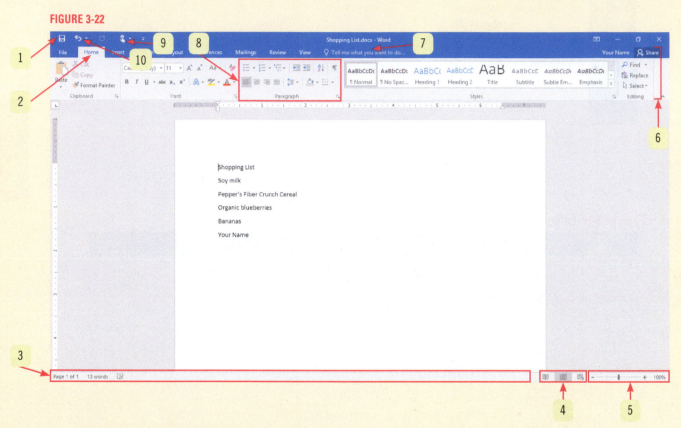

Match each of the following tasks with the most appropriate app for completing it.

11. Organize captured information for a research project
12. Create a newsletter containing text and graphics
13. Manage a large amount of product inventory information
14. Create a chart that shows sales of bestselling products
15. Create slides for a company meeting presentation

a. Word
b. OneNote
c. Access
d. PowerPoint
e. Excel

Creating a Document

CASE Jessica Ramos, the marketing director for Pepper's Green Basket, asks you to finish creating a letter to one of the winners of the Pepper's Green Basket recipe contest. Jessica has already created a document that contains part of the letter. You will open Jessica's letter; add, edit, and rearrange text in it; proof it for spelling errors; then print it.

Module Objectives

After completing this module, you will be able to:

- Create a new document from an existing file
- Enter text in a document
- Select and edit text
- Copy text
- Move text
- Find and replace text
- Format text using the Mini toolbar
- Check spelling and grammar
- Preview and print a document

Files You Will Need

4-1.docx	4-4.docx
4-2.docx	4-5.docx
4-3.docx	

Create a New Document from an Existing File

Sometimes it is useful to create a new document by adapting an existing one. For instance, suppose you need to write a memo that will include lots of information contained in a memo you already wrote. You can open the existing memo, and then, before making any changes, use the Save As command to save a copy of it with a new name. This keeps the original file intact in case you want to use it again, while saving you the trouble of creating the new memo from scratch. **CASE** *You need to complete Jessica's letter to the appetizer winner of the recipe competition. You need to open Jessica's document and save it with a different name, to keep Jessica's original letter intact.*

STEPS

1. **On the Windows taskbar, click the Start button ⊞, click All apps on the Start menu, scroll the list, then click Word 2016**

   The Word Start screen opens, as shown in Figure 4-1. You want to open an existing file.

2. **Click Open Other Documents at the bottom of the Recent pane on the left side of the Start screen**

   The Open screen appears in Backstage view and displays places where files are stored, including Recent (which is currently selected), and This PC (which is your computer as well as any external drives attached to it). If you are signed into a Microsoft account, then you will also see your OneDrive listed.

3. **Click Browse, navigate to the location where you store your Data Files, then double-click the Module 4 folder**

   The Data Files for Module 4 appear in the Open dialog box.

4. **Click 4-1.docx, click Open, then click Enable Editing if necessary**

   The yellow bar with the Enable Editing command appears any time you open an unfamiliar file; it's a safeguard to help protect you from malicious viruses that could harm your computer or compromise your data. Jessica's partially completed document is now open in the document window.

5. **Click the File tab, click Save As to open the Save As screen, then click Browse**

   The Save As dialog box opens, and displays the files in the Module 4 folder, as shown in **FIGURE 4-2**, and displays the contents of the Module 4 folder (the most recently opened folder). You use the Save As dialog box to create a copy of the document with a new name. The name in the File name text box is **selected**, or highlighted; any words you type replace the selected text.

6. **Type 4-Recipe Winner Letter**

   The File name text box now contains the new title you typed. Because the filename begins with "4-", you will be able to identify it as a file you created for Module 4 of this book.

7. **Click Save**

   Word saves the 4-Recipe Winner Letter file in the Module 04 folder. The title bar changes to reflect the new name, as shown in **FIGURE 4-3**. The file 4-1 closes and remains intact.

Creating a new document from a template

If you need to create a certain type of document, you might want to start from a template. A **template** is a file that contains predesigned formatting and text for common business documents such as letters, business cards, and reports. To create a document from a template, click the File tab, then click New to open the New screen in Backstage view, then click the template you want. A new document based on the template opens on your screen, ready for you to customize and save. To access a huge variety of templates, you can search online by typing keywords in the search box at the top of the New screen.

FIGURE 4-1: Word Start screen

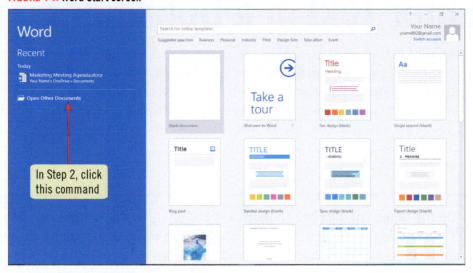

In Step 2, click this command

FIGURE 4-2: Save As dialog box

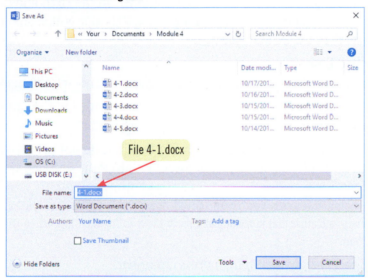

File 4-1.docx

FIGURE 4-3: 4-Recipe Winner Letter in Print Layout view

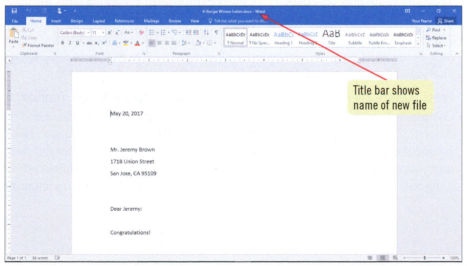

Title bar shows name of new file

Enter Text in a Document

Learning Outcomes
- Display formatting marks
- Enter text in Print Layout view
- Explain AutoCorrect

To add text to a document, you need to first position the insertion point where you want to insert text, and then start typing. Typing text is also called **entering** text. When you enter text into a document, it is a good idea to work in Print Layout view, which is the default view for entering and editing text. An advantage of Print Layout view is that you see exactly how the text will look when printed on paper. To help you in the editing process, turn on formatting marks so you can see blank spaces and paragraph marks as you work. **CASE** *Jessica's letter contains some text. You need to add a paragraph informing the recipient he won the contest.*

STEPS

QUICK TIP

The Show/Hide ¶ button is a toggle button: clicking it once turns it on to show formatting marks; clicking it again turns it off to hide formatting marks.

1. **On the Home tab, click the Show/Hide ¶ button ¶ in the Paragraph group**

   Your screen now displays formatting marks. Dots between words represent spaces, and a paragraph mark (¶) represents a paragraph return that Word inserts when you press [Enter]. Showing formatting marks when you write and edit makes it easier to see extra spaces, unintended paragraph returns, and other punctuation errors.

2. **Click to the right of the word "Congratulations!" in the sixth line of text**

   Clicking in this location sets the **insertion point**, the blinking vertical line on the screen that controls where text will be inserted when you type.

3. **Press ↓ two times**

   The insertion point is now next to the second paragraph mark below "Congratulations!".

4. **Type You won the Pepper's Green Basket recipe contest in the Appetizer category!**

   The insertion point moved to the right as you typed each word.

QUICK TIP

As you type, the word count indicator on the status bar displays the number of words your document contains. For more specific word-count information, click the indicator.

5. **Press [Spacebar], then type the following text, but do not press [Enter] when you reach the right edge of your screen: Your Sweet Potato Puffs received the highest scores from our judges.**

   At some point, the words you typed moved down, or **wrapped**, to the next line. This is known as **word wrap**, a feature that automatically pushes text to the next line when the insertion point meets the right margin.

6. **Press [Spacebar], type teh, then press [Spacebar]**

   Notice that even though you typed "teh", Word assumed that you meant to type "The" and automatically corrected it. This feature is called **AutoCorrect**.

7. **Type the following text exactly as shown (including errors): prizes listed beelow will be shipped to you soon soon:**

   You should see red wavy lines under the word "beelow" and the second instance of "soon." These red lines indicate the Spell Checker automatically identified these as either misspelled or duplicate words. Blue wavy lines indicate possible grammatical errors.

8. **Press [Enter], then click the Save button 🖫 on the Quick Access Toolbar**

   Compare your screen to **FIGURE 4-4**. Pressing [Enter] inserted a blank line and moved the insertion point down two lines to the left margin. Although you pressed [Enter] only once, an extra blank line was inserted because the default style in this document specifies to insert a blank line after you press [Enter] to start a new paragraph. **Styles** are settings that control how text and paragraphs are formatted. Each document has its own set of styles, which you can easily change. You will work with styles in a future module.

FIGURE 4-4: Letter with new text entered

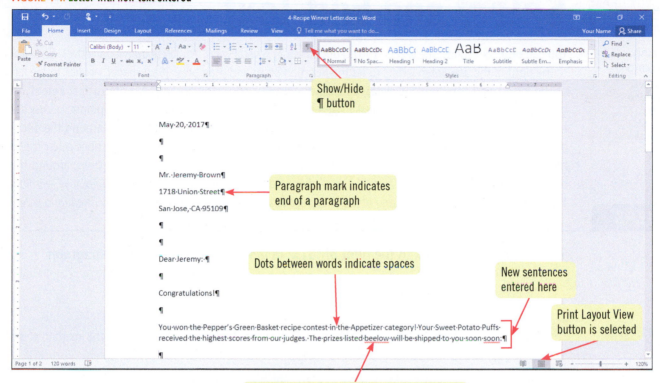

Show/Hide ¶ button

Paragraph mark indicates end of a paragraph

Dots between words indicate spaces

New sentences entered here

Print Layout View button is selected

Red wavy line indicates possible spelling error

Using AutoCorrect

The AutoCorrect feature works automatically to catch and correct incorrect spellings of common words as you type them. For example, if you type "comapny" instead of "company," as soon as you press [Spacebar], Word corrects the misspelling. After Word makes the correction, you can point to the word to make a small bar appear under the corrected text. If you place the pointer over this bar, the AutoCorrect Options button appears. Click the AutoCorrect Options button to display a list of options, as shown in **FIGURE 4-5**; then click an option.

You can change AutoCorrect settings in the AutoCorrect dialog box. To open this dialog box, click Control AutoCorrect Options on the AutoCorrect menu, or click the File tab, click

Options, click Proofing in the Word Options dialog box, then click AutoCorrect Options.

FIGURE 4-5: AutoCorrect Options menu

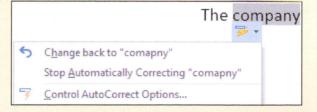

The company

↶ Change back to "comapny"

Stop Automatically Correcting "comapny"

⚡ Control AutoCorrect Options...

Select and Edit Text

You can **edit**, or modify, the text in a Word document in several ways. To delete individual letters, first click to the right of the unwanted letters to set the insertion point and then press [Backspace], or click to the left of the letters and then press [Delete]. To delete several words or paragraphs, you must first **select**, or highlight, the unwanted text, then press [Delete]. To select text, drag the I-beam mouse pointer across the text, then release the mouse button. To edit text, you need to move the insertion point around the document. You can do this by pointing and clicking or by using the keyboard. **TABLE 4-1** describes other useful methods for selecting text. **TABLE 4-2** describes keys you can use to move the insertion point around the document. **CASE** *You need to make some changes to the letter to correct errors and improve wording. You also decide to change the spacing of the document to single spaced, so it is properly formatted for a letter.*

STEPS

1. **Press the ↓, then click to the right of "$25" in the line of text below the paragraph you typed**

   The insertion point is just after the "5" in "25".

2. **Press [Backspace] twice**

   You deleted "25". Each time you pressed [Backspace], you deleted the character to the left of the insertion point.

3. **Type 150**

   The amount of the prize money now reads "$150", the correct amount.

4. **Double-click the second instance of soon in the second line of the new paragraph you typed**

   The word "soon" is now selected. Double-clicking a word selects the entire word and the leading space if there is one.

5. **Press [Delete]**

   The second instance of the word "soon" and the space before it are removed from the document. You could have deleted either instance of the duplicated word to remove the red wavy line and correct the error. The text after the deleted word wraps back to fill the empty space.

6. **Scroll to the end of the document if necessary, place the mouse pointer to the left of "Jessica Ramos" (the last line of the document) until the pointer changes to ⏋, then click**

   See **FIGURE 4-6**. The entire line of text ("Jessica Ramos") is selected, including the paragraph symbol at the end of the line. The area to the left of the left margin is the **selection bar**, which you use to select entire lines. When you place the mouse pointer in the selection bar, it changes to ⏋.

7. **Type your name**

   Your name replaces Jessica's name in the letter.

8. **Press [Ctrl][Home] to move the insertion point to the beginning of the document**

   Notice the line spacing of the letter is double spaced after each paragraph mark ¶. So that the letter is properly formatted, you want to change the line spacing to be single spaced. To do this, you first need to select all the text in the document.

9. **Press [Ctrl][A] to select the entire document, click the No Spacing button in the Styles group, click anywhere to deselect the text, then save your changes**

   The document is now single spaced after each paragraph mark. Compare your screen to **FIGURE 4-7**.

FIGURE 4-6: Selecting an entire line of text

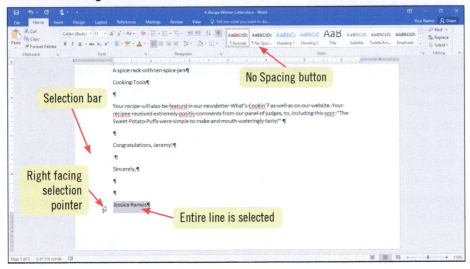

Selection bar

Right facing selection pointer

No Spacing button

Entire line is selected

FIGURE 4-7: Document after applying No Spacing style

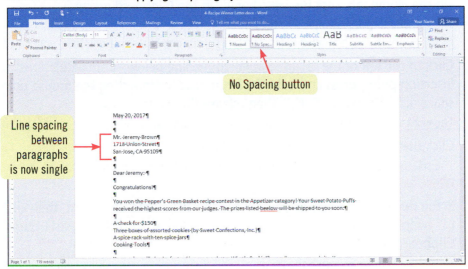

No Spacing button

Line spacing between paragraphs is now single

TABLE 4-1: Methods for selecting text

text to select	selection method
One word	Double-click the word
A paragraph	Triple-click in the paragraph
An entire document	Press [Ctrl][A]
A line of text	Position to the left of the line, then click

TABLE 4-2: Useful keyboard shortcuts for moving the insertion point

keyboard method	moves insertion point
↑ or ↓	Up or down one line
← or →	To the left or right
[Ctrl]→ or [Ctrl]←	One word to the right or left
[Home] or [End]	To the beginning or end of the line
[Ctrl][Home] or [Ctrl][End]	To the beginning or end of the document

Copy Text

Learning Outcomes
• Copy and paste text using the Office Clipboard
• Copy text using drag and drop

When editing a document, you often need to copy text from one place to another. **Copying** leaves the text in its original location, and **pasting** moves a duplicate of it to the location you specify. To copy and paste text, you first need to select the text you want to copy. Next, you use the Copy command to place a copy of the selected text on the **Windows Clipboard**, a temporary storage area in your computer's memory for copied or cut items. Finally, you use the Paste command to insert the copied text to a new location. If you need to copy multiple items, you can use the **Office Clipboard**, which works like the Windows Clipboard but stores up to 24 items at a time and is available only in Office programs. To use the Office Clipboard, you need to open the Clipboard task pane. You can also duplicate text using a technique called **drag and drop**, in which you select the text you want to copy, press and hold [Ctrl], and then use the mouse to drag a copy of the selected text to a new location. Items you copy using drag and drop do not get placed on the Windows or Office Clipboard. **CASE** *You decide to make further edits to the letter by copying and pasting text.*

STEPS

QUICK TIP
If your Clipboard is not empty, click Clear All on the task pane.

1. **On the Home tab, click the launcher ⬚ in the Clipboard group**

   The Clipboard task pane opens to the left of the document window. You use the Clipboard task pane to gather multiple cut and copied items. The task pane is empty because you have not copied or cut any text.

2. **Click to the left of the "S" in "Sweet" in the line below "Congratulations!" to set the insertion point, press and hold the left mouse button, drag the mouse pointer to the space after the word "Puffs", then release the mouse button**

   The words "Sweet Potato Puffs" and the space that follows are now selected.

QUICK TIP
To copy selected text using the keyboard, press [Ctrl][C]; to paste text, press [Ctrl][V].

3. **Click the Copy button in the Clipboard group**

   The selected text is copied to the Office Clipboard and appears in the Clipboard task pane, as shown in **FIGURE 4-8**.

QUICK TIP
You can also paste an item by clicking its name in the Clipboard task pane.

4. **Scroll down if necessary so you can see the end of the document, then click to the left of "recipe" in the first line of the last paragraph, then click the Paste button in the Clipboard group**

   The copied text is pasted into the document and also remains on the Office Clipboard, from which you can paste it as many more times as you like, as shown in **FIGURE 4-9**. The Paste Options button appears under the pasted text.

5. **Click the Paste Options button 📋 (Ctrl) ▾**

   The Paste Options menu opens and displays buttons for applying formatting to the pasted text. By default, the pasted text maintains its original formatting, which in this situation is fine, since it matches the text.

6. **Press [Esc] to close the Paste Options menu**

7. **Select Pepper's Green Basket and the space after it in the first line of the first paragraph**

QUICK TIP
If you don't press [CTRL] as you drag, the text will be removed from its original location as you drag it (and not duplicated).

8. **Press and hold [Ctrl], drag the selected text to the left of "Cooking Tools" four lines below the paragraph, release the mouse button, then release [Ctrl]**

   As you drag, the pointer changes to an indicator line that shows where the text will be inserted. This instance of "Pepper's Green Basket" does not get copied to the Clipboard, as shown in **FIGURE 4-10**.

9. **Click the Save button 💾 on the Quick Access Toolbar**

FIGURE 4-8: Selected text copied to the Office Clipboard

Copy button

Clipboard launcher

Clipboard task pane

Selected text copied to Office Clipboard

Selected text

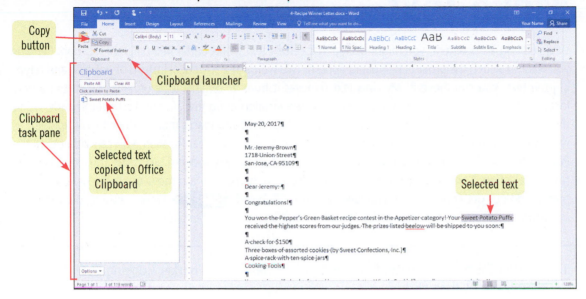

FIGURE 4-9: Text placed on the Office Clipboard

Pasted text remains on Office Clipboard and can be pasted again

Pasted text from Office Clipboard

Paste Options button

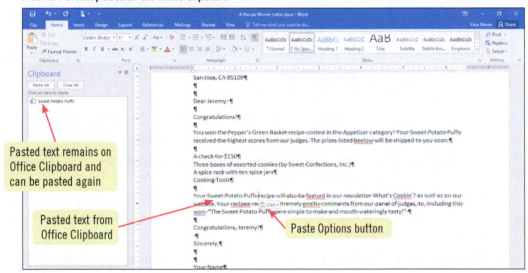

FIGURE 4-10: Dragged and copied text

Dragged text is not copied to Office Clipboard

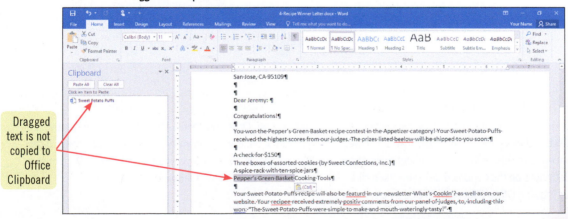

Creating a Document

Move Text

While editing a document, you might decide that certain text works better in a different location. Perhaps you want to switch the order of two paragraphs, or two words in a sentence. Instead of deleting and retyping the text, you can move it. **Moving** text removes it from its original location and places it in a new location that you specify. You can move text to a new location using the Cut and Paste commands. Using the **Cut** command removes selected text from your document and places it on the Windows Clipboard as well as the Office Clipboard if activated. To place the cut text in another location, you can either click the Paste button on the Home tab of the Ribbon or click the item in the Clipboard task pane. You can also move text by selecting it and then dragging it to a new location. Items that you move using the drag-and-drop method do not get copied to the Windows or Office Clipboard. **CASE** *While checking your letter, you decide that you want to rearrange the list of prizes so they appear in a different order.*

STEPS

1. **Position the mouse pointer to the left of "Pepper's Green Basket Cooking Tools" until it changes to ⌐, then click**

   The entire line, including the paragraph mark, is selected, as shown in **FIGURE 4-11**.

2. **On the Home tab, click the Cut button in the Clipboard group**

   The text is cut from the document and is now the first item in the Clipboard task pane. The last item you cut or copy becomes the first item in the task pane. If you cut or copy more than 24 items without clearing the task pane, the oldest item is deleted to make room for the new one.

3. **Click to the left of the "T" in "Three boxes of assorted cookies", then click the Paste button in the Clipboard group on the Ribbon**

   The text from the Clipboard is pasted to the new location, on the line below "A check for $150".

4. **Place the mouse pointer in the selection bar to the left of "A spice rack with ten spice jars" until it changes to ⌐, then click to select the entire line**

5. **Move the pointer over the selected text, drag it to the left of the "T" in "Three boxes of assorted cookies", then release the mouse button**

   As you drag, the pointer changes to ⌐, and an indicator line shows you where the text will be placed. Notice the dragged text does not appear as an item on the Clipboard. Now the prizes are listed in a new order, as shown in **FIGURE 4-12**.

6. **Click anywhere to deselect the text, then click the Close button ✕ on the Clipboard task pane**

   The task pane closes.

7. **Click the Save button 🖫 on the Quick Access Toolbar**

Activating the Office Clipboard

The Office Clipboard stores multiple items only if it is active. Opening the Clipboard task pane automatically makes it active. If you want to activate the Office Clipboard without showing the task pane, click Options on the Clipboard task pane, then click Collect Without Showing Office Clipboard. Click the option again to turn it off. Once you choose this option it remains active until you turn it off, even when you work in other documents. If the Office Clipboard is not active, you can only copy one item at a time using the Windows Clipboard.

FIGURE 4-11: Selecting a line of text

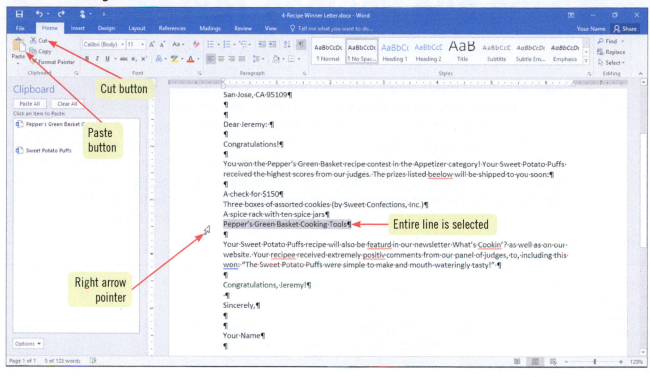

Cut button

Paste button

Right arrow pointer

Entire line is selected

FIGURE 4-12: Moving text by dragging it

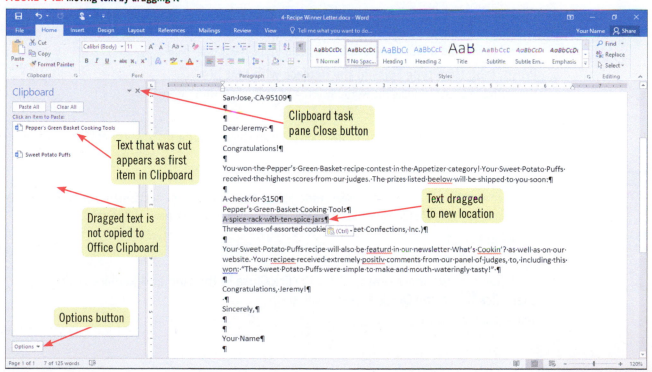

Clipboard task pane Close button

Text that was cut appears as first item in Clipboard

Text dragged to new location

Dragged text is not copied to Office Clipboard

Options button

Find and Replace Text

Once in a while you might need to make a global change in a document. For instance, suppose you are writing a novel about a character named Joe. After writing 50 pages, you decide to change the character's name to Sam. You could manually edit the document to change each occurrence of "Joe" to "Sam", but there is an easier, more automated method. The **Replace** command helps you quickly and easily substitute a new word or phrase for one or more occurrences of a particular word or phrase in a document. Choosing the Replace command opens the Find and Replace dialog box, which you use to specify the text you want to find and the text with which you want to replace it. You can replace every occurrence of the text in one action, or you can review each occurrence, choosing to replace or keep the text each time. You can also use the Navigation pane to quickly highlight all instances of specific text. **CASE** ▶ *Jessica just told you that the winning recipe name in the letter is incorrect. You need to replace all instances of the incorrect name with the correct name.*

STEPS

1. **On the Home tab, click Find in the Editing group**

   The Navigation pane opens on the left side of your screen and the insertion point appears in the Search box at the top of the pane. This pane makes it easy to see repeated instances of text and other elements, all in one organized list, and to move quickly from one to another.

2. **Type Sweet**

   All the instances of "Sweet" are now highlighted in yellow. You can quickly see there are four instances of "Sweet" in the document. See **FIGURE 4-13**. You can use the Find and Replace dialog box to fix the incorrect names. First you should move the insertion point to the top of the document.

3. **Close the Navigation pane, click anywhere in the document window, then press [Ctrl][Home]**

   Pressing [Ctrl][Home] moves the insertion point to the beginning of the document and deselects any text. This ensures that Word starts searching for occurrences of your specified text at the beginning of the document and checks the entire document.

4. **Click Replace in the Editing group**

   The Find and Replace dialog box opens, with the Replace tab in front. You can see that "Sweet" is already entered in the Find what box, because you typed it in the Navigation pane.

5. **Press [Tab], then type Spicy in the Replace with text box**

   You are ready to start finding the word "Sweet" and replacing it with "Spicy."

6. **Click Find Next**

   Word searches the document from the insertion point and highlights the first instance of "Sweet", as shown in **FIGURE 4-14**.

7. **Click Replace**

   Word replaces the first instance of "Sweet" with "Spicy", then moves to the next instance of "Sweet", which is the company name of the assorted cookies prize. You do not want to replace this instance.

8. **Click Find Next**

   Word locates the next instance of "Sweet".

9. **Click Replace two more times, click OK, click Close in the Find and Replace dialog box, then click 🔡 on the Quick Access Toolbar**

   Your changes are saved.

FIGURE 4-13: Finding text using the Navigation pane

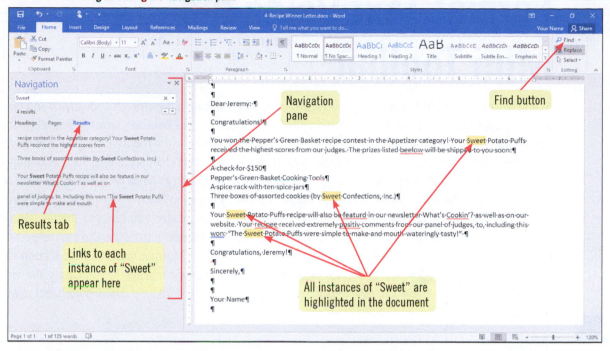

- Navigation pane
- Find button
- Results tab
- Links to each instance of "Sweet" appear here
- All instances of "Sweet" are highlighted in the document

FIGURE 4-14: Finding text using the Find and Replace dialog box

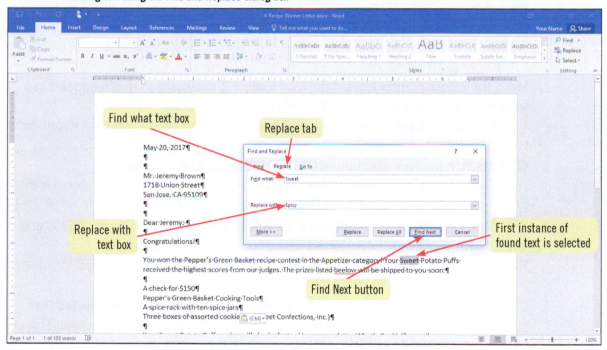

- Find what text box
- Replace tab
- Replace with text box
- First instance of found text is selected
- Find Next button

Using Insights for Office

As you create documents in Word, you can easily tap into contextual information from the web as you work using Insights for Office. Powered by Bing, Insights quickly pulls up information on any word or text you want, saving you time and providing a rich reading and writing experience. To use this feature, right-click a word or selected text, then click Smart Lookup. The Insights task pane opens, presenting rich content about the topic in a clean format. (The first time you use the feature, you might need to read the privacy statement and agree to the terms of use.) The Define link displays a definition from the Oxford dictionary; the Explore link displays several layers of information, including web links and images, if available. You can also open the Insights pane by clicking the Smart Lookup button on the Review tab.

Word 2016

Format Text Using the Mini Toolbar

Learning Outcomes
- Explain the Mini toolbar
- Apply formatting to text using the Mini toolbar

As you work in Word 2016, you will discover many tools for enhancing a document's appearance and readability by applying formatting. Perhaps the simplest of these is the **Mini toolbar**, which is a small toolbar that contains the most common formatting commands; it appears near the mouse pointer whenever you select text. The Mini toolbar is useful for making quick, basic formatting changes to text, such as changing the font of selected text. A **font** is the design of a set of characters, such as **Arial** or **Times New Roman**. You can also use the Mini toolbar to change the **font style** by applying bold, underline, or italic formatting, or to change the **font size** of selected text so it is larger or smaller. You can also format selected paragraphs as a bulleted list using the Mini toolbar. All of the Mini toolbar buttons are also available on the Home tab of the Ribbon, in the Font and Paragraph groups. You will format text using the Ribbon in a future module. **CASE** *You decide to enhance the appearance of the letter by formatting the word "Congratulations!" in a larger font size, formatting the prizes as a bulleted list, and applying italic font style to the newsletter title.*

STEPS

1. **Position the selection pointer ⤢ to the left of "Congratulations!" in the first paragraph, then click**

   The word "Congratulations" and the exclamation point and the paragraph mark (**¶**) that follow it are selected. The Mini toolbar appears near the selected text; moving the pointer away from the toolbar causes it to fade to a ghosted image.

2. **Move the mouse pointer toward the Mini toolbar if necessary so that it appears in a solid form, then click the Bold button B on the Mini toolbar**

   The selected text "Congratulations!" now appears in a darker and thicker font, which sets it apart from the other text in the letter.

3. **Click the Increase Font Size button A˙ on the Mini toolbar four times**

   The selected text grows in size from 11 to 18, as shown in **FIGURE 4-15**. The new font size appears in the Font Size box on the Mini toolbar. You measure font size using points. A **point** is 1/72", so a font size of 12 is 1/6".

4. **Select the four lines of text containing the prizes, starting with A check for $150 and ending with Three boxes of assorted cookies (by Sweet Confections, Inc.)**

   The four prizes are now selected. You can now apply formatting to the selected text. You decide to make the prizes look more ordered by formatting them as a bulleted list.

5. **Click the Bullets button ⊞ on the Mini toolbar, then click outside the selected text**

   Each prize is indented and preceded by a small round dot, or **bullet**. The listed prizes now stand out much better from the body of the letter and help create a more organized appearance.

6. **Select the text What's Cookin'? in the paragraph below the bulleted list, click the Italic button I on the Mini toolbar, then save your changes**

   The title of the Pepper's Green Basket newsletter, *What's Cookin'?*, now appears in italic. Compare your screen to **FIGURE 4-16**.

Creating a Document

FIGURE 4-15: Using the Mini toolbar to format text

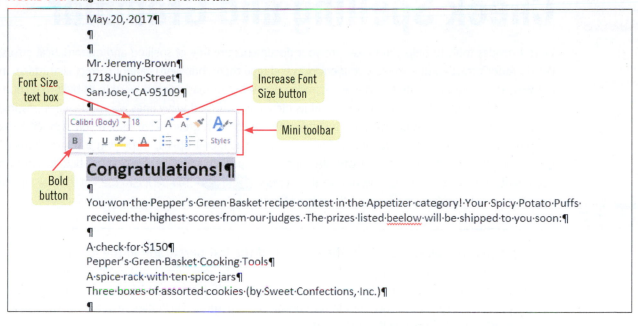

FIGURE 4-16: Letter with formatted text and bulleted list

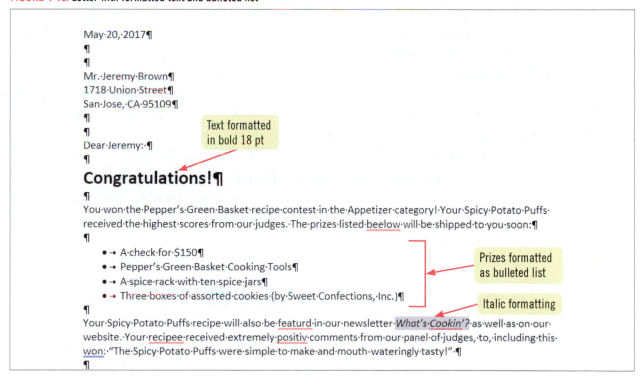

Check Spelling and Grammar

Word provides tools to help you make sure your documents are free of spelling and grammatical errors. Word's AutoCorrect feature corrects your errors as you type them, but Word cannot correct all mistakes in this way. The program identifies possible misspelled words by comparing each word to its built-in dictionary, then underlines any words that are not in its dictionary with red wavy lines. Word identifies possible grammatical errors such as passive voice by underlining them with green wavy lines. If you right-click the flagged misspelled words or grammatical errors, a shortcut menu opens, displaying a list of correctly spelled or phrased alternatives. You can also open the Spelling and Grammar dialog box to check a document for misspelled words and grammatical errors. **CASE** ▶ *You decide to use Word's spelling and grammar checking tools to ensure your letter is free of errors.*

STEPS

1. **Right-click the word featurd in the first line of the last paragraph in the letter**

   A shortcut menu opens, displaying a list of alternatives to the misspelled word, as shown in **FIGURE 4-17**. Other options you can choose in this menu include Ignore All (if you want Word to stop alerting you to the possible misspelling of this word in the document), and Add to Dictionary (if you want Word to add this word as spelled to its built-in dictionary).

2. **Click featured from the list at the top of the shortcut menu**

   The shortcut menu closes, and the word "featured" replaces the misspelled word.

3. **Click the Review tab on the Ribbon**

4. **Press [Ctrl][Home] to move the insertion point to the top of the letter, then click the Spelling & Grammar button in the Proofing group**

   The Spelling pane opens, as shown in **FIGURE 4-18**. The word "beelow" appears in bold at the top of the pane as a misspelled word, and suggested replacement words are listed below. The word "below" (the correct spelling) is highlighted and definitions are listed.

5. **Click Change**

   Word changes "beelow" to "below" and moves to the next possible error, which is the word "Cookin". This is part of the newsletter name, so you want to leave this as is.

6. **Click Ignore**

   Word advances to the next possible error, which is the misspelled word "recipee".

7. **Click Change, then click Change to correct the misspelled word "positiv"**

   The next error that is identified is a grammatical error. Even though "won" is not an incorrectly spelled word, Word is able to tell that it is used incorrectly in this context. The correct word should be "one".

8. **Click Change, then click OK in the alert box**

   Although the spelling and grammar check is complete, you should always do a final review to ensure that no errors remain.

9. **Select the word to in the last paragraph, type too, then save your changes**

FIGURE 4-17: Spelling shortcut menu with possible alternatives

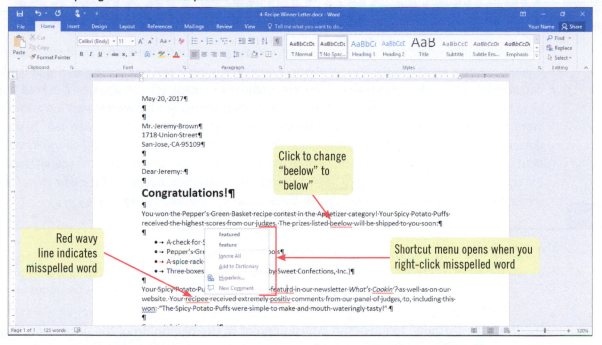

Click to change "beelow" to "below"

Red wavy line indicates misspelled word

Shortcut menu opens when you right-click misspelled word

FIGURE 4-18: Spelling task pane with possible spelling error flagged

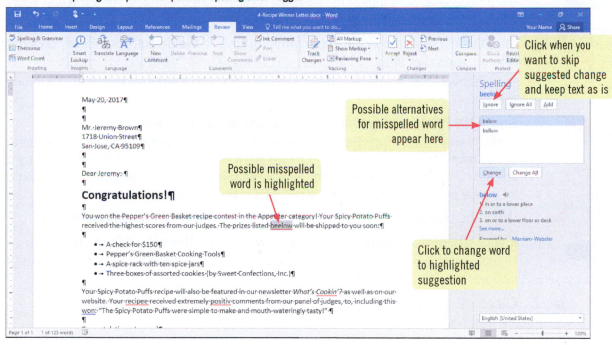

Click when you want to skip suggested change and keep text as is

Possible alternatives for misspelled word appear here

Possible misspelled word is highlighted

Click to change word to highlighted suggestion

Translating documents into other languages

Word 2016 has the ability to translate any word in your document, or even an entire document, into more than 43 different languages. To translate an entire document from one language to another, on the Review tab click the Translate button in the Language group, then click Translate Document. If you have not previously specified translation languages in Word, the Translation Language Options dialog box opens. In the Translation Language Options dialog box, specify the Translate from and Translate to languages, then click OK. An alert box opens, telling you the document will be sent over the Internet for translation. Click Yes to send the document, and seconds later your document appears in your browser window fully translated. Use the Views buttons in the Translator window to view the translated text in a separate pane above or beside the original text. To create a new document for the translation, select all of the translated content, copy it to the Clipboard, then paste it into a new Word document.

Preview and Print a Document

When you finish creating and editing a document, you can preview it to see exactly how it will look when printed. Seeing a preview of the document before printing it is useful and can save paper. If your finished document is going to be viewed primarily on screen (and not printed), you can also view it in Read Mode view, which is the ideal view for reading text on screen. There are many other ways to view a document in Word. See **TABLE 4-3** for a description of these views, which you can access on the View tab. To print a document, you use the Print screen in Backstage view. The tools on the Print screen let you specify various print settings, including the printer you want to use, how many copies to print, and the specific pages of the document you want to print. **CASE** *You are ready to preview and print the letter now. (Note: Many schools limit printing in order to conserve paper. If your school restricts printing, skip Step 6.)*

STEPS

1. **Click the View tab, then click One Page in the Zoom group**

   Now you can see the text of the letter is laid out on the page. Notice the text is bunched up at the top of the paper. You need to move it down to make room for the company letterhead, which is preprinted on your company paper.

2. **Press [Ctrl][Home] to move the insertion point to the beginning of the document, then press [Enter] seven times**

   You inserted seven blank lines at the top of the document. See **FIGURE 4-19**. The text is now positioned further down the page. You are ready to print the letter now.

3. **Click the 100% button in the Zoom group to restore the default zoom level, click the File tab, then click Print**

   The Print place opens in Backstage view, as shown in **FIGURE 4-20**. You can see a preview of the letter in the right pane.

4. **Notice the Printer and Settings options to the left of the Preview area**

   Adjust these options to specify your print settings. The option below Printer shows the default printer. The options below Settings let you specify which pages you want to print (if you do not want to print the entire document), the number of copies to print, the orientation of the document, the size of the paper on which the document will print, and more. The default settings are appropriate for the letter.

5. **Verify the button below Printer displays the name of the printer you want to use**

6. **If your school allows printing, click the Print button; otherwise, skip to Step 7**

   The document prints, Backstage view screen closes, and your screen displays your document with the Home tab open.

7. **Click Save on the File tab, then click the Word window Close button ✕**

   The letter is saved, and the document and Word both close.

Using research and writing tools

Besides the Insights pane, there are other writing and research tools you can tap into as you create documents in Word. For instance, if you click a word while pressing [Alt], the Research task pane opens and displays definitions for that word pulled from Bing. Synonyms for that word are listed below the definitions in the Thesaurus area. You can also view synonyms for any word without opening the Research task pane; just right-click the word, point to Synonyms, then click a synonym in the list to insert it.

FIGURE 4-19: Viewing the entire page of the completed letter

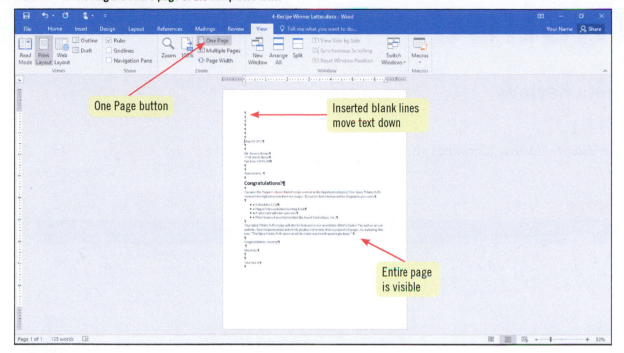

One Page button

Inserted blank lines move text down

Entire page is visible

FIGURE 4-20: Printing the final letter in Backstage view

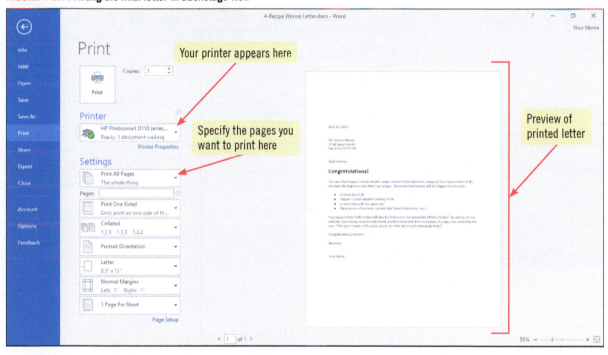

Your printer appears here

Specify the pages you want to print here

Preview of printed letter

TABLE 4-3: Available views in Word

view	how it displays a document	use for
Print Layout	Shows all elements of the printed page	Previewing the layout of printed page
Read Mode	Optimized for on-screen reading	Reading documents on a computer screen
Web Layout	As it would appear as a Web page	Creating a Web page
Outline	Shows only the headings in a document	Reviewing the structure of a document
Draft	Does not show all page elements	Typing, editing, and simple formatting

Creating a Document

Practice

Concepts Review

Label the Word window elements shown in FIGURE 4-21.

FIGURE 4-21

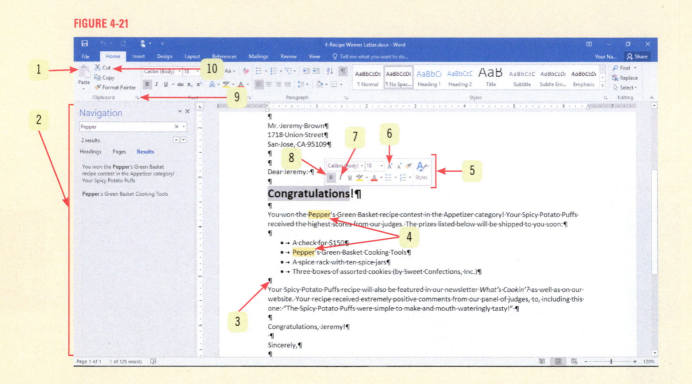

Match each of the items with its function.

11. [File]

12. [A⁺]

13. [⌐]

14. **No Spacing button in Styles group**

15. [✂]

a. Removes selected text and places it on the Clipboard, where you can paste it to a new location.

b. Increases the font size of selected text.

c. Changes the amount of space after a paragraph return to single space.

d. Opens Backstage view, where you can print a document.

e. Opens a dialog box where you can choose additional options and settings not available on the Ribbon.

Select the best answer from the list of choices.

16. Which of the following tasks can you complete using the Navigation pane?
   a. Moving a selected word from one location to another.
   b. Formatting all instances of a specific word in a certain way.
   c. Locating and highlighting all instances of a particular word.
   d. Replacing all instances of a particular word.

17. Which of the following is true when you open an existing file and save it with a new name?
   a. The file that you open is deleted when you save it with a new name.
   b. The file that you open remains intact and is saved to its original location.
   c. The file that you save contains no content.
   d. The file that you save must be saved to a different folder from the original file.

18. Which is the default view in Word?
   a. Draft
   b. Print Layout
   c. Read Mode
   d. Outline

19. Which of the following keyboard shortcuts moves the insertion point to the beginning of the current document?
   a. [Ctrl][Home]
   b. [Ctrl][Alt][Delete]
   c. [Ctrl][A]
   d. [Shift][Home]

20. When dragging text, which key should you hold down to copy the text as you drag?
   a. [Ctrl]
   b. [Shift]
   c. [Alt]
   d. [Ctrl][Shift]

Skills Review

1. Create a new document from an existing file.
   a. Start Word, then open the Open screen.
   b. Navigate to the location where you store your Data Files, then open 4-2.docx.
   c. Save the file as **4-Option One Event Planning** in the location where you save your Data Files.

2. Enter text in a document.
   a. Make sure formatting marks are displayed in the document.
   b. Switch to Draft view.
   c. Move the insertion point to the right of "-9985" (the end of the fax number at the end of the fourth line), then press [Enter] twice.
   d. Type the following text: **About Our Company**. Press [Enter].
   e. Type the following text: **Option One Event Planning, Inc. plans, creates, and executes events that reflect the missions and goals of our clients.** Press [Enter].
   f. Move the insertion point to the end of the paragraph below the heading "About Our Team", press [Spacebar], then type **Our supporting staff are service oriented and dedicated to ensuring our clients' satisfaction.**
   g. Save your changes.

3. Select and edit text.
   a. In the fourth line, replace the last four digits of the fax number (9985) with **3250**.
   b. In the heading "About Our Company", delete "Our Company" and replace it with **Option One**.
   c. Scroll down if necessary so you can see the paragraph under the heading Available Venues, then use the [Backspace] key to delete "examples" at the end of that paragraph.
   d. Type **venues we frequently use** so the last sentence of that paragraph reads "Here are some venues we frequently use:"

Skills Review (continued)

    e. Select the entire document, then click the No Spacing button in the Styles group.

    f. Save your changes.

4. Copy text.

    a. Open the Clipboard task pane. If there are entries on it, clear them.

    b. Select the text "Option One" in the first line of the document, then copy this text to the Clipboard.

    c. Delete "Our" in the heading "About Our Services".

    d. Paste the copied text where the deleted text used to be.

    e. Select the text "world-class" in the second line of text below "About Our Team".

    f. Drag a copy of the selected text to the left of "supporting staff" three lines below. (*Hint*: Press and hold [Ctrl] while dragging the selection.)

    g. Save your changes.

5. Move text.

    a. In the paragraph below the heading "Contact Us", select the text "We hope to hear from you soon!" and the space following it, then use the Cut command to move this text to the Clipboard.

    b. Paste the text you cut after the sentence "Call us today to start planning your next event" below the Contact Us heading.

    c. Scroll down if necessary so the bottom of the document is visible on your screen.

    d. Select the heading "Contact Us", the line below it, and the paragraph mark below the line, then drag the entire selection down to the end of the document.

    e. Close the Clipboard task pane, then save your changes.

6. Find and replace text.

    a. Find all the instances of "location".

    b. Move the insertion point to the beginning of the document.

    c. Use the Replace command to replace all instances of "location" with "venue".

    d. Close the Find and Replace dialog box. Close the Navigation pane.

    e. Save your changes.

7. Format text using the Mini toolbar.

    a. Change the view to Print Layout view.

    b. Select "Option One Event Planning, Inc." in the first line of the document, then use the Mini toolbar to apply bold formatting to this text.

    c. With the first line of text still selected, use a button on the Mini toolbar to increase the font size of "Option One Event Planning, Inc." to 24.

    d. Use the Mini toolbar to apply bold formatting to each of the following headings in the document: "About Option One", "About Our Team", "About Option One Services", "Available Venues", and "Contact Us".

    e. In the paragraph below the heading "About Our Team", use the Mini toolbar to apply italic formatting to the newspaper title "Event World".

    f. Scroll down if necessary so all the text under the heading "Available Venues" is visible, then select the list of venues starting with "Art galleries" and ending with "Waterfront properties".

    g. Use the Mini toolbar to format the selected text as a bulleted list.

    h. Save your changes.

8. Check spelling and grammar.

    a. In the paragraph below "About Option One", correct the spelling of the misspelled word "successs" by right-clicking and choosing the correct spelling from the shortcut menu.

    b. Move the insertion point to the beginning of the document.

    c. Click the tab on the Ribbon that contains the Spelling & Grammar button.

Skills Review (continued)

d. Open the Spelling pane.

e. Review each spelling and grammatical error that Word identifies, and correct or ignore the errors depending on what seems appropriate for this document.

f. Save your changes.

9. **Preview and print a document.**

a. View the document in Read Mode view. Then close Read Mode view, and view the document in Print Layout view. Finally, click the button in the Zoom group that lets you see the entire page.

b. Insert two line spaces above the first line of the document.

c. Move the insertion point to the end of the document, then type your name.

d. Preview the document again using the Print tab.

e. Save your changes, then submit your finished document to your instructor. Your final document should look like **FIGURE 4-22**.

f. Close the document, then exit Word.

FIGURE 4-22

Option One Event Planning, Inc.

225 Warren Ave.
Seattle, WA 98102
Phone: (206) 555-6657 Fax: (206) 555-3250

About Option One
Option One Event Planning, Inc. plans, creates, and executes events that reflect the missions and goals of our clients.

We pride ourselves on delivering exceptional meetings and events for product launches, private parties, weddings, company meetings, corporate events, and more. We work closely with our clients to ensure total success and satisfaction.

About Our Team
Our management team is led by our managing partners Jay Underwood and Fiona Waters, who founded the company with a vision of creating world-class events in the Pacific Northwest. Jolene Flanders, our Creative Director, recently profiled in *Event World*, is known for turning empty spaces into magnificent events. Our program managers, Charlize Redfield and Arnie Burns, work hard to ensure needs are met from start to finish. Our world-class supporting staff are service oriented and dedicated to ensuring our clients' satisfaction.

About Option One Services
At Option One Event Planning Inc., we work collaboratively with our clients to manage and oversee every aspect of planning and managing an event, including venue selection and design, invitation design menu planning, entertainment, transportation, security and more.

Available Venues
Seattle offers a wide variety of venues for events of any size. For corporate meetings, hotel venues are always an option, but we can also identify and secure local settings to make your event a bit different. Here are some venues we frequently use:

- Art galleries
- Restaurants
- The Space Needle
- Yacht clubs
- Theatres
- Sports venues
- Waterfront properties

Contact Us
Call us today to start planning your next event. We hope to hear from you soon!

Your Name

Independent Challenge 1

As the product director for the SunRay Auto Group, Inc., you are in charge of organizing a product launch event for the company's first solar-powered car. You need to create a memo notifying the product team of the launch date and providing key information they need to book flights for this important event. You have already created a partially completed version of this memo; now you need to make final edits to finish it.

a. Start Word, open 4-3.docx from the location where you store your Data Files, then save it as **4-Product Launch Memo**.

b. Select the entire document, then apply the No Spacing style to the whole document.

c. In the fourth line of text, replace the text "Your Name" with your name.

d. In the sixth line of text (which begins "The meeting date…"), change the text "meeting" to **product launch**.

e. Select the heading "Dates", then replace it with **When to Arrive and Depart**.

f. At the end of the paragraph under "When to Arrive and Depart," type the following text: **Please schedule your flights accordingly**.

g. In the first line of text under the heading "Other Trip Details", move the text "Please let me know if you have question or concerns." to the end of the paragraph.

h. Increase the font size of the word "Memo" in the first line of the document to 26, then apply bold formatting to it.

i. Apply bold formatting to the following headings in the memo: "When to Arrive and Depart", "About the Hotel and Conference Center", "Pre-Launch Setup", "Launch Agenda", and "Other Trip Details". Use a button on the Mini Toolbar to increase the font size of each heading to 14.

j. Below the heading "Launch Agenda", format the six lines of text beginning with "9:00-9:15" and ending with "12:00-1:30: Lunch…" as a bulleted list.

k. You suddenly learn that the Red Fox Hotel and Conference Center will not be able to accommodate the meeting. Fortunately, you are able to secure an alternate venue: the Blue Rattler Resort and Conference Center, also in Scottsdale. Replace all instances of "Red Fox Hotel" with **Blue Rattler Resort**.

l. Check the spelling and grammar in the document, and correct any errors as needed. Ignore any proper names (such as "SunRay") that are flagged as misspelled words.

m. Save your changes, then view the memo in Read Mode. Close Read Mode view, then view the document in Print Layout view, using the setting that lets you see the entire document on one page.

n. Insert one blank line above "Memo". Type your name at the bottom of the document. Change the view to 100%. Your finished document should look like **FIGURE 4-23**.

o. Close the document, then exit Word. Submit your completed document to your instructor.

FIGURE 4-23

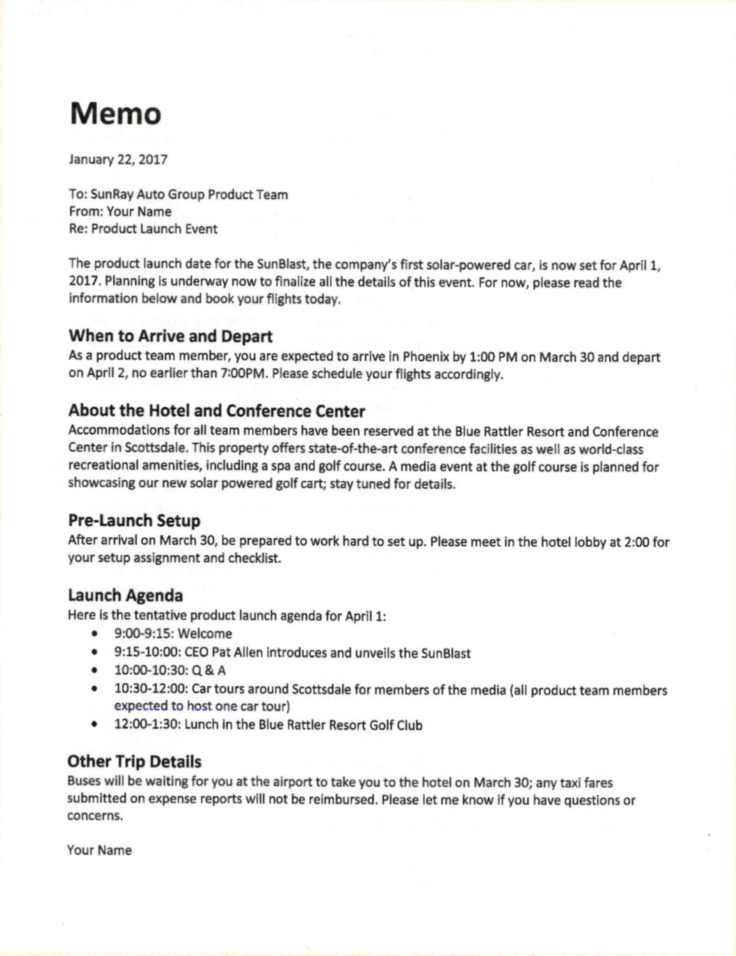

Memo

January 22, 2017

To: SunRay Auto Group Product Team
From: Your Name
Re: Product Launch Event

The product launch date for the SunBlast, the company's first solar-powered car, is now set for April 1, 2017. Planning is underway now to finalize all the details of this event. For now, please read the information below and book your flights today.

When to Arrive and Depart
As a product team member, you are expected to arrive in Phoenix by 1:00 PM on March 30 and depart on April 2, no earlier than 7:00PM. Please schedule your flights accordingly.

About the Hotel and Conference Center
Accommodations for all team members have been reserved at the Blue Rattler Resort and Conference Center in Scottsdale. This property offers state-of-the-art conference facilities as well as world-class recreational amenities, including a spa and golf course. A media event at the golf course is planned for showcasing our new solar powered golf cart; stay tuned for details.

Pre-Launch Setup
After arrival on March 30, be prepared to work hard to set up. Please meet in the hotel lobby at 2:00 for your setup assignment and checklist.

Launch Agenda
Here is the tentative product launch agenda for April 1:
- 9:00-9:15: Welcome
- 9:15-10:00: CEO Pat Allen introduces and unveils the SunBlast
- 10:00-10:30: Q & A
- 10:30-12:00: Car tours around Scottsdale for members of the media (all product team members expected to host one car tour)
- 12:00-1:30: Lunch in the Blue Rattler Resort Golf Club

Other Trip Details
Buses will be waiting for you at the airport to take you to the hotel on March 30; any taxi fares submitted on expense reports will not be reimbursed. Please let me know if you have questions or concerns.

Your Name

Independent Challenge 2

You manage an animal shelter that rescues stray cats and dogs and places them in loving homes. You need to create a questionnaire for volunteers to help understand their skills and interests so you can deploy them appropriately at the shelter. You have already started the questionnaire document but need to make some edits and formatting changes.

a. Start Word, open 4-4.docx from the location where you store your Data Files, then save it as **4-Volunteer Questionnaire**.

b. Select all the text in the document, then apply the No Spacing style to all the selected text.

c. In the fifth line of text, delete the blank underline next to Name: and replace it with your name. Then, replace the blank underline next to Phone number: with **(773) 555-0865**.

d. Apply bold formatting to "Question 1:" in the seventh line of text. Then, apply bold formatting to "Question 2:" and "Question 3:".

e. Below each of the three questions, format the list of answers as a bulleted list.

f. Reorder the bulleted items under Question 1 so they are in alphabetical order.

g. Copy Question 3 and its four bullets, then paste the copied text on the second line below the last bullet on the page.

h. Edit the pasted Question 3: so that it reads **Question 4:**.

i. Replace all instances of "dog" in Question 4 and its bullets with **cat**.

j. Increase the font size of the text in the first line of the document to 24 then apply bold and italic formatting to it.

k. Copy "(circle best answer)" at the end of Question 1, and paste it at the end of the other questions in the document.

l. Check the spelling and grammar, and correct all spelling and grammar errors. Ignore any flagged words that are spelled correctly.

m. Save your changes to the document. Use Print Preview to see how the printed questionnaire will look. Compare your document to **FIGURE 4-24**.

n. Submit your work to your instructor.

FIGURE 4-24

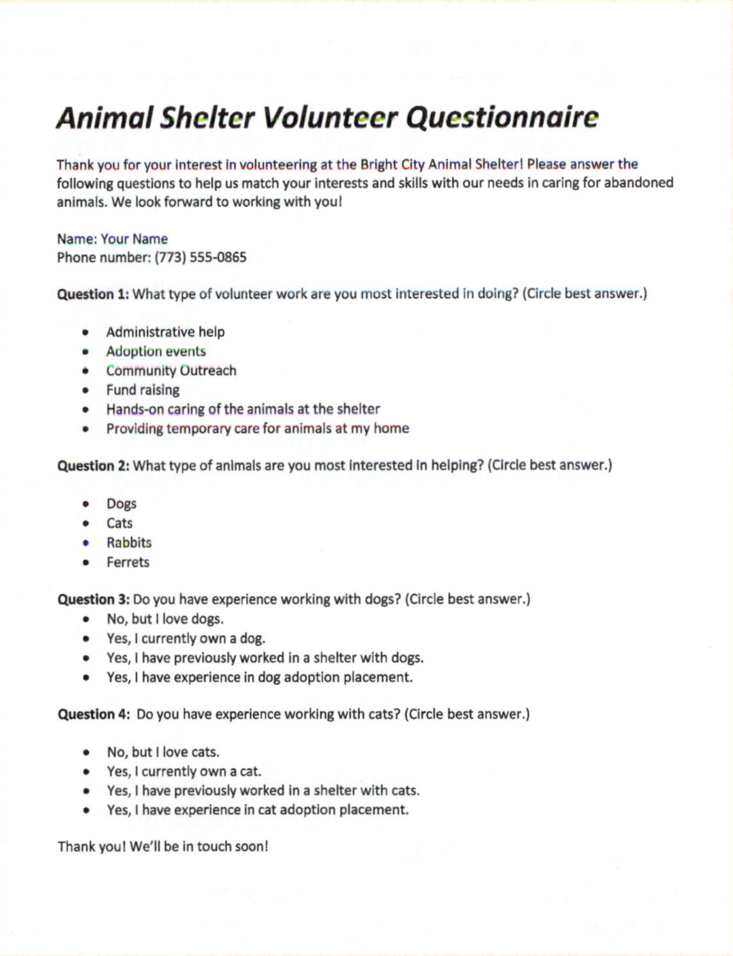

Animal Shelter Volunteer Questionnaire

Thank you for your interest in volunteering at the Bright City Animal Shelter! Please answer the following questions to help us match your interests and skills with our needs in caring for abandoned animals. We look forward to working with you!

Name: Your Name
Phone number: (773) 555-0865

Question 1: What type of volunteer work are you most interested in doing? (Circle best answer.)

- Administrative help
- Adoption events
- Community Outreach
- Fund raising
- Hands-on caring of the animals at the shelter
- Providing temporary care for animals at my home

Question 2: What type of animals are you most interested in helping? (Circle best answer.)

- Dogs
- Cats
- Rabbits
- Ferrets

Question 3: Do you have experience working with dogs? (Circle best answer.)
- No, but I love dogs.
- Yes, I currently own a dog.
- Yes, I have previously worked in a shelter with dogs.
- Yes, I have experience in dog adoption placement.

Question 4: Do you have experience working with cats? (Circle best answer.)

- No, but I love cats.
- Yes, I currently own a cat.
- Yes, I have previously worked in a shelter with cats.
- Yes, I have experience in cat adoption placement.

Thank you! We'll be in touch soon!

Independent Challenge 3

You work for Tanya Belle Watson, founding partner of Fame & Fortune Talent Agency, Inc. The agency is expanding its business and is actively seeking new talent. Tanya Belle has given you a draft of a press release announcing this news; she has asked you to finalize it by making some edits and formatting improvements.

a. Start Word, open 4-5.docx from where you store your Data Files, then save it as **4-Press Release**.

b. Select the first line of text, then use the Mini toolbar to increase the font size of the selection to 48.

c. Format the lines starting with "Adult Male Actors" and ending with "Voiceover Talent" as a bulleted list. Format the last four lines of text in the document as a bulleted list.

d. Use the Mini toolbar to apply bold formatting to each of the following headings in the document: "About the Agents", "About the Agency", "Now Accepting Submissions".

e. Move the heading "About the Agents" and the paragraph below it so they are located directly above the heading "Now Accepting Submissions".

f. Replace all instances of "Fame and Fortune" with **Fame & Fortune**.

g. Check the spelling and grammar in the document, and make all appropriate changes. Ignore any occurrences of sentence fragments that Word identifies. Type your name below the last line of the document.

h. Preview the document, then save and close the document.

i. Submit the document to your instructor, then exit Word.

Independent Challenge 4: Explore

You and your Italian cousin, Leonardo, are planning to meet in San Francisco for a short vacation. Leonardo, who speaks little English, wants to learn more about San Francisco. You agree to create a document that contains three facts about the city written in both English and Italian, and send it to him. You don't know much about San Francisco, either, so you will use Word's Insights feature to find the three facts. You want the document to look attractive, so you decide to use a template to create it.

a. Start Word.

b. In the Word Start screen, click in the Search for online templates box at the top of the screen, and type **Ion**. The thumbnail shown in FIGURE 4-25 should appear in the results. Click the thumbnail, read the description, then click Create.

c. Select "Title", delete it.

d. Select "Heading", then type **San Francisco**.

e. Select the placeholder text (starting with "To take advantage" and ending "get started."), then delete it.

f. Select San Francisco, right-click, then click Smart Lookup. Read the Wikipedia information in the Insights pane, then type three facts you learned from the information, pressing [Enter] after each fact.

g. Format the facts as a bulleted list.

h. Save the document as **4-San Francisco Facts** to the location where you store your Data Files.

i. Click the Review tab, click Translate in the Language group, then click Choose Translation Language. Adjust the Translate to: setting to Italian (Italy), then click OK.

j. Click the Translate button in the Language group, click Translate Document [English (United States) to Italian (Italy)], read the message in the dialog box, then click Yes. Your default browser opens with your English text side by side with the Italian translation.

FIGURE 4-25

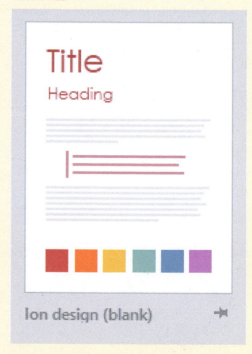

Ion design (blank)

Independent Challenge 4: Explore (continued)

k. In the browser window, select the Italian translated text, right-click to open a shortcut menu, then click Copy.

l. Close the browser and switch back the Word document.

m. Press [Enter] twice to move the insertion point down two lines, then click the Paste button. Make any formatting adjustments necessary to make the document look good. (*Hint*: if the Italian heading has a bullet, click the Bullets button to remove it.)

n. Preview the document using the One Page zoom setting. Your document should look similar to FIGURE 4-26 (although your facts should be different than those shown, since you wrote them).

o. Type your name in the last line of the document. Save and close the document, then submit it to your instructor.

FIGURE 4-26

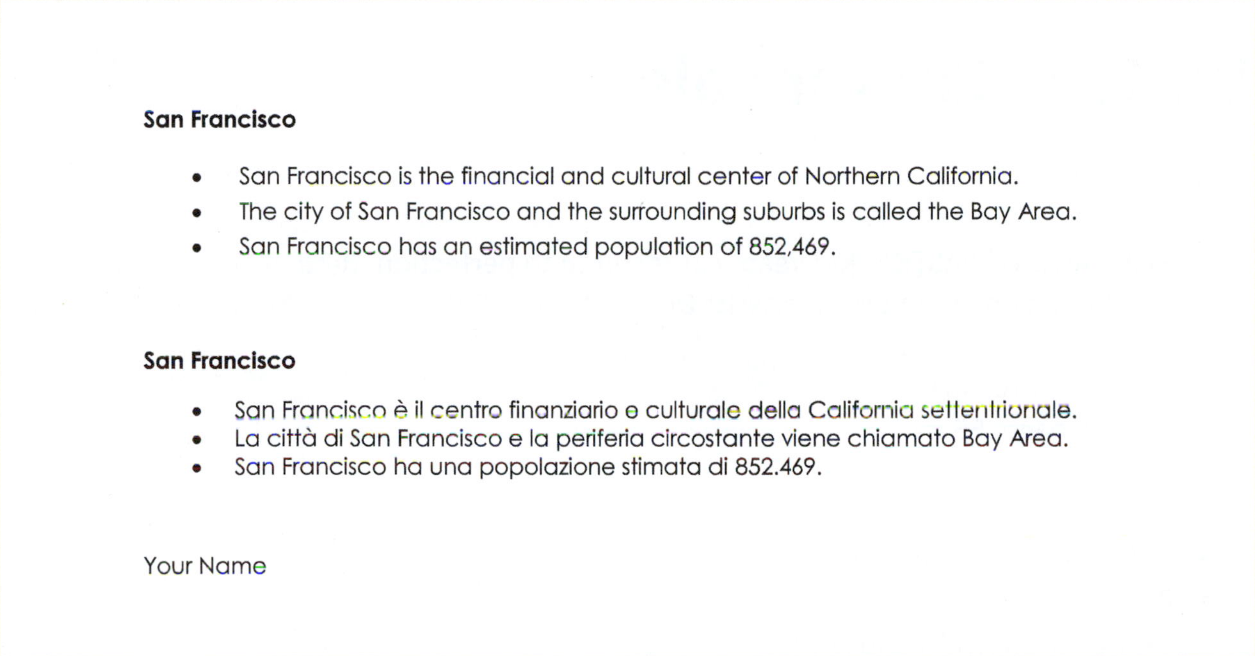

San Francisco

- San Francisco is the financial and cultural center of Northern California.
- The city of San Francisco and the surrounding suburbs is called the Bay Area.
- San Francisco has an estimated population of 852,469.

San Francisco

- San Francisco è il centro finanziario e culturale della California settentrionale.
- La città di San Francisco e la periferia circostante viene chiamato Bay Area.
- San Francisco ha una popolazione stimata di 852.469.

Your Name

Visual Workshop

Use the skills you have learned in this module to create the document shown in FIGURE 4-27. Start Word, use the Blank document command to create a new untitled document, then type and format the text as shown. (*Hint:* to create a new file, click the File tab, click New, then click Blank document in the New screen.) Set the font size of the heading to 36, set the font size of "Description:" to 18, and format the rest of the text with a font size of 16. Save the document as **4-Car Flyer** in the location where you store your Data Files. Check the spelling and grammar in the entire document, then save it. When you are finished, close the document, then exit Word. Submit your completed document to your instructor.

FIGURE 4-27

Vintage Car for Sale

Description:

1968 MUSTANG GT FASTBACK! Dream car restored to perfection. Rare opportunity to own an American classic. Drives like it's 1968!

- Beautifully restored
- Low Mileage: 55,876
- V-8 engine
- Power steering
- Automatic transmission
- Power disc brakes
- Deluxe white leather interior
- Candy red exterior
- Fold down rear seat
- Power steering
- Great investment

Asking price: $62,500

Too good to last! *For more details and to schedule a meeting and test drive, call Jerry at 773-555-1864*

Your Name

Enhancing a Document

CASE Jessica Ramos, marketing director for Pepper's Green Basket, needs you to finish a fact sheet for a new product offering: Pepper's Quick Meal Kits. Jessica asks you to format the information on the sheet so it is attractive and easy to read.

Module Objectives

After completing this module, you will be able to:

- Change font and font size
- Change font color, style, and effects
- Change alignment and line spacing
- Change margin settings
- Set tabs
- Set indents
- Add bulleted and numbered lists
- Apply styles

Files You Will Need

5-1.docx	5-5.docx
5-2.docx	5-6.docx
5-3.docx	5-7.docx
5-4.docx	

Change Font and Font Size

Learning Outcomes
• Change the font of selected text
• Adjust the font size of selected text

Choosing an appropriate font is an important part of formatting a document. The fonts you use help communicate the tone you want to set. For instance, if you are creating a report that describes harmful effects of toxins on the environment, you should choose a conservative, traditional font, such as Times New Roman. On the other hand, if you are creating a formal wedding invitation, you should choose a font that conveys a sense of elegance and celebration, such as French Script. **TABLE 5-1** shows some examples of fonts available in Word. You can use either the Home tab or the Mini toolbar to change the font and font size. You can change font and font size before you begin typing, or you can select existing text and apply changes to it.

CASE ▸ *All the text in the Quick Meals Kit fact sheet is the same font (Calibri) and size (11 point). You decide to change the font and font size of the first two lines so they stand out from the rest of the text in the document. First, you will open the document and save it with a new name to keep Jessica's original document intact.*

STEPS

1. **Start Word, open 5-1.docx from where you store your Data Files, save it as 5-Meal Kits Fact Sheet, then click Enable Editing if necessary**
   The 5-Meal Kits Fact Sheet document is now open in Print Layout view.

2. **Place the pointer in the selection bar to the left of Pepper's Green Basket in the first line until it changes to ⟋ then click to select the entire line**
   To format existing text, you must first select it.

3. **Click the Font Size list arrow in the Font group, then point to 18 as shown in FIGURE 5-1**
   Just by pointing to 18, the font size of the selected text increases in size on the page. You might have noticed that pointing to any other font size option instantly caused the selected text to change in size to reflect that point size. This feature is called **Live Preview**, and makes it possible to preview how a formatting option will look on the page before actually choosing that option. Live Preview is available in many formatting lists and galleries.

4. **Click 18**
   The Font Size list closes, and the selected text changes to 18 point. The first line of text is now much larger than the rest of the text in the document.

5. **Select Quick Meal Kits in the second line of the document, click the Font Size list arrow, then click 28**
   The second line of text increases in size to 28 point and is now larger than the first line.

6. **Select the first line of text, Pepper's Green Basket**

7. **Click the Font list arrow in the Font group on the Home tab, scroll in the Font list until you see Viner Hand ITC, then click Viner Hand ITC**
   The selected text changes to the Viner Hand ITC font.

8. **Select the second line of text, Quick Meal Kits, click the Font list arrow, scroll in the list until you see Britannic Bold, then click Britannic Bold as shown in FIGURE 5-2**
   The selected text changes to the Britannic Bold font.

9. **Click the Save button 🖫 on the Quick Access Toolbar to save your changes**

FIGURE 5-1: Changing the font size of selected text using the Font Size list

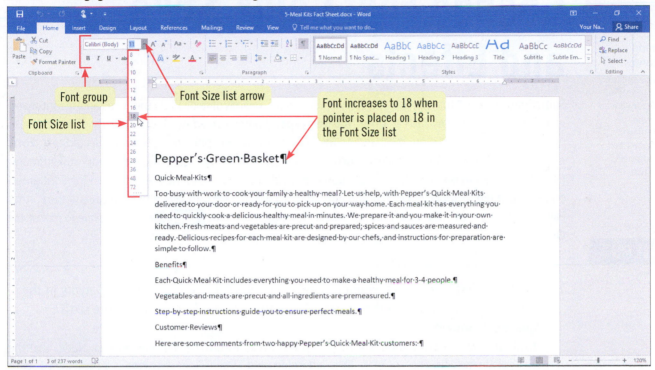

Font group

Font Size list arrow

Font Size list

Font increases to 18 when pointer is placed on 18 in the Font Size list

FIGURE 5-2: Changing the font type of selected text using the Font list

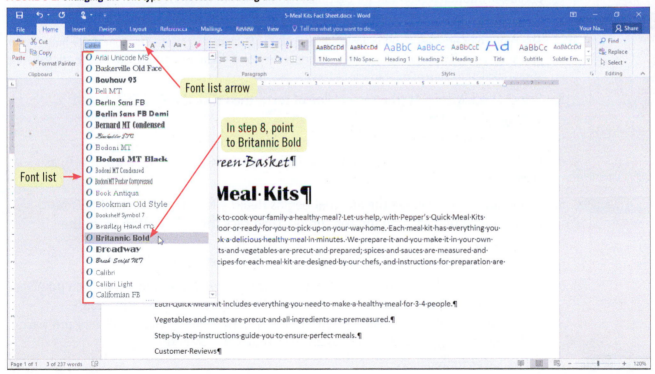

Font list arrow

In step 8, point to Britannic Bold

Font list

TABLE 5-1: Samples of fonts and font sizes

font formats	samples
Font	Times New Roman, *French Script*, **Impact**, ALGERIAN, **Broadway**, Chiller
Size	eight point, twelve point, fourteen point, eighteen point

Change Font Color, Style, and Effects

Learning Outcomes
- Change the font color and style
- Apply font effects
- Copy the formatting of selected text and apply it to other text

Sometimes you want to emphasize certain words, phrases, or lines of text. To do this, you can use font styles, which are font attributes such as **bold** (**darker type**), *italic* (*slanted type)*, and underline. You can also make certain words stand out by changing their color, or you can apply font effects to selected text. **Font effects** are special enhancements—such as shadow (**Shadow** looks like this) or strikethrough (~~strikethrough looks like this~~) that you can apply to selected text. You can use the buttons in the Font group on the Home tab to apply font effects and formatting to selected text. To save time, you can use the Format Painter button to copy the formatting of selected text to other text. **CASE** *You continue to format the Quick Meal Kits fact sheet by applying font styles, colors, and effects to certain words.*

STEPS

1. **Select the first line of text, Pepper's Green Basket, click the Font Color list arrow in the Font group, then point to the green color in the Standard Colors area (the sixth square), as shown in FIGURE 5-3**

   Thanks to Live Preview, you can see Pepper's Green Basket with the green color applied. Notice that the color palette includes Theme Colors, Standard Colors, and More Colors. A **theme** is a predesigned set of formatting elements, including colors, which you can use to achieve a coordinated overall look in your document. **Standard colors** are the basic hues red, orange, green, and so on.

   QUICK TIP
   To remove formatting from selected text, click the Clear All Formatting button ▧ in the Font group.

2. **Click the green color in the Standard Colors area (ScreenTip reads "Green")**

   The Font Color list closes, and Pepper's Green Basket is formatted in green. The Font Color button now displays a green stripe, indicating this is the current color. Clicking the Font Color button (not the list arrow) applies the current color to selected text.

3. **Select Quick Meal Kits (the second line of text), then click the Text Effects and Typography button Ⓐ in the Font group**

   The Text Effects and Typography gallery opens.

4. **Click the fifth option in the second row (Fill - Gray-50%, Accent 3, Sharp Bevel), as shown in FIGURE 5-4**

   QUICK TIP
   To underline text, click the Underline button ⓤ in the Font group.

5. **Scroll down until you see the line that begins Healthy & fast:, select Healthy & fast:, click the Bold button Ⓑ in the Font group, then click the Italic button Ⓘ in the Font group**

   "Healthy & fast:" is now formatted in bold and italic, and is still selected.

6. **Click the Format Painter button in the Clipboard group on the Home tab, then point (but do not click) anywhere over Saves time:, three lines below Healthy & fast**

   Notice that the pointer shape changes to ▧Ⅰ when you place it on the document, indicating that you can apply the formatting of the selected text to any text you click or select next.

   QUICK TIP
   Double-clicking the Format Painter button lets you apply the selected formatting multiple times.

7. **Select Saves time:**

   The bold and italic formatting is applied to "Saves time:".

8. **Click outside the selected text, then save your changes**

   See **FIGURE 5-5**.

FIGURE 5-3: Font Color list with Green color selected

Font Color list arrow

Bold button

Underline button

Italic button

Click this shade of green

In Step 1, select this text

FIGURE 5-4: Applying a text effect

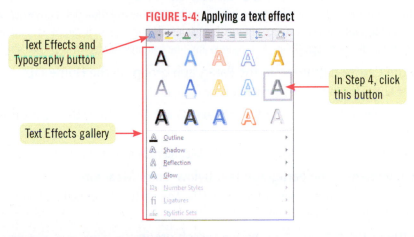

Text Effects and Typography button

In Step 4, click this button

Text Effects gallery

FIGURE 5-5: Bold and italic formatting applied to text

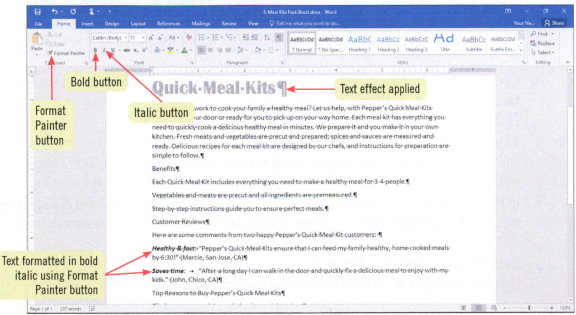

Bold button

Quick·Meal·Kits¶

Text effect applied

Italic button

Format Painter button

Text formatted in bold italic using Format Painter button

Word 2016

Change Alignment and Line Spacing

The amount of space between the edge of the page and your document text is called the **margin**. You can change the **alignment**, or position of text within a document's margins, using the alignment buttons in the Paragraph group on the Home tab. For example, titles are often centered, headings left-aligned, and paragraphs **justified** (aligned equally between the left and right margins). You can also adjust the spacing between lines using the Line and Paragraph Spacing button in the Paragraph group on the Home tab. **CASE** *All of the text in the Quick Meal Kits fact sheet is aligned along the left margin. You decide to center the first two lines and justify the descriptive paragraph. You also want to decrease the amount of spacing between the lines in the paragraph so they are single spaced, and increase the amount of space both above and below the paragraph.*

STEPS

1. **Press [Ctrl][Home] to move the insertion point to the beginning of the document**

   Although you need to select text to change character formats such as font size or font style, you can change most paragraph formatting, such as alignment, just by positioning the insertion point anywhere in the paragraph. In Word, a **paragraph** is any text that ends with a paragraph mark (¶), so it can be as short as a one-word title or as long as you like. A paragraph mark is inserted anytime you press [Enter]; this is also called a hard return.

2. **Click the Center button ≡ in the Paragraph group on the Home tab**

   The first line of text is centered between the two margins.

3. **Click anywhere in the second line of text (Quick Meal Kits), then click the Center button ≡**

   The second line of text is centered between the left and right margin. See **FIGURE 5-6**.

4. **Click anywhere in the paragraph text below Quick Meal Kits**

   The insertion point is now set in the paragraph. Any paragraph formatting you specify will affect the formatting of the entire paragraph.

5. **Click the Justify button ≡ in the Paragraph group**

   The paragraph's alignment changes to justified. When you select justified alignment, Word adds or reduces the space between each word so the text is aligned along both the right and left margins. This is different from **center-aligning** text, which centers text between the left and right margins, but does not adjust the spacing between words.

6. **Click the Line and Paragraph Spacing button ⇳≡▾ in the Paragraph group on the Home tab, then click 1.0, as shown in FIGURE 5-7**

   The paragraph is now both justified and single spaced.

7. **Click the launcher ⌐ in the Paragraph group**

   The Paragraph dialog box opens with the Indents and Spacing tab in front. This dialog box offers another way to change paragraph settings, including customizing the amount of space above and below a paragraph.

8. **In the Spacing section, click the Before up arrow twice to set spacing above the paragraph to 12 pt, then click the After up arrow twice to set spacing below the paragraph to 18 pt**

   See **FIGURE 5-8**.

9. **Click OK, then save your changes**

   Notice the spacing above and below the paragraph text increases to reflect the new settings.

FIGURE 5-6: Center-aligned text

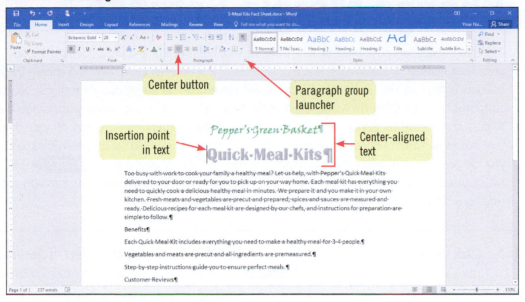

Center button

Paragraph group launcher

Insertion point in text

Center-aligned text

FIGURE 5-7: Paragraph with justified alignment and line spacing set to 1.0

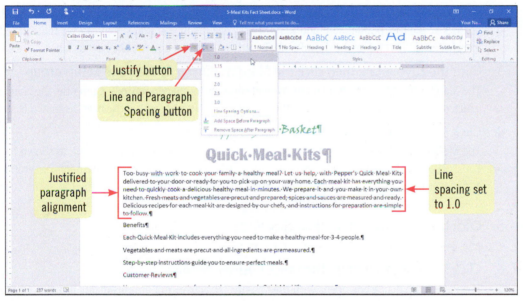

Justify button

Line and Paragraph Spacing button

Justified paragraph alignment

Line spacing set to 1.0

FIGURE 5-8: Indents and Spacing tab of Paragraph dialog box

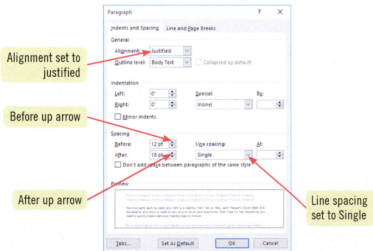

Alignment set to justified

Before up arrow

After up arrow

Line spacing set to Single

Word 2016

Change Margin Settings

By default, Word sets page margins at 1" from the top, bottom, left, and right sides of the page. Word also provides a number of additional preset margin settings that you can easily view and choose by clicking the Margins button on the Layout tab. If you do not like any of the preset margin settings, you can specify custom settings by using the Margins tab of the Page Setup dialog box. When you change the margins, Word automatically adjusts line wrapping and **repaginates** (renumbers the pages of) your document. To evaluate what margin settings to use in a specific document, you should set the zoom level to One Page so you can see and work with the actual margins as they will appear on the page. **CASE** ▶ *The Quick Meal Kits fact sheet is currently formatted with the default margins. You decide to explore other margin settings to see whether a different setting would make the document look better.*

STEPS

TROUBLE
If there is already a check mark in the Rulers check box, do not click it.

1. **Click the View tab, then click the Ruler check box to display the rulers, if necessary**
   The View tab is in front, and the horizontal and vertical rulers appear along the top and left edge of the document window.

2. **Click the One Page button in the Zoom group**
   You can now see your whole document in the document window, making it possible to see the margin settings at the top, bottom, left, and right of the page. Using the rulers, you can see that the left and right margins are 1". To change the default margin settings, you need to use the Layout tab.

3. **Click the Layout tab, then click the Margins button in the Page Setup group**
   The Margins list opens and displays ready-made options for margin settings. Currently, the Normal option is selected, which specifies a 1" margin at the top, bottom, left, and right of the page, as shown in **FIGURE 5-9**.

4. **Click Narrow in the Margins list**
   The Margins list closes, and the Narrow margins setting is applied to the document, as shown in **FIGURE 5-10**. You can see that there is only a ½" margin at the top, bottom, left, and right. This margin setting is too narrow and makes the text placement look unbalanced; all the text is stretched out at the top of the document, and there is a large blank space at the bottom.

QUICK TIP
To format selected text into multiple columns, click the Columns button in the Page Setup group, then click a column setting.

5. **Click the Margins button, then click Wide**
   The Wide margins setting is applied to the document.

6. **Click the Margins button, then click Custom Margins**
   The Page Setup dialog box opens with the Margins tab active. You use this dialog box to set specific margin settings. The first margin text box, Top, is currently selected.

7. **Press [Tab] twice**
   The Left text box is selected. Pressing [Tab] moves the insertion point from one text box to the next.

8. **Type 1.1 in the Left text box, then press [Tab]**
   The Left text box shows 1.1, and the Right text box is selected. The Preview box shows the new left margin.

QUICK TIP
Most printers require at least a 1/4" margin around the page.

9. **Type 1.1 in the Right text box, compare your screen to FIGURE 5-11, click OK, then save your changes**
   The left and right margins of the Quick Meal Kits fact sheet change to 1.1".

FIGURE 5-9: Margins list

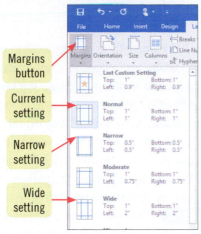

- Margins button
- Current setting
- Narrow setting
- Wide setting

FIGURE 5-10: Quick Meal Kits fact sheet with Narrow margins setting applied

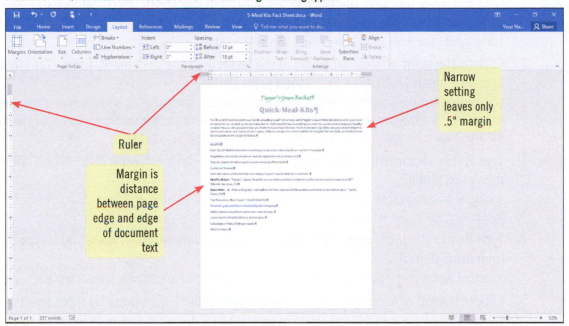

- Narrow setting leaves only .5" margin
- Ruler
- Margin is distance between page edge and edge of document text

FIGURE 5-11: Margins tab of Page Setup dialog box

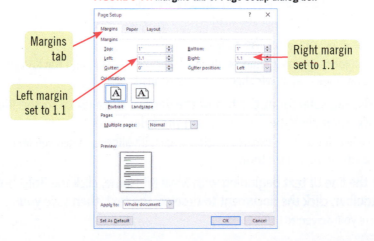

- Margins tab
- Left margin set to 1.1
- Right margin set to 1.1

Word 2016

Set Tabs

Learning Outcomes
- Explain tabs and tab stops
- Set left and right tab stops using the ruler
- Organize text into columns using tabs

You can improve the appearance of a document by using tabs to align text within a line at specific positions on the page. A **tab** is a set position where text following a tab character aligns. (When you press [Tab], Word inserts a tab character—a right-facing arrow—to indicate the presence of a tab.) The ruler makes it easy to set **tab stops** (locations the insertion point moves to when you press [Tab]) and to see immediately how they affect your document. By default, Word sets left-aligned tab stops every 1/2". Any tab stop you add to the ruler will appear as a tab icon on the ruler and will override the default tab stop settings to the left of it. By default, new tab stops that you set on the ruler are left-aligned and appear as a ⌐ on the ruler. You can use the **tab selector** on the ruler to align text differently, such as to the right or center of a tab stop. When you set tabs, they apply only to text you selected or, if no text is selected, to the paragraph containing the insertion point. **CASE** ▸ *You need to enter information about the subscription plans for the Quick Meal Kits at the bottom of the page. You will use tabs to align the information in columns.*

STEPS

QUICK TIP
The Page Width button increases the zoom so that the width of the page fills the width of your screen.

1. **Click the View tab, click the Page Width button in the Zoom group, then scroll down so the bottom of the document is visible**

   This is where you want to add the subscription plan details.

2. **Click to the right of Meal Kit Name in the last line of the document, press [Tab], type Kit Contains, press [Tab], type Price, then press [Enter]**

   You can see that the word "Kit," which follows the first tab, is left-aligned at the default 1" tab stop. The word "Price" is aligned at the 2" mark, also a default tab stop. Notice that the tab appears as a right-arrow in the text. Now you need to enter the product information below each heading.

TROUBLE
Don't worry that your text is not aligned yet; you will fix that in a later step.

3. **Type Family (Standard), press [Tab], type Four meals with meat, press [Tab], type $120.00, then press [Enter]**

   You typed information for the first plan. Notice that "Four" is not aligned with the "Kit Contains" heading above. Also, "$120.00" is not aligned with the "Price" heading.

4. **Type Family (Veggie), press [Tab], type Four meals without meat, press [Tab], type $95.00, then press [Enter]**

   Now that you've entered the subscription information, you need to select the lines of text you just typed.

5. **Click to the left of Meal Kit Name, press and hold [Shift], then press [↓] three times**

   The three lines of text are selected, as shown in **FIGURE 5-12**. Any tab stop changes you make will apply to all three selected lines.

TROUBLE
If you click the wrong place, drag the tab marker off the ruler to remove it, then try again.

6. **Notice the tab selector at the top of the vertical ruler**

   The tab selector currently displays an image of a left tab stop ⌐ . This means that clicking the ruler will add a left tab stop, which is what you want.

7. **Click the 2 ¼" mark on the ruler**

   The left-aligned tab stop appears on the ruler at the 2 ¼" mark, and the Kit Contains heading and the two items below it are now all left-aligned at the 2 ¼" mark.

QUICK TIP
To add dots (called "leaders") between tabs, click the Layout tab, click the Paragraph group launcher, click Tabs, click the option you want in the Leader section, then click OK.

8. **Click the tab selector at the top of the vertical ruler twice so the Right Tab icon ⌐ appears, then click the 5 ½" mark on the ruler**

   The Price heading and the two prices below it are right-aligned. When you arrange numbers in a column, it is a good idea to right-align them.

9. **Select the line of text beginning with Meal Kit Name, click the Bold button B on the Mini toolbar, click the document to deselect the text, then save your changes**

   Compare your screen to **FIGURE 5-13**.

FIGURE 5-12: Selected text with tabs inserted

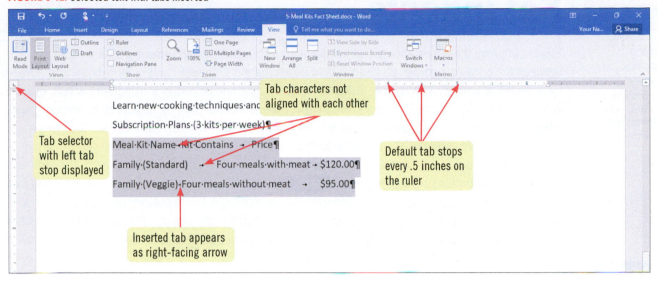

Tab characters not aligned with each other

Tab selector with left tab stop displayed

Default tab stops every .5 inches on the ruler

Inserted tab appears as right-facing arrow

FIGURE 5-13: Text arranged in columns with left and right tabs set

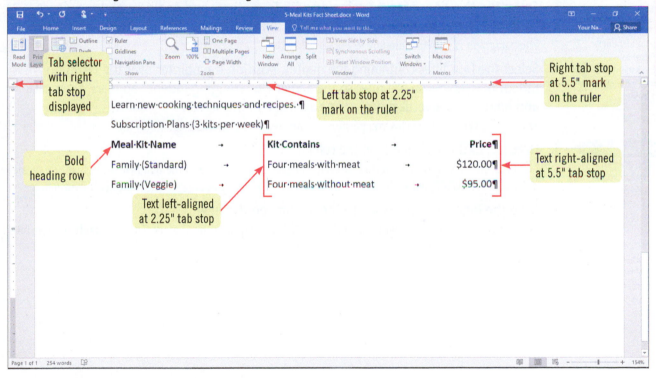

Tab selector with right tab stop displayed

Left tab stop at 2.25" mark on the ruler

Right tab stop at 5.5" mark on the ruler

Bold heading row

Text right-aligned at 5.5" tab stop

Text left-aligned at 2.25" tab stop

Enhancing a Document

Set Indents

You can improve the appearance of text on a page by setting indents. An **indent** is a set amount of space between the edge of a paragraph and the right or left margin. Different types of indents are appropriate for different situations. A **first line indent** indents the first line of text in a paragraph. A **left indent** indents the left edge of an entire paragraph; a **right indent** indents the right edge of an entire paragraph. A **hanging indent** is an indent where the first line of a paragraph is aligned flush left with the margin and all lines below it are indented. You can set indents using the sliding markers on the ruler. **TABLE 5-2** describes these markers. You can set left and right indents at 1/2" increments using the Increase Indent and Decrease Indent buttons on the Home tab. **CASE** *The text containing the customer quotes would look neater if it was aligned under the first word after the tab. To accomplish this, you decide to set a hanging indent. You also decide to set a left indent for the paragraph that describes the product. The fact sheet contains two customer comments. Each is preceded by a selling point in bold and a tab. You decide to indent both comments, and then set a hanging indent to align the quote text at a tab stop.*

STEPS

1. **Scroll up, then select the two lines of text beginning with** Healthy & fast: **and ending with** Marcie, San Jose, CA)

2. **Position the pointer over the** Left Indent marker ▢ **on the ruler until the ScreenTip "Left Indent" appears, then drag** ▢ **to the ½" mark on the ruler**
   The selected text is now indented by ½". You can also indent text using the Ribbon.

3. **Select the two lines of text beginning with** Saves time: **and ending with** John, Chico, CA) **click the** Home tab, **then click the** Increase Indent button ▤ **in the Paragraph group**
   The paragraph is now indented by ½". See **FIGURE 5-14**.

4. **Select the four lines containing the quotes, position the pointer over the** Hanging Indent marker △ **on the ruler so the ScreenTip "Hanging Indent" appears, then click and hold** △ **so a vertical dotted line appears on the screen**
   This dotted vertical line helps you position the marker in the desired location on the ruler.

5. **Drag** △ **to the 1 ½" mark on the ruler**
   The first line in each of the selected paragraphs remains flush left, and the text below the first line of each paragraph is now aligned at the 1 ½" mark on the ruler, where you dragged the Hanging Indent marker.

6. **Drag the** Right Indent marker **to the 6" mark on the ruler**
   The text is indented on the right side of the selected paragraphs at the 6" mark. The paragraphs are narrower now, because they are indented on both sides. See **FIGURE 5-15**.

7. **Save your changes**

FIGURE 5-14: Setting a left indent

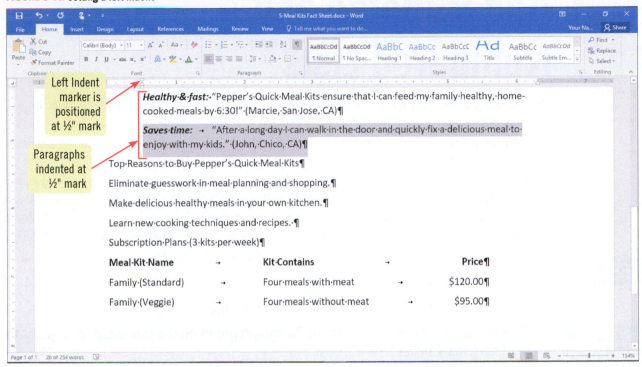

FIGURE 5-15: Setting a hanging indent

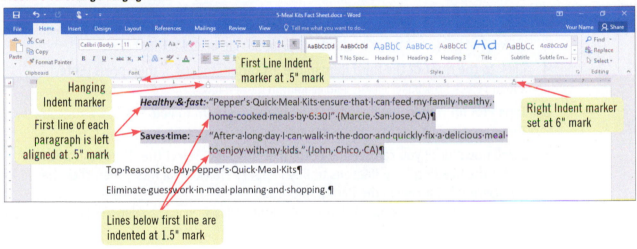

TABLE 5-2: Ruler markers used for setting indents

ruler marker name	ruler marker	indents
First Line Indent marker	▽	The first line of a paragraph
Hanging Indent marker	△	The lines below the first line of text in a paragraph
Left Indent marker	▢	The left edge of an entire paragraph
Right Indent marker	△	The right edge of an entire paragraph

Learning Outcomes
- Format paragraphs as a bulleted list
- Format paragraphs as a numbered list

Add Bulleted and Numbered Lists

Word provides many tools for organizing your text into a more orderly format. You can easily organize groups of related paragraphs into bulleted or numbered lists. You already learned how to create a bulleted list using the Bullets button on the Mini toolbar. The Bullets button is also available on the Home tab. When you apply the bullet format to a paragraph, Word sets off the paragraph with a bullet and automatically formats the text with a hanging indent. Use a numbered (ordered) list when you want to present items in a particular sequence, and use a bulleted (unordered) list when the items are of equal importance. There are many bullet and numbering styles to choose from when using the Bullets list and Numbering list on the Home tab, or you can create a custom style. **CASE** ▶ *You decide to add bulleted and numbered lists to the Quick Meal Kits fact sheet to make it easier to reference.*

STEPS

1. **Scroll up, then select the three lines of text under the heading Benefits**

QUICK TIP
With Live Preview, you can point to any format in the Bullet Library to see how the format will look if you apply it to the selected text.

2. **Click the Bullets list arrow ▤ in the Paragraph group on the Home tab, then point to the Check mark bullet style**

   The Bullets list opens and displays bullet formatting options in the Bullet Library. When you point to the Check mark bullet style, the text you selected appears as a bulleted list, with a check mark before each item, as shown in **FIGURE 5-16**.

3. **Click the Check mark bullet style**

   The Bullets list closes. Notice that each bullet in the list is indented and that there is a tab after each check mark. You can see by the ruler that a hanging indent has been automatically set. If any text in the bulleted list wrapped to a second line, it would align with the first line of text, not the bullet.

4. **Click to the right of the third item in the list (after "meals."), then press [Enter]**

   A fourth check mark bullet appears automatically in the new row.

5. **Type Pick up your kits at Pepper's or let us deliver them to you.**

   The text you typed is now formatted as a fourth item in the bulleted list.

6. **Scroll down until you can see the bottom of the page, select the three lines of text under the heading "Top Reasons to Buy Pepper's Quick Meal Kits", then click the Numbering list arrow in the Paragraph group**

   The Numbering list opens and displays the Numbering Library, containing different formatting options for a numbered list.

7. **Click the option shown in FIGURE 5-17 (the one with the parenthesis after each number), then save your changes**

   The selected text is now formatted as a numbered list.

FIGURE 5-16: Bullet library

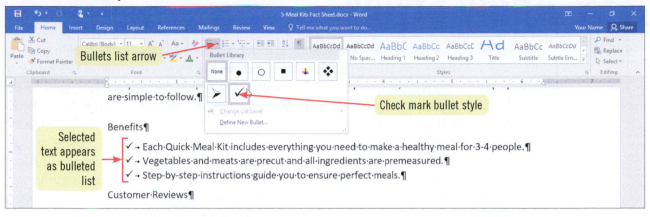

FIGURE 5-17: Quick Meal Kits fact sheet with bulleted and numbered lists

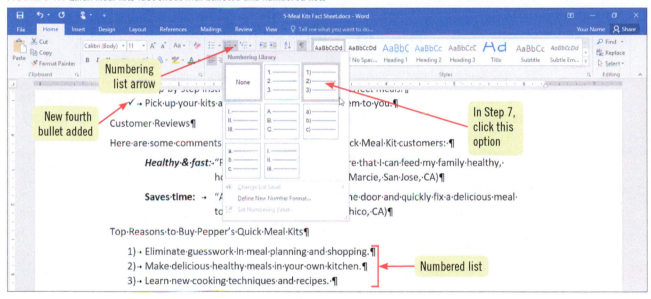

Creating a custom bullet

You can create a custom bullet using an image or symbol. To do this, click the Bullets list arrow in the Paragraph group, click Define New Bullet, then click Picture to open the Insert Pictures dialog box. To choose one of your own images, click Browse next to the From a file or the OneDrive options, navigate to the folder where your image is stored, click Insert, then click OK. Or, to create a bullet using an image from a website, type key words in the Bing Image Search text box, press [Enter], click the image you want, click Insert, then click OK.

Apply Styles

Learning Outcomes
- Explain styles and style sets
- Apply styles to text
- Change the style set and color palette

You can save a lot of formatting time and ensure that your document looks professional by applying styles to your document. A **style** is a set of predefined formatting attributes. For instance, the Normal Paragraph style (which is applied to any text you type in a new document) includes the Calibri 11-point font with 1.15 line spacing. Besides paragraph styles, you can also apply built-in styles for other types of text elements in your document, including headings, titles, and captions. To apply a style to a paragraph, click anywhere in the paragraph, then click the style you want in the Styles gallery, which is in the Styles group on the Home tab. Once you apply styles to your document, you can then change the look of the entire document in one click by applying a new style set. A **style set** is a group of professionally coordinated styles that look great together; applying a different style set changes all the styles in the document to a different overall look. CASE ▸ *You decide to use styles to complete the formatting of the Quick Meal Kits fact sheet.*

STEPS

1. **Scroll up, then click anywhere in Benefits in the line below the long paragraph**

   To apply a style to a paragraph, you first click in the paragraph to which you want to apply the style.

2. **In the Styles group on the Home tab, click the Heading 1 style in the Styles gallery**

   See **FIGURE 5-18**. The Benefits paragraph now has the Heading 1 style applied to it and is formatted in Calibri Light 18-point blue.

3. **Using the process you followed in Steps 1 and 2, apply the Heading 1 style to the following lines: Customer Reviews, Top Reasons to Buy Pepper's Quick Meal Kits, and Subscription Plans (3 kits per week)**

   All of the headings in the document now have the Heading 1 style applied.

4. **Scroll up if necessary to view the text below Customer Reviews, select the customer quote that begins "Pepper's Quick Meal Kits, then click the More button ⬇ in the Styles gallery**

   When you want to apply a style to only part of a paragraph, you need to first select the desired text before applying the style; otherwise, the style will be applied to the entire paragraph. The Styles gallery opens and displays all the styles you can apply to paragraphs or characters, as shown in **FIGURE 5-19**.

5. **Click the Quote style in the Styles gallery**

   The selected text is now formatted in italic, the preset formatting specifications for the Quote style. Because you selected text instead of clicking in the paragraph, the style was applied only to the characters you selected rather than to the whole paragraph.

6. **Select the customer quote that begins "After a long day... and ends (John, Chico, CA), click the Quote style in the Styles gallery, then deselect the text**

   Next, you decide to change the style set to change the overall look of the document.

7. **Click the Design tab, click the More button ⬇ in the Document Formatting group to open the Style Set gallery, then click the Minimalist thumbnail**

   The Minimalist style set is applied to the document. Each heading is now black and all capitals, and each has a short brown vertical rule at the left. Notice, too, that the quotes are no longer formatted in italic. You can see that changing a style set immediately changes the overall look of the document.

8. **Click the Colors button in the Document Formatting group, then click the Blue Warm color palette**

   Changing the color palette applies a new set of coordinated colors across the document.

9. **Press [Ctrl][End], type your name, save your changes, use the zoom slider to set the zoom to 60%, compare your screen to FIGURE 5-20, close the document, then exit Word**

   Submit your document to your instructor.

Enhancing a Document

FIGURE 5-18: Heading 1 style applied to paragraph

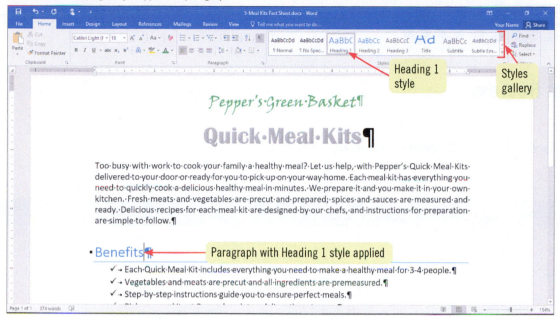

FIGURE 5-19: Styles gallery

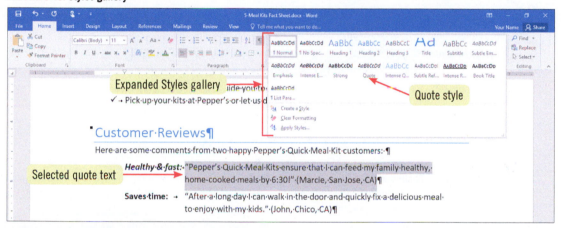

FIGURE 5-20: Completed 5-Meal Kits Fact Sheet at 60% zoom

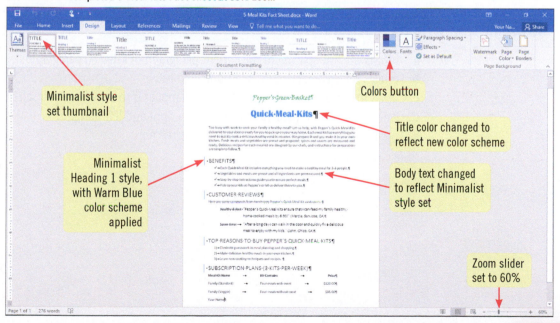

Practice

Concepts Review

Label the Word window elements shown in FIGURE 5-21.

FIGURE 5-21

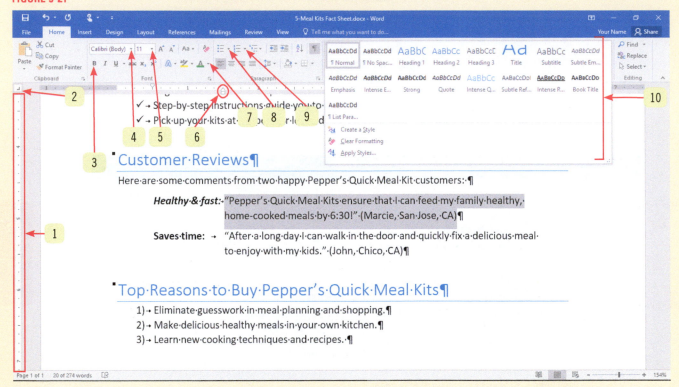

Match each button or icon with its function.

11.

12.

13.

14.

15.

a. Adjusts the line spacing of the current paragraph or selected paragraph(s).

b. Formats selected paragraphs as a numbered list.

c. Copies the formatting of selected text and applies it to other text you select.

d. Centers the current paragraph between the right and left margins.

e. Applies font and typography effects to selected text.

Select the best answer from the list of choices.

16. **Which of the following would you use to align text at multiple positions on the ruler?**
    a. Tab stops
    b. Left and right indent markers
    c. Hanging indent marker
    d. Preset margin settings

17. **Which setting would display the most white space on both sides of the page?**
    a. Narrow margin setting
    b. Wide margin setting
    c. Normal margin setting
    d. Custom margin setting with Left and Right settings set to .5"

18. **To specify a set amount of space before and after a paragraph, which of the following do you need to use?**
    a. Font dialog box
    b. Line Spacing list arrow
    c. Paragraph dialog box
    d. Ruler

19. **Which tool(s) would you use to apply a predefined set of formatting attributes such as headings, titles, and quotes to a paragraph?**
    a. Font group buttons
    b. Styles gallery
    c. Font list
    d. Paragraph group buttons

20. **Which alignment setting aligns a paragraph equally between the left and right margins, adjusting spacing between words as needed?**
    a. Center
    b. Align Right
    c. Align Left
    d. Justify

Skills Review

1. **Change font and font size.**
   a. Start Word, open 5-2.docx from the location where you store your Data Files, enable the content if necessary, then save it as **5-Baseball Tryouts**. If necessary, change the view to Print Layout view.
   b. Select the entire first line of the document.
   c. Change the font size to 16.
   d. Change the font to Trebuchet MS.
   e. Select the entire second line of the document, and then change the font size to 28. Change the font to Rockwell.
   f. Save your changes.

2. **Change font color, style, and effects.**
   a. Select the first line of the document, then change the font color to red (the second color under Standard Colors).
   b. Format the selected red text in bold.
   c. Select the second line of the document, open the Text Effects & Typography gallery, then apply the Gold, Accent 4, Soft Bevel Fill (fifth option in top row).
   d. Apply bold formatting to the text **Hector Garcia:** and **Stan Castillo:**.
   e. Select the text **Red Star Sports Academy** in the third line of the document, then apply bold formatting and change the font color to red.
   f. Use the Format Painter to apply the formatting of "Red Star Sports Academy" in the third line to the remaining unformatted instances of **Red Star Sports Academy** in the document. (*Hint*: There are three other instances.)
   g. Save your changes.

Skills Review (continued)

3. **Change alignment and line spacing.**
   a. Change the alignment of the paragraph located below "Baseball Tryouts" to justified.
   b. Change the line spacing of this paragraph to 1.15.
   c. Use the Paragraph dialog box to set 6 point spacing before and 12 point spacing after this paragraph.
   d. Center-align the first two lines of the document.
   e. Save your changes.

4. **Change margin settings.**
   a. Use a command on the View tab to adjust the view so you can see the whole page on the screen.
   b. Verify that the ruler is visible in the document window. If it is not visible, adjust your settings so it is visible.
   c. Apply the Narrow margins setting to the document.
   d. Apply the Wide margins setting to the document.
   e. Open the Page Setup dialog box with the Margins tab displayed, then set both the left and right margins to .9.
   f. Change the zoom level to Page Width.
   g. Save your changes.

5. **Set tabs.**
   a. Scroll down until you see the line of text that reads "Team Location Time".
   b. Select this line and the three lines below it (through the line that begins with **Red Stars**).
   c. Set a left tab stop at the 2 ½" mark on the ruler for the four selected lines.
   d. Set a right tab stop at the 5 ½" mark on the ruler for the four selected lines.
   e. Apply bold formatting to the line **Team Location Time**.
   f. Save your changes.

6. **Set indents.**
   a. Select the paragraph that starts with **Hector Garcia**, then use the ruler to set the left indent to 1/2".
   b. Select the paragraph that starts with **Stan Castillo**, then use a button on the Home tab to set the left indent to 1/2".
   c. Select the five lines of text that start with **Hector Garcia** and end with **off the field**.
   d. Set a hanging indent at the 1 ½" mark on the ruler for the selected lines of text.
   e. Set a right indent for these lines to the 6" mark on the ruler.
   f. Save your changes.

7. **Add bulleted and numbered lists.**
   a. Format the three lines beginning with **Yellow Stars** and ending with **Red Stars** as a bulleted list using the arrowhead bullet style.
   b. Format the last three lines of text in the document as a numbered list, choosing the style 1) 2) 3) (a number followed by a parenthesis).
   c. Save your changes.

8. **Apply Styles.**
   a. Apply the Heading 1 style to the text **Teams** (the seventh line in the document).
   b. Apply the Heading 1 style to the following headings: **Coaches**, **About the Tryouts**, **Tryout Times**, and **Tryout Requirements**.
   c. Use the Design tab to apply the Basic (Simple) style set to the document.
   d. Use the Colors button to change the color palette to Blue II.
   e. Type your name in the last line of the document. (*Note:* Make sure your name is not formatted as a numbered list. If you need to remove the numbered list format from any text in the document, click in the paragraph from which you want to remove it, then click the Numbering button.)

Skills Review (continued)

f. Save your changes.

g. Preview the document, compare your document with **FIGURE 5-22**, then exit Word. Submit your completed document to your instructor.

Independent Challenge 1

You work in the marketing department for the Blue Street Theatre in Bay Town, New Jersey. Audrey Chambers, the general manager, needs to create a one-page document that provides information about the theatre and upcoming shows in June. Audrey has already created a draft with all the necessary information; now she needs you to format it so that the information is presented effectively and looks attractive and professional.

a. Start Word, open 5-3.docx from the location where your Data Files are stored, enable the content, then save it as **5-June Events**.

b. Center-align the first four lines of the document.

c. Change the font of **June Events** to Broadway, increase the font size to 24, and change the font color to Blue, Accent 1.

d. Apply bold formatting to **Blue Street Theatre**, and increase the font size of this line and the two lines below it to 12 points.

e. Set the alignment of the first long paragraph (beginning "Now in its 5th Season") so it is justified, then set the line spacing to 1.0. Increase the space before and after this paragraph to 12 points, and apply italic formatting to it.

f. Apply the Heading 1 style to the following lines of text: **Open Mic Story Nights**, **June Shows**, and **Workshops**.

g. In the four lines of tabbed text below the heading "Open Mic Story Nights" and text describing the event, set two left tab stops—the first at 2" and the second at 4".

h. In the four lines of tabbed text below the heading "June Shows," set a left tab stop at 2", a second left tab stop at 3 ½", and a right tab stop at 5 ½". Apply bold formatting to the first row of tabbed text (which starts with "Dates").

i. Set the left and right page margins to .9.

j. Format the last three lines in the document as a bulleted list. Choose the open circle bullet style.

k. Apply the Lines (Stylish) style set to the document, then apply the Blue II color palette.

l. Type your name in the last line of the document, then center-align it.

m. Save your changes, close the document, then submit your document to your instructor.

FIGURE 5-22

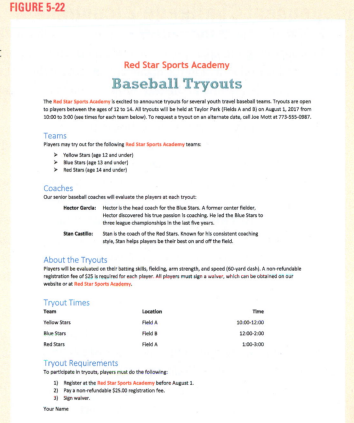

Independent Challenge 2

You are a marketing assistant at The Windy Bluff Inn, a family-owned and operated bed and breakfast on an island off the coast of Rhode Island. Olivia Griswold, one of the owners, has given you an unformatted document that provides information about the Inn for its guests. Olivia has asked you to format the document so it is attractive and easy to scan.

a. Open 5-4.docx from where you store your Data Files, enable the content, then save it as **5-Windy Bluff Inn**.

b. Center-align the first five lines of text in the document, which include the contact information.

Independent Challenge 2 (continued)

c. Format the name **Windy Bluff Inn** in the first line using any font, font style, or effects you like to make it look appealing and appropriate for a traditional family-owned business. Increase the font size to 26 pt.

d. Select all the other text in the document (except for the first line) and change the font to Franklin Gothic Book.

e. Apply italic formatting to the text in the second line ("Welcoming guests since 1925"). Increase the font size to 14 pt and apply a font color that you think looks good.

f. Apply the Narrow preset margin setting to the document.

g. Select the three lines 3 to 5 starting with 7 Sea Gull Road and ending with 773-555-0965, apply the No Space style to the selection, then center-align the selection.

h. Apply justified alignment to the first long paragraph (that begins "Welcome to the Windy Bluff Inn"). Increase the spacing before this paragraph to 12 pt and the spacing after it to 12 pt. Apply bold formatting to the text **Welcome to the Windy Bluff Inn** in the first line of the paragraph.

i. Select the quote that begins "We welcome all travelers…" (below the long paragraph), and set the left indent at the 1" mark and the right indent at the 6" mark. Center-align the selected text and apply italic formatting to it.

j. Apply the Heading 1 style to the following lines of text: **Our Family: Here to Serve You**, **Our Rooms**, and **Amenities**.

k. Under the heading "Our Family: Here to Serve You," select the four lines that provide information about each family member (beginning with "Brian Childress" and ending with "ext. 557"). Set a left tab stop for these lines at the 3" mark on the ruler, and a right-aligned tab stop at the 6" mark. Apply bold formatting to each person's name (Brian Childress, Laurie Childress, etc.).

l. Under the heading "Our Rooms," select the two paragraphs (four lines) describing the room types (beginning with "Studio Room:" and ending with "Internet access."). Set a hanging indent at the 1 ½" mark. Apply bold and italic formatting to **Studio Room:** and **Deluxe Suite:**.

m. Under the heading "Amenities," select the three lines of text, then set a left-aligned tab stop at the 2 ½" mark and a right-aligned tab stop at the 6" mark.

n. Apply the Casual style set to the document. Apply the Red color palette.

o. Add your name to the last line of the document, save your changes, preview the document, submit it to your instructor, then exit Word.

Independent Challenge 3

You are the director of training for Happy Family Dinner Haven, Inc. a restaurant chain based in Ohio. Your department designs and delivers employee training courses and programs. You have decided to start giving certificates of completion to each employee who completes a training. You have already created a document and entered the text for your first certificate; now you need to format it.

a. Open 5-5.docx from where you store your Data Files, enable the content, then save it as **5-Certificate**.

b. Apply the Narrow preset Margin setting to the document.

c. Center-align the first six lines of text. Change the font in the first line to Lucida Calligraphy 48 pt. Change the font in the second line to Copperplate Gothic Bold 14 pt.

d. Change the font in the third line to Lucida Calligraphy 22 pt and apply bold formatting to it.

e. Select the paragraph beginning "On April 5, 2017," and change the font to Gabriola 20 pt. Change the font color to Blue Accent 5, Darker 25%. Set the line spacing for this paragraph to 1.5, and specify spacing of 12 pt before and after it.

f. Change the paper orientation to Landscape. (*Hint*: To specify to print the document in landscape orientation, click the Layout tab, click the Orientation button in the Page Setup group, then click Landscape.)

g. In the line starting "Breads," insert a center-aligned tab stop at the 5" mark, and a right-aligned tab stop at the 9" mark. Set the left indent for this line at the 1" mark and set the right indent at the 9" mark. Format the text in this line to Gabriola 22 pt bold.

Independent Challenge 3 (continued)

h. For the last three lines, set the left indent at 5". Replace "Your Name" with your name and format it in Mistral 28 pt. Format the two lines below your name in Copperplate Gothic Bold 12 pt.

i. Save your changes, close the document, submit the file to your instructor, then exit Word.

Independent Challenge 4: Explore

You work for Joelle Swanson, the community relations commissioner of Oak City, New York. Joelle asks you to complete a flyer promoting the annual community yard sale. You have a document that contains all the text, you just need to enhance its appearance to attract customers.

a. Open 5-6.docx from where you store your Data Files, enable the content, then save it as **5-Yard Sale Flier.docx**.

b. Format the first line in Baskerville Old Face, 20 pt, Dark Red.

c. Apply the Title style to the line **Community Yard Sale**, and apply the Subtitle style to the third line, which begins "September 15."

d. Apply the Heading 1 style to the following lines of text: **Sample Items for Sale**, **Other Items**, and **Comments from Last Year's Participants**.

e. Select the three lines of text below the "Sample Items for Sale" heading, then set a right-aligned tab stop at the 6" mark on the ruler.

f. With the text still selected, position the mouse pointer over the selected text, right-click to open a shortcut menu, then click Paragraph to open the Paragraph dialog box. In the Paragraph dialog box, click Tabs to open the Tabs dialog box, click the 3 option in the Leader section, then click OK. Notice the dashed leader lines connecting each sample item to its associated price.

g. Select all the items below the "Other Items" heading (starting with **Bicycles** and ending with **Jewelry**). Click the Layout tab, click the Columns button in the Page Setup group, then click Three. Notice that all the sample items are now formatted into three columns.

h. Open the Design tab, then apply the Black and White (Capitalized) style set to the document. Apply the Blue color palette. Click the Fonts button in the Document Formatting group, scroll down, then click Arial. Notice that many of the fonts in the document are now different.

i. Under the "Comments from Last Year's Participants" heading, apply the Quote style to the three quotes and the names of the people being quoted. Indent the line below each quote (the quoted person's name) at the 2" mark.

j. Select the **Sample Items for Sale** heading, then change the color to Dark Red. With the heading still selected, click the Home tab, right-click the Heading 1 style in the Styles gallery, then click Update Heading 1 to Match Selection. All the headings in the document are now dark red. Compare your screen to **FIGURE 5-23**.

k. In the last line of the document, replace the text "Your Name" with your name. Preview, save, and close the document, then submit the file to your instructor. Exit Word.

FIGURE 5-23

Oak City Square's Annual

COMMUNITY YARD SALE
SEPTEMBER 15, 2017, 10:00 - 5:00

SAMPLE ITEMS FOR SALE
Lawn Mower: --- $60.00

Vacuum Cleaner: --- $25.00

Pine dining room set: --- $120.00

OTHER ITEMS

Bicycles	Toys	Luggage
Kitchen appliances	Sports equipment	Art
Yard tools	Video games	Home decor
Clothes	Electronics	Rugs
Furniture	Linens	Jewelry
Books	Pots and pans	

COMMENTS FROM LAST YEAR'S PARTICIPANTS

"I love this annual tradition! I always find something for my house!"

-Ann Johnson, longtime resident

"I outfitted our rec room with furniture bought at the community yard sale!"

-Luiz Hernandez, new homeowner

"I love the canoe that we bought at the community yard sale!"

-Erica Liu, mother of two

Your Name

Visual Workshop

Open 5-7.docx from where your Data Files are stored, enable the content, then save it as **5-Soup Menu**. Format the document so it appears as shown in FIGURE 5-24. (*Hint*: A different style set has been applied to the document, and the color palette was changed, so you will need to experiment with different combinations of styles, style sets, and color palettes until you find the right mix. For the title: apply the Title style but change the alignment.) Be sure to set tab stops for the tabbed column headings, prices, and fruits. Add your name at the bottom of the document, then preview the document. Close the document, then exit Word. Submit the document to your instructor.

FIGURE 5-24

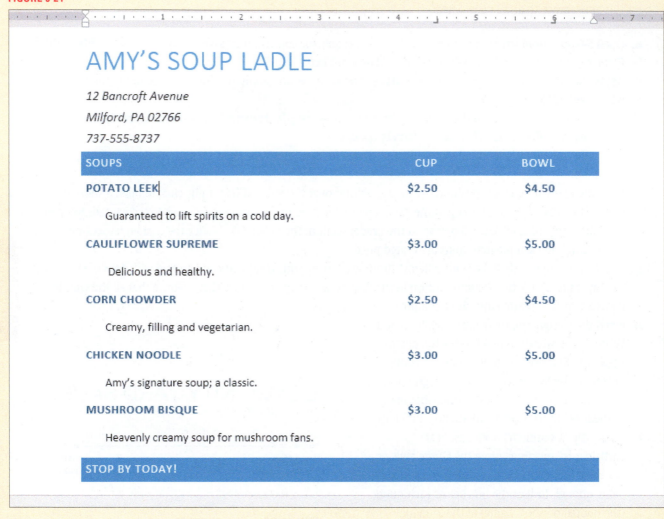

Adding Special Elements to a Document

CASE ▶ Jessica Ramos, marketing director for Pepper's Green Basket, has asked you to finish a report that recommends a plan for launching new community outreach initiatives at Pepper's Green Basket.

Module Objectives

After completing this module, you will be able to:

- Create a table
- Insert and delete table columns and rows
- Format a table
- Insert and format a picture
- Add footnotes and citations
- Insert a header or footer
- Add borders and shading
- Work with themes
- Format a research paper

Files You Will Need

6-1.docx	6-5.docx
6-2.docx	6-6.docx
6-3.docx	6-7.docx
6-4.docx	6-8.png

Create a Table

Learning Outcomes
• Insert a table
• Enter data into table cells
• Navigate a table

If you need to include detailed facts and figures in a document, you might want to use a table to organize the information. A **table** is a grid of rows and columns. The intersection of a row and column is called a **cell**. Cells can contain either text or graphics. You can insert a table using the Table button on the Insert tab. When you create a table, you specify the number of rows and columns; you can also add and delete rows and columns as you modify a table. You can also use tabs to organize text into rows and columns, but working with tables is often easier. **CASE** ▶ *Jessica gives you a file containing the content for the recommendation report. You begin by inserting a table to present the information about a new team organization.*

STEPS

TROUBLE
If the report does not open in Print Layout view, click the Print Layout button ▤ on the status bar.

1. **Start Word, open 6-1.docx from where you store your Data Files, then save it as 6-Community Outreach Report**

   The report opens in Print Layout view. The status bar indicates that there are four pages. You need to insert the table on page 3. You can use the Navigation pane to help you move to any page quickly.

2. **Click the Find button in the Editing group on the Home tab**

   The Navigation pane opens. The Headings tab displays links to all headings in the document.

TROUBLE
If your paragraph marks are not showing, click the Show/ Hide ¶ button ¶ in the Paragraph group.

3. **Click the Headings tab on the Navigation pane, then click the Community Outreach Teams heading in the Navigation pane**

   The insertion point moves to the Community Outreach Teams heading on page 4, as shown in **FIGURE 6-1**. You want to insert the table above the heading "Pepper's Green Basket Vision".

4. **Read the paragraph below the Community Outreach Teams heading, then click in the blank line below the last line of the paragraph**

5. **Click the Navigation Pane Close button ✕, click the Insert tab, then click the Table button in the Tables group**

   The Table menu opens and displays a grid for choosing the number of rows and columns for your table.

6. **Point to the third square in the third row of the grid, as shown in FIGURE 6-2, then click**

   A table with three rows and three columns appears below the paragraph, and the insertion point is in the first cell. Notice that two additional tabs now appear on the Ribbon: the Table Tools Design tab and the Table Tools Layout tab. These are **contextual tabs**, meaning they appear only when a particular type of object is selected and are not otherwise available.

QUICK TIP
You can also move to a different cell by clicking in the cell to where you want to move, or by using the arrow keys.

7. **Type Community Outreach Team, then press [Tab]**

   Pressing [Tab] moves the insertion point to the next cell. The symbol in each cell is an **end-of-cell mark**. The marks to the right of each row are **end-of-row marks**.

8. **Type Team Leader, press [Tab], type Department, then press [Tab]**

   Pressing [Tab] in the last cell of a row moves the insertion point to the first cell in the next row.

QUICK TIP
If you accidentally press [Tab] after the last entry and add a new row, click the Undo button ↺ to delete it.

9. **Type the text shown below in the rest of the table, pressing [Tab] after each entry to move to the next cell, but do not press [Tab] after the last entry**

Employment and Job Training	Lydia Barker	Human Resources
Charitable Causes	Jessica Ramos	Marketing

   All the cells in the table have data in them. Compare your screen to **FIGURE 6-3**.

10. **Click the Save button 🖫 on the Quick Access Toolbar**

    Notice that when you move the mouse pointer over the table, the Table Select handle ⊞ appears above the upper-left corner of the table. Clicking this icon selects the entire table.

Adding Special Elements to a Document

FIGURE 6-1: Using the Navigation pane to move to Community Outreach Teams heading

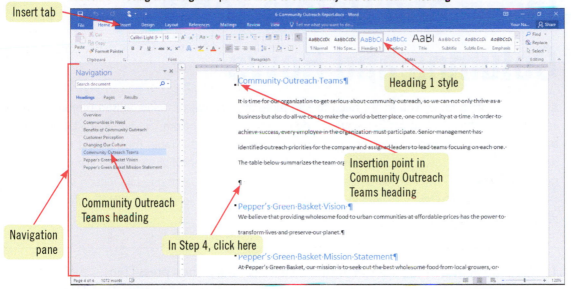

Insert tab

Heading 1 style

Insertion point in Community Outreach Teams heading

Community Outreach Teams heading

Navigation pane

In Step 4, click here

FIGURE 6-2: Inserting a 3 x 3 table

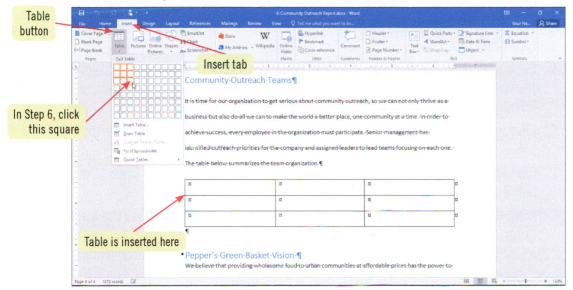

Table button

Insert tab

In Step 6, click this square

Table is inserted here

FIGURE 6-3: Table with all information entered

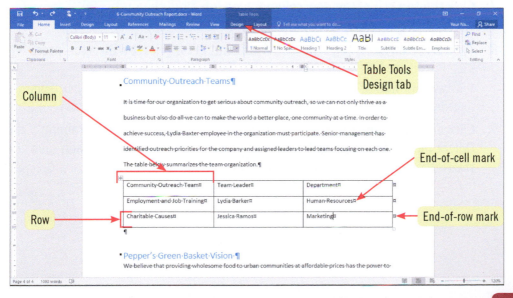

Table Tools Design tab

Column

End-of-cell mark

End-of-row mark

Row

Insert and Delete Table Columns and Rows

After you create a table, you might need to add more information or delete existing information. To accommodate the new information, you can add rows to the top, bottom, or middle of a table. You can add columns anywhere in a table, too. You can use commands on the Table Tools Layout tab to add or delete columns and rows, and you can also use the mouse and the Mini toolbar to accomplish these tasks. **CASE** ▶ *You need to add a new row in the middle of the table to add information about another team. You also need to add a column to the table that indicates each leader's job title. Finally, you need to delete one of the rows.*

STEPS

1. **Click Marketing in the last cell of the table if necessary, then press [Tab]**

   Pressing [Tab] in the last cell of a table inserts a new row at the bottom of the table. The table now has four rows, and the insertion point is in the first cell of the new row.

2. **Type Community Engagement Events, press [Tab], type Sophia Martin, press [Tab], then type Store Operations**

3. **Click any cell in the second row of the table, then click the Table Tools Layout tab**

   The Table Tools Layout tab displays tools and commands for adjusting settings in a table. Because the Table Tools Layout tab is a contextual tab, it appears only when you click in a table or select a table.

4. **Click the Insert Below button in the Rows & Columns group on the Table Tools Layout tab**

   A new empty row appears below the second row.

5. **Click the first cell of the new third row, type Customer Education, press [Tab], type Jamal Williams, press [Tab], then type Human Resources**

6. **Point to the upper left corner of the Department column, until you see the Insert Control ⊕, then click the Insert Control ⊕**

   A new empty column is added between the Team Leader and Department columns. Compare your screen to **FIGURE 6-4**. Notice that Word automatically narrowed the existing columns to accommodate the new column.

7. **Click the top cell of the new column, type Job Title, then press [▼]**

   The insertion point moves down to the second row in the third column.

8. **Type Director, press [▼], type Vice President, press [▼], type Director, press [▼], then type Vice President**

   You have just learned that the Customer Education and Employment and Job Training teams will be combined into one. You need to delete the Employment and Job Training team row.

9. **Click any cell in the row that begins with "Employment and Job Training", click the Delete button in the Rows & Columns group, click Delete Rows, then save your changes**

   The entire row is deleted, and the other rows move up to close up the space. Compare your screen to **FIGURE 6-5**.

FIGURE 6-4: Table with new column and rows added

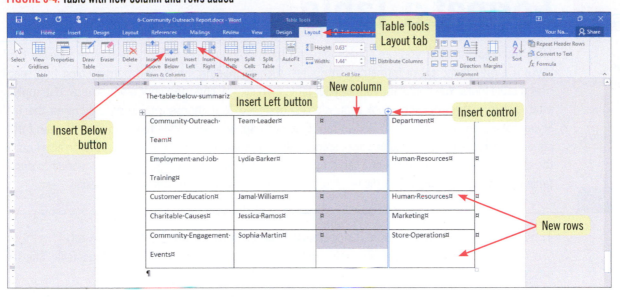

FIGURE 6-5: Table after deleting row

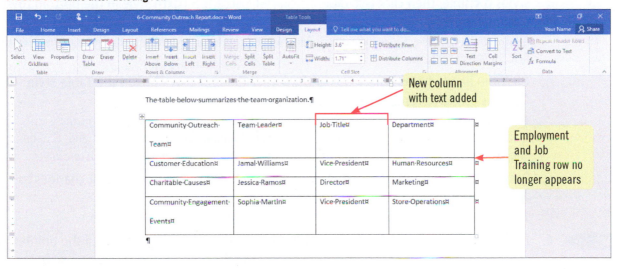

Other ways to create tables

The Insert Table menu provides other commands for creating tables. Click the Insert Table command to open a dialog box, where you can specify the number of rows and columns for a new table, and set AutoFit behaviors. Need to quickly create a specific type of table? Click the Quick Tables option on the Insert Table menu to open a gallery of preformatted tables designed for specific purposes, including calendars. Click a thumbnail in the gallery to insert that table. You can also create a table by drawing it. Click Draw Table on the Insert Table menu, then drag the ✏ pointer in a diagonal motion to create the outside border of the table. To add columns, drag vertically from the top border down; to add rows, drag horizontally from the right border to the left border. Press [Esc] to turn off the Draw Table feature.

Format a Table

Learning Outcomes
- Preview and apply table styles
- Select and resize columns
- Add table borders

After you create a table, you can quickly format it by applying one of many built-in table styles. A **table style** is a predefined set of formatting attributes, such as shading, fonts, and border color, that specify how a table looks. You could also format your table manually by choosing your own settings, but applying a table style makes your table look professionally designed. You choose a table style by using the Table Styles gallery on the Table Tools Design tab. Once you apply a table style that you like, you can further enhance and customize your table's appearance using the Shading and Borders tools. You can also improve the appearance and readability of a table by adjusting column widths. **CASE** *You decide to apply a table style to the table and adjust the width of the first column so all team names fit on one line.*

STEPS

1. **Click anywhere in the table if necessary, then click the Table Tools Design tab**
   The Table Tools Design tab is now active and displays tools and buttons for formatting a table. The Table Styles group displays thumbnails of preset styles that you can apply to your table.

2. **Point to each Table Style visible in the Table Styles group, then observe the change**
   With Live Preview, the table in the report changes to display a preview of each style as you move the mouse from one style to the next. You can view all available table styles by clicking the More button ▼ at the right end of the Table Styles group.

3. **Click the More button ▼ in the Table Styles group, scroll down so the bottom row of styles is visible, then click List Table 7 Colorful - Accent 5 (sixth style in the bottom row), as shown in FIGURE 6-6**
   All the text in the table is now formatted in blue, and there is a border below the first row and between the first and second columns.

4. **Click the Banded Rows check box and the First Column check box in the Table Style Options group to remove the check marks from these boxes**
   The data in the first column is no longer formatted differently from the other data in these rows. The shading is also removed from the table. Notice that "Community Outreach Team" and "Community Engagement Events" in the first column wrap to two lines. You want both items to fit on one line.

5. **Position the mouse pointer just above Community Outreach Team until it changes to ↓, then click**
   The first column is now selected, making it easy to see the right edge of the first column.

6. **Position the mouse pointer on the right edge of the selected column until the pointer changes to +‖+, drag the pointer to the right about ½", then release the mouse button**
   The width of the first column increases, and now the text in each first column cell fits on one line instead of two. The second column is now narrower.

7. **Point to the upper-left corner of the table until the ⊹ pointer appears, then click**
   The entire table is selected. Any formatting settings you choose at this point will be applied to all the cells in the table. You decide that you want to add column gridlines to the table. First you need to choose a blue border style.

8. **Click the Border Styles list arrow in the Borders group, then click the Single solid line, 1/2 pt, Accent 1 (second style in the first row) as shown in FIGURE 6-7**
   You chose a blue border style that matches the table color.

9. **Click the Borders button list arrow in the Borders group, click All Borders as shown in FIGURE 6-8, then save your changes**
   Blue gridlines now outline all of the cells in the table.

Adding Special Elements to a Document

FIGURE 6-6: Applying a table style

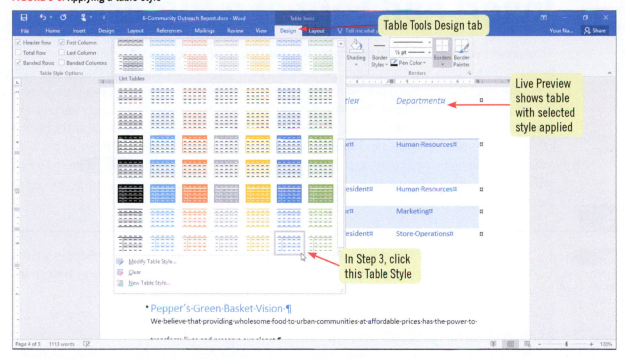

FIGURE 6-7: Choosing a Border Style

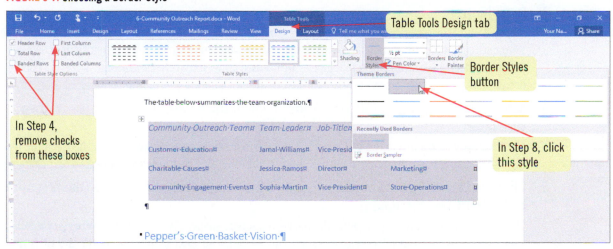

FIGURE 6-8: Formatted table with table style and borders added

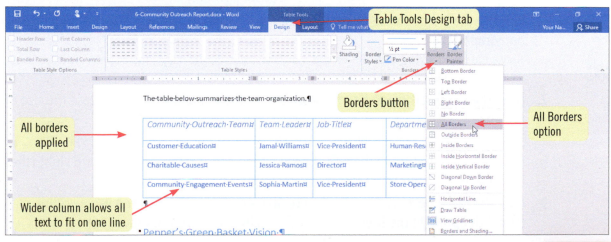

Adding Special Elements to a Document

Insert and Format a Picture

Pictures can help illustrate a point or enhance the visual appeal of a document. The Illustrations group on the Insert tab has tools for adding shapes, pictures, and other graphics. Clicking the Online Pictures button opens the Insert Pictures dialog box, where you can search for images from Bing or other sites, or insert a picture stored on your OneDrive. Be aware that any image you find online might be owned by an individual or organization, and rights to use it may be restricted, so before using an image check the rights information to make sure you are compliant. Once you insert a picture, you can move or resize it, or enhance it by applying picture styles, or changing the way text wraps around it. **CASE** *You decide to add a picture to the document. Note: To complete the steps below, your computer must be connected to the Internet.*

STEPS

1. **Scroll to the end of the document, click to the left of the first line below Pepper's Green Basket Mission Statement, click the Insert tab, then click the Online Pictures button in the Illustrations group**

   The Insert Pictures dialog box opens.

2. **In the Bing Image Search box, type openclipart.org basket**

   Entering "openclipart.org" and "basket" tells Bing to look for images of baskets from the openclipart.org site, which provides images that can be used freely by anyone without restriction.

3. **Press [Enter]**

   Thumbnails of images associated with the word "basket" appear in the search results, most of which are fed from openclipart.org. **Clip art** is a type of pre-made image you can use to illustrate any document. Notice the yellow banner, which informs you that images are licensed under **Creative Commons**, which is a copyright license that allows image owners to share their work with the public for most non-commercial uses.

4. **Scroll down to locate and then click the image of the basket shown in FIGURE 6-9, then click Insert**

   The image is inserted before the first word in the paragraph, creating an awkward space between the heading and paragraph. It is currently an **inline image**, meaning it is positioned as if it were a text character.

5. **Click the Layout Options button 🖼 next to the image, then click Square (the first option below With Text Wrapping)**

   The paragraph text now wraps around the image in a square shape. Choosing a **wrapping style** lets you adjust how text flows in relation to a graphic. An anchor icon next to the image indicates it is now a **floating image**, which is one that can be placed anywhere in a document. The paragraph might look better if the image were moved to the right of the paragraph text.

6. **Point to the image so the pointer changes to ⬍, then drag the image to the right of the paragraph text**

   Notice the round **sizing handles** on the corners and sides of the image; these appear when an image is selected. Dragging a corner sizing handle resizes an image without distorting it.

7. **Drag the lower-left sizing handle down and to the left about ¼" to increase the size of the image**

   The Picture Tools Format tab, which is active, contains tools to enhance the appearance of graphics.

8. **Click the Color button in the Adjust group, then click Green, Accent color 6 Light (the last option in the bottom row), as shown in FIGURE 6-10**

9. **Click the More button ⬇ in the Picture Styles group, click Reflected Bevel, White (the fifth option in the fourth row) as shown in FIGURE 6-11, then save your work**

Adding Special Elements to a Document

FIGURE 6-9: Insert Pictures dialog box with "basket" search results

Bing Image Search box

In Step 4, click this image

FIGURE 6-10: Applying a new color to an image using the Color Styles gallery

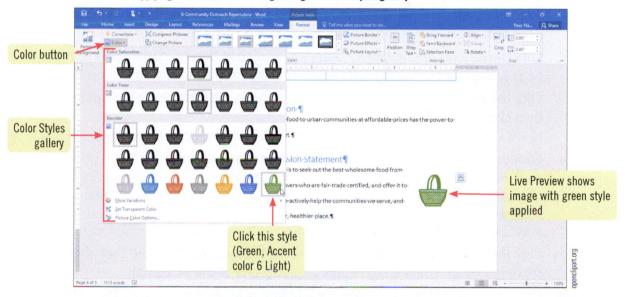

Color button

Color Styles gallery

Click this style (Green, Accent color 6 Light)

Live Preview shows image with green style applied

opencliparts.org

FIGURE 6-11: Resized basket image with text wrapping, color, and picture styles applied

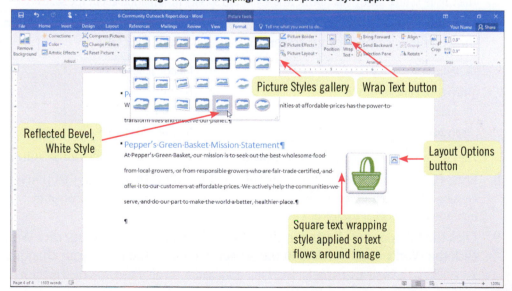

Picture Styles gallery

Wrap Text button

Reflected Bevel, White Style

Layout Options button

Square text wrapping style applied so text flows around image

Adding Special Elements to a Document

Add Footnotes and Citations

If your document includes quotes or paraphrased material from another source, you need to credit that source by inserting a citation. A **citation** is a reference to a source that usually includes the author's name and the page number of the referenced material. There are different styles for using citations; MLA style is often used for research papers. Citations that follow MLA guidelines appear in parentheses after a quote or paraphrase. If a document contains citations, it must also include a **bibliography**, which is a listing of detailed source information for citations in the document. The References tab in Word contains tools to manage sources, insert citations, and add a bibliography. You can also use the References tab to add footnotes. A **footnote** is a comment that appears at the bottom of a document page; it consists of two linked parts: the reference mark in the body of the document and the corresponding note text. **CASE** ▸ *You need to add a footnote to the report that comments on attendance at an open house. You also need to add a new source and citation, and insert a bibliography.*

STEPS

1. Click the Home tab, click the Find button in the Editing group, then in the Navigation pane click the Headings tab

2. Click the Benefits of Community Outreach heading in the Navigation pane to move to page 2, then click to the right of initiatives in the first line of the second paragraph

3. Click the References tab, click the Style list arrow in the Citations & Bibliography group, then click MLA if necessary

   MLA is a popular standard for citations and is often required for writing research papers.

4. Click the Insert Footnote button in the Footnotes group, then type In the prior year, at least 24 initiatives were launched. as shown in FIGURE 6-12

   After you clicked the Insert Footnote button, a superscript "1" appears after the word "initiatives." Also, the insertion point moved to the footnote area, and that's where the text you typed was entered. Now you need to add a citation to the quote at the end of the Customer Perception paragraph.

5. Click the Customer Perception heading in the Navigation pane, then click after the space following "community, Pepper's?" at the end of the paragraph

6. Click the Insert Citation button in the Citations & Bibliography group, then click Add New Source

   The Create Source dialog box opens, where you can specify information about the source.

7. Click the Type of Source list arrow, click Article in a Periodical, enter the information shown below, compare your screen to FIGURE 6-13, then click OK

Author: Sally Chambers	Month: January
Title: A Community in Need	Day: 10
Periodical title: Neighborhood Weekly	Pages: 7-8
Year: 2017	Medium: Magazine

   The Create Source dialog box closes. A reference to the source you added is inserted as "(Chambers)".

8. Press [Ctrl][End] to move to the end of the document, then press [Ctrl][Enter]

   Pressing [Ctrl][Enter] inserted a **hard page break**, which is a page break inserted by a user. Now the insertion point is set at the top of a new page.

9. Click the Bibliography button in the Citations & Bibliography group, click Works Cited, click the Works Cited heading in the Navigation pane, then save your changes

   See FIGURE 6-14. Word inserts the bibliographic information for all the sources cited in the report.

FIGURE 6-12: Footnote added to document

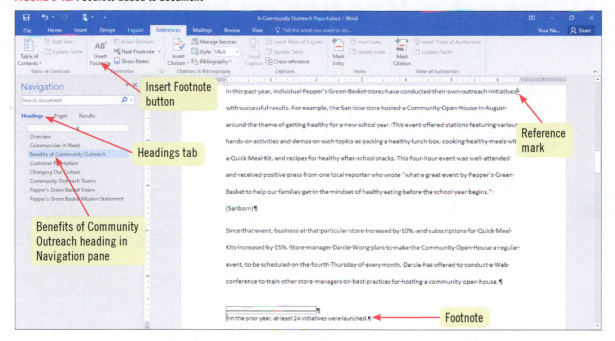

Insert Footnote button

Headings tab

Benefits of Community Outreach heading in Navigation pane

Reference mark

Footnote

FIGURE 6-13: Create Source dialog box with source information added

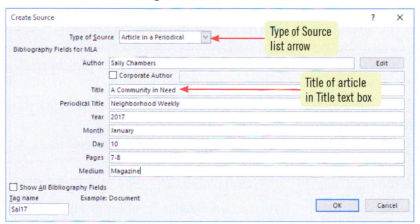

Type of Source list arrow

Title of article in Title text box

FIGURE 6-14: Report with bibliography added

Style list with MLA style selected

Insert Citation button

Bibliography button

New source added

Bibliography inserted in MLA style; includes all sources cited in this report

Word 2016

Insert a Header or Footer

Learning Outcomes
• Insert a footer or header
• Add elements to a footer or header
• Hide footers and headers on first page

When you create a document that contains several pages, you might want to add page numbers and other information to the top or bottom of every page. You can do this easily by adding headers or footers. A **header** is text that appears in the top margin of a page, and a **footer** is text that appears in the bottom margin of a page. Headers and footers usually repeat from page to page. In addition to page numbers, headers and footers often contain such information as the date, the document author's name, or the filename. You add headers and footers using the Header and Footer buttons on the Insert tab. You can format header and footer text in the same way you format regular text, and you can even add graphics. **CASE** ▸ *You decide to add a header and footer to the report.*

STEPS

1. **Click the Navigation Pane Close button ⊠, click the Insert tab, click the Footer button in the Header & Footer group, then click Blank**

   The footer area is now active. The [Type here] placeholder is selected. You want to replace the placeholder with the current date.

2. **Click the Date & Time button in the Insert group**

   The Date and Time dialog box opens, displaying several preset date formats. The first option in the list is selected, as shown in **FIGURE 6-15**, and is the one that is most appropriate for the report.

3. **Click OK, then save your changes**

   The current date now appears left-aligned in the footer.

QUICK TIP

You can open the header or footer by double-clicking in the header or footer area in a document in Print Layout view.

4. **Click the Insert tab, click the Header button, then click Blank (Three Columns)**

   The insertion point moves to the header area, which contains three placeholders into which you can click and type text. The Header & Footer Tools Design tab is now open and contains buttons and tools for working with headers and footers. Notice the other text on the Works Cited page is dimmed.

5. **Click the left-aligned [Type here] placeholder, press [Delete], click the center-aligned [Type here] placeholder, then press [Delete]**

   You deleted two of the three placeholders. You can replace the third placeholder with your name and the page number.

6. **Click the right-aligned [Type here] placeholder, type your name, then press [Spacebar]**

7. **Click the Page Number button in the Header & Footer group, point to Current Position, then click Plain Number**

   The header now contains your name and the page number, as shown in **FIGURE 6-16**. This header will appear at the top of every page in the report. You do not want it to appear on the first page.

8. **Click the Different First Page check box in the Options group on the Header & Footer Tools Design tab to add a check mark**

   This option applies the current header and footer to all pages in the document except the first page.

QUICK TIP

You can see headers and footers only in Print Layout view and in Print Preview; you cannot see headers and footers in Read Mode view or Draft view.

9. **Click the File tab, click Print, then click the Previous Page button ◂ at the bottom of the Print Preview pane four times to view each page of the report**

   Notice the header and footer appear on all pages except page 1. **FIGURE 6-17** shows page 3.

FIGURE 6-15: Date and Time dialog box

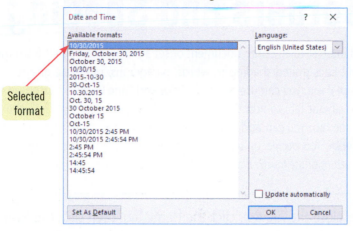

Selected format

FIGURE 6-16: Header with name and page number

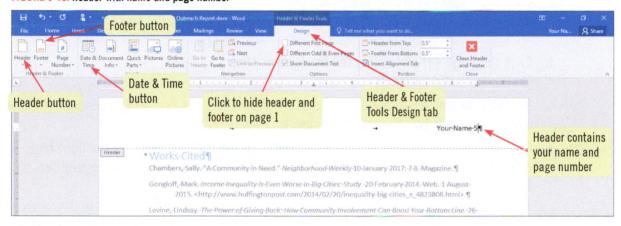

Footer button

Header button

Date & Time button

Click to hide header and footer on page 1

Header & Footer Tools Design tab

Header contains your name and page number

FIGURE 6-17: Report in Print Preview showing header and footer on third page

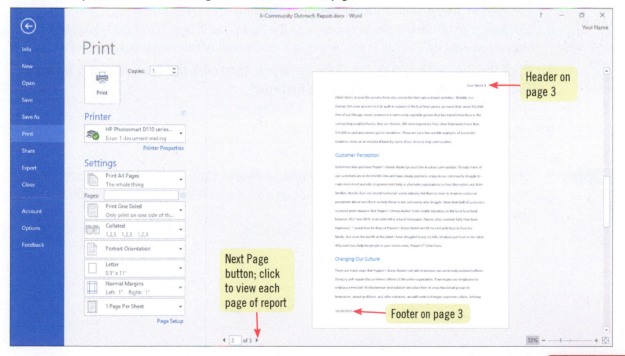

Header on page 3

Next Page button; click to view each page of report

Footer on page 3

Adding Special Elements to a Document

Add Borders and Shading

You can add visual interest to an entire document or set a block of text apart from the rest of the page by adding borders and background shading to words, paragraphs, graphics, or entire pages. To add these elements to an entire page, you can use the Page Color and Page Borders buttons in the Page Background group on the Page Layout tab; to add them to selected text, it is easiest to use the Shading and Borders buttons on the Home tab. You can add borders at the top, bottom, left, or right edges of text, or around a graphic. **CASE** ▶ *You decide to add a border and shading to the "Pepper's Green Basket Vision" paragraph at the bottom of the fourth page to set it off from the rest of the report's text.*

STEPS

1. **Press [Esc] to close the File tab, click the Home tab, then click the Find button in the Editing group**

   The Navigation pane opens. The Pages tab lets you jump quickly to a specific page in the document.

2. **Click the Pages tab in the Navigation pane**

   The Pages tab displays small thumbnails of each page in the document. The page 5 thumbnail is selected because page 5 is the current page. You can jump to any page by clicking the thumbnail for that page.

3. **Click the page 4 thumbnail in the Navigation pane**

   The insertion point moves to the top of page 4.

4. **Scroll to the bottom of page 4 if necessary, then select the Pepper's Green Basket Vision heading and the two lines of text below it**

5. **Click the Shading button list arrow in the Paragraph group, then click the light blue color in the second row of Theme colors (ScreenTip reads "Blue, Accent 5, Lighter 80%"), as shown in FIGURE 6-18**

   The selected text now has blue shading applied to it. Notice the Shading button displays the blue shade you applied. If you wanted to apply this shade of blue somewhere else, you could simply select the text and click the Shading button instead of the Shading list arrow.

6. **Click the Navigation Pane Close button ⊠, click the Borders list arrow ⊞ ▾ in the Paragraph group, then click Borders and Shading**

   The Borders and Shading dialog box opens, with the Borders tab in front. This tab lets you specify a border color, width, and style, as well as choosing from a pre-designed setting such as Box and Shadow.

7. **Click the Box setting, click the Color list arrow, then click the Blue, Accent 5 square in the Theme colors (ninth shade in the first row)**

   The preview area shows the shaded text with a blue border.

8. **Click the Width list arrow, then click 1 pt**

   Compare your screen to FIGURE 6-19.

9. **Click OK, click anywhere in the document to deselect the text, then save your changes**

   The Pepper's Green Basket Vision heading and paragraph are now shaded in a blue box with a blue border. Compare your screen to FIGURE 6-20.

Adding Special Elements to a Document

FIGURE 6-18: Live Preview of paragraph with light blue shading applied

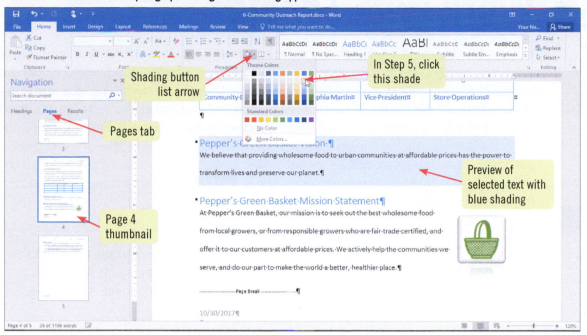

FIGURE 6-19: Borders tab of Borders and Shading dialog box

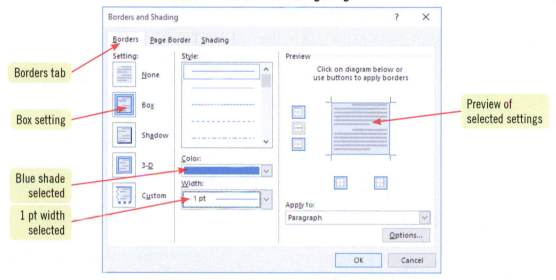

FIGURE 6-20: Paragraphs with a box border and shading applied

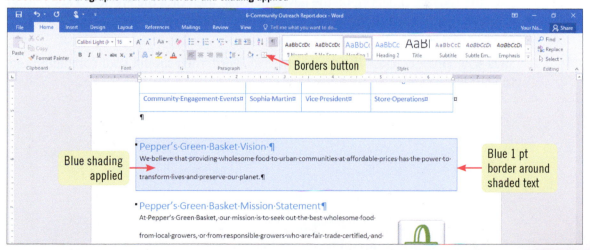

Work with Themes

You have learned how to format individual document elements, such as a text selection or an object, and also how to use styles to change multiple formatting attributes in a paragraph. A powerful tool for making multiple formatting changes at once is the Themes feature. Changing the **theme** applies a coordinated set of colors, fonts, and effects to your entire document, updating any styles applied. Themes ensure your document has a consistent and professional look. To apply a theme, use the Themes button in the Document Formatting group of the Design tab. You can vary a theme's fonts and colors by applying different sets of theme fonts and theme colors. Themes are available throughout Office, so you can produce many different documents and ensure that they all have a consistent, branded look. **CASE** ▶ *You decide to change the overall look of the report by applying a theme to it.*

STEPS

1. **Click the View tab, click the Multiple Pages button in the Zoom group, then click the Zoom Out button on the Zoom slider as needed until the zoom level is set at 30%**

    With the zoom set at 30%, all five pages of the report are visible on screen, so you can see at a glance how your changes will affect the whole document.

2. **Click the Design tab, then click the Themes button in the Document Formatting group**

    The Themes gallery opens and displays thumbnails of available themes, as well as other options, such as resetting your document to the original theme and browsing for more themes on your computer.

3. **Point to each theme in the gallery, then observe the change in the document window**

    With Live Preview, you can see how the colors and fonts in each theme would affect the document if applied. Notice the change in colors, including the background color in the image, and how the text wraps differently depending on the theme. The Organic theme keeps the report to five pages.

4. **Click the Organic theme**

    The Themes gallery closes, and the Organic theme is applied to the report.

5. **Click the Colors button in the Document Formatting group**

    The Theme Colors gallery opens and displays a list of all the sets of theme colors. You want to apply the Blue II theme colors to the report.

6. **Point to each set of Theme Colors to preview the effect in the report, then click Blue II, as shown in FIGURE 6-21**

    By applying a different theme and customizing it with different theme colors, you have completely transformed the look of the report in just a few clicks.

7. **Click the File tab, click Print on the navigation bar, then click the Previous Page button ◀ to preview each page of the report in the Preview pane**

    Compare your report to FIGURE 6-22.

8. **Save your changes, close the document, exit Word, then submit your completed report to your instructor**

QUICK TIP

Every template has a theme applied to it by default. If you apply a theme to a document but then decide you want to go back to the original template theme, click the Themes button, then click Reset to Theme from Template.

QUICK TIP

To create your own customized themes, change the formatting of any element you want (such as the font used in headings), click the Themes button, click Save Current Theme, type a name for the theme, then click Save. The new theme will appear in the Themes gallery under Custom.

Adding Special Elements to a Document

FIGURE 6-21: Theme Colors gallery with Blue II theme colors selected

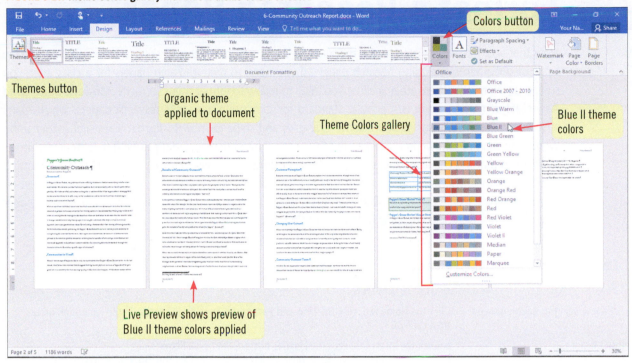

FIGURE 6-22: Finished report with Organic theme and Blue II theme colors applied

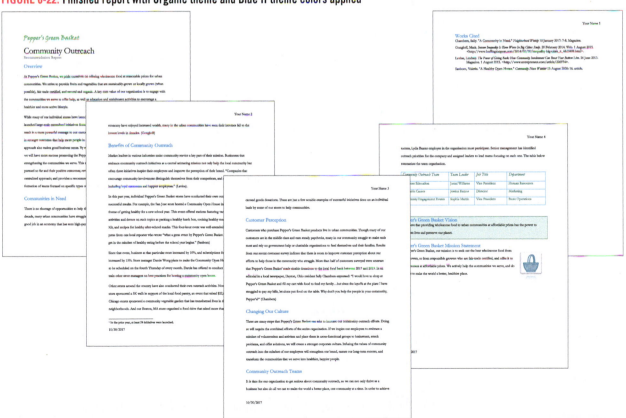

Format a Research Paper

Learning Outcome
• Format a research paper

Now that you have completed all the modules on Word, you have learned skills to help you create many kinds of documents, including research papers. If you need to write research papers for a class, then you should be aware that there are guidelines you need to follow to format them correctly. **Modern Language Association (MLA) style** is a popular standard for formatting academic research papers, which many schools require. This lesson provides some examples and steps for how to format a research paper using Word. The example shown in FIGURE 6-23 and FIGURE 6-24 is formatted according to MLA style. TABLE 6-1 shows steps for formatting the first page of a research paper using MLA style. TABLE 6-2 shows steps for formatting the whole paper. The steps and example shown here will just get you started; for detailed information on MLA guidelines, search online or ask your school librarian for help. (*Note*: You can format the research paper shown in this lesson by completing Independent Challenge 4: Explore in this module.)

TABLE 6-1: Steps for formatting the first page of a research paper

step	task	quick reference
1	Set line spacing to double-spaced	Click the **Home tab**, click the **Line and Paragraph Spacing list arrow** in the Paragraph group, then click **2.0**
2	Insert header	a. Click the **Insert tab**, click the **Header button**, then click **Blank** b. Type your name, press [**Spacebar**], click the **Page Number button**, click **Current Position**, then click **Plain Number** c. Click the **Home tab**, then click the **Align Right button** in the Paragraph group
3	Type your name	At the top of the page (below the header), type your name; make sure it is left-aligned
4	Type your professor's name	Press [**Enter**], then type your professor's name
5	Type the course number	Press [**Enter**], then type the course number
6	Type the title	a. Press [**Enter**] then type the title of your paper b. Select the title, then click the **Align Center button** in the Paragraph group on the Home tab
7	Type the body text	Press [**Enter**], click the **Align Left button** in the Paragraph group, press [**Tab**], then begin typing the body text of the paper

TABLE 6-2: Steps for formatting whole research paper

step	task	quick reference
1	Set line spacing for the entire document	a. Press [**Ctrl**][**A**] to select all the text in the document b. Click the **Home tab**, click the **Line and Paragraph Spacing list arrow** in the Paragraph group, then click **2.0**
2	Set margins to Normal (1" on all margins)	Click the **Layout tab**, click the **Margins button**, then click **Normal**
3	Set indents	Press [**Tab**] at the start of a new paragraph OR Press [**Ctrl**][**A**] to select the entire document, then drag the first line indent marker to the 1/2" mark on the ruler
4	Specify the font	Click the **Home tab**, click the **Font list arrow**, then click **Times New Roman**
5	Set the font size	Click the **Font Size list arrow** on the **Home tab**, then click **12**
6	Insert header	See "Insert header" in Table 6-1
7	Insert citations	a. Click where you want to place the citation b. Click the **References tab**, click the **Insert Citation button**, then click the **source name** or click **Add New Source** to add source information
8	Insert Works Cited page	a. Click at the end of the document b. Press [**Ctrl**][**Enter**] c. Click the **References tab**, click the **Bibliography button**, then click **Works Cited**

FIGURE 6-23: First page of research paper formatted

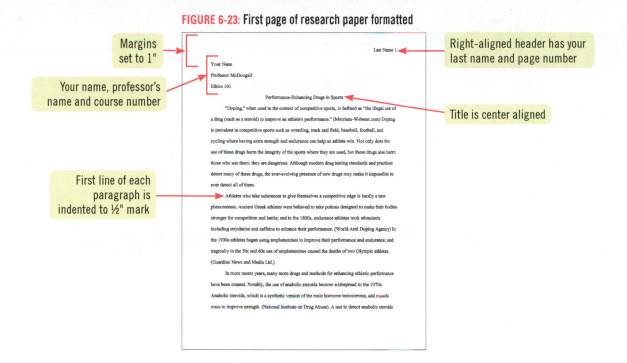

Margins set to 1"

Your name, professor's name and course number

First line of each paragraph is indented to ½" mark

Right-aligned header has your last name and page number

Title is center aligned

FIGURE 6-24: Page 2 of research paper and Works Cited page

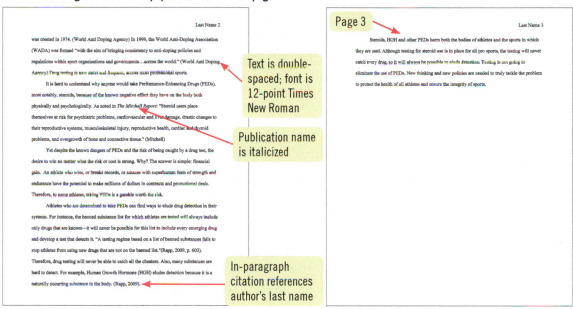

Page 3

Text is double-spaced; font is 12-point Times New Roman

Publication name is italicized

In-paragraph citation references author's last name

Works Cited page includes all sources referenced in the paper

Word 2016

Practice

Concepts Review

Label the Word window elements shown in FIGURE 6-25.

FIGURE 6-25

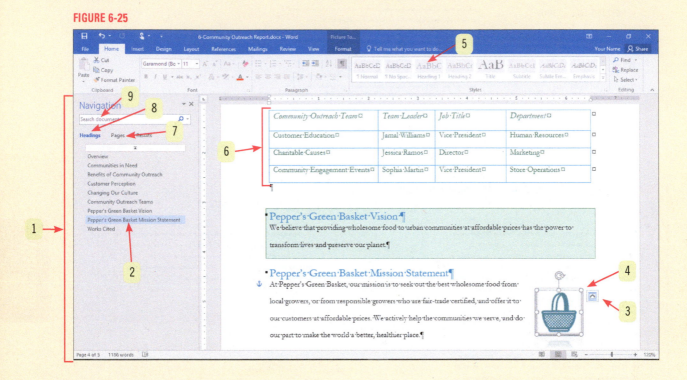

Select the best answer from the list of choices.

10. **Which tab on the Ribbon should you use to add a table to a document?**
    - **a.** Table Tools Design tab
    - **b.** Insert tab
    - **c.** Table Tools Layout tab
    - **d.** View tab

11. **Which of the following actions adds a new row to a table when the insertion point is in the last cell of a table?**
    - **a.** Pressing [Tab]
    - **b.** Pressing [Enter]
    - **c.** Pressing [Shift][Tab]
    - **d.** Pressing [↓]

12. **The Insert Online Pictures dialog box lets you search for online images using which Search engine?**
    - **a.** Ask.com
    - **b.** Google
    - **c.** Bing
    - **d.** Yahoo!

13. **A reference to a source that is inserted within a report or research paper, and that usually includes the author's name and page number, is called a(n) _____.**
    - **a.** bibliography
    - **b.** footnote
    - **c.** endnote
    - **d.** citation

14. Which of the following statements is NOT true about applying a theme?

   a. Themes ensure a consistent look across a document.

   b. You can apply a theme to part of a document.

   c. You use the Design tab to apply a theme.

   d. You can choose different theme colors or fonts when you apply a theme.

15. Repeated text that appears on every page in a document in the bottom margin is called a _____.

   a. heading   **c.** header

   b. footnote text   **d.** footer

Skills Review

NOTE: To complete the steps below, your computer must be connected to the Internet.

1. Create a table.

   a. Start Microsoft Word, open 6-2.docx from where you store your Data Files, then save it as **6-Aquatics Center Report**.

   b. Open the Navigation pane and display the headings of the document in it. Use the Navigation pane to move to the heading "Recommendations." Set the insertion point in the blank line above "Office of the Mayor" at the bottom of page 2. Close the Navigation pane.

   c. Insert a table that is four columns wide and four rows high.

   d. Enter the information shown in the table below into the table you created.

Committee	Chair	Report Due
Property Acquisition	Maria Fernandez	March 1, 2017
Construction	Frank Richardson	March 8, 2017
Community Involvement	Anne Ridgeway	March 18, 2017

   e. Save your changes to the document.

2. Insert and delete table columns and rows.

   a. Insert a new row as the last row in the table.

   b. Enter the following information into the cells in the new row:

Staffing and Programming	Lucinda Jones	March 25, 2017

   c. Insert a new row below the row that contains "Construction", then enter the following information into the new cells:

Maintenance	Joe Blakely	March 22, 2017

   d. Delete the row that contains "Community Involvement".

   e. Insert a new column to the right of the Chair column.

   f. Enter the information from the table below into the new column.

Co-Chair
Sheila Brown
George Owen
Phil Rushton
Sam Presley

   g. Save your changes.

Skills Review (continued)

3. Format a table.

  a. Format the table by applying the List Table 2 - Accent 5 Table Style.

  b. Adjust the Table Style Options so there are no banded rows and so the first column does not display special formatting.

  c. Increase the width of the second column so "Staffing and Programming" fits on one line.

  d. Apply borders to all the cells in the table, using the Single solid line, 1 ½ pt, Blue, Accent 1 style.

  e. Save your changes.

4. Add and format a picture.

  a. Use the Navigation pane to move to the heading "Benefits of an Aquatic Center." Close the Navigation pane. Set the insertion point before the first word in the paragraph text below the heading "Benefits of an Aquatic Center" ("There").

  b. Use the Online Pictures button to open the Insert Pictures dialog box. Search for a public domain image of **swimming** in the Bing Image Search box.

  c. Insert the image shown in FIGURE 6-26, or a similar one that is in the public domain.

  d. Reduce the size of the image so it is approximately 1 ½" wide and 1" tall. (*Hint*: Use the ruler as a guide to help you size it, and drag a corner sizing handle so that the image resizes proportionally.)

  e. Set the wrapping style of the image to Square.

FIGURE 6-26

George Hoden www.publicdomainpictures.net

  f. Drag the image so it is positioned to the right of the paragraph, with the right side of the image at the 6.5" mark on the ruler. Move the image down slightly if necessary so its top edge is aligned with the top of the first line of paragraph text. The first few lines of the paragraph should flow around the image.

  g. Recolor the image with the Blue, Accent color 1 Dark color.

  h. Apply the Simple Frame, Black Picture Style to the image.

  i. Save your changes.

5. Add footnotes and citations.

  a. Use the Headings tab of the Navigation pane to navigate to the heading "Aquatics Today in East Sandburg."

  b. Set the insertion point to the right of the word "survey" (just before the comma) in the second line below the "Aquatics Today in East Sandburg" heading.

  c. Insert a footnote.

  d. Type the following text as footnote text: **Survey was conducted in September 2016 and completed by 5,327 residents**.

  e. Use the Navigation pane to move to the subheading "Community Support."

  f. Confirm that MLA is set as the current Citation Style, scroll to the end of the paragraph under the subheading, set the insertion point after the closing quotation mark that follows the word "**months**" at the end of the paragraph, then use the Insert Citation button to add a new source.

  g. Enter the following information in the Create Source dialog box:

Type of Source:	Article in a Periodical
Author:	Francis Burns
Title:	Swimming Year Round in East Sandburg?
Periodical Title:	East Sandburg Weekly Herald
Year:	2017
Month:	September
Day:	7
Pages:	2-3
Medium:	Newspaper

Skills Review (continued)

h. Close the Create Source dialog box, use the Navigation pane to move to the heading "Recommendations", then set the insertion point in the blank line below the table.

i. Set the insertion point in the blank line just below the table, insert a page break, then insert a bibliography using the Works Cited style. Use the Navigation pane to move to the "Works Cited" heading.

j. Save your changes.

6. Insert a header or footer.

a. Insert a footer using the Blank option.

b. Replace the [Type text] placeholder with the current date, specifying the format that displays the date as Day Month Year (for example, 15 September 2017).

c. Insert a header using the Blank (Three Columns) option.

d. Delete the left-aligned and the center-aligned [Type text] placeholders. Replace the right-aligned [Type text] placeholder with your name. Insert a space after your name, then insert the page number after the space, choosing the Plain Number style.

e. Specify that the header and footer be different on the first page.

f. Close the header, then save your changes.

7. Add borders and shading.

a. Use the Navigation pane to move to the "Works Cited" heading, or press [Ctrl][End] to move to the end of the document.

b. Select the last four lines of text starting with **Office of the Mayor** and including the contact information, then apply Gold, Accent 4, Lighter 80% paragraph shading to the selection.

c. Use the Borders tab of the Borders and Shading dialog box to apply a box border around the selection with the Blue, Accent 1 color and a weight of 2 ¼.

d. Save your changes.

8. Work with themes.

a. Adjust your view of the report using the Multiple Pages button so all three pages are visible, then use the Zoom slider to set the zoom to 30%.

b. Apply the Facet theme to the document.

c. Apply the Blue Warm theme colors to the document.

d. Open the Print screen, then use the navigation buttons to view each page of the report. Compare your finished report with **FIGURE 6-27**, then close the document and exit Word. Submit your report to your instructor.

FIGURE 6-27

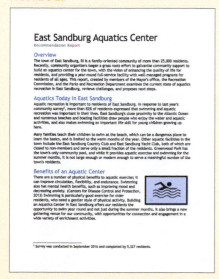
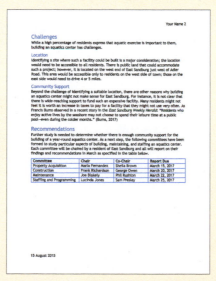

Independent Challenge 1

You are the new manager at Brill Brothers Home Remodeling, a full service contractor specializing in kitchen and bathroom remodels. You need to create a one-page information sheet that describes the company, promotes a special offer to attract new customers, and includes quotes from happy customers. You have a partially completed document that you need to finish. You will add a table to organize the information on the Spring special. You will also add shading and borders to the customer quotes so they stand out more. You will also apply a theme.

a. Open 6-3.docx from where you store your Data Files, then save it as **6-Contractor Info Sheet**.

b. Click in the blank line below the "Spring Special!" heading, then insert a 3 x 2 table.

c. Insert the text shown below into the table:

The Deal	The Details	The Price
Custom Kitchen Design with Full Set of Plans	Includes dimensions, cabinet sizing, and full 3D drawing	$49

d. Apply the List Table 3 - Accent 1 table style to the table. Make sure the First Column check box and the Header Row check box have check marks in them.

e. Select the table if necessary, then apply a single solid line, 1 ½ pt., Green, Accent 6 Box border to the table. Select the first row of the table, then apply Center alignment (*Hint*: on the Home tab, click the Center button in the Paragraph group.) Center-align **$49** in the third column, too.

f. If there are blank lines between the table and the "Testimonials" heading, delete them.

g. Under the "About Brill Brothers Home Remodeling" heading, insert an online image appropriate for a home construction firm (make sure to check for any copyright restrictions), apply the Tight text wrapping style to it, and position it to the right of the paragraph. Resize the image so it fits well and looks good in the space next to the paragraph. Recolor the picture with a shade of your choosing, and apply a picture style that looks good.

h. Insert a footer using the Blank (Three Columns) style. Replace the center-aligned placeholder with your name, and replace the right-aligned placeholder with the date, using the format month/day/year (for example, 3/1/2017). Delete the left-aligned placeholder.

i. Select the first paragraph below the "Testimonials" heading. Apply Blue, Accent 5, Lighter 80% shading to it. Apply a box border around the shaded text, using Green for the border color, and a line weight of 1½ pt. Apply the same shading and border formatting to the other two paragraphs below the Testimonials heading. (Be sure to leave the blank lines with no formatting between each paragraph.)

j. Apply the Damask theme to the document.

k. Apply the Green theme colors to the document.

l. Save your changes, preview the document, and compare your finished document to **FIGURE 6-28** (your image will differ). Close the document and exit Word. Submit your completed document to your instructor.

FIGURE 6-28

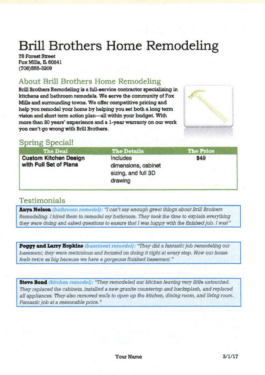

Brill Brothers Home Remodeling

78 Forest Street
Fox Mills, IL 60541
(708)555-3209

About Brill Brothers Home Remodeling

Brill Brothers Remodeling is a full-service contractor specializing in kitchens and bathroom remodels. We serve the community of Fox Mills and surrounding towns. We offer competitive pricing and help you remodel your home by helping you set both a long term vision and short term action plan—all within your budget. With more than 20 years' experience and a 1-year warranty on our work you can't go wrong with Brill Brothers.

Spring Special!

The Deal	The Details	The Price
Custom Kitchen Design with Full Set of Plans	Includes dimensions, cabinet sizing, and full 3D drawing	$49

Testimonials

Anya Nelson *(bathroom remodel)*: "I can't say enough great things about Brill Brothers Remodeling. I hired them to remodel my bathroom. They took the time to explain everything they were doing and asked questions to ensure that I was happy with the finished job. I was!"

Peggy and Larry Hopkins *(basement remodel)*: "They did a fantastic job remodeling our basement; they were meticulous and focused on doing it right at every step. Now our house feels twice as big because we have a gorgeous finished basement."

Steve Bond *(kitchen remodel)*: "They remodeled our kitchen leaving very little untouched. They replaced the cabinets, installed a new granite countertop and backsplash, and replaced all appliances. They also removed walls to open up the kitchen, dining room, and living room. Fantastic job at a reasonable price."

Your Name   3/1/17

Independent Challenge 2

You are the event coordinator at The Lazy Days Spa and Resort, located in Scottsdale, Arizona. You are in charge of coordinating an offsite retreat for the senior management team at Fast Lane Industries, Inc. The goal of the retreat is to provide a day of guided activities to help the senior management team learn relaxation techniques to make them more creative, insightful, and balanced. You need to create a one-page schedule for Jenna Brooks, the Human Resources Director at Fast Lane Industries, that shows the times and locations for each of the day's activities as well as the contact person in charge of each.

a. Open 6-4.docx from where you store your Data Files, then save it as **6-Spa Schedule**.

b. Replace the date in the document with today's date.

c. In the line below "To: Jenna Brooks", type your name to the right of "From:".

d. In the blank line below the paragraph ending in "today's activities.", insert a table containing the information shown below.

Time	Room	Contact Person	Description
8:00	Canyon Terrace	Li Wong	Welcome and Warm-up Exercises
9:00	Red Rock Room	Juanita Gomez	Relaxation Seminar
12:00	Canyon Terrace	Li Wong	Lunch
1:30	Red Rock Room	Pradeep Kumar	Meditation for Executives
3:00	Yoga Studio	Linda Radley	Yoga and Closing

e. Insert a row in the table between the 9:00 and 12:00 time slot. Enter the information shown in the following table into the new row.

11:00	Coyote Room	Emily Rowley	Visualization Techniques

f. Resize the width of the columns as needed so that all cell entries fit on one row.

g. Apply a table style of your choosing to the table.

h. Insert a citation after the quotation mark following the word "productivity." in the main paragraph. Add a new source (MLA style) for the book *Luanne's Lazy Days Philosophy*, by Luanne Braxton. This book was published by Blue Coyote Press, located in Tucson, in 2017; the quote appeared on page 2. (*Hint*: To add the page number, check the "Show All Bibliography Fields" check box, then enter 2 in the Pages box.) Insert a bibliography in the blank line at the bottom of the page choosing the References style.

i. Insert a footnote to the right of "Lunch" in the table. Type the following text for the footnote: **Box lunches will be provided so that teammates can choose to eat by the pool or other locations**. Format this footnote text in italic.

j. Insert a picture that relates to the theme of the offsite retreat (make sure to check for any copyright restrictions). Resize it so that it is no more than an inch or two wide or tall. Apply the Tight text wrapping style then move it to the right of the paragraph. Recolor it and apply a picture style of your choosing.

k. Insert a footer that contains your name, right-aligned.

l. Apply a theme to the document that you think looks good and is appropriate for this type of document. Choose a theme that keeps the document to one page.

m. Add a border around the Our Mission Statement heading and the paragraph below it using a border setting that you like. Add shading to this selection, using a color that looks good with the border you picked. Format the text in this shaded box using fonts, formatting, alignment, and font styles to make it look attractive.

n. Save and close the document. Submit the document to your instructor.

Independent Challenge 3

Serena Johnson in the Human Resources Department at Simonson Glass & Steel has asked you to create a one-page flyer for the annual Company Bake Off event, a fun employee social event. You have a partially completed document with some of the information already provided. You need to add a table that lists the baked good categories, the category host, and the room location. You also need to enhance the appearance of the document so it is eye-catching, and motivates employees to join in the fun.

a. Open 6-5.docx from where you store your Data Files, then save it as **6-Bake Off**.

b. Apply shading to the first paragraph in the document (the line "Simonson Glass & Steel"), using a fill color and font that look good together.

c. At the end of the document, insert a table containing the information shown in the table below.

Category	Category Host	Location
Cakes	Susan Michaelson	Steel Room
Pies	Alea McDonald	Cafeteria
Cookies	Audrey Francesca	Iron Room
Tarts	Paul McTibbers	Glass Room
Muffins	Jose Luega	Fire Room
Bread	Butch Givens	Water Room

d. Format the table using a table style of your choosing.

e. Format the text in the document so it reflects a friendly and fun mood; you want the flyer to convey that the event will be rewarding and enjoyable. Apply your choice of fonts, font sizes, and formatting attributes to make the key information stand out.

f. Insert an appropriate image for the event (make sure to check for any copyright restrictions). The image should convey the idea of baking. Apply a text wrapping style of your choosing that causes the text to flow attractively around the image. Resize and position the image so that the flyer looks balanced. Apply a picture style to the image.

g. Insert a footer that contains your name, center-aligned.

h. Apply a theme and theme colors to the flyer.

i. Save your changes, preview the flyer, then close the document. **FIGURE 6-29** shows one possible solution; yours will vary depending on the formatting choices you made and the image you chose. Submit your flyer to your instructor.

FIGURE 6-29

SIMONSON GLASS & STEEL

Company Bake Off!

November 18
4:00-6:00

Don't miss the chance to show off your baking skills at the pre-Thanksgiving Company Bake Off on November 18! This is your chance to sharpen your baking skills, taste delicious baked goods, and socialize with your colleagues. Bring your prize-worthy home-made baked item to the room listed below by noon on November 18. Prizes awarded to the winners; fun provided for all. Contact the category host with questions.

Category	Category Host	Location
Cakes	Susan Michaelson	Steel Room
Pies	Alea McDonald	Cafeteria
Cookies	Audrey Francesca	Iron Room
Tarts	Paul McTibbers	Glass Room
Muffins	Jose Luega	Fire Room
Bread	Butch Givens	Water Room

Your Name

Independent Challenge 4: Explore

Research papers are frequently assigned for history and English classes in college. Knowing how to format a research paper according to standards is extremely important. A common standard used for writing and formatting research papers is MLA. Another popular standard is APA. If your professor assigns a research paper, he or she will probably specify that you write and format your paper according to MLA or APA standards. In this Independent Challenge, you will create a research paper and format it according to MLA guidelines. So you do not have to actually research and write the paper, you will use text from an existing file for the paper. Before completing the steps below, review the lesson Formatting a Research Paper located just before the end-of-module exercises.

a. Open 6-6.docx from where you store your Data Files, then save it as **6-Research Paper**.

b. With the insertion point set before the first line of text in the document, type your name.

c. Press [Enter], type **Professor McDougall**, then press [Enter].

d. Type **Ethics 101**, then press [Enter].

e. Center-align the title of the paper, "Performance-Enhancing Drugs in Sports."

f. Find "The Mitchell Report" on page 1 in the text. Format this text in italic.

g. Immediately following the Mitchell Report quote (that ends "…connective tissue."), insert a citation to Mitchell, George. (*Hint*: To choose this source, click Insert Citation, then click Mitchell.)

h. Press [Ctrl][A] to select all the text in the document. Set the line spacing to double-spaced (2.0).

i. Change the font for all the selected text to Times New Roman, then change the font size to 12 point.

j. Indent the beginning of each paragraph of body text in the paper to the ½" mark on the ruler. (*Hint*: You can either press [Tab] before the first character in the paragraph or create a first line indent by dragging the First Line Indent marker to the ½" mark on the ruler.)

k. Create a header that contains your last name followed by the page number. Right-align the header. Change the font in the header to 12-point Times New Roman if necessary.

l. Move the insertion point to the end of the document. Insert a page break. Insert a bibliography using the Works Cited option. Format all the text in the Works Cited section in 12-point Times New Roman, double-spaced. Center-align the Works Cited heading.

m. Save your changes. Compare your research paper to the one shown the lesson "Format a Research Paper" earlier in this module, in FIGURES 6-23 and 6-24.

Visual Workshop

Open 6-7.docx from where you store your Data Files, then save it as **6-Cabin For Sale.docx**. Use the skills you learned in this module to create the flyer shown in **FIGURE 6-30**. (*Hints*: Apply the Headlines theme. Insert the picture shown using the Insert Picture command on the Insert tab. Browse for the Data File named 6-8.jpg, then click Insert. The Square text wrapping style was applied. The paragraph text is 14 point and the size of the first line text is 48 point. Bold formatting is applied to some text. The style of the table is shown in the figure.) Type your name in the footer as shown, save your changes, preview the flyer, and then submit it to your instructor.

FIGURE 6-30

Cabin

For Sale by Owner

Get back to nature in this inviting cabin nestled in the woods close to Turtleback Lake! This modern yet cozy 3-bedroom cabin includes two full bathrooms, and an updated kitchen. With floor to ceiling windows

let the sunshine or starlight pour in while you enjoy solitude or entertain family and friends. Three expansive decks and extra sleeping areas allow plenty of room for entertaining. Perfect weekend getaway or rental property. Lovingly maintained by same family for 45 years. Many updates including new windows, flooring, heaters, bathroom and kitchen fixtures. Only 90 minutes from Portland!

Property Details

County	Clatshop
Price	225,000$
Taxes	$2,134
Square ft	1446
Beds	3
Bath	2
Year Built	1968

For more details, contact:

Theresa Lohman
4478 Briarwood Rd.
Portland, OR
Phone: (773) 555-9531

Your Name

Photo credit: Iriana Shiyan/Shutterstock.com.

Creating a Worksheet

CASE ▶ Jessica Ramos, the marketing director for Pepper's Green Basket, asks you to help her create a worksheet that shows estimated sales for a new product line of all-natural sauces that will be released in May. You will create a new Excel workbook, enter values and labels into a worksheet, create formulas to make calculations, format the worksheet, and prepare it for printing.

Module Objectives

After completing this module, you will be able to:

- Navigate a workbook
- Enter labels and values
- Work with columns and rows
- Use formulas

- Use AutoSum
- Change alignment and number format
- Enhance a worksheet
- Preview and print a worksheet

Files You Will Need

No files needed.

Navigate a Workbook

Learning Outcomes
- Start Excel and open a blank workbook
- Identify Excel interface elements
- Navigate a worksheet and select cells
- Add a new sheet

Microsoft Excel is a powerful program you can use to organize and analyze data. An Excel **worksheet** is an electronic grid consisting of rows and columns in which you can perform numeric calculations. Similar to a Word table, the intersection of a row and column is called a **cell**. You can use a worksheet for many purposes, such as analyzing sales data, creating a budget, or displaying data in a chart. An Excel file, called a **workbook**, can contain one or more worksheets. Each new workbook you create contains just one worksheet, but you can easily add more. People sometimes refer to a worksheet or a workbook as a **spreadsheet**. **CASE** *You decide to start Excel, familiarize yourself with the workbook window, and save a blank workbook.*

STEPS

1. **On the Windows taskbar click the Start button ⊞, click All apps on the Start menu, scroll the list, then click Excel 2016**

   Excel starts and the Excel Start screen displays thumbnails of different templates you can create using Excel.

2. **Click Blank workbook**

   A blank workbook opens, as shown in **FIGURE 7-1**. Excel contains elements that are in every Office program, including the Ribbon, the File tab, the Quick Access Toolbar, a status bar, and View buttons.

QUICK TIP
You can quickly move the cell pointer to cell A1 by pressing [Ctrl][Home].

3. **Look at the worksheet window**

   The cell with the dark border in the upper left corner of the worksheet is called the **active cell**. The dark border surrounding the active cell is the **cell pointer**. You must click a cell to make it active before entering data. Every cell in a worksheet has a unique **cell address**, which is the specific location of a cell in a worksheet where a column and row intersect. A cell address consists of a column letter followed by a row number (such as B33). When you first start Excel, the active cell in the new workbook (Book1) is cell A1.

QUICK TIP
To navigate quickly to a specific cell, press [Ctrl][G] to open the Go To dialog box, type the cell address you want to navigate to in the Reference text box, then click OK.

4. **Click cell D5**

   Cell D5 becomes the active cell. Clicking a cell selects it and makes it active. **TABLE 7-1** lists several methods for selecting cells with the mouse or keyboard. Notice the column and row headings of the active cell (column D and row 5) appear in a contrasting color. The **name box** shows the address of the selected cell, and the **formula bar**, located just above the column headings, shows the contents of the selected cell (it is currently empty). The mouse pointer changes to ✛ when you move it over any cells in the workbook.

5. **Press [→], press [↓], then press [Tab]**

   Cell F6 is now the active cell. You can move to and select a cell by clicking it, by using the arrow keys, or by pressing [Tab] (to move one cell to the right), [Shift][Tab] (to move one cell to the left), or [Enter] (to move one cell down).

6. **Click the New sheet button ⊕ at the bottom left of the worksheet just above the status bar**

   A new worksheet named Sheet2 opens on your screen and is now the active sheet. You can tell it is the active sheet because Sheet2 is in bold on the sheet tab. Notice that cell A1 is the active cell. To work with different sheets in a workbook, you click the sheet tab of the sheet you want to see.

7. **Drag the ✛ pointer from cell A1 to cell D8**

   Cells A1 through D8 are selected, as shown in **FIGURE 7-2**. A group of selected cells that share boundaries is called a **cell range**. To reference a cell range, use the cell address of the first cell in the range followed by a colon and the cell address of the last cell in the range. The cell range you selected is A1:D8.

8. **Click the Sheet1 sheet tab, then press [Ctrl][Home]**

   Clicking the sheet tab returns you to Sheet1, and the keyboard shortcut returns the cell pointer to cell A1.

9. **Click the Save button 🖫 on the Quick Access Toolbar to open the Save As screen, navigate to where you store your Data Files, then save the file as 7-Sauce Sales Estimates**

Creating a Worksheet

FIGURE 7-1: Excel program window

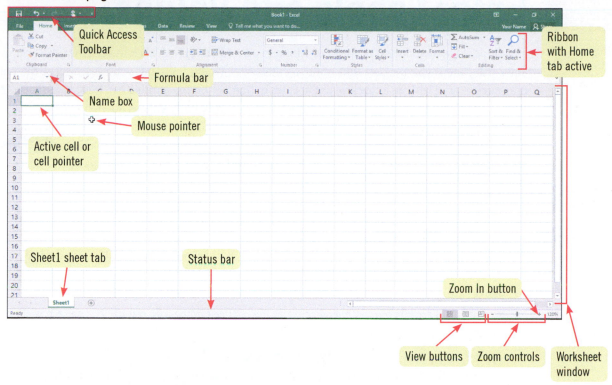

FIGURE 7-2: Selecting a range of cells in Sheet2

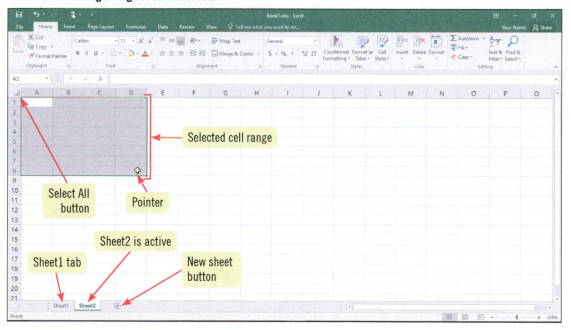

Excel 2016

TABLE 7-1: Methods for selecting worksheet cells

to select	with the mouse	with the keyboard
A cell	Click the cell	Use arrow keys
A row	Click the row heading	Select a cell in the row, then press [Shift][Spacebar]
A column	Click the column heading	Select a cell in the column, then press [Ctrl][Spacebar]
A cell range	Drag across the cells	Press [Shift], then press the arrow keys
A worksheet	Click the Select All button to the left of column heading A	Press [Ctrl][A]

Creating a Worksheet

Excel 181

Enter Labels and Values

Entering data in a worksheet is similar to typing in a Word table. First, click the cell in which you want to enter data, then type the data you want to enter. After typing the data, you must accept the entry by pressing [Enter], [Tab], an arrow key, or the Enter button ☑ on the formula bar. Most worksheets contain labels and values. A **label** is text that describes data in a worksheet. **Values** are numeric data that can be used in calculations. You can edit a cell entry by double-clicking the cell to put the cell in Edit mode. In Edit mode, select the part of the cell entry you do not want, then type your corrections. **CASE** ▷ *This worksheet needs to show the names, prices, and estimated first year units for six new, all-natural sauces. To get started, you decide to enter the labels first and then enter the values.*

STEPS

1. **In cell A1, type Sauce**

   As you type, the text appears in cell A1 and in the formula bar, as shown in **FIGURE 7-3**. The text you typed is a label that describes the first column of data in the worksheet.

2. **Press [Tab]**

   Pressing [Tab] accepts your entry and activates the next cell in the row, cell B1. The name box shows B1 as the active cell. You need to type two more labels.

3. **Type Price, press [Tab], then type Estimated Year 1 Units**

   "Estimated Year 1 Units" is too long to fit in cell C1; although it extends into cell D1, it is actually contained only in cell C1. If cell D1 contained data, only the part of the label that fits in C1 would appear.

4. **Press [Enter]**

   Pressing [Enter] moved the cell pointer down to the first cell of the next row. Cell A2 is now the active cell. You need to type a sauce name in this cell.

5. **Type Peach Mango Barbecue, then press [↓]**

   Cell A3 is now the active cell. Pressing [↓] accepted the cell entry and moved the cell pointer to the cell below.

6. **Type Texas Style BBQ, press [Enter], type Traditional Teriyaki, press [Enter], type Sweet Pepper & Tomato, press [Enter], type Zach's Old Style Barbecue, press [Enter], type Creamy Alfredo, then press [Enter]**

   You have typed all the sauce names. Cell A8 is the active cell. You need to make an edit to the Zach's Old Style Barbecue name.

7. **Double-click cell A6**

   Double-clicking the cell put cell A6 in Edit mode. Notice the insertion point is flashing in cell A6. You can now select part of the cell entry to edit it.

8. **Double-click Style type Time, then press [Enter]**

   Cell A6 now contains the label "Zach's Old Time Barbecue."

9. **Click cell B2, type 2.95, then press the Enter button ☑ on the formula bar**

   Unlike pressing [Enter] on the keyboard, clicking the Enter button keeps the same cell active. Notice that some of Peach Mango Barbecue is cut off in cell A2 because cell B2 now contains data.

10. **Press [→], type 65000, then press ☑**

    You entered the value for Estimated Year 1 Units for the Peach Mango Barbecue sauce in cell C2.

11. **Enter the values shown in FIGURE 7-4 for the range B3:C7, then save your changes**

FIGURE 7-3: Worksheet text in active cell and formula bar

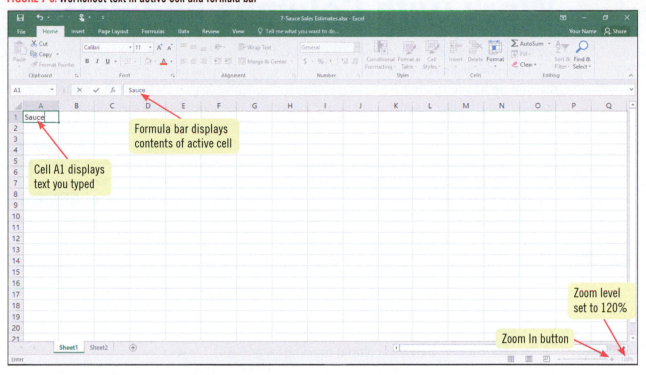

Formula bar displays contents of active cell

Cell A1 displays text you typed

Zoom level set to 120%

Zoom In button

FIGURE 7-4: Worksheet after entering labels and values

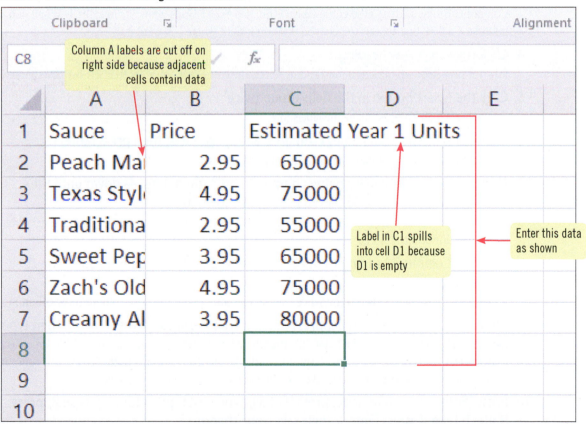

Column A labels are cut off on right side because adjacent cells contain data

Label in C1 spills into cell D1 because D1 is empty

Enter this data as shown

	A	B	C	D	E
1	Sauce	Price	Estimated Year 1 Units		
2	Peach Ma	2.95	65000		
3	Texas Styl	4.95	75000		
4	Traditiona	2.95	55000		
5	Sweet Pep	3.95	65000		
6	Zach's Old	4.95	75000		
7	Creamy Al	3.95	80000		
8					
9					
10					

Creating a Worksheet

Work with Columns and Rows

You can adjust the width of a column or the height of a row using the mouse, Ribbon, or shortcut menu. To increase the width of a column using the mouse, you position the mouse pointer on the right edge of the **column heading**, which is a rectangle above the worksheet column that contains a capital letter, and double-click. The column width automatically adjusts to fit the longest entry in that column. You can also resize a column width by dragging the right edge of a column heading to the desired width. To resize a row using the mouse, you drag the bottom edge of the row heading to the desired height. **Row headings** are the boxes containing numbers that run along the left edge of the worksheet. Using the mouse is a quick and easy method when you do not need an exact width or height. You can also insert or delete columns and rows using the Insert and Delete buttons in the Cells group on the Home tab. **CASE** *You need to increase the width of column A and column C so all the labels fit. You also need to insert two rows above the labels and enter a worksheet title in the new top row.*

STEPS

QUICK TIP

To use AutoFit on more than one column at a time, drag to select all the column headings of the columns you want to widen, then double-click any column boundary in the selection.

1. **Position the mouse pointer on the column boundary between column heading A and column heading B so the pointer changes to ↔**

   Compare your screen to **FIGURE 7-5**.

2. **Double-click ↔ between column headings A and B**

   Double-clicking a column boundary automatically widens or narrows it to fit the longest entry in the column using a feature called **AutoFit**. The sauce names in cells A2:A7 are now fully visible.

3. **Point to the column boundary between columns C and D, then drag ↔ to the right of the "s" in "Units" in row 1**

   Column C is now wider, so the entire label "Estimated Year 1 Units" now fits in cell C1. When you drag a boundary, a dark line appears to help you position it right where you want it.

4. **Click the row 1 row heading**

   Row 1 is now selected. Clicking a row heading selects the entire row. You want to insert two rows above row 1.

5. **Click the Insert button in the Cells group twice**

   Two new rows are inserted above the labels row.

6. **Click cell A1, type Year 1 Sales Estimates: Sauce Products, then press [Enter]**

   The worksheet title now appears in cell A1. The active cell is now cell A2.

TROUBLE

To change the row height you can also select the row, click the Format button in the Cells group, click Row Height, type the row height measurement, and then click OK.

7. **Point to the row boundary between rows 2 and 3, then drag ↕ down until the ScreenTip reads Height: 30.00 (40 pixels), as shown in FIGURE 7-6**

   The height of row 2 changes to 30 points (40 pixels). The extra space creates a visual separation between the worksheet title and the labels.

8. **Click the Column B heading to select column B, then click the Insert button in the Cells group**

   A new column is added between the Sauce column (column A) and the Price column (now column C).

9. **Click cell B3, type Sauce Type, press [Enter], type Barbecue, press [Enter], then type B**

   Even though you typed only the letter "B", the whole word "Barbecue" appears in cell B5. Excel "guesses" that you want to type the same word beginning with "B" that you typed in another cell in this column. This feature, called **AutoComplete**, can save you time in entering data in a worksheet.

10. **Press [Enter], type Marinade, press [Enter], type Pasta, press [Enter], type B, press [Enter], type P, press [Enter], then save your changes**

    Compare your worksheet to **FIGURE 7-7**.

FIGURE 7-5: Changing column width in the worksheet

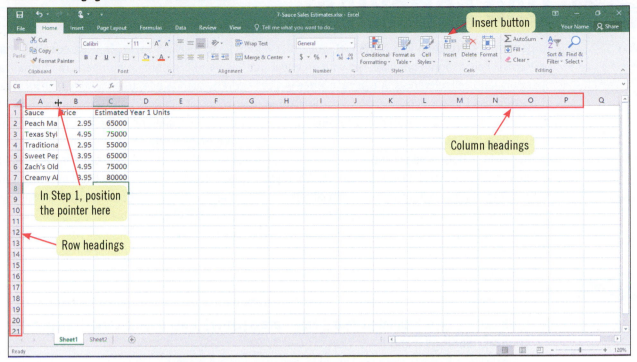

Insert button

Column headings

In Step 1, position the pointer here

Row headings

FIGURE 7-6: Changing row height in the worksheet

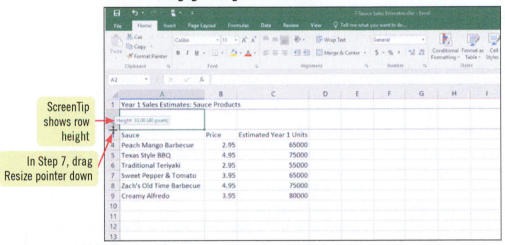

ScreenTip shows row height

In Step 7, drag Resize pointer down

FIGURE 7-7: Worksheet with new column and row added

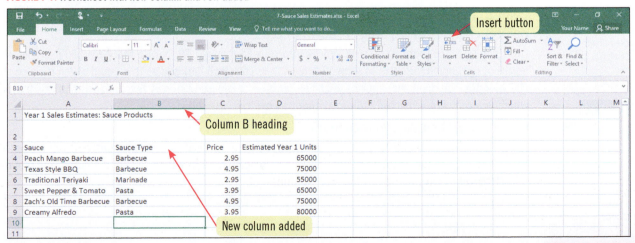

Insert button

Column B heading

New column added

Use Formulas

To perform a calculation in a worksheet, you enter a formula in a cell. A **formula** is an equation that performs a calculation. Formulas start with an equal sign (=) and can contain numbers, mathematical operators, and cell references. A **cell reference** is a cell address, such as E44, that identifies the location of a value used in a calculation. **TABLE 7-2** lists some mathematical operators and sample formulas. If more than one operator is used in a formula, Excel performs the calculations in the order listed in the table, which is a standard order used in math called the **order of precedence**. For example, in formulas that include both multiplication and addition, multiplication will occur first. You can copy and move formulas just like other data in a worksheet. When you copy a formula to a new cell, Excel automatically replaces the original cell references with cell references that are in the *same relative position* as those in the original formula. This is called **relative cell referencing.** **CASE** ▶ *In the sauce sales estimates worksheet, you need to create a formula that calculates the Year 1 estimates for each sauce which is the price multiplied by the Year 1 units. You first create a formula that calculates the Year 1 sales for the first sauce, then copy the formula to the other cells.*

STEPS

1. **Click cell E3, type Estimated Year 1 Sales, press [Enter], then double-click ✛ between column headings E and F**

   Estimated Year 1 Sales is now a label in cell E3, and the active cell is now E4. The Estimated Year 1 Sales label fits in cell E3 because you widened the column.

2. **Type =**

   The equal sign (=) indicates that you are about to enter a formula in cell E4. Everything you enter in a cell after the equal sign, including any numbers, mathematical operators, cell references, or functions, is included in the formula.

3. **Click cell C4**

   A dotted border appears around cell C4, and C4 now appears in both the formula bar and cell E4.

4. **Type * (an asterisk), then click cell D4**

   See **FIGURE 7-8**. In Excel, the asterisk symbol is the operator for multiplication. When Excel calculates the formula, it will multiply the value in cell C4 by the value in cell D4. Using cell references ensures that the formula will automatically be updated if the values in C4 and D4 change.

5. **Click the Enter button ✓ on the formula bar**

   The result of the formula (191750) appears in cell E4. Notice that although the formula's result appears in cell E4, the formula =C4*D4 still appears in the formula bar. To save time, you can copy the formula in E4 to cells E5:E9.

6. **Point to the small dark square in the lower-right corner of cell E4, then when the pointer changes to ✛, drag ✛ down to cell E9**

   Excel copies the amount formula in cell E4 into cells E5 through E9. Notice that cells E5:E9 display the results of the copied formulas, as shown in **FIGURE 7-9**. The small dark square that you dragged is called the **fill handle**. The icon that appears after you release the mouse button is the Auto Fill Options button, which you can click to choose additional options when copying cells.

7. **Click cell E6, then save your changes**

   The formula bar shows the formula =C6*D6. Notice that the copied formula uses different cell references than those used in the original formula. When Excel copied the formula to cell E6, it adjusted the original cell references relative to the new formula location.

Creating a Worksheet

FIGURE 7-8: Entering a formula

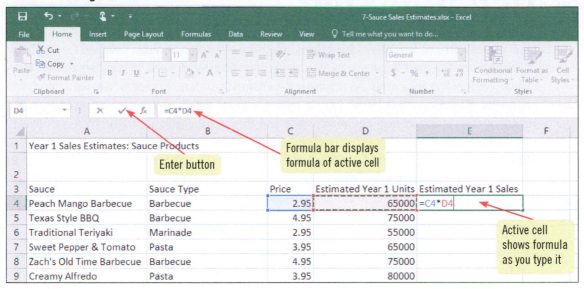

FIGURE 7-9: Worksheet after using fill handle to copy formulas to cells E5:E9

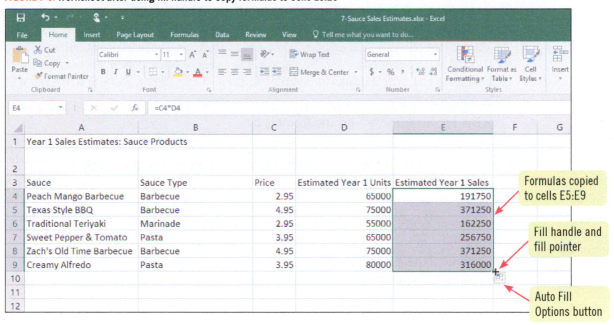

TABLE 7-2: Useful mathematical operators and sample formulas listed in order of precedence

operator	description	sample formula	result	sample worksheet (used in sample formulas)
( )	Parentheses	=(A2*B2)*3	1500	
^	Exponent	=B2^2	10,000	
*	Multiplication	=B2*2	200	
/	Division	=B2/2	50	
+	Addition	=B2+10	110	
–	Subtraction	=B2–20	80	

Sample worksheet:

	A	B	C
1	Price	Quantity	
2	$ 5.00	100	
3			

Excel 2016

Use AutoSum

Excel comes with a wide variety of **functions**, which are prewritten formulas designed for particular types of calculations. The most frequently used worksheet function, **SUM**, totals all numbers and cell references included as function arguments. An **argument** is information a function needs to make a calculation, and can consist of values (such as 100 or .02), cell references (such as B3), or range references (such as A9:G16). Functions save time and help ensure accuracy, and they are available for both simple calculations and extremely complex ones. Each Excel function has a name that you usually see in all capital letters, such as AVERAGE or DATE. Because the SUM function is so commonly used, it has its own button—the AutoSum button—on the Home tab. **CASE** *You are now ready to add up the Estimated Year 1 Units and Estimated Year 1 Sales columns. You decide to use the AutoSum button.*

STEPS

1. **Click cell A10, type Total, then press [Enter]**
   This new label makes it clear that values in this row are total amounts.

2. **Click cell D10**
   Cell D10 is now the active cell. You want D10 to display the total Year 1 units for all of the sauce products, which is the sum of the range D4:D9.

3. **Click the AutoSum button in the Editing group on the Home tab**
   A moving dotted border appears around the cells in the range D4:D9, as shown in **FIGURE 7-10**, indicating that these are the cells that Excel assumes you want to add together. The function =SUM(D4:D9) appears in cell D10 and in the formula bar, ready for you to edit or accept. When you use a function, Excel suggests a cell or range to add. With AutoSum, it is usually the group of cells directly above or to the left of the cell containing the function.

4. **Click the Enter button ☑ on the formula bar**
   Excel accepts the formula and the result, 415000, appears in cell D10.

5. **Click cell E10, click the AutoSum button in the Editing group, then click ☑**
   The sum of the range E4:E9 (1669250) appears in E10. See **FIGURE 7-11**. When you clicked the AutoSum button, Excel guessed (correctly) that you wanted to calculate the sum of cells E4:E9, the cells directly above cell E10. You just learned that the price of the Peach Mango Barbecue sauce is actually $4.95. You need to correct this.

6. **Click cell C4, type 4.95, then click ☑**
   Changing the value in cell C4 automatically changed the formula results in cell E4 (for the Peach Mango Barbecue sauce Estimated Year 1 Sales) and also for the total estimated sales of all the sauces in cell E10, as shown in **FIGURE 7-12**, because these formulas use the value in cell C4. The Estimated Year 1 Sales for the Peach Mango Barbecue sauce increased to 321750.00, an increase of 130,000. This increase is also reflected in cell E10, the total Estimated Year 1 Sales number. You can see what a valuable tool Excel is; changing one value in a cell changes the results in any cell that contains a cell reference to that cell.

7. **Save your changes**

Viewing sum data on the status bar

If you want to know the sum of a range of cells without creating a formula or using AutoSum, you can use the status bar. To do this, select the range of cells that you want to total; the sum of the selected range will appear at the right end of the status bar, along with the average value of the selected range. The status bar also displays a value for Count, which represents the number of cells in the selected range.

FIGURE 7-10: Using the AutoSum button

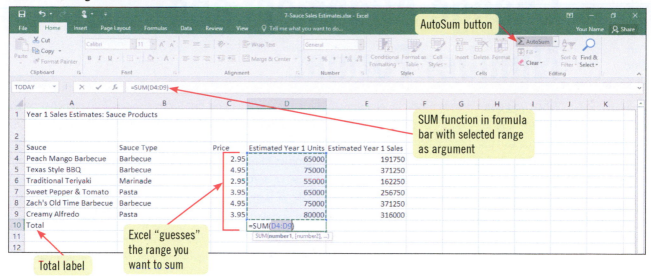

AutoSum button

SUM function in formula bar with selected range as argument

Excel "guesses" the range you want to sum

Total label

FIGURE 7-11: Worksheet with totals calculated using the SUM function

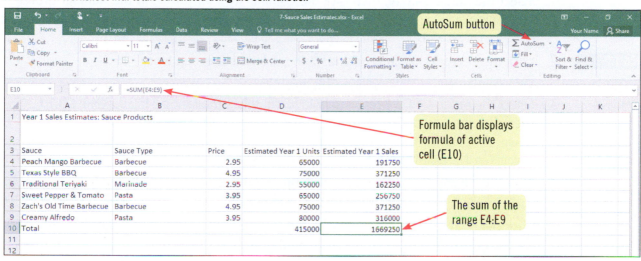

AutoSum button

Formula bar displays formula of active cell (E10)

The sum of the range E4:E9

FIGURE 7-12: Worksheet after changing the price in cell C4

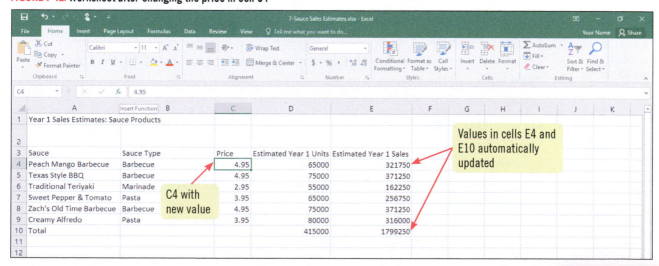

Values in cells E4 and E10 automatically updated

C4 with new value

Change Alignment and Number Format

Learning Outcomes
• Change cell alignment
• Apply number formats

When you enter data in a cell, Excel automatically left-aligns text and right-aligns values. You can change the alignment to left-, right-, or center-align cell contents using the buttons in the Alignment group on the Home tab. You can also use the Merge & Center button to merge several cells into one cell and center the text in the merged cell. You can also change the format of numbers to make your worksheet easier to read using the buttons in the Number group. For instance, you can quickly format a value or range as currency or as a date, or format numbers so they contain commas, decimals, or both. You can also insert rows and columns in your worksheet; when you do so, any cell references are updated to reflect the change. **CASE** ▸ *You decide to apply number formats and adjust alignments to improve the worksheet's appearance. You also need to add a new column that includes the in-store date for each sauce, format the column labels in bold, and merge and center the worksheet title.*

STEPS

1. **Select the range D4:D10, then click the Comma Style button** 🔢 **in the Number group**
   The numbers in column D are now formatted with a comma and include two decimal places. The decimal places are not necessary for the unit estimates, since all the values are whole numbers.

2. **Click the Decrease Decimal button** 🔢 **in the Number group twice**
   The numbers in column D now appear without decimals.

   > **QUICK TIP**
   > To increase the number of digits following a decimal point, click the Increase Decimal button 🔢 in the Number group.

3. **Select the range C4:C9, press and hold [Ctrl], select the range E4:E10, release [Ctrl], then click the Accounting Number Format button** 💲 **in the Number group**
   Pressing and holding [Ctrl] when you select cells lets you select nonadjacent cell ranges. The Price values in column C and Estimated Year 1 Sales values in column E are now formatted as currency, as shown in **FIGURE 7-13**.

4. **Click the column D heading, then click the Insert button in the Cells group**
   A new column is inserted to the left of the Estimated Year 1 Units column. You need to enter a label in cell D3.

5. **Click cell D3, type In Store Date, click the Enter button** ✓ **on the formula bar, then click the Wrap Text button** 📑 **in the Alignment group**
   Clicking the Wrap Text button wrapped the In Store Date text to two lines. Now the entire label is visible in cell D3.

   > **QUICK TIP**
   > When a cell displays ### it means the cell is not wide enough to display the numeric value contained in the cell. Widen the column to view the cell contents.

6. **Click cell D4, type May 2, 2017 click** ✓**, then widen column D so the date fits in cell D4**
   Excel recognized that you typed a date in cell D4 and changed the format to 2-May-17.

7. **Click the Number Format list arrow, as shown in FIGURE 7-14, then click Short Date**
   The date format in cell D4 is now 5/2/2017. You can copy this date to the other cells in column D.

8. **Click the Copy button in the Clipboard group, select the range D5:D9, then click the Paste button in the Clipboard group**
   Now all cells in the range D5:D9 display the date 5/2/2017.

9. **Click the row 3 heading, click the Center button** ☰ **in the Alignment group, click the column B heading, then click** ☰
   Each label in row 3 is now center-aligned, and the sauce type values in column B are also center-aligned.

   > **QUICK TIP**
   > The Orientation button 📐 in the Alignment group lets you align cell contents at any angle you specify.

10. **Select the range A1:F1, click the Merge & Center button in the Alignment group, then save your changes**
    As shown in **FIGURE 7-15**, the worksheet title is centered across the six selected cells, which have merged into one cell. Note that the cell address for this cell is still A1.

FIGURE 7-13: Worksheet after using the Accounting Number Format, Comma Style, and Decrease Decimal buttons

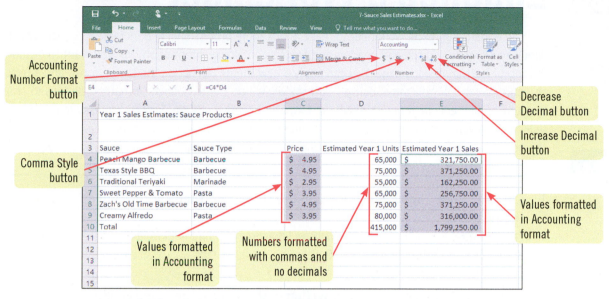

Accounting Number Format button

Comma Style button

Decrease Decimal button

Increase Decimal button

Values formatted in Accounting format

Values formatted in Accounting format

Numbers formatted with commas and no decimals

FIGURE 7-14: Applying a date format using the Number Format list

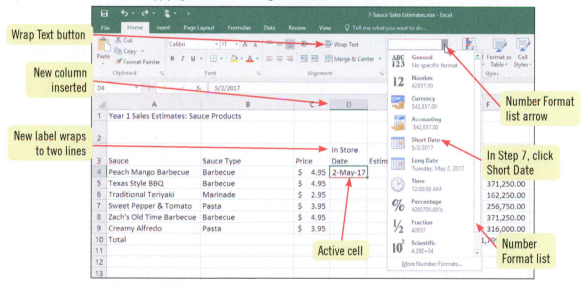

Wrap Text button

New column inserted

New label wraps to two lines

Number Format list arrow

In Step 7, click Short Date

Number Format list

Active cell

FIGURE 7-15: Worksheet after changing alignment and number formats

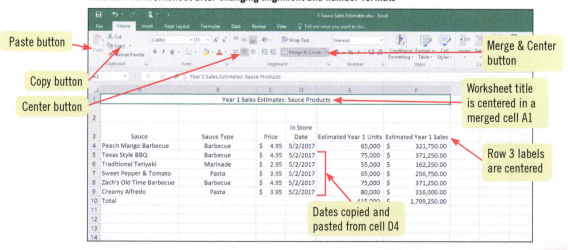

Paste button

Copy button

Center button

Merge & Center button

Worksheet title is centered in a merged cell A1

Row 3 labels are centered

Dates copied and pasted from cell D4

Enhance a Worksheet

You can enhance an Excel worksheet to make it look more professional and increase its visual appeal. In Page Layout view, you can add headers and footers containing information that you want to include at the top or bottom of each page. You can apply a new theme to change the colors, fonts, and effects of an entire workbook. You can also apply **cell styles**, which are predefined formatting options to ensure that similar elements in your worksheet are formatted consistently. **CASE** ▶ *You need to add a header that contains your name, and a footer that contains the date and file name. To enhance the appearance of the worksheet, you decide to apply a theme and apply cell styles to the title, header row, labels, and values.*

STEPS

1. **Click the Page Layout button 🔳 on the status bar, then click Add header in the header**

   The worksheet is now in Page Layout view, and the insertion point is above the worksheet title in the middle of the header's three sections. In this view, you can see that the worksheet columns do not all fit on one page; you will fix this later.

2. **Press [Tab] to move to the right section of the header, then type your name**

   Your name appears in the right section of the header, right-aligned, as shown in **FIGURE 7-16**. The Header & Footer Tools Design tab is now active on the Ribbon.

3. **Click the Go to Footer button in the Navigation group**

4. **Click the left section of the footer, then click the Current Date button in the Header & Footer Elements group**

   Excel inserts the code "&[Date]" into the left section of the footer. When you click outside of this section, the actual date will appear here.

5. **Click the right section of the footer, click the File Name button in the Header & Footer Elements group, then click any cell in the worksheet above the footer**

   The filename appears on the right end of the footer, and the date is in the left side, as shown in **FIGURE 7-17**.

6. **Click the Normal view button 🔳 on the status bar, then press [Ctrl][Home]**

   Cell A1 is now active, and the worksheet appears in Normal view. The vertical dotted line to the right of column E indicates the page break line. This line is helpful to see if your worksheet contains many columns and you need to fit all columns on one page.

7. **Click the Page Layout tab, click the Themes button in the Themes group, then click the Berlin theme**

   The Berlin theme is applied to the worksheet. You decide to apply cell styles to enhance the worksheet title and the column headings.

8. **Click the Home tab, click cell A1, click the Cell Styles button in the Styles group, then click Title in the Titles and Headings section**

   The title in cell A1 is now formatted in 18 point, dark brown.

9. **Select the range A3:F3, click the Cell Styles button in the Styles group, click Accent4, select cells A4:F10, click the Cell Styles button, click Output as shown in FIGURE 7-18, then save your changes**

   Cells A3:F3 now have a blue cell background color and white text, and cells A4:F10 have light gray shading and black borders.

Creating a Worksheet

FIGURE 7-16: Header with text added

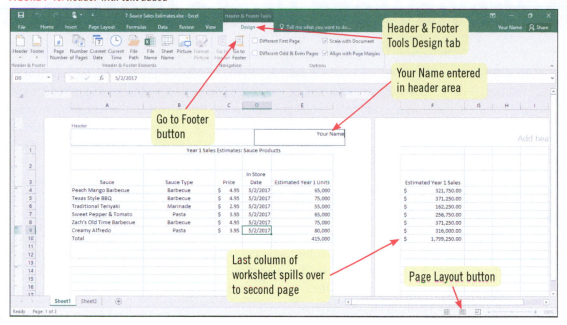

Header & Footer Tools Design tab

Go to Footer button

Your Name entered in header area

Last column of worksheet spills over to second page

Page Layout button

FIGURE 7-17: Footer with current date and file name added

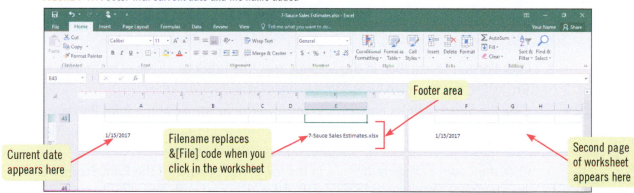

Footer area

Current date appears here

Filename replaces &[File] code when you click in the worksheet

Second page of worksheet appears here

FIGURE 7-18: Worksheet with Berlin theme and cell styles applied

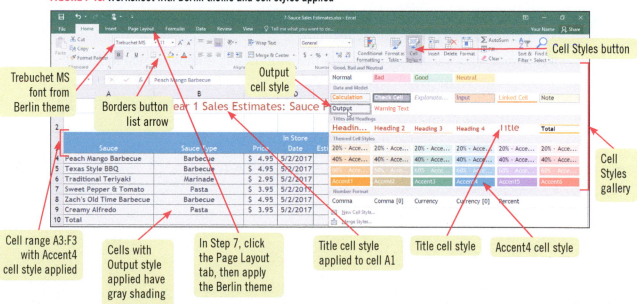

Cell Styles button

Trebuchet MS font from Berlin theme

Borders button list arrow

Output cell style

Cell Styles gallery

Cell range A3:F3 with Accent4 cell style applied

Cells with Output style applied have gray shading

In Step 7, click the Page Layout tab, then apply the Berlin theme

Title cell style applied to cell A1

Title cell style

Accent4 cell style

Creating a Worksheet

Preview and Print a Worksheet

When you finish working with a worksheet and have saved your work, you are ready to print it. Just like in Word, you can use the Print screen in Backstage view to preview the printed worksheet and specify settings. If the columns or rows do not fit on one page you can adjust the scaling to reduce the size of the columns and rows enough to fit. You can also change the orientation, adjust margins, specify the printer, specify the paper size, and more. **CASE** ▸ *You have finished working with the worksheet and are ready to preview and print it. (Note: Many schools limit printing in order to conserve paper. If your school restricts printing, skip Steps 6 and 7.)*

STEPS

1. **Click the File tab, then click Print**

   The Print screen opens in Backstage view, and the sales estimates worksheet appears in the Print Preview area, as shown in **FIGURE 7-19**. Notice the header and footer text appear at the top and bottom of the page. The worksheet is set to print in **portrait orientation** (where the page is taller than it is wide). This orientation is too narrow, and some of the columns are cut off. You can ensure that all of the columns fit by adjusting the scaling in the Settings area.

2. **Click No Scaling at the bottom of the Settings area, then click Fit Sheet on One Page**

   The preview of the worksheet shows the columns all now fit on one page. Adjusting the scaling resulted in squeezing down the width of each column proportionally so all columns fit on one page. You decide to change the orientation to **Landscape** (where the page is wider than it is tall) so there will be more room for all the columns.

3. **Click Portrait Orientation in the Settings area, then click Landscape Orientation**

   The Print Preview area shows the worksheet in landscape orientation, as shown in **FIGURE 7-20**.

4. **Click the Show Margins button ⊞ in the lower-right corner of the Print Preview area**

   Lines appear on the worksheet indicating the location of the margins at the Normal setting. The margins look fine at the Normal setting, so there is no need to change this setting.

5. **Click the Zoom to Page button ⊡ in the lower-right corner of the Print Preview area**

   The worksheet appears up close in the Print Preview area, giving you a magnified view of the worksheet data, as shown in **FIGURE 7-21**. These are toggle buttons; clicking once turns the setting on, and clicking it again turns the setting off.

6. **Verify that your printer is on and connected to your computer, and that the correct printer appears in the Printer text box**

7. **If your school allows printing, click the Print button; otherwise, skip to Step 8**

   The document prints, and the Home tab opens.

8. **Save your changes, click the File tab, click Close, then click the Close button ☒ in the Excel window title bar**

   The worksheet is saved, and the worksheet and Excel both close.

9. **Submit your completed worksheet to your instructor**

FIGURE 7-19: Worksheet in Print Preview in Backstage view, portrait orientation

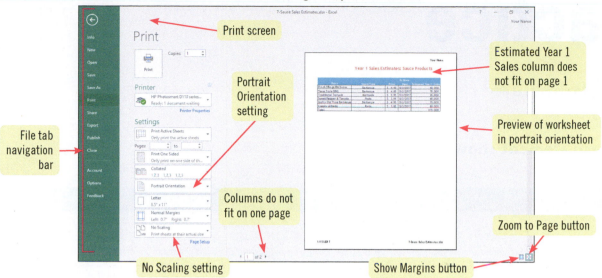

Print screen

Estimated Year 1 Sales column does not fit on page 1

File tab navigation bar

Portrait Orientation setting

Preview of worksheet in portrait orientation

Columns do not fit on one page

Zoom to Page button

No Scaling setting

Show Margins button

FIGURE 7-20: Worksheet in Print Preview in Backstage view, Landscape Orientation

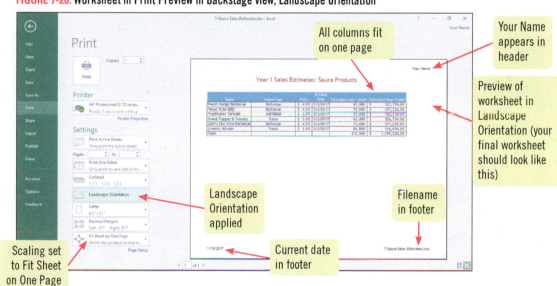

All columns fit on one page

Your Name appears in header

Preview of worksheet in Landscape Orientation (your final worksheet should look like this)

Landscape Orientation applied

Filename in footer

Scaling set to Fit Sheet on One Page

Current date in footer

FIGURE 7-21: Zooming in on the worksheet in Print Preview

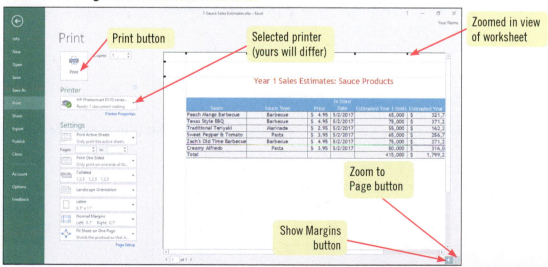

Print button

Selected printer (yours will differ)

Zoomed in view of worksheet

Zoom to Page button

Show Margins button

Creating a Worksheet

Practice

Concepts Review

Label each element shown in FIGURE 7-22.

FIGURE 7-22

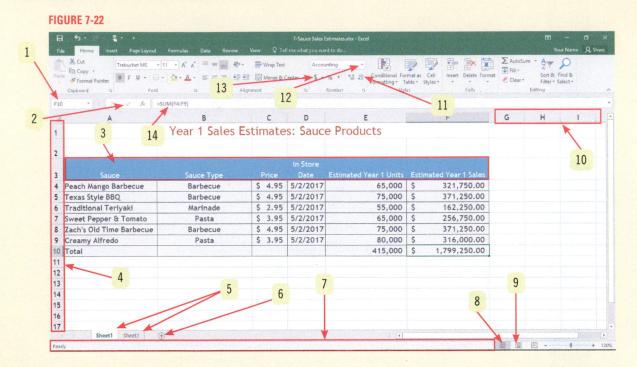

Match each icon with its appropriate use.

15. ✛
16. ⸖
17. ✚
18. ⊕
19. $
20. ✓

a. Button used to add a new sheet to a workbook
b. Button used to accept the contents of an entry
c. Button used to format a number with a comma
d. Button used to apply the Accounting Number format
e. Pointer used to resize a row
f. Pointer when it is positioned over a fill handle

Select the best answer from the list of choices.

21. Which of the following is the correct cell reference for the cell that is in the 23rd row of column B?

   a. 23B
   b. 23-B
   c. B23
   d. B-23

22. A formula always begins with which of the following characters?

   a. *
   b. =
   c. &
   d. -

23. In the formula =C7*595, which of the following best describes what C7 is?

a. a label

b. a value

c. function

d. a cell reference

24. Text that describes data in a worksheet is called a _____

a. function.

b. label.

c. header.

d. footer.

25. For which of the following tasks would you be able to use the fill handle?

a. Copying a formula from cell E4 to the range E5:E8

b. Copying a formula from cell D2 to the range A5:B8

c. Copying a label from cell D22 to B7

d. Copying a formula from cell A2 to D7

Skills Review

1. Navigate a workbook.

a. Start Microsoft Excel and open a new blank workbook.

b. Identify the Excel screen elements without referring to the lesson material.

c. Click cell B13, then click cell F5.

d. Insert a new sheet, then in Sheet2, select the range A2:H8.

e. Switch to Sheet1, then use the keyboard to place the cell pointer in cell A1.

f. Save the workbook as **7-Cottage Rental Revenue** in the location where you store your Data Files.

2. Enter values and labels.

a. Starting in cell A1, type the following labels in the range A1:D1:

Cottage Name	Weeks Rented	Weekly Rental Rate	Total Rental Revenue

b. Enter the following labels for Cottage Name in the range A2:A8: **Cozy Hideaway**, **Swan Haven**, **Bear claw Hut**, **Deer Lodge**, **Wooded Chalet**, **Robin's Nest**, and **Hilltop Retreat**.

c. Use the table below as a guide to enter the values for Weeks Rented (in the range B2:B8) and the values for Weekly Rental Rate (in the range C2:C8):

Weeks Rented	Weekly Rental Rate
12	895
10	895
9	695
12	1095
14	695
10	1095
10	895

3. Work with columns and rows.

a. Increase the size of column A by dragging the appropriate column boundary so the column is wide enough to fit all the labels in the range A1:A8.

b. Increase the width of columns B and C by double-clicking the appropriate column boundary for each.

c. Insert two rows above row 1.

d. Enter the label **Cottage Rental Revenue: Summer Season** in cell A1.

e. Increase the height of row 2 to 30.00 (40 pixels) using the dragging method. (If you have trouble dragging the row to the exact height, click the Format button in the Cells group, click Row Height, type **30**, then click OK.)

Skills Review (continued)

f. Insert a new column between column A and column B. Type **Cottage Type** in cell B3. Enter the following in cells B4:B10:

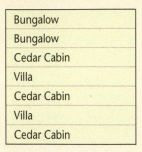

Bungalow
Bungalow
Cedar Cabin
Villa
Cedar Cabin
Villa
Cedar Cabin

g. Adjust the width of column B by double-clicking the column boundary between columns B and C, then save your changes.

4. Use formulas.

a. Type a formula in cell E4 that multiplies the value in cell C4 by the value in cell D4, then use a button on the formula bar to accept the entry.

b. Type a formula in cell E5 that multiplies cell C5 by cell D5, then use a keyboard command to accept the entry.

c. Use the fill handle to copy the formula you entered in cell E5 to the range E6:E10, then save your changes.

5. Use AutoSum.

a. In cell A11, enter **Total**.

b. Use the AutoSum button to enter a formula in C11 that adds the values in the cell range C4:C10.

c. Use the AutoSum button to enter a formula in E11 that adds the values in the cell range E4:E10.

d. Change the Weeks Rented value for Robin's Nest to **14**, then view the changes in cells E9, C11, and E11, then save your changes.

6. Change alignment and number format.

a. Apply the Accounting number format to the cell range D4:E11. Use a button to remove the decimals for the selected range.

b. Insert a column to the left of column E. Enter the label **Season End Date** in cell E3. Format this cell so the label wraps to two lines in the cell.

c. Enter **September 15, 2017** in cell E4. Use the Number Format list arrow to apply the Short Date format to this cell. Copy the date in cell E4, then paste it to the range E5:E10. If you see the error message ##### in the range E4:E10, the column is too narrow; widen column E so the full date is visible.

d. Center the labels in the range A3:F3.

e. Merge and center cells A1:F1, then save your changes.

7. Enhance a worksheet.

a. Switch to Page Layout view.

b. Type your name in the left section of the header.

c. Switch to the footer, then insert a code for the filename in the left section of the footer. Insert a code for the current date in the right section of the footer.

d. Click in any worksheet cell, and look at the footer you entered. Move the cell pointer to cell A1, then switch to Normal view.

e. Apply the Wood Type theme to the worksheet. If any of the cells display #####, widen the necessary column.

f. Apply the Title cell style to cell A1.

g. Apply the Accent2 cell style to the labels in row 3 (range A3:F3).

h. Apply the Output cell style to the range A4:F11.

i. Save your changes.

Skills Review (continued)

8. **Preview and print a worksheet.**

a. Preview the worksheet using the Print tab in Backstage view.

b. Change the scaling to Fit Sheet on One Page.

c. Change the orientation to Landscape.

d. Use a button to view the margin rules on the worksheet.

e. Use a button to zoom in on the worksheet.

f. If your school permits printing, verify that the printer settings are correct, then print the worksheet. Compare your completed worksheet to **FIGURE 7-23**.

g. Save your changes, close the workbook, exit Excel, then submit your completed workbook to your instructor.

FIGURE 7-23

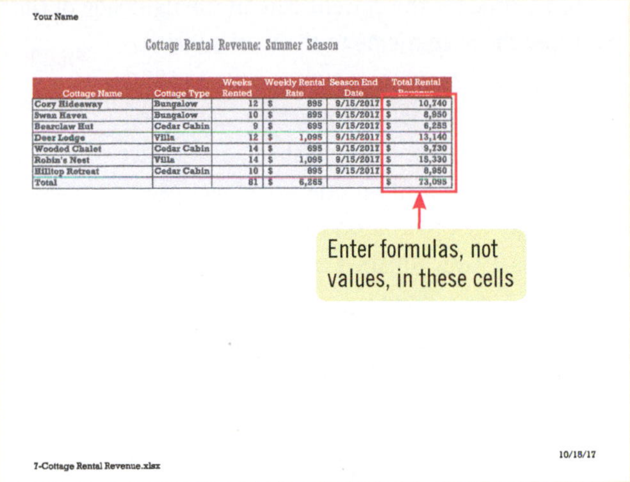

Enter formulas, not values, in these cells

Independent Challenge 1

You are the administrative assistant at the Red Tree Art Gallery in San Francisco, California. Your manager, Larry Bond, has asked you to create a worksheet that summarizes art sales in August. The worksheet needs to include the name of each piece of art, its art type, the sale price, the amount due the artist, and the commission amount for the gallery. The split for each art piece sold is 40% to the gallery and 60% to the artist. You need to create formulas to calculate the amount due to the artist and the gallery commission.

a. Create a new workbook, then save it as **7-August Art Gallery Sales** in the location where you store your Data Files.

b. Enter the title **Red Tree Art Gallery: August Sales** in cell A1.

c. Enter the information shown in the table below, starting in cell A3.

Artwork Name	Artwork Type	Sale Price	Date Sold
City at Dusk	Oil on Canvas	5000	8/1/2017
Children at Play	Photograph	3500	8/5/2017
Blue Cow	Sculpture	6000	8/8/2017
Foggy Bay	Oil on Canvas	4200	8/12/17
City Plaza	Photograph	3750	8/19/2017

d. Widen each column as necessary so all the labels and data in the range A3:D8 fit completely in their cells.

e. Apply the Accounting Number format to the ranges C4:C8. Apply the Short Date format to cells D4:D8.

f. Add the label **Artist Amount Due** in cell E3. Widen column E so the entire label fits in cell E3.

g. Enter a formula in cell E4 that multiplies cell C4 by 60%, then use the fill handle to copy the formula to cells E5:E8.

h. Add the label **Gallery Commission** in cell F3. Widen column F so the entire label fits in cell F3.

i. Enter a formula in cell F4 that multiplies cell C4 by 40%, then use the fill handle to copy the formula to cells F5:F8.

j. Use the AutoSum button to enter a formula in cell E9 that adds the values in the range E4:E8.

k. Use the fill handle to copy the formula in cell E9 to cell F9. Copy the formula in cell F9 and paste it in cell C9 (widen column C if necessary).

l. Add the label **Total** to cell A9.

m. Increase the row height of row 2 to 24.00. Merge and center cells A1:F1. Apply the Title cell style to cell A1.

n. Apply the Total cell style to cells A9: F9. Apply the Heading 2 cell style to the labels in row 3 (A3:F3). Widen columns A through F as needed to accommodate the larger font size of each label with the Heading 1 style applied.

Independent Challenge 1 (continued)

o. Add your name in the left section of the header. Add a code for the filename in the middle section of the header. Add a code for the current date in the right side of the header.

p. Apply the Slice theme to the workbook.

q. Apply the 20%-Accent4 style to cells A4:F8.

r. Open the Print tab in Backstage view. Look at the preview of the worksheet, and notice that it does not fit on one worksheet page. Change the orientation to Landscape. Compare your finished worksheet to **FIGURE 7-24**.

s. Save your changes, close the workbook, exit Excel, then submit the workbook to your instructor.

FIGURE 7-24

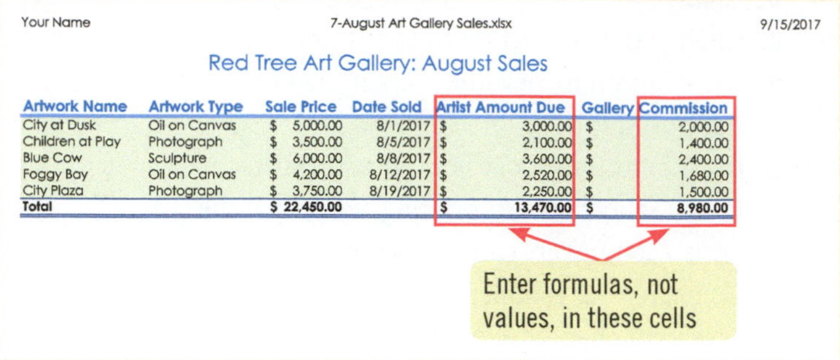

Red Tree Art Gallery: August Sales

Artwork Name	Artwork Type	Sale Price	Date Sold	Artist Amount Due	Gallery Commission	
City at Dusk	Oil on Canvas	$ 5,000.00	8/1/2017	$ 3,000.00	$ 2,000.00
Children at Play	Photograph	$ 3,500.00	8/5/2017	$ 2,100.00	$ 1,400.00
Blue Cow	Sculpture	$ 6,000.00	8/8/2017	$ 3,600.00	$ 2,400.00
Foggy Bay	Oil on Canvas	$ 4,200.00	8/12/2017	$ 2,520.00	$ 1,680.00
City Plaza	Photograph	$ 3,750.00	8/19/2017	$ 2,250.00	$ 1,500.00
Total		$ 22,450.00		$ 13,470.00	$ 8,980.00

Enter formulas, not values, in these cells

Independent Challenge 2

You are the national sales manager for Hodges & Greenwood Medical Supplies, a national company with sales teams in five territories across the country. You need to create a worksheet that analyzes second quarter results of each territory. Your worksheet needs to compare second quarter sales of each territory to the first quarter, and also compare second quarter actual sales to the second quarter sales forecast. Because it is a new, growing business, each territory was forecast to meet a sales increase of 3% over the first quarter.

a. Create a new workbook, then save it as **7-Q2 Sales Analysis** in the location where you store your Data Files.

b. Enter the company name **Hodges & Greenwood Medical Supplies** in cell A1, then enter **Q2 Sales Analysis** in cell A2.

c. Enter the information shown in the table below in the worksheet, starting with the **Territory** label in cell A4. First type the values, then apply the proper number formatting and adjust decimal places so the data in your worksheet matches the table.

Territory	Q1 Sales	Q2 Sales
New England	$1,986,433	$1,765,433
Mid Atlantic	$1,546,780	$1,865,334
Midwest	$2,876,987	$2,876,445
Southeast	$786,322	$902,334
West	$2,087,432	$2,217,876

d. Insert a column to the left of column A. Add **Sales Manager** as a label in cell A4, then add the following labels in cells A5:A9: **Johnson**, **Rodriguez**, **Chung**, **Lipinski**, **Warren**.

e. Enter **Change** in cell E4, then enter a formula in cell E5 that calculates the change in sales in Q2 Sales over Q1 Sales for the New England territory (*Hint*: The formula should subtract cell C5 from cell D5.) Notice the value in E5 appears in parentheses. This means the value is a negative number; Q2 sales for the New England Territory were lower than Q1 Sales.

f. Copy the formula in cell E5 to cells E6 through E9.

g. Enter **Q2 Forecast** in cell F4, then enter a formula in cell F5 that multiplies the Q1 Sales by 1.03. Copy this formula to cells F6 through F9.

h. Enter the label **Actual vs. Forecast** in cell G4. Format the label so it wraps to two lines. Enter a formula in cell G5 that subtracts the Q2 Forecast amount in cell F5 from the Q2 Sales amount in cell D5. Copy this formula to cells G6:G9.

i. Enter **Totals** in cell A10, then use AutoSum to enter a formula in cell C10 that calculates the total of cells C5 through C9. Copy this formula to the range D10:G10.

Independent Challenge 2 (continued)

j. Increase the row height of row 3 to 33.00 (44 pixels). Center-align the labels in row 4.

k. Merge and center cells A1:G1 so the worksheet title is centered in the merged cell A1. Merge and center cells A2:G2 so the worksheet subtitle is centered in the merged cell A2.

l. Apply the Title cell style to cell A1. Apply the Heading 2 cell style to cell A2.

m. Apply the Dividend theme to the workbook. Apply the Heading 4 cell style to cells A4:G4. Apply the Total cell style to cells A10:G10. Apply the Bad cell style to any cells in column E or G that contain negative values (values in parentheses). Widen columns as needed so that all values fit in the cells.

n. Insert your name in the left section of the header.

o. Preview the worksheet in Backstage view. Set the scaling to Fit Sheet on One Page. Keep the orientation as Portrait. Compare your worksheet to **FIGURE 7-25**. Save your changes, close the workbook, then exit Excel. Submit your completed workbook to your instructor.

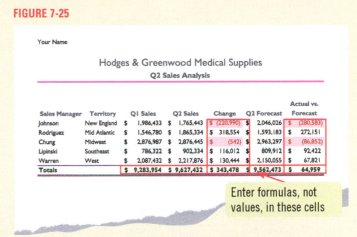

FIGURE 7-25

Independent Challenge 3

You are the administrative assistant for Pike Brothers Piano Restoration, a new small business that buys old pianos, restores them, and sells them at a profit. George Pike has asked you to create a spreadsheet that shows sales and profits for the first year. The spreadsheet needs to list each piano purchased, the cost to buy and restore it, and its sale price. It also needs to include formulas that calculate the amount of profit for each restored piano sold.

a. Create a new workbook, then save it as **7-Piano Profits** in the location where you store your Data Files.

b. Enter the company name **Pike Brothers Piano Restoration** in cell A1. Enter **First Year Profits** in cell A2.

c. Enter the labels and data shown in the table below, starting in cell A4. Use Accounting number formatting for the cells that contain dollar amounts.

Piano Model	Purchase Price	Restoration Cost	Sale Price	Date Sold
Steinway Upright	$12,500.00	$6,250.00	$29,500.00	2/7/2017
Yamaha Baby Grand	$9,200.00	$1,259.00	$32,750.00	3/15/2017
Steinway Grand	$25,750.00	$12,653.00	$58,950.00	4/7/2017
Baldwin Upright	$2,575.00	$3,287.00	$21,750.00	8/8/2017
Kawai Upright	$7,250.00	$3,250.00	$15,895.00	9/15/2017

d. Insert a new column to the left of "Sale Price". Enter the label **Total Investment** in cell D4. Make adjustments so that the Restoration Cost and Total Investment labels both wrap to two lines.

e. Adjust the width of the other columns as necessary, so that all the labels are visible.

f. Enter a formula in cell D5 that sums cells B5 and C5.

g. Copy the formula in cell D5 to cells D6:D9.

h. Type the label **Profit** in cell G4. Enter a formula in cell G5 that calculates the total profit for the Steinway Upright. (*Hint:* The formula needs to subtract the value in the Total Investment cell from the Sale Price cell.)

i. Copy the formula in cell G5 to cells G6:G9.

j. Add the label **Total** to cell A10. Enter a formula in cell B10 that sums cells B5:B9. Copy this formula to cells C10:E10 and to cell G10.

Independent Challenge 3 (continued)

k. Center-align the labels in row 4. Apply bold formatting to row 10.

l. Change the number format of the Date Sold values to the Short Date format.

m. Format the worksheet by applying a theme of your choosing. Apply cell styles that you think enhance the worksheet's appearance and make it easier to read.

n. Add your name to the center section of the header. Add a code for the filename in the right section of the header. Save your changes.

o. Preview the worksheet in Backstage view. Change the orientation to Landscape. Save your changes. FIGURE 7-26 shows the completed worksheet with possible formatting options applied.

p. Close the workbook, exit Excel, then submit your completed workbook to your instructor.

FIGURE 7-26

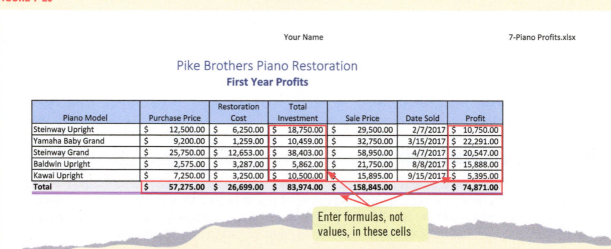

Independent Challenge 4: Explore

A long-lost relative has died and left you a five-bedroom house. You are happy to have a big house to live in, but you are a recent college graduate and are concerned about expenses. The annual property taxes for your big house are $8,244.00; you will need to calculate a monthly amount to put aside, to ensure you can pay the full amount. You want to rent out some or all of your four extra bedrooms to provide an income stream to pay your new expenses. You decide to create a worksheet to determine how many rooms you will need to rent to pay the bills. The worksheet will also need to include your other monthly expenses as well as your monthly salary.

a. Start Excel, then save a new workbook as **7-House Expenses and Income** in the location where you store your Data Files.

b. Enter the title **House Expenses and Income** in cell A1. Apply the Title cell style to this cell.

c. In cell A3, enter the label **Annual Property Taxes**. Apply the Heading 2 cell style. In cell B3 enter **$8,244**.

d. In cell A5, enter **Monthly Housing Expenses**. Apply the Heading1 cell style to A5, then merge and center cells A5 and B5. Apply a fill color to the merged cell, choosing Blue, Accent 5, Lighter 80% from the Theme Colors (*Hint*: Click the cell, click the Fill Color button list arrow in the Font group, then click the ninth shade in the second row under Theme Colors.)

e. In cells A6:A9, enter the following labels: **Property Taxes**, **Utilities**, **Maintenance**, **Total**. In cell B6, enter a formula that calculates the amount you will need to put aside for your property taxes. (*Hint*: The formula should divide the total tax amount in cell B3 by 12.)

f. Enter **$225** in cell B7 (Utilities) and enter **$150** in B8 (Maintenance). Apply the Accounting format to these cells. Enter **Total** in cell A9, then use AutoSum to calculate the total monthly expenses in cell B9.

g. In cell A11, enter **Other Expenses**. Apply the Heading1 cell style to A11, then merge and center cells A11 and B11. Apply the same fill color to this merged cell that you applied to cell A5. (*Hint*: Click the cell, then click the Fill Color button in the Font group.)

h. Enter the labels and values shown below into cells A12: B18. Apply the Accounting format to the cells that contain values.

Car Payment	$250.00
Car Insurance	$110.00
Gas/Parking	$75.00
Student Loan	$150.00
TV/Internet	$75.00
Phone	$120.00
Food	$400.00

i. Enter **Total** in cell A19, then use AutoSum to calculate the total for all other expenses in B19.

j. Merge and center cells A21:B21. Enter **Total Expenses** in the merged cell. Format cell A21 so that it has the same formatting as cell A11.

k. In cell A22, enter **Housing + Other**. Enter a formula in cell B22 that calculates the sum of total House Expenses and total Other Expenses.

l. Apply the Total cell style to cells A9:B9, A19:B19, and A22:B22.

m. In cell D5, enter **Income Sources**. Apply the Heading 1 cell style to D5, then merge and center cells D5 and E5. Apply a light green fill color to the merged cell.

n. Enter the labels and values shown below into cells D6:E10. Apply the Accounting Number format to the cells that contain values.

Salary	**$1,250.00**
Room #1	$500.00
Room #2	$500.00
Room #3	$500.00
Room #4	$500.00

o. Enter the label **Total** in cell D11, then in E11, enter a formula using AutoSum that calculates the total of all income sources in E6:E10.

p. In cell D14 enter the label **Income after Expenses**. Apply the Heading 1 style to D14, then merge and center cells D14:E14. Apply the same fill color to D14 that you applied to cell D5.

q. In cell D15, enter **Total**. In cell E15, enter a formula that subtracts the total expenses (B22) from the total income sources (E11). Notice the result in cell E15, indicating you will have $1,008 after paying your monthly bills if you rent out 4 rooms.

r. Delete the value for Room #4 in cell E10 and observe the change in cell E15. Then delete the value for Room #3 and observe E15 again. Now you will barely have enough to pay your bills, but it would be nice to rent only two rooms. Increase the rent for Room #1 and Room #2 to $600.00 each. This amount gives you some extra padding, so this seems like a good plan.

s. Apply a theme of your choosing to the worksheet. Make adjustments to alignments, row heights, and column widths as necessary so that all the labels and values are visible.

t. Insert a header that contains your name, centered, and a code for the current date, left-aligned. Save the worksheet, submit it to your instructor, then exit Excel.

Visual Workshop

Create the worksheet shown in **FIGURE 7-27**. Use formulas where indicated for totals (remember that you can use the AutoSum button to speed up this process). Apply the theme shown. Apply the Title cell style to cell A1, then use the Increase Font Size button to increase the font size to 36. Use the Heading 1 style for cell A2. (*Hint*: For the Large Boxes label, enter **Large Boxes** in cell A7, click the Orientation button list arrow in the Alignment group, then click Rotate Text Up. Next, select A7:A12, click the Merge & Center list arrow in the Alignment group on the Home tab, then click Merge Cells. Apply the Heading 2 cell style to the selection. Follow the same process to create the Medium Boxes and Small Boxes labels. To apply the borders, select the cells that need borders, click the Borders button list arrow in the Font group, then click All Borders.) Save the workbook as **7-September Sales Results** in the location where you store your Data Files, with your name in the left section of the header. Save and preview the worksheet, then submit it to your instructor.

FIGURE 7-27

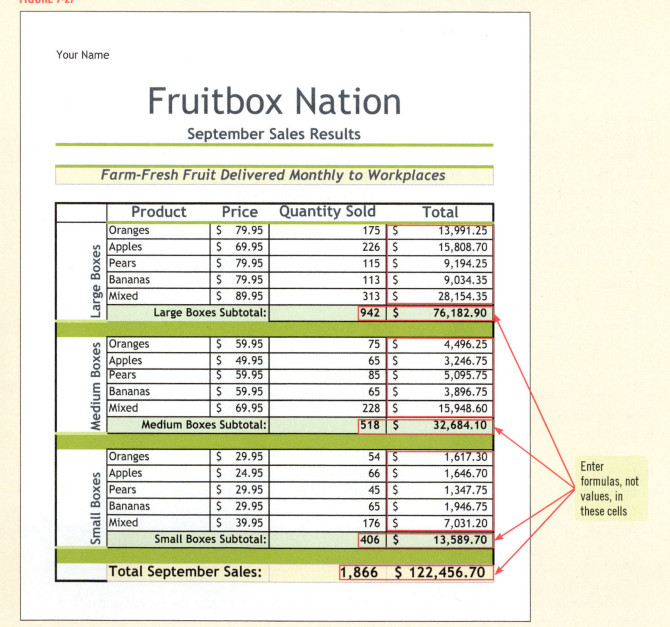

Using Complex Formulas, Functions, and Tables

CASE David LeBlanc, vice president of merchandising at Pepper's Green Basket, has given you a worksheet that shows first quarter sales of the Quick Meal Kits in the Northeastern region. David has asked you to perform some calculations on the data, highlight certain information, sort the information in a certain way, and filter it to show only information that meets specific criteria.

Module Objectives

After completing this module, you will be able to:

- Create complex formulas
- Use absolute cell references
- Understand functions
- Use date and time functions
- Use statistical functions
- Apply conditional formatting
- Sort rows in a table
- Filter table data

Files You Will Need

8-1.xlsx	8-4.xlsx
8-2.xlsx	8-5.xlsx
8-3.xlsx	8-6.xlsx

Create Complex Formulas

When you create worksheets that contain many calculations, you might need to create formulas that contain more than one mathematical operator. For instance, to calculate profits for a particular product, a formula would first need to calculate product sales (product price multiplied by number of products sold) and then subtract costs from that result. Formulas that contain more than one operator are called **complex formulas**. When a formula contains multiple operators, Excel uses the **order of precedence** rule to determine which calculation to perform first. Calculations in parentheses are always evaluated first. Next, exponential calculations are performed, then multiplication and division calculations, and finally addition and subtraction calculations. If there are multiple calculations within the parentheses, they are performed according to this same order. **TABLE 8-1** lists the common mathematical operators and the order in which Excel evaluates them in a formula. **CASE** *Stores in the Northeast region began selling Quick Meal Kits in January. As part of the promotion, customers can return any kit if they are not 100% satisfied. David provides you with a worksheet that shows first quarter sales, as well as returns. He asks you to add a new column that calculates the adjusted sales total for all three months.*

STEPS

1. **Start Excel, open 8-1.xlsx from where you store your Data Files, then save it as 8-Quick Meal Kit Sales**

   A copy of David's partially completed worksheet is open and saved with a new name.

2. **Click cell G6**

   You need to enter a formula in this cell that calculates total sales for the Brooklyn store for January (cell C6), February (cell D6), and March (cell E6), and then subtracts Brooklyn's returns (cell F6).

3. **Type =, click cell C6, press +, click cell D6, press +, click cell E6, press -, click cell F6, then click the Enter button ✔ on the formula bar**

   See **FIGURE 8-1**. The formula bar displays the formula =C6+D6+E6-F6, and cell G6 displays the formula result, $138,096. This formula added the values in cell C6 (Brooklyn's January sales), D6 (Brooklyn's February sales) and E6 (Brooklyn's March sales), then subtracted the value in cell F6 (Brookyn's returns). In effect, Excel added $38,400, $45,600 and $55,200, and then subtracted $1,104. Now you need to copy the formula to the range G7:G13, to calculate the Total Sales Less Returns for the other stores in the region.

4. **In cell G6, drag the fill handle pointer ✛ down through cell G13 to copy the formula in cell G6 to the range G7:G13**

   The results of the copied formula appear in cells G7 through G13, as shown in **FIGURE 8-2**.

5. **Click the Save button 🖫 on the Quick Access Toolbar**

   Excel saves your changes to the workbook.

Using the Clear button

Clicking the Clear button in the Editing group displays commands you can use to delete everything in a selected cell, or only specific aspects of the cell's contents and formatting. For instance if a cell contains $1,500.00, clicking Clear All will remove both the value (1500) and all its formats (red, bold, Accounting format). Clicking Clear Formats would keep the value but remove the formatting, so the cell contents would appear as 1500. Clicking Clear Contents would remove the value (1500) but leave the formatting, so any new value entered in that cell (such as 22) would be formatted in red, bold with Accounting format applied ($22.00). To remove comments from a cell, click Clear Comments; to remove a hyperlink but leave the linked text or URL, click Clear Hyperlinks.

FIGURE 8-1: Complex formula and its returned value

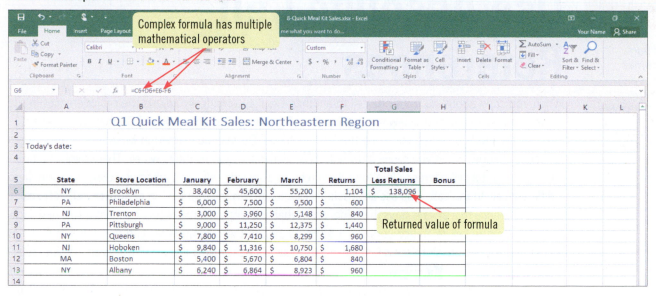

Complex formula has multiple mathematical operators

Returned value of formula

FIGURE 8-2: Copying a formula to a range of cells

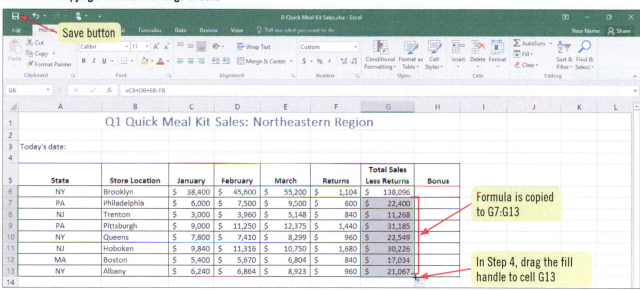

Save button

Formula is copied to G7:G13

In Step 4, drag the fill handle to cell G13

TABLE 8-1: Review of order of operations

order of operations	operators
1. Calculate items in parentheses	( )
2. Calculate exponents	^
3. Multiply or divide (from left to right)	* or /
4. Add or subtract (from left to right)	+ or -

Use Absolute Cell References

When you copy a formula from one cell to another, Excel automatically adjusts the cell references in the copied formula to reflect the new formula location. For example, a formula in cell D5 that reads "=B5*C5" changes to "=B6*C6" when you copy the formula to cell D6. As you learned in Module 7, a relative cell reference changes when you move it, to reflect its relative location to the new cell. There might be times when you want a cell reference in a formula to refer to a specific cell, even when you copy the formula to a different cell. In this case, you use an absolute cell reference in the formula. An **absolute cell reference** is a cell reference that always stays the same, even when you copy a formula that contains it to a new location. An absolute cell reference contains a $ symbol before the column letter and row number (such as $A$1). To insert an absolute cell reference in a formula, click the cell you want to use as an absolute reference, then press [F4]. **CASE** *As an incentive to promote the Quick Meal Kits, each store manager will receive a 3% bonus on Quick Meal Kit sales in Q1 for that store. You need to create a formula for the cells in the Bonus column that multiplies the bonus rate in cell B16 (3%) by the Total Sales Less Returns value in column G. You need to use the absolute cell reference $B$16 for the bonus rate in the formula.*

STEPS

1. **Click cell H6**

   You need to enter a formula in this cell that calculates the Brooklyn store manager's bonus. The formula needs to multiply the bonus rate contained in cell B16 (3%) by the Total Sales Less Returns value in cell G6. You begin by entering the absolute cell reference $B$16.

2. **Type =, click cell B16, then press [F4]**

   The formula bar and cell H6 display =$B$16. Pressing [F4] automatically added two $ symbols to the B16 cell reference to format it as an absolute cell reference. Now you need to complete the formula.

3. **Type *, then click cell G6**

   The formula bar and cell H6 display the formula =$B$16*G6, as shown in **FIGURE 8-3**. Cells B16 and G6 are highlighted because they are referenced in the formula.

4. **Click the Enter button ✓ on the formula bar**

   Cell H6 shows the formula result of $4,143, the bonus amount for the Brooklyn store manager. You need to copy the formula to the range H7:H13, to calculate the bonus amounts for the other stores.

5. **Double-click the cell H6 fill handle ■ to copy the formula to H7:H13**

   Double-clicking the fill handle automatically filled cells H7:H13. Double-clicking a fill handle automatically fills adjacent cells down a column or across a row; this method can be faster and more efficient than dragging the fill handle. Now cells H6:H13 display the bonus amounts for all the stores.

6. **Click the Decrease Decimal button ⬚ twice to remove the decimal places from the range H6:H13**

7. **Click cell H7, then save your changes**

   As shown in **FIGURE 8-4**, the formula bar displays =$B$16*G7, which is the formula for cell H7. Notice that the formula contains the absolute cell reference $B$16; it was copied exactly from cell H6. The other cell reference in the formula, G7, is a relative cell reference, which changed when the formula was copied to cell H7. Cell H7 displays the value $672, the bonus for the Philadelphia store manager.

Using Complex Formulas, Functions, and Tables

FIGURE 8-3: Using an absolute cell reference in a formula

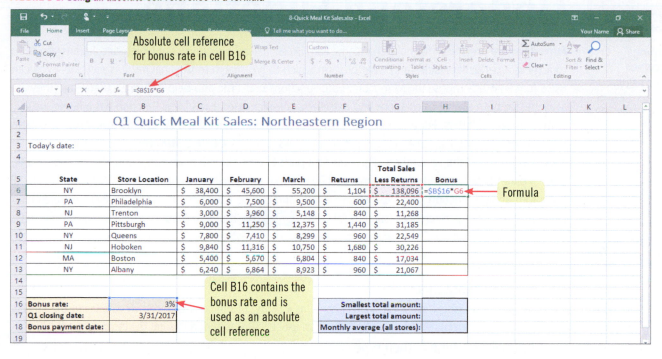

FIGURE 8-4: Viewing an absolute cell reference in a copied formula

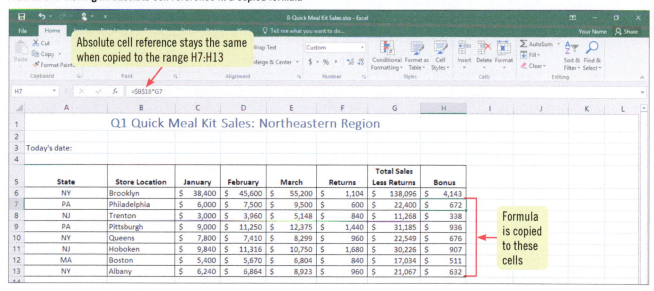

Excel 2016

Understand Functions

Functions are prewritten formulas that come with Excel. Instead of figuring out which calculations you need to achieve a particular result—and what order in which to type them so the final result is accurate—you can use a function to compose the formula for you. Functions save time and help ensure accuracy, and they are available for both simple calculations and extremely complex ones. Each Excel function has a name, usually written in capital letters. For example, the **SUM function** adds values, the **AVERAGE function** calculates the average value of a specified range of cells or values, and the **COUNT function** counts the number of cells in a range containing numbers. There are four parts to every function: an equal sign, the function name, a set of parentheses, and arguments separated by commas and enclosed in parentheses. **Arguments** are all the information a function needs to perform a task, and can be values (such as 100 or .02), cell references (such as B3), or range references (such as A9:G16). **CASE** ▶ *You need to familiarize yourself with functions so you can use them in the Quick Meal Kit Sales worksheet.*

STEPS

1. **Click the Sheet2 sheet tab**

   The Sheet2 worksheet opens. This sheet contains a listing of ingredients and their calories in the Stir Fry Chicken and Vegetables Quick Meal Kit. You can use the SUM function to total the calories in cell B12.

2. **Click cell B12, type =, then type s**

   See **FIGURE 8-5**. A list of functions beginning with the letter "S" appears below cell B12. Anytime you type an equal sign followed by a letter, a list of valid functions and names beginning with that letter appears. This feature is called **Formula AutoComplete**. Notice that the first function in the AutoComplete list, SEARCH, is selected, and that a description of it appears in a ScreenTip to help guide you.

3. **Type u**

   Typing the letter "U" shortens the list, so only the functions beginning with "SU" are listed. The SUM function is one of the most commonly used functions.

4. **Double-click SUM in the list of functions**

   Now SUM is entered into cell B12 along with an open parenthesis. A ScreenTip appears below cell B12 showing the proper structure for the SUM function. The placeholders, number1 and number2, indicate arguments, which should be separated by commas; you can insert values, cell references, or ranges. The ellipsis (...) indicates that you can include as many arguments as you wish.

5. **Select cells B5:B11, then click the Enter button ☑ on the formula bar**

   The formula bar displays the function =SUM(B5:B11), and cell B12 displays the value 445, which is the result of the function. Notice that Excel automatically added a closing parenthesis for the formula, as shown in **FIGURE 8-6**.

6. **Click the Formulas tab**

   The Formulas tab contains commands for adding and working with formulas and functions. The Function Library group lets you choose a function by category or by using the Insert Function command. In cell B13, you need to use a function that returns the number of cells that contain ingredients for this Quick Meal Kit.

7. **Click cell B13, click the AutoSum button arrow in the Function Library group, then click Count Numbers**

   Notice that all the cells containing numbers directly above cell B13 are highlighted. Excel is "guessing" that you want to reference all of these cells because they are adjacent to the active cell. You do not want to select the total in cell B12, so you need to select just the cells with prices.

8. **Select the range B5:B11, then click ☑**

   Cell B13 displays 7. The formula bar contains the formula =COUNT(B5:B11). See **FIGURE 8-7**.

9. **Click the Sheet1 tab, then save your changes**

   The Sheet1 worksheet containing the Quick Meal Kit sales information is open on your screen.

Using Complex Formulas, Functions, and Tables

FIGURE 8-5: Entering a formula using Formula AutoComplete

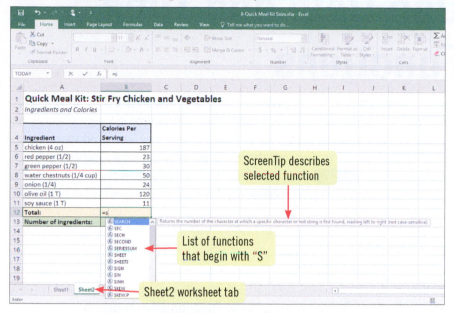

ScreenTip describes
selected function

List of functions
that begin with "S"

Sheet2 worksheet tab

FIGURE 8-6: Completed formula containing the SUM function

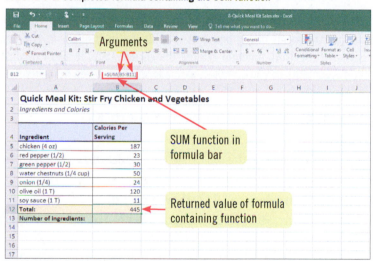

Arguments

SUM function in
formula bar

Returned value of formula
containing function

FIGURE 8-7: Completed formula containing the COUNT function

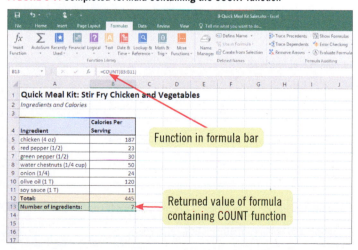

Function in formula bar

Returned value of formula
containing COUNT function

Using Complex Formulas, Functions, and Tables

Use Date and Time Functions

Learning Outcomes
- Explain date and time functions
- Use the TODAY function

There are many categories of functions in Excel. See **TABLE 8-2** for a list of common ones. The Excel date and time functions let you display the current date and/or time in your worksheet, and they can help you calculate the time between events. Some date and time functions produce recognizable text values that you can display "as is" in your worksheets. Other date and time functions produce values that require special formatting. **CASE** *You need to use the TODAY function to enter the current date in the worksheet. You also need to use a formula to calculate the date that bonus payments will be made.*

STEPS

1. **Click cell B3**

   This cell is to the right of the label "Today's date." You want to enter a function in this cell that returns today's date.

2. **Click the Date & Time button in the Function Library group**

   The list of date and time functions opens. You can point to any item to view a ScreenTip that describes the purpose of that function.

3. **Point to TODAY in the list of functions, as shown in FIGURE 8-8, then click it**

   The Function Arguments dialog box opens, as shown in **FIGURE 8-9**. The description in the dialog box explains that the TODAY function returns the current date. It also explains that the TODAY function requires no arguments, so you do not need to add values between the parentheses in the formula.

4. **Click OK**

   The result of this function, the current date, appears in cell B3.

5. **Click cell B18**

   You want to enter a formula in this cell that returns the date that is 30 days from the date in cell B17, which is the closing date Q1.

6. **Type =, press [↑] to select cell B17, then type +30**

   The formula you entered, =B17+30, calculates the day when commission checks are issued, which is 30 days after the date in cell B17.

7. **Click the Enter button ✓ on the formula bar, then save your changes**

   The bonus payment date (4/30/2017) appears in cell B18, as shown in **FIGURE 8-10**.

TABLE 8-2: Categories of common worksheet functions

category	used for	includes
Financial	Loan payments, appreciation, and depreciation	PMT, FV, DB, SLN
Logical	Calculations that display a value if a condition is met	IF, AND, NOT
Text	Comparing, converting, and reformatting text strings in cells	FIND, REPLACE
Date & Time	Calculations involving dates and times	NOW, TODAY, WEEKDAY
Lookup & Reference	Finding values in lists or tables or finding cell references	ADDRESS, ROW, COLUMN
Math & Trig	Simple and complex mathematical calculations	ABS, ASIN, COS

Using Complex Formulas, Functions, and Tables

FIGURE 8-8: Inserting the TODAY function

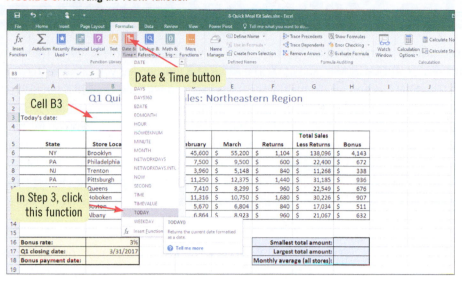

FIGURE 8-9: Function Arguments dialog box

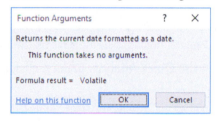

FIGURE 8-10: Quick Meal Kit worksheet after adding date functions

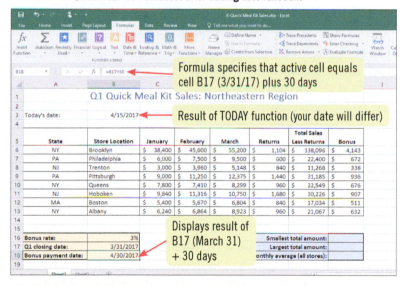

Understanding how dates are calculated using serial values

When you enter a date in a worksheet cell, the date appears in a familiar format (such as May 20, 2017), but it is actually stored as a serial value. A **serial value** is a number in a sequential series of numbers. Date serial values represent the number of days since January 1, 1900. Dates are stored as serial values so they can be used in calculations. For example, in this lesson, you added 30 days to the date March 31, 2017. To Excel, the formula in cell B18 (shown in **FIGURE 8-10**) is

really =42825+30. This is useful to know if you remove formatting from a cell previously formatted as a date, or apply the General format to a cell containing a date. Instead of displaying the date, Excel displays the serial value that represents that date. To make the cell contents recognizable again, right-click the cell, click Format Cells to open the Format Cells dialog box, click Date in the Category list, choose a date format in the Type list, then click OK.

Using Complex Formulas, Functions, and Tables

Use Statistical Functions

Excel includes many statistical functions that let you analyze numeric data. Three common statistical functions are AVERAGE, MIN, and MAX. The **AVERAGE** function lets you calculate the average of a range of cells. The **MIN** function returns the smallest value in a range of cells. The **MAX** function returns the highest value in a range of cells. You can access these functions quickly using the AutoSum list menu on the Formulas tab, or by using the Quick Analysis gallery, which provides easy access to common functions and formatting tools. To access all statistical functions, click More Functions in the Function Library group on the Formulas tab, then click Statistical. **CASE** David wants you to insert formulas in row 14 to calculate the averages for each column. He also wants you to identify the stores that had the biggest and smallest totals and the monthly average for all stores. You also need to add shading and borders to make the worksheet look good.

STEPS

1. **Type the label** Average: **in cell B14, click the Enter button** ✓ **on the formula bar, select the range** C6:C13, **then click the Quick Analysis button** 📊 **that appears just below and to the right of cell C13**

   The Quick Analysis gallery opens, with the Formatting tab active. The Quick Analysis button appears whenever you select a range of two or more cells and gives you easy access to frequently used tools for formatting cells or analyzing data. Common functions are available on the Totals tab.

2. **Click the** Totals tab **in the Quick Analysis gallery, click the** Average button **as shown in** FIGURE 8-11, **then click cell** C14

   The value $10,710 now appears in cell C14, and the formula bar contains the function AVERAGE(C6:C13).

3. **Drag the cell** C14 fill handle **to the range** D14:H14

   You copied the formula in cell C14 to the cells in the rest of the row. Now you need to enter a formula in cell H16 that identifies the smallest sales amount.

4. **Click cell** H16, **click the** AutoSum button list arrow **in the Function Library group, then click** Min

   Notice that Excel automatically highlights H6:H15. Excel is guessing that you want to look for the smallest value in the cells directly above the active cell (H6:H15). This is not what you want to do; you want to find the lowest sales amounts in the range G6:G13.

5. **Select the range** G6:G13, **as shown in** FIGURE 8-12, **then click** ✓

   The formula =MIN(G6:G13) is entered in the formula bar. The active cell (H16) displays the result of the formula ($11,268). This is the smallest value contained in the range G6:G13 and tells us that the Trenton store had the lowest Total Sales Less Returns amount.

6. **Click cell** H17, **click the** AutoSum button list arrow **in the Function Library group, click** Max, **select the range** G6:G13, **then click** ✓

   The formula =MAX(G6:G13) appears in the formula bar. The active cell H17 displays the formula's result ($138,096). This amount, found in cell G7, is the Total Sales Less Returns amount for the Brooklyn store. Next you need to enter a function in cell H18 that calculates the monthly average of all the stores in Q1.

7. **Click cell** H18, **click the** AutoSum button list arrow **in the Function Library group, click** Average, **select the range** C6:E13, **then click** ✓

   Cell H18 displays the formula's result ($12,594), which is the average sales amount per month for all stores.

8. **Click the** Home tab, **select the range** A14:H14, **click the** Fill Color button list arrow **in the Font group, click the** lightest shade of green **(second row, 10th color), click the** Borders button list arrow **in the Font group, click** All Borders, **click cell** H18, **then click** 💾

   Row 14 now has light green shading and borders around each cell. Compare your screen to FIGURE 8-13.

Using Complex Formulas, Functions, and Tables

FIGURE 8-11: Inserting the AVERAGE function using the Quick Analysis gallery

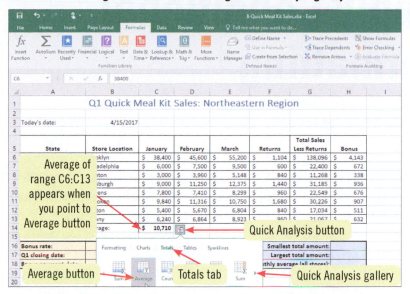

Average of range C6:C13 appears when you point to Average button

Quick Analysis button

Average button · Totals tab · Quick Analysis gallery

FIGURE 8-12: Using the MIN function

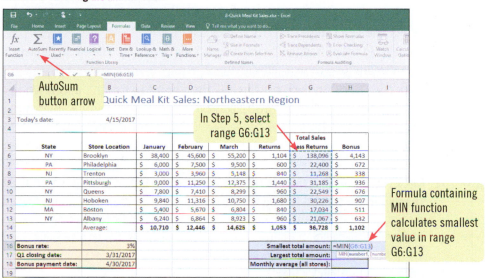

AutoSum button arrow

In Step 5, select range G6:G13

Formula containing MIN function calculates smallest value in range G6:G13

FIGURE 8-13: Worksheet with functions added and borders and shading applied

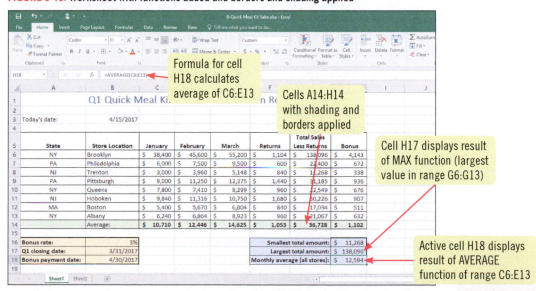

Formula for cell H18 calculates average of C6:E13

Cells A14:H14 with shading and borders applied

Cell H17 displays result of MAX function (largest value in range G6:G13)

Active cell H18 displays result of AVERAGE function of range C6:E13

Excel 2016

Apply Conditional Formatting

Learning Outcomes
- Explain conditional formatting
- Apply conditional formatting to selected cells
- Identify color scales, data bars, and icon sets

Sometimes you might want to highlight certain cells in a worksheet that contain significant data points. For instance, if your worksheet shows product sales, you could highlight cells containing the highest and lowest amounts. Instead of manually formatting each highlighted cell, you can use conditional formatting. Excel applies **conditional formatting** to cells when specified criteria are met. For instance, you could apply green, bold formatted text as conditional formatting to all product sales greater than $100,000. You can specify your own customized conditional formats, or you can use one of the built-in conditional formatting options available in Excel such as data bars, color scales, and icon sets. The Quick Analysis gallery contains popular conditional formatting options that you can apply quickly. The Conditional Formatting gallery on the Home tab offers a wider variety of conditional formatting styles. **CASE** *David wants the worksheet to highlight all sales amounts above $10,000 for Jan, Feb, and March. He also wants the worksheet to highlight the varying values in the Total Sales Less Returns cells. You explore different conditional formatting options to find the right effect.*

STEPS

1. **Select the cell range** G6:G13

   You selected the cells in the Total Sales Less Returns column. These cells display the total Quick Meal Kit sales amounts for each store (minus returns).

2. **Click the Quick Analysis button** 📊**, then point to Color... as shown in** FIGURE 8-14

   Color scales are shading patterns that use two or three colors to show the relative values of a range of cells. The selected cells now contain shading gradations of different red and green shades. The green shades highlight the values that are above average; the red shades highlight the values that are below average. The darkest shades are the highest and lowest values. You decide to remove this shading so you can explore other conditional formats.

3. **Click the Data Bars button on the Formatting tab of the Quick Analysis gallery**

   The cells in the selected range now contain blue shading. The cells with the highest values have the most shading, and the cells with the lowest values have the least. **Data bars** make it easy to quickly identify the large and small values in a range of cells and also highlight the relative value of cells to one another. You decide to clear the blue data bars and explore other options.

4. **Click** 📊**, then click Clear...**

   With the conditional formatting rules cleared, the blue data bars no longer appear in the selected cells.

5. **Click the Conditional Formatting button in the Styles group on the Ribbon, point to Data Bars, then click the Orange Data Bar option in the Gradient Fill section, as shown in** FIGURE 8-15

   The orange data bars are lighter than the blue data bars were, so it's easier to see the values in each cell. You can see the Conditional Formatting gallery in the Styles group has a lot more options than the Quick Analysis gallery.

6. **Select cells C6:E13, click the Conditional Formatting button, point to Highlight Cells Rules, then click Greater Than**

   The Greater Than dialog box opens. You want to highlight values greater than $10,000.

7. **Type 10000 in the Format cells that are GREATER THAN text box, click the list arrow in the text box on the right, click Green Fill with Dark Green Text, compare your screen to** FIGURE 8-16**, click OK, then save your changes**

   The cells containing values greater than $10,000 in cells C6:E13 are now shaded in green. It is now easy to see that Brooklyn's sales for all three months were greater than $10,000; and Pittsburgh and Hoboken had sales greater than $10,000 in February and March.

8. **Save your changes to the worksheet**

Using Complex Formulas, Functions, and Tables

FIGURE 8-14: Applying Color Scales conditional formatting using the Quick Analysis gallery

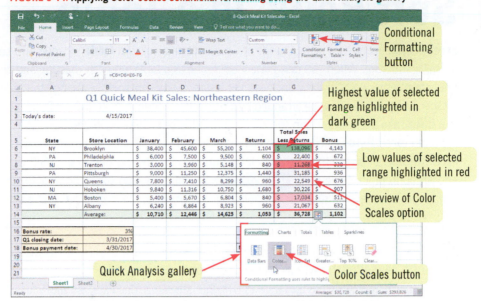

FIGURE 8-15: Applying data bars to selected cells

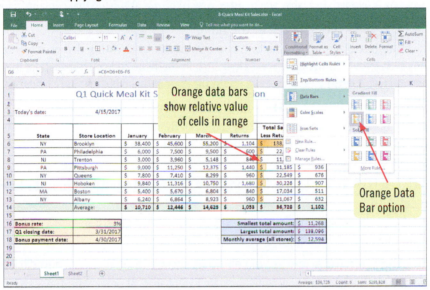

FIGURE 8-16: Greater Than dialog box with conditional format rules specified

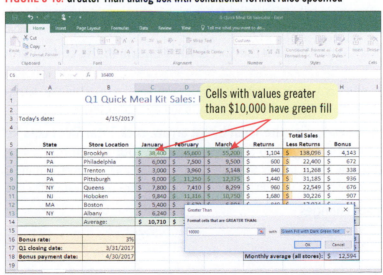

Excel 2016

Sort Rows in a Table

Excel lets you analyze a separate range of worksheet data called a **table**, or rows and columns of data with a similar structure. When you designate a cell range as a table, you can manage and analyze its data separately from other parts of the worksheet. For instance, you can **sort**, or change the order of the table rows, by specifying that the rows be arranged by a particular column in the table. An Excel table is similar to a table in a **database** because you can sort data in much the same way. As in database tables, Excel table columns are often called **fields** (such as a Last Name field), and rows of data are called **records** (such as a record for each customer). You use the Format as Table button in the Styles group to specify the cell range for the table and an appropriate table style. **CASE** *David wants the data sorted by state—alphabetically—and then within each state by total sales amount from largest to smallest. You format the data as a table in order to sort it.*

STEPS

1. **Click cell A5, click the Format as Table button in the Styles group, then click Table Style Light 14 (seventh style in the second row), as shown in FIGURE 8-17**

   A dotted border surrounds the range A5:H13; this is the range that Excel assumes you want to format as a table. The Format As Table dialog box is also open, with the range $A$5:$H$13 specified. The My table has headers check box is selected. In a table, the **header row** is the row at the top that contains column headings.

2. **Click OK, then click any cell in the table**

   The dialog box closes, and the range is now defined as a table. Notice that each cell in the header row contains a list arrow. On the Table Tools Design tab in the Table Style Options group, the Total Row check box is deselected. A **total row** is an extra row at the bottom of a table that Excel adds.

3. **Click the Total Row check box in the Table Style Options group**

   Row 14 now contains a Total label (in cell A14). By default, the last cell in the Total row contains the SUBTOTAL function, which calculates the sum total of the table's last column of data. Cell H14 now shows the subtotal of the Bonus cells (for the range H6:H13).

4. **Click cell H14, point to the fill handle ▪ in cell H14 until it changes to +, then drag + to cell C14**

   You copied the formula that summed cells H6:H13 from cell H14 to cells C14:G14. Now cells C14:G14 display the sum totals for the data in columns C through G.

5. **Click the State list arrow ▾ in cell A5 as shown in FIGURE 8-18, then click Sort A to Z**

   The items in the table are now sorted by state in alphabetical order, with the Massachusetts store (Boston) at the top and the Pennsylvania stores at the bottom. Notice that there is now a small Up arrow to the right of the list arrow in cell A5, indicating this column is sorted in ascending order (or smallest to largest). David also wants the list to be sorted by totals within each state, from largest to smallest.

6. **Click the Home tab, click the Sort & Filter button in the Editing group, then click Custom Sort**

   The Sort dialog box opens. Because you already performed one sort on this data, your sort criteria is listed in the dialog box. You can use this dialog box to sort up to three levels.

7. **Click Add Level, click the Then by list arrow, click Total Sales Less Returns, click the Order list arrow, click Largest to Smallest, compare your screen to FIGURE 8-19, then click OK**

   The list is now sorted first by the State column in alphabetical order. Within each State listing, the cells containing the highest value in the Total Sales Less Returns column are listed first, as shown in FIGURE 8-20.

8. **Save your changes**

Using Complex Formulas, Functions, and Tables

FIGURE 8-17: Choosing a table style and defining a table range

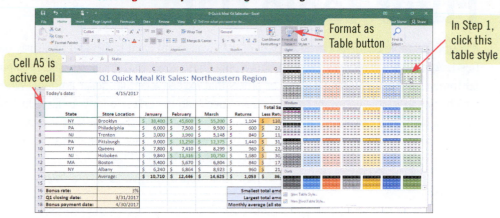

- In Step 1, click this table style
- Format as Table button
- Cell A5 is active cell

FIGURE 8-18: Sorting a list from A to Z

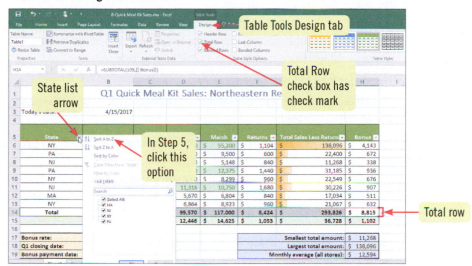

- Table Tools Design tab
- Total Row check box has check mark
- State list arrow
- In Step 5, click this option
- Total row

FIGURE 8-19: Sort dialog box

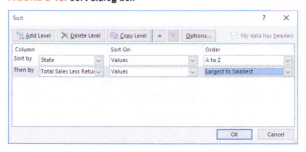

FIGURE 8-20: Table sorted by two sort criteria

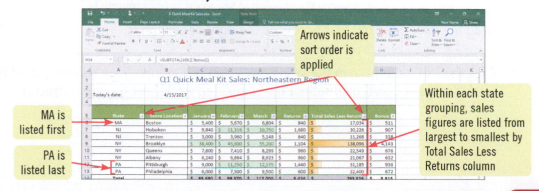

- Arrows indicate sort order is applied
- MA is listed first
- PA is listed last
- Within each state grouping, sales figures are listed from largest to smallest by Total Sales Less Returns column

Filter Table Data

If your Excel table contains a large amount of data, you might want to **filter** it to display only the data you need. Applying a filter tells Excel to show only those rows that meet specific requirements, such as customers with a particular zip code, or orders that exceed a certain dollar amount. When you tell Excel which rows in a table you want to see, you are specifying the **criteria** for your filter. Just as when you sort data in a table, you can apply a filter to a table by using the filter list arrows that appear to the right of each column heading. Unlike a sort, a filter does not change the order of the items in your table; instead, it temporarily hides the rows that do not meet your criteria. **CASE** *David wants you to filter the table data so it shows only the sales stores in New Jersey and Pennsylvania whose sales amounts are less than $25,000.*

STEPS

1. **Click the State list arrow ▾ in cell A5**

   The filter drop-down list opens and displays the list of available filters for this column. Excel creates filters for each of the values in the column, plus filters to automatically select all values, custom values, specified text, or numeric values. You can even filter a table by cell color.

2. **Click the (Select All) check box**

   The check marks are now removed from all the check boxes. You want the rows containing NJ and PA in the States column to be displayed.

   > **QUICK TIP**
   > To remove an applied filter, click the Sort & Filter button in the Editing group, then click Filter.

3. **Click the NJ check box, click the PA check box, compare your screen to FIGURE 8-21, then click OK**

   You have applied a filter that shows only the rows that contain the values NJ and PA in the State column (four locations). You can tell that the table is filtered because the arrow in the column header contains a filter icon ▾, and the row numbers have breaks in their numeric sequence.

4. **Click the Total Sales Less Returns list arrow in cell G5, point to Number Filters, then click Less Than**

   The Custom AutoFilter dialog box opens. You use this dialog box to specify one or more criteria for a filter. The list box below Total Sales Less Returns displays "is less than," and the insertion point is in the box where you need to specify an amount.

   > **QUICK TIP**
   > To change a table back to a normal range, right-click anywhere in the table, point to Table, click Convert to Range, then click Yes.

5. **Type 25000, compare your screen to FIGURE 8-22, then click OK**

   The table is filtered to show stores in NJ and PA whose Total Sales Less Returns amounts are less than $25,000, as shown in FIGURE 8-23. Now the table displays only two rows. By using the filter drop-down arrows in succession like this, you can apply more than one criterion to the same data in your table.

6. **Type your name in cell A22, then click ✓**

7. **Click the View tab, then click Page Break Preview**

   The worksheet now appears in Page Break Preview. You can see in this view that not all the columns fit on page 1. You can fix this by dragging the blue dotted line to the right of column H.

8. **Drag the Page 1 dotted blue border to the right of column H**

   Now all of the columns fit on one page. See FIGURE 8-24.

9. **Click the Normal button in the Workbook Views group, save your changes, close the worksheet, exit Excel, then submit the completed worksheet to your instructor**

FIGURE 8-21: Applying filters to the State column

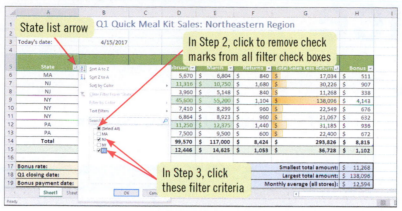

FIGURE 8-22: Custom AutoFilter dialog box

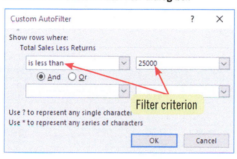

FIGURE 8-23: Worksheet with two filters applied

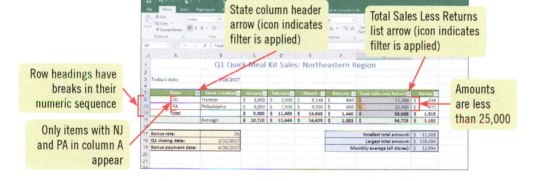

FIGURE 8-24: Worksheet in Page Break Preview

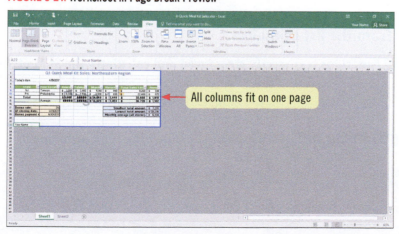

Excel 2016

Practice

Concepts Review

Label each of the elements of the Excel worksheet window shown in FIGURE 8-25.

FIGURE 8-25

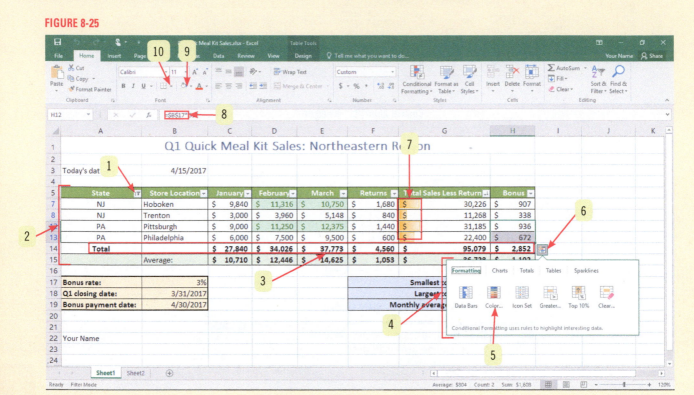

Match components of the formula =AVERAGE(B7:B12,C7:C12) with their descriptions.

11. =

12. C7:C12

13. B7:B12

14. AVERAGE

15. ,

a. Function name

b. Symbol that indicates beginning of a formula

c. First argument in the function

d. Symbol that separates arguments in functions

e. Second argument in the function

Select the best answer from the list of choices.

16. **Which of the following functions is correctly structured and calculates the SUM of 10 plus the values in cells H12, C3, and E7?**

   a. =SUM(10,H12,C3,E7)

   b. =SUM(10,C3:E7)

   c. =SUM(10+H12+C3+E7)

   d. =SUM(10,C3:H12)

17. **In the formula =SUM(B32:B36,E2,D7:D10), which of the following is an argument?**

   a. SUM

   b. ()

   c. E2

   d. B32+B36

18. **Which of the following keys should you press to convert a relative cell reference to an absolute cell reference?**

   a. [Shift]
   c. [Ctrl]
   b. [F4]
   d. [F1]

19. **In the formula =(7-1)*A8/A2*44-2, which of the following is evaluated first?**

   a. (7-1)
   c. A2*44
   b. A8/A2
   d. 44-2

20. **Which of the following functions would you use to determine the number of values in a specified range?**

   a. AVERAGE
   c. MAX
   b. SUM
   d. COUNT

21. **What value would Excel return in calculating the formula =SUM(10,MIN(1,2,4))?**

   a. 11
   c. 40
   b. 17
   d. 12

22. **Which function would you use to identify the smallest value in a range of cells?**

   a. MIN
   c. MAX
   b. COUNT
   d. SUM

Skills Review

1. **Create complex formulas.**
   a. Start Excel, open 8-2.xlsx from where your Data Files are stored, and then save it as **8-August Services and Payments**.
   b. Enter a complex formula in cell G6 that calculates the sum of cells D6 and E6 minus the value in cell F6.
   c. Copy the formula from cell G6 to the range G7:G14, then save your changes.

2. **Use absolute cell references.**
   a. In cell H6, enter a formula that multiplies the value in cell D6 by the value in B17, using an absolute cell reference for B17.
   b. Use the fill handle to copy the formula in cell H6 to cells H7:H14.
   c. Click cell H7. Look at the formula bar and notice the absolute reference to cell B17 is in the formula.
   d. Change the value in cell B17 to **20%**. Notice that all values in the range H6:H14 increased to reflect the new percentage in cell B17.

3. **Understand functions.**
   a. Click the Sheet2 worksheet tab. Notice the list of Lawn Care Services with listing services and prices.
   b. Click cell B11, type **=**, type **su** to display a list of functions beginning with "su", then double-click SUM.
   c. Select cells B5:B10, then click the Enter button on the formula bar. Notice the Total amount of all the prices in cell B11.
   d. Click the Formulas tab, then click cell B12, which is where you need to enter a formula that counts the number of items in the Lawn Care Services list.
   e. Click the AutoSum button list arrow in the Function Library group, click Count Numbers, select the range B5:B10, then click the Enter button.
   f. Click the Sheet1 tab, then save your changes.

4. **Use date and time functions.**
   a. Use the TODAY function to enter today's date in cell B19.
   b. Enter a formula in cell J6 that calculates the date that is 30 days later than the Service Date for Raymond Smith.
   c. Use the fill handle to copy the formula in cell J6 to cells J7:J14. Save your changes.

5. **Use statistical functions.**
   a. Enter the label **Average:** in cell C15.
   b. Select the range D6:D14, open the Quick Analysis gallery, then click the Average button on the Totals tab.

Skills Review (continued)

   c. Copy the formula in cell D15 to the range E15:H15 using the D15 fill handle.

   d. Enter a formula in J17 that calculates the largest service amount billed in the range D6:D14.

   e. Enter a formula in cell J18 that determines the smallest service amount billed in the range D6:D14.

   f. Enter a formula in cell J19 that calculates the average labor costs amount for the range H6:H14.

   g. Make the Home tab active, then apply Orange, Accent 6, Lighter 80% shading to the range C15:H15. Apply borders to the range C15:H15 using the All Borders setting. Apply bold formatting to the Average: label in cell C15. Save your changes.

6. Apply conditional formatting.

   a. Select the range D6:D14.

   b. Open the Quick Analysis gallery, then preview the Color Scales conditional format. (*Hint:* Scroll down if necessary so that the Quick Analysis gallery opens below the selected range.)

   c. Apply the Data Bars conditional format to the selected range.

   d. Clear the Data Bars conditional formatting using a button in the Quick Analysis gallery.

   e. Open the Conditional Formatting gallery in the Styles group, then apply the Green Data Bar conditional format from the Gradient Fill section to the selected range (D6:D14).

   f. Select the range G6:G14, then apply conditional formatting to the cells in this range, specifying that all cells containing values greater than 200 be formatted in Light Red Fill with Dark Red Text. Save your changes.

7. Sort rows in a table.

   a. Format the cell range A5:J14 as a table with headers, then apply the Table Style Light 9 style (blue style in second row of Table Styles gallery).

   b. Use a button on the Table Tools Design tab to add a Total row to the table. Delete the value in cell J15 of the Total row (because it is a date). Click cell D15, click the cell D15 down arrow, then click Sum.

   c. Drag the cell D15 fill handle to cell H15.

   d. Sort the table in alphabetical order by Town.

   e. Use the Sort dialog box to sort the list data first by Town in alphabetical order, then by Service Amount Billed in largest to smallest order. Save your changes.

8. Filter table data.

   a. Apply a filter so only the rows containing Betcherfield and Springtown appear.

   b. Apply a custom filter to the filtered table that displays only those items whose Balance Due amount is greater than $200. Enter your name in cell A23 of the worksheet.

   c. Click the Page Layout tab, click the Orientation list arrow in the Page Setup group, then click Landscape.

   d. View the worksheet in Page Break Preview. Drag the dotted blue bar to the right so all the columns in the table fit on one page. Change the view to Normal.

   e. Compare your completed worksheet to FIGURE 8-26, then view the worksheet in Print Preview.

   f. Save your changes, close the workbook, then exit Excel. Submit your completed workbook to your instructor.

FIGURE 8-26

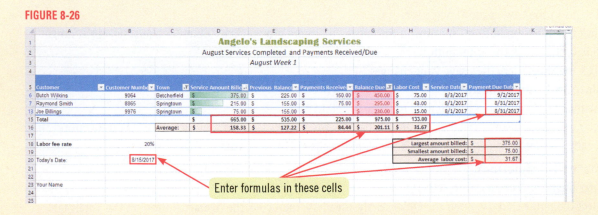

Independent Challenge 1

You are the sales manager for the Northeast region at Blue Fox Foods, Inc. You need to complete a worksheet that analyzes sales Q2 results for each state in your region. In addition, you need to highlight the total sales, the average sales, and the best and worst performing sales regions. You also need to calculate the bonuses for each sales rep.

a. Start Excel, open 8-3.xlsx from where you store your Data Files, then save it as **8-Blue Fox Q2 Sales**.

b. In cell E5, enter a formula that subtracts the value in D5 (Q2 Sales Prior Year) from the value in cell C5 (Q2 Sales). Use the fill handle to copy the formula to cells E6:E15.

c. Enter a formula in cell F5 that calculates the percentage that Q2 Sales increased over Q2 Sales in the prior year. (*Hint:* Your formula needs to divide the value in cell E5 by the value in cell D5.) Use the fill handle to copy the formula to cells F6:F15.

d. In cell B17, use the AVERAGE function to compute the average sales total for all states. (*Hint:* Specify the range C5:C15.)

e. In cell B18, use the MAX function to identify the largest Q2 sales amount in the range C5:C15.

f. In cell B19, use the MIN function to identify the smallest Q2 sales amount in the range C5:C15.

g. Define the range A4:F15 as a table, and apply Table Style Medium 6. Include a Total row. Delete the value in cell F16. Click cell E16, click the down arrow in cell E16, then click Sum. Drag the E16 fill handle to cells D16:C16.

h. Sort the data in the table by the Sales Rep column (column B) in order from A to Z. Using the Custom Sort dialog box, apply a second sort level that sorts by Q2 Sales from largest to smallest.

i. In cell B22, use the AVERAGE function to compute the average Q2 percentage increase for Avery Wood's states. (*Hint:* Use the range F5:F7.)

j. In cell B23, use the AVERAGE function to compute the average Q2 increase for Maria Ortiz's states. (*Hint:* Use the range F8:F12.)

k. In cell B24, use the AVERAGE function to compute the average Q2 increase (as a percentage) for Samantha Brown's states. (*Hint:* Use the range F13:F15.)

l. Apply Green Data Bar Solid Fill conditional formatting to the range E5: E15.

m. Enter a formula in cell F22 that calculates Avery Wood's bonus amount. (*Hint:* The formula needs to multiply cell F19 by the sum of cells C5:C7.)

n. Enter a formula in cell F23 that calculates Maria Ortiz's bonus amount. (*Hint:* The formula needs to multiply cell F19 by the sum of cells C8:C12.)

o. Enter a formula in cell F24 that calculates Samantha Brown's bonus amount. (*Hint:* The formula needs to multiply cell F19 by the sum of cells C13:C15.) Enter your name in cell A26.

p. Apply a filter so only the rows containing Maria Ortiz appear.

q. Apply a custom filter to the filtered table that displays only those rows where the percentages in the Q2 Sales vs. Prior Year Q2 (%) column is greater than 7%.

r. Preview the worksheet in Backstage view. Change the orientation to landscape. View the worksheet in Page Break Preview and, if necessary, adjust the page breaks so all columns fit on one sheet.

s. Save your changes, close the workbook, then exit Excel. Submit your completed worksheet to your instructor.

Independent Challenge 2

You are the administrative assistant to Camilla Jordan, the sales director at Phillips-Margolis Uniforms, Inc., a company that offers uniform products to a wide variety of service industries. Camilla has given you a partially completed worksheet containing data for the first week of May. Camilla wants you to calculate the commission amount for each account manager, which is 3% of the order amount, and then show the order amount less the commission for each order. She also wants you to sort the orders, in alphabetical order by account manager and then from smallest to lowest within each account manager grouping. You also need to highlight orders greater than $7,500 using conditional formatting, and use functions to make key calculations to determine a few statistics for the week, including the highest and lowest individual orders, the averages for each account manager who got the highest and lowest orders, and the number of total orders for the week.

Independent Challenge 2 (continued)

a. Open the file 8-4.xlsx from where you store your Data Files, then save it as **8-May Account Manager Report**.

b. Enter a formula in cell E7 that calculates the commission owed to account manager Marco Gonzales. (*Hint:* Multiply cell D7 by the absolute reference B4.) Use the fill handle to copy the formula to cells E8:E39.

c. Create a formula in cell F7 that subtracts the account manager's commission in cell E7 from the order amount in cell D7.

d. Copy the formula in cell F7 to the range F8:F39.

e. Enter the label **Average:** in cell C40. Select the range D7:D39, then use the Quick Analysis gallery to enter a formula in cell D40 that calculates the average of the selected range. Use the fill handle to copy the formula in D40 to cells E40:F40.

f. Create a table from the range A6:F39. Apply the table style Table Style Dark 11 to it. Include a Total row. Use the fill handle to copy the formula in cell F40 to cells E40:D40.

g. Sort the table first by Account Manager (A to Z) and then by Order Amount (Smallest to Largest).

h. Enter a formula in cell C43 that calculates the number of orders for this sales period. (*Hint:* Use the COUNT function and the range D7:D39.)

i. Select cell C44, then enter a formula that uses the MAX function to identify the highest order amount. Apply the Accounting number format to cell C44 with no decimal places. Locate this order amount in the Order Amount column. What is the name of the account manager who got this order? Enter his or her name in cell C45.

j. Enter a formula in cell C46 that calculates the average order amounts for the account manager you entered in cell C45. (*Hint:* The range in this formula should be the range containing the order amounts for this account manager.) Apply the Accounting Number format, and remove all decimals.

k. Select cell C47, then enter a formula that uses the MIN function to identify the lowest order amount. Apply the Accounting Number format to cell C47 with no decimal places. Locate this order amount in the Order Amount column. What is the name of the account manager who got this order? Enter his or her name in cell C48.

l. Enter a formula in cell C49 that calculates the average order amounts for the account manager you entered in cell C48. Apply the Accounting Number format, and remove all decimals.

m. Use conditional formatting to highlight in green shading with dark green text all the orders that are above $7,500 in the range D7:D39.

n. Apply light orange shading (Orange, Accent 6, Lighter 80%) to cells C41:F41. Enter your name in cell F1.

o. View the worksheet in Page Break view. Adjust the page breaks so the whole worksheet fits on one sheet in portrait orientation.

p. Save your changes, close the workbook, then exit Excel. Submit your completed worksheet to your instructor.

Independent Challenge 3

You own and operate a pizzeria called Pete's Perfect Pizzas. You are building an Excel spreadsheet to calculate your profits for the previous year. You have entered sales and most of the expense data in the worksheet. Now you need to enter the necessary formulas to calculate the delivery costs and the profits for each month.

a. Open 8-5.xlsx from where you store your Data Files, then save it as **8-Pizza Profits**. Enter your name in cell A26.

b. Pete's Perfect Pizzas pays for food deliveries through a delivery service, which charges a flat fee per delivery, shown in cell B20. Enter a formula in cell I5 that calculates the cost of deliveries for the month of January. (*Hint:* The formula needs to multiply cell H5—the cell that contains the number of deliveries for January—by cell B20, with B20 as an absolute cell reference.)

c. Enter a complex formula in cell J5 that calculates profits for January. The formula should subtract the sum total of cells C5:G5 and cell I5 from B5 (Sales for January). (*Hint:* Start the formula with B5 followed by the – mathematical operator, followed by the SUM function to add cells C5:G5 and I5.)

Independent Challenge 3 (continued)

d. Select cells I5 and J5, then use the fill handle in cell J5 to copy the formulas down the columns.

e. Enter a formula in cell B21 that identifies the highest profit amount.

f. Enter a formula in cell B22 that identifies the smallest profit amount.

g. Enter a formula in cell B23 that calculates the average monthly profit for all the months.

h. Apply Blue Data Bars Solid Fill conditional formatting to the cells J5:J16.

i. Format the range A4:J16 as a table, choosing any table style you like. Add a Total row. Use the fill handle to copy the formula in cell J17 to cells I17:B17. (*Note:* If any cells display #####, increase column widths until all cells display numbers.) Apply the General number format to cell H17. (*Hint:* Click the Home tab, click the Number Format list arrow in the Number group, then click General.)

j. Sort the table by the Profits column (Largest to Smallest).

k. Apply shading of your choice to cells A21: B24. Apply All borders around the shaded cells.

l. Preview the worksheet in Backstage view. Change the orientation to landscape, then adjust the scaling so all columns fit on one sheet.

m. Save your changes, close the workbook, then exit Excel. Submit your completed worksheet to your instructor.

Independent Challenge 4: Explore

Instead of building a worksheet from scratch, you can start by using a template, which you can choose on the New screen in Excel. You can choose from hundreds of templates designed for particular types of tasks to help you with school, work, and life. For example, you can find templates for creating invoices, budgets, calendars, and time sheets. You can even find templates for helping you plan a party, keep track of weight loss, or plan a move. You have volunteered to manage an upcoming talent show to raise money for a cause that is important to you. You have a budget of $1,000 and your fundraising goal is $3,000. In this Independent Challenge, you use an event planning template to budget expenses, and plan a ticket price strategy that meets your goal. This Independent Challenge requires an Internet connection.

a. Start Excel. The Start screen displays a selection of templates you can download.

b. Click in the Search for online templates text box at the top of the Start screen, type **event budget**, then press [Enter].

c. Click the Event Budget template, read the description, then click Create.

d. Save the workbook as **8-Talent Show** where you save your Data Files.

e. The first tab of the workbook, named Dashboard, is currently active and displays a summary of estimated and actual income, expenses, and profit in cells C6:D8. This information is pulled from the sample data entered in the other two sheet tabs: Expenses and Income. You need to edit the data in these two tabs for the talent show event.

f. In cell B2, replace [Event Name] with **Talent Show**.

g. Switch to the Expenses sheet. Replace any sample data that is entered into the Estimated column with appropriate data for this project; you do not need to enter data in all expense cells. Enter amounts only into expense cells that make sense for a talent show event—for example, it would be logical to enter an amount into the Room and hall fees cell, but would not make sense to budget for speakers or hotels. Your total amount for Estimated expenses must equal $1,000. You can check your estimated total by looking at the Estimated amount in cell G5. Adjust amounts as needed so that the total equals $1,000.

h. Open the Income tab. Delete all sample data in Column B (Estimated) and in Column C (Actual).

i. In the Admissions section, enter the number of adult tickets you expect to sell in cell B8. Enter the ticket price for one adult ticket in cell E8.

j. Open the Dashboard tab and view the summary of your total income, total expenses and total profit. Does your total profit exceed $3,000? If it doesn't, you need to lower your expenses or increase your ticket sales.

k. Make adjustments to your ticket sales and your expenses as needed to increase your profit to at least $3,000.

l. Enter your name in cell D3.

m. Save your changes, then preview each tab of the worksheet in Backstage view. Close the workbook, exit Excel, then submit the workbook to your instructor.

Visual Workshop

Open 8-6.xlsx and save it as **8-Art School Profits** in the location where you store your Data Files. Modify the worksheet so it contains all the formulas, functions, and formatting shown in FIGURE 8-27. The Total Student Fees cells need to include formulas that multiply the number of students by the student fee by the number of classes. The Instructor Cost cells need to include formulas that multiply the number of classes by the Instructor fee ($125.00) in cell B19. (Use an absolute cell reference.) The Profit cells need to subtract the Instructor Cost from the Total Student Fees. Enter appropriate formulas in the range H19:H20. Convert the range A4:H17 to a table, then resize column widths to match the figure. Sort and filter the table and add a Total row as shown. Change alignments and apply formatting to match the figure. Add your name to cell A22. Adjust the print settings to landscape orientation, and adjust page breaks so that all columns fit on one page. Save and close the workbook, exit Excel, then submit your finished workbook to your instructor.

FIGURE 8-27

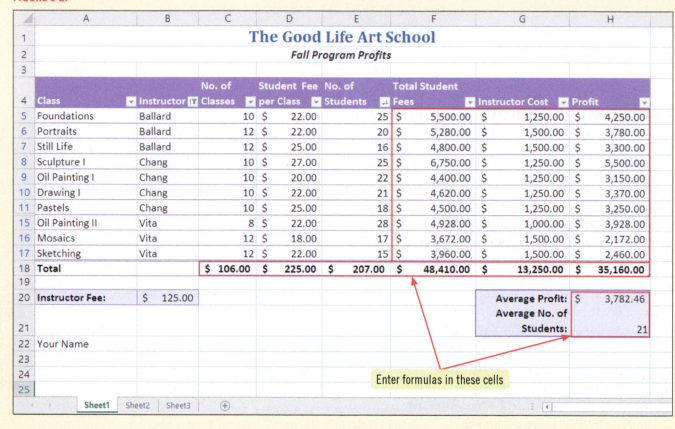

Using Complex Formulas, Functions, and Tables

Working with Charts

CASE ▶ David LeBlanc, vice president of merchandising at Pepper's Green Basket, has asked you to create a chart from worksheet data that shows sales of organic fruits and vegetables in the California stores. You will create and customize two different types of charts for David. You will also add sparklines, which are miniature charts, to help illustrate the sales trends for each store in the worksheet.

Module Objectives

After completing this module, you will be able to:

- Understand and plan a chart
- Create a chart
- Move and resize charts and chart elements
- Apply chart layouts and styles
- Customize chart elements
- Enhance a chart
- Create a pie chart
- Create sparklines

Files You Will Need

9-1.xlsx	9-5.xlsx
9-2.xlsx	9-6.xlsx
9-3.xlsx	9-7.xlsx
9-4.xlsx	

Understand and Plan a Chart

Learning Outcomes
- Define chart
- Interpret charts
- Identify chart elements and purpose of each
- Identify common chart types and purpose of each
- Organize a worksheet for a chart

A worksheet is great for presenting and summarizing data, but interpreting numbers in rows and columns takes time and effort. A much more effective way to communicate worksheet data to an audience is to present the data as a chart. A **chart** is a visual representation of worksheet data. For example, a chart can illustrate the growth in sales from one year to the next in a format that makes it easy to see the increase. Excel provides many tools for creating charts to help you communicate key trends and facts about your worksheet data. Before you create a chart, you need to understand some basic concepts about charts. You also need to determine what data you want your chart to show and what chart type you want to use. **CASE** *Before you create the chart that David has requested, you decide to review your data and think about which chart type best represents the information you want to convey.*

DETAILS

In planning and creating a chart, it is important to:

- ### Understand the different parts of a chart

  The chart in **FIGURE 9-1** shows sales of organic produce at each California store for January, February, and March. This chart is based on the range A3:D7 in the worksheet. Like many charts, the one shown here is two-dimensional, meaning it has a horizontal axis and a vertical axis. The **horizontal axis** (also called the **x-axis**) is the horizontal line at the base of the chart that shows categories. The **vertical axis** (also called the **y-axis**) is the vertical line at the left edge of the chart that provides values. The vertical axis is sometimes called the **value axis**. In the figure, the vertical axis provides values for sales, and the horizontal axis shows months. The **axis titles** identify the values on each axis. The green, blue, and yellow bars each represent a data series.

  A **data series** is a sequence of related numbers that shows a trend. For example, the blue data series shown in the figure represents organic produce sales for the San Francisco store. A **data marker** is a single chart symbol that represents one value in a data series. For example, the green data marker on the far right of the chart represents the organic produce sales in March for the San Diego store. A chart **legend** identifies what each data series represents. The **gridlines** in the chart are vertical and horizontal lines that help identify the value for each data series. The **plot area** is the part of the chart contained within the horizontal and vertical axes; in the figure, the plot area is light blue. The **chart area** is the entire chart and all the chart elements.

- ### Identify the purpose of the data and choose an appropriate chart type

  You can use Excel to create many different kinds of charts; each chart type is appropriate for showing particular types of data. Before you create a chart, decide what aspect of your data you want to emphasize, such as making a comparison between two categories, so you can choose the appropriate chart type. **TABLE 9-1** provides a listing of common Excel chart types and their uses, and shows a graphic of each. Be sure to study the information in this table so you can identify the appropriate chart types to use for specific needs. As the chart in the figure demonstrates, column charts are good for comparing values over time. This chart shows that three of the four stores had increased sales in February. It also shows the San Diego store (represented by the dark green bars) had the highest overall sales for all months, and that the San Francisco store (represented by blue bars) had decreased sales in February.

- ### Design the worksheet so Excel creates the chart you want

  Once you have decided on the chart type that best conveys your meaning, you might want to arrange your rows and columns so the chart data illustrates the points you want to make. David arranged the data series in the underlying worksheet so the store with the lowest total sales (Oakland) would appear on the left of each cluster, and the region with the highest total sales (San Diego) would appear on the right.

FIGURE 9-1: Example of a column chart

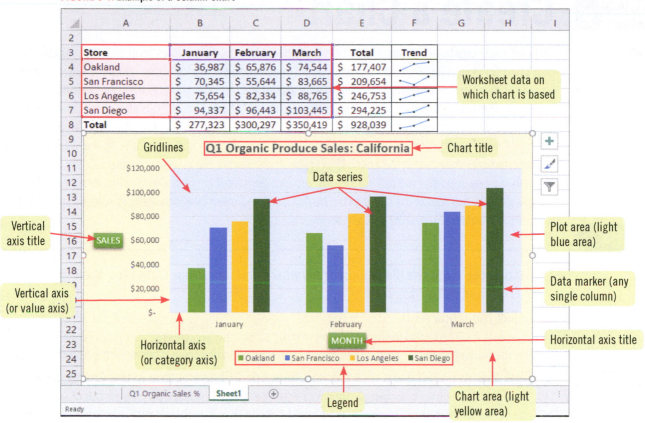

TABLE 9-1: Common chart types in Excel

chart type	used for	example
Area	Showing relative importance of values over a period of time	
Bar	Comparing values across categories, with minimal emphasis on time	
Column	Comparing values across categories over time	
Line	Showing trends by category over time	
Pie	Showing the relationship of parts to the whole	
Scatter	Showing the relationship between two kinds of related data	
Hierarchy	Comparing categories within a hierarchy level	
Waterfall	Tracking a running total and showing impact of negative and positive values on it	

Interpreting charts

A key reason charts are so useful is they make it easy to see trends and draw conclusions from the underlying worksheet data. Take a moment to look at the chart in **FIGURE 9-1** and identify key information it is conveying. See if you can answer the questions below by looking at the chart:

- Which month had the highest sales for all four stores?
- Which month showed a bigger jump in sales for the Oakland store—February or March?

- Which store had a decrease in sales in February?
- Which store had the lowest sales in January and March?
- Based on the data in the chart, do you think any of the stores is in trouble? Why do you think so?
- Which store had the most solid sales performance? Why do you think so?

Create a Chart

Learning Outcomes
• Insert a recommended chart in a worksheet
• Change a chart to a different chart type
• Insert a column chart

You can easily create Excel charts based on worksheet data. Excel provides tools to help you choose the best chart for your data. To create a chart, you first need to select the cells that contain the data you want to chart. Once you have selected the cells in your worksheet, you can then click the Recommended Charts button on the Insert tab to choose from a selection of chart types, or you can click one of the chart type buttons on the Insert tab. After you insert a chart, you can easily change the chart type by clicking the Change Chart Type button on the Chart Tools Design tab. Any changes you make to the worksheet data are automatically reflected in the chart. **CASE** ▶ *At the start of the new year, Pepper's Green Basket stores in California began purchasing all their organic produce from local farmers. David wants to see how this new organic produce has sold in the first quarter. He has given you a worksheet that shows sales by store location; you need to create a chart based on the worksheet data.*

STEPS

1. **Start Excel, open the file 9-1.xlsx from where you store your Data Files, then save it as 9-Q1 Organic Produce Sales**

2. **Select the range A3:D7**
   The range A3:D7 contains the data you want to chart. Notice that you selected the row and column labels but not the column totals. For most charts, you should avoid including totals when selecting worksheet cells.

3. **Click the Insert tab, then click the Recommended Charts button in the Charts group**
   The Insert Chart dialog box opens, as shown in **FIGURE 9-2**. The left pane displays thumbnails of recommended chart types for the data you selected. The Clustered Column chart type thumbnail is selected; there is a preview of this chart in the main area of the dialog box. You decide to explore other recommended charts.

4. **Click the second chart thumbnail (Stacked Column)**
   A preview of this chart appears in the main area of the dialog box. Each stacked column represents the total sales for one store, with each colored segment representing a month. On the Oakland column, you can see that the gray segment is almost twice as large as the blue segment, which tells you that March (represented by gray) had the most sales for the Oakland store. You decide to insert this chart.

5. **Click OK**
   The stacked column chart is inserted into the current worksheet, as shown in **FIGURE 9-3**. The dark border and sizing handles around the chart indicate that the chart is selected. Notice the Chart Tools Design and Chart Tools Format tabs are available on the Ribbon; these contextual tabs become available when a chart is selected. You decide to try another chart type.

6. **Click the Change Chart Type button in the Type group on the Chart Tools Design tab**
   The Change Chart Type dialog box opens. The left pane displays each chart category. The Column category is currently selected because the selected chart is a stacked column chart. You decide to insert the Line chart type.

7. **Click the Line category in the left pane, as shown in FIGURE 9-4, then click OK**
   A line chart is inserted into the current worksheet. Colored lines representing the sales data for January, February, and March appear in the chart. This chart type is a little harder to interpret; you decide to change the chart type to a column chart. You can change the chart type by clicking a different chart type button in the Charts group on the Insert tab.

8. **Click the Insert tab on the Ribbon, click the Insert Column or Bar Chart button** 📊 **in the Charts group, click the Clustered Column option as shown in FIGURE 9-5, then save your changes**
   The chart in the worksheet changes to a clustered column chart, with three data series (blue, orange, gray) representing January, February, and March sales for each California store.

FIGURE 9-2: Insert Chart dialog box

Clustered Column chart type

In Step 4, click this option (Stacked Column)

Left pane displays thumbnails of recommended chart types

Preview of clustered column chart

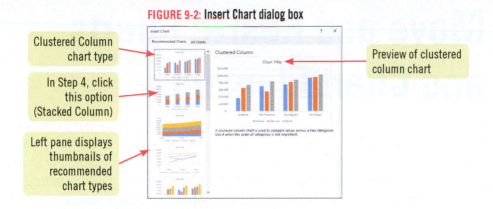

FIGURE 9-3: Stacked column chart in the worksheet

Change Chart Type button

Chart Tools Design and Format tabs are available when chart is selected

Sizing handles

Stacked column chart in worksheet

Each stacked column represents total sales for one store

Each colored segment represents a month's sales for a store

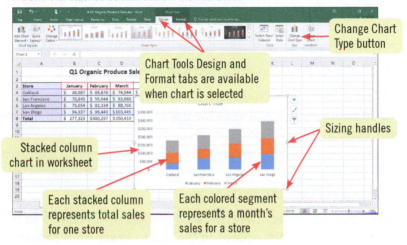

FIGURE 9-4: Change Chart Type dialog box

Line category

Preview of Line chart

Each line represents sales for a particular month

FIGURE 9-5: Inserting a clustered column chart using the Insert Column or Bar Chart button

Insert Column or Bar Chart button

In Step 8, click this option

Inserted clustered column chart

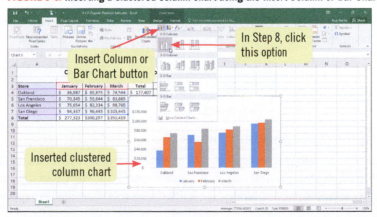

Working with Charts

Move and Resize Charts and Chart Elements

Learning Outcomes
- Move a chart by dragging it
- Resize a chart
- Move a chart element using the Chart Elements menu

You can easily move a chart if it obscures your worksheet data, or resize it if it is too large or too small. You can also move or resize many of the individual components of a chart—called **chart elements** or **chart objects**—such as the chart background or the legend. To move a chart or chart element, select it and drag it to a new location. To resize a chart or chart element, drag one of its sizing handles. The Chart Elements menu lets you choose which chart elements to show or hide; and it also lets you change their locations. **CASE** *To improve the overall appearance of the worksheet, you decide to move the chart below the worksheet data and make it bigger. You also decide to move the legend so it is at the top of the chart.*

STEPS

> **TROUBLE**
> To move the chart, make sure you drag the chart edge but not a sizing handle; dragging a sizing handle will resize the chart rather than move it.

1. **If the chart is not selected, click the chart border to select it**

2. **Point to the top edge of the chart so the pointer changes to 🔲, drag the chart so its upper-left corner is aligned with the upper-left corner of cell A9, then release the mouse button**

   The chart is now directly below the worksheet data. As you dragged the chart, an image of the chart moved with the pointer.

3. **Scroll down until you can see row 26**

> **QUICK TIP**
> If you make a mistake when moving or resizing a chart, click the Undo button on the Quick Access Toolbar, then try again.

4. **Position the pointer over the chart's lower-right sizing handle so the pointer changes to 🔲, drag the sizing handle down so the chart's lower-right corner is aligned with the lower-right corner of cell H25, as shown in FIGURE 9-6, then release the mouse button**

   The chart enlarges to the new dimensions. If you drag a corner sizing handle, you increase or decrease a chart's height and width simultaneously. To increase or decrease only the height or width of a chart, drag a top, bottom, or side sizing handle.

5. **Click the Chart Elements button ➕ to the right of the chart**

   The Chart Elements menu opens, listing all the individual chart elements. You use this menu to hide or show chart elements. Elements that have check marks next to their names are showing; elements that are not checked are hidden. You can also use this menu to change the position of elements. You want to move the legend to the top of the chart.

> **QUICK TIP**
> To move the legend manually, select it, then drag any border.

6. **Point to Legend on the Chart Elements menu, click the arrow ▶ that appears on the right, then click Top as shown in FIGURE 9-7**

   The legend is now positioned above the chart and below the Chart Title placeholder.

> **QUICK TIP**
> To delete a chart or chart element, select it, then press [Delete].

7. **Press [Esc] to close the Chart Elements menu and deselect the chart, then save your changes**

Creating a chart using the Quick Analysis tool

You can create a chart very quickly using the Quick Analysis tool. To do this, select the worksheet cells on which you want your chart to be based, then click the Quick Analysis button 📄 to open the Quick Analysis tool. Click the Charts tab to view recommended chart types, then click the chart you want. The chart is instantly inserted into your worksheet.

FIGURE 9-6: Resizing a chart

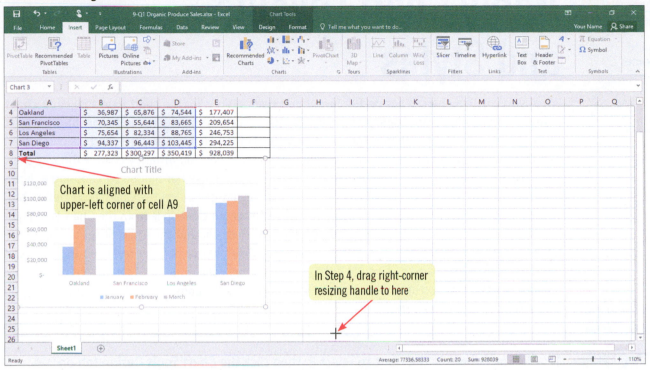

FIGURE 9-7: Using the Chart Elements menu to move the legend to the top of the chart

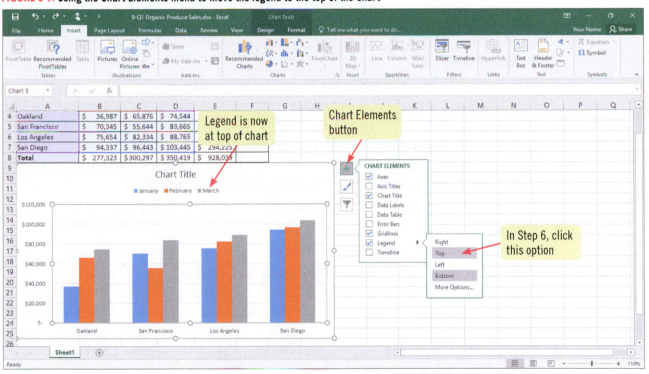

Apply Chart Layouts and Styles

When you create a chart, it has default layout and style settings for the chart type applied. A **chart layout** is a predefined arrangement of chart elements, such as the legend and chart title. A **chart style** is a predefined set of chart colors and fills. Instead of modifying individual chart elements, such as moving the legend or changing the color of a data series, you can instantly change the way chart elements are positioned and whether certain elements are displayed or hidden by choosing a different layout. Chart layouts are available from the Quick Layout gallery on the Chart Tools Design tab. You can change fill colors and textures and fonts by choosing a chart style from the Chart Styles gallery that you can access on the Chart Tools Design tab, or by clicking the Chart Styles button to the right of a selected chart. You can also get a different view of your data by reversing the rows and columns. **CASE** ▶ *David asks you to change the rows and columns in the chart so the columns are grouped by month instead of by store. You also want to improve the appearance of your chart by applying a different chart layout and style.*

STEPS

1. **Click anywhere in the chart to select it, then click the Chart Tools Design tab on the Ribbon**

   The Chart Tools Design tab displays commands for changing the appearance of a chart.

2. **Click the Switch Row/Column button in the Data group**

   See **FIGURE 9-8**. The chart now shows only three clusters of data series (instead of the original four), one for each month. Each data series now represents a store (instead of a month), and there are four data markers for each month cluster (instead of three for each store cluster). The horizontal axis labels now list the three months of the first quarter (instead of the four store locations). This view of the data more clearly shows the sales for each month.

3. **Click the Quick Layout button in the Chart Layouts group**

   The Quick Layout gallery displays an assortment of thumbnails of different layouts. Some have gridlines, some have data labels, and a few have chart and axis titles. You want a layout that has a chart title and axis titles.

4. **Click Layout 9 (third layout in third row) as shown in FIGURE 9-9**

   Your chart now has placeholder text for a chart title, a vertical axis title, and a horizontal axis title. You need to replace the placeholder text for these titles with appropriate text for your chart.

5. **Click Chart Title, type Q1 Organic Produce Sales: California, then press [Enter]**

6. **Click Axis Title in the vertical axis, type Sales, then press [Enter]**

   The vertical axis label now reads "Sales," clarifying that each data series represents sales figures.

7. **Scroll down, if necessary, click Axis Title in the horizontal axis, type Month, then press [Enter]**

   The horizontal axis label changes to "Month." The chart and axis titles make it easier to interpret the meaning of the chart.

8. **Click the Chart Styles button 🖌 to the right of the chart to open the Chart Styles gallery, then click the second thumbnail**

   The new style is applied to the chart, as shown in **FIGURE 9-10**. This style shows data labels at the top of each data marker, making it easy to see the exact sales amount for January, February, and March for each store.

9. **Click in any worksheet cell to close the Chart Elements menu, then save your changes**

FIGURE 9-8: Chart with rows and columns switched

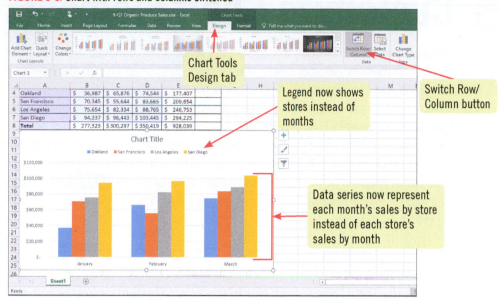

Chart Tools Design tab

Legend now shows stores instead of months

Switch Row/ Column button

Data series now represent each month's sales by store instead of each store's sales by month

FIGURE 9-9: Applying a chart layout

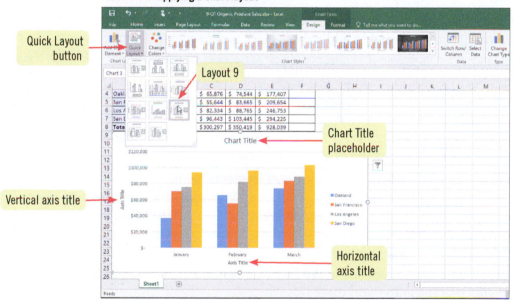

Quick Layout button

Layout 9

Chart Title placeholder

Vertical axis title

Horizontal axis title

FIGURE 9-10: Applying a chart style using the Chart Styles gallery

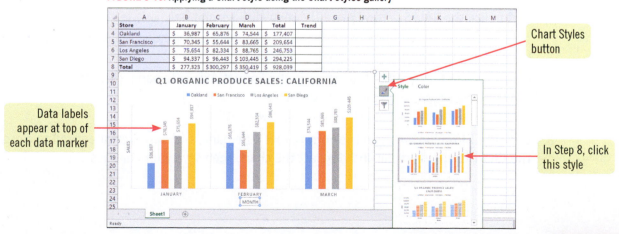

Store	January	February	March	Total	Trend
Oakland	36,987	65,876	74,544	177,407	
San Francisco	70,345	55,644	83,665	209,654	
Los Angeles	75,654	82,334	88,765	246,753	
San Diego	94,337	96,443	103,445	294,225	
Total	277,323	300,297	350,419	928,039	

Chart Styles button

Data labels appear at top of each data marker

In Step 8, click this style

Customize Chart Elements

Although Excel's chart layouts and styles are professionally designed and look great, you can still make changes to them to suit your needs. You can add, remove, or change the positioning of chart elements using the Chart Elements menu. If you want to modify the formatting or alignment of a chart element, you can use the Format pane, which displays settings unique to each chart element that you can adjust. To open a chart element's Format pane, right-click the chart element, then click Format *chart element name*. Chart elements that can be modified include the chart title, axis titles, legend, data labels, axes, gridlines, plot area, and data table. A **data table** in a chart is a grid containing the chart's underlying worksheet data, which is added below the x-axis in certain types of charts. **CASE** *David asks you to remove the data labels from the chart and add the vertical axis values. You also decide to explore other options to improve the chart's appearance.*

STEPS

1. **Click the chart to select it, click the Chart Elements button ➕ next to the chart, then click the Data Labels check box in the Chart Elements menu to remove the check mark**

   The data labels no longer appear on the chart. Next you want the vertical axis to show dollar amounts along its edge.

2. **Point to Axes in the Chart Elements menu, click the arrow ▶ that appears next to it, then click Primary Vertical to add a check mark as shown in FIGURE 9-11**

   Dollar amounts in increments of $20,000 now appear along the vertical axis. Now you need to add horizontal gridlines.

3. **Point to Gridlines in the Chart Elements menu, click the arrow ▶ that appears next to it, then click Primary Major Horizontal**

   Horizontal gridlines now appear in the chart, making it easier to identify the value for each store's monthly sales. Next you want to experiment by adding a data table.

4. **Click the Data Table check box in the Chart Elements menu**

   See FIGURE 9-12. A data table is inserted below the chart, with a legend in the first column that identifies the data series in each row. Data tables are helpful when you want to show both the chart and the underlying worksheet data. Because this worksheet already includes the data for the chart, you don't need the data table here; it looks better without it.

5. **Click the Data Table check box in the Chart Elements menu to remove the check mark, then click any cell in the worksheet**

   The data table is removed, and the Chart Elements menu closes. Next you want to change the orientation of the Sales axis title so it is horizontal. You can do this using the Format pane.

6. **Right-click the SALES vertical axis title, then click Format Axis Title in the shortcut menu**

   The Format Axis Title pane opens, with options for modifying the fill and border settings. The text alignment settings you need to adjust are not available on this tab.

7. **Click the Size & Properties button 🔲 in the Format Axis Title pane, click the Text direction list arrow, then click Horizontal**

   The SALES axis title is now positioned horizontally. See FIGURE 9-13.

8. **Click the Close button ✖ in the Format Axis Title pane, click any worksheet cell to close the Chart Elements menu and deselect the chart, then save your changes**

FIGURE 9-11: Selecting the Primary Vertical axis option on the Chart Elements menu

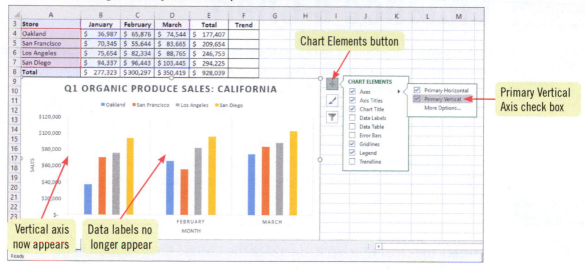

Chart Elements button

Primary Vertical Axis check box

Vertical axis now appears

Data labels no longer appear

FIGURE 9-12: Data table in chart

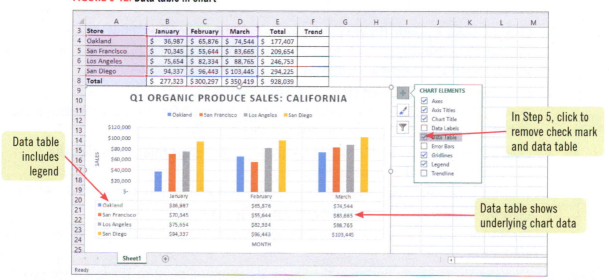

Data table includes legend

In Step 5, click to remove check mark and data table

Data table shows underlying chart data

FIGURE 9-13: Format Axis Title pane with Text direction setting set to Horizontal

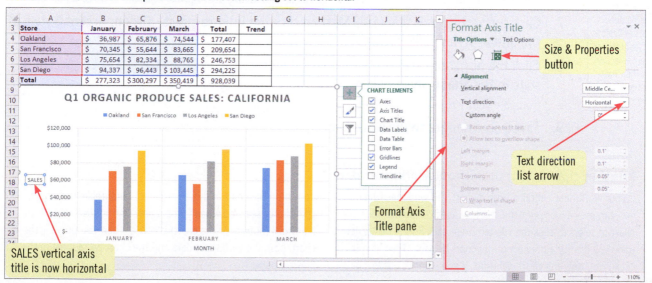

Size & Properties button

Format Axis Title pane

Text direction list arrow

SALES vertical axis title is now horizontal

Enhance a Chart

Excel provides many tools for enhancing the appearance of a chart so it looks just the way you want it to. You can quickly change the colors in a chart by applying a different color palette. You can apply special effects, styles, and formatting to any chart element by choosing from a wide variety of tools on the Chart Tools Format tab. For instance, you can apply a shape style to a chart title or axis title and then adjust the fill, outline, and shape effect to your liking. You can also click a WordArt style to apply special effects to selected text. You can also align and reposition multiple elements. To format an element, you first must select it. **CASE** *You decide to enhance the visual appeal of the chart by changing its colors, and applying a shape style and outline style to the chart title. You also decide to apply the same shape style to the axis titles so they are easier to see.*

STEPS

1. **Click the chart to select it, then click the Change Colors button in the Chart Styles group on the Chart Tools Design tab**

   The Chart Colors gallery opens, showing four Colorful palette options and several other Monochromatic palette options.

2. **Click the Color 4 palette (fourth palette in the Colorful section), as shown in FIGURE 9-14**

   The chart colors change to reflect the new color set you applied. Notice that Oakland and San Diego data series are now shades of green; San Francisco is blue, and Los Angeles is yellow.

3. **Click the Chart Tools Format tab**

   The Chart Tools Format tab is active. This tab contains many buttons and tools for enhancing the appearance of chart elements. You want to format the chart title; first you need to select it.

4. **Click Q1 ORGANIC PRODUCE SALES: CALIFORNIA (the chart title), then click the More button ⮟ in the Shape Styles gallery**

   The Shape Styles gallery opens and displays several shape styles you can apply to the selected chart title.

5. **Click the Intense Effect - Green, Accent 6 style, as shown in FIGURE 9-15**

   The chart title is now formatted with a three-dimensional green background and white font. You decide to add a shadow special effect to it.

6. **Click the Shape Effects button in the Shape Styles group, point to Shadow, then click the Offset Right style in the Outer category**

   The chart title now has a shadow along its right edge, enhancing the impression that it is three dimensional.

7. **Click the vertical axis title (SALES), then click the Intense Effect - Green, Accent 6 style in the Shape Styles gallery**

8. **Click the horizontal axis title (MONTH), then click the Intense Effect - Green, Accent 6 style in the Shape Styles gallery**

   Compare your screen to FIGURE 9-16.

9. **Save your changes to the worksheet**

Printing charts with or without worksheet data

If your worksheet contains both a chart and worksheet data, you can preview or print the chart by itself. To do this, click the chart to select it, click the File tab, then click Print. The Preview pane will display a preview of the chart by itself. Then, if you click Print, only the chart will print. If you want to preview or print both the chart and the worksheet data, make sure the chart is not selected when you preview or print the worksheet. If any cell (outside of the chart) is active when you preview the chart, both the worksheet data and the chart will appear in the Preview pane.

FIGURE 9-14: Changing the colors of a chart using the Change Colors button

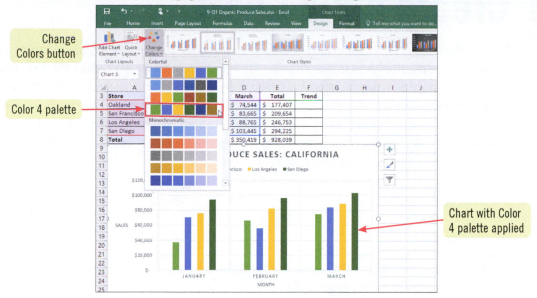

Change Colors button

Color 4 palette

Chart with Color 4 palette applied

FIGURE 9-15: Applying a shape style to a chart element

Chart Tools Format tab

Shape Styles gallery

Chart title with shape style applied

Intense Effect - Green, Accent 6

FIGURE 9-16: Completed chart with formatting enhancements

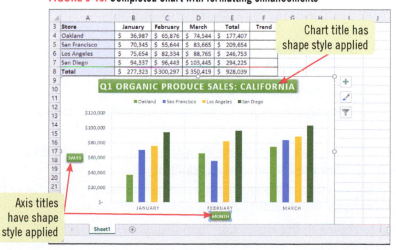

Chart title has shape style applied

Axis titles have shape style applied

Create a Pie Chart

Column charts are great for comparing values across categories, but they are not very useful for comparing percentages or parts to a whole. For instance, the column chart does not convey the San Diego store's percentage of total first-quarter sales. A pie chart is an effective tool for comparing the relative values of parts to a whole. Just like any other type of chart, you can add it to a worksheet, or you can add it on a separate chart sheet. A **chart sheet** is a sheet in a workbook that contains only a chart; it contains no worksheet cells. **CASE** ▸ *David wants you to create a pie chart on a separate chart sheet that compares total first-quarter organic produce sales by store.*

STEPS

1. **Scroll up so the top of the worksheet is visible, select the range A4:A7, press and hold [Ctrl], then select the range E4:E7**

   You selected two nonadjacent ranges (the store locations and total first-quarter sales for each store); this is the only worksheet data you want reflected in the pie chart. You want to create a pie chart that shows each store's percentage of total sales.

2. **Click the Insert tab, click the Insert Pie or Doughnut Chart button 🔵▾ in the Charts group, then click the 3-D Pie option as shown in FIGURE 9-17**

   A 3D-style pie chart now appears in the worksheet and covers part of the column chart. The pie chart shows that the yellow pie wedge (representing the San Diego store) is slightly bigger than the others, and the blue pie wedge (representing the Oakland store) is the smallest. You decide to move the pie chart to a new chart sheet in the workbook, so it can be viewed separately from the column chart.

3. **Click the Chart Tools Design tab, then click the Move Chart button in the Location group on the Chart Tools Design tab**

   The Move Chart dialog box opens.

4. **Click the New sheet option button, type Q1 Organic Sales % in the New sheet text box as shown in FIGURE 9-18, then click OK**

   The pie chart moves to a new chart sheet called "Q1 Organic Sales %."

5. **Click the Quick Layout button 📊 in the Chart Layouts group, then click Layout 1**

   Each pie slice in the chart now contains a label for the store location and for the store's percentage of total sales. A chart title placeholder is displayed above the chart.

6. **Click the Chart Title placeholder, type Q1 Organic Produce Sales by Store (California), then press [Enter]**

   Notice that the data labels are formatted in very small type and are hard to read. You can change the font formatting of data labels using buttons on the Home tab.

7. **Click San Diego on the yellow pie slice**

   Clicking just one data label selected all of the data labels. Any formatting changes you make will apply to all of the data labels.

8. **Click the Home tab, click the Increase Font Size button 🅐 seven times to increase the font size to 18, click the File tab, then click Print**

   A preview of the chart sheet is displayed in the preview area in Backstage view. Notice that the orientation is set to Landscape, the default setting for chart sheets. Compare your screen to FIGURE 9-19.

9. **Press [Esc] to return to the Home tab, then save your changes**

FIGURE 9-17: Creating a pie chart

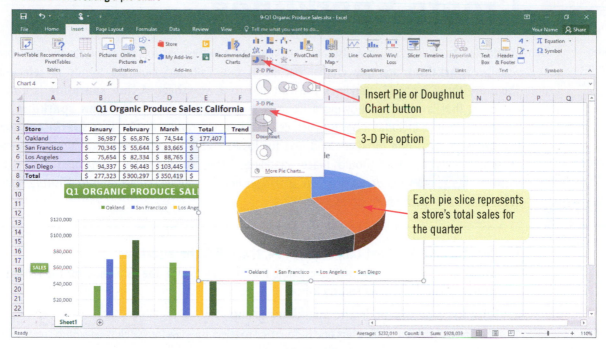

FIGURE 9-18: Move Chart dialog box

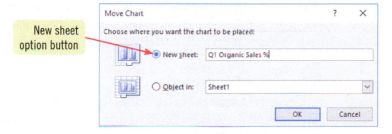

FIGURE 9-19: Preview of completed pie chart in Backstage view

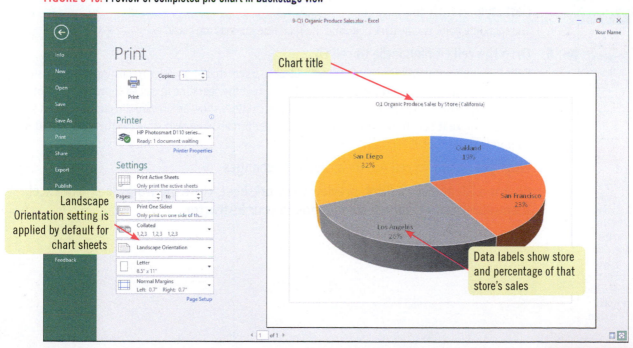

Excel 2016

Create Sparklines

In addition to charts, you can also add sparklines to a worksheet to communicate patterns or trends visually. **Sparklines** are tiny charts that fit in one cell and illustrate trends in selected cells. There are three types of sparklines you can add to a worksheet. A **line sparkline** is a miniature line chart that is ideal for showing a trend over a period of time. A **column sparkline** is a tiny column chart that includes a bar for each cell in a selected range. A **win/loss sparkline** shows only two types of bars: one for gains and one for losses. TABLE 9-2 provides descriptions and examples of sparkline types. You should place sparklines close to the cells containing the data they illustrate. **CASE** *You decide to create sparklines next to your worksheet data to illustrate sales trends in the quarter for each of the stores.*

STEPS

1. **Click the Sheet1 sheet tab, click cell F4, then click the Insert tab**

   This is where you need to insert a sparkline for the range B4:D4, the data series for the Oakland store's organic produce sales from January to March.

2. **Click the Line button in the Sparklines group**

   The Create Sparklines dialog box opens. You need to select the cells for which you want to create a sparkline: the three months of sales for the Oakland store.

   > **TROUBLE**
   > If the Create Sparklines dialog box is blocking the range you want to select, drag it out of the way.

3. **Select the range B4:D4, compare your screen to FIGURE 9-20, then click OK**

   Cell F4 now contains a sparkline that starts in the bottom left of the cell and slants upward to the upper-right corner, indicating an increase from cell B4 to C4 to D4. At a glance, the sparkline communicates that sales increased steadily from January to March. You can add markers on the line to indicate values for each cell in the selected range.

   > **QUICK TIP**
   > To change the color of sparklines or sparkline markers for selected cells, click the Sparkline Color arrow or the Marker Color arrow in the Style group, then click the color you want.

4. **Click the Markers check box in the Show group**

   The sparkline now displays three tiny red markers. The left marker represents the Oakland store's January sales (B4), the middle marker represents the Oakland store's February sales (C4), and the far-right marker represents the Oakland store's March sales (D4). You want to change the sparkline to a different color.

   > **QUICK TIP**
   > To change the sparkline type, select the cell(s) containing the sparkline, then click a different option in the Type group on the Sparkline Tools Design tab.

5. **Click the More button ▼ in the Style group, then click Sparkline Style Dark #6 (last style in fifth row)**

   The sparkline color is now dark blue, and the sparkline markers are black.

6. **Drag the cell F4 fill handle to cell F8**

   Cells F5:F8 now contain blue sparklines with black markers that show sales trends for the other stores, as well as the total sales, as shown in FIGURE 9-21. Notice that the sparkline in cell F5 shows a sharp downward trend from the first to the second marker. All other sparklines show an upward direction. You can see how sparklines make it easy to see at a glance the sales performance of each store for the quarter and for the California stores overall.

   > **TROUBLE**
   > If the chart is selected when you preview the worksheet in Backstage view, only the chart will appear in the Preview pane. Click any cell in the worksheet outside of the chart to preview and/or print the worksheet with the chart.

7. **Enter your name in cell A2, then save your changes**

8. **Click the File tab, click Print, preview the worksheet, close the worksheet, exit Excel, then submit your completed workbook to your instructor**

FIGURE 9-20: Create Sparklines dialog box

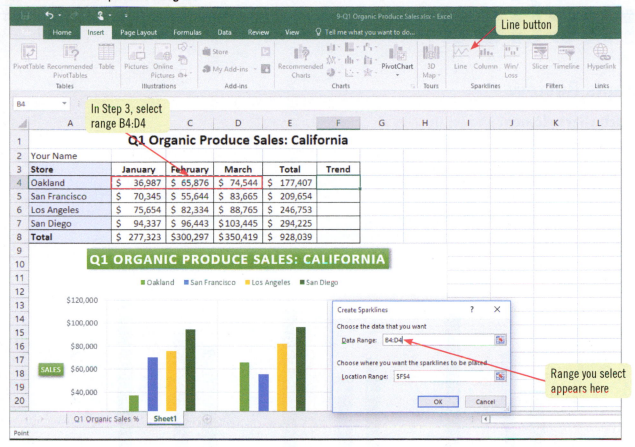

FIGURE 9-21: Completed worksheet with sparklines added

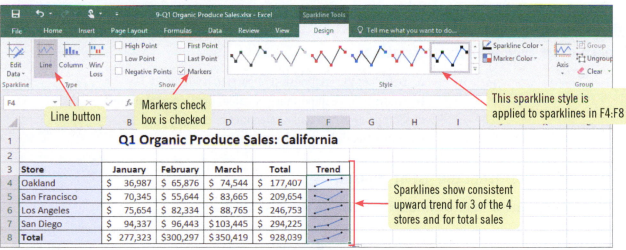

TABLE 9-2: Sparkline types and their uses

sparkline type	used for	example
Line	Showing trends over time	
Column	Comparing values over time	
Win/Loss	Showing gains and/or losses over time	

Practice

Concepts Review

Label each chart element shown in FIGURE 9-22.

FIGURE 9-22

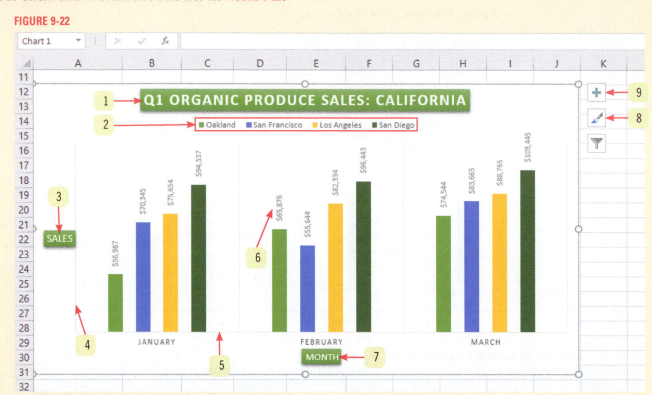

Match each chart type with its description.

10.
11.
12.
13.

a. Describes the relationship of parts to a whole
b. Shows relative importance of values over a period of time
c. Compares values across categories over time
d. Shows trends by category over time

Select the best answer from the list of choices.

14. In a chart, a sequence of related values that shows a trend is called a _____.
   a. data series
   b. data marker
   c. data table
   d. legend

15. Which of the following items identifies what each data series in a chart represents?
   a. Value axis
   b. Legend
   c. Plot area
   d. Data point

16. You just completed a fundraiser with five other people, and want to create a chart that shows the amounts of money raised by each teammate in relation to the whole amount raised. Which of the following charts would be best to use?
   a. Column chart
   b. Bar chart
   c. Pie chart
   d. Line chart

17. Which of the following tools would you use to add a data table to a chart?

    a. Quick Layout button   **c.** Chart Tools Design tab

    b. Insert tab   **d.** Chart Elements menu

18. A tiny chart that fits in a cell and is used to show trends in a nearby cell range is called a _____.

    a. plot area   **c.** sparkline

    b. data line   **d.** data table

Skills Review

1. Understand and plan a chart.

    a. Open 9-2.xlsx from where you store your Data Files, then save it as **9-Q2 Custom Windows Sales**.

    b. Examine the worksheet data, then consider which Excel chart types would best help viewers interpret this information.

    c. Is the worksheet designed in such a way that it will be easy to create a chart? Why or why not?

2. Create a chart.

    a. Select the range A4:D9.

    b. Display the tab on the Ribbon that contains commands for inserting charts, then choose a command on this tab that recommends chart types for the selected range.

    c. Examine the different chart types that are recommended, then insert a Stacked Column chart.

    d. Change the chart type to a Line chart using a button on the Chart Tools Design tab.

    e. Change the chart type to a Clustered Column chart, using the Insert tab.

    f. Save your changes to the workbook.

3. Move and resize charts and chart elements.

    a. Drag the chart so the upper-left corner of the chart is aligned with the upper-left corner of cell A12.

    b. Use a corner sizing handle to align the lower-right corner of the chart with the lower-right corner of cell G28.

    c. Move the legend to the top of the chart, using the Chart Elements menu.

    d. Save your changes.

4. Apply chart layouts and styles.

    a. Open the Chart Tools Design tab, if necessary.

    b. Use a button on the Chart Tools Design tab to reverse the column and row data. Examine the chart, and identify what new meaning this new structure conveys.

    c. Apply the Layout 9 Quick Layout to the chart.

    d. Replace the chart title placeholder with **Q2 Sales by State (West Region)**.

    e. Replace the vertical axis title placeholder text with **Sales**.

    f. Replace the horizontal axis title placeholder text with **Month**.

    g. Apply the Style 4 chart style to the chart.

    h. Save your changes.

5. Customize chart elements.

    a. Display the Chart Elements menu, then remove the data labels from the chart.

    b. Adjust the settings to specify that the primary vertical axis shows on the chart.

    c. Add primary major vertical gridlines to the chart.

    d. Display a data table on the chart. Notice how this looks on the chart, then remove the data table from the chart.

    e. Open the Format Axis Title pane. Change the text direction of the vertical axis title (Sales) to horizontal. Close the Format Axis Title pane.

    f. Save your changes.

6. Enhance a chart.

    a. Select the chart if necessary, then make sure the Chart Tools Design tab is active.

    b. Change the chart colors to the Color 3 palette (in the Colorful category).

    c. Select the chart title, then open the Chart Tools Format tab, and apply the Moderate Effect – Orange, Accent 2 shape style to the chart title. Apply this same effect to the two axis titles.

    d. Apply a Bevel shape effect to the chart title, using the Bevel Circle effect.

    e. Save your changes.

7. Create a pie chart.

    a. Select cells A5:A9, then press and hold [Ctrl] while selecting cells E5:E9.

    b. Insert a pie chart, choosing the 3-D Pie option.

    c. Move the pie chart to a new sheet in the workbook. Name the new sheet **Q2 Sales by State (West) %**.

    d. Apply the Layout 6 Quick Chart layout to the chart.

    e. Increase the font size of the percentage amounts on the pie slices to 24. Select the legend, then increase the font size of the legend to 14. (*Hint*: Click to select the whole legend; you don't need to select the text for each legend item.)

    f. Click the chart title placeholder, type **Q2 Sales by State (West)**, then press [Enter].

    g. Preview the chart in Backstage view. Press [Esc] to exit Backstage view. Save your changes.

FIGURE 9-23

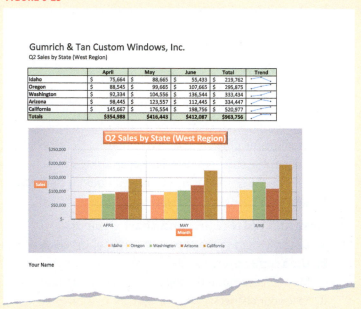

8. Create sparklines.

    a. Click the Sheet1 sheet tab to return to this worksheet.

    b. Add a Line sparkline to cell F5 that is based on the data range B5:D5.

    c. Specify to add markers to the sparkline.

    d. Apply Sparkline Style Dark #6 to the sparkline.

    e. Use the fill handle to copy the sparkline in cell F5 to the range F6:F10.

    f. Enter your name in cell A30. Save your changes.

    g. Preview the worksheet in Backstage view. Change the scaling setting to Fit Sheet on One Page, exit Backstage view, then save your changes. Compare your completed worksheet and chart sheet to **FIGURE 9-23** and **FIGURE 9-24**. Close the workbook, exit Excel, then submit your completed workbook to your instructor.

FIGURE 9-24

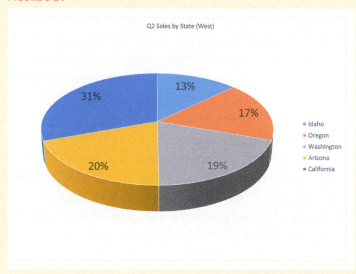

Independent Challenge 1

You are the assistant to Julia Maggio, owner of Red Raccoon Gourmet Gifts, Inc., based in Madison, Wisconsin. The company packages and markets a variety of high-end food products as gifts for special occasions and holidays and sells them locally to businesses and consumers. Julia has created a worksheet that contains sales data for the five product categories sold by the company for the last four months of the year. She has asked you to create a chart using the worksheet data to show the results for each month.

a. Open 9-3.xlsx from where you store your Data Files, then save it as **9-Red Raccoon Sales Results**.

b. Create a stacked area chart based on the data in the range A4:E9.

c. Change the chart type to a stacked column chart. (*Hint*: Click the Column category in the Change Chart Type dialog box, click the Stacked Column button at the top of the All Charts tab, verify that the first Stacked Column thumbnail is selected, then click OK.)

d. Make sure the months (September, October, November, and December) appear on the x-axis. (If the months do not appear along the x-axis, click the Switch Row/Column button.)

e. Move the chart so it is positioned directly below the worksheet data, then enlarge it so the bottom-right corner of the chart is aligned with the bottom-right corner of cell G29.

f. Apply the Layout 3 Quick Layout to the chart, then apply Chart Style 6. Add data labels to the chart.

g. Remove the Primary Vertical axis.

h. Replace the chart title placeholder with **Product Sales, September – December**.

i. Add the vertical axis title **Sales** and the horizontal axis title **Month**.

j. Apply the Subtle Effect - Gold, Accent 4 shape style to the chart title and axis titles.

k. Change the colors of the chart to the Color 8 palette (in the Monochromatic section).

l. Open the Format Plot Area pane. (*Hint*: Right-click anywhere on the plot area, then click Format Plot Area.) Adjust the Fill Settings to specify a solid fill. Set the fill color to White, Background 1, Darker 5%.

m. Insert a line sparkline in cell G5 for the range B5:E5; choose the Sparkline Style Dark #4. Add markers to the sparkline. Copy the sparkline to the range G6:G10.

n. Create a 3-D pie chart by selecting the noncontiguous ranges A5:A9 and F5:F9. Move the pie chart to a separate chart sheet named **Sales by Product Type**. Apply the Layout 1 chart layout to the pie chart. Apply Style 2 to the chart. Change the chart title to **Sales by Product Type**. Increase the font size of the percentage amount labels on each pie slice to 16, and apply bold formatting to them. If any label is outside the pie, drag it onto its associated wedge. Increase the font size of the chart title to 20.

o. Open Sheet1, then type your name in cell A31.

p. Preview the Sheet1 worksheet in Backstage view. Change the scaling settings to Fit Sheet on One Page, then save your changes. Compare your finished chart to **FIGURE 9-25**.

q. View Sheet1 and the Sales by Product Type chart sheet in Backstage view. Close the workbook, exit Excel, then submit your completed workbook to your instructor.

FIGURE 9-25

Working with Charts

Excel 249

Independent Challenge 2

You are the marketing director of The Lazy Days Spa. You have created an Excel worksheet that shows sales results for the spa specials offered in February. To better understand and visualize the results, you decide to create a chart in the worksheet that shows the percentage of total sales each spa special represents.

a. Open the file 9-4.xlsx from where your Data Files are located, then save it as **9-Spa Sales**.

b. Create a pie chart using the data in the noncontiguous ranges A4:A9 and D4:D9. Choose the 2-D Pie option.

c. Move the chart below the worksheet data.

d. Resize the chart so its lower-right corner is aligned with the lower-right corner of cell G29.

e. Change the value in cell B6 (the number of Enzyme Facials sold) to **124**. Observe the change in the chart.

f. Apply Chart Style 12. Change the chart title text to **February Sales by Treatment**. Apply a shape style that you like to the chart title.

g. Right-click in the chart area (the white space outside the pie), then click Format Chart Area to open the Format Chart Area pane. Click Fill to display fill options, then click Solid fill. Click the Color button, then click Green, Accent 6, Lighter, 80%. Close the Format Chart Area task pane.

h. Use the Chart Elements button to add percentages to the data labels. (*Hint*: Open the Format Data Labels pane, then in the Label Options pane, click the Percentage check box and the Show Leader Lines check box to add check marks.) Increase the font size of the labels and percentage amounts to 11.

i. Format the worksheet data and worksheet title using fonts, font sizes, borders, alignments, and shading to make the worksheet look professional, visually pleasing, and easy to understand. Choose formatting options that are complementary to the colors and style of the chart. Make any other formatting enhancements to the chart to make it attractive and more professional looking. Enter your name in cell A31 in the worksheet.

j. Preview the worksheet and chart in Backstage view. Close the workbook, exit Excel, then submit your completed workbook to your instructor.

Independent Challenge 3

You work for Brendan McFarlan, the director of Thrill-Land Water Park. In June, the park opened a new 10-story waterslide and an indoor arcade. Thanks to an effective ad campaign and increased media exposure, attendance increased dramatically in that month. Brendan is preparing to meet with the park's board of directors to discuss the increased attendance. He has asked you to create a chart that shows the number of people who visited the park from June through September. He also needs the chart to show a breakdown of children, adults, and seniors who attended. The underlying data you need in order to create the chart has already been entered into a worksheet.

a. Open 9-5.xlsx from where you store your Data Files, then save it as **9-Water Park Attendance**. Enter your name in cell A10, then format the cell if necessary to remove bold and fill color formatting. (*Hint*: Use a button in the Editing group on the Home tab to Clear Formats.)

b. Create a 2D line chart of all four customer categories during the months June through September. Choose the 2-D Line with Markers chart type (the fourth subtype in this category). Apply Chart Style 7.

c. Move the chart to a new chart sheet in the workbook. Name the chart sheet **Water Park Attendance June-Sept**.

d. Replace the chart title placeholder with **Water Park Attendance, June-September**. Add axis titles, then replace the vertical axis title with **Number of Visitors**. Replace the horizontal axis title with **Month**.

Independent Challenge 3 (continued)

e. Apply a solid color fill to the plot area, choosing the color Blue, Accent 1, Lighter 80%. (*Hint*: Right-click the plot area, then click Format Plot Area to open the Format Plot Area pane, click the Solid fill option, click the color button list arrow, then click Blue, Accent 1, Lighter 80%.)

f. Apply a shape style of your choosing to the chart title and axis titles. **FIGURE 9-26** shows one possible example of the completed chart.

g. Save your changes, preview the worksheet and chart sheet, close the workbook, then exit Excel. Submit your completed workbook to your instructor.

FIGURE 9-26

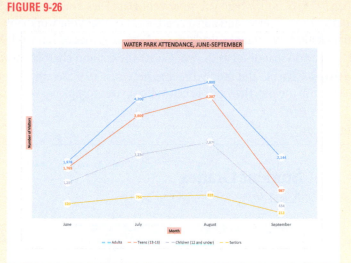

Independent Challenge 4: Explore

You recently organized a ballroom dance contest. One of the judges provided you with a spreadsheet containing the scores for each dance team, and you want to visually illustrate these results. You decide to add a bar chart showing the scores for each dance team. You also decide to add a pie chart showing the percentage of audience votes that each dance team got.

a. Open 9-6.xlsx from where you store your Data Files, then save it as **9-Dance Contest Results**.

b. Enter your name in cell A2.

c. Insert a Clustered Column chart based on the range A4:G9. Reposition the chart so that its upper-left corner is in cell A10. Resize the chart so that the lower-right corner is in cell I27. Switch the columns and rows so that the dance teams are shown on the horizontal axis, and the scores are shown on the vertical axis.

d. Change the chart title to **Dance Team Scores**. Add axis titles. Rename the vertical axis title **Score**. Rename the horizontal axis **Dance Team**. Apply a shape style that you like to the chart title and axis titles.

e. Insert a pie chart that shows the numbers of audience votes that each dance team got. (*Hint*: You need to select two non-contiguous ranges, one for the dance teams and one for the Audience votes.) Apply Chart Style 3.

f. Move the chart to a separate chart sheet named **Audience Votes %**. Change the chart title to **Audience Votes by Dance Team**. Increase the font size of the data labels to 12 point.

g. Format the data labels to add category names. (*Hint*: Open the Format Data Labels pane, then in the Label Options tab, click the Category Name check box under Label Options to add a check mark.)

h. Select the chart, then click the Chart Filters button to the right of the chart. Point to each category in the menu, and observe what happens to the chart. Click the Smith & Johnson check box to remove the check mark, click Apply, and notice that the chart now shows all teams except for Smith & Johnson. Notice how all the remaining pie slices got bigger. Click the Smith & Johnson check box again to add a check mark, then click Apply. Click outside the chart to close the Chart Filters menu.

i. Save your changes, preview the chart sheet, preview Sheet1, change the scaling to Fit Sheet on One Page, close the file, then exit Excel. Submit your completed workbook to your instructor.

Visual Workshop

Open 9-7.xlsx from where you store your Data Files, then save it as **9-Student Grades**. Enter your name in cell G1. Modify the worksheet and add a chart sheet so that your workbook looks like **FIGURE 9-27**. You need to add a formula to the Final Grade column that calculates the average grades of Term 1-4. You also need to use the AVERAGE formula in cells B16:E16. Add sparklines as shown. Create the column chart as shown, moving it to a separate chart sheet named **Student Grades Chart**, and modifying it as necessary to match the figure. Save your changes, preview the worksheet and chart sheet, close the file, then exit Excel. Submit your completed workbook to your instructor.

FIGURE 9-27

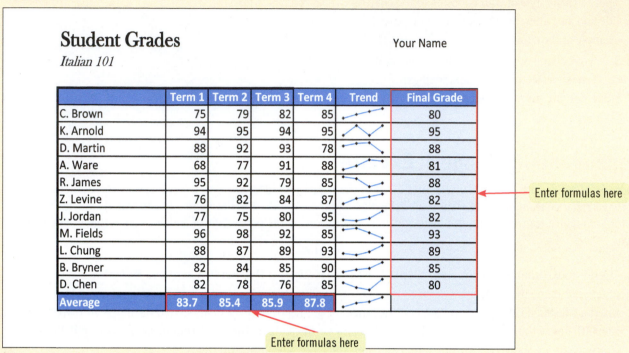

	Term 1	Term 2	Term 3	Term 4	Trend	Final Grade
C. Brown	75	79	82	85		80
K. Arnold	94	95	94	95		95
D. Martin	88	92	93	78		88
A. Ware	68	77	91	88		81
R. James	95	92	79	85		88
Z. Levine	76	82	84	87		82
J. Jordan	77	75	80	95		82
M. Fields	96	98	92	85		93
L. Chung	88	87	89	93		89
B. Bryner	82	84	85	90		85
D. Chen	82	78	76	85		80
Average	83.7	85.4	85.9	87.8		

Enter formulas here

Enter formulas here

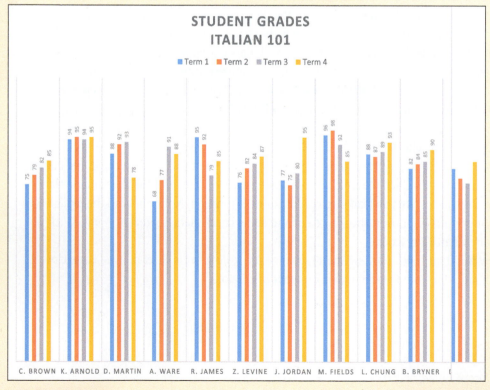

Creating a Database

CASE David LeBlanc, vice president of merchandising at Pepper's Green Basket, has asked you to create a database that helps keep track of stores and regional managers. First, you want to get familiar with basic database concepts, then you'll build the database.

Module Objectives

After completing this module, you will be able to:

- Understand databases
- Create a database
- Create a table in Datasheet view
- Create a table in Design view

- Modify a table and set properties
- Enter data in a table
- Edit data in Datasheet view
- Create and use a form

Files You Will Need

No files needed.

Understand Databases

You can use Microsoft Access to create a database to help you manage and track a large collection of related data. A **database** is an organized collection of related information. A database can contain information of any kind, such as sales and financial records for a business, products in a warehouse, or employee information. Access is a **database management system** (**DBMS**), a powerful tool for storing, organizing, and retrieving information. **CASE** Before you start using Access, you need to know some basic concepts about databases and database management systems.

DETAILS

Databases can help you:

- **Store information**

  A database stores data in one or more spreadsheet-like lists called **tables**. For instance, one table in a database might store all the data about a company's products, another table might store data about the company's customers, and another might store data about the company's orders. A database containing just one table is called a **simple database**, and one that contains two or more tables of related information is called a **relational database**. **FIGURE 10-1** shows the Stores table you will create in this module, which will be used to keep track of store information. Each row in the table is called a **record**. Records consist of **fields**, which contain information about one aspect of a record, such as the store's city location, or its prior year sales. The column headings in the table are called **field names**. Because entering data in the rows and columns of a table is tedious, you can create a form to make data entry easier. A **form** is a user-friendly window that contains text boxes and labels that let users easily input data, usually one record at a time. Each text box in a form corresponds with a field in a table. **FIGURE 10-2** shows the form you will create in this module that is based on the Stores table.

- **Retrieve information**

  Once you add data to a database, you can use Access queries or reports to retrieve or display all or part of the information in meaningful ways. A **query** extracts data from one or more database tables according to criteria that you set. For instance, at Pepper's Green Basket, you could create a query that displays all the stores in California. You can also create reports that print selected information from the database. A **report** is a summary of information pulled from the database, specifically designed for printing. Tables, forms, queries, and reports are app components called **objects**. **TABLE 10-1** provides a summary of common database objects.

- **Connect information**

  As a relational database management system, Access is particularly powerful because you can enter data once and then retrieve information from all or several tables as you need it. For example, **FIGURE 10-3** shows a report that contains fields from two related tables, Regional Managers and Stores. Each table has mostly unique information, but they share Reg Mgr ID as a common field. Because the Regional Manager ID field is shared by both tables, the tables can be linked, allowing you to pull information from both at once. Also, if you make changes to the data in a particular field in a table, any other object (such as a report or a query) that contains that field will automatically be updated to reflect the new value. For instance, in the example shown in **FIGURE 10-3**, imagine that regional manager Wanda Breslow changes her name to Wanda Jones. If you delete "Breslow" from the Last Name field in the Regional Managers table and replace it with "Jones," the report at the top of the figure would automatically be updated to show the regional manager's name as "Wanda Jones."

FIGURE 10-1: Stores table

- Field names
- Record (each row is a record)
- Prior Year Sales field (each column is a field)

FIGURE 10-2: Stores form

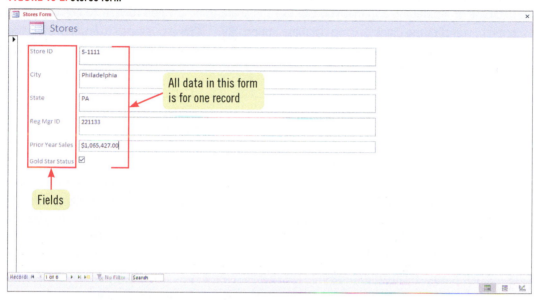

- All data in this form is for one record
- Fields

FIGURE 10-3: Report in a relational database containing fields from two related tables

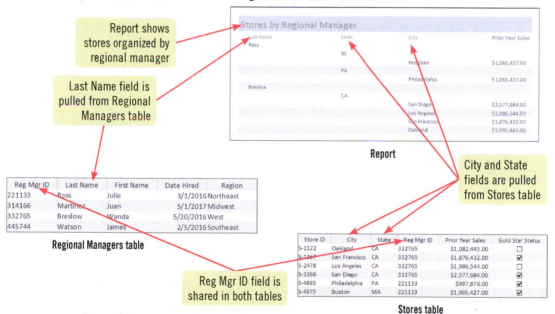

- Report shows stores organized by regional manager
- Last Name field is pulled from Regional Managers table
- City and State fields are pulled from Stores table
- Reg Mgr ID field is shared in both tables
- Regional Managers table
- Stores table
- Report

TABLE 10-1: Common database objects in Access

objects	description
Table	A list of data organized in rows (records) and columns (fields)
Query	A set of criteria you specify to retrieve data from a database
Form	A window that lets you view, enter, and edit data in a database one record at a time
Report	A summary of database information designed specifically for distributing or printing

Create a Database

You can create a database in Access in two ways: by starting with a blank database or from a template. Creating a database from a template can save time, as it contains ready-made database objects, such as tables structured with field names appropriate to a particular type of database. By using a template, you can focus on entering data instead of designing appropriate database objects. When you first start Access, the Start screen opens and displays a variety of templates you can use to create a specific type of desktop database or a database app that you can use and share using a web browser. To create a database from scratch, you click the Blank desktop database option. **CASE** *You're ready to begin creating the database that will be used to track stores and regional managers at Pepper's Green Basket. You need to start Access, specify a name and location for the database file, and then create the database.*

STEPS

1. **On the Windows taskbar, click the Start button** ⊞
   The Start menu opens.

2. **Click All apps, then click Access 2016**
   Access starts and displays the Access Start screen as shown in **FIGURE 10-4**. The Recent pane lists any recent database files you have opened. The large pane on the right displays thumbnails of different types of templates you can use to create specific types of databases. There is also a thumbnail for creating a custom web app, which allows you to create databases that can be viewed and accessed by others over the web. You want to start a new blank database.

3. **Click Blank desktop database**
   The Blank desktop database dialog box opens. You need to specify a name for your new database in it.

4. **Click in the the File Name box to select the temporary file name, then type 10-PGB**

5. **Click the Browse for a location to put your database button** 🗁 **to the right of the File Name text box**
   The File New Database dialog box opens. Like the Save As dialog box in Excel and Word, you use this dialog box to specify the folder and drive where you want to save the database file.

6. **Navigate to where you store your Data Files, then click OK**
   The dialog box closes. Notice that the path to the database under the File Name text box in the Blank desktop database dialog box now shows the drive and folder location you specified, as shown in **FIGURE 10-5**.

7. **Click Create**
   The Access app window opens in Datasheet view with the Table Tools Fields tab in front, as shown in **FIGURE 10-6**. Below the Ribbon are two panes. In the right pane, a blank table datasheet with the temporary name Table1 is open. The left pane is the **Navigation pane**; this is where all database objects for the open database are listed. Table1 is the only object listed.

Creating databases and Access apps from templates

You can create a powerful database quickly by choosing a template from the Access Start screen. Like ready-made templates for Word or Excel, Access templates are files designed for specific types of tasks, such as managing all your contacts, or tracking inventory, or keeping track of all the tasks in a large-scale project. In a database created from a template, the structure of the database is already set, with tables, queries, forms, and reports all pre-built. All you have to do is name and save the database, then enter the data you want. You can also customize the database by adding additional tables or other objects to suit your needs. You can also use templates to create a web-based database app, called an Access app, that you can share with colleagues. The advantage of an Access app is that users can access it from any location using a web browser. To create a database app, you need a SharePoint server or an Office 365 site (which comes included with an Office 365 business subscription) to host it.

FIGURE 10-4: Access Start screen

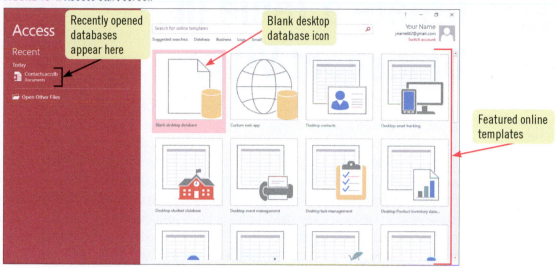

Recently opened databases appear here

Blank desktop database icon

Featured online templates

FIGURE 10-5: Blank desktop database dialog box showing path to where database file is stored

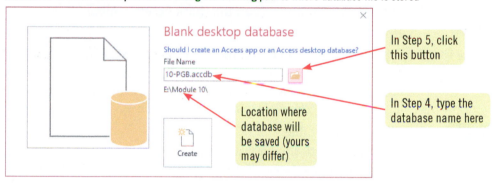

In Step 5, click this button

In Step 4, type the database name here

Location where database will be saved (yours may differ)

FIGURE 10-6: Blank table datasheet

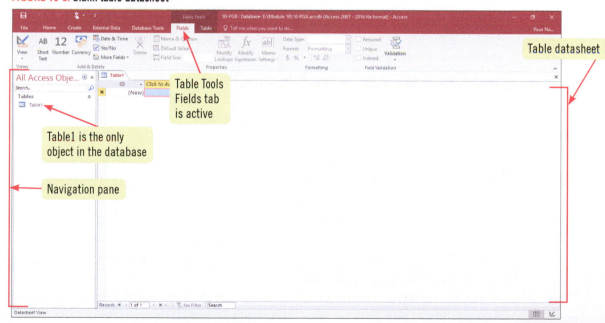

Table datasheet

Table Tools Fields tab is active

Table1 is the only object in the database

Navigation pane

Create a Table in Datasheet View

When you start working in a new database, a blank table opens in Datasheet view. In **Datasheet view**, you can add fields to a table and view any data that the table contains. Before you begin adding fields to the table, it is a good idea to save the table with an appropriate name. Although you already saved the database, you also need to save each object you create within it, including tables. To add a field to a table, you need to specify its data type (such as Date or Currency) and then specify a name. See **TABLE 10-2** for a description of field data types you can use. Every table in a database must contain one field that is designated as the **primary key field**, which uniquely identifies each record among all other records in a database. By default, every blank new table in Access includes a blank ID field, which is automatically designated the primary key field. **CASE** *You need to save the blank table with the name Regional Managers. Then, before you add new fields, you need to change the ID field data type to Short Text. Finally, you need to specify names and data types for new fields in the table.*

STEPS

1. **Click the Save button 🔲 on the Quick Access toolbar**

   The Save As dialog box opens. You need to specify a name for the new table.

2. **Type Regional Managers in the Table Name text box, then click OK**

   The Regional Managers table is saved to the PGB database. The name "Regional Managers" now appears under the Tables heading in the Navigation pane and in the tab above the datasheet. Notice the ID field. In this table, the ID field name can be used to store each regional manager's ID number.

3. **Click ID in the table**

   The ID field is selected. Notice that the Data Type text box in the Formatting group indicates that the field has the AutoNumber data type applied to it. The **AutoNumber** data type assigns a unique number for each record in the table, starting with 1 and increasing sequentially by 1 for each record. You need to change the data type to Short Text, because regional manager ID numbers are unique numbers that need to be entered individually.

4. **Click the Data Type list arrow in the Formatting group as shown in FIGURE 10-7, then click Short Text**

   The ID field now has the Short Text data type applied to it. The Short Text data type is appropriate here because it lets you enter text (such as names), numbers that do not require calculations (such as phone numbers), or combinations of text and numbers (such as street addresses).

5. **Click Click to Add in the second field in the table**

   A menu of available field types opens, as shown in **FIGURE 10-8**. You want to apply the Short Text data type to this field because it will be used for manager last names.

6. **Click Short Text**

   The Short Text data type is now applied to the second field, and the temporary field name Field1 is selected. You can now type the name for this field.

7. **Type Regional Manager Last Name, then press [Tab]**

   The second field in the table now displays the name "Regional Manager Last Name". The Data Type list is now open for the third field in the table, which you need to use for regional manager first names.

8. **Click Short Text, type Regional Manager First Name, click Click to Add, click Short Text, type Region, then save your changes**

   You entered the Regional Manager First Name field name and the Region field name and applied the Short Text data type for each. The table now contains four text fields, as shown in **FIGURE 10-9**.

Creating a Database

FIGURE 10-7: Applying the Short Text data type to the ID field

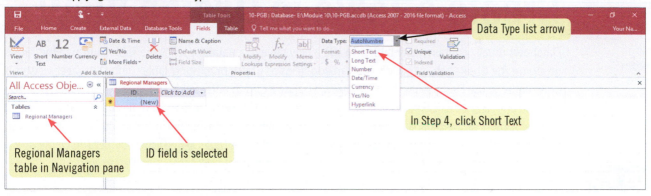

FIGURE 10-8: Specifying a data type for a new field

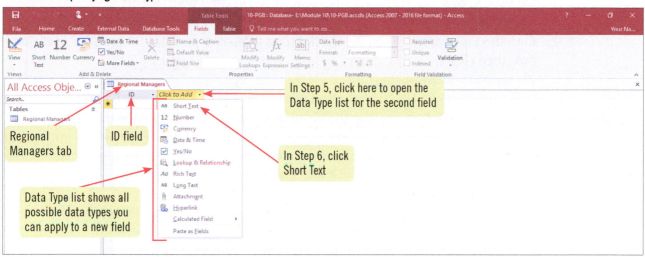

FIGURE 10-9: Regional Managers table with four fields

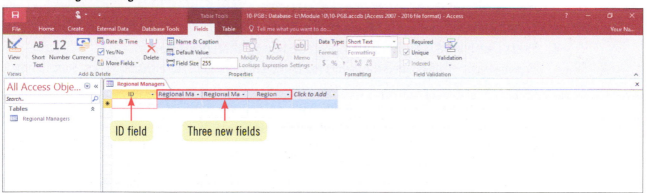

TABLE 10-2: Common field data types

data type	description
Short Text	A word or string of words, numbers that do not require calculations, or a combination of text and numbers
AutoNumber	Unique sequential numbers that Access assigns to each new record, which cannot be edited
Number	Numeric data to be used in calculations
Currency	Currency values and numeric data used in calculations
Date/Time	Date and time values
Yes/No	Values that can be only Yes or No; used to identify the presence or absence of specific criteria
Long Text	Lengthy text (which can also contain numbers that do not require calculations)
Calculated	Displays a value that is the result of a formula that includes field values

Create a Table in Design View

Databases usually contain many tables. To add a new table to a database, click the Table button in the Tables group on the Create tab. Although you can add fields to a new or existing table using Datasheet view, it is often easier to use Design view. In Design view, you use a grid to enter fields and specify field data types. You can also add field descriptions to fields in Design view. A **field description** identifies the purpose of a field and helps users of the database understand the information that the field is meant to contain. You can also use Design view to view and change the primary key field in a table. **CASE** *You need to create a new table that contains information about the stores. You decide to create this table using Design view.*

STEPS

1. **Click the Create tab, then click the Table button in the Tables group**

   A new blank table with the temporary name Table1 opens in Datasheet view.

2. **Click the Save button 🖫 on the Quick Access toolbar, type Stores in the Save As dialog box, then click OK**

   The Stores table is saved to the PGB database. The name "Stores" now appears under the Tables heading in the Navigation pane and in the tab above the datasheet, next to the Regional Managers tab.

   > **QUICK TIP**
   > You can also change to Design view by clicking the Design View button 🖉 on the status bar.

3. **Click the View button arrow in the Views group, then click Design View**

   The main window now displays a grid with the headings Field Name, Data Type, and Description (Optional). The ID field is listed as the first field; the key icon to the left of "ID" indicates this is the primary key field. You want to change the name of the ID field to Store ID.

4. **Type Store ID, then press [Tab]**

   The ID field name is changed to Store ID. This field currently has the AutoNumber data type applied to it. You want to change the data type to Short Text because each store is assigned a unique Store ID.

5. **Click the AutoNumber arrow in the Data Type column as shown in FIGURE 10-10, then click Short Text**

   The Store ID field now has the Short Text data type. You need to enter a description for this field, which will appear in the status bar and help users understand what type of data should be entered for this field.

6. **Press [Tab], type 4-digit number preceded by S-, then press [Enter]**

   Pressing [Tab] or [Enter] moves the pointer to the next cell in the grid. The blank field below Store ID is now active and ready for you to type a new field name in it.

7. **Type City, press [Enter] three times, type State, press [Enter] three times, type Reg Mgr ID, then press [Enter] three times**

   You entered three new fields and specified the data types for each as Short Text. If you specify no particular data type, the Short Text data field is automatically applied.

8. **Type Prior Year Sales, press [Enter], click the Data Type list arrow, click Currency, then press [Enter] twice**

   You applied the Currency data type to the Prior Year Sales field. The Currency data type is appropriate because this field will contain the dollar amount of a store's sales for the prior year. Any numbers entered in this field will automatically be formatted as currency.

   > **QUICK TIP**
   > To show the description message in the status bar wherever the Gold Star Status field is used, click the Property Update Options button below the Description you typed, then click Update Status Bar Text everywhere Gold Star Status is used.

9. **Type Gold Star Status, press [Enter], type Y, press [Enter], type Yes if store met sales, profitability, and community goals in prior year, press [Enter], then save your changes**

   Typing the letter "Y" in the Data Type column applied the Yes/No data type for the Gold Star Status field. In Datasheet view, any field with a Yes/No data type will contain a check box; a check mark in a field check box indicates a Yes value for the field. The description you typed in the Description column will let users know to mark this field as Yes if the store met sales, profitability, and community goals in the prior year. Compare your screen to FIGURE 10-11.

Creating a Database

FIGURE 10-10: Specifying a data type for the Store ID field in Design view

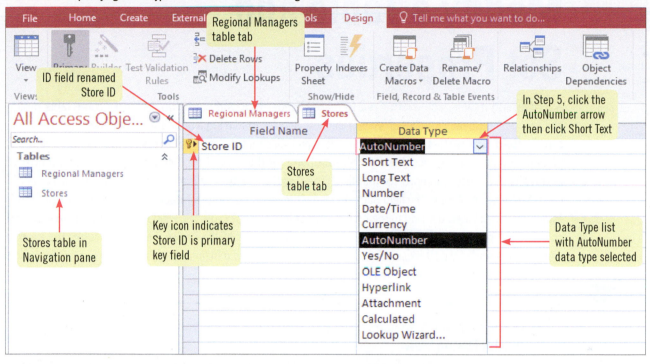

FIGURE 10-11: Stores table with six fields in Design view

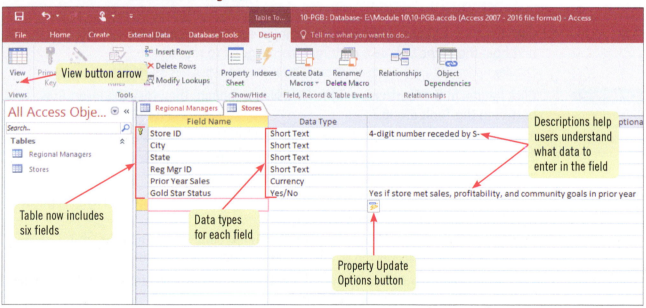

Access 2016

Modify a Table and Set Properties

After creating a table, you might need to make changes to it. Although you can make some table design changes in Datasheet view, Design view is the best view for modifying a table's structure. In Design view, you can set **field properties**, which are data characteristics that dictate how Access stores, handles, and displays field data. For instance, the Field Size property for the Short Text data type specifies the number of characters that a user can enter for that field. The **Caption property** is a label that appears in a form or in Datasheet view in place of the field name to clarify the field's contents for data entry or interpretation; this is especially useful when the field name itself is long or technical. You use the Field Properties pane to view and change field properties. **CASE** *You need to make changes to the Regional Managers table. You need to change the name of the ID field, limit its field size, and add a field description. You also need to add captions to two fields and insert a new Date Hired field.*

STEPS

1. **Click the Regional Managers table tab, click the View button arrow in the Views group, then click Design View**

   The Regional Managers table opens in Design view. You want to change the name of the ID field to "Reg Mgr ID". The ID field is selected, so you are ready to type the new name.

2. **Type Reg Mgr ID**

   The field name is changed to "Reg Mgr ID". The Field Properties pane at the bottom of the screen displays the field properties for the Reg Mgr ID field. The settings reflect the default settings for the Short Text data type. By default, Short Text fields have a limit of 255 characters.

3. **Double-click 255 in the Field Size text box in the Field Properties pane, then type 6**

   Users will not be able to enter more than six characters for this field, as shown in **FIGURE 10-12**.

4. **Click Reg Mgr ID in the Field Name column, press [Tab] twice to move to the Description text box, then type Unique 6-digit number assigned to reg mgr**

   This description will appear in the status bar in Datasheet view when this field is active.

5. **Click Region in the fourth row of the Field Name column, then click the Insert Rows button in the Tools group**

   A new, blank row is inserted between "Regional Manager First Name" and "Region".

6. **Type Date Hired, press [Enter], click the Data Type arrow, then click Date/Time**

   You added a new Date Hired field and specified its data type as Date/Time.

7. **Click Regional Manager Last Name, click in the Caption text box in the Field Properties pane, type Last Name, then press [Enter]**

   The caption for the Regional Manager Last Name field is now "Last Name". This means that "Last Name" will appear as the field name for this field in Datasheet view and in any form that includes this field.

8. **Click Regional Manager First Name, click in the Caption text box in the Field Properties pane, type First Name, then press [Enter]**

   You specified the caption for the Regional Manager First Name field as "First Name", as shown in **FIGURE 10-13**.

9. **Save your changes, then click the View button in the Views group**

   The view changes to Datasheet view, as shown in **FIGURE 10-14**. Notice that the Regional Manager Last Name and Regional Manager First Name fields now appear as "Last Name" and "First Name".

FIGURE 10-12: Changing the Field Size property for the Reg Mgr ID field in Design view

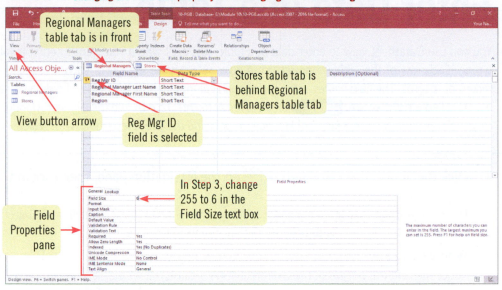

FIGURE 10-13: Regional Managers table in Design view after adding a field and changing properties

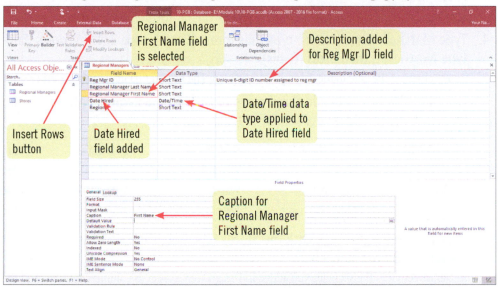

FIGURE 10-14: Regional Managers table in Datasheet view after changes

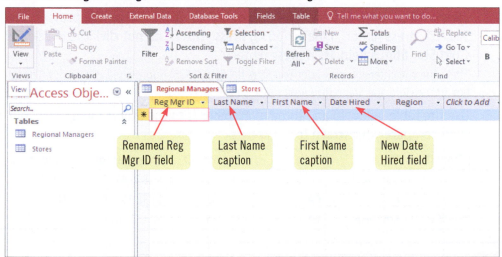

Enter Data in a Table

Learning Outcome
• Add records in Datasheet view

You can use Datasheet view to enter data in a table; just click where you want to enter a value and start typing. Each row of the table is one record. A **row selector** to the left of each record lets you select a record or records. The field names at the top of each column identify the fields. The data you enter in each field is called a **field value**. **CASE** ▶ You are ready to enter records into the Regional Managers and Stores tables. You need to enter four Regional Manager records and the Stores records for West region.

STEPS

QUICK TIP
You can also press [F11] to open or close the Navigation pane.

1. **Click the Shutter Bar Close button ⊲⊲ on the Navigation pane, then click in the Reg Mgr ID field**

   The Reg Mgr ID field name is highlighted, indicating it is selected. A star in the first row selector indicates it is a new record. The Reg Mgr ID field description appears in the status bar.

QUICK TIP
A pencil icon appears in the row selector for the first record, indicating that this record is being edited.

2. **Type 2211337**

   Notice the field will not accept the seventh digit (7) because you set the Field Size property to six. The Reg Mgr ID for this record is actually 221133, so you can move on to the next field.

3. **Press [Enter]**

   Pressing [Enter] or [Tab] accepts your entry and moves the insertion point to the next field.

QUICK TIP
You can also enter a date by clicking the calendar icon that appears when you click in a field formatted as a date, then using the calendar window to complete the entry.

4. **Type Marshall, press [Enter], type Julie, press [Enter], type 3/1/16, press [Enter], type Northeast, then press [Enter]**

   Access changed the date to the date format 3/1/2016. The Reg Mgr ID field in the second record is now active.

5. **Use the table below to add three more records to the Regional Managers table, press [Enter], then compare your screen to FIGURE 10-15**

Reg Mgr ID	Last Name	First Name	Date Hired	Region
314166	Lo	Wendell	4/5/2015	Midwest
332765	Breslow	Wanda	5/20/2016	West
445744	Your last name	Your first name	2/5/2016	Southeast

6. **Click the Save button 🖫, click the Stores table tab, then click the Datasheet View button 🖽 on the status bar**

   In Datasheet view, the six fields you added in Design view appear as column headings, and the Store ID field is active. You need to enter the records for the stores in the West region, managed by Wanda Breslow. Wanda's manager ID is 332765.

QUICK TIP
To indicate No in a Yes/No field, no action is required; just press [Enter] or [Tab] to skip to the next field. If you inadvertently add a check mark, click it again to remove the check mark.

7. **Type S-1122, press [Enter], type Oakland, press [Enter], type CA, press [Enter], type 332765, press [Enter], type 1075533, press [Enter], do not click the check box in the Gold Star Status field, then press [Enter]**

   The value you entered for the Prior Year Sales field (1075533) is formatted as currency. The unchecked check box in the Gold Star Status field indicates a No value.

QUICK TIP
To delete a record, click the row selector for the record, then press [Delete].

8. **Use the table below to add three more records to the Stores table, save your changes, then compare your screen to FIGURE 10-16**

Store ID	City	State	Reg Mgr ID	Prior Year Sales	Gold Star Status
S-1367	San Francisco	CA	332765	$1,876,432.00	Y
S-2478	Los Angeles	CA	332765	$1,986,544.00	N
S-3366	San Diego	CA	332765	$2,577,684.00	Y

Creating a Database

FIGURE 10-15: Field values entered in the Regional Managers table in Datasheet view

Shutter Bar Open/Close button

Regional Managers table tab

Reg Mgr ID	Last Name	First Name	Date Hired	Region	Click to Add
221133	Marshall	Julie	3/1/2016	Northeast	
314166	Lo	Wendell	4/5/2015	Midwest	
332765	Breslow	Wanda	5/20/2016	West	
445744	Your last name	Your first name	2/5/2016	Southeast	

Four records added

Row selectors for bottom three records

Your first and last name should appear here

Star icon indicates next new blank record

Field description for Reg Mgr ID field appears in status bar

Record: 5 of 5   No Filter   Search

Unique 6-digit ID number assigned to reg mgr

FIGURE 10-16: Field values entered in the Stores table in Datasheet view

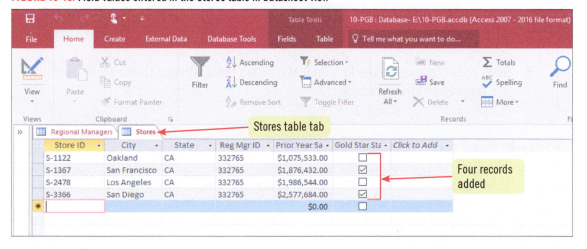

Stores table tab

Store ID	City	State	Reg Mgr ID	Prior Year Sa	Gold Star Sta	Click to Add
S-1122	Oakland	CA	332765	$1,075,533.00	☐	
S-1367	San Francisco	CA	332765	$1,876,432.00	☑	
S-2478	Los Angeles	CA	332765	$1,986,544.00	☐	
S-3366	San Diego	CA	332765	$2,577,684.00	☑	
*				$0.00	☐	

Four records added

Creating a Database

Edit Data in Datasheet View

Learning Outcomes
- Edit field values in Datasheet view
- Resize columns in Datasheet view

To keep a database current, you regularly need to add and delete records and make edits to individual fields. You can edit the data in a table in Datasheet view using the editing skills you learned for Word and Excel. To edit a field value, you need to select either the entire field value or the part of it you want to edit, then type the replacement data. As you make edits in a datasheet, you might find it helpful to resize columns to make the data easier to see. To resize a column to fit its contents, double-click the line between the column headings. To resize a column to a specific width, drag the line between the column headings to the desired width. **CASE** *A new regional manager, Juan Martinez, was just hired to manage the Midwest region. Also, Julie Marshall changed her last name. And the Prior Year Sales value for the Oakland store is incorrect. You need to edit records in both tables to reflect these changes.*

STEPS

1. **Click the Regional Managers table tab, click Lo in the second row, then press [F2]**

   Pressing [F2] selects the entire field value Lo, the last name of the current regional manager.

   > **QUICK TIP**
   > If you start editing a field and realize you want to keep the original entry, press [Esc] to undo the edit.

2. **Type Martinez, press [Enter], type Juan, press [Enter], type 5/1/2017, then press [Enter]**

   The text you typed replaced the original field values for the Last Name, First Name, and Date Hired fields for the second record. You can also edit text by selecting it and then typing new text.

3. **In the Last Name field for the first record, double-click Marshall, type Ross, then press [Enter]**

   See **FIGURE 10-17**. The field value in the Last Name field for the first record now reads Ross, reflecting the new last name of the Northeast regional manager. Using the [Backspace] key is another useful method for editing field values in a datasheet.

   > **QUICK TIP**
   > To move to the previous field in a datasheet, press [Shift][Tab].

4. **Click the Stores table tab, in the Prior Year Sales field for the first record click to the right of $1,075,533.00, press [Backspace] nine times, type 92445, then press [Enter]**

   The value in the Prior Year Sales field for the first record now reads $1,092,445.00.

   > **QUICK TIP**
   > You can also resize columns by dragging the column separator to the width you want.

5. **Point to the border between the Prior Year Sales and the Gold Star Status field names until the pointer changes to ↔ as shown in FIGURE 10-18, then double-click**

   The Prior Year Sales column widened just enough to fit the entire field name. The border between the field names that you clicked is called the **column separator**. Double-clicking the column separator automatically resizes a column to make it larger or smaller to fit the widest field name or field contents.

6. **Double-click the column separator between each of the field names in the field name row**

   Each column is now resized, as shown in **FIGURE 10-19**.

   > **QUICK TIP**
   > You can also save or close a table by right-clicking its tab, then clicking Save or Close.

7. **Save your changes to the Stores table, then click the close button ✕ for the Stores table**

   The Stores table closes.

8. **Save your changes to the Regional Managers table, then click the close button ✕ for the Regional Managers table**

   The Regional Managers table closes.

Printing objects in Access

If you want to print information from a database, you would usually create a report that includes selected fields, then print it. However, there might be times when you want to print a datasheet or form. To print any object in Access, select the object in the Navigation pane, click the File tab, then click Print. The Print page opens in Backstage view and displays three print options. Click Quick Print to print the object using default print settings. Click Print to open the Print dialog box, which lets you adjust print settings. Click Print Preview to preview the object with its default settings. In Print Preview, you can use the tools on the Print Preview tab to adjust settings, then click the Print button when you are ready to print.

FIGURE 10-17: Edited records in the Regional Managers Table in Datasheet view

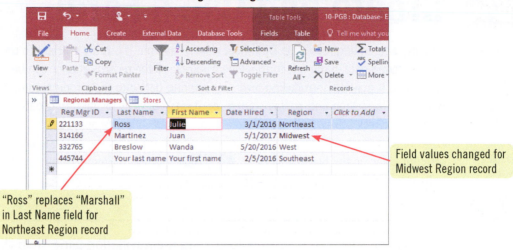

"Ross" replaces "Marshall" in Last Name field for Northeast Region record

Field values changed for Midwest Region record

FIGURE 10-18: Resizing a column in Datasheet view

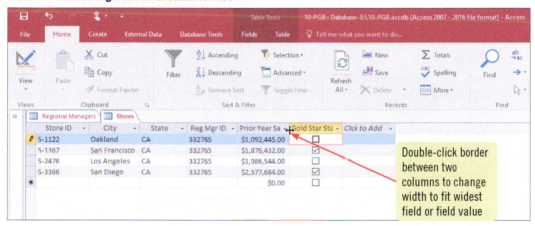

Double-click border between two columns to change width to fit widest field or field value

FIGURE 10-19: Edited records in the Stores Table in Datasheet view

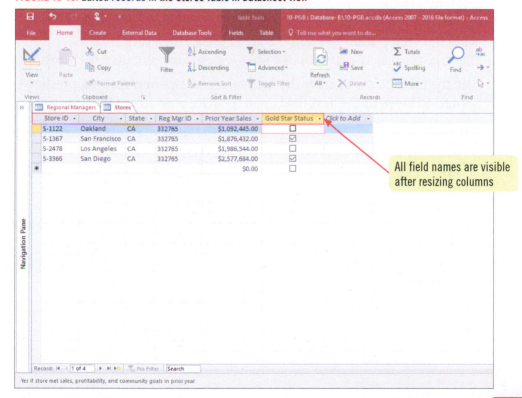

All field names are visible after resizing columns

Create and Use a Form

Entering and editing records in Datasheet view is easy, but it is more efficient to use a form. In Datasheet view, entering data in the grid format where you see all the records at once can be tedious and cause eye-strain, and it may risk introducing errors by entering data into the wrong record. A form usually displays one record at a time and contains **form controls**—devices for inputting data, such as text boxes, list arrows, or check boxes. You can create a form using a variety of approaches; the simplest is to click the Form button on the Create tab, which creates a form based on the open database table or the currently selected object in the Navigation pane. **CASE** ▶ *You need to create a form based on the Stores table, and enter records for some of the stores in the Northeast region.*

STEPS

1. **Click the Shutter Bar Open button ⯈⯈ in the Navigation pane, then click the Create tab**
   The Navigation pane is now open and lists the Regional Managers table and the Stores table. The Create tab allows you to add new objects to your database.

2. **Click the Stores table in the Navigation pane, then click the Form button in the Forms group**
   A new form based on the Stores table opens in Layout view, as shown in **FIGURE 10-20**. You use Layout view to change the structure of the form. The data for the first record (Oakland) is shown in the form. In Layout view, you can view records but cannot add, delete, or edit records. To view different records, you use the buttons on the **navigation bar**.

3. **Click the Next record button ▶ twice on the navigation bar**
   The record for Los Angeles (record 3 of 4) is now open.

4. **Click the Previous record button ◀ on the navigation bar**
   The record for San Francisco (record 2 of 4) is now open.

5. **Click the New (blank) record button ▶⁕ on the navigation bar**
   A blank form for a new record opens. To enter data in a form, you must switch to Form view.

6. **Click the View button arrow in the Views group, then click Form View**
   The form is now displayed in Form view, which you use to add, edit, and delete records.

7. **Use the table below to enter the field values for two new records, pressing [Tab] or [Enter] to move to the next field, then compare your screen to FIGURE 10-21**

Store ID	City	State	Reg Mgr ID	Prior Year Sales	Gold Star Status
S-4895	Philadelphia	PA	221133	$997,876	Yes
S-4975	Boston	MA	221133	$1,065,427	Yes

8. **Click the Save button 🖫 on the Quick Access toolbar, click OK in the Save As dialog box to save the form with the name Stores, then click the close button ✕ for the Stores table**
   The Stores form closes. You are now ready to close the 10-PGB database and exit Access.

9. **Click the File tab, click Close as shown in FIGURE 10-22, then click the Access window close button ✕**
   The PGB database and Access both close. Submit your database to your instructor.

FIGURE 10-20: New form in Layout view

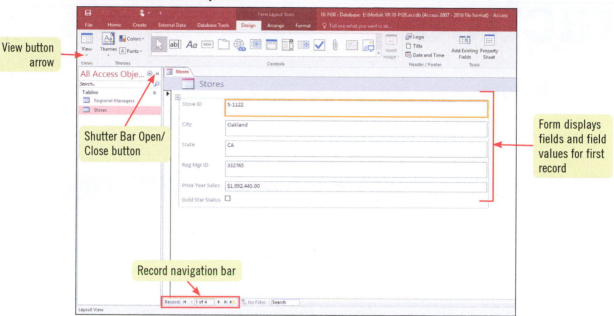

View button arrow

Shutter Bar Open/Close button

Form displays fields and field values for first record

Record navigation bar

FIGURE 10-21: New record added to the Stores table in Form view

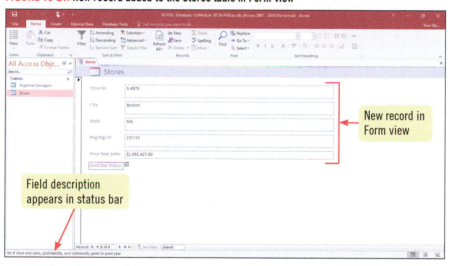

New record in Form view

Field description appears in status bar

FIGURE 10-22: Closing the database and exiting Access

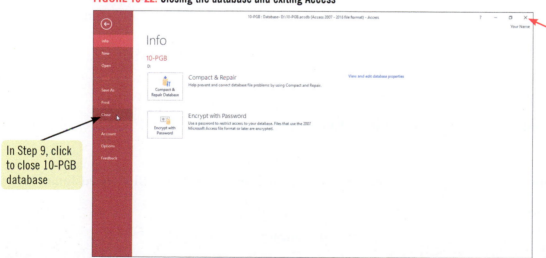

In Step 9, click to exit Access

In Step 9, click to close 10-PGB database

Practice

Concepts Review

Label the elements of the Access window shown in FIGURE 10-23.

FIGURE 10-23

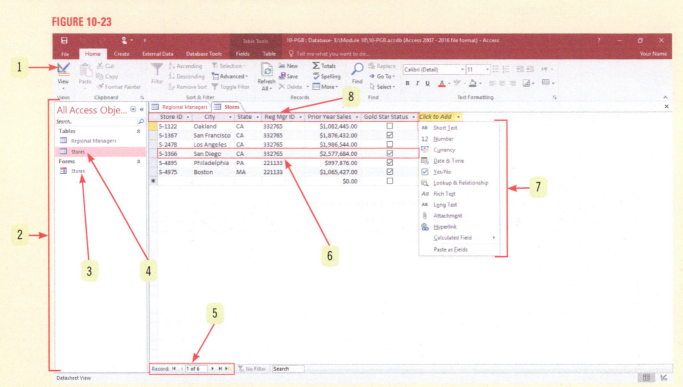

Match each term with the statement that best describes it.

9. **Database**
10. **Object**
11. **Form**
12. **Record**
13. **Table**
14. **Field**

a. One row of data in a database table
b. Information about one item in a particular record in a database
c. An app component, such as a table or form that is saved in a database
d. A collection of information organized in columns and rows and stored electronically in a file
e. An app component in a database that is used to store, view, enter, and edit data in a gridlike format
f. Window containing text boxes and labels used for entering data.

Select the best answer from the list of choices.

15. **Which of the following views can you use to add a description to a field?**
   a. Form Layout
   b. Table Design
   c. Form
   d. Form Design

16. **Which of the following data types would be most appropriate for a field that will store customer last names?**
   a. Long Text
   b. Short Text
   c. Yes/No
   d. Currency

17. Which of the following activities is NOT possible to do in Design view?

a. Add or edit a record.

c. Specify the data type for a field.

b. Edit a field name.

d. Specify a caption for a field.

18. In an Access table, one row of data is called a _____.

a. record

c. caption

b. field

d. property

19. In Datasheet view, the headings at the top of the table are called _____.

a. records

c. field names

b. queries

d. properties

20. Where does a field description appear in Form view?

a. Next to the field in the form window.

c. In the status bar.

b. In the record navigation bar.

d. In the Field Properties pane.

21. Which of the following is NOT a database object?

a. Query

c. Table

b. Field

d. Form

22. A form object is used primarily for which of the following tasks?

a. Viewing all table data at once.

c. Entering data.

b. Setting field properties.

d. Specifying field data types.

Skills Review

1. Understand databases.

a. Explain the purpose of Microsoft Access; what type of business tasks is it designed to perform?

b. Without referring to the lesson material, define database, table, fields, records, forms, reports, and queries.

c. What are the common database objects in Access? What is the purpose of each?

2. Create a database.

a. Start Access.

b. Create a new, blank desktop database with the name **10-Instrument Rentals**.

c. Save the new database where you store your Data Files.

3. Create a table in Datasheet view.

a. Save the blank table that is open in Datasheet view with the name **Instruments**.

b. Use a button on the Ribbon to change the data type of the ID field to Short Text.

c. Use the table below to add fields to the table.

Field name	Data Type
Instrument Type	Short Text
Rental Rate	Currency
Rent to Own	Yes/No
Data Entered By	Short Text

d. Save your changes to the table.

4. Create a table in Design view.

a. Create a new table, and save it as **Rental Orders**.

b. View the Rental Orders table in Design view, then change the name of the ID field name to **Rental ID**. Change the data type for the Rental ID field to Short Text.

    c. Use the table below to add fields to the Rental Orders table.

Field Name	Data Type
Rental Date	Date/Time
Customer Last Name	Short Text
Customer First Name	Short Text
Instrument ID	Short Text
Months Committed	Number
Data Entered By	Short Text

    d. Save your changes to the table.

5. Modify a table and set properties.

    a. Open the Instruments table in Design view, then change the ID field name to **Instrument ID**.

    b. Change the Field Size property for the Instrument ID field to **5**.

    c. Add a new field between Instrument Type and Rental Rate. Rename the new field **Date Purchased**, and apply the Date/Time data type to it.

    d. Add the following description to the Rental Rate field: **Rental rate is for one month of use**.

    e. Change the Caption property for the Rental Rate field to **Rate**.

    f. Add the following description to the Rent to Own field: **Specify Yes if allowable for customer to apply monthly payments toward purchase**.

    g. Save your changes to the table.

6. Enter data in a table.

    a. View the Instruments table in Datasheet view.

    b. Using the table below, enter the three records shown into the Instruments table in Datasheet view, then save the Instruments table. (*Note:* Enter your name in each Data Entered By field.)

Instrument ID	Instrument Type	Date Purchased	Rate	Rent to Own	Data Entered By
11226	Saxophone	1/7/2017	$50.00	Yes	Your Name
77643	Trombone	1/15/2016	$40.00	Yes	Your Name
88543	Cello	1/25/2016	$75.00		Your Name

    c. View the Rental Orders table in Datasheet view.

    d. Using the table below, enter the three records shown into the Rental Orders table in Datasheet view.

Rental ID	Rental Date	Customer Last Name	Customer First Name	Instrument ID	Months Committed	Data Entered By
R-2255	8/1/2017	Martin	Howard	11226	12	Your Name
R-2256	9/2/2017	Gupta	Pradeep	45612	9	Your Name
R-2578	9/3/2017	Lim	Molly	33511	10	Your Name

    e. Save your changes to the Rental Orders table.

7. Edit data in Datasheet view.

    a. In the Instruments table, change the Rate field value for the Trombone to **$50.00**.

    b. In the Instruments table, edit the Instruments Type field value for the Saxophone so it reads **Tenor Saxophone**.

Skills Review (continued)

c. Adjust all the column widths in the Instruments table datasheet for best fit, save your changes to the table, then compare it to **FIGURE 10-24**.

FIGURE 10-24

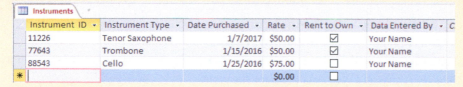

Instrument ID	Instrument Type	Date Purchased	Rate	Rent to Own	Data Entered By	C
11226	Tenor Saxophone	1/7/2017	$50.00	☑	Your Name	
77643	Trombone	1/15/2016	$50.00	☑	Your Name	
88543	Cello	1/25/2016	$75.00	☐	Your Name	
*			$0.00	☐		

d. In the Rental Orders table, in the third record, change the Months Committed field value to **6**.

e. Adjust all the column widths in the Rental Orders table datasheet for best fit.

f. Save your changes to the Rental Orders table, then compare it to **FIGURE 10-25**.

FIGURE 10-25

Rental ID	Rental Date	Customer Last Name	Customer First Name	Instrument ID	Months Committed	Data Entered By
R-2255	8/1/2017	Martin	Howard	11226	12	Your Name
R-2256	9/2/2017	Gupta	Pradeep	45612	9	Your Name
R-2578	9/3/2017	Lim	Molly	33511	6	Your Name
*					0	

8. Create and use a form.

a. Create a new form based on the Instruments table.

b. In Layout view, view each record one by one using the Previous and/or Next buttons on the navigation bar.

c. Switch to Form view, then add a new record using the information in the table below:

Instrument ID	Instrument Type	Date Purchased	Rate	Rent to Own	Data Entered By
89622	Upright Piano	6/26/2016	$60.00	Yes	Your Name

d. Save the form as **Instruments**, then compare your screen to **FIGURE 10-26**.

FIGURE 10-26

e. Close the database, then exit Access.

f. Submit your completed database to your instructor.

Independent Challenge 1

You own and run a photo agency. Clients call you when they need a photographer for a variety of needs, such as a wedding, sporting event, or if they need a headshot or a photo of their child or pet. Your job is to book appropriate photographers for each need. You also sell the work of the photographers you represent. You need to create a database to manage all this information. Your database needs to contain a table that includes information about each photographer and a table that keeps track of photographs.

a. Create a new, blank desktop database named **10-Photo Agency** where you store your Data Files.

b. Save the blank table that appears in Datasheet view as **Photographs**.

c. View the table in Design view. Change the ID field name to **Photo ID**, and keep its data type as AutoNumber. Use the table below to enter the field names and their data types for the table.

Field	Data Type
Photo Description	Short Text
Date Taken	Date/Time
Price for single use	Currency
Photographer Last Name	Short Text
Data Entered By	Short Text

d. Save your changes. Create a new table, save it as **Photographers**, then enter the following fields into it in Design view. (For the Photographer ID field, replace the ID field.)

Field Name	Data Type
Photographer ID	AutoNumber
Photographer Last Name	Short Text
Photographer First Name	Short Text
Photographer Phone	Short Text
Uses Subcontractors	Yes/No
Photographer City	Short text
Photographer State	Short text
Data Entered By	Short text

e. Add the following field description to the Uses Subcontractors field: **Yes if photographer works with other photographers**.

f. Specify the Field Size property for the Photographer State field to **2**. For the Photographer Last Name field, specify the caption as **Last Name**. For the Photographer First Name field, specify the caption as **First Name**. Save your changes.

g. View the Photographers table in Datasheet view, then enter the records shown below into it. (*Hint*: Press [Tab] to accept the AutoNumber in the Photographer ID field.)

Photographer ID	Last Name	First Name	Photographer Phone	Uses Subcontractors	Photographer City	Photographer State	Data Entered By
1	Chung	Rayleen	(773)555-2332	Yes	St. Louis	MO	Your name
2	Radcliffe	Dexter	(773)555-3477	No	Chicago	IL	Your name
3	Moore	Deion	(773)555-7566	Yes	Boston	MA	Your name

h. View the Photographs table in Datasheet view, then enter the records shown below into it.

Photo ID	Photo Description	Date Taken	Price for Single Use	Photographer Last Name	Data Entered By
1	Boys playing soccer	4/5/17	$1,500	Chung	Your name
2	Aerial view of Chicago	5/7/17	$750	Radcliffe	Your name
3	Boston at night	6/1/17	$450	Moore	Your name

Independent Challenge 1 (continued)

i. In the record for Rayleen Chung, change the Photographer City field value to **Madison** and the Photographer State field value to **WI**. Adjust the column widths in the datasheet for best fit. Compare your datasheet to FIGURE 10-27, then save and close the table.

FIGURE 10-27

Photographer ID	Last Name	First Name	Photographer Phone	Uses Subcontractors	Photgrapher City	Photographer State	Data Entered By
1	Chung	Rayleen	(773)555-2332	☑	Madison	WI	Your Name
2	Radcliffe	Dexter	(773)555-3477	☐	Chicago	IL	Your Name
3	Moore	Deion	(773)555-7566	☑	Boston	MA	Your Name
(New)				☐			

j. Create a form based on the Photographs table, then save the form as **Photographs Form**. View each record using the record navigation bar.

k. Switch to Form view, than add the following record:

Photo ID	Photo Description	Date Taken	Price for Single Use	Photographer Last Name	Data Entered By
4	Children playing on beach	6/26/17	$750	Moore	Your Name

l. Close all open objects and close the database, then exit Access. Submit your completed database to your instructor.

Independent Challenge 2

You provide administrative help to the owners of The Windy Bluff Inn, a family-owned and operated bed and breakfast on an island off the coast of Rhode Island. Olivia Griswold, one of the owners, has asked you to create a database to store and track information about the inn. To start off, you decide to create a table to track information about each room.

a. Create a new, blank database with the name **10-Windy Bluff Inn**, and save it where you store your Data Files.

b. Save the blank new table as **Rooms**. Switch to Design view, then rename the ID field **Room ID**. Change the data type for the Room ID field to Short Text. Then, enter the fields and data types shown in the table below.

Field Name	Data Type
Room Name	Short Text
Room Type	Short Text
Rental Rate	Currency
Times Rented	Number
Bed Size	Short Text
Ocean View	Yes/No
Data Entered By	Short Text

c. Add the following description to the Rental Rate field: **Rate is 25% higher during first week of July**. Add the following description to the Ocean View field: **Yes if room faces south**.

d. Set the Caption property for the Rental Rate field to **Rate**. For the Room ID field, set the Field Size property to **5**. Save your changes to the Rooms table, then close it.

e. Create a form based on the Rooms table using the Form tool. Click the Themes button arrow, then click the Wisp theme thumbnail.

Independent Challenge 2 (continued)

f. Save the form as **Rooms**, then switch to Form view.

g. Add the following records to the form:

Room ID	Room Name	Room Type	Rate	Times Rented	Bed Size	Ocean View	Data Entered By
11267	Robin's Nest	Studio	$169.00	42	Queen	No	Your Name
22558	Honeymoon Hideaway	Deluxe	$219.00	61	King	Yes	Your Name
33567	Bay Suite	Deluxe	$219.00	85	King	Yes	Your Name

h. Save and close the form. Open the Rooms table in Datasheet view. Change the Room Name field value for Robin's Nest so it reads **The Robin's Nest**. Resize all the column widths of the table for best fit. Compare your finished datasheet to FIGURE 10-28.

i. Close the database, then exit Access. Submit your completed database to your instructor.

FIGURE 10-28

Rooms

Room ID	Room Name	Room Type	Rate	Times Rented	Bed Size	Ocean View	Data Entered By
11267	The Robin's Nest	Studio	$169.00	42	Queen	☐	Your Name
22558	Honeymoon Hideaway	Deluxe	$219.00	61	King	☑	Your Name
33567	Bay Suite	Deluxe	$219.00	85	King	☑	Your Name
*			$0.00	0		☐	

Independent Challenge 3

As part of a marketing strategy at the Twirl Dance Academy you decide to create a database that contains names, addresses, and other information about people who have participated in your classes. You will use the database to promote future classes.

a. Create a new, blank database named **10-Dance Academy**, and save it where you store your Data Files.

b. Save the blank open table as **Students**, then switch to Design view.

c. Use Design view to design your table. Keep the ID field name and data type the same, and keep it as the primary key field.

d. Add at least seven fields that seem appropriate for this type of database. Of those fields, you must include **Last Name** and **First Name**. Include at least one field with a Date/Time data type and at least one with a Yes/No data type.

e. If your first seven fields do not include one, add a field called **Data Entered By** that has the Short Text data type.

f. Add at least one description for one of the fields.

g. Save the table.

h. View the table in Datasheet view. Resize all columns for best fit. Close the table.

i. Use the Form tool to create a form based on the Students table. In Layout view, apply a theme that you like, then save the form with the name **Students**.

j. Switch to Form view, then add three fictional records. Enter your name in the Data Entered By field. Save and close the form and table.

k. Close the database, then exit Access. Submit your completed database to your instructor.

Independent Challenge 4: Explore

Access comes with a number of ready-made templates that you can use to organize specific types of projects or information. For instance, there is an asset tracking template you can use to keep track of business or personal inventory, and there is a task management template you can use to keep track of projects. In this Independent Challenge, you will use an Access template to track your contacts. *Note:* To complete this Independent Challenge, your computer must be connected to the Internet.

a. Start Access.

b. On the Start screen, locate the Contacts template. (Note that the word "Updated" before a template name means Microsoft has recently updated the template.) Click the template, then create the database. Save the database as **10-Contacts** in the location where you store your Data Files.

c. Notice the security warning below the Ribbon. Since this database is one that you downloaded from Microsoft you can feel confident that it is safe to use. Click Enable Content. If the Welcome to the Contacts Database window opens, take a few minutes to watch the video that teaches how to use the Contacts Management database. When you have finished watching the video, close the video window, click the Access icon on the taskbar to return to the Access program window, then click the Get Started button.

d. Look at the Navigation pane; notice that there are two tables (Contacts, Settings), and three forms (Contact Details, Contact List, and Welcome). There are also Queries and Reports (which you will learn about in later modules), as well as Macros and Modules.

e. Notice that the Contact List form is open now. This form looks more like a table, but you can tell it is a form because of the form icon in the tab and because the name Contact List appears under Forms in the Navigation pane.

f. Click New in the first row of the form to open a Contact Details window. Enter the information for Jack Wilson shown in FIGURE 10-29, into the appropriate fields. Enter the phone number into the Business Phone field. Click the Category list arrow, then click Business. (*Note:* You will need to leave some of the fields blank, since the figure shows information only for selected fields.)

FIGURE 10-29

```
Jack Wilson, Account Manager
Power Spoon Corporate Catering
55 West Elm Street
Ridgewood, NJ 07450
(773)555-7777
jack@powerspooncatering.com
```

g. Click Save and New to move to a new blank record, then enter the information for Ellen Weintraub, shown in FIGURE 10-30. Notice that when you type the first letter of Power Spoon Corporate Catering in the Company field, the full name of the company is automatically entered. Access "guesses" that you want to enter the name of the company from an existing contact. For the Category field, choose Business.

FIGURE 10-30

```
Ellen Weintraub, Owner
Power Spoon Corporate Catering
55 West Elm Street
Ridgewood, NJ 07450
(773)555-7778
ellen@powerspooncatering.com
```

h. Click Save and New, then enter one more contact record. For this record, enter your first name and your last name. Populate the other fields for this contact using the other field values for Ellen Weintraub or Jack Wilson (your choice). For the email address, enter your first name@powerspooncatering.com (use your first name, followed by "@powerspooncatering.com"). Save and close the Contact Details form and the Contact List form.

i. Double-click Directory in the Navigation pane. The Directory report opens and lists the three contact names you entered in an easy-to-reference report format. Open the Phone Book report; notice that this report shows only the names and phone numbers of Jack, Ellen, and you. Close the Phone Book report and the Directory report.

j. Close the database and exit Access. Submit your completed database to your instructor.

Visual Workshop

Create the database form shown in **FIGURE 10-31**. (*Hint*: First create a new, blank database called **10-Antiques Business** where you store your Data Files, then create the table and form shown in the figure. Assign appropriate data types for each field in the table. Set the Field Size property to **4** for the Est'd Year Made field. Enter the data shown in the figure into the form. Save and close the form, close the database, then exit Access. Submit your completed database to your instructor.

FIGURE 10-31

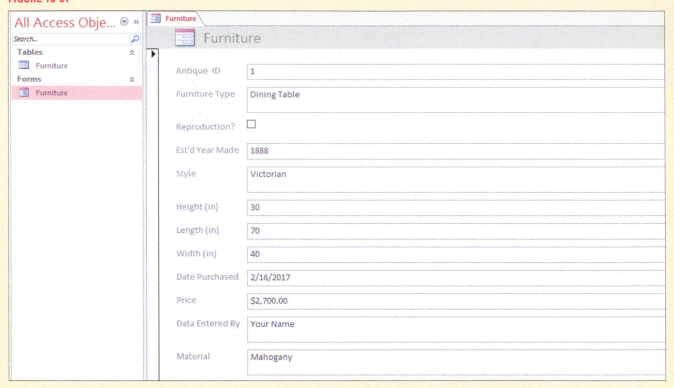

Working with Data

CASE David LeBlanc, vice president of merchandising at Pepper's Green Basket, has given you a database that contains two tables. He asks you to sort and filter the data so that it is more useful. He also needs you to retrieve some information from these tables by using queries. Finally, he wants you to add a calculated field to one of the tables.

Module Objectives

After completing this module, you will be able to:

- Open an existing database
- Sort records in a table
- Filter records in a table
- Create a query
- Modify a query in Design view
- Relate two tables
- Create a query using two tables
- Add a calculated field to a table

Files You Will Need

11-1.accdb	11-5.accdb
11-2.accdb	11-6.accdb
11-3.accdb	11-6a.docx
11-4.accdb	11-7.accdb

Open an Existing Database

**Learning
Outcomes**
• Open a database
• Enable content in
 a database
• Save a database
 with a new name

After you enter data into a database, you can pull out information you need by filtering and querying the data and by sorting it in useful ways. In this module, you will work with an existing database that contains two tables. First you need to open it. Opening an existing Access database is similar to opening a Word or Excel file. From the Access Start screen, you click the Open Other Files command to open the Open screen, navigate to the folder where the file is located, then double-click the file you want. (If you worked with the file recently, you can click its name in the Recent list in the Start screen.) One difference between opening an Access database and opening a file in Word or Excel is that you can only open one Access database file at a time. If you want two databases open at once, you need to start an additional session of Access, then open the additional database in that second session. **CASE** ▶ *To get started on your project for David, you decide to open the database and then save it with a new name, so the original database will remain intact. Then, you decide to view the tables it contains in Datasheet view.*

STEPS

1. **Start Access**

   The Access Start screen is displayed on your screen.

2. **Click Open Other Files at the bottom of the Recent list on the Start screen**

   The Open screen opens in Backstage view and displays a list of recently opened files.

3. **Click Browse to open the Open dialog box, navigate to the drive and folder where you store your Data Files, click 11-1.accdb, then click Open**

   The database opens, as shown in **FIGURE 11-1**, displaying the Security Warning in the yellow bar. Unless you change the standard default settings in Access, this security warning appears any time you open an existing database.

4. **Click the File tab, then click Save As**

   The Save As screen opens. Notice that Save Database As is selected in the File Types section and that Access Database (*.accdb) is selected in the Save Database As section. See **FIGURE 11-2**. These settings are appropriate; you want to save the file as an Access database file.

QUICK TIP
When you save to a
network location,
Access allows you to
make it a trusted
location; clicking No
means you may need
to enable the content
again in the future;
clicking Yes means
you won't need to
do so, as long as the
database remains in
the trusted location.

5. **Click Save As**

   The Save As dialog box opens.

6. **Type 11-PGB in the File name text box, navigate to the folder where you save your Data Files, if necessary, then click Save**

   The copy of the database opens with the new name 11-PGB.accdb. The Security Warning appears below the Ribbon again, as Access recognizes this is a database file you have not opened before.

7. **Click Enable Content in the Security Warning bar, click Yes to make this a trusted document if necessary, then double-click the Products table in the Navigation pane**

   The Products table opens in Datasheet view, as shown in **FIGURE 11-3**. You can see in the navigation bar at the bottom of the screen that this table contains 182 records.

TROUBLE
If your Navigation
pane is closed, click
the pane's Shutter
Bar Open button
⟩⟩ to open it.

8. **Double-click the Suppliers table in the Navigation pane**

   A new tab opens in the database window and displays the Suppliers table, as shown in **FIGURE 11-4**. This table has only eight records (one for each supplier) and contains eight fields (Supplier ID, Supplier, Contact Last Name, Contact First Name, Address, City, State, and Zip). Note that the Supplier ID is the primary key field. You will use this table later in the module, but you do not need it now.

9. **Click the Suppliers table Close button ☒ in the database window**

FIGURE 11-1: Database open with Security Warning

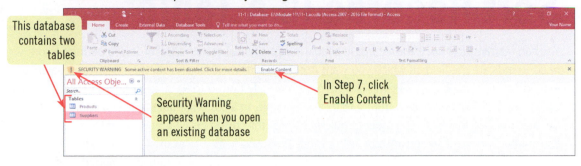

This database contains two tables

Security Warning appears when you open an existing database

In Step 7, click Enable Content

FIGURE 11-2: Save As screen

FIGURE 11-3: Products table in Datasheet view

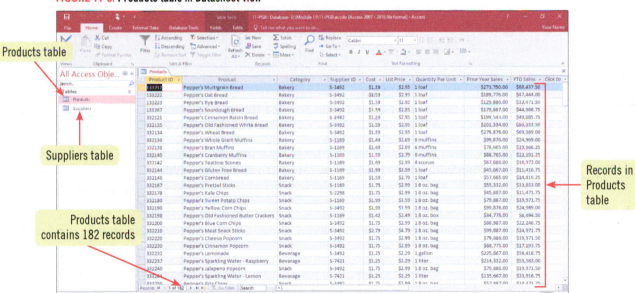

Products table

Suppliers table

Products table contains 182 records

Records in Products table

FIGURE 11-4: Suppliers table in Datasheet view

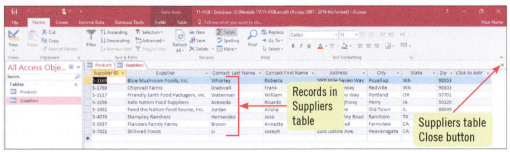

Records in Suppliers table

Suppliers table Close button

Sort Records in a Table

Learning Outcomes
- Sort records in ascending or descending order
- Sort records by two different fields
- Remove a sort order setting

You can rearrange, or **sort**, the records in a table in alphabetical or numerical order. To perform a sort, you need to indicate the field on which you want Access to sort, then specify whether to sort the database in ascending order (alphabetically from A to Z or numerically from 0 to 9) or descending order (alphabetically from Z to A or numerically from 9 to 0). For example, in a customer database, you could sort records by the Sales field in descending order to quickly identify the customers who purchased the most products. You might also want to sort records using more than one field. For example, you might wish to sort primarily by state but also by customer name, so that the records for each state are grouped together, with customers listed in alphabetical order within each state grouping. **CASE** *David asks you to create a sorted list that groups the records first by Category and then, within each Category grouping, by YTD Sales in descending order. First, you experiment with sorting in different ways.*

STEPS

1. **Click the Shutter Bar Close button ⌧ in the Navigation pane**

   The database window now displays the Customers table with all its fields in view. Just to experiment, you decide to sort the table in ascending order by product name.

2. **Click any value in the Product column**

   Before performing a sort, you need to select the field by which you want to sort.

3. **Click the Ascending button in the Sort & Filter group on the Home tab**

   The table is now sorted by product name in ascending alphabetical order, with Alaskan Cod Fillet listed first. Notice there is a small upward-pointing arrow to the right of the Product column header, indicating that the table is sorted in ascending order by this field, as shown in **FIGURE 11-5**.

   > **QUICK TIP**
   > If you select two columns in a table, click either the Ascending or the Descending button—Access will first sort the records in the left column, then sort the records in the right column.

4. **Click the Descending button in the Sort & Filter group on the Home tab**

   The table is now sorted by product name in descending alphabetical order (Z to A), with Yellow Onion listed first. Notice the downward-pointing arrow in the Product column heading, indicating the records in the table are sorted in descending order by this field.

5. **Click the Remove Sort button in the Sort & Filter group**

   The table is now ordered in its original order, with Pepper's Multigrain Bread listed first in the Product column.

6. **Click any value in the YTD Sales column, click the Descending button in the Sort & Filter group, then widen the column if necessary to see all the values**

   The records are now sorted in descending order by year-to-date sales amounts. You see that Grass Fed Ground Beef has sold the most this year, with $1,385,830.00 in the YTD Sales field.

   > **QUICK TIP**
   > To capture a screenshot of your sorted table after Step 7, follow the instructions in the yellow box below.

7. **Click any value in the Category column, then click the Ascending button in the Sort & Filter group**

   The records in the Products table are now sorted first by Category in ascending order and then, within each Category grouping, by YTD Sales amounts in descending order, as shown in **FIGURE 11-6**.

8. **Click the Remove Sort button in the Sort & Filter group**

   The table reverts to its original order.

Capturing a screenshot of your sorted table

Your instructor might ask you to capture a screenshot of the sorted Products table and submit it. To do this, start Microsoft Word, open a new blank document, click the Insert tab, click the Screenshot button, then click the image of the Access window in the Available Windows menu. The screenshot of your sorted table is pasted into the new Word document. Save this document as Module 11-Screenshot, and submit it to your instructor. Click the Access program button on the taskbar to return to Access.

FIGURE 11-5: Products table in alphabetical order by product

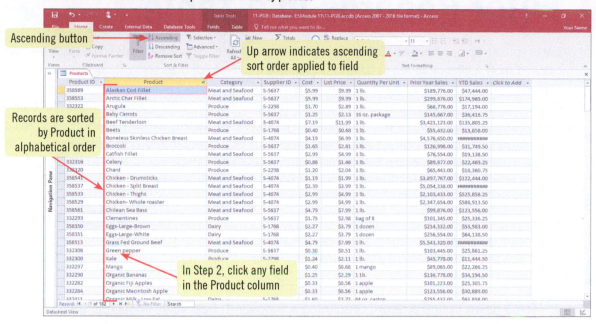

Ascending button

Up arrow indicates ascending sort order applied to field

Records are sorted by Product in alphabetical order

In Step 2, click any field in the Product column

FIGURE 11-6: Records sorted by two different fields

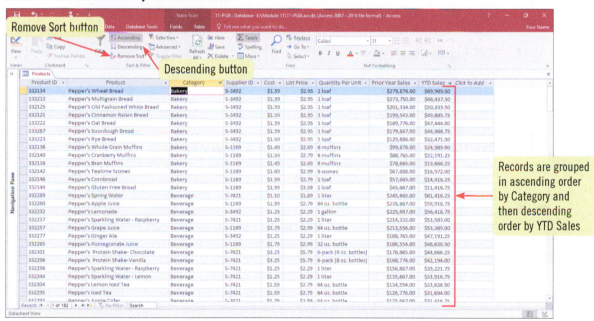

Remove Sort button

Descending button

Records are grouped in ascending order by Category and then descending order by YTD Sales

Access 2016

Sorting on multiple fields

Before you sort records in a table by two different fields, you first need to decide which field you want to be the primary sort field and which field you want to be sorted within the primary field grouping. The field that is the primary sort field is called the outermost sort field, and the field that is the secondary sort field is called the innermost sort field. For example, in **FIGURE 11-6**, the Category field is the outermost sort field, and the YTD Sales field is the innermost sort field; the records are first sorted by Category in ascending order, then by YTD Sales in descending order. Ironically, to get the results you want, you need to first sort the records by the innermost field and then sort by the outermost field. This may be counterintuitive; thus, it is important that you understand these rules before you sort on two fields.

Filter Records in a Table

Learning Outcomes
- Filter a table by selection
- Toggle a filter to remove it and reapply it
- Apply a number filter

Just as you can apply a filter to an Excel worksheet to display only the information that you want to see, you can also apply a filter to an Access table to display only those records that meet criteria that you specify. **Criteria** are conditions that must be met for a record to be displayed. For example, you might want to filter a database to see only the records for customers who are located in New York, or only for customers who made a purchase within the past 6 months. The simplest way to filter a table is to select a field value that matches your criterion (for instance, a State field value of NY), and then use the Equals command to display those records that match the selection. You can also apply a Number Filter to a selected field to filter records that are greater than, less than, or equal to a specific number, or between two different numbers. You cannot save a filter as a database object, but you can save it as part of the table or form you are working on and reapply it the next time. You can also print the results of a filter. **CASE** *David needs you to identify customers whose prior year sales were greater than $100,000 for supplier Chipwell Farms. You decide to apply filters to display records that meet these criteria.*

STEPS

1. **Scroll down to find a record containing a Supplier ID field value of S-1768, then click any value of S-1768**

   This Supplier ID number (S-1768) is the ID number for Chipwell Farms.

2. **Click the Selection button in the Sort & Filter group**

   The Selection menu opens and displays four commands. These commands let you filter records that are equal or not equal to the selected field value, or that do or do not contain the selected value.

3. **Click Equals "S-1768"**

   Twenty-seven records containing S-1768 in the Supplier ID field appear in the datasheet window, as shown in **FIGURE 11-7**. These records are all products that were produced and distributed by Chipwell Farms. Notice that a filter icon appears to the right of the Supplier ID column heading, indicating that a filter is applied to this field.

4. **Click the Toggle Filter button in the Sort & Filter group**

   The filter is removed, and all the records in the table appear again. Clicking the Toggle Filter button once removes the filter; clicking it again reapplies it.

QUICK TIP

When a filter is applied to a table, the word "Filtered" appears in the record navigation bar; when you click the Toggle Filter button, the navigation bar displays "Unfiltered." If no filter is applied, the navigation bar displays "Unfiltered."

5. **Click the Toggle Filter button**

   The filter is reapplied, so that only the 27 product records for supplier S-1768 (Chipwell Farms) appear.

6. **Click any value in the Prior Year Sales field, then click the Filter button in the Sort & Filter group**

   The Filter menu opens and displays commands for filtering and sorting records specific to the Prior Year Sales field. The bottom of the list displays all the specific values for the Prior Year Sales field, with check boxes next to each. To show only records with one of these specific values, you can click the check box next to that value. You want to display records that are greater than $100,000 so you need to use a Number Filter command.

QUICK TIP

To capture a screenshot of your filtered table after Step 7, follow the steps in the yellow box in the previous lesson.

7. **Point to Number Filters in the Filter list, click Greater Than, type 100,000 in the Custom Filter dialog box, compare your screen to FIGURE 11-8, then click OK**

   The filtered list now shows fifteen records, with two filter criteria applied. All the records contain S-1768 in the Supplier ID field, and all the values in the Prior Year Sales field are greater than $100,000, as shown in **FIGURE 11-9**.

8. **Click the Toggle Filter button, then save your changes**

   The filter is removed, and your changes are saved.

Working with Data

FIGURE 11-7: Filtered Customers table with one filter applied

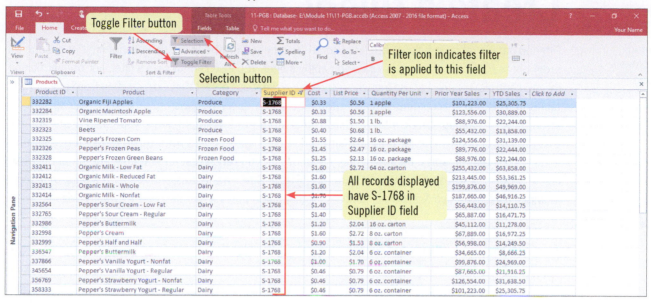

FIGURE 11-8: Custom Filter dialog box

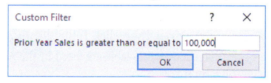

FIGURE 11-9: Products datasheet with two filters applied

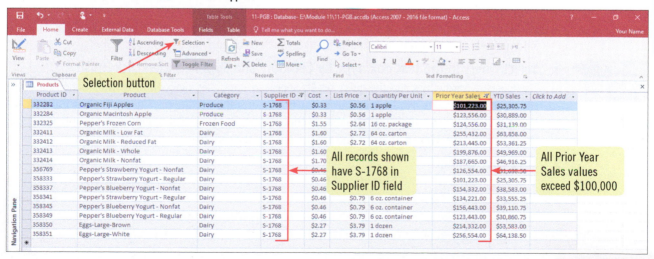

Create a Query

Filtering data in tables is helpful, but it has some limitations. For one thing, you cannot limit or change the order of the fields Access displays when you apply a filter. You also cannot save a filter. For greater flexibility and control, you need to use a query. A **query** is a database object that extracts data from one or more tables in a database according to criteria that you set. A query displays only the fields you specify. For instance, in a database that contains 10 fields that store product information, you could create a query that displays only the fields for product names and prices. You can also use a query to pull together information from several tables. Because a query is an object, you can save it for later use. The simplest way to create a query is to use the Query Wizard. **CASE** ▶ *David wants to see a view of the data that shows products, categories, and Supplier ID numbers. To accomplish this, you decide to use the Query Wizard.*

STEPS

1. **Click the Products table Close button ☒ in the database window, then click the Shutter Bar Open button »**

   You need to close a table before creating a query that is based on it. The Navigation pane is now open.

2. **Click the Create tab, then click the Query Wizard button in the Queries group**

   The New Query dialog box opens, as shown in **FIGURE 11-10**, where you select the type of Query Wizard you want to use. By default, Simple Query Wizard is selected. This wizard creates a **select query**, a query that retrieves or selects data from one or more tables or queries according to your criteria. This is the most commonly used type of query and is the one you want to create.

3. **Click OK**

   The Simple Query Wizard dialog box opens. First you need to specify the table or query from which you want to select fields for your query.

4. **Click the Table/Queries list arrow, then click Table: Products**

   Notice that all the fields from the Products table are listed in the Available Fields list. You now need to choose the fields you want from this list.

5. **Click Product in the Available Fields list, then click the Select Single Field button >**

   The Product field moves to the Selected Fields list. You can move fields back and forth between the Available Fields list and the Selected Fields list using the buttons shown in **TABLE 11-1**.

6. **Click Category if necessary to select it, click >, click Supplier ID if necessary, then click >**

   Now the Product, Category, and Supplier ID fields are listed in the Selected Fields area, as shown in **FIGURE 11-11**.

7. **Click Next**

   In this dialog box, you specify a name for the query. Unless you specify otherwise, the Query Wizard will automatically name the query "Products Query", which is currently in the text box.

8. **Select Query in the text box, type by Category and Supplier, then click Finish**

   The Query Wizard closes and the query results appear in Datasheet view, showing the Product, Category, and Supplier ID fields. Notice that the Products by Category and Supplier query is now listed in the Navigation pane below the Suppliers table, as shown in **FIGURE 11-12**. This query contains only fields that David needs to see. He can now sort and apply filters to the query to get just the information he needs.

9. **Save your changes**

FIGURE 11-10: New Query dialog box

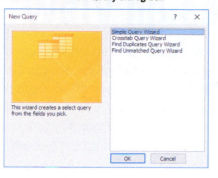

FIGURE 11-11: Specifying a table and fields for a simple query

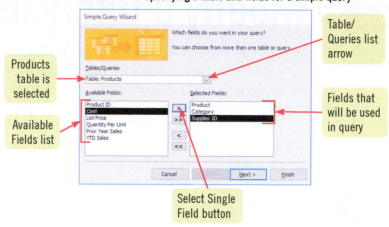

FIGURE 11-12: Products by Category and Supplier query results

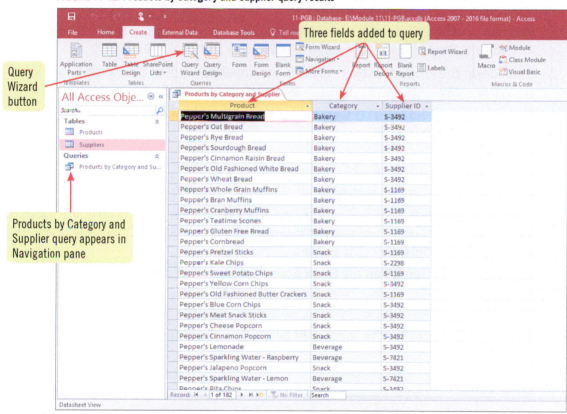

TABLE 11-1: Select Field buttons in Query Wizard

button	use to
>	Move a single field to the Selected Fields area
>>	Move all available fields to the Selected Fields area
<	Remove a single field from the Selected Fields area and restore it to the Available Fields list
<<	Remove all fields from the Selected Fields area and restore them to the Available Fields list

Modify a Query in Design View

You can modify an existing query if you need to make changes to it using Design view. In Design view, you can add or delete fields, specify a sort order for one or more fields, or specify criteria for fields. You can also use Design view instead of Query Wizard to create a query. **CASE** *David asks you to modify the Products by Category and Supplier query so it includes the YTD Sales field. He also wants the results to be sorted by YTD Sales in descending order. In addition, he wants you to create another query based on the Products by Category and Supplier query that displays products produced by one of the suppliers. You decide to create this new query in Design view.*

STEPS

1. **Click the Home tab, then click the View button in the Views group**

   The database window displays the Products by Category and Supplier query in Design view, and the Query Tools Design tab is active. In Design view, the database window is divided into two panes. The upper pane displays the Products table field list. The lower pane is the query design grid. You use the cells in this grid to specify fields and their criteria for the current query. The query design grid currently contains the three fields in the Products by Category and Supplier query (Product, Category, and Supplier ID).

2. **Scroll down the Products table field list in the upper pane, then double-click YTD Sales**

   The YTD Sales field is now added to the query design grid and appears in the fourth column.

3. **Click the Sort cell for the YTD Sales field in the query design grid, click the Sort list arrow, then click Descending**

   See **FIGURE 11-13**.

4. **Click the View button in the Results group, then widen the YTD Sales column, if necessary, so that all data is visible**

   The query results appear in Datasheet view, and the records are sorted by the YTD Sales field in descending order. As you modify a query, it is convenient to switch back and forth between Design view and Datasheet view to see the modified query results, as shown in **FIGURE 11-14**.

5. **Click the Save button 🔲 on the Quick Access Toolbar, then click the View button in the Views group**

   The changes you made to the query are saved, and the query appears in Design view.

6. **Click the Criteria cell for the Supplier ID field in the query design grid, type S-1169, then press [Enter]**

   After you press [Enter], quotation marks appear around your entry. The criteria "S-1169" specifies that the query results should only display records that contain the characters "S-1169" in the Supplier field.

7. **Click the View button in the Results group**

   The query results appear in Datasheet view, as shown in **FIGURE 11-15**. The results show fifteen records that contain "S-1169" in the Supplier field. The records are sorted in descending order by YTD Sales.

8. **Click the File tab, click Save As, click Save Object As, click Save As, type Blue Mushroom Foods Products in the Save 'Products by Category and Supplier' to text box in the Save As dialog box, then click OK**

   The modified query is saved as Blue Mushrooms Foods Products and appears in the Navigation pane.

9. **Click the Close 'Blue Mushroom Foods Products' button ⊠**

   The Blue Mushroom Foods Products query closes.

FIGURE 11-13: Adding a field to the Products by Category and Supplier query in Design view

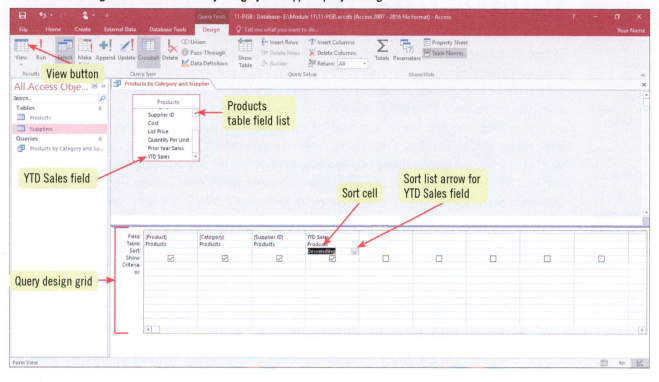

FIGURE 11-14: Modified Products by Category and Supplier query results in Datasheet view

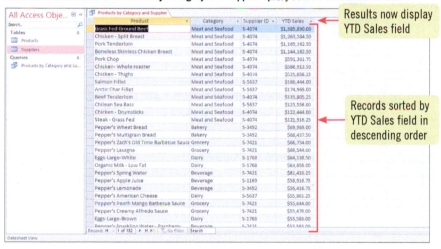

FIGURE 11-15: Modified query in Datasheet view

Relate Two Tables

To take advantage of the full power of Access, you can create queries that pull fields from more than one table. For instance, the query you created in the previous lesson pulls from a single table, the Products table, but it might be helpful to also include the Contact Last Name field, which is in the Suppliers table. This is possible if you first **relate** the two tables, or specify a relationship between them. To do so, your tables must share a common field, and that shared field must be the primary key field in one of the tables. You use the Relationships window to specify a relationship between two or more tables. The most common type of relationship to set up is a **one-to-many relationship**, in which the primary key field in one table is associated with multiple records in a second table. **CASE** *You need to specify a one-to-many relationship between the Suppliers table and the Products table so you can create queries that pull fields from both tables.*

STEPS

1. **Click the Database Tools tab, then click the Relationships button in the Relationships group**

   The Relationships window opens. To set up relationships, you first need to choose the tables you want to relate. Notice the Show Table dialog box shown in **FIGURE 11-16**. You use this dialog box to add specific tables or queries to the Relationships window so you can specify relationships among them. Notice the Products table is selected in the Tables tab of the dialog box.

2. **Click Suppliers in the Show Table dialog box, click Add, click Products, click Add, then click Close**

   The Show Table dialog box closes, and the Relationships window displays the Suppliers and Products tables. Notice that in the Suppliers table, the Supplier ID field is the primary key field, but in the Products table, the Supplier ID field is *not* the primary key field. This is appropriate; in order to relate two tables, the shared field must be a primary key field in *only* the first table. In the second table, the common field shared with the first table is called the **foreign key**. To create a one-to-many relationship, you need to drag the primary key from the first table to the foreign key in the second table.

3. **Point to the lower-right corner of the Products table until the ⬉ pointer appears, then drag ⬉ down to increase the height of the table until all the fields are visible**

   You should be able to see the YTD Sales field in the Products table now.

4. **Drag the Supplier ID field from the Suppliers table to the Supplier ID field in the Products table**

   The Edit Relationships dialog box opens. The current settings reflect the relationship you just specified by dragging. The Supplier ID field from the Suppliers table is on the left, and the Supplier ID field from the Products table is on the right. At the bottom, the Relationship Type is listed as One-To-Many. These settings are exactly what you want; one supplier is associated with multiple products but each product is associated with a single supplier. Therefore, it makes sense to set up a one-to-many relationship with the Supplier ID field in the Suppliers table on the "one" side of the relationship, and the Supplier ID field in the Products table on the "many" side.

5. **Click the Enforce Referential Integrity check box to add a check mark**

   Selecting this check box tells Access to reject any attempts to enter data that would be inconsistent. For instance, if a user entered "777" as a Supplier ID number in the Products table, Access would reject the entry because that Supplier ID number does not exist in the Suppliers table. See **FIGURE 11-17**.

6. **Click Create**

   A relationship line now connects the Supplier ID field in the Suppliers table and the Supplier ID field in the Products table, as shown in **FIGURE 11-18**. Note that there is a 1 at the top of the line and an infinity symbol at the bottom of the line, indicating that these two fields have a one-to-many relationship.

7. **Click the Save button 🔲 on the Quick Access Toolbar, then click the Close button ⊠ in the Relationships window**

FIGURE 11-16: Show Table dialog box

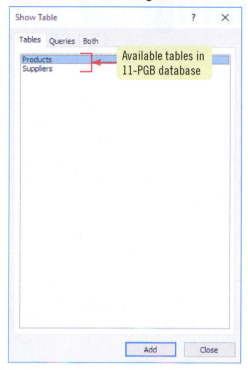

Available tables in 11-PGB database

FIGURE 11-17: Edit Relationships dialog box

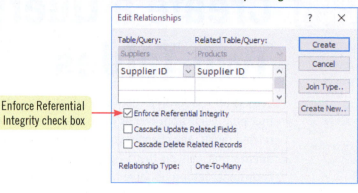

Enforce Referential Integrity check box

FIGURE 11-18: Relationships window with a one-to-many relationship established

Relationship line indicates one-to-many relationship

Infinity symbol

Understanding good database design

Creating a well-designed database requires careful planning. First, decide on the main goals of the database. What is its purpose? What data will it store? Once you decide this, you need to organize the database into categories of data. For instance, if your database will track information about your sports league, you might have categories called Teams, Players, Coaches, and Games. You can then turn each of these categories into tables in your database. Then, you need to define fields and the data types for each table. Remember that each table must have a primary key field that uniquely identifies each record from any other in the database. Once you have created your tables, you need to decide how each table relates to the others in the database and set up appropriate relationships between them. You might need to add new fields to the tables to create these relationships. Creating a well-designed structure for your database will ensure that your data is easy to access, maintain, and update.

Create a Query Using Two Tables

Setting up relationships between tables offers many advantages. One is that you can create a query that pulls fields from two or more related tables. Also, if you specify to enforce referential integrity in related tables, any changes you make to fields in one table are instantly reflected in all related tables or queries that contain that field. This is a huge benefit and ensures that the data in your database is consistent. Setting up table relationships also ensures that your data is valid and accurate. Access will prohibit any attempt to enter data in the foreign key field that is not consistent with the data in the primary key field. **CASE** *David would like a view of the data that shows products whose year-to-date orders exceed $50,000. Because you have set up a one-to-many relationship between the Suppliers table and the Products table, you can create a query that contains the information David needs.*

STEPS

1. **Click the Create tab, then click the Query Design button in the Queries group**

   A new blank query opens in Design view, and the Show Table dialog box opens with the Products table selected.

2. **On the Tables tab of the Show Table dialog box, click Suppliers, click Add, click Products, click Add, compare your screen to FIGURE 11-19, then click Close**

   The field lists for the Suppliers table and the Products table appear. Notice the relationship you created between the Supplier ID field in the Suppliers table and the Supplier ID field in the Products table is shown.

3. **In the Suppliers field list, double-click Supplier**

   The Supplier field is added to the query design grid.

4. **In the Products field list, double-click Product, double-click Category, scroll down in the Products field list, then double-click YTD Sales**

5. **Click the Sort cell for the YTD Sales field, click the Sort list arrow, then click Descending**

6. **In the query design grid, click in the Criteria cell for the YTD Sales field, then type >50000**

   This criteria specifies that the query results should only display records whose YTD Sales field value is greater than $50,000. The greater than symbol (>) is one type of operator you can use in the Criteria cell to return the query results that you want. **TABLE 11-2** displays useful comparison operators.

7. **Click the Sort cell for the Supplier field, click the Sort list arrow, click Ascending, then compare your screen to FIGURE 11-20**

8. **Click the View button in the Results group, then widen columns as needed so that all data is visible**

   The query results appear in Datasheet view, as shown in **FIGURE 11-21**. The results are grouped first by Supplier in alphabetical order, then by YTD Sales in descending order. There are 30 records displayed.

9. **Click the Save button 🖫 on the Quick Access Toolbar, type Top Products by Supplier in the Save As dialog box, click OK, then close the Top Products by Supplier query**

   The query is saved as Top Products by Supplier and appears in the Navigation pane below Queries.

Working with Data

FIGURE 11-19: Adding tables in Design view

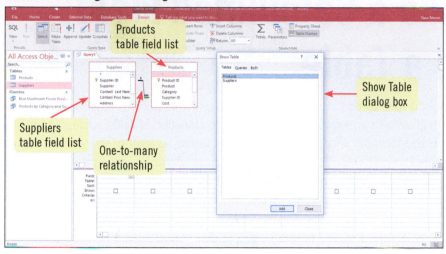

FIGURE 11-20: Query with specified fields, sorts, and criteria in Design view

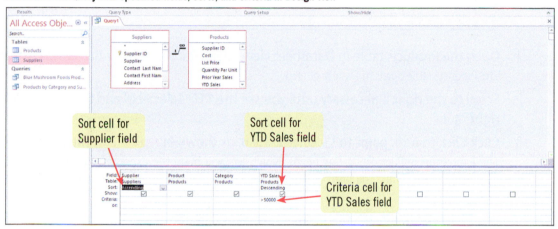

FIGURE 11-21: Query results in Datasheet view

TABLE 11-2: Comparison operators

operator	description
>	Greater than
<	Less than
=	Equals
<>	Not equal to

Working with Data

Access 2016

Add a Calculated Field to a Table

Learning Outcomes
- Explain what a calculated field is
- Add a calculated field to a table in Datasheet view
- Set the data type for a calculated field

You might want to add a calculated field to a table if the table contains values. A **calculated field** is a field that contains an **expression**, which is a combination of fields, values, and mathematical operators (similar to a formula). A calculated field is useful when you want to show the results of calculations based on values in certain fields. For instance, in a products table that contains a field for net price, you could add a calculated field for determining the sales tax; the expression would multiply the net price field by .08 (or the appropriate tax percentage). Calculated fields have the Calculated data type. Choosing a Calculated data type opens the Expression Builder dialog box, where you can easily build the expression you want by specifying fields, values, and operators. **CASE** *David asks that you add a field to the Products table that shows the total sales for each customer. You need to create a calculated field that adds the Prior Year Sales field to the YTD Sales field.*

STEPS

1. **Open the Products table in Datasheet view, then click the Shutter Bar Close button** ❮❮
   The Products table opens in Datasheet view.

2. **Scroll to the right if necessary until you see the YTD Sales field and the blank field to the right of it**

3. **Click Click to Add, point to Calculated Field, as shown in FIGURE 11-22, then click Currency**
   The Expression Builder dialog box opens, which lets you build the expression using fields, values, and mathematical operators. You need to build an expression that sums the Prior Year Sales field and the YTD Sales field.

   > **QUICK TIP**
   > Unlike Excel formulas, expressions do not start with an equal sign (=).

4. **Double-click Prior Year Sales in the Expression Categories section**
   The Prior Year Sales field appears in the top part of the dialog box in brackets. This field is the first part of your expression. Next you need to enter the addition operator.

5. **Type +**
   You typed the plus sign (the addition operator). You can now add the YTD Sales field to complete the expression.

   > **QUICK TIP**
   > Note that a calculated field in a table can only include field references to fields in that table.

6. **Double-click YTD Sales in the Expression Categories section**
   The top section of the dialog box shows the completed expression, as shown in FIGURE 11-23.

7. **Click OK**
   The new column (next to YTD Sales) is now populated with currency values, which are the result of the expression you built (Prior Year Sales + YTD Sales). You need to type a label for this field. The placeholder label is selected, so you can simply start typing.

8. **Type Total Sales, then press [Enter]**
   The field name "Total Sales" now appears as the last field name in the table, as shown in FIGURE 11-24.

9. **Select Pepper's Multigrain Bread (the field value for the Product in the first record), type your name, click 💾, click the File tab, click Close, click the Access window Close button, then submit your database to your instructor**
   The Products table, the database, and Access all close.

FIGURE 11-22: Adding a calculated field to a table

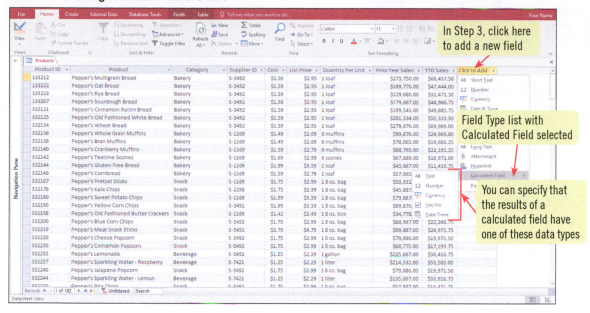

FIGURE 11-23: Building an expression using the Expression Builder dialog box

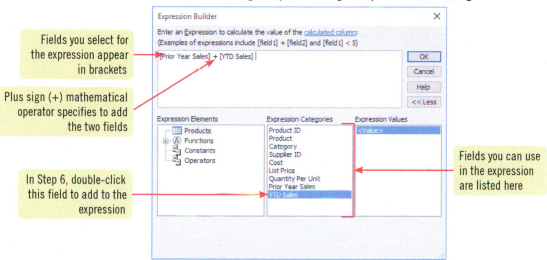

FIGURE 11-24: Products table with new calculated field added

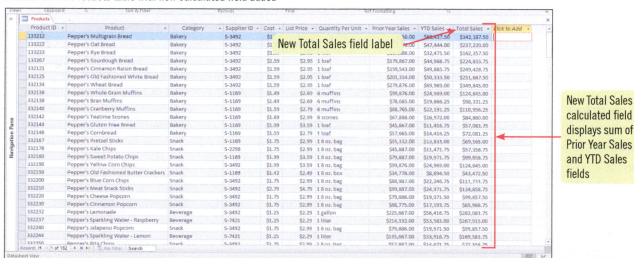

Practice

Concepts Review

Label the elements of the Access window shown in FIGURE 11-25.

FIGURE 11-25

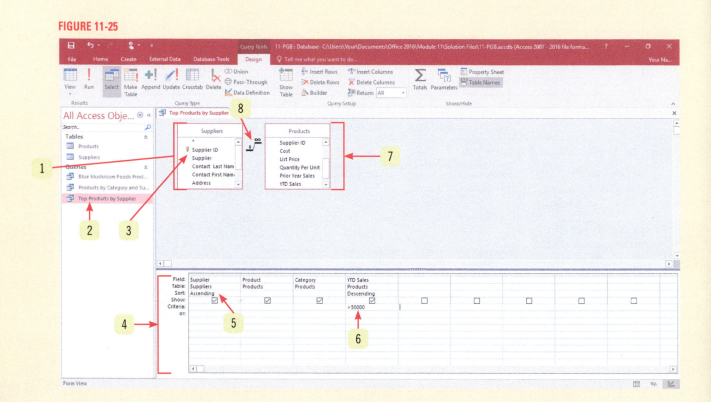

Match each term with the statement that best describes it.

9. **Calculated field**

10. **Filter**

11. **Primary key**

12. **Foreign key**

13. **Sort**

14. **Query**

a. A specified arrangement of records, in ascending or descending order

b. A field in a table that contains a combination of fields, values, and mathematical operators

c. A database object that extracts data from one or more tables in a database according to criteria that you set

d. A field in a table that uniquely identifies a record

e. A field in a table that is also the primary key field in a related table

f. A view of a table that displays only fields that meet specified criteria

Select the best answer from the list of choices.

15. **Which of the following is an Access object that can be saved?**
    a. Filter
    b. Expression
    c. Sort
    d. Query

16. **To create a query that contains fields from two different tables, the tables must be:**
    a. Sorted in ascending order.
    b. Related.
    c. In different databases.
    d. Filtered.

17. **Which of the following shows how the Sales field would appear in an expression?**
    a. (Sales)
    b. <Sales>
    c. [Sales]
    d. =Sales

18. **To apply a filter that displays all the records that contain Purple in the Color field, which of the following actions would you take?**
    a. Click a Purple field value in the table, click the Selection button, then click Equals Purple.
    b. Click any field in the table, click the Selection button, then click Equals Purple.
    c. Click the Filter button, then type Purple.
    d. Click the Color field name in the column heading, click the Selection button, then click Equals Purple.

19. **Which of the following cannot be included in an expression?**
    a. Values
    b. Mathematical operators
    c. Fields
    d. Captions

20. **You manage a database for a summer camp that contains two tables, one called Counselors and one called Campers. Both tables contain the common field Counselor ID. Which of the following statements about these tables is NOT true?**
    a. In the Counselors table, the shared field (Counselor ID) is the primary key.
    b. In the Campers table, the shared field (Counselor ID) is the primary key.
    c. The Counselor ID field is the foreign key in the Campers table.
    d. One record in the Counselors table is related to many records in the Campers table.

Skills Review

1. **Open an existing database.**
    a. Start Access.
    b. Open 11-2.accdb from the drive and folder where you store your Data Files.
    c. Save the database as a new database with the name **11-Photo Agency**. Enable the content and if desired, click Yes to make this a trusted document.
    d. Open the Photographers table in Datasheet view, and review the fields and records it contains. View the Photographs table in Datasheet view, and review its fields and records.
    e. View each table in Design view. Note the number of fields in each table and the data type assigned to each.
    f. Close the Photographers table.

2. **Sort records in a table.**
    a. View the Photographs table in Datasheet view. Close the Navigation pane.
    b. Sort the table by the Photo Name field in ascending order. What is the Photo ID of the first record in the sorted list? Reverse the sort order so the records are sorted in descending order by Photo Name. What is the Photo ID of the first record now?
    c. Clear all sorts, so the records appear in their original order.
    d. Sort the table by the Sale Price field in descending order. What is the Photo Name of the first record? Without removing the first sort, sort the table by the Subject field in ascending order. Now what is the Photo Name for the top record in the sorted list?

Skills Review (continued)

    e. Select the first Photo ID value (11280), then enter your name. If your instructor asks you to provide a screenshot of your sort results, follow the instructions in the yellow box on page 282.

    f. Remove the sort.

3. Filter records in a table.

    a. Apply a filter to the Photographs table to show only records that contain the field value **Sports** in the Subject field. How many records are displayed with the filter applied? What is the Photo Name of the first record?

    b. Remove the filter using a button on the Home tab.

    c. Apply a Number filter to show only records with values greater than 400 in the Sale Price. How many records are displayed with the filter applied? What is the Photo Name for the last record?

    d. Save your changes. If your instructor asks you to provide a screenshot of your sort results, follow the instructions in the yellow box on page 282. Remove the filter, then save your changes.

4. Create a query.

    a. Close the Photographs table, then open the Navigation pane. Create a new query using the Simple Query Wizard.

    b. Base the query on the Photographs table, and include the Photo Name, Subject, and Sale Price fields in the query. Specify to create a detail query.

    c. Name the query **Photos by Subject**, then finish the Wizard and view the query results in Datasheet view.

    d. Sort the query in ascending order by the Subject field.

    e. Save your changes.

5. Modify a query in Design view.

    a. View the Photos by Subject query in Design view.

    b. Add the Size field to the query design grid.

    c. Set the sort order to Descending for the Sale Price field.

    d. Use the query design grid to enter the criteria **nature** for the Subject field. Set the criteria to **large** for the Size field cell.

    e. View the query results in Datasheet view. Save the modified query object as **Large Nature Photos Sold**. Compare your datasheet to FIGURE 11-26.

    f. Close the Large Nature Photos Sold query.

FIGURE 11-26

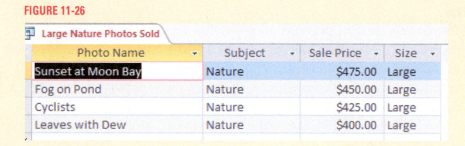

Photo Name	Subject	Sale Price	Size
Sunset at Moon Bay	Nature	$475.00	Large
Fog on Pond	Nature	$450.00	Large
Cyclists	Nature	$425.00	Large
Leaves with Dew	Nature	$400.00	Large

6. Relate two tables.

    a. Open the Relationships window.

    b. Add the Photographers table to the Relationships window, then add the Photographs table to the Relationships window. Close the Show Tables dialog box.

    c. Drag the Photographer ID field from the Photographers table to the Photographer ID field in the Photographs table.

    d. Specify to enforce referential integrity, then create the relationship.

    e. View the tables in the Relationships window, and make sure there is a one-to-many relationship between the Photographer ID fields.

    f. Save your changes, then close the Relationships window.

    Working with Data

Skills Review (continued)

7. Create a query using two tables.

a. Create a new query in Query Design view.

b. Use the Show Table dialog box to add the Photographers table and the Photographs table to the upper pane of the query design window. Close the Show Table dialog box.

c. Notice the relationship line between the Photographers table and the Photographs table.

d. Add the Photo Name and Sale Price fields from the Photographs table to the query design grid. (*Hint*: Scroll down in the field list as necessary to locate the Sale Price field.)

e. Add the Photographer Name from the Photographers table to the query design grid.

f. In the Criteria cell for the Sale Price field, enter an operator and value that will return records with values greater than 450.

g. Set the Sale Price sort order to Descending.

h. View the query results in Datasheet view. Resize columns as needed so that all data is visible. Select Dexter Radcliffe in the Photographer Name cell for the Grand Central Station record, type your name, then press [Enter] twice. Notice that your name now appears as the artist name in five different rows in the query. This is because of referential integrity: When you replaced Dexter Radcliffe with your name, all other records containing Dexter Radcliffe in the Photographer Name field changed immediately to reflect the edit. Save the query as **Top Photos by Photographer**. Compare your datasheet to FIGURE 11-27. Close the query.

i. Open the Photographers table. Again, notice that due to referential integrity, the field value for the Photographer Name for the second row has been updated with your name. Close the Photographers table.

FIGURE 11-27

Top Photos by Photographer		
Photo Name	Sale Price	Photographer Name
Grand Central Station	$550.00	Your Name
Tightrope Walker	$525.00	Felix Marotta
Catching a Football	$500.00	Your Name
Aerial View of Chicago	$485.00	Your Name
Sky Diving at Dusk	$485.00	Your Name
Aerial View of San Francisco	$475.00	Your Name
London Bridge	$475.00	Rayleen Chung
Sunset at Moon Bay	$475.00	Deion Moore

8. Add a calculated field to a table.

a. Open the Photographs table in Datasheet view, then close the Navigation pane.

b. Add a calculated field to the table with the Currency data type.

c. In the Expression Builder dialog box, enter an expression that subtracts the Cost field from the Sale Price field. Click OK to close the Expression Builder dialog box.

d. Enter the field name **Profit** for the new field. Sort the table by the Profit field in descending order.

e. Compare the first several records in your table to FIGURE 11-28. Save your changes, close the Photographs table, then close the database. Exit Access. Submit your completed database to your instructor.

FIGURE 11-28

Photo ID	Photographer ID	Photo Name	Subject	Size	Cost	Sale Price	Profit
11239	P-1217	Grand Central Station	City Living	Large	200.00	$550.00	$350.00
Your Name	P-1217	Aerial View of Chicago	Aerial View	Large	150.00	$485.00	$335.00
11278	P-1217	Sky Diving at Dusk	Sports	Large	150.00	$485.00	$335.00
11237	P-1225	Sunset at Moon Bay	Nature	Large	150.00	$475.00	$325.00
11275	P-1217	Aerial View of San Francisco	Aerial View	Large	150.00	$475.00	$325.00
11256	P-1235	Tightrope Walker	Performing Arts	Large	200.00	$525.00	$325.00
11254	P-1213	London Bridge	City Living	Large	150.00	$475.00	$325.00
11235	P-1225	Fog on Pond	Nature	Large	150.00	$450.00	$300.00
11241	P-1235	Dancing Feet	Performing Arts	Large	150.00	$450.00	$300.00

Independent Challenge 1

You are the marketing coordinator Twirl Dance Academy. Registration forms have just started coming in for fall classes. Your manager created a database to manage the data about dance teachers and students. She wants you to answer some questions about the students and teachers so she can make appropriate plans for fall classes.

a. Start Access, then open 11-3.accdb from the drive and folder where you store your Data Files. Save the database as **11-Dance Academy**, and enable the content. Open the Classes table and the Students table, and review the fields and records of each.

b. View the Classes table in Datasheet view. In the Tap – Level 1 record, replace "Jordan" in the Teacher field with your first and last name. Close the Classes table.

c. View the Students table in Datasheet view, then sort the table by the Age field in ascending order. Which student appears in the top row? Now sort by the Age field in descending order. Which student appears in the first row? Remove the sort.

d. Apply a filter to the Students table so that the table displays records of students who are age 25 or younger. How many records are displayed now? Apply a second filter to show only the students who are defined as Intermediate for the Dance Level. If your instructor asks you to provide a screenshot of your results, follow the instructions in the yellow box on page 282. Save your changes. Close the Students table.

e. Create a simple query using the Query Wizard. Base the query on the Students table, and include the fields Last Name, First Name, and Class ID. Name the query **Students by Class ID**. In Datasheet view, sort the query results in ascending order by the Last Name field. Replace the last name of the first student with your first and last name. Save your changes.

f. Open the Students by Class ID query in Design view. Add the Dance Level field to the query. Add appropriate criteria to one of the cells in the query design grid specifying to show only the records containing Beginner in the Dance Level field. Specify to sort the records by the Class ID field in ascending order. View the query results in Datasheet view, then save the modified query as **Beginner Students by Class ID**. Close the query.

g. Open the Relationships window, then show the Classes table and the Students table in the window.

h. Drag the Class ID field from the Classes table to the Class ID field in the Students table. (*Hint*: Remember that you can enlarge a field list by dragging its bottom edge or bottom corner to resize it.) In the Edit Relationships dialog box, specify to enforce referential integrity, then create the relationship.

i. Save the layout of the relationship, then close the Relationships window.

j. Open the Classes table. Add a Calculated field with a data type of Currency. The field should multiply the Number of Classes field by the Fee Per Class field. Name the field **Fee Per Student**. Save and close the Classes table.

k. Create a new query in Query Design view. Add the Classes table and the Students table to the grid. Use the appropriate tables to add the following fields to the query design grid in this order: First Name, Last Name, Class, Teacher, Day and Time, Studio, Fee Per Student.

l. Set the criteria for the Class field to **Tap - Level 1**

m. Save the query as **Tap Level 1 Schedule and Fees**. View the query results in Datasheet view. Who is the teacher for this class? Compare your screen to FIGURE 11-29, then close the Tap Level 1 Schedule and Fees query.

n. Close the database, then exit Access. Submit your completed database to your instructor.

FIGURE 11-29

First Name	Last Name	Class	Teacher	Day and Time	Studio	Fee Per Student
Fred	Your Name	Tap - Level 1	Your Name	Monday 7:00-9:00	A	$240.00
Sherry	Hwang	Tap - Level 1	Your Name	Monday 7:00-9:00	A	$240.00
Bethany	Maggio	Tap - Level 1	Your Name	Monday 7:00-9:00	A	$240.00
Arshad	Talluh	Tap - Level 1	Your Name	Monday 7:00-9:00	A	$240.00
Raul	Jordan	Tap - Level 1	Your Name	Monday 7:00-9:00	A	$240.00
Mae	Parker	Tap - Level 1	Your Name	Monday 7:00-9:00	A	$240.00
Lexi	Starbird	Tap - Level 1	Your Name	Monday 7:00-9:00	A	$240.00
Nathan	Tandy	Tap - Level 1	Your Name	Monday 7:00-9:00	A	$240.00

Independent Challenge 2

You own a small business that provides personal assistant services to busy families. You employ five personal assistants who go to clients' homes and perform such tasks as running errands, doing light housekeeping, preparing meals, and driving children to after-school activities. You've created a database to help you manage information about your clients and your personal assistants. You now need to create two queries that show scheduling information for the assistants, both of which pull information from two tables in your database. You also need to add a calculated field to one table to show the weekly fee each client owes.

a. Start Access, then open 11-4.accdb from the drive and folder where you store your Data Files. Save the database as **11-Personal Assistants Business**, and enable the content.

b. Open each table in Design view, and review the fields and field types each contains. Note which fields are the primary key fields. Get a sense of the information that each table contains. Close both tables when you have finished reviewing them.

c. Open the Relationships window, then establish a one-to-many relationship between the Assistant ID field in the Assistants table and the Assistant ID field in the Clients table. Specify to enforce referential integrity. Save the relationship, then close the Relationships window.

d. Open the Assistants table. Replace Mary Jones in the Assistant Name field for the first record with your name. Close the table.

e. Open the Clients table, then add a calculated field in the table that has the Currency data type. Build an expression for this field that multiplies the Hours per Week field by the Hourly Fee field. Name the field **Weekly Fee**. Close the Clients table.

f. Create a new query in Query Design view. Use the Show Table dialog box to open the field lists for the Assistants table and the Clients table, then close the Show Table dialog box. Save the query as **Soloski Weekly Schedule**.

g. Add the following fields in the order listed to the query design grid: Assistant Name, Client Last Name, Street Address, Hours per Week, Visit Time, and Service Notes.

h. Enter **Greta Soloski** as the criteria for the Assistant Name field. Sort the query in ascending order by Visit Time. Save your changes.

i. View the query results in Datasheet view. Enter your first and last name in the Client Last Name field.

j. Switch back to Query Design view. Delete "Greta Soloski" in the Criteria cell for the Assistant Name field. Enter **9:00 AM** in the criteria field for the Visit Time field, then save the query as **Morning Assignments**. Sort the query in ascending order by Client Last Name. (Remove the sort setting from the Visit Time field.) View the query in Datasheet view, widen columns if needed so that all field values and headings are visible, then save and close the query.

k. Close the database, then exit Access. Submit your database to your instructor.

Independent Challenge 3

You are the tour coordinator for a company that offers summer bike tours for teens in various regions of the world. You have created an Access database to manage information about upcoming tours and customers who have signed up for a tour. In preparation for coordinating the tours, you want to filter and query the data.

a. Start Access, then open 11-5.accdb from the drive and folder where you store your Data Files. Save the database as **11-Tour Company**. Enable the content.

b. Open the Customers table in Datasheet view, then filter the data to show customers who are signed up for the tour with Tour ID 112. Sort the filtered results in alphabetical order by the Last field. Type your name in the Data Entered By field for the first filtered record, then save your changes. If your instructor asks you to provide a screenshot of your results, follow the instructions in the yellow box on page 282. Remove the filter, then close the table.

Independent Challenge 3 (continued)

c. Use the Relationships window to create a one-to-many relationship from the Tours table to the Customers table using the Tour ID field. Specify to enforce referential integrity in the Edit Relationships dialog box. Save the relationship, then close the Relationships window.

d. Open the Tours table. Add a calculated field to the table that has the Currency data type. Build an expression for this new field that adds the Price field and the Air Fare field. Name the field **Total Price**. Save and close the Tours table.

e. Create a new query in Query Design view. Use the Show Table dialog box to open both the Tours table field list and the Customers table field list. Close the Show Table dialog box.

f. Add the following fields from the appropriate table to the query design grid: First, Last, Tour Name, Tour Leader, Start Date, Duration, and Total Price. (Remember that you can resize a field list as needed to see all available fields.)

g. Set the sort order to Ascending for the Tour Name field. Save the query with the name **Customer List by Tour**. View the query in Datasheet view.

h. Return to Design view, then set the criteria for the Tour Name field as **California Coast**. Set the sort order to Ascending for the Last field. Save the modified query as **California Coast Customer List**. View the query results in Datasheet view.

i. Open the Tours table in Datasheet view. Select Tsai in the Tour Leader for the California Coast tour, then type your name.

j. Save and close the Tours table. Now look at the California Coast Customer List query in Datasheet view, and observe the change in the Tour Leader field. Close the California Coast Customer List query.

k. View the Customer List by Tour query in Datasheet view. Observe your name in the Tour Leader field for the California Coast Tour. Close the query.

l. Close the database, then exit Access. Submit your database to your instructor.

Independent Challenge 4: Explore

In this Independent Challenge, you work with a database to help you keep track of data for a new dog grooming business. This database contains three tables: one for dogs, one for owners, and one for services. One of these tables contains Attachment and Hyperlink field data types, which you have not worked with before. You will add records to all three tables and set up relationships among them. Then you will create a query using fields from all three tables. *Note:* To complete the Independent Challenge, your computer must be connected to the Internet.

a. Start Access, then open 11-6.accdb from the drive and folder where you store your Data Files. Save the database as **11-Dog Grooming Business**. Enable the content.

b. Open all three tables in Design view, and review the fields and data types for each.

c. View the Dogs table in Datasheet view. Double-click the paper clip icon in the first row of the table to open the Attachments dialog box, click Add to open the Choose File dialog box, navigate to where you store your Data Files, double-click file 11-6a.docx, then click OK.

d. Double-click the paper clip icon in the first row again, click file 11-6a if necessary to select it, then click Open to open the file in Word. As you can see, this document contains special grooming instructions for the first dog in the Dogs table. Close the document, quit Word, then close the Attachments dialog box.

Independent Challenge 4: Explore (continued)

e. Add a new field to the Dogs table named **Link**. Assign the Hyperlink data type to this field. Save your changes to the table. Open your favorite search engine in your browser, then search for information about grooming cocker spaniels. When you find a webpage you like, right-click the URL in the address bar, then click Copy to copy the link. Return to the Dogs table in Access. In Datasheet view, right-click the Links field for the first record, then click Paste. Widen the column if you wish to see the entire link. Notice the blue line under the text you just typed, indicating it is a live link. Click the link to view the page. Close your browser window.

f. Add two appropriate records to the Dogs table, using the Dog IDs D-4 and D-5, the Owner IDs O-4 and O-5, and fictional data that you make up. Then, add two fictional records to the Owners table, using the Dog IDs from the new records you added to the Dogs table. For Owner O-5, enter your name in the Data Entered By field. Widen columns as necessary to ensure that all field names and field values are visible on the screen. Save your changes, then close both tables.

g. Open the Services table. Add two fictional records to this table, using the two new Dog IDs you added in Step f.

h. Open the Relationships window. Show the Services table, the Dogs table, and the Owners table (in that order). Create a one-to-many relationship between the Dog ID field in the Dogs table and the Dog ID field in the Services table. Enforce referential integrity. Then create a one-to-many relationship between the Dog ID field in the Dogs table and the Dog ID field in the Owners table. Enforce referential integrity. Save your changes, then close the Relationships window.

i. Create a new query in Design view. Show the Services table, the Dogs table, and the Owners table (in that order). Save the query as **Dogs and Services**.

j. Add the following fields to the query design grid in the order specified: Dog Name, Breed, Last Name, Service Date, Service Description, and Data Entered By. Set a sort order on the Service Date field that lists the records from newest to oldest. Save your changes, then view the query in Datasheet view.

k. Close all open objects, then exit Access. Submit your completed database to your instructor.

Visual Workshop

Open 11-7.accdb from the drive and folder where you store your Data Files, then save it as **11-Lazy Days Spa**. Enable the content. Set up the relationships shown in FIGURE 11-30. Create the query shown in FIGURE 11-31, using fields from the four related tables in the database. Specify the appropriate sort order for the Appointment Date field. View the query in Datasheet view, then replace the name Jessica in the Treatment Provider Name column with your name. Save the query as **Client Treatments**. Close the database, then exit Access. Submit your completed database to your instructor.

FIGURE 11-30

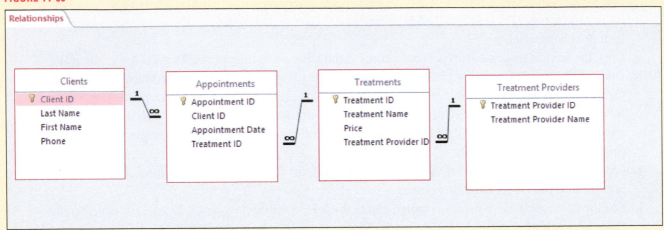

FIGURE 11-31

First Name	Last Name	Appointment Date	Treatment Name	Treatment Provider Name	Price
Claire	Wood	2/1/2017	Swedish Massage	Debra	$90.00
Heather	Khan	2/2/2017	Signature Facial	Jessica	$55.00
Lauren	Taylor	2/2/2017	Deep Tissue Massage	Debra	$80.00
Henry	Kirk	2/2/2017	Foot Reflexology	Marcie	$50.00
Sara	Cow	2/2/2017	Facial	Marcie	$45.00
Riley	Lorenzo	2/2/2017	European Facial	Jessica	$75.00
Sylvia	Zimmer	2/3/2017	Signature Facial	Jessica	$55.00
Rachel	Carpenter	2/3/2017	Spa Manicure	Rebecca	$20.00
Virginia	Williams	2/3/2017	European Facial	Jessica	$75.00
Mike	Clark	2/3/2017	Deep Tissue Massage	Debra	$80.00
Cynthia	Cohn	2/3/2017	Deep Tissue Massage	Debra	$80.00
Paula	Cooper	2/3/2017	Facial	Marcie	$45.00
Riley	Lorenzo	2/7/2017	Organic Facial	Jessica	$60.00
Fatima	Thayer	2/8/2017	Signature Facial	Jessica	$55.00
Eric	Clayton	2/8/2017	European Facial	Jessica	$75.00
Missy	Ergood	2/8/2017	Swedish Massage	Debra	$90.00

Creating Database Reports

CASE David LeBlanc, vice president of merchandising at Pepper's Green Basket, has asked you to create a series of reports containing information from the PGB database. The first report needs to show products, organized by supplier and category, with total sales for each. The second report needs to show the year-to-date sales for an important PGB supplier, Stampley Ranchers. You also need to create some mailing labels for an upcoming promotion.

Module Objectives

After completing this module, you will be able to:

- Create a report using the Report Wizard
- View a report
- Modify a report
- Add a field to a report
- Apply conditional formatting to a report
- Add summary information to a report
- Create mailing labels

Files You Will Need

12-1.accdb	12-5.accdb
12-2.accdb	12-6.accdb
12-3.accdb	12-7.accdb
12-4.accdb	

Create a Report Using the Report Wizard

A **report** is a summary of database information designed specifically for printing. Report data can be pulled from one database object, such as a table, or from multiple database objects. You can create new reports quickly using the **Report Wizard**, which automatically creates a report based on settings that you specify and displays it in Print Preview. You can save reports as objects in a database, so that you can open or print them anytime. All reports are composed of sections, each of which contains specific information. **CASE** *David asks you to create a report that shows products, listed by supplier and grouped by category, that displays year-to-date sales of each product. You decide to use the Report Wizard to create this report.*

STEPS

1. **Start Access, open** 12-1.accdb **from the location where you store your Data Files, then save the database as** 12-PGB

2. **Enable the content, click the** Create tab, **then click the** Report Wizard button **in the Reports group**

   The first dialog box of the Report Wizard opens. You use this dialog box to choose the **record source(s)**—that is, the database object(s) from which a report gets its data, and to specify the fields you want to include in the report.

3. **Click the** Tables/Queries list arrow, **click** Table: Suppliers, **click** Supplier **in the Available Fields list, then click the** Select Single Field button >

   The Supplier field now appears in the Selected Fields list.

4. **Click the** Tables/Queries list arrow, **click** Table: Products, **double-click** Product **in the Available Fields list, double-click** Category, **double-click** Cost, **then double-click** Total Sales

   The Product, Category, Cost, and Total Sales fields are added to the Selected Fields list, as shown in **FIGURE 12-1**.

5. **Click** Next

   The next dialog box lets you organize records in the report so they are grouped by a recommended field (in this case, the Supplier field in the Suppliers table) or ungrouped. **Grouping** organizes a report by field or field values. You want to group the records by Supplier, which is the current setting.

6. **Click** Next

   This dialog box lets you specify additional grouping levels in the report.

7. **Click** Category, **click** > , **notice that Category now appears in blue below the Supplier grouping as shown in** FIGURE 12-2, **then click** Next

   The records will be grouped by Category within each Supplier grouping. The next dialog box sets the sort order.

8. **Click the** Sort list arrow **for the first field, then click** Product

   This specifies to sort the records in ascending order by Product.

9. **Click** Next, **verify the** Stepped Layout option button **is selected, verify the** Portrait option button **is selected, verify the** Adjust the field width so all fields fit on a page check box **is selected, then click** Next

10. **Select** Suppliers **in the What title do you want for your report? text box, type** Products by Supplier and Category **as the report title, verify the** Preview the report option button **is selected, then click** Finish

    The Report opens in Print Preview, as shown in **FIGURE 12-3**.

Creating Database Reports

FIGURE 12-1: Report Wizard dialog box

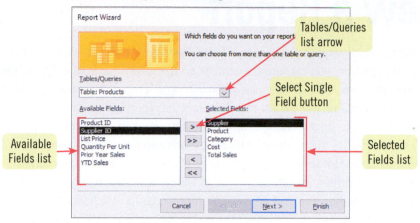

Tables/Queries list arrow

Select Single Field button

Available Fields list

Selected Fields list

FIGURE 12-2: Setting a second grouping level

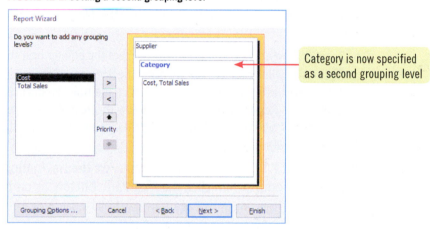

Category is now specified as a second grouping level

FIGURE 12-3: Products by Supplier and Category report in Print Preview

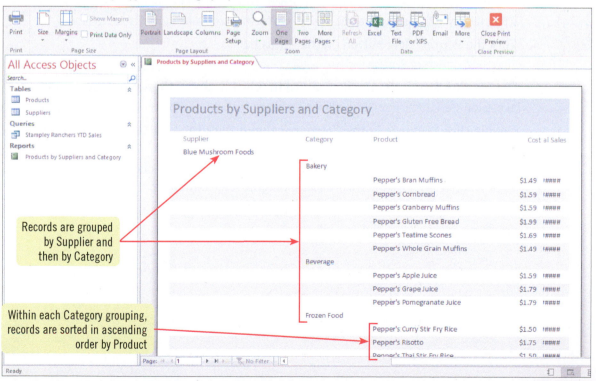

Records are grouped by Supplier and then by Category

Within each Category grouping, records are sorted in ascending order by Product

View a Report

**Learning
Outcomes**
• View a report in
Print Preview,
Design view, and
Report view
• Apply a filter by
selection in Report
view
• Remove a filter

Access offers several ways to view a report. **Print Preview** shows you exactly how the printed report will look. In Print Preview, you can use the buttons on the record navigation bar to view each page of the report. **Report view** is the default view when you open a report from the Navigation pane. Report view looks similar to Print Preview, except that it displays the report in a continuous flow, without page breaks. If you need to make layout changes to your report, you can use either Design view or Layout view. **Design view** includes many powerful tools for modifying a report; however, it can be a difficult view in which to work because it shows only the structure of the report, not the data contained in it. **Layout view** does not include as many modification tools as Design view, but it shows you report data as you work. **TABLE 12-1** describes the views that are available for reports. To switch views, click the View buttons on the status bar. **CASE** ▸ *You decide to view the report in Print Preview, Design view, and Report view.*

STEPS

QUICK TIP
Clicking on the report when the Zoom In pointer 🔍 is active will cause the view to zoom in again.

1. **Click the Shutter Bar Close button ≪ on the Navigation pane, then click 🔍 anywhere on the report**

   The Zoom Out pointer 🔍 appears when you place the pointer over the report. Clicking the report when the 🔍 is active will let you see the full page. The first page of the report is now fully visible on the screen in Print Preview, as shown in **FIGURE 12-4**. Notice the title "Products by Supplier and Category" appears at the top in the **Report Header** section. Below the Report Header, the **Page Header** section contains all the fields you selected in the wizard. Also notice the report is first grouped by Supplier and then by Category in alphabetical order.

2. **Click the Next Page button ▶ three times on the navigation bar to view the first four pages of the report, then click the First Page button ◀ on the navigation bar**

   Notice that each page contains a **Page Footer**, which contains the date and the page number.

TROUBLE
If the report opens in a different view, click the View list arrow in the Views group, then click Design view.

3. **Click the Close Print Preview button in the Close Preview group**

   See **FIGURE 12-5**. The report appears in **Design view**, which you can use to make formatting and layout changes and to modify the structure of the report. Design view does not display any records; instead, the screen displays all six sections of the report, each of which contains controls you can modify.

4. **Click the Report View button on the status bar**

   The report appears in Report view.

5. **Double-click Muffins in the first record to select it, then attempt to type Bagels**

   As you can see, it is not possible to edit data in Report view. You can, however, sort and filter in Report view.

6. **Double-click Beverage in the Category column, click the Selection button in the Sort & Filter group, then click Equals "Beverage"**

   See **FIGURE 12-6**. You just applied a filter to the report specifying to show only records that have "Beverage" in the Category field. You can remove a filter using the Toggle Filter button.

7. **Click the Toggle Filter button in the Sort & Filter group, then save your changes**

   The filter is removed, and all the records reappear.

FIGURE 12-4: Page 1 of Products by Supplier and Category report in Print Preview

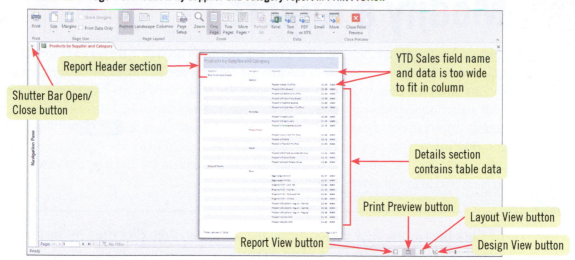

Report Header section

Shutter Bar Open/Close button

YTD Sales field name and data is too wide to fit in column

Details section contains table data

Print Preview button

Layout View button

Report View button

Design View button

FIGURE 12-5: Report in Design view

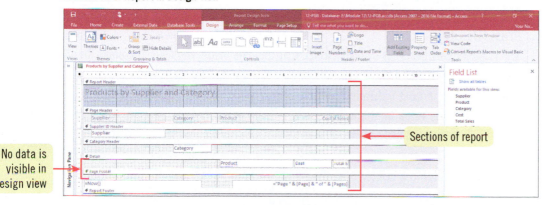

Sections of report

No data is visible in Design view

FIGURE 12-6: Filtering a report in Report view

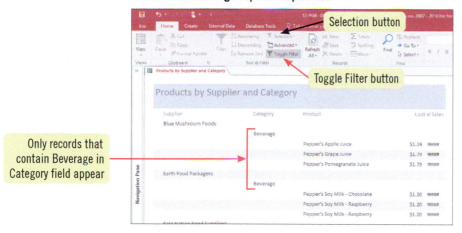

Selection button

Toggle Filter button

Only records that contain Beverage in Category field appear

TABLE 12-1: Available report views in Access

button	view	use to
	Print Preview	See exactly how your report will look when printed
	Report view	View records in a report; apply a filter; copy data to the clipboard
	Design view	Add or edit controls; change properties; view the underlying report structure (but not its data)
	Layout view	Add or delete fields; resize, move, or delete columns while also viewing records; add grouping levels; change sort order

Modify a Report

After you create a report using the Report Wizard, you might need to make layout changes to improve its appearance. For instance, sometimes columns are not wide enough to display field names or values, or they are either too close together or too far apart. You might need to move or resize columns so all the fields and data are visible and look good on the page. You might also decide to delete columns that aren't necessary. You can use Layout view to resize, move, and delete columns. **CASE** *You need to delete the Cost field, which is not necessary for this report. You then need to widen the Product column so all product names are visible. You also need to widen the Total Sales column so the field label and values are visible. You decide to work in Layout view to make these changes.*

STEPS

1. **Click the Layout View button ☰ on the status bar, then click the Cost heading**

   The view changes to Layout view, which at first glance looks very much like Report view. However, you can see a dotted border around the outside edge of the report as well as an orange border around the Cost column heading, indicating that it is selected.

2. **Press [Delete]**

   The Cost column header is deleted. Notice that the data below the deleted column header is still in the report; you need to select field value cells separately from the column header.

3. **Click $1.49 (the cost value in the first record)**

   Clicking the first value in this column selected the entire column of Cost field values, as shown in **FIGURE 12-7**. Notice the first cell ($1.49) is outlined in orange and the other cells are outlined in yellow.

4. **Press [Delete]**

   The Cost data column is deleted from the report.

5. **Click the Product column heading, press and hold [Shift], then click Pepper's Bran Muffins (the first product name below the Product heading)**

   The Product column heading and all the data in the Product column are selected. You need to widen this column by dragging its right edge to the right so all product names are fully visible.

6. **Position the ↔ pointer on the right edge of the orange border that surrounds Pepper's Bran Muffins, then drag to the right about ½"**

   The Product column is now 1/2" wider, as shown in **FIGURE 12-8**. All of the product names should now be entirely visible. Notice that the Total Sales column header (the last column in the report) is only partially visible, and the field values below it appear as ## characters because the column is too narrow. You need to increase the width of the column and column heading.

7. **Click the Total Sales column heading, press and hold [Shift], then click the first instance of ## below the Total Sales column header**

   The entire Total Sales column is now selected.

8. **Position the ↔ pointer over the left border of the orange Total Sales column header, then drag approximately ½" to the left**

   The Total Sales column header and all the values in the column are now visible. Compare your screen to **FIGURE 12-9**.

9. **Save your changes**

FIGURE 12-7: Selecting a field in Layout view

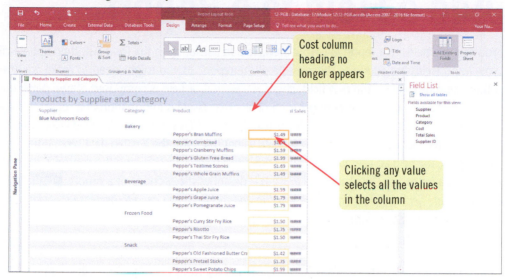

Cost column heading no longer appears

Clicking any value selects all the values in the column

FIGURE 12-8: Report in Layout view after widening the Product column

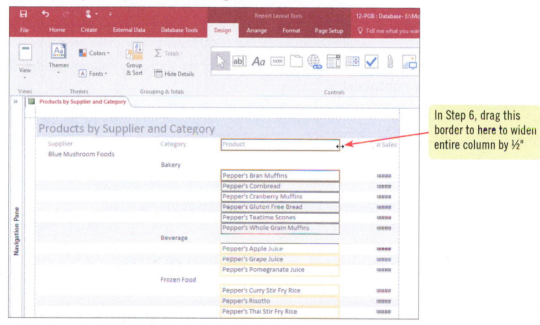

In Step 6, drag this border to here to widen entire column by ½"

FIGURE 12-9: Report after widening Total Sales column

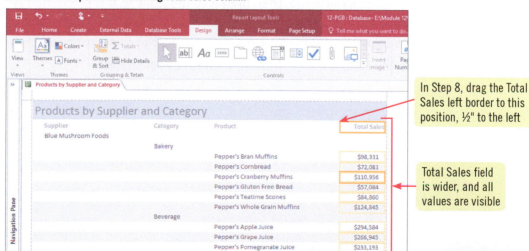

In Step 8, drag the Total Sales left border to this position, ½" to the left

Total Sales field is wider, and all values are visible

Creating Database Reports

Add a Field to a Report

You can add fields to a report in Layout view. To add a field, open the Field List, then double-click the field you want. Fields are added to the left side of the report, so you might need to make adjustments to the other columns to place the new field where you want it. A field is composed of two parts: the field label, and its associated control. A **control** is an object that displays information in a report. Different controls are used for each data type. For instance, a text box control is used to display field values that have the Text data type; a check box control is used for field values that have the Yes/No data type. When you add a field to a report, the field label is automatically added to a header section, and the control is added to either the Group Header or the Detail section. **TABLE 12-2** describes the sections of a report. **CASE** *You need to add the State field to the report. Before you can add this field, you need to decrease the width of the Category column to create space for the new field.*

STEPS

1. **Click the Category column header, press and hold [Shift], then click Bakery**

   You selected both the Category field label and the first text box control for the Category field (which displays "Bakery"). Clicking the first text box control in the column selected all the controls in that column. So, now the Category field label and all the category names below it are selected. You can now resize the column by dragging the left border to the right to make room for the new field.

2. **Place the ↔ pointer on the left side of the Category column header, then drag ↔ to the right about ¾"**

   The Category column is now narrower. Because the text in the column is left aligned, the text is now closer to the Product column. Resizing the column opened up a space on the left of the report, as shown in **FIGURE 12-10**. There is now room to fit the State field.

3. **Look at the Field List pane on the right side of the screen**

   The Field List pane displays the fields that are used in the open report.

4. **Click the Show all tables link at the top of the Field List**

   All the fields from the two tables in the database are now displayed in the Field List. The State field is in the Suppliers table.

5. **Double-click the State field in the Field List task pane**

   Access automatically places the new State field and field control in the far left of the report. You need to move it to the empty space between the Supplier column and the Category column.

6. **With the State column heading and column values still selected, position the ⬚ pointer over the State heading, then drag it to the right so it is positioned between the Supplier column and the Category column**

   You might need to do this a few times to place it just right. Compare your screen to **FIGURE 12-11**.

7. **Click the Field List close button, then save your changes**

FIGURE 12-10: Report after resizing the Category column

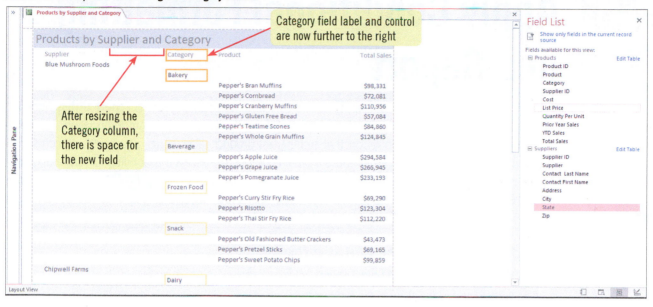

FIGURE 12-11: Adding the State field using the Field List

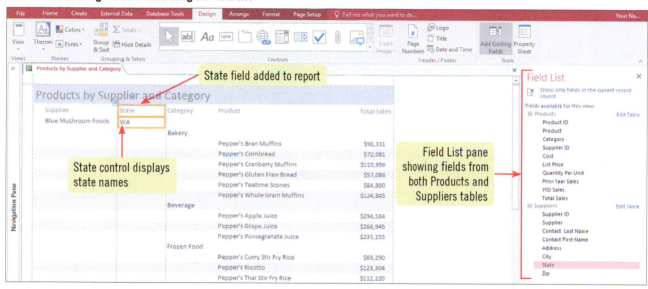

TABLE 12-2: Report sections

section	description
Report Header	Contains the report name or company logo and appears only at the top of the first page of the report
Page Header	Contains field labels and appears at the top of every page (but below the Report Header on the first page)
Group Header	Contains the chosen group field name and appears at the beginning of a group of records ("Group" is replaced by the chosen field name)
Detail	Usually contains bound controls and appears once for every record in the underlying datasheet
Group Footer	Contains the chosen group field name and appears at the end of every group of records ("Group" is replaced by the chosen field name)
Page Footer	Usually contains the current date and page number and appears at the bottom of every page
Report Footer	Appears at the end of the last page of the report, just above the page footer

Apply Conditional Formatting to a Report

As in an Excel worksheet, you can apply conditional formatting in an Access report to highlight key information. Applying conditional formatting is a great way to draw attention to information that meets specific criteria. For instance, in a report that summarizes product sales results, you could use conditional formatting to highlight in yellow results above a certain number. You access the Conditional Formatting Rules Manager dialog box from the Report Layout Tools Format tab in Layout view. **CASE** *You want to apply conditional formatting to the report to highlight Total Sales values that exceed $200,000.*

STEPS

1. **Click any field value in the Total Sales column**

2. **Click the Report Layout Tools Format tab**

   The Report Layout Tools Format tab is now active.

3. **Click the Conditional Formatting button in the Control Formatting group, then click the New Rule button in the Conditional Formatting Rules Manager dialog box**

   The New Formatting Rule dialog box opens. It displays options for specifying one condition and setting a format, but you can click the Add button to set additional conditions and formats.

4. **Click the between list arrow, then click greater than**

5. **Press [Tab] to move to the next text box, then type 200000**

   You have set the conditions for which the conditional formatting will take effect: the value in the Total Sales field must be greater than $200,000. Now you need to specify formatting to apply if these conditions are met.

6. **Click the Bold button B , click the Font color list arrow, then click the green square in the bottom row (Screen tip reads "Green")**

   Compare your screen to **FIGURE 12-12**.

7. **Click OK twice**

   All values greater than $200,000 in the Total Sales column appear in green bold.

8. **Click Products by Supplier and Category in the Report header, press [F2], press [Spacebar], type (Your Name), then press [Enter]**

   Pressing [F2] activated Edit Mode and placed the insertion point after the last character in the Report Header. Your name, enclosed in parentheses, now appears in the report title.

9. **Click the Report Layout Tools Design tab, click the Themes button, click the Retrospect theme as shown in FIGURE 12-13, then save your changes**

10. **Click the Print Preview button ⊡ on the status bar, click the Next Page button ▶ twice on the Navigation bar to view pages 1-3 of the report, compare your screen to FIGURE 12-14, click the Close Print Preview button, then close the report**

    The Products by Supplier and Category report closes.

FIGURE 12-12: New Formatting Rule dialog box

In Step 4, set this to greater than

In Step 5, type 200000 here

In Step 6, click the Bold button and set the font color to Green

FIGURE 12-13: Applying the Retrospect theme to the report

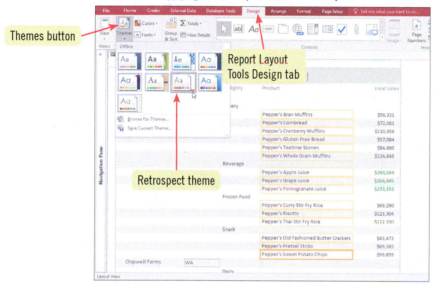

Themes button

Report Layout Tools Design tab

Retrospect theme

FIGURE 12-14: Products by Supplier and Category report with Retrospect theme and conditional formatting applied

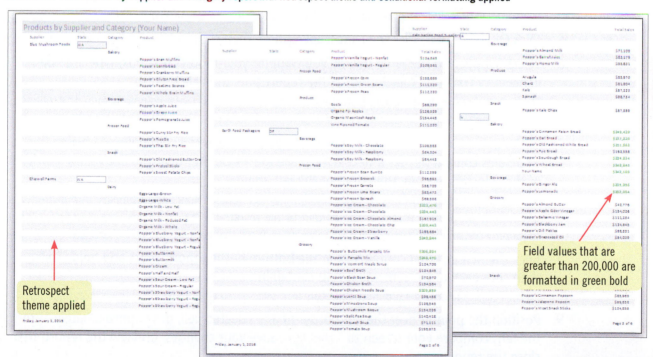

Retrospect theme applied

Field values that are greater than 200,000 are formatted in green bold

Add Summary Information to a Report

Summary information in a report displays statistics about one or more fields in a database. Summaries can include statistics for the sum, average, minimum, or maximum value in any numeric field. **TABLE 12-3** describes the five summary calculations you can use in your database reports. You can add summary information to a report while creating the report with the Report Wizard. **CASE** *David has asked you to create a new report that shows YTD Sales for products produced by Stampley Ranchers, a supplier of organic meat products. David wants to see average sales for Stampley products, as well as their total sales and other statistics. The record source for this report is a query that David created.*

STEPS

1. **Click the Shutter Bar Open button on the Navigation pane, click the Stampley Ranchers YTD Sales query in the Navigation pane, click the Create tab, then click the Report Wizard button in the Reports group**

   The Report Wizard dialog box opens. "Query: Stampley Ranchers YTD Sales" appears in the Tables/Queries list box because you selected it in the Navigation pane before starting the Report Wizard.

2. **Click the Select All Fields button** >>

   All the fields from the Stampley Ranchers YTD Sales query now appear in the Selected Fields list.

3. **Click Next three times to accept the settings in the next three dialog boxes, then click Summary Options**

   The Summary Options dialog box opens. Of the fields you selected for this report, summary options are available only for the YTD Sales field because this is the only field containing numeric values.

4. **Click the Sum check box, click the Avg check box, click the Min check box, click the Max check box, click the Detail and Summary option button if necessary, then click the Calculate percent of total for sums check box**

   You specified to include all of the summary values in the dialog box, as shown in **FIGURE 12-15**.

5. **Click OK, click Next, click the Landscape option, then click Next**

6. **Select Suppliers in the What title do you want for your report? text box, type Stampley Ranchers YTD Sales (Your Name) as the report title, then click Finish**

   The report opens in Print Preview. Notice that ## appears in the YTD Sales column because the column is not wide enough to display the values. You need to switch to Layout view and widen this column.

7. **Click the Layout View button on the status bar, click any cell containing ## below the YTD Sales column header if necessary, place the ↔ pointer over the left yellow border of the selected column, then drag to the left about 1"**

   All of the field values in the YTD Sales column are now visible. Notice the summary information you specified in the Report Wizard at the bottom of the report. The ## characters appear in the column containing the summary values. You need to widen each cell that contains these ## characters.

8. **Click the first cell that contains ## at the bottom of the report, press and hold [Shift], then click each of the remaining cells containing ##**

   All the cells containing the summary values are now selected, so you can resize all the cells at once.

9. **Position the pointer over the left border of any selected cell, drag approximately 1" to the left, compare your screen to FIGURE 12-16, save your changes, preview the report, then close the report**

FIGURE 12-15: Summary Options dialog box

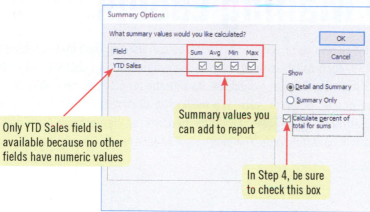

Only YTD Sales field is available because no other fields have numeric values

Summary values you can add to report

In Step 4, be sure to check this box

FIGURE 12-16: Report in Layout view after widening columns

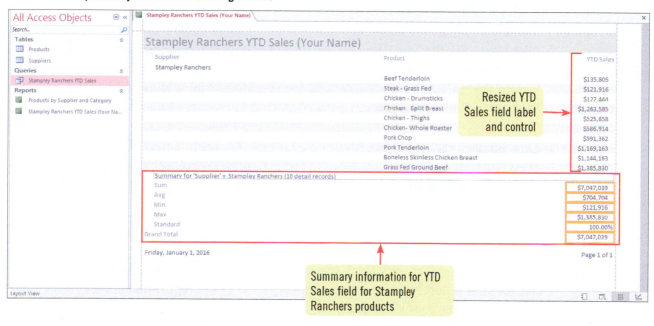

Resized YTD Sales field label and control

Summary information for YTD Sales field for Stampley Ranchers products

TABLE 12-3: Common summary calculations available in database reports

summary	statistic	calculates
SUM	Sum	Total of all values in the field
AVG	Average	Average of all values in the field
COUNT	Count	Number of records in the database
MIN	Minimum	Smallest value in the field
MAX	Maximum	Largest value in the field

Create Mailing Labels

You don't have to print all reports on sheets of paper. You can use the data in a database to create other forms of printed output, such as labels or envelopes. Access includes a Label Wizard to help you create labels containing data from any fields in a database. As with the reports you have already created, you can create labels based on queries or tables, such as a mailing to all customers in California or all employees in the Marketing Department. **CASE** ▶ *David has asked you to create labels for a mailing to suppliers informing them of new branding standards. The mailing will be sent to all PGB suppliers.*

STEPS

1. **Click Suppliers in the Navigation pane, click the Create tab, then click the Labels button in the Reports group**

   The first dialog box of the Label Wizard opens.

2. **Click the Filter by manufacturer list arrow, click Avery if necessary, then click C2163 in the Product number list**

   This option has two labels that are each 1½" × 3⁹⁄₁₀" aligned across a sheet.

3. **Click Next, click the Font name list arrow, click Bodoni MT, click the Font Size list arrow, click 12, set the Font weight to Normal, verify the Text color is set to black, then click Next**

   In this dialog box, you choose which fields you want to include on the label and how to arrange them. You select each field from the Available Fields list in the order in which you want it on the label. You need to enter any spaces, punctuation, or hard returns using the keyboard.

4. **Click Supplier, click the Select Single Field button ▷ , press [Enter], double-click Address, press [Enter], double-click City, type , (a comma), press [Spacebar], double-click State, press [Spacebar], then double-click Zip**

   Your screen should look similar to **FIGURE 12-17**.

5. **Click Next**

   In this dialog box, you specify how you want to sort the records when you print them.

6. **Double-click Supplier, click Next, select Labels Suppliers in the What name would you like for your report? text box, type Supplier Labels as the report name, click Finish, then click the Shutter Bar Close button**

   The labels appear in Print Preview. They are sorted alphabetically by Supplier. Notice that the labels are sorted going across the page in rows rather than down the page in columns.

7. **Click the Design View button 🗠 on the status bar**

8. **Position the pointer over the bottom of the Page Footer bar until it changes to ✛, drag down ½", click the Label button 🗛 in the Controls group, click the left side of the Page Footer section, type your name, then press [Enter]**

   See **FIGURE 12-18**. You added your name as a label to the Page Footer section, which will appear at the bottom of the report.

9. **Click the Print Preview button 🖾 on the status bar, then click the report to zoom out**

   Your name appears in the Page Footer section. Compare your labels with **FIGURE 12-19**.

10. **Save your changes, close the 12-PGB database, exit Access, then submit your database to your instructor**

Creating Database Reports

FIGURE 12-17: Label Wizard dialog box

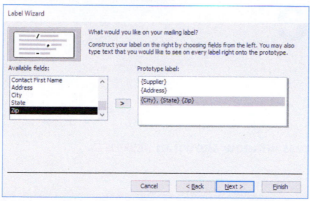

FIGURE 12-18: Adding a label to the Page Footer section in Design view

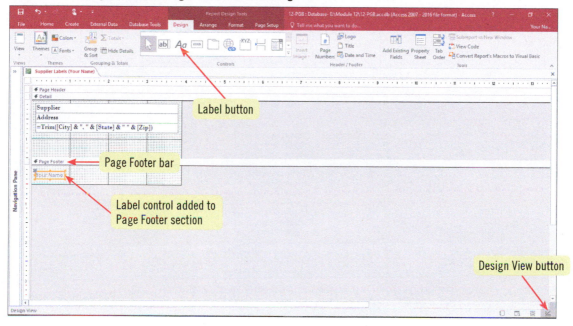

FIGURE 12-19: Supplier Labels report in Print Preview

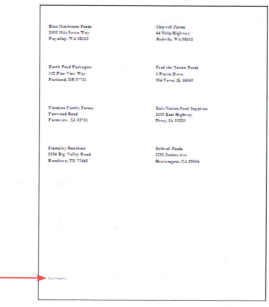

Practice

Concepts Review

Label the elements of the Access window shown in FIGURE 12-20.

FIGURE 12-20

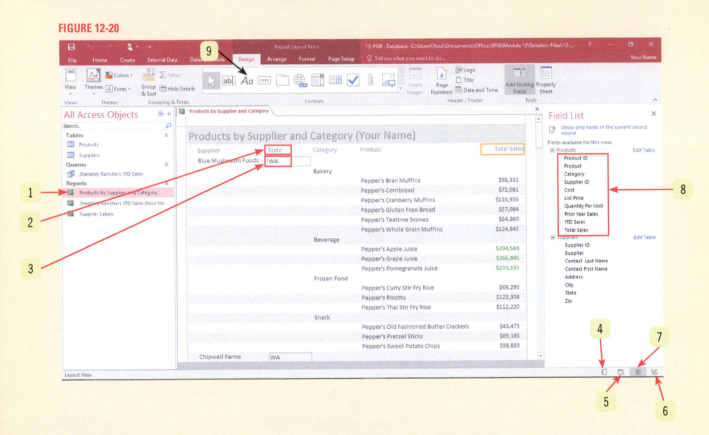

Match each view description with the correct view.

10. Report view
11. Design view
12. Layout view
13. Print Preview

a. Shows the individual pages of a report
b. Displays a report with data and lets you make formatting changes
c. Shows records but not individual pages of a report
d. Displays only the structure of a report and not the data in it

Select the best answer from the list of choices.

14. Which of the following views could you use to move, delete, or widen a column?
   a. Layout view
   b. Report view
   c. Print Preview
   d. None of the above

15. Which of the following tasks can you accomplish using Report view?
   a. Edit a field value
   b. Apply a theme
   c. Apply a filter
   d. View page numbers

16. In a report, a field consists of two parts: a field label and a _____.
    a. control
    b. sort specification
    c. filter
    d. calculated field
17. Which of the following is a summary option you can choose to include in a report?
    a. Average
    b. Hyperlink
    c. Title
    d. Header

Skills Review

1. **Create a report using the Report Wizard.**
   a. Start Access, then open the database 12-2.accdb from where you store your Data Files. Save the database as a new database with the name **12-Photo Agency**. Enable the content.
   b. Use the Report Wizard to create a new report. Display the Photographers table, then select the Photographer Name field. Display the Photos table, then select the Photo Name, Subject, Size, and Sale Price field.
   c. Specify to view the data by Photographer Name in the Photographers table, then specify to group the data by Subject. Specify to sort in ascending order by Photo Name. Select the Stepped layout and Portrait orientation.
   d. Type **Photos by Photographers** as the report title.
   e. Finish the report and view it in Print Preview.

2. **View a report.**
   a. Close the Navigation pane, then zoom out in Print Preview to see the full first page.
   b. Close Print Preview to view the report in Design view.
   c. View the report in Report view.
   d. Filter the report to show only records containing **Felix Marotta** in the Photographer Name field. If your instructor asks you to provide a printout of your filtered results, follow the instructions in the yellow box on page 282. Toggle the filter off.

3. **Modify a report.**
   a. View the report in Layout view.
   b. Delete the Size field and field values from the report.
   c. Increase the width of the Photo Name column by using the [Shift] key to select both the column header and any value in the column, then dragging the right border of the selection to the right approximately 1".
   d. Increase the width of the Sale Price column by selecting both the column header and any value in the column then dragging its left border to the left approximately ½". Make sure all the Sale Price values are visible, and that no ## symbols appear.
   e. Save your changes.

4. **Add a field to a report.**
   a. Use the [Shift] key to select the Photo Name column heading and any value in the column, so the entire column is selected.
   b. Drag the left border of the selected column to the right about an inch to make room for a new field.
   c. Open the Field List pane if necessary, then show all tables in the list.
   d. Add the Photo ID field to the report. Close the Field List.
   e. Move the Photo ID column heading and field values so the column positioned between the Subject and Photo Name columns. Make sure the new column does not overlap with the adjacent columns; make adjustments as needed to position it just right.
   f. Save your changes.

5. **Apply conditional formatting to a report.**
   a. Select one of the Sale Price values in the report.
   b. Open the Conditional Formatting Rules Manager dialog box, then create a new rule.

c. Set the conditions as greater than 350, then specify green bold formatting.

d. Close the Conditional Formatting dialog boxes.

e. Display the Report Layout Tools Design tab. Apply the Organic theme to the report. Preview the report in Print Preview. Compare your report to **FIGURE 12-21**.

f. Save and close the report.

6. Add summary information to a report.

a. Open the Navigation pane. Use the Report Wizard to create a new report based on the Moore Photos query.

b. Select all the fields, then accept the suggested grouping level of Photographer Name in the Photographers table.

FIGURE 12-21

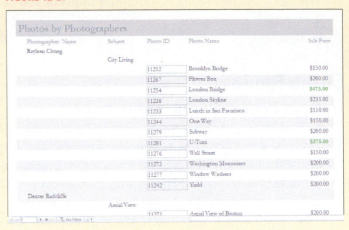

c. Open the Summary Options dialog box, then specify to add the Sum, Avg, Min, and Max summary values for the Total Sales field. Also, specify to calculate percent of total for sums.

d. Sort in ascending order by the Photo Name field, choose the Stepped layout, choose Landscape orientation, and type **Moore Photos** as the report title.

e. Preview the report. If necessary, use Layout view to adjust the column widths of the field values and the summary information columns so all information is visible and the page looks balanced.

f. Preview and print the report, compare your screen to **FIGURE 12-22**, then save and close the report.

7. Create mailing labels.

a. Create a new report using the Label Wizard, based on the Photographers table.

b. Choose Avery in the Filter by manufacturer list, then choose label C2160.

FIGURE 12-22

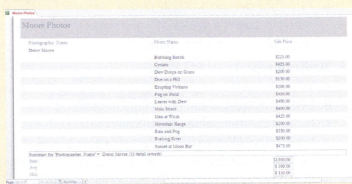

c. Choose font settings of black 11-point Arial, Normal font weight, with no italic or bold formatting.

d. Set up the label as shown in **FIGURE 12-23**.

FIGURE 12-23

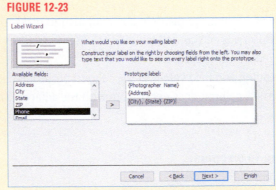

Skills Review (continued)

e. Sort the records by ZIP in ascending order. Title the report **Photographer Labels**.

f. Preview the labels, then switch to Design view. Add your name as a label to the Page Footer section, then preview the labels. Compare your labels to **FIGURE 12-24**.

g. Save the labels, close the report, then exit Access. Submit your completed database to your instructor.

FIGURE 12-24

Independent Challenge 1

You are the marketing coordinator for the Twirl Dance Academy. You need to distribute information about this fall's classes to the dance teachers. You also need to create labels to affix to each student's welcome packet. You decide to create reports to compile and present this information.

a. Start Access, then open the file 12-3.accdb from where you store your Data Files. Save the database as **12-Dance Academy**. Enable the content.

b. Create a report using the Report Wizard based on the Classes and Students tables. Include the Class, Day and Time, Studio, and Teacher fields from the Classes table, then include the First Name, Last Name and Dance Level fields from the Students table.

c. Specify to view the data by Classes, then specify to group the data by Teacher. Sort the records by Last Name in ascending order. Choose the Stepped Layout style and Portrait orientation. Title the report **Classes by Teacher**.

d. View the report in Layout view. Delete the Dance Level column heading and field values. Resize and move the remaining columns if necessary so that all field names and field values are visible, and so the columns look balanced on the page.

e. Apply the Slice theme to the report.

f. Add your name after the report title in parentheses. Save your changes. View the report in Print Preview, then compare your finished report to **FIGURE 12-25**. Close the report.

g. Create labels for all Students based on the Student Labels query. Use Avery label C2242, and choose Cambria for the font, 12 for the font size, Normal for the font weight, and black for the font color. Place the fields for the label as shown in **FIGURE 12-26**. Be sure to type the additional text shown in the figure. Sort the labels first by Class, then by Last Name. Save the report as **Student Labels**, then preview it.

h. View the labels in Design view, then add your name as a label to the Page Footer section. Save your changes.

i. Preview the first page of the labels, close the Student Labels report, then exit Access. Submit your completed database to your instructor.

FIGURE 12-25

Teacher	Class	Day and Time	Studio	Last Name	First Name
Ballard					
	Tap - Level 1	Monday 7:00-9:00	A		
				Black	Fred
				Hwang	Sherry
				Jordan	Raul
				Maggio	Bethany
				Parker	Mae
				Starbird	Lexi
				Talluh	Arshad
				Tandy	Nathan
	Tap - Level 2	Wed 7:00-9:00	A		
				Gordon	Kelvin
				Lozinski	Mary
				Roman	Kathrina
				Rupp	Harvey
				Soler	Ricardo
				Yao	Nancy
Monroe					

Classes by Teacher (Your Name)

FIGURE 12-26

Prototype label:

{Last Name}, {First Name}
Class: {Class}
Teacher: {Teacher}

Access 2016

Independent Challenge 2

You own a small business that provides personal assistant services to busy families. You employ five personal assistants who go to clients' homes and perform such tasks as running errands, doing light housekeeping, preparing meals, and driving children to after-school activities. You've created a database to help you manage information about your clients and your personal assistants. You need to create a report that shows a listing of all your clients, grouped by assistant. You will create this report from existing tables in the database. You need to create a second report based on a query that shows weekly client fees.

a. Start Access, then open the database 12-4.accdb from where you store your Data Files. Save the database as **12-Personal Assistants Business**.

b. Use the Report Wizard to create a report based on the Assistants and Clients tables. Include the Client Last Name, Street Address, Visit Time, Service Notes, and Hours per Week fields from the Clients table. Include the Assistant Name field from the Assistants table. Specify to view the data by the Clients table, then group the fields by Assistant Name.

c. Sort the records by the Visit Time field in ascending order, and choose the Stepped layout with Landscape orientation. Type **Clients by Assistants** as the report title.

d. View the report in Layout view. Delete the Hours per Week field and field values. Resize and move the Service Notes column and other column as needed so the field names and field values are all visible and the report looks balanced.

e. Add the Weekly Fee field to the report. Resize and move columns so there is room for this new column on the far right side of the report, then move the Weekly Fee column to the far right side of the report.

f. Add your name in parentheses to the Report Header after the title, preview the report, save the report, then close the report.

g. Create a report using the Report Wizard based on the query Client Fees. Include all the fields from the query in the report. Do not specify a grouping level. Sort the records by the Weekly Fee field in descending order. Set the orientation to Landscape and choose the Tabular layout. Save the report with the name **Client Fees (Your Name)**.

h. View the report in Layout view. Set a new conditional formatting rule to apply green bold formatting to Weekly Fee field values that are greater than 250. Apply the Integral theme. If necessary, resize any columns so all information is visible and the columns are balanced. View the report in Print Preview, then close the report.

i. Close the database. Exit Access. Submit your completed database to your instructor.

Independent Challenge 3

You are the tour coordinator for a company that offers summer bike tours for teens in various regions of the world. You have created an Access database to manage information about upcoming tours and customers who have signed up for a tour. You created a query that shows customers who have signed up for the tours to England and Scotland in June. You have decided to create a report based on this query that shows the total amounts paid for the tours so far. You will need to use summary information in this report.

a. Start Access, then open the file 12-5.accdb from where you store your Data Files. Save the database as **12-Tour Company**. Enable the content.

b. Use the Report Wizard to create a report based on the England and Scotland Tours query. Specify to include all the fields from the query in the report. Specify to view the data by Customers, and group by Tour Name. Specify to sort by the Last field in ascending order. Specify to add summary information for Sum, Avg, Min, and Max summary values for the Total Price field. Choose the Stepped layout and Landscape Orientation. Save the report with the name **England and Scotland Tours**, then click Finish.

c. View the report in Layout view. Delete the Tour ID field. (*Hint*: This may be difficult if it is overlapped with the Total Price field; drag it to the left before deleting, to make sure you delete the right field.) Resize the Total Price column heading and field values so that all values are visible. In the Summary section of the report, increase the width of each field value cell so that all values are visible.

Independent Challenge 3 (continued)

d. Adjust the widths of the other values in the report as needed so that the report looks balanced and all values are visible.

e. Switch to Design view. Drag the lower edge of the Report Header bar down ½", then use the Label button to add your name as a label to the Report Header section. Save your changes. Preview the report, then close the report.

f. Exit Access. Submit your completed report to your instructor.

Independent Challenge 4: Explore

In this Independent Challenge, you create a report that presents information about your dog grooming business. This database contains four tables for dogs, owners, appointments, and services. You need to create a report that shows appointments that occurred for the current month. After you create and save the report you will save it as a PDF file, which is a format that preserves formatting and allows viewing on multiple devices.

a. Start Access, then open the database 12-6.accdb from where you store your Data Files. Save the database as **12-Dog Grooming Business**. Enable the content.

b. Open the Dogs, Owners, Appointments, and Services tables in Datasheet view. Review the fields contained in each table, and identify the field types for each.

c. Open the Relationships window and view the relationships among all tables.

d. Create a report using the Report Wizard that is based on all four tables. Include the following fields: Appointment Date, Service, Service Amount, Dog Name, Breed, and Last Name. Specify to group the report by Service. Sort the report by Service Amount in ascending order. Open the Summary Options dialog box, and include all four summary values. Specify to calculate percent of total for sums. Choose the Stepped layout and specify Landscape orientation. Save the report with the name **Feb Appointments (Your Name)**.

e. View the report in Layout view. Resize and move the columns as necessary so all the data is visible and so the report looks balanced.

f. Click in the Report Header section ("Feb Appointments (Your Name)"). Click the Report Layout Tools Design tab, then click Date and Time in the Header/Footer group. In the Date and Time dialog box, click OK to accept the default settings. Notice that today's date and the current time are added to the Report Header and are right aligned.

g. Apply a Theme that you like to the report. Click the Colors button in the Themes group, then apply a different color palette (any one that you like). Click the Fonts button in the Themes group, then click a different Font set that you like.

h. Adjust the widths of the columns as necessary to ensure all information is visible and the page looks balanced. Save and close the report.

i. Click the Feb Appointments report in the navigation bar, then click the External Data tab. This tab lets you import data into your database or export it into different formats. You will export your report into a PDF file, which is a file format that is easily viewed on many devices. Click PDF or XPS in the Export group. In the Publish as PDF or XPS dialog box, navigate to the location where you store your Data Files, click Publish, then click Close. (*Note*: If the Feb Appointments file opens on your screen after you click Publish, close the file.)

j. Exit Access. Using Windows Explorer, open the folder where you store your Data Files, then double-click Feb Appointments (Your Name).pdf to view your report. Close the file, then submit the PDF file to your instructor.

Visual Workshop

Open the Data File 12-7.accdb from the drive and folder where you store your Data Files, then save it as **12-Lazy Days Spa**. Enable the content. Create the report shown in FIGURE 12-27, based on the Treatments by Anna query. (*Hints*: In the Report Wizard, choose the fields shown, view by Appointments, and group by Treatment Provider Name. Sort as shown, and be sure to add the Summary Information shown. Use your own name in the header.) Specify the Block layout and Landscape orientation. Save the report as **Anna Appointments**. Adjust the column widths as needed. Apply the theme shown. Preview the report in Print Preview, then close the database and exit Access.

FIGURE 12-27

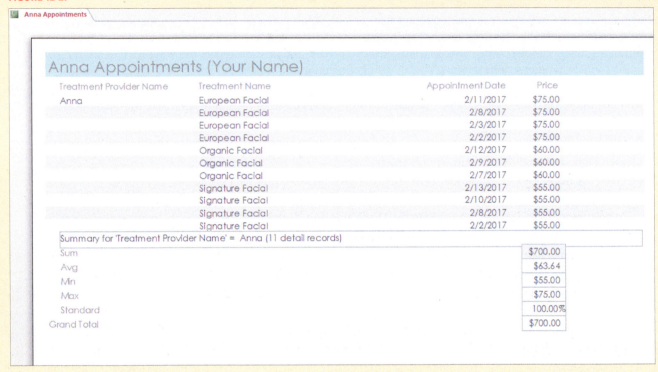

Creating a Presentation

CASE Justin Ramirez, vice president of finance for Pepper's Green Basket, has asked you to create a presentation for a local bank, to support a loan application. He wants the presentation to explain the company's goals and values and summarize the funding plan.

Module Objectives

After completing this module, you will be able to:

- Open and view a presentation
- Create a new presentation
- Enter and format slide text
- Apply a theme

- Add and modify an online image
- Add and modify shapes
- Create SmartArt
- Insert a table

Files You Will Need

13-1.pptx	13-3.pptx
13-2.pptx	13-4.pptx

Open and View a Presentation

Learning Outcomes
• Start PowerPoint
• Use presentation views

PowerPoint is a **presentation graphics app** that allows you to create dynamic **slides**, which are on-screen pages you use in a slide show. A **slide show** displays a sequence of full-screen slides on a computer. Slides can combine text, graphics, sound, and video. PowerPoint includes several ways to view a presentation. When you open a presentation in PowerPoint, the workspace opens in **Normal view** and is divided into two **panes**, or areas. The larger pane on the right, the **Slide pane**, shows the full slide, and the smaller **Thumbnail pane** on the left shows **thumbnails**, or small versions, of the slides. You can also switch to other views. **Outline view** shows slide text instead of thumbnails in the left pane, in an indented format. **Slide Sorter view** shows only thumbnails of the entire presentation and is useful for reordering and deleting slides. You can switch to **Slide Show view** to view the slide show as your audience will see it, or **Reading view**, to view it full screen but also see the status bar. PowerPoint also includes **Notes Page view**, where you can see your slide and any notes you have made, plus three master views you can use to change multiple slides in a presentation. **CASE** *Before you create the new presentation, you view a presentation about the partnership between Pepper's Green Basket and a local community college.*

STEPS

1. **On the Windows taskbar click the** Start button ⊞, click All apps **on the Start menu, scroll the list, then click** PowerPoint 2016

   The PowerPoint Start screen opens, as shown in **FIGURE 13-1**.

2. **Click** Open Other Presentations **on the left side of the screen**

   The Open screen appears, allowing you to open a presentation from your OneDrive or from your computer.

3. **Click** Browse

   The Open dialog box opens.

QUICK TIP

To resize the panes, point to the gray border between the two panes, then when the pointer changes to ⟷ drag the pane border left or right.

4. **Navigate to the location where you store your Data Files, click** 13-1.pptx, **then click** Open

   A presentation about the partnership with Brook Community College opens, as shown in **FIGURE 13-2**. When you start PowerPoint, the workspace opens by default in Normal view.

5. **Click the** Next Slide button ⬇ **at the bottom of the vertical scroll bar**

   Slide 2 appears on the screen, and the Slide 2 thumbnail is highlighted in orange. You can move to the next or previous slide by clicking the Next Slide button ⬇ and Previous Slide button ⬆, or by pressing [▲], [▼], [Page Up], or [Page Down] on the keyboard.

QUICK TIP

To move a slide in Slide Sorter view, drag it to a different position.

6. **Click the** View tab, **then click the** Slide Sorter button **in the Presentation Views group**

   The view changes to Slide Sorter view, as shown in **FIGURE 13-3**. The slide thumbnails are arranged in rows across the window. The currently selected slide, Slide 2, is highlighted in orange.

7. **Click the** Outline View button **in the Presentation Views group**

   The View tab contains buttons that let you change how the presentation appears on the screen. In Outline View, the Thumbnail pane changes to display only the text on each slide, arranged in indented form, like an outline. The status bar also contains view buttons.

8. **Click the** Slide Show button 🖵 **on the status bar, then press** [Spacebar] **until you reach the end of the presentation**

   The slide show advances and then ends with a black screen. Pressing [Spacebar] again (or clicking the black screen) returns you to Outline view. You can also advance a slide show by clicking the screen, or pressing [Enter], [Page Down], or [▼].

9. **Click the** File tab, **then click** Close, **clicking** No **if asked to save your changes**

   The 13-1.pptx file closes.

FIGURE 13-1: PowerPoint Start screen

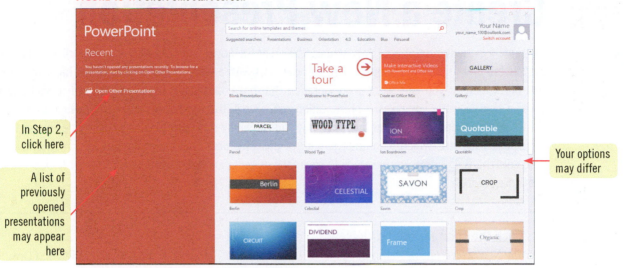

In Step 2, click here

A list of previously opened presentations may appear here

Your options may differ

FIGURE 13-2: Presentation open in Normal view

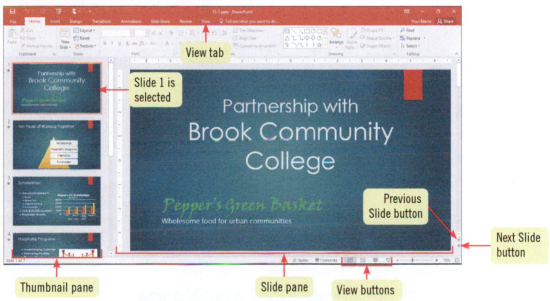

View tab

Slide 1 is selected

Previous Slide button

Next Slide button

Thumbnail pane

Slide pane

View buttons

FIGURE 13-3: Presentation in Slide Sorter view

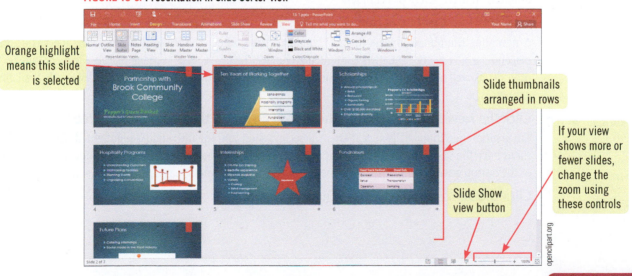

Orange highlight means this slide is selected

Slide thumbnails arranged in rows

If your view shows more or fewer slides, change the zoom using these controls

Slide Show view button

Creating a Presentation

Create a New Presentation

To create a presentation of your own, you can begin at the PowerPoint Start screen or by clicking New on the File tab any time PowerPoint is open. You can start with a blank presentation, which has white slides and black text, or you can select a presentation that has coordinated fonts, colors, and special effects, called a **theme**. After you create a presentation, you save it, then add slides and content such as text and graphics. A new presentation has one slide, but you can easily add more. For each new slide you add, you can select a **layout**, which is an arrangement of **placeholders** that can hold text, graphics, and other slide content. **CASE** ▶ *You are ready to create the presentation Justin requested. You want to begin with a blank presentation.*

STEPS

1. **Click the File tab, then click New**

   The New screen opens, shown in **FIGURE 13-4**. Here you can choose from themes such as Ion and Organic, templates with preformatted content, such as Create an Office Mix (which incorporates interactive video), or simply a blank presentation. If you choose a blank presentation now, you can easily add a theme later.

2. **Click Blank Presentation**

   A new, blank presentation opens. The Thumbnail pane contains a thumbnail representing one blank slide. Because it is the only slide, it is highlighted. The Slide pane shows the slide's placeholders. The **title placeholder** contains the text "Click to add title", and the **subtitle placeholder** contains the text "Click to add subtitle". You'll add text to these placeholders in the next lesson.

3. **Click the File tab, click Save As, click Browse, navigate to where you store your Data Files, type 13-Funding Plan in the File name text box, click Save, then click the Home tab if it isn't already in front**

   The Save As dialog box closes, and the presentation is saved to the location you chose. The new filename, 13-Funding Plan.pptx, appears in the title bar. The Home tab is now active, showing the most frequently used presentation command buttons. Before adding slide content, you'll add slides to the presentation. When you add a slide, you can choose a layout. Each layout contains formatting for placeholders. For example, the slide in your new presentation is based on the **Title slide layout**, which contains a placeholder with larger, centered text for a title, and another placeholder below it with smaller centered text for a subtitle.

4. **Click the New Slide button arrow in the Slides group**

   The New Slide gallery opens, showing nine available layouts. See **FIGURE 13-5**. Each layout contains a different arrangement of placeholders.

5. **Click the Two Content layout**

   A new slide thumbnail appears in the Thumbnail pane, under the first slide. The new slide has a title placeholder at the top, and two content placeholders below it. The content placeholders contain text prompts as well as six icons you can click to add other types of content. **TABLE 13-1** lists each available content type.

6. **Click the New Slide button (not the button arrow) in the Slides group three times**

   Three more slide thumbnails appear after the second slide, and the fifth slide is highlighted. The three new slides have the same Two Content layout as the second one. When you click the New Slide button instead of the button arrow, PowerPoint adds a new slide with the same design as the slide before it.

7. **Click the Save button 🖫 on the Quick Access Toolbar**

FIGURE 13-4: PowerPoint New screen

FIGURE 13-5: New Slide gallery

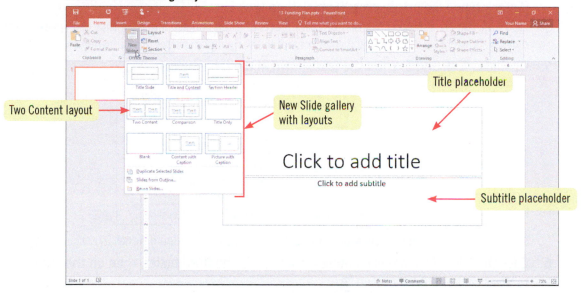

TABLE 13-1: Content placeholder icons

icon	name	lets you add
	Insert Table	A table with the number of rows and columns you specify
	Insert Chart	A chart using any Excel chart type
	Insert a SmartArt Graphic	A predesigned SmartArt diagram you can customize
	Pictures	A picture stored on your computer or on a network location
	Online Pictures	A picture from the web, your OneDrive, Facebook, and/or other selected locations
	Insert Video	A video file stored on your computer or from the web

Creating a Presentation

Enter and Format Slide Text

Learning Outcomes
• Enter slide text
• Change font appearance

You can enter text on a slide in the Slide pane or in Outline view. Working in the Slide pane shows you exactly how the text will look on the slide, while Outline view can be useful when you have a lot of text to edit and rearrange. A placeholder containing text, a graphic, or a table is an editable **object** on the slide that you can move and resize. **CASE** ▶ *You begin the presentation by adding text to the title slide.*

STEPS

QUICK TIP

Clicking a slide thumbnail is another way to move to a slide in the Slide pane. To display a thumbnail that is hidden, use the vertical scroll bar in the Thumbnail pane.

1. **Click the Slide 1 thumbnail, position the mouse pointer over the title placeholder in the Slide pane until it changes to I, then click once**

   A **selection box** surrounds the title placeholder, the prompt text "Click to add title" is no longer visible, and a blinking vertical insertion point indicates where the new text will be entered.

2. **Type Funding Plan, click the subtitle placeholder, then type Pepper's Green Basket**

   The title text appears in the title font and style, and the subtitle text appears in the subtitle font and style.

3. **Click the Slide 2 thumbnail, click the Click to add title placeholder in the Slide pane, then type Why Pepper's Green Basket?**

4. **Click the prompt text Click to add text in the left placeholder, type High quality, press [Enter], type Low prices, press [Enter], then type Local**

   Each time you press [Enter], the insertion point moves to a new bulleted line. Your slide text appears on the slide, as shown in **FIGURE 13-6**. You'll enter content in the right placeholder in a future lesson.

TROUBLE

There's no need to manually type an accent for the word Café; when you type the word, PowerPoint automatically adds the accent over the last letter.

5. **On Slides 3, 4, and 5, enter the text shown in the table below:**

slide #	title	bullets in left placeholder
3	Our Values	Sustainable Fair Trade Natural or organic
4	Our Plan	New classes Hire outreach coordinator Café expansion
5	Funding Needed: $300,000	[No bullet text on this slide]

   Each completed slide thumbnail displays the added text. The presentation now has five slides.

6. **Click the Slide 2 thumbnail, double-click Local in the third bullet, then on the Mini toolbar click the Bold button** B

7. **Click Slide 1, click the subtitle Pepper's Green Basket, click the edge of the subtitle placeholder with the ⬚ pointer so that its edges become solid lines, click the Font list arrow in the Font group, scroll down and click Viner Hand ITC, click the Font Size list arrow in the Font group, then click 40**

   Clicking the edge of the placeholder so that its edges become solid lines selects the entire placeholder. Any formatting you apply after that applies to everything inside the placeholder.

8. **Click the Font Color button arrow** A ▾ **in the Font group, then under Standard Colors click the Green color square**

   The company name text is now green, the color of the company logo.

9. **Click in the title placeholder, click its edge, click the Align Text button in the Paragraph group, click Middle, click the Font Size list arrow, click 80, click a blank area of the slide, then save your changes**

   See **FIGURE 13-7**.

FIGURE 13-6: Entering bulleted text

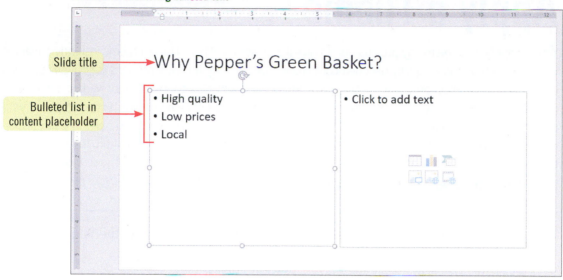

Slide title

Bulleted list in content placeholder

FIGURE 13-7: Completed title slide

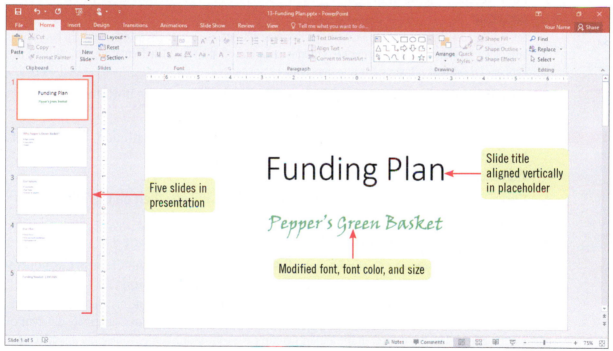

Slide title aligned vertically in placeholder

Five slides in presentation

Modified font, font color, and size

Indenting and unindenting text

When you enter text in a bulleted list placeholder, it is automatically formatted as a Level 1 bullet, meaning that it starts at the left side of the placeholder. However, you can "demote" a bullet so it is indented from the left side, indicating it is a subbullet of the previous one. Click just before the first character in the bullet you want to demote, then press [Tab]. After you type the Level 2 bullet text and press [Enter], the next bullet will also be a Level 2 bullet. To raise a bullet to Level 1, click before the first character, then press [Shift][Tab].

You can also use the ruler to control text indents, just as you do in Microsoft Word. The ruler shows the indents for the text containing the insertion point. In any text placeholder, drag the **First line indent marker** ▽ to set the indent for the first line of the current paragraph. Drag the **Hanging indent marker** △ to set the indent for the second and subsequent lines of the current paragraph.

Apply a Theme

Learning Outcomes
• Apply a theme
• Apply a theme variant

You can apply a theme to any presentation to give it a professional look. Using a theme instantly enhances your work with a professionally designed combination of colors, graphics, fonts, and special effects, such as shadows and reflections. Once you apply a theme, you can also choose a color variant for a more distinctive appearance. Choose a theme that matches your presentation content. For example, if your presentation is related to nature, you might want to choose a theme with greens and blues as a suggestion of trees or plants. Although you can choose a theme when you first create a presentation, it is often helpful to first create your slide content, then try out several different themes to see which one looks best with your content. **CASE** ▶ *You decide to apply a theme that complements the content of your presentation.*

STEPS

1. **Click the Design tab, click the More button ⟱ in the Themes group, then point to (but don't click) the theme under "This Presentation"**
   Clicking the More button opens the full Themes gallery. Although you clicked Blank Presentation when creating this file, the ScreenTip for the highlighted icon at the top of the gallery shows that Office is the actual name of this theme, which is plain, having no special graphics or colors.

2. **Point to each theme in the gallery, then observe the presentation after you point to each one**
   See **FIGURE 13-8**. As you point to each theme, its name appears in a ScreenTip, which can help you refer to it later. Live Preview shows you what each theme looks like on the slide. The formatting you applied to the Pepper's Green Basket text on the title slide remains unchanged.

3. **Click the Retrospect theme (white background, brown bar at the bottom)**
   Your presentation slides are now formatted with the Retrospect theme.

4. **Click the Slide Show button 🖵 on the status bar, view the presentation, then return to Normal view**
   The bullet text is a bit small.

5. **Click Slide 2 in the Thumbnail pane, select the three bullets, then on the Mini toolbar click the Increase Font Size button until the text is 28 pt**

6. **Repeat Step 5 for the bullets on Slides 3 and 4, then return to Slide 1**

7. **Drag to select Pepper's Green Basket, click the Home tab, click the Change Case button in the Font group, click Capitalize Each Word, then click the Design tab**
   The Retrospect theme changed the text to uppercase. Now the company name matches how it appears in other marketing materials. Each theme lets you choose one of several **variants**, which are different color combinations. The first variant in the Variants group has a contrasting border, indicating it is selected. You decide to experiment with the other three variants of the Retrospect theme.

8. **Click the second, third, and fourth variants in the Variants group on the Design tab, observing the title slide and the slide thumbnails**
   The second variant has a green bar, which is appropriate for the company's goals.

9. **Click the second variant, click a blank area of the slide, then save your changes**
   See **FIGURE 13-9**.

FIGURE 13-8: Themes gallery

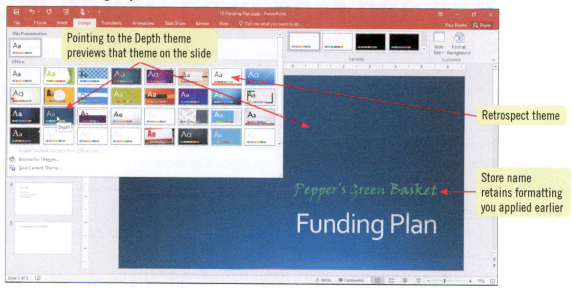

Pointing to the Depth theme previews that theme on the slide

Retrospect theme

Store name retains formatting you applied earlier

FIGURE 13-9: Theme with second variant applied

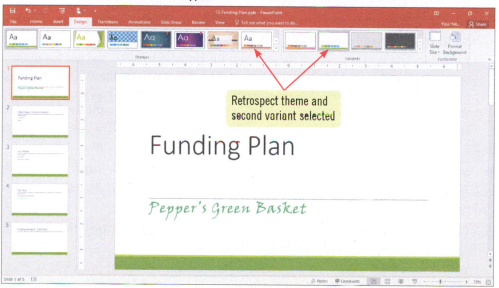

Retrospect theme and second variant selected

Using templates

While a theme is a combination of colors, graphics, fonts, and effects that can add visual interest to your presentations, a **template** has all these elements plus content and/or guidance for specific types of presentations you might want to create. You can use a template as a basis for creating your own presentation. Templates, along with themes, are organized into categories. For example, the Sales and marketing presentation template shown in **FIGURE 13-10** contains suggestions relevant to this topic. You select templates when you first create your presentation. At the New screen, click a category near the top of the screen, such as Business or Education, or use the Search text box. The templates and themes available in that category appear. Click a template or theme, then in the Preview window, click the More Images arrows to view that layout with sample text and graphics and

content guidance, if any. When you find one you want to use, click Create to create a new presentation based on that template or theme.

FIGURE 13-10: Sales and marketing presentation template

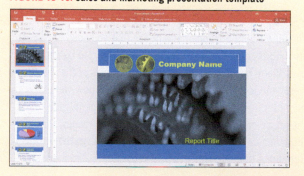

Add and Modify an Online Image

Learning Outcomes
- Add an online image
- Resize an image
- Add a shadow to an image

You can add predesigned photos and illustrations anywhere on a slide. You'll find countless images available online. To find images directly from within PowerPoint, you can click the Online Pictures icon in a content placeholder or click the Online Pictures button in the Images group on the Insert tab. You can search for images using **keywords**, words that you type into the Bing Image Search text box to locate items related to a topic. You can also apply special effects to enhance appearance of any image. **CASE** ▶ *You decide to add an image to the second slide, then format it to give it a shadow. Note: To complete the steps below, your computer must be connected to the Internet.*

STEPS

1. **Click the Slide 2 thumbnail**

   You'll insert the image in the content placeholder on the right side of the slide.

   > **TROUBLE**
   > Be sure you click the Online Pictures icon, not the Pictures icon, to its left.

2. **Click the Online Pictures icon 🖼 in the content placeholder**

   The Insert Pictures dialog box opens, as shown in **FIGURE 13-11**. You can use this dialog box to search the web using Bing Image Search, to select a picture from a social site such as Flickr, or to insert one from your OneDrive (if you are signed in with your Microsoft account).

   > **TROUBLE**
   > To show all web images, you can click the CC Only list arrow, then click All Images.

3. **Click in the Bing Image Search text box if necessary, type carrot, press [Enter], then point to any image**

   PowerPoint searches for images on the web using the Bing search engine, and displays thumbnail images of carrots. See **FIGURE 13-12**. A band near the bottom of the dialog box and the CC Only in the search box indicate that the images are licensed under a Creative Commons license. When you point to an image, its size and source appear in a screentip below the image. You can also click the Report Image button to tell Microsoft about an image that is irrelevant or inappropriate. See the yellow box at the bottom of this page for more information about using images.

4. **Scroll down, click the carrot image of your choice, then click Insert**

   The image you selected is inserted on the slide, and the Picture Tools Format tab appears and becomes active in the Ribbon.

5. **Click the Height text box in the Size group, type 3, press [Enter], then drag the carrot image so it is centered in the blank area**

   When you adjust the height, the width adjusts automatically to keep the image's proportions the same. As you drag the picture, you will see positioning lines called Smart Guides that help you align the object.

6. **Click the Picture Effects button in the Picture Styles group, point to Shadow, scroll down if necessary, then click the second effect in the first row under Perspective (ScreenTip reads "Perspective Diagonal Upper Right"), as shown in FIGURE 13-13**

   The carrot image now has a shadow under it, to its right.

7. **Save your changes**

Using online images legally

The Bing dialog box includes a notice that you need to respect an image's copyright. Many images are protected by copyright laws. If you find an image you want to use, check the source website to locate its **terms of use**, which tell how you are permitted to use it. You may need to request permission from the image creator or pay a **royalty** fee. Some images, such as those in a default Bing Image Search, carry a **Creative Commons license**, which allows free use of material under certain conditions. Go to creativecommons.org for more information. Images in the **public domain** are those that have passed out of copyright and are generally free to use. **Stock image** agencies such as iStockphoto and Shutterstock make photos and illustrations available for a fee that varies, depending on the image size and how the image is used. Openclipart.org is a good source for royalty-free clipart you can use for commercial and noncommercial purposes.

FIGURE 13-11: Insert Pictures dialog box

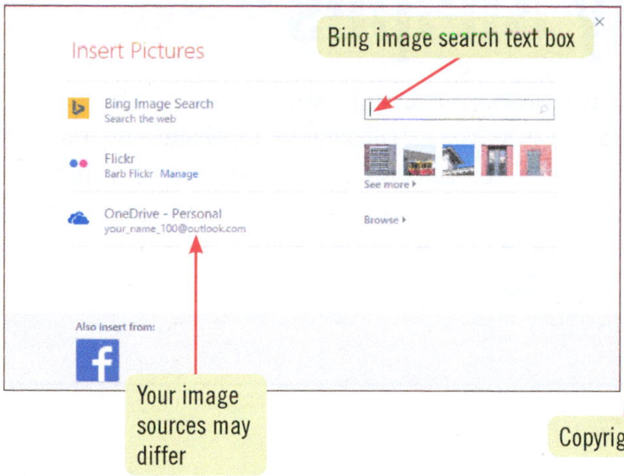

FIGURE 13-12: Found images for "carrot" search

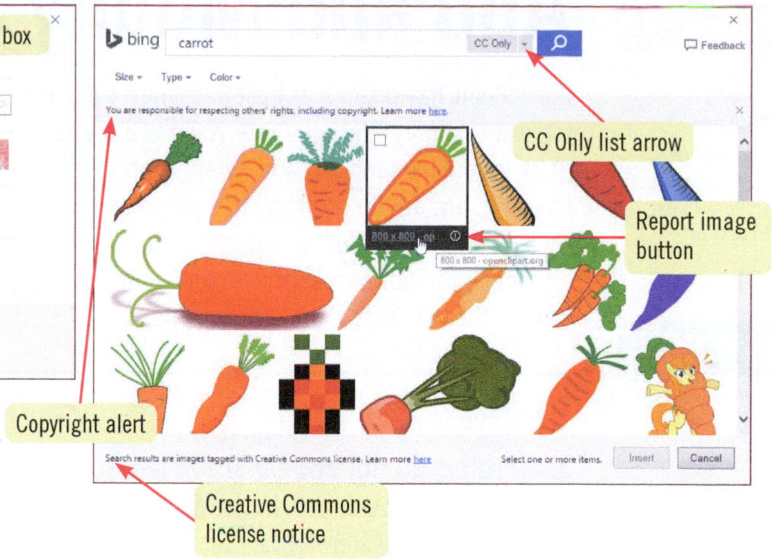

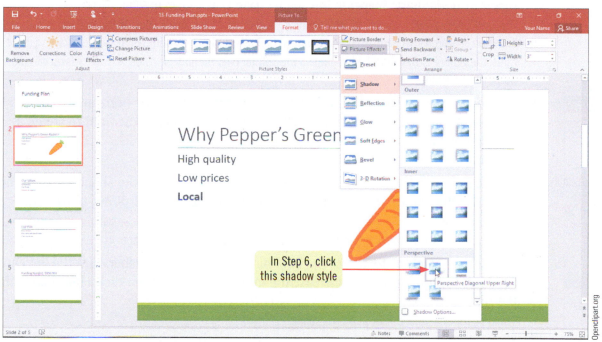

FIGURE 13-13: Selecting a shadow effect

In Step 6, click this shadow style

Understanding picture effects

PowerPoint contains many editing features that let you change the look of your pictures. First, select the picture to activate the Picture Tools Format tab. The Corrections button in the Adjust group lets you change the picture's color, brightness, and contrast. The Artistic Effects button lets you make your picture look like a painting or drawing. You can see a Live Preview of each effect before applying it. See **FIGURE 13-14**. Not all features are available for each file type.

FIGURE 13-14: Viewing picture corrections and artistic effects

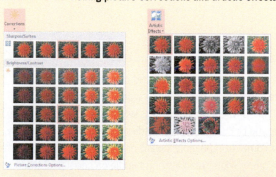

PowerPoint 2016

Add and Modify Shapes

PowerPoint has dozens of built-in shapes, such as squares, circles, and stars, which can help add visual interest to a presentation. Once you add a shape to a slide, you can change its appearance by modifying its style, outline, and fill, and by applying shape effects. You can also instantly add text to a shape and format it, just as you do with other presentation text. As you work with shapes, it's often helpful to display the PowerPoint horizontal and vertical rulers above and to the left of a slide, which can help you to insert a shape in the same location on multiple slides. **CASE** *You want to add a shape to call attention to the year on the title slide, so you add a shape and format it.*

STEPS

1. Move to Slide 1

2. If rulers do not appear above and to the left of the slide, click the View tab, then click the Ruler check box in the Show group to select it

   The horizontal and vertical rulers appear.

3. Click the Insert tab, click the Shapes button in the Illustrations group, then click the Bevel shape ☐ under Basic Shapes in the Shapes gallery, as shown in FIGURE 13-15

   You can select from a variety of shape styles, including Lines, Rectangles, Basic Shapes, Block Arrows, Equation Shapes, Flowcharts, Stars and Banners, Callouts, and Action Buttons. After you click the shape you want, the gallery closes and when you move the pointer over the slide, it changes to ✛ so you can draw the shape on the slide.

4. Position ✛ so it aligns with the 2" mark on the right side of the horizontal ruler and the 3" mark at the top of the vertical ruler, then drag down and to the right to create a bevelled box about 2" wide and 1" tall

   A bevelled box shape appears on the slide.

5. On the Drawing Tools Format tab, click the More button ▼ in the Shape Styles group, then click the Light 1 Outline, Colored Fill - Green, Accent 4 (third row, third from right), as shown in FIGURE 13-16

   The style is applied to the shape. You can type to add text to any selected shape on a slide.

6. Type 2017, select the text, click the Bold button on the Mini toolbar, click the Increase Font Size button Ａ˄ twice to increase the font size to 24 pt, then click a blank area of the slide

   The text appears bold and 24 pt on the shape.

7. Compare your screen to FIGURE 13-17, then save your changes

---

Resizing graphics and images

You can modify shapes, photos, and other images using the Picture Tools Format tab or the Drawing Tools Format tab, which opens whenever an image is selected. To resize a selected image, you can drag its sizing handles: To resize it proportionally, drag a corner sizing handle inward or outward; to resize only the height or width, drag a sizing handle on one side of the image. For additional size and position options, click the launcher 🖿 in the Size group to open the Format pane. In the category list, click ▷ next to Size for options to adjust its size, scale, and rotation. Click ▷ next to Position to see options to enter a specific location on the slide. Use Text Box options to set the text alignment, direction, behavior, and margins.

FIGURE 13-15: Selecting a shape from the Shapes gallery

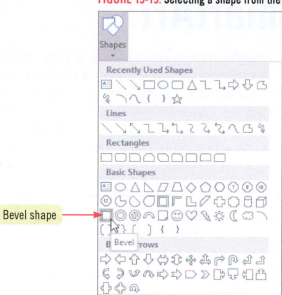

FIGURE 13-15: Selecting a shape from the Shapes gallery

Bevel shape

FIGURE 13-16: Applying a Shape Style

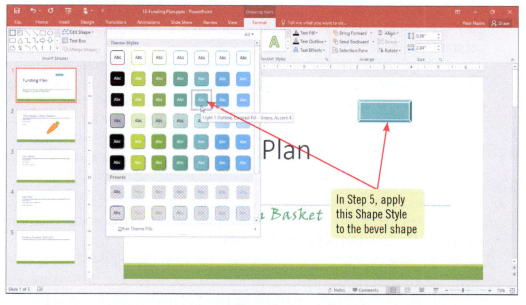

In Step 5, apply this Shape Style to the bevel shape

FIGURE 13-17: Title slide with formatted bevel shape

Shape with Shape Style and formatted text

Create SmartArt

You can use **SmartArt** to instantly create professional-looking diagrams to quickly communicate relationships and concepts. SmartArt includes many layouts from which to choose, organized by category, as listed in **TABLE 13-2**. For example, you can show proportional or hierarchical relationships, processes, and directional flows. You can also convert existing text to SmartArt. Once you create a SmartArt graphic, you can modify its style just as you can with any object. **CASE** ▶ *You want to emphasize the company's values and decide to use SmartArt to create a diagram to help illustrate them. You then convert new slide text to SmartArt.*

STEPS

1. **Click Slide 3 in the Thumbnail pane, then in the right placeholder click the Insert a SmartArt Graphic icon** 🖼

   The Choose a SmartArt Graphic dialog box opens, as shown in **FIGURE 13-18**. The dialog box consists of three panes. The left pane lists the SmartArt categories, the middle pane shows thumbnails of SmartArt layouts in the selected category, and the right pane shows a preview of the selected layout and a description of how to use it.

2. **Click Process, click several Process layouts observing the preview and description of each one, scroll down to and click the Circle Arrow Process (fifth row from the bottom, second from the left), then click OK**

   A blank SmartArt object with the Circle Arrow Process layout appears on the slide, using the current theme colors. The SmartArt Tools Design tab is active, as shown in **FIGURE 13-19**. The SmartArt object may also show a text pane on its left side that you can use to enter SmartArt text. Depending on your settings, the text pane might open or it might be closed and display only the text pane button on the left side of the object. You'll be entering text directly on the SmartArt objects, instead of using the text pane.

3. **Click the text placeholder in the top SmartArt object, then type Nourish**

   The text automatically resizes to fit the text box.

4. **Click the middle text placeholder, type Sustain, click the third text placeholder, type Protect, drag the SmartArt object to the left to center it in the white space, then click outside of the SmartArt object to deselect it**

   The SmartArt object is complete. The existing Slide 4 text about planning would look better as a SmartArt diagram.

5. **Click the Slide 4 thumbnail, on the Home tab click the Layout button in the Slides group, click Title and Content, then click anywhere in the bulleted text**

6. **Click the Convert to SmartArt button in the Paragraph group, click Pyramid List (bottom row, second from left), then click a blank area of the slide**

   The bulleted list is converted into a SmartArt graphic using the Pyramid List design.

FIGURE 13-18: Choose a SmartArt Graphic dialog box

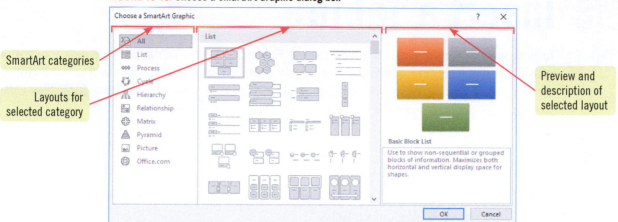

FIGURE 13-19: SmartArt inserted on a slide

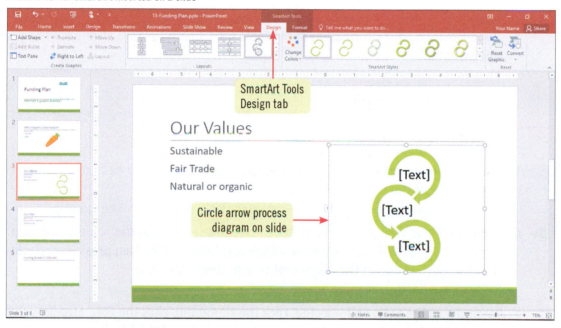

TABLE 13-2: Uses for SmartArt categories

type	use	type	use
List	Nonsequential information	Matrix	Complex relationships relating to a whole
Process	Directional flow and connections between parts of a process	Pyramid	Proportional or hierarchical relationship
Cycle	Repeating or circular processes	Picture	Highlight photos with or without text
Hierarchy	Decision tree, chain of command, and organizational chart	Office.com	Layouts downloadable online at Office.com
Relationship	Connections between two or more sets of information		

Insert a Table

Learning Outcomes
• Insert a table
• Format a table
• Add footer information

To summarize information efficiently, you can use PowerPoint tables. **Tables** are rows and columns of information and appear in PowerPoint just as they do in Word. You enter information and format them the same way. As in Word, a PowerPoint table is an object you can format, modify, and move. **CASE** *Justin asks you to use a table to summarize the three areas needing funding, and then format it.*

STEPS

1. Go to Slide 5, click the Home tab if necessary, click the Layout button in the Slides group, then click Title and Content

2. In the content placeholder click the Insert Table icon ⊞
   The Insert Table dialog box opens.

3. Replace 5 in the Number of columns text box with 2, replace 2 in the Number of rows text box with 4, then click OK
   A blank table appears on the page with the insertion point in the left header row cell.

4. Type the following information in the table cells, pressing [Tab] after each entry, except the last one:

Need	Cost
Classes	$50,000
Coordinator	$50,000
Café Expansion	$200,000

5. Move the pointer over the edge of the table, until the pointer becomes ⬍, then click once to select the entire table object
   Now any formatting you select will apply to the entire table, instead of just one part of it.

6. Click the Table Tools Layout tab, click the Height text box in the Table Size group, type 2, then press [Enter]; click the Width text box, type 6, then press [Enter]; click the Cell Margins button in the Alignment group, then click Wide
   Wide cell margins make the table data easier to read.

7. With the entire table still selected, click the Home tab, click the Font Size list arrow, click 28, then drag the table by its edge to the center of the blank area
   The completed table appears in **FIGURE 13-20**.

8. Click the Insert tab, click the Header & Footer button in the Text group, select the Footer check box, type your name in the Footer text box, then click Apply to All

9. Save your changes, click the Slide Sorter button ⊞ on the status bar, compare your completed presentation with **FIGURE 13-21**, close the presentation, exit PowerPoint, then submit your presentation to your instructor

FIGURE 13-20: Table with increased height and wide cell margins

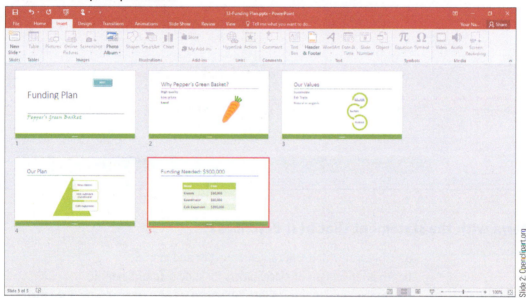

Funding Needed: $300,000

Need	Cost
Classes	$50,000
Coordinator	$50,000
Café Expansion	$200,000

FIGURE 13-21: Completed presentation

Slide 2: Openclipart.org

Adding slide footers

You can add a **footer** to appear at the bottom of one or more slides, containing such information as the date and time, the slide number, or specific text you enter. If you only want the footer to appear on certain slides, select the first slide, press and hold [Ctrl], then click the others. Click the Insert tab, then click the Header & Footer button in the Text group. In the Header and Footer dialog box, shown in **FIGURE 13-22**, click the Slide tab, and click the check boxes next to the items you want to include. You can select a date that updates automatically every time the presentation is opened, or a fixed date that you enter. Then click Apply to add the footer to the selected slides, or click Apply to All to add it to all the slides in your presentation.

FIGURE 13-22: Slide tab in Header and Footer dialog box

Practice

Concepts Review

Label each of the elements shown in FIGURE 13-23.

FIGURE 13-23

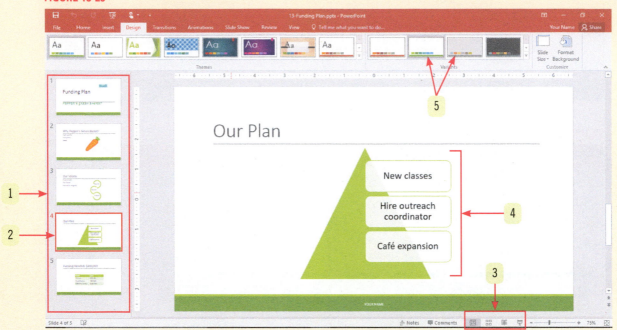

Match each term with the statement that best describes it.

6. **SmartArt**
7. **Placeholder**
8. **Slide Show view**
9. **Layout**
10. **Template**

a. Object in which you can enter text or add graphics
b. An arrangement of placeholders for slide text and graphics
c. Displays presentation slides full screen, as an audience would see them
d. Predesigned diagrams you can add to a slide
e. A combination of colors, graphics, fonts, effects, and content guidance, which you can use to create a presentation

Select the best answer from the list of choices.

11. **Which view allows you to see slide thumbnails arranged in rows?**
    a. Normal view
    b. Slide Sorter view
    c. Slide Show view
    d. Outline view

12. **Which view shows only slide text in the left pane, in an indented format?**
    a. Reading view
    b. Slide Show view
    c. Outline view
    d. Normal view

Skills Review

This Skills Review requires an Internet connection.

1. **Open and view a presentation.**
   a. Start Microsoft PowerPoint, then open the presentation file 13-2.pptx.
   b. Use the Next Slide button on the scroll bar to view each slide in Normal view.
   c. View the presentation in Outline view.
   d. View the presentation in Slide Sorter view.
   e. View the presentation in Slide Show view, viewing each slide.
   f. Return to Normal view.
   g. Close the presentation, clicking No if you are asked to save changes.

2. **Create a new presentation.**
   a. Create a new blank presentation, and save it as **13-Study Abroad**.
   b. Add three new slides using the Two Content layout.
   c. After the fourth slide, add one new slide with the Title and Content layout.
   d. Save your changes.

3. **Enter and format slide text.**
   a. Go to Slide 1, then type **Study Abroad** in the title placeholder.
   b. Type **Learn the World!** in the subtitle placeholder.
   c. In the title placeholder on Slide 2, type **Summer Programs**.
   d. On Slide 2, type the following bullets in the left content placeholder: **Earn college credit**, **Explore a country**, and **Go international!**.
   e. Add the information shown in the table to Slides 3, 4, and 5.
   f. Go to Slide 3, and apply bold formatting to the text "Live with families."
   g. Go to Slide 1 and select the title placeholder by clicking its border. (*Hint*: Click once in the placeholder first, then click its edge; verify that its border becomes a solid line.)

Slide	Title	Bullets in left placeholder
3	Semester Programs	• Learn language • Stay four months • Live with families
4	Internships	• Earn while you learn • Build your resume • Boost your language skills
5	Special Programs	[No bullet text on this slide]

   h. Format the selected placeholder text with the Arial Rounded MT Bold font, 60 pt, and the Blue font color in the Standard Colors row of the Font Color palette.
   i. Change the vertical alignment of the title text to Middle, then save your changes.

4. **Apply a theme.**
   a. Apply the Berlin theme to the presentation. (*Hint*: It has an orange gradient background.)
   b. Apply each of the four variants of the Berlin theme to the presentation, then return to the original (orange) variant.
   c. View the presentation in Slide Show view, then save your changes.

5. **Add and modify an online image.**
   a. Go to Slide 2, Summer Programs.
   b. Use the Online Pictures icon to insert the online picture of your choice from Bing Image Search. (*Hint*: Try search text such as "summer study abroad," "study abroad," or "travel.") Before you insert an image, select it and read its source information.
   c. Use the Shape Height and Shape Width text boxes in the Size group of the Picture Tools Format tab to resize the image so it fits well on the slide.
   d. Use the Picture Effects button to apply a shadow; in the Perspective section, choose the Perspective Diagonal Upper Left option.
   e. Save your changes.

Skills Review (continued)

6. Add and modify shapes.

   a. Go to Slide 3, and click the edge of the right content placeholder to select it.

   b. Press [Delete] to delete the placeholder.

   c. Display the horizontal and vertical rulers, if they are not already displayed.

   d. Draw a Left-Right arrow (in the Block Arrows group of the Shapes gallery) on the right side of the slide, starting at the 1" mark on the left side of the horizontal ruler and the 1" mark at the top of the vertical ruler, and dragging down approximately two inches and to the right approximately five inches, so it is approximately centered in the blank area to the right of the bulleted list.

   e. Enter the text **Live and Learn**, then format the text in 28 pt bold.

   f. Save your changes.

7. Create SmartArt.

   a. Go to Slide 4, and use the Insert a SmartArt Graphic icon to insert a Pyramid List diagram, from the Pyramid group.

   b. In the three text boxes, insert the words **Language**, **Business**, and **Culture**.

   c. Click Slide 5, then add a new slide to the end of the presentation, using the Title and Content layout.

   d. Add a slide title **APPLY NOW!** to the new slide, and add three bullets to the content placeholder: **Excellent reviews**, **Scholarships available**, and **Our 20th year**.

   e. Select the content placeholder, then convert it to SmartArt, using the Vertical Block List SmartArt design. (If the text pane opens, close it.)

   f. Save your changes.

8. Insert a table.

   a. On Slide 5, Special Programs, insert a table with 2 columns and 4 rows. Enter the information shown on the right into the table:

Country	Program
Brazil	Business
Spain	Language Studies
France	Culinary Arts

   b. Click the edge of the table to select the entire object, then use commands on the Table Tools Layout tab to add wide cell margins and increase the height of the table to 4".

   c. Verify that the table is selected, then use the Home tab to increase the font size to 28 points.

   d. Use the Table Tools Design tab to apply the Themed Style 1 - Accent 1 table style. (*Hint*: The style is in the first row of the Best Match for Document section of the gallery.)

   e. Adjust the width of both columns to fit the text attractively. (*Hint*: To adjust the width of the right column, you can change the Table Column Width setting in the Cell Size group on the Table Tools Layout tab.)

   f. Position the table in the center of the blank area. (*Hint*: Move the mouse pointer over the edge of the table and drag it, or use the Align Center command in the Arrange group of the Table Tools Layout tab.)

   g. Add your name to the slide footer and apply the footer to all slides. Save your changes, go to Slide Sorter view, then compare your screen to **FIGURE 13-24**.

   h. Save your changes, close the presentation, then exit PowerPoint. Submit your completed presentation to your instructor.

FIGURE 13-24

Slide 2: Openclipart.org

Independent Challenge 1

You volunteer at your town's community center, which presents activities to enrich the lives of residents, such as open mic nights and community suppers. To help promote community health, the board has recently decided to offer healthy cooking classes to residents at a reasonable cost. To help market your new class, you create a presentation that will play in the lobby of the club at the next open mic night.

a. Start PowerPoint, open 13-3.pptx from where you store your Data Files, then save it as **13-Cooking Class**.

b. Apply the Depth theme to the presentation, then apply the fourth variant of the Depth theme.

c. On Slide 1, add the subtitle text **To your health!**, change its font color to yellow from the Standard Colors palette, then apply bold formatting to it.

d. On Slide 2, add the following two bullets to the content placeholder: **Quick meal preparation** and **Health on a budget**, and apply bold formatting to "budget."

e. On Slide 2, add a right-pointing block arrow shape, then adjust its size to 2" high by 3" wide.

f. On Slide 3, add six bullets to the left placeholder: **Saturdays at noon**, **April and May**, **In our kitchen**, **36 Apple Street**, **Side entrance**, and **10 people maximum**.

g. Indent the fourth and fifth bullets as subbullets under the third bullet, "In our kitchen."

h. In the right placeholder, insert an online picture related to cooking by searching Bing Image search. Verify that the Bing search results state that the image has a Creative Commons license.

i. Apply the Perspective Diagonal Upper Right shadow to the picture.

j. Adjust the height of the picture to 4", then drag it to center it on the right side of the slide.

k. On Slide 4, use a placeholder icon to create a table with the following information:

Sign up	Where
Our website	www.communitycenter.org
Call Rhonda	222-555-0011
Take a form	Front desk

l. Double-click the right border at the first column to fit the text; adjust the width of the right column using the Table Tools Layout tab if necessary.

m. Select the entire table, make the table 3" high and 7" wide, and make the cell margins wide.

n. Apply the Themed Style 1 - Accent 4 style to the table. (*Hints*: It's in the Best Match for Document section of the gallery. If the web address was automatically formatted as a hyperlink, right-click it, then click Remove Hyperlink.)

o. Use a command on the Table Tools Layout tab to center all of the table text vertically within each cell.

p. Enlarge the table text to 24 pt, and adjust column widths as necessary so everything is ready to read. Center the table object on the slide.

q. Add your name to the footer on all slides. Spell-check your work, save your changes, then view the presentation in Slide Show view and compare your results to **FIGURE 13-25**. Close the presentation, exit PowerPoint. Submit your completed presentation to your instructor.

FIGURE 13-25

Independent Challenge 2

You work for Eco-Dunebugs, Inc., a company that rents eco-friendly electric dune buggies. You will be attending a Chamber of Commerce open house next month, and you will be in charge of the Eco-Dunebugs booth. You need to create a PowerPoint presentation that will run in the booth. The presentation will summarize the services the company offers.

a. Start PowerPoint, create a new presentation, then save it as **13-Eco-Dunebugs** in the location where you store your Data Files.

b. Add four more slides after the title slide, using the Two Content layout.

c. Enter the following slide information:

Slide	Title text	Subtitle text	Bullets in left placeholder
1	Sand Adventures	Eco-Dunebugs, Inc	
2	Kind to Nature		Electric Eco-friendly Quiet
3	Find Adventure Here!		Constructed dunes only Cape Beach Ocean Beach Sand Trail
4	Our Electric Buggies		ATVs Two-seaters Four-seaters
5	Call Today!		First-timer discount Driver tours available Call 555-3030

d. Save your work, then apply the Slice theme and the third variant to the presentation.

e. Select the bulleted list placeholders on slides 2, 3, 4, and 5 and enlarge the text to 28 pt. Save your work, then view the presentation in Outline View, Slide Sorter view, and Slide Show view. Return to Normal View.

f. Format the subtitle text on Slide 1 with bold formatting, enlarge the text to 32 pt, and change its font color to Orange, Text 2, Lighter 60%.

g. On Slide 3, select the right placeholder and delete it, add a triangle shape that's 4 inches wide, then type the following three text items on it, each on a separate line: **Families**, **Day Trippers**, **Thrill Riders**.

h. Adjust the triangle text size to 24 pt, and adjust the triangle width so none of the items wraps to two lines.

i. Apply the Shape Style of your choice to the triangle.

j. Go to Slide 4, and insert an online picture of a beach, using Bing Image Search. Verify that the Bing search results state that the image has a Creative Commons license.

k. Apply the artistic effect of your choice to the picture. (*Hint*: On the Picture Tools Format tab, use a command in the Adjust group.) Resize and reposition the image appropriately.

l. Go to Slide 2, change the layout to Title and Content, then convert the list to SmartArt, using the Pyramid List design. Resize and reposition the SmartArt object as necessary.

m. Go to the title slide, then add the Sun shape with your name in it anywhere on the slide.

n. Save your work, view the presentation in Slide Show view, close the presentation, then exit PowerPoint. Submit your completed presentation to your instructor.

Independent Challenge 3

You handle marketing for an art gallery that sells artwork made entirely of recycled ocean debris. You are working on a presentation that you will show at a local organization's meeting to acquaint them with the gallery's objectives and work.

a. Start PowerPoint, open 13-4.pptx from where you store your Data Files, then save it as **13-Art Gallery**.

b. Apply a theme and variant of your choice to the presentation, then move any objects on the slides if necessary so that all text is visible.

Independent Challenge 3 (continued)

c. On Slide 3, add an appropriate SmartArt design to the right placeholder, using the text **Reuse**, **Rethink**, and **Renew**. Position and size it so it looks attractive on the slide.

d. On Slide 5, add an online picture related to the slide content. Verify that the search results state that the image has a Creative Commons license. Apply picture corrections and artistic effects of your choice.

e. On Slide 6, add a table with the information on the right:
Format the table style, size, and margins using any options you choose, then resize and align the table appropriately on the slide.

When	Where
June 15	Eastern University
September 1	State Bank
November 1	Concert Hall

f. Apply text formatting of your choice to any other text in the presentation that you think should be emphasized. Check the size and position of all slide objects, resizing and moving them as necessary. Check your spelling.

g. Add your name to the footer on the title slide only.

h. Save your changes, view the presentation in Slide Show view, close the presentation, then exit PowerPoint. Submit your completed presentation to your instructor.

Independent Challenge 4: Explore

You are a marketing assistant for a computer parts dealer. You have been asked to prepare a presentation giving an overview of QDrives, a new line of portable solid state drives. You will use a PowerPoint template to create a presentation using the information below. You have been given the following information. The drives:

- Store data on electronic memory instead of spinning disk drives
- Are thin, lightweight, and durable
- Have no moving parts, so are less likely to be damaged when being carried around
- Transfer data more quickly than a traditional disk drive
- Consume less power than hard disk drives
- Are reliable and quiet, and feature no startup time
- Are available at the company website, qdrives.net, at the following sizes and prices: 250GB ($125) and 512GB ($225) and 1 TB ($450) of data

a. Start PowerPoint. At the Start screen, in the Search for online templates and themes box, type **Product Overview**, then press [Enter].

b. In the search results, click the Product overview presentation, then click Create. Save the presentation where you store your Data Files as **13-Drives**. (*Note:* If this template is not available, choose another product overview template and adjust your work in Steps d through g accordingly.)

c. Review the template content suggestions by viewing the presentation in Slide Show view.

d. Using the product information above, replace the slide content suggestions with content that gives an overview of the company's solid state drives. The presentation should have at least four slides. Delete any slides or placeholders you don't want to use (but do not delete Slide 3, Features and Benefits, or Slide 6, Pricing). Feel free to adapt or add slides and change their layouts as necessary.

e. On the Features and Benefits slide, add an online picture from Bing Image Search. Verify that the image has a Creative Commons license. Resize it and add any special effects that you feel are effective.

f. Adjust the theme and variant as necessary. Add shapes to any slides, adding QuickStyles and text as necessary to enhance their appearance.

g. On the Pricing slide, delete the placeholder content and create a table with the size and price information provided above.

h. Review your work, and move or resize objects and text as necessary.

i. Add SmartArt (or convert existing bullets to SmartArt) on any slides you feel are necessary.

j. Add your name to the footer of all slides, save your work, view the presentation in Slide Show view, then close the presentation and exit PowerPoint. Submit your completed presentation to your instructor.

Visual Workshop

Using the skills you have learned in this module, create and format the slides shown in **FIGURE 13-26**. Create a new, blank, presentation with three slides, and save it where you store your Data Files as **13-Your Stuff**. Use the Main Event theme with the third variant. The online art on Slide 1 is from Bing Image Search; if this image is unavailable, choose a different one. The SmartArt on Slide 2 is in the List category; the text is 44 pt., and the object has been narrowed. The bullet text on Slide 3 is 32 pt. The square shape on Slide 3 has a Perspective Diagonal Upper Left shadow. Place your name in the footer of the title slide only. Save the presentation, view it in Slide Show view, close it, then exit PowerPoint. Submit your completed presentation to your instructor.

FIGURE 13-26

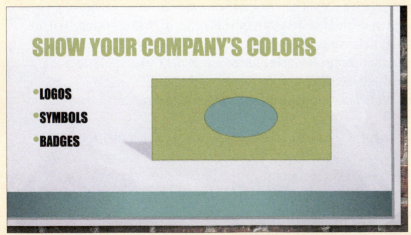

Polishing and Running a Presentation

CASE ▶ Jessica Ramos, marketing director, has asked you to help with a presentation for Pepper's Green Basket, which describes classes in healthy cooking that the store is offering during the summer. You will polish the presentation by adding pictures, sound, and video. Then you will set slide show transitions and animations, add speaker notes, print handouts, and review the presentation for effectiveness.

Module Objectives

After completing this module, you will be able to:

- Add pictures
- Add sound
- Add video
- Set slide transitions and timing

- Animate slide objects
- Use speaker notes and Notes Page view
- Print handouts and notes pages
- Design effective presentations

Files You Will Need

14-1.pptx	Erica.mp4
Kale Leaf.png	Benny and Griff.mp4
Dinner Bell.mp3	14-5.pptx
Dinner Bell.png	Truck Horn.aiff
Stir-Fry.mp4	Ice Cream Garnish.avi
14-2.pptx	Sundae.jpg
14-3.pptx	14-6.pptx
Lagoon Nebula.jpg	Seagull.wav
Saturn Radio	Lighthouse.jpg
Waves.mp3	Paths.jpg
Spiral Galaxy.jpg	Port.jpg
Star Cluster.mp4	Seals.jpg
14-4.pptx	Leaves.jpg
Laughter.wav	Drumsticks.png
Comedy.png	Mallets.png

Add Pictures

In PowerPoint, a picture might be a photograph, a shape you draw, a piece of clip art, or an illustration created using a graphics app. PowerPoint lets you insert pictures in many different file formats, including JPEG, PNG, GIF, TIFF, and BMP. After you insert a picture into your presentation, you can use features on the Picture Tools Format tab to **crop**, or cut off, portions of a picture to keep the parts you want and remove the picture background. **CASE** ▶ *You insert a photograph relating to an upcoming cooking class on a slide, crop it, then modify its background and its position on the slide.*

STEPS

1. **Start PowerPoint, open 14-1.pptx from the location where you store your Data Files, then save it as 14-Summer Cooking Classes**

2. **Go to Slide 3, then click the Pictures button 🖻 in the placeholder**
   The Insert Picture dialog box opens.

3. **Navigate to where you store your Data Files, click Kale Leaf.png, then click Insert**
   A picture of a kale leaf is inserted on the right side of the slide, and because the picture is selected, the Picture Tools Format tab appears on the Ribbon. You decide to crop off some of the wood-textured background on either side.

4. **Click the Crop button in the Size group, drag the left and right cropping handles toward the center, so your graphic looks like FIGURE 14-1, then click the Crop button in the Size group again**
   Clicking the Crop button again completes the crop. You have reduced the wood-textured area around the leaf using the **cropping handles**, which appear on each corner and side of the image so you can drag to indicate which areas you want to crop. However, you want to make the leaf stand out even more, so you decide to remove its background.

5. **Click the Remove Background button in the Adjust group**
   The area behind the kite image turns magenta, which represents the program's best "guess" at the areas to delete, and the Background Removal tab opens on the Ribbon, containing tools that let you fine-tune the removal areas if necessary. See FIGURE 14-2. For this picture, the entire wood background is magenta, so you know that all of the wood background will be removed. You need to adjust the borders so they don't cut off the top and bottom of the leaf.

6. **Drag one or more white selection handles away from the leaf, so the entire leaf appears in green, then click the Keep Changes button in the Close group**
   The background is removed, and only the leaf is visible. It needs to be larger.

7. **Move the mouse pointer over the picture's upper-right corner until the pointer changes to ⬈, then drag up and to the right about 1"**
   The picture is larger, but it would look better if it were centered.

8. **Move the mouse pointer over the picture until the pointer changes to ⬩, then drag the picture so it's centered horizontally in the white space**

9. **Click the Align button in the Arrange group of the Picture Tools Format tab, click Align Middle, click on a blank area of the slide, compare your screen to FIGURE 14-3, then save your changes**
   Now the picture is also centered vertically on the slide.

FIGURE 14-1: Cropping a picture

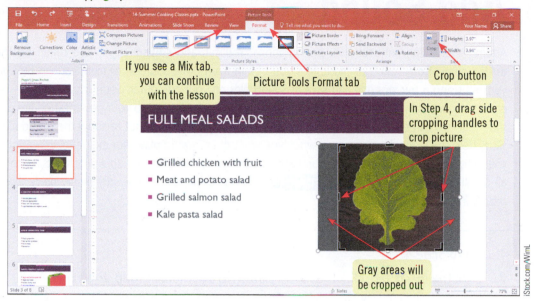

If you see a Mix tab, you can continue with the lesson

Picture Tools Format tab

Crop button

In Step 4, drag side cropping handles to crop picture

FULL MEAL SALADS

- Grilled chicken with fruit
- Meat and potato salad
- Grilled salmon salad
- Kale pasta salad

Gray areas will be cropped out

iStock.com/WimL

FIGURE 14-2: Removing a picture background

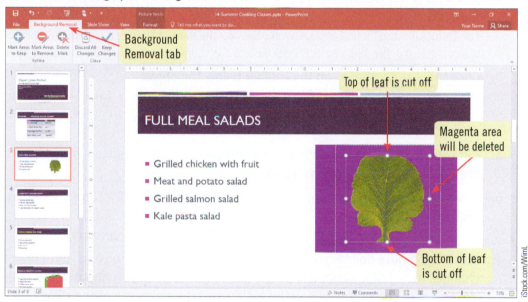

Background Removal tab

Top of leaf is cut off

FULL MEAL SALADS

Magenta area will be deleted

- Grilled chicken with fruit
- Meat and potato salad
- Grilled salmon salad
- Kale pasta salad

Bottom of leaf is cut off

iStock.com/WimL

FIGURE 14-3: Resized and repositioned picture

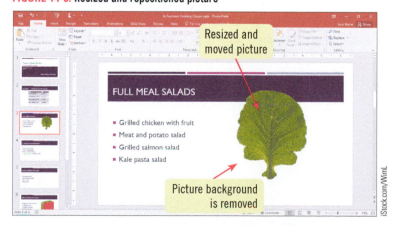

Resized and moved picture

FULL MEAL SALADS

- Grilled chicken with fruit
- Meat and potato salad
- Grilled salmon salad
- Kale pasta salad

Picture background is removed

iStock.com/WimL

Polishing and Running a Presentation

Add Sound

Adding sound can enhance your presentations. You can add **sound clips**, also called **audio files** or **audio clips**, from sound or music files you obtain from other sources, or from sounds that you record yourself using a microphone and save as sound files on your computer. Sounds can include short sound effects or complete musical selections. Like pictures, sounds you add to your presentation are objects on a slide that you can move and modify. You can also specify whether or not to show the sound file icon on a slide, how the icon will appear, and when you want the sound to play—for example, you might want the sound to play when you click the sound object during a presentation, when a slide starts, or to play across all the slides in your presentation. **CASE** ▶ *You add a sound to the healthy dinner party slide, and then modify it.*

STEPS

1. Go to Slide 4

2. Click the Insert tab, click the Audio button in the Media group, then click Audio on My PC

   The Insert Audio dialog box opens, as shown in **FIGURE 14-4**, letting you select an audio file from your computer or from an online source such as OneDrive.

3. Navigate to the location where you store your Data Files if necessary, click Dinner Bell.mp3, then click Insert

   The Dinner Bell.mp3 sound appears as an object on the slide, as shown in **FIGURE 14-5**. Because the sound object is selected, the Audio Tools Format tab and the Audio Tools Playback tab appear on the Ribbon.

4. Click the Play button ▶ on the toolbar below the object

   The audio file plays. The Start option in the Audio Options group reads "On Click," indicating that when you run the slide show, the sound will play only when you click the icon, not automatically when the slide appears. You decide to replace the sound icon with a picture.

5. Click the Audio Tools Format tab, click the Change Picture button in the Adjust group, then click Browse next to From a file

6. Navigate to where you store your Data Files if necessary, click Dinner Bell.png, then click Insert

   The dinner bell picture appears in place of the sound icon, though it is currently too small.

7. Move the mouse pointer over the lower-right corner of the picture, until the pointer changes to ↘, drag down and to the right until the object is about 2" tall, then drag the object to center it between the bullets and the right side of the slide

8. Click the Slide Show button 🖵 on the status bar, move the mouse pointer over the dinner bell image, click the Play button ▶ on the image as shown in **FIGURE 14-6**, press [Esc], then save your work

   After the slide appears, the sound plays only after you click the Play button under the sound object on the slide.

FIGURE 14-4: Insert Audio dialog box

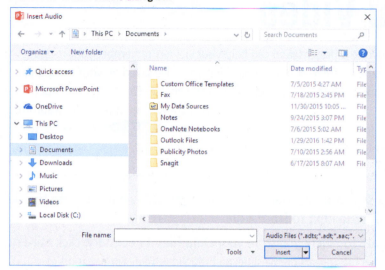

FIGURE 14-5: Inserted sound object on the slide

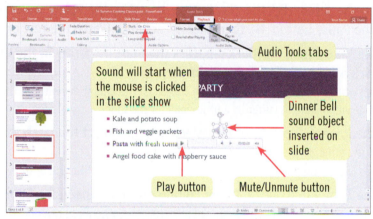

FIGURE 14-6: Playing the sound clip during the slide show

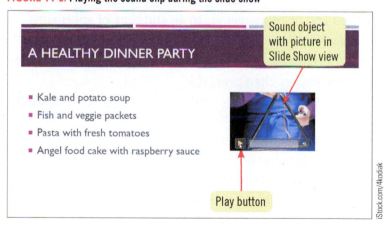

Adjusting sound playback during a slide show

You can change the way a sound plays back during the slide show by using the commands on the Audio Tools Playback tab. Using the tools in the Editing group, you can trim the beginning or end of an audio clip using the Trim Audio button, or have the sound fade in and out by using the Fade Duration controls. You can also control when and how the audio clip plays during the slide show by using the tools in the Audio Options group. To have a selected sound play in the background of the entire presentation, click the Play in Background button in the Audio Styles group. To reset a clip's playback settings to the default settings, click the No Style button in the Audio Styles group.

Add Video

Learning
Outcomes
• Insert a video clip
• Trim a video clip

Adding video to a presentation can help your viewers remember your message. You can insert a video file from an online resource or from a collection you have saved on your computer or an online location. After you insert a video into your presentation, you can use features on the Video Tools Playback tab to adjust how and when the video plays during the slide show. See TABLE 14-1 for a summary of how to insert media objects on slides without using slide placeholders. **CASE** *You decide to add a video of stir frying to support the information on the Simple Veggie Stir Fries page.*

STEPS

1. **Go to Slide 5 if necessary, click the Insert Video button** ⊞ **in the right placeholder, then click Browse next to From a file**

2. **Navigate to where you store your Data Files if necessary, click Stir-Fry.mp4, then click Insert**
   The video file appears on the slide, and the Video Tools Format and Video Tools Playback tabs appear on the Ribbon.

3. **Point to the video, click the Play button** ▶ **below the video, watch for a few seconds, press the Pause button** ‖ **, then click** ▶ **again to watch the rest of the video**

4. **Click the Video Tools Playback tab, click the Start list arrow in the Video Options group, then click Automatically as shown in FIGURE 14-7**
   The video will now start as soon as the slide appears in the slide show, without the presenter having to click it first. The video image is currently a little small for the slide.

5. **Drag the lower left corner of the selected video object to match the size and location shown in FIGURE 14-8**
   The video is a bit long, so you decide to remove a segment from the end of the video.

6. **Click the Trim Video button in the Editing group on the Video Tools Playback tab**
   The Trim Video dialog box opens, as shown in FIGURE 14-9, where you can drag the green start point and red end point markers to shorten the video from the beginning or the end. You want to shorten the video.

7. **Drag the red End point marker** ▮ **to an end time of approximately 10 seconds**
   The video will end at the point you set. You decide to preview the movie in Slide Show view.

8. **Click OK, click the Slide Show button** 🖵 **on the status bar, view the slide until the video finishes playing, then press [Esc]**
   The current slide plays automatically, from the start point to the end point you set, as soon as the slide appears. You decide to preview the slide show as your audience will see it.

9. **Click the Slide Show tab, click the From Beginning button in the Start Slide Show group, press [Spacebar] to view the slide show, clicking the Play button below the audio object on Slide 4 and viewing the video object as it plays on Slide 5, then save your changes**
   The sound plays after you click the audio object on Slide 4, and the movie plays as soon as Slide 5 appears.

TABLE 14-1: Inserting media objects using the Insert tab

to add	from this group	use command(s)
Images from your computer	Images	Pictures
Images from Bing image search	Images	Online Pictures
Sounds from your computer	Media	Audio > Audio on My PC...
Video from your computer	Media	Video > Video on My PC...
Video from YouTube	Media	Video > Online Video...

FIGURE 14-7: Setting the video to start automatically

Start list arrow

FIGURE 14-8: Resized video in new location

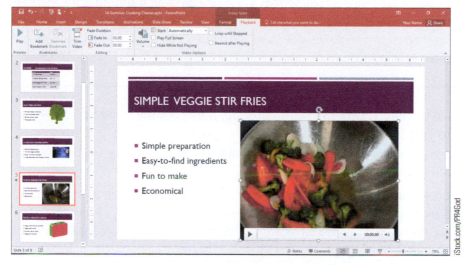

iStock.com/PR4God

FIGURE 14-9: Trim video dialog box

Start point marker

Timebar

End point marker

iStock.com/PR4God

Formatting sound and video objects

You can change the way a sound or video object appears on a slide. For example, you can adjust its color or brightness, just as you can with a picture. You can also apply a style, such as a frame, or a shape, border, or effect, as well as crop and rotate the object. For example, **FIGURE 14-10** shows a video in an oval shape with a shadow effect. To copy formatting from one sound or video object to another, click the object whose formatting you want to copy, click the Format Painter button in the Clipboard group on the Home tab, then click the second object.

FIGURE 14-10: Applying styles to objects

Video courtesy of Michele Miller

Set Slide Transitions and Timing

Learning Outcomes
• Add slide transitions
• Add slide timings

There may be times when you want to run a presentation automatically, without manually controlling when each slide appears. For example, you might want the presentation to run unattended at a booth or kiosk. You might also want to customize how slides appear in a slide show. To do this, you can set slide transitions and timings in PowerPoint. A **transition** is a special effect that determines how a slide appears as it enters or leaves the screen, such as a fade or a dissolve. A **timing** is the number of seconds a slide remains on the screen before advancing to the next one. **CASE** *Jessica wants to concentrate on her message instead of running the slide show. You decide to set the transitions and timings, and add an audio transition to the last slide.*

STEPS

1. **Go to Slide 1, click the Transitions tab, then click the More button ⤓ in the Transition to This Slide group**

   A gallery shows transition effects in three categories: Subtle, Exciting, and Dynamic Content. You decide to add an Exciting transition to Slide 1.

2. **Click the Cube transition in the Exciting section, as shown in FIGURE 14-11**

   You see a preview of the Cube transition on Slide 1. When a slide has a transition applied to it, or has a video like the one you inserted in Slide 5, a small transition icon ★ appears under the slide number in the Thumbnail pane, alerting you that a transition has been applied to this slide. Now you want to apply the same transition to all the slides.

3. **Click the Apply To All button in the Timing group**

   The transition you applied to Slide 1 is now applied to all slides in the presentation. The transition icon appears under every slide number in the Thumbnail pane. You now want to set the slide show to advance automatically after a set amount of time.

4. **In the Timing group, click the Advance Slide After up arrow until 00:08.00 appears, then click the Apply To All button**

   Each slide will remain on the screen for 8 seconds before automatically advancing to the next one. But you can override these settings during the presentation by pressing [Spacebar] or any other slide advance technique, because the On Mouse Click check box is still selected.

5. **Click the Slide Sorter button ▦ on the status bar, then adjust the zoom using the status bar controls so you can see all the slides**

   The transition icon and slide timing appear beneath each thumbnail.

6. **Click Slide 7, click the Sound list arrow in the Timing group, click Whoosh, compare your screen to FIGURE 14-12, then click the Preview button in the Preview group**

   The Whoosh sound plays during the transition to Slide 7. Finally, you decide to view the entire presentation with the transitions and timings you have set. Instead of using Slide Show view, you decide to use Reading view, which lets you see a presentation in full screen but also gives you status bar controls that are useful for reviewing a presentation.

7. **Click Slide 1, click the Reading View button ▤ on the status bar, allow the presentation to play for the first three slides, then use [Spacebar] to advance the remaining slides**

   The slide transitions, timing, animation, and sounds play in the slide show until the end, then you return to Slide Sorter view. You decide to remove the slide timings so it's a little easier to work with the presentation.

8. **In Slide Sorter view, click Slide 1, press and hold [Shift], click Slide 8, click the Transitions tab if necessary, click the After check box in the Timing group to deselect it, then save your changes**

FIGURE 14-11: Applying the cube transition

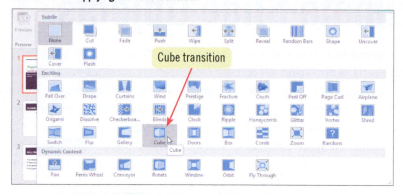

Cube transition

FIGURE 14-12: Timing and a transition applied in Slide Sorter view

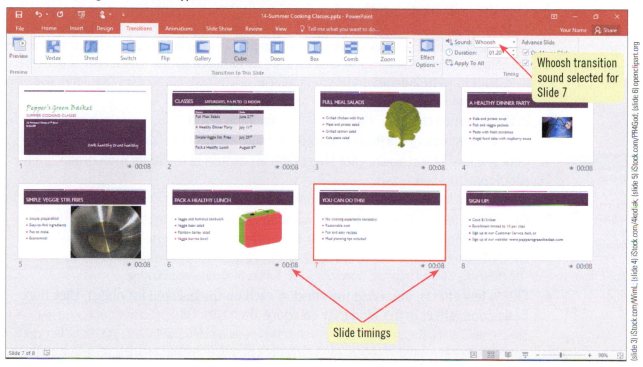

Whoosh transition sound selected for Slide 7

Slide timings

Using slide masters

There may be times when you want to make a design change to all the slides in your presentation, such as changing the alignment or font size of text, or adding a logo to every slide. Instead of making the change on each slide, you can change the slide master. A **slide master** contains the layouts, design elements, and other formatting for a presentation. Every slide you create is based on a slide master. A slide master has a number of supporting **layouts**, or arrangements of slide placeholders, such as a Title slide layout, which has placeholders for a presentation title and subtitle, or a Title and Content layout, which has placeholders for a slide title and for slide content. You can customize a slide master, or any supporting layout, and save it for future use. See **FIGURE 14-13**. To modify a slide master, click the View tab, then click the Slide Master button in the Master Views group. Click to select a master in the Thumbnail pane, then use the buttons on the Slide Master tab to apply a theme, change its background, or add placeholders. To create a new slide master, click the Insert Slide Master button in the Edit Master group, then customize the new slide master or one of its supporting layouts.

FIGURE 14-13: Adding a logo to the Title and Content layout master

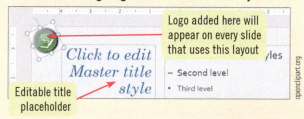

Logo added here will appear on every slide that uses this layout

Editable title placeholder

openclipart.org

Polishing and Running a Presentation

Animate Slide Objects

Learning Outcomes
• Animate slide graphics
• Animate slide text
• Copy animation effects

Once you have added text and graphics to a presentation, you can add interest to them by applying animation effects. **Animation effects** are movements or changes in appearance that you can apply to any text placeholder or graphic, including clip art, photos, and illustrations. For example, you can have a graphics "fly in" from the top or bottom of the slide, or "bounce out." You can also call attention to a slide object by having it "grow," "pulse," or "spin." Once you have animated an object, you can use the Animation Painter to apply those same settings to other objects. **CASE** ▶ *You decide to animate the graphic on Slide 3 and the bulleted text in Slide 8. Then you copy the text animation to the text in Slide 7.*

STEPS

1. **Double-click Slide 3 to display it in Normal view, then click the kale image to select it**

2. **Click the Animations tab, then click the More button ▼ in the Animation group**
   A gallery opens, showing animation effects in four categories. See **FIGURE 14-14**. **Entrance animations** determine how an object appears on the slide, **Emphasis animations** show various ways you can emphasize an object that's already on the slide, and **Exit animations** determine how an object leaves the slide. **Motion path animations** let you move slide objects from one location to another along paths formed by lines or shapes.

3. **In the Entrance category, click the Fly In animation effect**
   The slide shows a preview of the kale "flying in" from the bottom of the slide.

QUICK TIP
To slow down an animation effect for a selected object, click the Duration up arrow in the Timing group.

4. **Click the kale object again, click Effect Options button in the Animation group, then click From Top-Left**
   Now the kale flies in from the upper-left corner of the slide.

5. **Go to Slide 8, click the bulleted list placeholder, click the Animation More button ▼, then click More Entrance Effects near the bottom of the gallery**
   The Change Entrance Effect dialog box opens, showing a larger gallery of entrance effects. See **FIGURE 14-15**. The effects are divided into four categories: Basic, Subtle, Moderate, and Exciting.

6. **Click a few effects, observing the effect of each on the bulleted list object, click the Basic Zoom effect in the Moderate category, then click OK**
   The preview behind the dialog box shows each bullet appearing individually. After the dialog box closes, an **animation order number** appears in an orange box next to each bullet on the slide, indicating the order in which it will play, as shown in **FIGURE 14-16**. You decide to have the bullets appear all at the same time.

QUICK TIP
The Animation Painter copies animation effects just as the Format Painter copies formatting of text and graphics. To copy to two or more slides, double-click the Animation Painter button, click the item on each slide, then press [Esc].

7. **Click the Effect Options button in the Animation group; in the Sequence category click All at Once, then click the Preview button in the Preview group**
   The animation previews, and the numbers next to each bullet change to "1"s, indicating that all the bullets appear at the same time. Now you decide to copy the animation effect to Slide 7.

8. **Click the bulleted list placeholder on Slide 8 to select it, click the Animation Painter button in the Advanced Animation group, go to Slide 7, then click the bulleted list placeholder**

9. **Save your work, go to Slide 1, then click the Slide Show button on the status bar and view the slide show, pressing [Spacebar] to advance the slides; play the sound on Slide 4, then play the rest of the show**

Working with motion paths

After you apply a motion path animation to an object, dotted lines appear that tell you the movement path the object will take. For line, arc, and turn animations, green and red triangles indicate the animation's starting and ending point. If you click the dotted line for these animations, a second image of the object appears to show you its ending position. Custom Path animations let you click and drag to create your own customized path.

FIGURE 14-14: Selecting an animation

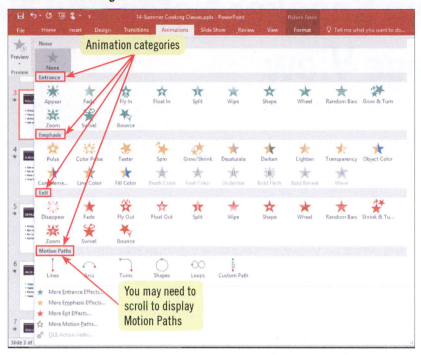

FIGURE 14-15: Change Entrance Effect dialog box

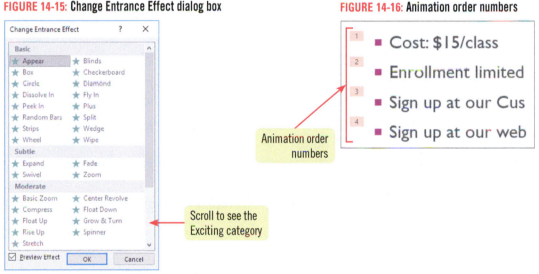

Scroll to see the Exciting category

FIGURE 14-16: Animation order numbers

Animation order numbers

1 ■ Cost: $15/class
2 ■ Enrollment limited
3 ■ Sign up at our Cus
4 ■ Sign up at our web

Adding animations using the Animation pane

You can add more than one animation to an object and control when each animation occurs using the Animation pane. Select an object to which you've applied one animation, then click the Add Animation button in the Advanced Animation group and select another animation, such as an Exit animation. Click the Animation Pane button in the Advanced Animation group. The Animation Pane opens to the right of the slide, and lists the two animations in order. Click the list arrow to the right of a selected animation to see options for changing that animation's timing or behavior. See **FIGURE 14-17.** Drag an animation up or down in the list to change its order. To delete an animation effect, click its list arrow, then click Remove.

FIGURE 14-17: Using the Animation Pane

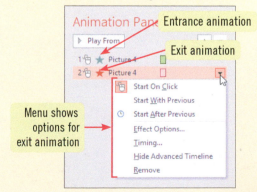

Use Speaker Notes and Notes Page View

Learning Outcomes
• Add speaker notes
• View slides in Notes Page view

When you show your presentation to others, you might need to use notes to remind yourself of important points you want to make. You can add **speaker notes** to any slide using the **Notes pane**, which appears below the slide window in Normal view. Then you can view your slides and notes in **Notes Page view**, print a copy of your slides with their notes, and refer to them during the presentation. **CASE** ▶ *Jessica asks you to mention more about the store's cooking classes, so you insert notes about them and then run the presentation.*

STEPS

1. **Go to Slide 1 if necessary, click the View tab, then click the Notes button in the Show group**
   The Notes pane appears below the slide, with the prompt text "Click to add notes." Although the pane appears to be small, it can hold multiple lines of text.

2. **Click in the Notes pane, then type This is our second year of classes., as shown in FIGURE 14-18**

3. **Enter the following slide notes:**

Slide 2	Customers prefer morning classes.
Slide 3	These are all super easy to prepare.
Slide 4	You can make these ahead of time.

4. **Click the Notes Page button in the Presentation Views group, click the Zoom button in the Zoom group, type 120% in the Percent box, then click OK**

5. **Scroll up if necessary to display the entire slide, then press [▲] and [▼] on the keyboard to view the slides and the notes**
   Notes Page view shows a reduced image of your slides with your notes below it. See **FIGURE 14-19**, which shows the notes for Slide 1.

6. **Click the Normal View button in the Presentation Views group, then save the presentation**

FIGURE 14-18: Speaker notes

This is our second year of classes.

Speaker notes in
the Notes pane

FIGURE 14-19: Notes Page view

Pepper's Green Basket

SUMMER COOKING CLASSES

36 Prospect Street, 2nd floor
Briarcliff

Cook healthy to eat healthy

This is our second year of classes.

Using Presenter view

It's often helpful to use **Presenter view**, a special view you use when showing your presentation using an external monitor or projection screen. In Presenter view, the slide show appears on the projected screen for the audience to view, but on your computer screen you see the slide, your speaker notes, and the next slide, all at the same time. To enter Presenter view, click the Slide Show view button on the status bar. If you are using an external monitor, Presentation view starts automatically. To practice a presentation in Presenter view with only your computer, go to Slide Show view, then right-click the first slide. Left-click Show Presenter View, and you see your presentation in three panes, shown in **FIGURE 14-20**. The current slide is on the left, a preview of the next slide is on the right, and your speaker notes are below the preview. Each time you click the Next Slide button at the bottom of the screen, you see the next slide or the next action. Tools under the left slide let you annotate a slide, navigate to a different slide,

zoom in, blacken a slide, or see a list of keyboard navigation commands.

FIGURE 14-20: Presenter view

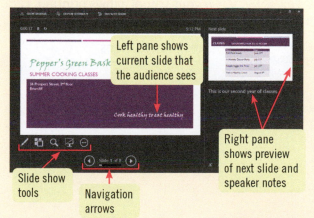

Left pane shows
current slide that
the audience sees

Right pane
shows preview
of next slide and
speaker notes

Slide show
tools

Navigation
arrows

Print Handouts and Notes Pages

Learning Outcomes
• Print handouts
• Print Notes pages

When you give a presentation, you may also want to give a printed copy to your audience so they can use it to take notes. You may also want a printed copy of your slides with speaker notes that you can refer to during the presentation. You can print **handouts**, which contain one or more slides per page, and you can include blank lines for audience members to use for notes. **Notes pages** contain a thumbnail of each slide plus any speaker notes you added in the Notes pane, as well as header and footer information. Before printing any document, it is always a good idea to preview it. *Note:* Many schools limit printing in order to conserve paper. If your school restricts printing, skip Steps 5 and 7. **CASE** *You preview the handout pages, add information to the handout header, and print the handouts for Jessica to review. Then you print Notes pages she can refer to during the presentation.*

STEPS

1. **Click the File tab, click Print, click the Full Page Slides list arrow; in the Handouts section click 2 Slides, then click the page navigation buttons to view the handout pages**

   You see a preview of the handouts showing two slides per page. The date appears in the **handout header**, the area at the top of every page. You want to add the presentation name to the header.

   QUICK TIP
   If you do not have a color printer selected, the preview will appear in grayscale, showing shades of gray, and the Color list arrow will be the Grayscale list arrow.

2. **Click Edit Header & Footer at the bottom of the Settings section, then click the Notes and Handouts tab in the Header and Footer dialog box if necessary**

3. **Click the Header check box to select it, click the Header text box, type Summer Cooking Classes, then click Apply to All**

   The text you typed now appears in the upper-left corner of all the handout pages. See **FIGURE 14-21**.

4. **Click the Color list arrow, then click Pure Black and White**

   Using the Pure Black and White option is the most economical way to print because it prints object outlines and does not print colors or background shading, saving toner.

   QUICK TIP
   To select all, current, or a range of slides to print, click Print All Slides, then select the option you want.

5. **If your school allows printing, click the Print button in the Print section to print the handouts (if you don't print, click the Back button ⬅ to return to the Home tab)**

   You return to the Home tab. Next, you print the Notes pages.

6. **Click the File tab, click Print, click the 2 Slides list arrow, click Notes Pages, navigate to page 1 if necessary, compare your screen to FIGURE 14-22, then click ▶ to see the notes pages**

   You see a preview of the Notes pages, with the header information you entered. Each notes page contains one slide as well as any speaker notes. The preview shows that the pure black-and-white setting you chose for the handouts also applies to the notes pages.

   QUICK TIP
   To select another printer, click the selected printer in the Printer section, then click a different printer.

7. **If your school allows printing, click the Print button in the Print section to print the handouts (if you don't print, click ⬅ to return to the Home tab)**

8. **Save your changes**

FIGURE 14-21: Preparing to print handouts with headers

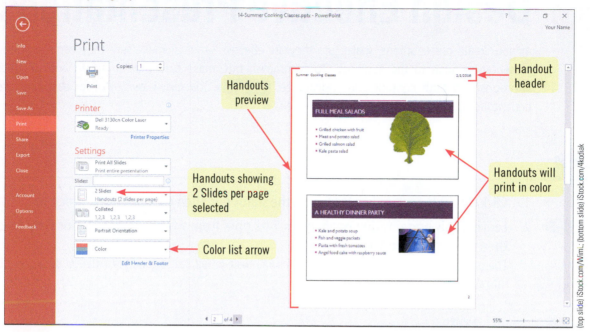

FIGURE 14-22: Preparing to print Notes pages with headers

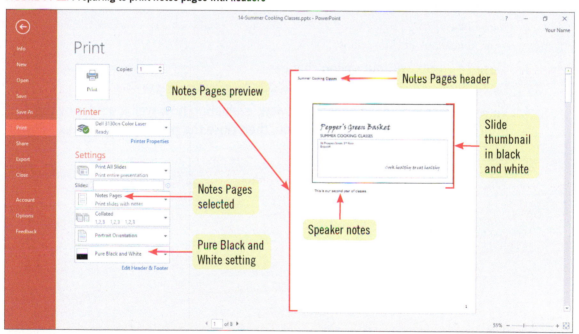

Printing presentation slides

You might want to print each of your presentation slides on a separate page, adding header and footer information such as the date and slide number. Click the File tab, click Print, click the Notes Pages (or the previously selected print option) list arrow, then click Full Page Slides. The first slide appears in the preview area. To add a header and footer, click Edit Header & Footer, click the Date and time check box to select it, and select the Update automatically or Fixed option. Click the Slide number check box to print the slide number on each slide, and click the Footer check box to select it and then enter footer text. If you don't want the header or footer information to print on the title slide, select the Don't show on title slide check box. Then click Apply to put the header and footer information on the current slide only, or click Apply to All to have the information appear on all presentation slides. Click the Next Page button ▶ to view the slides with the header and footer information you added. When you return to your presentation slides, you'll see the header and footer information on the slide or slides you specified.

Design Effective Presentations

**Learning
Outcomes**
• Follow effective
  presentation
  guidelines
• Evaluate a
  presentation

As you create presentations, make sure they are effective—that is, make sure they communicate your presentation goals to the audience. To accomplish this, make sure that your text and graphics are appropriate in both content and appearance. **CASE** ▶ *You review guidelines for designing effective presentations, then review your own presentation.*

STEPS

1. **Click the Slide Sorter view button on the status bar, then compare your screen to FIGURE 14-23**

QUICK TIP

The slides advance
automatically.

2. **Leaving this presentation open, open 14-2.pptx from where you store your Data Files, then view it in Slide Show view**

   The presentation (see **FIGURE 14-24**) outlines some basic principles of good presentation design, organized into six sections:
   1. Content
   2. Design
   3. Text
   4. Graphics
   5. Colors
   6. Animations and Transitions

3. **Close 14-2.pptx without saving changes**

   The Summer Cooking Classes presentation remains open on your screen.

4. **View the presentation in Slide Show view, evaluating how well it abides by the principles of good presentation design, then close the presentation and exit PowerPoint**

Creating interactive content with Office Mix

Office Mix is an auxiliary program called an **add-in**, also called **plug-in**, that you add to PowerPoint. **Office Mix** lets you create interactive online presentations, called **Mixes**, that you can make available to others on the web. A Mix can contain audio or video recordings, screen recordings, animations, and narrations. You can also include free-form screen inking to annotate important points on the screen. In addition, you can create interactive lessons, quizzes, and polls. After creating a Mix and sending it to the Office Mix portal, you can share the link with others so they can access the Mix using a web browser. They don't even have to have Windows or PowerPoint. You can then view statistics showing how many people viewed it, how long they stayed, and their quiz results. To get Office Mix, close PowerPoint, go to mix.office.com, click the Get Office Mix button, then log into your Microsoft account. After the add-in downloads to your computer, follow the onscreen instructions to install it. When the installation is completed, start PowerPoint and display the Mix tab if it does not appear (click the Customize Quick Access Toolbar button, click More Commands, click Customize Ribbon, click the Mix check box in the list on the right, then click OK.) Use the commands on the Mix tab and the information in the Welcome task pane to create a Mix.

FIGURE 14-23: The final presentation

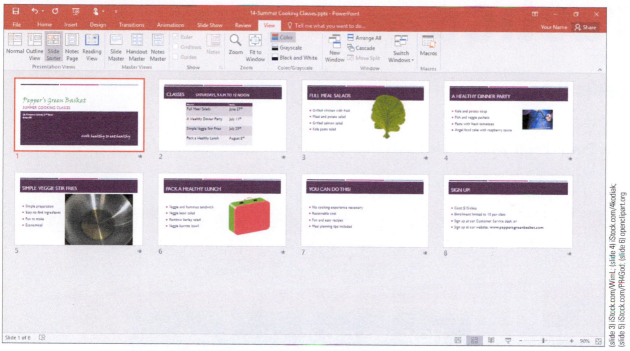

FIGURE 14-24: Viewing a presentation on design

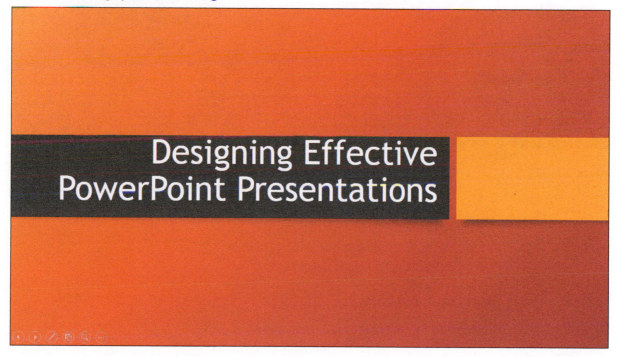

Practice

Concepts Review

Label the PowerPoint window elements shown in FIGURE 14-25.

FIGURE 14-25

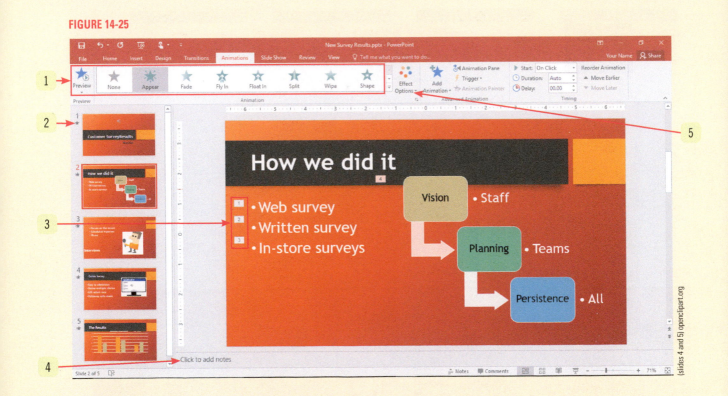

Match each term with the statement that best describes it.

6. **Animation**
7. **Transition**
8. **Crop**
9. **Slide master**
10. **Sound clip**
11. **Serif**

a. A small, decorative stroke at the top and bottom of letters
b. A special effect that determines how a slide enters or leaves the screen
c. Audio file that you can insert on a slide
d. Movement or change in appearance
e. Every slide is based on one of these
f. To remove part of a picture

Select the best answer from the list of choices.

12. **To copy a movement or change in appearance to another object, use the:**
    a. Sounds clips.
    b. Handouts.
    c. Animation Painter.
    d. Transitions.

13. **Which animation type calls attention to an object that's already on a slide?**
    a. Entrance animation
    b. Transition
    c. Exit animation
    d. Emphasis animation

14. Which of these ensures greater readability in a presentation?

a. Sans serif fonts

b. Serif fonts

c. Lots of bright yellow

d. Text under 22 pt in size

15. Which PowerPoint view shows slide thumbnails as well as speaker notes?

a. Presenter view

b. Notes Page view

c. Normal view

d. Slide Show view

Skills Review

1. Add pictures.

a. Start PowerPoint, open 14-3.pptx from the location where you store your Data Files, then save it as **14-Space Studies**.

b. Play the presentation in Reading view to get an idea of the content, then return to Normal view.

c. On Slide 1, insert the picture **Lagoon Nebula.jpg** from the location where you store your Data Files, using the Pictures command on the Insert tab.

d. Crop the picture from both sides so it's approximately a square.

e. Resize and reposition the picture so it fits above the slide title and is centered. (*Hint*: Use the Align > Align Center command in the Arrange group of the Picture Tools Format tab.)

2. Add sound.

a. On Slide 7, insert the audio file **Saturn Radio Waves.mp3**, then play the sound. Move it to the top of the slide, next to the title.

b. Verify the inserted sound object is set to play when you click it during the slide show. (*Hint*: Select the sound object if necessary, then on the Audio Tools Playback tab, verify the Start option is set to On Click in the Audio Options group.)

c. With the sound object still selected, use the Change Picture command on the Audio Tools Format tab to replace the speaker graphic with **Spiral Galaxy.jpg** from where you store your Data Files.

d. Enlarge the sound file object so it's approximately 1 inch square, then position it next to the title.

3. Add video.

a. Go to Slide 2, insert the video file **Star Cluster.mp4** from the location where you store your Data Files, then play the video.

b. Set the video to play automatically, as soon as the slide appears. (*Hint*: Use the Video Tools Playback tab.)

c. Use the Video Tools Playback tab to trim off approximately the last 3 seconds of the video.

d. Resize and reposition the video object so it fits to the right of the bulleted text, then play the video again.

e. Save the presentation, go to Slide 1, then view the presentation in Slide Show view; watch the Slide 2 video start automatically, and on Slide 7, click the Play button on the audio file to play it (be sure to point to the sound file first, to see the button).

4. Set slide transitions and timings.

a. Switch to Slide Sorter view and apply the Conveyor transition to all the slides. (*Hint*: It's in the Dynamic Content category.)

b. Go to Slide 1, then view the presentation in Reading view, watching the video on Slide 2 and playing the sound on Slide 7.

c. Adjust the slide timing so each slide stays on the screen for 2 seconds before automatically moving to the next one.

d. View the presentation in Slide Show view.

e. Remove the timing setting, ensuring that the slides will now advance when you click the mouse button during the presentation.

f. In Slide Sorter view, select Slide 7, then apply the Chime transition sound. (*Hint*: Use the Sound list arrow in the Timing group on the Transitions tab.)

g. Preview the sound transition on the slide.

Skills Review (continued)

5. **Animate slide objects.**

   a. Switch to Normal view, go to Slide 3, then animate the picture with the Shape entrance animation effect.

   b. Set the Effect Options so the animation uses the Box shape.

   c. Go to Slide 2, then apply the Grow & Turn Entrance animation to the bulleted list.

   d. Use the Animation Painter to copy the animation effect of this bulleted list to the bulleted list on Slide 3.

   e. View the presentation in Slide Show view, pressing [Spacebar] as necessary to view the slide objects, and clicking the Play button on the audio object on Slide 7.

6. **Use speaker notes and Notes Page view.**

   a. In Normal view, display the Notes pane if necessary.

   b. On Slide 1, enter the following slide note: **A variety of available jobs**.

   c. On Slide 2, enter the following slide note: **Be on the forefront of new technology**.

   d. On Slide 3, enter the following slide note: **Salaries can be highly competitive**.

   e. Save your work, then view the presentation in Notes Page view from Slide 1 and observe the slide notes on the first three slides.

7. **Print handouts and notes pages.**

   a. Set printing options to print the presentation as handouts, showing two slides per page. View the preview of all the handout pages.

   b. Edit the Notes and Handouts header so it includes the text **Space Studies** and apply it to all the pages. Preview each page.

   c. Change the handout print color to Pure Black and White.

   d. Set printing options to print the presentation as Notes pages, verifying that you can see the slide notes on Slides 1, 2, and 3.

   e. Print the Notes pages if desired, return the printing option to Color, then save your work.

8. **Design effective presentations.**

   a. Add your name to the footer of all slides using the Header & Footer command on the Insert tab. (Notice that it appears on the top right side of the title slide.)

   b. View the presentation in Slide Sorter view, comparing your screen to **FIGURE 14-26**.

   c. Evaluate the presentation content, design, text, graphics, colors, and animations and transitions.

   d. Save your changes, submit your finished presentation to your instructor, then exit PowerPoint.

FIGURE 14-26

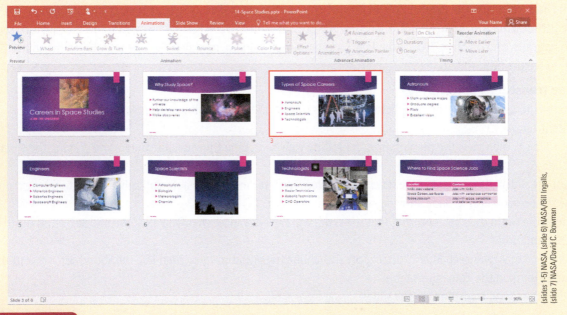

(slides 1-5) NASA, (slide 6) NASA/Bill Ingalls, (slide 7) NASA/David C. Bowman

Independent Challenge 1

A friend of yours owns a comedy club, and you have volunteered to help her with marketing. She is making a presentation at a business association meeting. She has given you a PowerPoint presentation she has started, so you are ready to make it more exciting by adding images, sounds, and video.

a. Start PowerPoint, open 14-4.pptx from where you store your Data Files, then save it as **14-Comedy Club**.

b. Play the presentation in Slide Show view.

c. Go to Slide 1, then insert the sound file **Laughter.wav** from where you store your Data Files. Change its picture from the speaker icon to an image of your choosing that you find in Bing Image Search. (Make sure to check the licensing information before downloading.) Resize and reposition the object so it is above the presentation title and centered horizontally on the slide. Have the sound start automatically when the presentation begins.

d. Go to Slide 2, then insert the picture **Comedy.png** from where you store your Data Files. Crop off the extra space to the right of the microphone.

e. Remove the picture's background. You can leave the circular shadow behind the microphone or use the Mark Areas to Remove tool to drag across any background you want to remove.

f. Size and position the image so it fits well to the right of the bulleted list. Center it vertically on the slide.

g. Go to Slide 4, then remove the background from the image. (*Hint:* If there is an area in magenta that you want to keep, click the Mark Areas to Keep button and drag across the area.)

h. Go to Slide 5, then insert the video **Erica.mp4** from where you store your Data Files. Play the video, then resize and reposition it appropriately. Have it play only when clicked during the slide show.

i. Go to Slide 6, then insert the video **Benny and Griff.mp4** from where you store your Data Files. Play the video, then resize and reposition the object appropriately. Have it play only when clicked during the slide show.

j. Go to Slide 1 and play the presentation in Slide Show view, playing the videos on Slides 5 and 6, then make any necessary adjustments.

k. Add the following speaker notes:

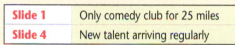

Slide 1	Only comedy club for 25 miles
Slide 4	New talent arriving regularly

l. Apply the transition of your choice to all the slides.

m. Animate the picture on Slide 2 using the Grow & Turn entrance effect.

n. Save your work, then view the presentation in Slide Show view again.

o. Preview the Notes Pages for the presentation, verifying that your speaker notes appear.

p. Preview the handouts, at 9 slides (Horizontal) per page, add your name to the handout header, set the handouts to print in Pure Black and White, then print the handouts, if desired.

q. Add your name to the footer of all slides, return to color, save your changes, review the presentation for effectiveness, submit your finished presentation to your instructor, then exit PowerPoint.

Independent Challenge 2

You and your friend want to start a gourmet ice cream truck business. Your friend has started making a presentation to potential funders, but it needs more visual interest. She has given you the basic presentation, so you need to polish it.

a. Start PowerPoint, open 14-5.pptx from where you store your Data Files, then save it as **14-Ice Cream Truck**.

b. View the presentation in Slide Show view.

c. On Slide 3, insert the sound file **Truck Horn.aiff** from where you store your Data Files. Trim the audio so it plays only the second honking sound, then have the sound play automatically in the slide show.

d. Change the sound's picture to an image of your choosing from Bing image search, using the search text "honk." (Be sure to check its licensing information before downloading.) Then resize and reposition the sound file image so it's to the right of the slide title.

Independent Challenge 2 (continued)

e. On Slide 4, insert the video **Ice Cream Garnish.avi** from where you store your Data Files. Play the video, resize it so it fits well next to the bulleted list, then trim it to remove approximately the last two seconds.

f. On Slide 5, insert the picture **Sundae.jpg**, enlarge it, then remove its background. Resize, crop, and reposition it so it fits well to the right of the bulleted list.

g. On Slide 2, use the Online Pictures command on the Insert tab to insert an image of your choice from Bing Image Search, sizing and positioning it appropriately. Be sure to check its licensing information before downloading.

h. Apply the transition and timing of your choice to all slides.

i. Animate the truck image on Slide 3 with the animation effect and an effect option of your choice, if one is available for the animation you chose. If you wish, change the Start, Duration, and Delay setting for the animation. Preview the animation to make sure it looks the way you want.

j. Add the following speaker notes:

Slide 3	It's in great condition
Slide 6	Thank them for their consideration

k. Remove the slide timings, save your work, then view the presentation in Slide Show view, playing the sound file and watching the animation on Slide 3 and watching the video on Slide 4.

l. Evaluate the presentation for effectiveness.

m. Preview the presentation as handouts, 3 slides to a page, and add the footer **Ice Cream Truck**, followed by a hyphen and your name, to the footer for all pages of the Notes and Handouts. Add your name to the footer of all slides. Preview the Handouts pages using the 6 slides horizontal layout, and using Pure Black and White. Return the setting to color.

n. Save you work, view the presentation in Slide Show view once more to view the slide footers, comparing your presentation to **FIGURE 14-27** (your graphics on Slides 2 and 3 may differ), submit your final presentation to your instructor, then exit PowerPoint.

FIGURE 14-27

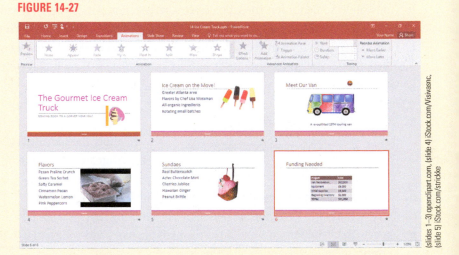

(slides 1–3) openclipart.com, (slide 4) iStock.com/Visivasnc, (slide 5) iStock.com/strickke

Independent Challenge 3

You own a bike touring business called Maine Bike Tours. You've created a presentation to show to local hotel owners, advertising your bike tours. You've developed the slide text, but now you need to complete the presentation by making it more eye-catching. You decide to do this using graphics, transitions, sound, and animations.

a. Start PowerPoint, open 14-6.pptx from where you store your Data Files, then save it as **14-Maine Bike Tours**. View the presentation in Slide Show view.

b. Using commands on the Insert menu, add the sound **Seagull.wav** from the location where you store your Data Files to any appropriate slide, play the sound, then change its picture to one that you select from Bing Image Search. (Be sure to check its licensing information before downloading.) Size and position it attractively on the slide. Have the sound play automatically when the slide appears in Slide Show view.

c. Add the images **Lighthouse.jpg**, **Paths.jpg**, **Port.jpg**, **Seals.jpg**, and **Leaves.jpg** to the slides of your choice (excluding Slide 6). Size and position them appropriately.

Independent Challenge 3 (continued)

   d. On Slide 6, add an image of a van from Bing Image Search, remove its background if necessary, then size and position it appropriately. (Be sure to check its licensing information before downloading.)

   e. Add appropriate transitions to all slides.

   f. Add an appropriate animation option to one of the images, and have the animation start automatically after the slide appears. Use the Animation Painter to apply the same animation to all the other images.

   g. Add any speaker notes you choose to three of the slides.

   h. Save your work, then run the slide show, evaluating it for effectiveness.

   i. Set printing options for the handouts to 2 slides per page, then add a header that reads **Maine Bike Tours** and a footer with your name, and apply the header and footer to all pages.

   j. Preview the Notes pages and Handouts, printing them if you wish.

   k. Save your changes, submit your finished document to your instructor, then close the presentation and exit PowerPoint.

Independent Challenge 4: Explore

In this Independent Challenge, you learn more about Office Mix, install the Office Mix add-in if instructed, and then explore the process of creating your own Mix. (*Note*: Check with your Instructor or lab manager before installing this or any add-in.)

   a. Close PowerPoint, then go to the Office Mix portal at mix.office.com.

   b. Click the Gallery link, then scroll down the gallery to view the different categories. Click to view three of the Mixes posted there that interest you.

   c. If Office Mix is not installed on your computer, return to mix.office.com, click the Get Office Mix link, then sign in using one of the sign-in options shown. The Mix add-in downloads to your computer. When it has finished downloading, you see a message near the bottom of the screen.

   d. Click Run. Agree to the license terms, click Install, then click Yes. After installation is complete, click Close in the message box. PowerPoint starts, displaying the Mix tab on the Ribbon.

   e. Start a new blank PowerPoint presentation.

   f. Click the Mix tab on the Ribbon if necessary, then click the Using Mix button in the Tutorials group. The Welcome pane opens on the right side of the screen.

   g. Click the links at the bottom of the Welcome pane to view Mix presentations about Mix. After the first Mix runs, return to PowerPoint and click the next link.

   h. If you feel ready after viewing the tutorials, scroll down in the pane and click the Create Your First Mix button. Follow the instructions for starting a slide recording, and record a simple screen drawing on the "Create your first Mix recording" screen, using the tools on the right side of the screen. (Note that you can have only one recording per slide.)

   i. Enter your name in the footer on the first slide, save your work, then click the Upload to Mix button in the Mix group. When the upload process is complete, click Show me my Mix, then click the Play button to view your Mix.

   j. Save the presentation as **14-Trying Mix**, submit the document to your instructor, close the presentation, then exit PowerPoint.

Visual Workshop

Start a new, blank presentation and save it where you store your Data Files as **14-Drumsticks**, then create the presentation shown in FIGURE 14-28. Use the Organic theme (make sure to choose the correct variant). Increase the font sizes of the subtitle on Slide 1 to 28 pt and both bulleted lists to 32 pt. On Slides 2 and 3, insert Drumsticks.png and Mallets.png from the location where you store your Data Files. Apply the Shape animation in the shape of a diamond to the Slide 2 image, then use the Animation Painter to apply the same animation to the Slide 3 image. Add your name to the slide footer of all slides, view the presentation in Slide Show view, save your work, then submit the presentation to your instructor.

FIGURE 14-28

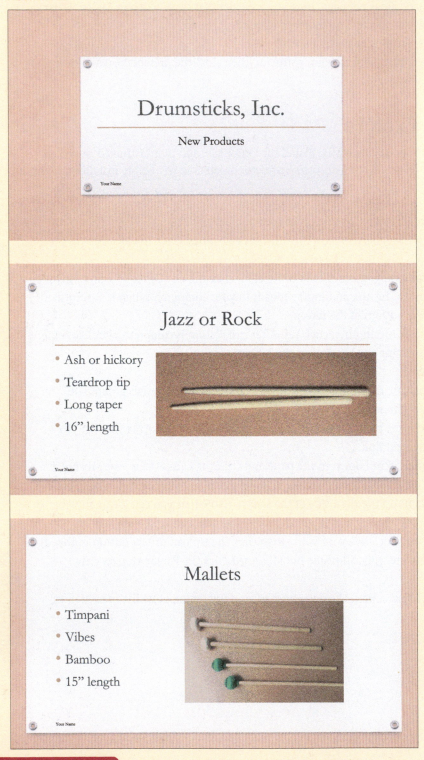

Integrating Office 2016 Programs

CASE ▶ David LeBlanc, Vice President of Merchandising for Pepper's Green Basket, needs you to insert an Excel chart into a presentation he developed, create slides from a Word outline, and insert a screenshot into a slide. He also has a letter to several potential suppliers; he needs you to paste a linked chart into the letter, and then send it out as a mail merge form letter.

Module Objectives

After completing this module, you will be able to:

- Insert an Excel chart into a PowerPoint slide
- Create PowerPoint slides from a Word document
- Insert screen clips into a Word document
- Insert text from a Word file into an open document
- Link Excel data to a Word document
- Update a linked Excel chart in a Word document
- Insert merge fields into a Word document
- Perform a mail merge

Files You Will Need

15-1.pptx	15-13.accdb
15-2.docx	15-14.pptx
15-3.pptx	15-15.docx
15-4.docx	15-16.docx
15-5.docx	15-17.docx
15-6.xlsx	15-18.docx
15-7.accdb	15-19.xlsx
15-8.pptx	15-20.accdb
15-9.docx	15-21.xlsx
15-10.docx	15-22.docx
15-11.docx	15-23.docx
15-12.xlsx	

Insert an Excel Chart into a PowerPoint Slide

Learning Outcomes
- Create an embedded chart on a slide
- Edit an embedded chart on a slide

When you want to show a simple chart to your audience in PowerPoint, you can enter the data and select a chart type using an Excel spreadsheet within PowerPoint. When you create a chart in PowerPoint, you **embed** data into the presentation, meaning that the chart is part of the presentation but you can edit it using Excel spreadsheet tools. Once you've created an embedded chart, you can edit and format it using the Chart Tools Design and Chart Tools Format tabs in PowerPoint. **CASE** *David has given you a presentation he created for the next sales meeting and a hard copy of the sales figures. You need to insert a chart comparing sales, so you decide to embed the chart directly in PowerPoint.*

STEPS

1. **Start PowerPoint, open 15-1.pptx from the location where you store your Data Files, then save it as 15-Projections**

2. **Move to Slide 2, then click the Insert Chart icon ▮▮ in the content placeholder**
   The Insert Chart dialog box opens, as shown in **FIGURE 15-1**.

3. **Verify the Clustered Column chart style is selected, then click OK**
   An Excel spreadsheet with sample data opens on top of a chart based on the sample data, as shown in **FIGURE 15-2**. The Chart Tools Design tab is active. You replace the sample data in the spreadsheet with figures from David's report.

4. **Replace the data in the spreadsheet with the data in the following table (including the commas):**

	A	B	C
1		2017	Projected 2018
2	Southeast	930,000	1,500,000
3	Northeast	780,000	960,000
4	Midwest	850,000	980,000
5	West	1,900,000	2,500,000

   As you enter the data in the spreadsheet, the chart in the slide updates automatically.

5. **Drag the lower right corner of the selected range to the left, so the range includes only columns A through C, then click the Close button ✕ on the spreadsheet window**
   The chart with the new data appears on the slide. The embedded data is saved as part of the presentation. You learn that one of the projection numbers has changed, so you need to edit the chart.

6. **Click the chart to select it if necessary, then on the Chart Tools Design tab click the Edit Data button in the Data group**
   The spreadsheet reopens.

7. **Click cell C4, type 1,200,000, press [Enter], click the spreadsheet window Close button ✕, click the chart title, then press [Delete]**
   The bar representing the Midwest Projected sales adjusts to represent the new figure.

8. **On the Chart Tools Design tab, click Style 2 in the Chart Styles group, click the Change Colors button in the Chart Styles group, click Color 4 (the fourth row of colors), then save your changes**
   Your completed chart appears as shown in **FIGURE 15-3**.

FIGURE 15-1: Choosing a chart style in the Insert Chart dialog box

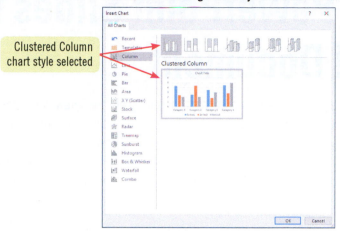

Clustered Column chart style selected

FIGURE 15-2: Spreadsheet with sample data on top of chart

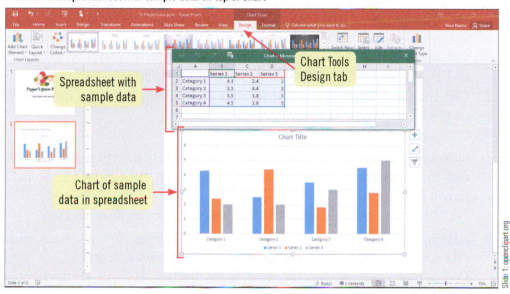

Chart Tools Design tab

Spreadsheet with sample data

Chart of sample data in spreadsheet

FIGURE 15-3: Completed chart

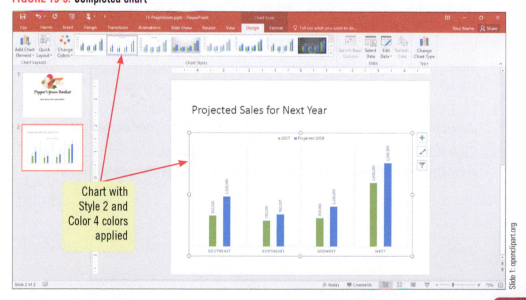

Chart with Style 2 and Color 4 colors applied

Create PowerPoint Slides from a Word Document

**Learning
Outcomes**
• Insert slides from a Word outline
• Reset a slide's theme

You can use an outline that was created in Word as a starting point for a new PowerPoint presentation, or you can use it to add slides to an existing presentation. Word Outline view makes it easy to see how a document is organized. When you insert a Word outline into PowerPoint, lines that are formatted as Level 1 in the outline appear as slide titles, and lower-level text appears as bulleted text. **CASE** *David wants you to incorporate one of his outlines as new slides in the presentation. First, you want to view the document in Word.*

STEPS

1. **Start Word, then open 15-2.docx from where you store your Data Files**

2. **Click the View tab, then click the Outline button in the Views group**

   The document appears in Outline view, and the Outlining tab opens on the Ribbon. See **FIGURE 15-4**. The text appears in a hierarchical structure using headings and subheadings. The insertion point is in the first slide title, "Southeast Region," and the Outline level in the Outline Tools group shows "Level 1." Because the text is organized into outline levels, it will be just right for importing into PowerPoint.

3. **Click the Close Outline View button in the Close group, then click the Close button ☒ on the Word program window**

   The document and the Word program close.

4. **In PowerPoint, verify that Slide 2 is selected in the Thumbnail pane, click the Home tab, click the New Slide button arrow in the Slides group, then click Slides from Outline, as shown in FIGURE 15-5**

   The Insert Outline dialog box opens. The new slides will appear after the selected slide.

5. **Navigate to the location where you store your Data Files, click 15-2.docx, click Insert, click Slide 3 if necessary, then scroll down to view Slides 3, 4, and 5**

   Three new slides are inserted into the presentation, as shown in **FIGURE 15-6**. The new slides are formatted in the theme font from the Word document.

6. **Verify that Slide 3 is selected in the Thumbnail pane**

   The slide title, "Southeast Region", was formatted as Level 1 in the Word outline, and it appears as the slide title in the first imported slide.

7. **With Slide 3 selected, press and hold [Shift], click Slide 5, release [Shift], then click the Reset button in the Slides group**

   The newly added slides are formatted in the theme of the presentation.

8. **Click the Insert tab, click the Header & Footer button in the Text group, click the Footer check box to select it, click the Footer text box, type your name, then click Apply to All**

9. **Click the Slide Show tab, click the From Beginning button in the Start Slide Show group, view the presentation, save your changes, then close the presentation**

FIGURE 15-4: Viewing a Word document in Outline view

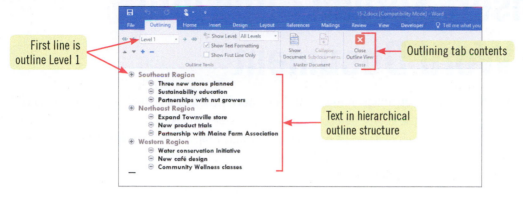

First line is outline Level 1

Outlining tab contents

Text in hierarchical outline structure

FIGURE 15-5: Inserting slides from a Word outline

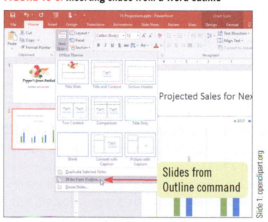

Projected Sales for Nex

Slides from Outline command

Slide 1: openclipart.org

FIGURE 15-6: PowerPoint slides created from Word outline text

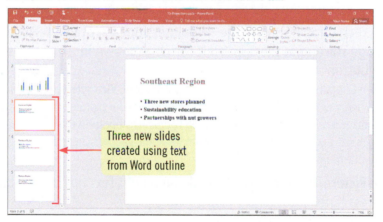

Three new slides created using text from Word outline

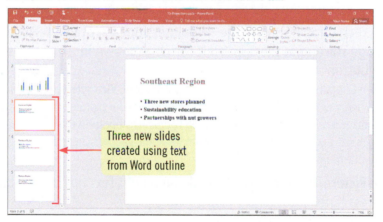

Using outlines in Word and PowerPoint

If you want to create an outline in Word that you can use as the basis for a PowerPoint presentation, it is best to use Word outline levels in your text. Start a new document in Word, click the View tab, then click the Outline button in the Views group. As you type your outline text, use the Outline Level list arrow in the Outline Tools group to apply a level for each line. Use the Level 1 style for slide titles, Level 2 for the first level of indented text, and so on. In Normal view, use the Heading styles, which correspond to the Level styles in Outline view. The styles determine the structure of the outline when it is imported into PowerPoint. You can adjust the outlining structure in Outline view by clicking the Promote, Demote, and Move Up or Move Down buttons. You can change the the amount of detail to show by clicking in a heading that has levels below it, and then clicking the Expand or Collapse buttons in the Outline Tools group. When the outline is complete, save and close the Word document.

You can also save a PowerPoint presentation in outline format and then open it in Word. To save a PowerPoint outline, click the File tab, click Save As, click Browse, click the Save as type list arrow, then click Outline/RTF (*.rtf). Next, open the document in Word, then reformat the text as necessary using Word commands.

Insert Screen Clips into a Word Document

Learning Outcomes
• Insert a screen clip into a document
• Center a screen clip in a document

When you need to place an image from another open document into a PowerPoint presentation or Word document, you can use the PowerPoint Screenshot feature. You can take a screenshot of an entire window or part of a window, which gives you a quick way to include graphics or data. **CASE** ▶ *David wants to include a screenshot from a PowerPoint presentation in a letter to potential suppliers. You use the Screenshot tool to capture a clip of the slide in Normal view.*

STEPS

1. **In PowerPoint, open 15-3.pptx from the location where you store your Data Files**

2. **Start Word, open 15-4.docx from where you store your Data Files, then save it as 15-Supplier Letter**

3. **Press [Ctrl][Home] to make sure the insertion point is at the top of the document, press [Enter] to insert a new line, then press [↑] to move up a line**

4. **Click the Insert tab, then click the Screenshot button in the Illustrations group**

   Thumbnails of open programs that are not minimized to the taskbar appear in the list, as shown in **FIGURE 15-7**. To insert a full screen, you would click a thumbnail in the Available Windows section. You want to capture just the Pepper's name and graphic from the screen. When you use the Screen Clipping option, Word automatically switches to the previous window, which is the first thumbnail shown in the Available Windows section. If you have multiple programs open and maximized or in Restore Down mode, be sure that the window from where you want to capture a clip is the first thumbnail. In this case, the slide you want to clip is the only one, but you only want part of the slide, so you use screen clipping.

TROUBLE
You may need to wait a few moments for ✚ to appear before you can drag to select the screen clip.

5. **Click Screen Clipping; when the ✚ pointer appears, drag a selection box around the image starting at the upper-left corner as shown in FIGURE 15-8, then release the mouse button**

   The Screen Clipping feature switches to the PowerPoint Slide View screen, where you can select any area on the screen. When you release the mouse button, Word inserts the captured screen image into the document. The inserted image is selected, and the Picture Tools Format tab appears in the Ribbon. You can use this tab to adjust the image's size and apply effects to it. The image of the Pepper's Green Basket logo is too large for the letter, so you decide to resize it.

QUICK TIP
To save the screen clip as a new file, right-click the image, click Save as Picture from the menu, type a name, select a file type, then click Save.

6. **On the Picture Tools Format tab, click the Height text box in the Size group, type 1.5, then press [Enter]**

   The image would look better if it were centered.

7. **Click the Home tab, then click the Center button ≣ in the Paragraph group**

   The image is centered on the page, as shown in **FIGURE 15-9**. You can adjust the image and apply styles and effects to it as you would any photograph.

TROUBLE
When capturing a screen clip from the Internet, assume the content is protected by copyright.

8. **Save your changes to the Word document, close the PowerPoint presentation, then exit PowerPoint**

FIGURE 15-7: Screenshot options

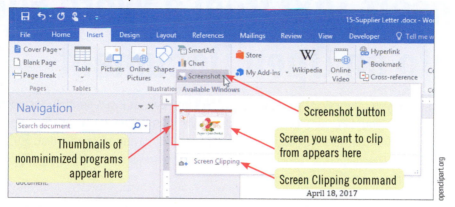

FIGURE 15-8: Capturing a screen clip

FIGURE 15-9: Screen clip inserted and centered in a Word document

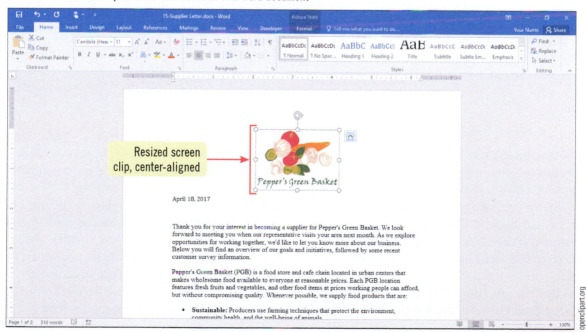

Insert Text from a Word File into an Open Document

Learning Outcomes
- Import a Word text object
- Format imported text

As you work, you might want to combine two files into one, or insert another document into the current one. Although you can easily copy and paste information between two or more open documents, it is sometimes easier to insert the contents from a file without having to open it first. **CASE** *David wants you to include Descriptions of current offerings from another document in the letter to potential suppliers that you have been working on.*

STEPS

1. **In the Supplier Letter document in Word, scroll down to the end, position the insertion point at the top of page 2, on the blank line above "Very truly yours,", click the Insert tab, click the Object button arrow in the Text group, then click Text from File**
   The Insert File dialog box opens.

2. **Navigate to where you store your Data Files if necessary, click 15-5.docx as shown in FIGURE 15-10, then click Insert**
   The contents of the file, consisting of three paragraphs of text describing current offerings at Pepper's Green Basket, are inserted at the bottom of the letter, as shown in FIGURE 15-11.

3. **Select the three paragraphs of text you just inserted, click the Home tab, click the Bullets button arrow ⊞ ▾ in the Paragraph group, then point to the square bullet style, as shown in FIGURE 15-12**

4. **Click the square bullet style**
   The current offerings text is formatted in a bulleted list.

5. **Save your changes to the document**

Placing an Access table in a Word document

In addition to inserting a Word file into a Word document, you can insert data from other applications, such as Access. You can insert an Access table into a Word document by various methods. You can copy the entire table or individual records and paste them into a Word document. You can also use the Export feature in Access to export objects, such as a table, query, report, or form. To export from Access, open the database, enable content if necessary, open the Navigation pane, then select the object you want to export. Click the External Data tab, click the More button in the Export group, click Word, choose the format to which you want to export, click OK in the dialog box, then click Close. Note that Access always exports to a new Rich Text Format (RTF) file; you cannot export to an open Word document. In Word, insert the RTF file using the Object command on the Insert tab. Click the Create from File tab, click the Browse button and locate the file. The inserted Access object in Word is a standard table; it does not link back to the Access database. So any modifications you make to a table in Word affect only the Word document. Depending on the number of fields and the length of their content, you may need to reformat the table in Word.

FIGURE 15-10: Insert File dialog box

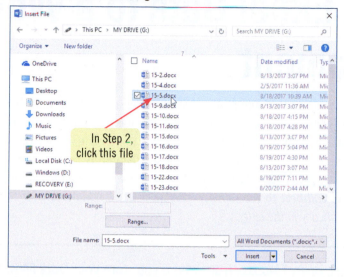

FIGURE 15-10: Insert File dialog box

FIGURE 15-11: File text inserted into letter

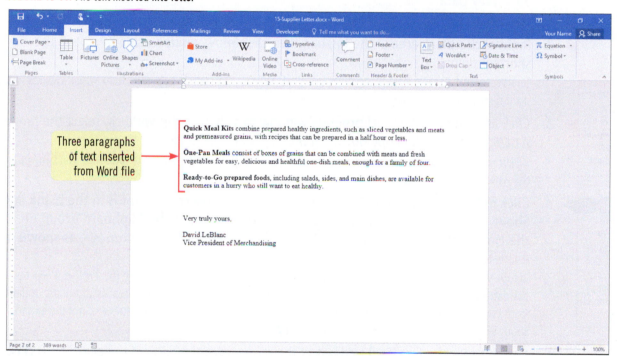

FIGURE 15-12: Formatting bulleted text

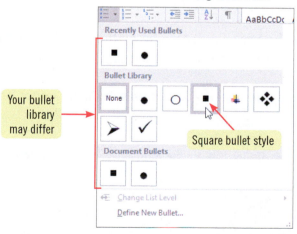

Link Excel Data to a Word Document

Learning Outcomes
- Link an Excel range to a Word document
- Link an Excel chart to a Word document

Linking data shares updated information between files and programs. A **link** displays information from a **source file** (which is the original file containing the data) in the **destination** file (the location to which that data is copied or moved). In a Word document, linked data looks just like inserted or embedded data. However, you can edit the linked data in its original program by right-clicking it and clicking Edit Data. **CASE** *David wants to add data from the survey to the supplier letter. You decide to link the Excel spreadsheet to the supplier letter so if David updates any of the data, the changes will be updated automatically in the letter.*

STEPS

TROUBLE
If you have other windows open, close them, then repeat Step 2.

1. **Start Excel, open 15-6.xlsx from where you store your Data Files, then save it as 15-Survey Data**
   The worksheet contains data and a chart.

TROUBLE
If necessary, you can drag the Word and Excel title bars to the left and right sides of the screen, respectively, to view them side by side.

2. **Right-click a blank area of the taskbar, then click Show windows side by side in the shortcut menu**
   The Word and Excel program windows are tiled, so you can switch between them while viewing both documents.

3. **Click anywhere in the Excel program window to switch to this window, select the range A1:D6, then click the Copy button in the Clipboard group on the Home tab**
   When windows are tiled, clicking anywhere in an inactive program window activates it so you can work in the window. The cells are copied to the clipboard.

QUICK TIP
Whether you are pasting a chart or copied cells, you can select a paste option that includes source or destination formatting, and embed or link options.

4. **Click in the Word window to activate it, verify the insertion point is in the blank line above "Very truly yours,", click the Paste button arrow in the Clipboard group on the Home tab, then click the Link & Keep Source Formatting button 📋, as shown in FIGURE 15-13**
   Before you click the button, a Live Preview of the copied cells appears. Using the Link & Keep Source Formatting option automatically applies the current Excel style to the table and permits automatic updating from Word or Excel. This is useful if you want to paste the same data in multiple files and not have to worry about updating each file every time the data changes.

5. **Switch to Excel, press [Esc] to deselect the range, click the edge of the chart, then click the Copy button in the Clipboard group**
   The chart object is copied to the clipboard.

6. **Switch to Word, click the Maximize button ◻ on the program window title bar, press [Enter], click the Paste button arrow, then click the Use Destination Theme & Link Data button**
   The chart appears in the Supplier letter as a linked chart object in the current Word theme, as shown in FIGURE 15-14.

7. **Save your changes**
   In the next lesson, you'll test the link between the Word letter and the Excel workbook.

FIGURE 15-13: Selecting a paste option for copied Excel cells

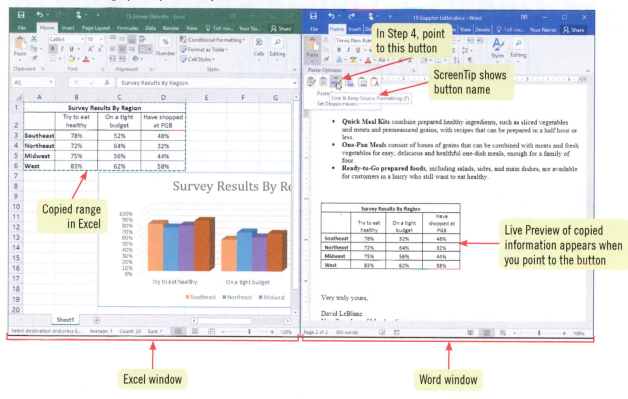

FIGURE 15-14: Excel chart pasted as a link in Word

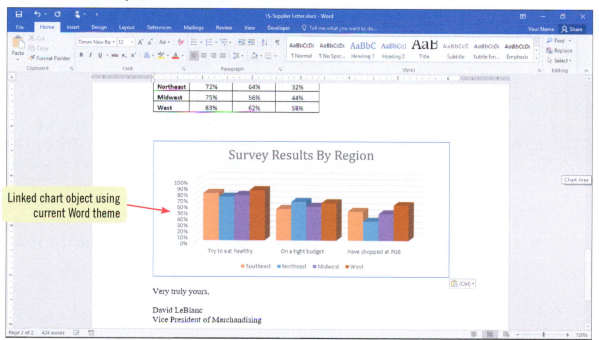

Integration
Module 15

Learning
Outcomes
• Edit a source file
• Update a
  linked file

Update a Linked Excel Chart in a Word Document

Linked files save time and help ensure accuracy in your documents, because when you update a source file, linked objects in destination files can be updated automatically. You can also update a linked object manually by right-clicking it and clicking Update Link, or by selecting the linked object and pressing [F9]. The [F9] key updates links in any Office application. **CASE** *David just received updates to the survey data for the West region. You make the changes in Excel, and view the updated results in the linked Word document.*

STEPS

1. **Right-click a blank area of the taskbar, then click Show windows side by side in the shortcut menu**

QUICK TIP

If the charts in Excel and Word don't update automatically, right-click each chart and click Update now.

2. **Switch to Excel, edit the data in the Survey Results workbook to match that in the following table, then click an empty cell:**

Cell	Data
B6	90%
C6	71%
D6	65%

The chart columns in Excel and in Word change as you enter new figures, as shown in **FIGURE 15-15**. However, the linked table in Word does not update automatically, which you'll fix in a moment.

3. **Maximize the Excel program window, select the range A1:D6, click the Fill Color button arrow 🖌 in the Font group, then click the Dark Blue, Text 2, Lighter 80% color (in the fourth column, second row)**
The cells are shaded in blue.

QUICK TIP

When you open a Word document that contains linked data, Word prompts you to update links.

4. **Switch to Word, right-click the table, compare your screen to FIGURE 15-16, then click Update Link**
The table is updated with the content and format changes you made in Excel.

5. **Switch to Excel, save your changes, close the worksheet, then exit Excel**

6. **Maximize the Word program window, click the edge of the chart object, click the Chart Tools Design tab, click the More button ▾ in the Chart Styles group, then click Style 5 (in the fifth column, first row)**
The chart style is changed. Because you selected to paste the chart with the destination style, any style changes you make in the future to the chart in Excel will not be reflected in the Word document.

7. **Click a blank area in the window, compare your screen to FIGURE 15-17, then save your changes to the document**

FIGURE 15-15: Viewing updated chart data from a linked file

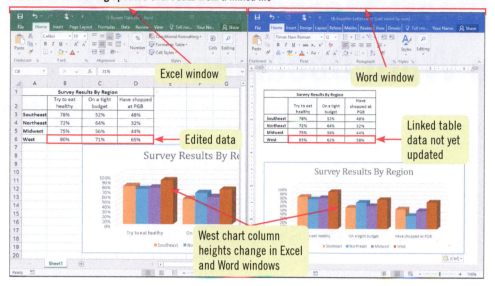

Excel window

Word window

Edited data

Linked table data not yet updated

West chart column heights change in Excel and Word windows

FIGURE 15-16: Updating data in Word

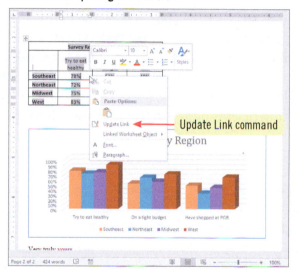

Update Link command

FIGURE 15-17: Updated objects in Word

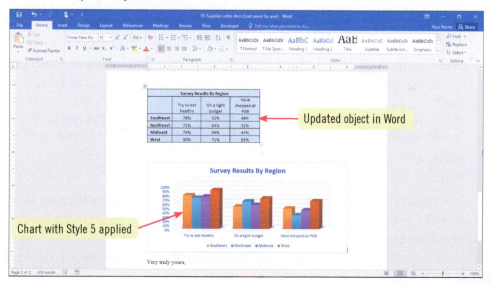

Updated object in Word

Chart with Style 5 applied

Integration
Module 15

Learning
Outcomes
• Start a mail merge
• Insert merge fields

Insert Merge Fields into a Word Document

A **form letter** is a document that contains standard body text and a custom heading containing the name and address for one of many recipients. The letter, or **main document**, is usually created in Word; the data for the custom heading, also known as the **data source**, is usually stored in a table, a worksheet, or a database such as Access. From these two files—the main document and the data source—you can print your merged documents, or create a third file, a **merged document**, consisting of multiple personalized letters. This process is called **mail merge**. Before performing a mail merge, you add **merge fields** to the main document, which are placeholders to indicate where the custom information from the data source should appear. **CASE** ▶ *David asks you to send the supplier letter to four potential suppliers who have contacted PGB, and he gives you a file containing their names and addresses. First, you insert merge fields.*

STEPS

1. **In Word, press [Ctrl][Home], then click the** blank line **below the date**

2. **Click the** Mailings tab, **click the** Start Mail Merge button **in the Start Mail Merge group, compare your screen to** FIGURE 15-18, **then click** Letters

   The document is now identified as a main document in a Letter mail merge and is ready for you to add merge fields, such as names, addresses, and salutations, from the data source. You can also perform a mail merge for email messages, address labels, envelopes, or a catalog or directory.

3. **Click the** Select Recipients button **in the Start Mail Merge group, then click** Use an Existing List

   The Select Data Source dialog box opens, with the My Data Sources folder as the default data source location. Your data source is in your Data Files folder. You can select from a variety of data sources, such as an Outlook address book, data from an Excel spreadsheet, or a Word document or an HTML file that contains a single table. Your data source is an Access database.

4. **Navigate to where you store your Data Files, click** 15-7.accdb, **then click** Open

   The Select Data Source dialog box closes. Although the Access database file is designated as the data source, Access does not need to be open in order to use the data.

5. **Click the** Edit Recipient List button **in the Start Mail Merge group**

   The Mail Merge Recipients dialog box opens, as shown in FIGURE 15-19. Here you can view the records in the data source file and select, filter, and sort data so you can send the mail merge letter to specific recipients. You want to include all the recipients in the database, so you do not need to make changes to this dialog box.

6. **Click** OK, **then click the** Address Block button **in the Write & Insert Fields group**

   The Insert Address Block dialog box opens, where you can select the format for the address block and preview it. The address block is created using the Title, First Name, Last Name, Address 1, Address 2, City, State, and Postal Code fields from the Access database file. Word automatically arranged the fields as shown in the Preview window because this is a common format for fields in a mail merge letter.

7. **Click** OK

   The block field <<AddressBlock>> appears in the document.

8. **Press [Enter] twice, click the** Greeting Line button **in the Write & Insert Fields group, click** OK **in the Insert Greeting Line dialog box, compare your screen to** FIGURE 15-20, **then save your changes**

   The greeting line field <<GreetingLine>> is inserted into the document. You will complete the mail merge in the next lesson.

FIGURE 15-18: Selecting the Letters Mail Merge option

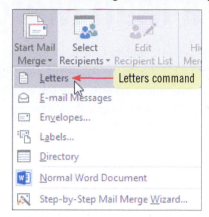

Letters command

FIGURE 15-19: Mail Merge Recipients dialog box

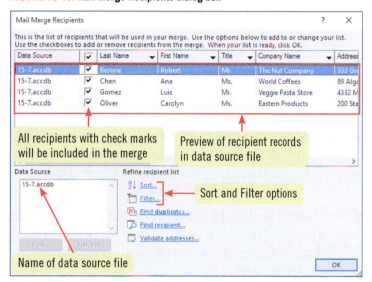

All recipients with check marks will be included in the merge

Preview of recipient records in data source file

Sort and Filter options

Name of data source file

FIGURE 15-20: Viewing inserted merge fields

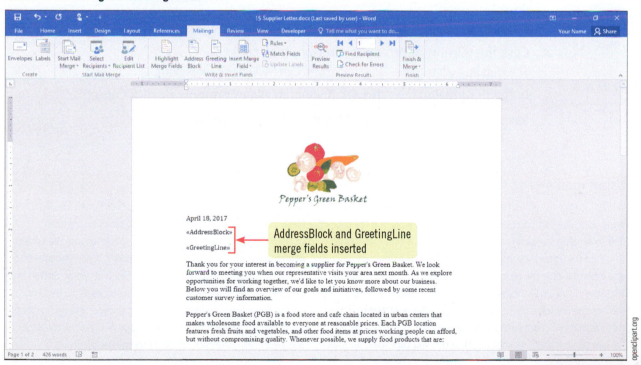

AddressBlock and GreetingLine merge fields inserted

Perform a Mail Merge

Learning Outcomes
- Highlight merged fields
- Preview merged data
- Merge a document with a data source

After you set up a main document, specify a data source, and insert merge fields, you are ready to merge, or combine, the standard text with the custom heading information to create personalized documents. You can preview the mail merge to ensure all the information will appear properly in the final document. **CASE** *Now that the main document—the supplier letter—has merge fields inserted, you are ready to preview and then merge it with the data source to create the final mail merge letters. You also want to print one of the merged letters for David's review.*

STEPS

QUICK TIP

You can also perform a mail merge using step-by-step instructions by clicking the Start Mail Merge button in the Start Mail Merge group, then clicking Step-by-Step Mail Merge Wizard.

1. **Click the Highlight Merge Fields button in the Write & Insert Fields group, then compare your screen to FIGURE 15-21**

   The merge fields <<AddressBlock>>, which includes all the necessary name and address fields from the data source, and <<GreetingLine>> are shaded in gray, making it easy to see where merged data will be inserted into the letter. Other commands in the Write & Insert Fields group include the Insert Merge Field button, which lets you insert any field from the data source document; the Rules button, which lets you select records that meet certain conditions; and the Match Fields button, which lets you match or map fields in a data source.

2. **Click the Highlight Merge Fields button in the Write & Insert Fields group to turn off highlighting, then click the Preview Results button in the Preview Results group**

   The name, address, and salutation for the first recipient in the data source file replace the fields in the document. See **FIGURE 15-22**.

3. **Click the Next Record button ▶ in the Preview Results group three times**

   The data from each record appears in its respective letter. You can use buttons in the Preview Results group to move backward or forward through records, find a particular record, and check for errors. You can click Check for Errors to have Word automatically check each document for errors.

TROUBLE

To add custom text to individual letters, click Edit Individual Documents, move to the individual letters you want to customize, then type the desired text.

4. **Click the Finish & Merge button in the Finish group as shown in FIGURE 15-23, then click Print Documents**

   The Merge to Printer dialog box opens, where you choose the records you want to print.

5. **Click the Current record option button, then click OK**

   The Print dialog box opens. The letter to Mrs. Carolyn Oliver is set to print.

6. **In the Print dialog box, click OK if your lab allows printing, or click Cancel**

7. **Save your changes, close the document, then exit Word**

Using mail merge to send personalized email messages

While it is easy to send an email message to several recipients at once using the carbon copy (Cc) feature in Outlook, you are limited to sending the same message to everyone. Using mail merge to create the email message enables you to personalize messages, ensuring that only the recipient's email address appears in the To: text box in the email message. The steps for creating an email mail merge are basically the same as for a letter mail merge. The main document can be a Word document, and the data source file can be your Outlook contact list. When you click the Start Mail Merge button to begin the mail merge, click E-mail Messages. Next, click the Select Recipients button, click Choose from Outlook Contacts, then follow the prompts to choose the correct address book and import the contacts folder. When you are ready to merge the final document, click the Finish & Merge button in the Finish group, then click Send Email Messages. Note that you cannot add a recipient to the Cc (carbon copy) or Bcc (blind carbon copy) fields. If you want to receive a copy of the email message, add your email address to the Mail Merge Recipients list.

FIGURE 15-21: Viewing highlighted merge fields

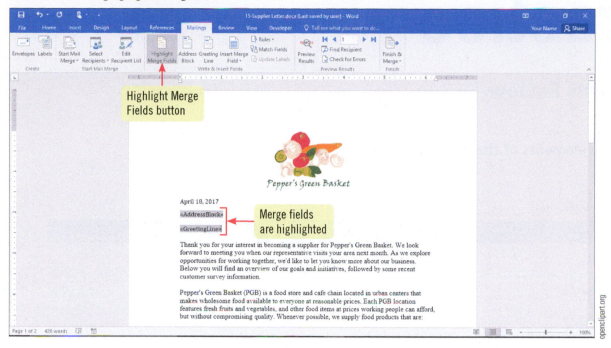

Highlight Merge Fields button

Merge fields are highlighted

FIGURE 15-22: Previewing merged file

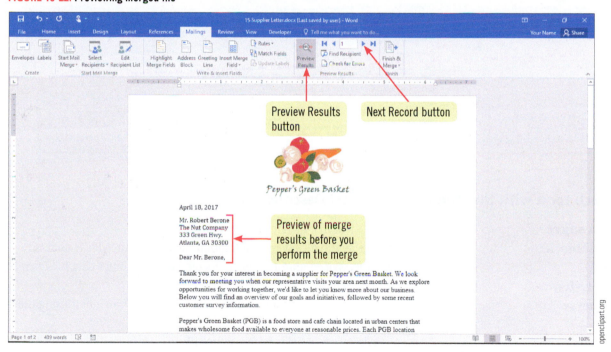

Preview Results button

Next Record button

Preview of merge results before you perform the merge

FIGURE 15-23: Printing merged letters

In Step 4, click here

Print Documents command

Practice

Concepts Review

Label the elements of the Word window shown in FIGURE 15-24**.**

FIGURE 15-24

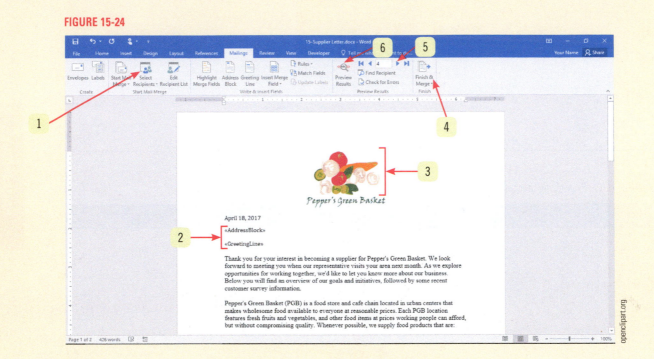

Match each term with the statement that best describes it.

7. **Linked object**
8. **Address block**
9. **Embed**
10. **Outline view**
11. **Mail merge**

a. Presents text in a hierarchical structure
b. Updates automatically in a destination file when source file is updated
c. The process of combining a main document and a source data file to create custom documents
d. Places an object into another document, where you can edit it using the source program's tools
e. A combination of fields from a source file

Select the best answer from the list of choices.

12. **When you create a chart in PowerPoint, which of the following describes the chart?**
    a. It cannot be formatted.
    b. It is an embedded object on the slide.
    c. It cannot be edited.
    d. It is a linked object on the slide.

13. **When you insert a Word outline into a PowerPoint presentation, the Level 1 outline headings become what in PowerPoint?**
    a. Slide titles
    b. Bulleted text
    c. Graphics
    d. Charts

14. **Receiving a prompt to update data in a document indicates that:**
    a. The document has been published to the web.
    b. The document contains a linked object.
    c. The document has an embedded object.
    d. The document is a mail merge source document.

15. **Which of the following indicates a merge field?**
    a. ""AddressBlock""
    b. --AddressBlock--
    c. << AddressBlock >>
    d. [[AddressBlock]]

Skills Review

1. **Insert an Excel chart into a PowerPoint slide.**
   a. Start PowerPoint, open the file 15-8.pptx from the location where you store your Data Files, then save it as **15-AfterSchool Arts**. (*Hint*: Throughout this exercise, maximize windows as necessary.)
   b. Move to Slide 2, then use the content placeholder to insert a 3-D pie chart. (*Hint*: Click Pie on the left side of the dialog box, then click the 3-D Pie option.)
   c. Enter the following data in the spreadsheet:

	A	B
1		# of Students
2	Music	54
3	Dance	78
4	Art	37
5	Drama	68

   d. Close the spreadsheet.
   e. Reopen the spreadsheet, edit the number of Music students to **63** then close the spreadsheet.
   f. With the chart selected, apply Chart Style 5 and change the chart colors to Color 2.
   g. Save your changes.

2. **Create PowerPoint slides from a Word document.**
   a. Start Word, then open the file 15-9.docx from the location where you store your Data Files.
   b. View the document in Outline view.
   c. Close the document, and exit Word.
   d. In PowerPoint, insert the file 15-9.docx after Slide 2 using the Slides from Outline command.
   e. Select the four new slides, then use a button in the Slides group on the Home tab to reset the new slides to the presentation theme.
   f. Add your name to the slide footer (*Hint:* Use the Insert tab and open the Header and Footer dialog box), apply it to all slides, move to Slide 1, then save your changes.

Skills Review (continued)

3. **Insert screen clips into a Word document.**
   a. Start Word.
   b. Open the file 15-10.docx from the location where you store your Data Files, then save it as **15-AfterSchool Arts Overview**.
   c. Verify the insertion point is at the top of the page, then use the Screenshot button on the Insert tab to select Screen Clipping.
   d. In PowerPoint, drag to select the image on Slide 1.
   e. In Word, apply the Compound Frame, Black picture style to the clip.
   f. Change the Shape Height of the clip to **1"** in the Size group, save your changes in Word, then switch to PowerPoint and exit the program.
   g. In the Word document, use a command on the Home tab to center the image horizontally, add a blank line below it, then save your changes.

4. **Insert text from a Word file into an open document.**
   a. Position the insertion point at the end of the line that reads "In our 35-year history, AfterSchool Arts students have gone on to become:", press [Enter] twice, then insert the file 15-11.docx from the location where you store your Data Files as Text from File. (*Hint*: Click a button arrow on the Insert tab.)
   b. Delete the extra line after the inserted text, select the three lines of text you just inserted from the file, then format them as a bulleted list using a hollow bullet style.
   c. Save your changes.

5. **Link Excel data to a Word document.**
   a. Start Excel, open the file 15-12.xlsx, then save it as **15-AfterSchool Arts Approval Ratings**.
   b. Show Word and Excel side by side.
   c. Switch to Excel, then select and copy the range A2:E4.
   d. Switch to Word, click before the paragraph that begins "We thank you", insert a blank line, use the Paste button arrow to insert the copied range, using the Link & Keep Source Formatting option. Adjust spacing so there is one blank line above and below the inserted object.
   e. Switch to Excel, then copy the chart.
   f. Switch to Word, insert another blank line after the inserted cells, use the Paste button arrow to insert the copied chart using the Use Destination Theme & Link Data option.
   g. Save your changes.

6. **Update a linked Excel chart in a Word document.**
   a. In Excel, change cell B4 to **30%** and cell D4 to **28%**.
   b. Switch to Word, then update the document with data from the linked file. (*Hint*: Right-click a cell in the table, then click Update Link.) Verify the chart in both the Word document and the Excel workbook were updated.
   c. In Excel, select the range B2:E2, then format the text in white and the cell fill in black.
   d. In the Word document, update the linked table, verify that the formatting updates to show your latest changes, then save the file.
   e. Switch to Excel, save and close the workbook, exit Excel, then maximize the Word window.

7. **Insert merge fields into a Word document.**
   a. Move to the top of the document, then insert two blank lines below the date.
   b. Start a letters mail merge.
   c. Designate file 15-13.accdb as the selected recipient list from the location where you store your Data Files.
   d. Open the Mail Merge Recipients dialog box, review the recipient list, then close the dialog box, accepting the defaults.
   e. Insert an address block, accepting the default block shown in the dialog box, then insert one more blank line in the document.

Skills Review (continued)

f. Use a command on the Mailings tab to insert a greeting line that uses the Greeting line format of just first name and leaves the default format for any invalid recipient names, then insert one blank line after this line. (*Hint*: In the Insert Greeting Line dialog box, click the Greeting line format name list arrow, scroll down the list of greetings, then click "Joshua.")

g. Save your changes.

8. Perform a mail merge.

a. Use a command on the Mailings tab to highlight the merge fields, then turn off highlighting.

b. Preview your mail merge results, reviewing each record in the merge.

c. Preview the document, adjust the size of the chart, the graphic at the top of the page, and the top and bottom margins as necessary so your document matches **FIGURE 15-25**.

d. Finish the mail merge using the Print Documents command, printing the current record if your lab allows it.

e. Save and close the document and exit Word.

FIGURE 15-25

Independent Challenge 1

You are working as a managerial trainee at PearTree Wildlife Rescue, a nonprofit organization that treats injured animals so they can be returned to the wild. You're working on a fundraising presentation that you will give at a meeting of a charitable organization. You also need to send personalized form letters to donors who have already made contributions to the organization.

a. Start PowerPoint, open 15-14.pptx from the location where you store your Data Files, then save it as **15-PearTree Presentation**.

b. On Slide 2, insert a pie chart using the 3-D Pie style.

c. In the spreadsheet, enter the following data:

	A	B
1	Animals	Number Rescued
2	Birds	254
3	Reptiles	125
4	Bears	64
5	Deer	97

Independent Challenge 1 (continued)

d. Delete the chart title, close the spreadsheet, then choose Chart Style 3.

e. Following Slide 2, insert slides from the outline contained in the file 15-15.docx, then select the new slides and reset their design.

f. Add your name to the footer of all slides except the title slide (*Hint*: Use a check box in the Header and Footer dialog box), then view the slide show from the beginning, save your changes, close the file, and exit PowerPoint.

g. Start Word, open the file 15-16.docx from the location where you store your Data Files, then save it as **15-PearTree Letter**. Replace the Your Name text at the end of the letter with your name.

h. Move the insertion point to the top of the page, insert a blank line and move the insertion point to the blank line, open 15-17.docx, return to the letter, then use the Screen Clipping feature to insert the image from the 15-17.docx file at the top of the page. Center the image, and resize it to one inch in height. Close 15-17.docx.

i. Move the insertion point to the space below the second paragraph of body text (after "our goals are:"), insert a blank line, insert the text from the file 15-18.docx, format the inserted text as a bulleted list, using the default bullet style, then save your work.

j. Start Excel, open the file 15-19.xlsx from the location where you store your Data Files, save it as **15-PearTree Data**, then add your name to the footer.

k. Copy the range A1:B5, switch to Word, then paste the data in the blank line following the paragraph that begins "As a contributor," as a link keeping the source formatting. Adjust column widths as necessary. (*Hint*: You can use the AutoFit button in the Cell Size group on the Table Tools Layout tab).

l. Return to Excel, copy the chart, then paste it in the letter, in the blank line after the paragraph that begins "As you can see…", using the destination theme and linking the data, and adjust its height to 2.5".

m. In Excel, adjust the amount for the State grants to **$60,000**. Return to Word, and update links as necessary. If necessary, re-adjust the columns widths of the table.

n. Move to the top of the first page of the letter, place the insertion point on the second blank line below the date, then create a letters mail merge that uses file 15-20.accdb as the data source file and includes the Address Block and Greeting Line fields, using the field formats of your choice. Preview the results, and adjust spacing as necessary.

o. Finish the merge by creating a new file containing all records (*Hint*: Use the Edit Individual Documents command), save the new file as **15-PearTree Merged Letters**, then print the third record if your lab allows it.

p. Close the merged document, save the 15-PearTree Letter document, preview it, compare your document to FIGURE 15-26, then close it.

q. Save and close any open files, then exit all open programs.

FIGURE 15-26

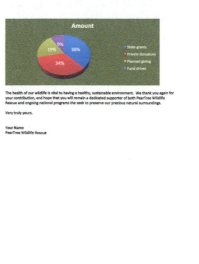

Independent Challenge 2

You and your business partner are planning to open a new outdoor adventure company called Outdoor Touring. It will take customers on outdoor adventures such as river rafting, nature walks, and mountain climbing. You need to apply for a start-up loan to get Outdoor Touring going. Your first task is to write a cover letter that will accompany your loan request to several banks.

a. Start Word, then write a letter that you can send to banks along with the loan package. You will add recipient information in a future step; for now, write the body of the letter, including the name and location of your new company, why you are applying for the loan, why the business will be successful, and how much you would like to borrow.

b. Save the letter as **15-Outdoor Loan Letter** in the location where you store your Data Files.

c. Start Excel, open the file 15-21.xlsx from the location where you store your Data Files, then save it as **15-Outdoor Sales Comparison**. This chart shows the success of current tours in comparable cities, and the increase in advance sales for next year's tours.

d. Modify the chart so that it includes all three types of activities shown in the worksheet data.

e. Change the chart style, chart layout, or individual chart elements as desired, then copy the chart object.

f. In Word, insert the chart, keeping source formatting and linking data.

g. Start a letters mail merge, then create a new recipient list with at least three entries. To create the list, click the Select Recipients button in the Start Mail Merge group, then click Type a New List. Enter at least three names and addresses in the New Address List dialog box, clicking New Entry as needed. When the list is complete, click OK, then save the file where you store your Data Files as **15-Outdoor List**.

h. Above the letter body text, insert Address Block and Greeting Line fields, using the options of your choice. Insert blank lines as appropriate. Insert a blank footer and add your name, left-aligned, then save the document.

i. Open a new, blank PowerPoint presentation, then apply the Blank layout to the slide. Insert up to four photos (your own or those you find using Bing Image Search, making sure to check the licensing information). Arrange them to form an attractive collage, then save the presentation as **15-Outdoor Collage**.

j. Go to the Loan Letter document in Word, then use screen clipping to insert the collage at the top of the letter. Save your work. Preview the mail merge, then complete the merge, printing the first record if your lab allows it. **FIGURE 15-27** shows one possible solution; your content will differ. Save and close the document.

k. Save and close any open files, then exit any open programs.

FIGURE 15-27

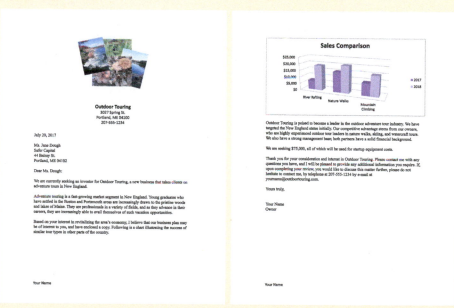

Independent Challenge 3

The Denver Community Development Association is organizing its annual Food Festival, which generates proceeds for the benefit of local shelters. The organization's president has asked you to create a PowerPoint presentation that includes information about the event, including financial information, for potential sponsors and participants.

a. Start PowerPoint, create a new, blank presentation using any theme and variant you like, customizing the title slide with appropriate text and clip art, then save it as **15-Food Festival Presentation** in the location where you store your Data Files.

b. Add another slide that lists important dates, including deadlines for vendor registration and ticket sales and the date of the event itself.

c. Use the Slides from Outline command to insert content from the file 15-22.docx into the presentation, after the second slide. Add your name to the footer of all slides except the title slide.

d. Adjust formatting as needed for the newly added slides. Insert clip art and/or photographs as desired.

e. At the end of the presentation, add a new slide with a title-only layout titled **Financials**, start Excel, then create a worksheet in the style of your choice that shows the amount of income for the last three years and three expense categories (such as Equipment, Traffic Control, and Security). Chart the expense categories.

f. Add a chart title, and format it as you wish.

g. Save the worksheet as **15-Food Festival Financials** where you store your Data Files, then copy the chart you created.

h. In PowerPoint, paste the Excel chart you copied, linked with either source or destination formatting.

i. Go to the Excel file, change one of the expense figures, then verify that the linked data updated in PowerPoint, then save the presentation.

j. Start Word, then create an informal confirmation letter to vendors who register for the event. Write at least two short paragraphs for the letter body text, confirming that the vendor is registered for the event. Add your name at the end of the letter. Save the document as **15-Food Festival Confirmation Letter**.

k. Find an image to use as the organization's logo (making sure to check the licensing information), and insert it at the top of the letter using the Picture command in the Illustrations group on the Insert tab.

l. Start a mail merge. Create a Mail Merge Recipients list in Word with at least three records. (*Hint*: Use the Type a New List command.) Include fields for Title, First Name, Last Name, Address 1, City, State, and ZIP Code. Save the data as **15-Food Festival Registrations**.

m. Below the heading at the top of the document, insert address block and greeting line fields. Preview your results and adjust spacing as necessary.

n. Finish the mail merge by merging to the printer, then print the second letter if your lab allows printing.

o. Close any open files, then exit all programs.

Independent Challenge 4: Explore

Think of an organization you either work for now or would like to work for, in either a paid or volunteer position. You'll create a letter, which could be an appeal for donations, a thank-you letter, or some kind of business communication for an event. In the content, you'll include a place to insert a table of names and email addresses, as well as text that introduces the table. (For example, your table might be a list of names and email addresses of participants or others who have volunteered to help out.) You'll create a table in Access with this information, then export it to an RTF document that you'll insert into your Word letter.

a. Start Word, then save a new document as **15-My Letter** in the location where you store your Data Files.

b. Type the letter text, including the table introduction. Add clip art or photographs if desired. Include your name as the signer of the document.

c. Start Access, then open a blank desktop database named **15-My Database**. Create a table containing fields for First Name, Last Name, and Email Address, giving the table an appropriate name, and add at least four records.

d. Export the Access table to an RTF file named **15-My Export**. (*Hint*: Use a command on the External Data tab, in the Export group. Do not save export steps. Save the file in the same location as your other files for this exercise.) Close the database and exit Access.

e. In the Word document, insert the exported RTF file in the appropriate location using the Text from File command. Delete the ID column, then format the inserted table any way you wish. (*Hint*: You may wish to use the Header Row check box in the Table Style Options group.)

f. Make any final formatting changes, then save and close the letter.

g. Open a new Word document, and type a short email message to the four participants, reminding them of the date or another relevant fact about your organization, perhaps an upcoming event. Save the file as **15-My Email text**.

h. Start a mail merge, using the E-mail Messages selection, and use 15-My Database as the data source.

i. Use the Insert Merge Field button to insert each recipient's email address at the top of the message.

j. Finish the merge, using the Edit Individual Documents command. Rather than sending the email messages, save the merged document as **15-My Merged Emails**.

k. Save and close all documents and programs.

Visual Workshop

Using the skills you learned in this module, create the PowerPoint slides shown in FIGURE 15-28. Create a new presentation and save it as **15-Dream Vacation.pptx** in the location where you store your Data Files. Enter the text shown for Slide 1. For the text on Slides 2 and 3, insert the Word outline file 15-23.docx. Search the web for an appropriate nature image of your choice, then use screen clipping to insert the image on Slide 3. (Be sure to check its licensing information before clipping the image.) Create the chart within PowerPoint, adjusting the slide layout as necessary and using the categories and values shown in the second slide. Use Quick Layout 1 and Chart Style 5, and delete the chart legend. (*Hints*: The bullet text on Slide 3 is 28 pt, and the theme is Retrospect.) Add your name to the footer of all slides.

FIGURE 15-28

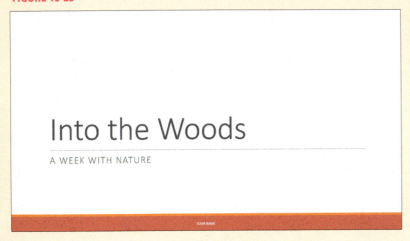

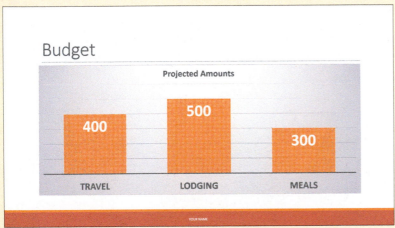

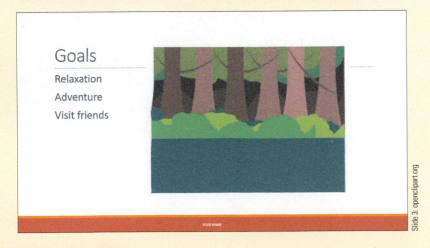

Slide 3: openclipart.org

Index

SPECIAL CHARACTERS
() (parentheses), EX 187
/ (forward slash), EX 187
– (minus sign), EX 187
< (left angle bracket), AC 293
= (equal sign), AC 293, EX 186
* (asterisk), EX 186, EX 187
^ (caret), EX 187
+ (plus sign), EX 187
# (hash mark), EX 190
> (right angle bracket), AC 293

A

absolute cell references, EX 208–209
accessibility
  computers, ECC 13
  video recordings, PA 11
active cell, EX 180
active window, WIN 44
Add Chart Element button, EX 238
add-ins, PA 10. *See also specific add-ins*
addition operator (+), EX 187
add-ons, PPT 366
address(es), WIN 58
Address bar, WIN 38, WIN 58
adware, ECC 20
aligning pictures, PPT 352
alignment
  text, WD 132, WD 133
  worksheets, EX 190, EX 191
animation effects
  slides, PPT 360–361
  speed, PPT 360
animation order numbers, PPT 360
Animation pane, PPT 361
annotating webpages, PA 15
anti-spyware software, ECC 20
antivirus software, ECC 20, ECC 21
application software (apps), ECC 24–25, WIN 36
  Access, creating from templates, AC 256
  common elements, OFF 86–87
  desktop, WIN 40
  inserting in slides, PA 12
  Office. *See* Office apps
  starting, WIN 40–41
  universal, WIN 40–41

architecture, computers, ECC 6
area charts, EX 231
arguments, functions, EX 188, EX 210
Arial, WD 112
Ascending button, AC 282
assistive devices, ECC 13
asterisk (*), multiplication operator, EX 186, EX 187
audio files (audio clips), PPT 354–355
AutoComplete feature, EX 184
AutoCorrect feature, WD 102, WD 103
AutoFill feature, formulas, EX 186
AutoFit feature, EX 184
AutoNumber data type, AC 258, AC 259
AutoSum, EX 188–189
AVERAGE function, EX 210, EX 214, EX 215
AVG calculations, reports, AC 317
axes, charts, EX 230
axis titles, EX 230

B

Backstage view, OFF 92
  Print screen, EX 194
backups, WIN 68
  off-site, ECC 11
bar charts, EX 231
basic input/output system (BIOS), ECC 8
bibliographies, WD 160
binary digits, ECC 17
BIOS (basic input/output system), ECC 8
bits, ECC 17
bits per second (bps), ECC 19
Blank desktop database dialog box,
  AC 256, AC 257
Bluetooth, ECC 14, ECC 18
Blu-ray discs, ECC 10
bold type, WD 130
boot process, ECC 8
booting up, ECC 8
borders, WD 164, WD 165
  applying around selected cells, EX 192
  windows, WIN 44
Borders and Shading dialog box, WD 164, WD 165
bps (bits per second), ECC 19
bridging, ECC 18
broadband connections, ECC 19

browsers, ECC 20
built-in graphics cards, ECC 14
bullet(s), custom, WD 141
Bullet Library, WD 140, WD 141
bulleted lists, WD 140, WD 141
buttons, WIN 38. *See also specific buttons*
   adding to taskbar, WIN 36
   dialog boxes, WIN 47
   groups, WIN 42
   Query Wizard, AC 287
   taskbar, WIN 37
   using, WIN 46
byte, ECC 17

C

cables, ECC 16
Calculated data type, AC 259
calculated fields, adding to tables,
   AC 294–295
calculations
   dates, using serial values, EX 213
   summary, in reports, AC 316, AC 317
   using total row cells, EX 218
Caption property, AC 262
cards, ECC 6
   Sway, PA 6
caret (^), exponent operator, EX 187
Cascading Style Sheets (CSS), ECC 24
case sensitivity, passwords, WIN 34
CD(s) (compact discs), ECC 10
CD-ROMs, ECC 10
cell(s), ECC 24
   tables, WD 152
   worksheets. *See* cell(s), worksheets
cell(s), worksheets, EX 180
   active, EX 180
   displaying formulas in, EX 186
   selected, applying borders around, EX 192
   selecting, EX 181
   too narrow to display values, EX 190
cell address, EX 180
cell pointer, EX 180
cell ranges, EX 180
   selecting, EX 181
cell references, EX 186
   absolute, EX 208–209
   entering in formulas, EX 186
cell styles, worksheets, EX 192, EX 193
center-aligning text, WD 132, WD 133
centering tables on slides, PPT 342
central processing unit (CPU).
   See **microprocessors**
Change Entrance Effect dialog box, PPT 360, PPT 361
channels, ECC 16

chart(s), EX 229–245
   chart layouts, EX 236, EX 237
   chart styles, EX 236, EX 237
   colors, EX 240, EX 241
   creating, EX 230, EX 232–233, EX 234
   customizing, EX 238
   elements, EX 230
   enhancing, EX 240–241
   inserting, EX 232, EX 233
   inserting Excel charts into PowerPoint slides, INT 376–377
   interpreting, EX 231
   moving, EX 234, EX 235
   planning, EX 230
   printing with or without worksheet data, EX 240
   resizing, EX 234, EX 235
   shape styles, EX 240, EX 241
   sparklines, EX 244–245
   trendlines, EX 238
   types, EX 230, EX 231
chart area, EX 230
chart elements (chart objects)
   customizing, EX 238–239
   deleting, EX 234
   moving, EX 234, EX 235
   removing formatting, EX 240
   resizing, EX 234, EX 235
   selecting, EX 240
Chart Filters button, EX 238
chart layouts, EX 236, EX 237
chart sheets, EX 242
   adding text, EX 242
chart styles, EX 236, EX 237
Chart Title placeholder, EX 236
Chart Tools Design tab, EX 236
Chart Tools Format tab, EX 240
check boxes, dialog boxes, WIN 47
Choose a SmartArt Graphic dialog box, PPT 340, PPT 341
circuit(s), ECC 6
circuit board, ECC 6
citations, WD 160, WD 161
Clear button, EX 206
clearing the Windows Clipboard, WD 106
clicking, WIN 39
client/server networks, ECC 18
clip(s), PA 11
   audio, PPT 354–355
   screen, INT 380
   sound. *See* sound clips
   video, capturing, PA 11
clip art, WD 158
clipboard, WIN 68
clock speed, ECC 7
Close button, OFF 96, OFF 97, WIN 42
closing
   Start menu, WIN 36
   text pane, PPT 340

cloud, OFF 82
   syncing notebooks to, PA 2–3
cloud computing, ECC 2
cloud storage, ECC 11
   locations, WIN 67
clustered column charts, EX 232, EX 233
collaboration, OFF 86
color(s)
   fonts, WD 130, WD 131
   icons, EX 216
   SmartArt graphics, PPT 340
   sparklines, EX 244
   standard, WD 130
color scales, EX 216
Color Styles gallery, WD 158, WD 159
column(s)
   datasheets, resizing, AC 266
   multiple, WD 134
   reports, resizing, moving, and deleting, AC 310, AC 311
   tables. *See* column(s), tables
   worksheets. *See* column(s), worksheets
column(s), tables
   automatically resizing, PPT 342
   deleting, WD 154, WD 155
   inserting, WD 154, WD 155
column(s), worksheets, EX 184, EX 185
   selecting, EX 181
column charts, EX 231
column headings, EX 184
column separator, AC 266
column sparklines, EX 244, EX 245
commands, ECC 6, OFF 86, WIN 38. *See also specific commands*
   groups, OFF 86
   Ribbon, OFF 88
compact discs (CDs), ECC 10
comparison operators, AC 293
complementary metal oxide semiconductor (CMOS)
   memory, ECC 8
complex formulas, EX 206–207
computer(s), ECC 4
   architecture (configuration), ECC 6
   information flow through, ECC 6, ECC 7
   types, ECC 4–5
computer accessibility, ECC 13
computer systems, ECC 6
   components, ECC 6–7
conditional formatting, EX 216–217
   reports, AC 314–315
configuration, computers, ECC 6
connectors, USB, ECC 16
content, adding to build story, PA 7
content placeholder icons, PPT 331
contextual tabs, WD 152
control(s)
   dialog boxes, WIN 47
   forms, AC 268
   reports, AC 312–313

controller cards, ECC 16
copying
   files, WIN 68–69
   text, WD 106–107
copyright, screen clips, INT 380
Cortana, PA 14–15, WIN 48, WIN 49
COUNT calculations, reports, AC 317
COUNT function, EX 210, EX 211
CPU (central processing unit). *See* microprocessors
CPU cache, ECC 8, ECC 9
Create Source dialog box, WD 160, WD 161
Create Sparklines dialog box, EX 244, EX 245
Create tab, AC 268
Creative Commons licenses, PA 7, PPT 336, WD 158
criteria
   filtering records in tables, AC 284
   filtering table data, EX 220
   multiple, AC 292
   search, WIN 72
cropping handles, PPT 352
cropping pictures, PPT 352, PPT 353
CSS (Cascading Style Sheets), ECC 24
Currency data type, AC 259
Custom AutoFilter dialog box, EX 220, EX 221
custom bullets, WD 141
Custom Filter dialog box, AC 284, AC 285
custom formatting, EX 216
customizing
   chart elements, EX 238–239
   charts, EX 238
   Details view, WIN 65
   Quick Access Toolbar, OFF 90, OFF 91
Cut command, WD 108
cutting files, WIN 70, WIN 71
Cycle SmartArt graphics, PPT 341

D

data, ECC 6
data bars, EX 216
data buses, ECC 16
data communications, ECC 16–17
data files, ECC 10
data markers, EX 230
data series, EX 230
   changing color, EX 240
   displaying/hiding, EX 238
data sources, INT 388
data types, fields, AC 258, AC 259
database(s), AC 254, ECC 24, EX 218
   creating, AC 256–257
   existing, opening, AC 280–281
   good design, AC 291
   queries. *See* queries
   reports. *See* report(s)

tables. *See* table(s)
uses, AC 254, AC 255
database management software, ECC 24. *See also*
Microsoft Access
database management systems (DBMSs), AC 254
database objects, AC 255. *See also* form(s); queries;
report(s); table(s)
datasheet(s), moving to previous field, AC 266
Datasheet view
creating tables, AC 258–259
editing data, AC 266–267
date(s)
calculation using serial values, EX 213
entering in tables, AC 264
Date and Time dialog box, WD 162, WD 163
date functions, EX 212, EX 213
Date/Time data type, AC 259
DBMSs (database management systems), AC 254
decimal points, number of digits following, EX 190
default, WIN 46, WIN 60
Delete File dialog box, WIN 74, WIN 75
deleting. *See also* **removing**
charts and chart elements, EX 234
columns in reports, AC 310, AC 311
fields from queries, AC 292
fields from tables, AC 258, AC 262
files, WIN 74, WIN 75
records, AC 264
table columns and rows, WD 154, WD 155
depth axis, EX 230
Descending button, AC 282
Design view, AC 308, AC 309
creating tables, AC 260–261
modifying queries, AC 288–289
desktop apps, WIN 40
desktop computers, ECC 4, ECC 5
desktop publishing program. *See* **Microsoft Publisher**
destination file, INT 384
Detail section, AC 313
Details view, customizing, WIN 65
device drivers, ECC 16
dialog box(es), OFF 86
using, WIN 46, WIN 47
dialog box launcher, OFF 86
digital video interface (DVI), ECC 16
digital world, ECC 2–3
display, ECC 14, ECC 15
display resolution, ECC 14
displaying. *See also* **viewing**
formulas in cells, EX 186
grid of clickable or tappable letters, WIN 36
Notes pane, PPT 362
password characters, temporarily, WIN 34
taskbar, WIN 36
division operator (/), EX 187

DNS servers, ECC 20
Docs.com public gallery, PA 8
document(s)
creating from an existing file, WD 100–101
creating from templates, WD 100
entering text, WD 102–103
main, INT 388
previewing, WD 116, WD 117
printing, WD 116, WD 117
removing from Recent Documents list, OFF 96
saved, sharing, OFF 97
translating into other languages, WD 115
document production software, ECC 24. *See also*
Microsoft Word
document window, OFF 86
dot leaders, WD 136
dots per inch (dpi), ECC 14
double-clicking, WIN 38, WIN 39
dpi (dots per inch), ECC 14
Draft view, WD 117
dragging, WIN 39
indent markers, WD 138
text, WD 108, WD 109
dragging and dropping, WD 106, WD 107, WIN 75
drawing canvas, PA 3
drivers, ECC 16
DSL (digital subscriber line), ECC 19
dual-core processors, ECC 7
DVI (digital video interface), ECC 16

E

Edge. *See* **Microsoft Edge**
Edit Relationships dialog box, AC 290, AC 291
editing
data in Datasheet view, AC 266–267
files, WIN 66, WIN 67
text, WD 104, WD 105
email, ECC 2
sending personalized email messages, INT 390
emailing files, WD 116
embedding Excel charts into PowerPoint slides, INT 376–377
emphasis animations, PA 8, PPT 360
end-of-cell marks, WD 152
end-of-row marks, WD 152
entering text in documents, WD 102–103
entrance animations, PPT 360
equal sign (=)
equal operator, AC 293
formulas, EX 186
ergonomic keyboards, ECC 12, ECC 13
Ethernet ports, ECC 16, ECC 17
executable files, ECC 10
exit animations, PPT 360

exiting
  Office apps, OFF 96–97
  Windows 10, WIN 50–51
expansion cards, ECC 16
expansion ports, ECC 16
expansion slots, ECC 16
exploding pie slices, EX 242
exponent operator (^), EX 187
Expression Builder dialog box, AC 294, AC 295

F

[F4] key, EX 208
field(s)
  adding to reports, AC 312–313
  adding to tables, AC 306
  calculated, adding to tables, AC 294–295
  data types, AC 258, AC 259
  databases, AC 254, ECC 24
  deleting, AC 258, AC 262
  deleting from queries, AC 292
  multiple, sorting on, AC 283
  renaming, AC 258, AC 262
  selecting, AC 286
  tables, EX 218
field descriptions, AC 260
field names, AC 254
field properties, AC 262, AC 263
Field Properties pane, AC 262
field values, AC 264
file(s), ECC 10, WIN 36
  changing sort order, WIN 65
  copying, WIN 68–69
  creating, WIN 60, WIN 61
  cutting, WIN 70, WIN 71
  deleting, WIN 74, WIN 75
  editing, WIN 66, WIN 67
  emailing, WD 116
  existing, creating new documents from, WD 100–101
  filtering, WIN 65
  moving, WIN 70, WIN 71, WIN 75
  opening, WIN 66, WIN 67
  pasting, WIN 70, WIN 71
  renaming, WIN 70, WIN 71
  restoring, WIN 74, WIN 75
  saving, OFF 92–93, WIN 60, WIN 61, WIN 66, WIN 67
  searching for, WIN 72–73
  selecting, WD 100, WIN 75
File Explorer button, WIN 37, WIN 58, WIN 62, WIN 63
  Search Tools tab, WIN 73
file extensions, OFF 92, WIN 60
file hierarchy, WIN 58, WIN 59
  navigating, WIN 62, WIN 63
File list, WIN 58

file management, WIN 57–75
file organization, planning, WIN 59
file syncing, WIN 67
File tab, OFF 86, OFF 96
  navigation bar, OFF 92
  Print button, WD 162
filenames, OFF 92
fill handles, EX 186
filtering
  files, WIN 65
  records in tables, AC 284–285
  removing applied filters, EX 220
  table data, EX 220–221
financial functions, EX 213
Find and Replace dialog box, WD 110, WD 111
finding text, WD 110–111
firewalls, ECC 20
firmware, ECC 8
firmware updates, ECC 8
first line indent(s), WD 138, WD 139
First line indent marker, PPT 333
flash drives, ECC 10, ECC 11, WIN 60
  security risk, ECC 10
flash memory, ECC 10, ECC 11
flash memory cards, ECC 10, ECC 11
flat panel monitors, ECC 14, ECC 15
floating images, WD 158
folders, WIN 36, WIN 58
  chafing sort order, WIN 65
  new, creating, WIN 68
  searching for, WIN 72–73
font(s), ECC 24, WD 112
  changing, WD 128, WD 129
  color, WD 130, WD 131
  samples, WD 129
  style sets, changing, WD 142
  styles, WD 130, WD 131
font effects, WD 130, WD 131
font size, WD 112
  changing, WD 128, WD 129
  samples, WD 129
font style, WD 112
footers
  inserting, WD 162, WD 163
  opening, WD 162
  showing on every slide except title slide, INT 378
  slide, PPT 343
  viewing, WD 162
  worksheets, EX 192, EX 193
footnotes, WD 160, WD 161
form(s), AC 254, AC 255
  creating, AC 268, AC 269
  split, AC 268
  themes, AC 268
  using, AC 268, AC 269

form controls, AC 268
form letters, INT 388
Format Painter button, WD 130
Format pane, EX 238
formatting
  applying multiple times, WD 130
  conditional, EX 216–217
  custom, EX 216
  pictures, WD 158, WD 159
  removing from selected text, WD 130
  sound clips, PPT 357
  tables, WD 156–157
  text. *See* formatting text
  video objects, PPT 357
formatting marks, hiding/displaying, WD 102
formatting text
  Mini toolbar, WD 112–113
  multiple columns, WD 134
  research papers, WD 168–169
  slides, PPT 332, PPT 333
formula(s), EX 186–187. *See also* function(s)
  absolute cell references, EX 208–209
  AutoFill to adjacent cells, EX 186
  complex, EX 206–207
  displaying in cells, EX 186
  entering cell references, EX 186
Formula AutoComplete, EX 210, EX 211
formula bar, EX 180
Formulas tab, EX 210
forward slash (/), division operator, EX 187
free-response quizzes, inserting in slides, PA 12
function(s), EX 188–189, EX 210–215
  categories, EX 213
  date and time, EX 212–213
  statistical, EX 214–215
Function Arguments dialog box, EX 212, EX 213

GBs (gigabytes), ECC 17
gestures, ECC 4, WIN 34
GHz (gigahertz), ECC 7
gigabytes (GBs), ECC 17
gigahertz (GHz), ECC 7
grammar, checking, WD 114, WD 115
graphical user interfaces (GUIs), ECC 22
graphics. *See also* picture(s)
  resizing, PPT 338
  SmartArt, PPT 340–341
graphics cards, ECC 14
graphics processors, ECC 14
graphics software, ECC 24

Greater Than dialog box, EX 216
greater than operator (>), AC 293
gridlines, charts, EX 230
group(s)
  buttons, WIN 42
  commands, OFF 86
Group Footer section, AC 313
Group Header section, AC 313
grouping records, AC 306
GUIs (graphical user interfaces), ECC 22

handout(s), printing, PPT 364, PPT 365
handout headers, PPT 364
handwriting, converting to text, PA 3–4
hanging indent(s), WD 138, WD 139
Hanging indent marker, PPT 333
hard copy, ECC 14
hard disk drives (HDDs) (hard disks; hard drives), ECC 10
hard page breaks, WD 160
hardware, ECC 6
  specifications, ECC 6
  Windows 10 requirements, ECC 23
hash mark (#), cell to narrow to display value, EX 190
HDDs (hard disk drives; hard disks; hard drives), ECC 10
HDMI (high-definition multimedia interface), ECC 16
header(s)
  inserting, WD 162, WD 163
  opening, WD 162
  viewing, WD 162
  worksheets, EX 192, EX 193
Header and Footer dialog box, PPT 343
header row, tables, EX 218
headings
  reordering in Navigation pane, WD 160
  worksheet rows and columns, EX 184
headphones, ECC 14
help
  Cortana, WIN 48, WIN 49
  online, WIN 48, WIN 49
hiding, Notes pane, PPT 362
hierarchy charts, EX 231
Hierarchy SmartArt graphics, PPT 341
high-definition multimedia interface (HDMI), ECC 16
highlighted icons, WIN 38
Home tab, OFF 86
horizontal axis, EX 230
HTML (Hypertext Markup Language), ECC 24
Hub, Edge, PA 14
Hypertext Markup Language (HTML), ECC 24

I

icons
   colors, EX 216
   highlighted, WIN 38
   placeholder, PPT 331
   selecting, WIN 38
images
   online, slides, PPT 336–337
   resizing, PPT 338
   stock, PPT 336
inactive window, WIN 44
indent(s), WD 138–139
indent markers, dragging, WD 138
indenting text, PPT 333
information and task management software, ECC 24. *See also* Microsoft Outlook
information collection tool and organizer. *See* **Microsoft OneNote**
information manager, ECC 24. *See also* Microsoft Outlook
infrared technology, ECC 18
Ink to Text button, PA 3
inked handwriting, PA 3
Inking toolbar, PA 15
inkjet printers, ECC 14, ECC 15
inline images, WD 158
input, ECC 6
input and output (I/O), ECC 22
input devices, ECC 6, ECC 12
   types, ECC 12–13
Insert Audio dialog box, PPT 354, PPT 355
Insert Chart dialog box, EX 232, EX 233, INT 376, INT 377
Insert File dialog box, INT 382, INT 383
Insert Pictures dialog box, PPT 336, PPT 337, WD 158, WD 159
Insert tab
   Header button, WD 162
   inserting media, PPT 356
   Table button, WD 152
Insert Table menu, WD 155
insertion point, OFF 86, WD 102
   keyboard shortcuts for moving, WD 105
Insights for Office, WD 111
insights pane, OFF 94
interactive presentations, creating with Office Mix, PPT 366
interface cards, ECC 16
Internet, ECC 18
   digital world, ECC 2–3
   lasting repercussions of activities on, ECC 3
italic type, WD 130

J

justification, WD 132, WD 133

K

keyboard(s), ECC 12, ECC 13
   adding new slides, PPT 330
keywords, OFF 94, PPT 336
kilobytes (KBs or Ks), ECC 17

L

label(s), entering in worksheets, EX 182, EX 183
Label Wizard, AC 318, AC 319
LAN(s) (local areal networks), ECC 16, ECC 18
landscape orientation, EX 194
languages, translating documents, WD 115
laptop computers, ECC 4, ECC 5
laser printers, ECC 14, ECC 15
launcher, OFF 86
layout(s)
   chart layouts, EX 236, EX 237
   displaying files and folders, WIN 64, WIN 65
   presentations, PPT 330
   slide masters, PPT 359
Layout view, AC 308, AC 309
   modifying reports, AC 310–311
LCD (liquid crystal display) technology, ECC 14, ECC 15
lectures, recording, PA 4
LED printers, ECC 14
LED (light emitting diode) technology, ECC 14
left angle bracket (<), AC 293
left indents, WD 138, WD 139
legends, charts, EX 230
less than operator (<), AC 293
light emitting diode (LED) technology, ECC 14
line charts, EX 231
line sparklines, EX 244, EX 245
link(s), INT 384
linking
   Excel data to Word documents, INT 384–385
   updating linked Excel charts in Word documents, INT 386–387
liquid crystal display (LCD) technology, ECC 14, ECC 15
list(s)
   bulleted, WD 140, WD 141
   numbered, WD 140, WD 141
list boxes, dialog boxes, WIN 47
List SmartArt graphics, PPT 341
Live Preview, OFF 94, WD 128
live tiles, WIN 36
local areal networks (LANs), ECC 16, ECC 18
lock screens, WIN 34, WIN 35
logging in (logging on), ECC 22, WIN 34
logging out, WIN 50–51
logical functions, EX 213
Long Text data type, AC 259
lookup & reference functions, EX 213

M

Macs, ECC 4
magnetic storage devices, ECC 10
mail merge, INT 388–391
  inserting merge fields into Word documents, INT 388–389
  performing, INT 390–391
  sending personalized email messages, INT 390
Mail Merge Recipients dialog box, INT 388, INT 389
mailing labels, AC 318–319
main documents, INT 388
mainframe computers, ECC 4
malware, ECC 20
margins, WD 132
  changing settings, WD 134–135
  worksheets, changing, EX 194
Margins list, WD 134, WD 135
math & trig functions, EX 213
mathematical operators, EX 186, EX 187
Matrix SmartArt graphics, PPT 341
MAX calculations, reports, AC 317
MAX function, EX 214
Maximize button, WIN 42
MBs (megabytes), ECC 17
megabytes (MBs), ECC 17
megahertz (MHz), ECC 7
memory, ECC 8
  capacity, ECC 8
  flash, ECC 10, ECC 11
  types, ECC 8–9
memory RAM, ECC 8, ECC 9, WIN 60
menus, WIN 42
  using, WIN 46, WIN 47
merge fields, inserting into Word documents, INT 388–389
merged documents, INT 388
metric units, mailing labels, AC 318
MHz (megahertz), ECC 7
microphones, ECC 12
microprocessors, ECC 6
  speed, ECC 7
Microsoft Access, OFF 82
  placing Access tables in Word documents, INT 382
  printing objects, AC 266
Microsoft accounts, WIN 34
Microsoft Edge, PA 14–16, WIN 38, WIN 73
  annotating webpages, PA 15
  browsing the web, PA 14
  locating information with Cortana, PA 14–15
Microsoft Edge button, WIN 37
Microsoft Excel, OFF 82
  inserting Excel charts into PowerPoint slides, INT 376–377
  linking Excel data to Word documents, INT 384–385
  updating linked Excel charts in Word docs, INT 386–387
Microsoft Office, editions, OFF 84
Microsoft Office Home & Student, OFF 84

Microsoft Office Mix, PA 10–13
  adding to PowerPoint, PA 10
  capturing video clips, PA 11
  inserting quizzes, live webpages, and apps, PA 12
  overview, PPT 366
  sharing presentations, PA 12
Microsoft Office Online, OFF 84, OFF 92
Microsoft Office 365 Home, OFF 84
Microsoft Office 365 Personal, OFF 84
Microsoft OneDrive, OFF 82, OFF 86, OFF 92, WIN 67
Microsoft OneNote, OFF 82, PA 2–5
  converting handwriting to text, PA 3–4
  creating notebooks, PA 2
  recording lectures, PA 4
  syncing notebooks to cloud, PA 2–3
  taking notes, PA 3
Microsoft OneNote Mobile app, PA 2
Microsoft Outlook, OFF 82
Microsoft PowerPoint, OFF 82
  adding Office Mix, PA 10
  creating PowerPoint slides from a Word doc, INT 378–379
  inserting Excel charts into PowerPoint slides, INT 376–377
  inserting screen clips into Word documents, INT 380–381
  using Word outlines in PowerPoint, INT 379
Microsoft Publisher, OFF 82
Microsoft Sway, OFF 82, PA 6–9
  adding content, PA 7
  creating presentations, PA 6–7
  designing presentations, PA 8
  publishing presentations, PA 8
  sharing presentations, PA 8
Microsoft Word, OFF 82
  creating PowerPoint slides from a Word doc, INT 378–379
  inserting merge fields into Word documents, INT 388–389
  inserting screen clips into Word documents, INT 380–381
  inserting text from Word files into open documents, INT 382–383
  linking Excel data to Word documents, INT 384–385
  placing Access tables in Word documents, INT 382
  updating linked Excel charts in Word docs, INT 386–387
  using Word outlines in PowerPoint, INT 379
MIN calculations, reports, AC 317
MIN function, EX 214, EX 215
Mini toolbar, formatting text, WD 112–113
Minimize button, WIN 42
minimizing, Ribbon, OFF 88
minus sign (–), subtraction operator, EX 187
Mixes, PPT 366
MLA (Modern Language Association) style, WD 168–169
modems, ECC 16
Modern Language Association (MLA) style, WD 168–169
monitors, ECC 14, ECC 15
motherboard, ECC 6, ECC 7
  installing RAM, ECC 9
motion path(s), PPT 360
motion path animations, PPT 360

mouse, ECC 12, ECC 13
Move Chart dialog box, EX 242, EX 243
moving
    chart elements, EX 234, EX 235
    charts, EX 234, EX 235
    columns in reports, AC 310, AC 311
    files, WIN 70, WIN 71, WIN 75
    insertion point, keyboard shortcuts for, WD 105
    items using touch-screen devices, WIN 39
    to previous field in datasheets, AC 266
    selected objects, WIN 46
    to slides in Slide plane, PPT 332
    slides in Slide Sorter view, PPT 328
    between table cells, WD 152
    text, WD 108–109
multimedia authoring software, ECC 24
multimedia presentation tool. *See* **Microsoft Sway**
multiplication operator (*), EX 186, EX 187

N

name box, EX 180
navigating
    file hierarchy, WIN 62, WIN 63
    Start menu, WIN 36, WIN 37
    up/down, WIN 58
    Windows 10 desktop, WIN 36, WIN 37
    workbooks, EX 180–181
    worksheets, EX 180
navigation bar, AC 268
    File tab, OFF 92
Navigation pane, AC 256, WIN 58
    Pages tab, WD 164
    reordering headings, WD 160
network(s), ECC 18
    components, ECC 18, ECC 19
    types, ECC 18, ECC 19
network interface cards (NICs), ECC 18, ECC 19
network software, ECC 18
New Formatting Rule dialog box, AC 314, AC 315
New Query dialog box, AC 286, AC 287
NICs (network interface cards), ECC 18, ECC 19
nodes, ECC 18
nonvolatile memory, ECC 8
Normal view, PPT 328
not equal to operator (<>), AC 293
note(s), PA 2. *See also* Microsoft OneNote
    annotating webpages, PA 15
    speaker, PPT 362–363
    taking, PA 3
notebook(s), PA 2. *See also* Microsoft OneNote
notebook computers, ECC 4
Notes button, PPT 362
Notes page(s), printing, PPT 364, PPT 365
Notes Page view, PPT 328, PPT 362, PPT 363
Notes pane, speaker notes, PPT 362–363

Notification area, WIN 36
Number data type, AC 259
number format, worksheets, EX 190, EX 191
numbered lists, WD 140, WD 141

O

objects, AC 254, PPT 332
OCR (optical character recognition) software, ECC 12
Office apps, OFF 82
    exiting, OFF 96–97
    Office Online apps, OFF 83
    starting, OFF 84–85
    suites, OFF 82
Office Clipboard, WD 106, WD 107
    activating, WD 108
Office Mix, PPT 366
Office Online apps, OFF 83
Office.com SmartArt graphics, PPT 341
off-site backup, ECC 11
OneDrive. *See* **Microsoft OneDrive**
OneNote. *See* **Microsoft OneNote**
one-to-many relationships, AC 290
online images
    legal use, PPT 336
    slides, PPT 336–337
Online Pictures button, WD 158
opening
    existing databases, AC 280–281
    files, WIN 66, WIN 67
    footers, WD 162
    headers, WD 162
    presentations, PPT 328, PPT 329
    Start menu, WIN 36
operating environments, ECC 22
operating systems, ECC 22, WIN 34
optical, ECC 10
optical character recognition (OCR) software, ECC 12
option boxes, dialog boxes, WIN 47
order of precedence, EX 186, EX 206, EX 207
Orientation button, EX 190
outline(s), Word, using in PowerPoint, INT 379
Outline view, PPT 328, WD 117
output, ECC 6
output devices, ECC 6, ECC 14
    types, ECC 14–15
Overtype mode, WD 104

P

page break(s)
    inserting using Ribbon, WD 160
    verifying, EX 194
Page Break Preview button, EX 194
Page Footer section, AC 313

Page Header section, AC 313
  reports, AC 308
Page Setup dialog box, WD 134, WD 135
Page Width button, WD 136
pages per minute (ppm), ECC 14
panes, PPT 328
  resizing, PPT 328
  windows, WIN 58
PANs (personal area networks), ECC 18
paragraph(s), WD 132
Paragraph dialog box, WD 132, WD 133
parentheses (()), formulas, EX 187
passwords, ECC 22, WIN 34, WIN 35
  case sensitivity, WIN 34
  strong, ECC 22
  temporarily displaying characters, WIN 34
pasting
  files, WIN 70, WIN 71
  text, WD 106, WD 107
paths, WIN 58
PCs, ECC 4
peer-to-peer networks, ECC 18
pencil icon, AC 264
peripheral devices, ECC 6
permanent memory, ECC 8
personal area networks (PANs), ECC 18
personal computers, ECC 4, ECC 5
pharming, ECC 20
phishing, ECC 20
photo-editing software, ECC 24
picture(s). *See also* **graphics**
  aligning, PPT 352
  cropping, PPT 352, PPT 353
  formatting, WD 158, WD 159
  inserting, WD 158, WD 159
  presentations, PPT 352–353
picture effects, PPT 337
Picture SmartArt graphics, PPT 341
pie charts, EX 231
  creating, EX 242–243
pinching, OFF 96
pixels, ECC 14
placeholder(s), PPT 330
  slide layouts, PPT 356
placeholder icons, PPT 331
playback volume, PPT 354
plot area, charts, EX 230
plug-ins, PPT 366
plus sign (+), addition operator, EX 187
pointers, ECC 12, WIN 38
  shapes, WIN 38
pointing, WIN 39
pointing devices, ECC 12, WIN 38–39
  actions, WIN 38, WIN 39

portrait orientation, EX 194
PowerPoint Start screen, PPT 328, PPT 329
ppm (pages per minute), ECC 14
presentation(s). *See also* **slide(s); slide shows**
  effective, designing, PPT 366–367
  interactive, creating with Office Mix, PPT 366
  layouts, PPT 330
  new, creating, PPT 330–331
  Office Mix, sharing, PA 12
  opening, PPT 328, PPT 329
  pictures, PPT 352–353
  sound, PPT 354–355
  speaker notes, PPT 362–33
  Sway. *See* Microsoft Sway
  templates, PPT 330, PPT 335
  themes, PPT 330, PPT 334–335
  video, PPT 356–357
  viewing, PPT 328, PPT 329
presentation graphics apps, PPT 328. *See also* Microsoft
  PowerPoint
presentation graphics programs. *See* **Microsoft**
  PowerPoint
presentation software, ECC 24. *See also* Microsoft PowerPoint
Presenter view, PPT 363
previewing
  documents, WD 116, WD 117
  worksheets, EX 194, EX 195
primary key field, AC 258
Print dialog box, WIN 46, WIN 47
Print Layout view, WD 117
Print Preview, AC 308, AC 309, EX 194, EX 195
Print screen, Backstage view, EX 194
printers, ECC 14, ECC 15
  selecting, PPT 364
printing
  documents, WD 116, WD 117
  handouts, PPT 364, PPT 365
  Notes pages, PPT 364, PPT 365
  objects in Access, AC 266
  slides, PPT 365
  worksheets, EX 194, EX 195
Process SmartArt graphics, PPT 341
processing, ECC 6
processors. *See* **microprocessors**
program(s), ECC 6, WIN 34. *See also* software;
  specific programs
  suites, OFF 82
programming languages, ECC 22
properties, tables, setting, AC 262, AC 263
protocols, ECC 16
public domain, PPT 336
publishing Sways, PA 8
pulling out pie slices, EX 242
Pyramid SmartArt graphics, PPT 341

Q

quad-core processors, ECC 7
queries, AC 254, AC 255
　adding fields to query design grid, AC 288–289
　creating, AC 286–287
　creating using two tables, AC 292–293
　deleting fields, AC 292
　modifying in Design view, AC 288–289
　select, AC 286
　specifying multiple criteria for a field, AC 292
　viewing results, AC 292, AC 293
Query Wizard, AC 286–287
　buttons, AC 287
Quick Access area, WIN 58
Quick Access Toolbar, OFF 86, OFF 90–91, WIN 42, WIN 43
　customizing, OFF 90, OFF 91
　Save button, OFF 96
　Undo button, WD 104
Quick Access view, WIN 64
　disabling, WIN 63
　using, WIN 63
Quick Action buttons, WIN 64
Quick Analysis tool, creating charts, EX 234
quizzes, inserting in slides, PA 12

R

RAM. *See* **random access memory (RAM)**
RAM cache, ECC 8, ECC 9
random access memory (RAM), ECC 8, WIN 60
　adding, ECC 8
　installing on motherboard, ECC 9
　upgrading, ECC 9
Read Mode view, WD 117
Reading view, PA 14, PPT 328
read-only memory (ROM), ECC 8
receiver, ECC 16
Recent Documents list, removing documents, OFF 96, OFF 97
record(s)
　creating, AC 268
　databases, AC 254, ECC 24
　deleting, AC 264
　grouping, AC 306
　tables, EX 218
　tables, sorting, AC 282–283
record source(s), AC 306
recording lectures, PA 4
recordings
　screen, PA 11
　slide, PA 11
Recycle Bin, WIN 36, WIN 38, WIN 39, WIN 74, WIN 75
relational databases, AC 254
Relationship SmartArt graphics, PPT 341
relative cell referencing, EX 186

removing. *See also* **deleting**
　documents from Recent Documents list, OFF 96
　formatting from chart elements, EX 240
　formatting from selected text, WD 130
　transitions, PPT 358
renaming
　fields, AC 258, AC 262
　files, WIN 70, WIN 71
repagination, WD 134
Replace command, WD 110
replacing text, WD 110–111
report(s), AC 254, AC 255, AC 305–319
　adding fields, AC 312–313
　conditional formatting, AC 314–315
　controls, AC 312–313
　creating using Report Wizard,
　　AC 306–307
　modifying, AC 310–311
　Page Header section, AC 308
　Report Header section, AC 308
　sections, AC 313
　summary information, AC 316–317
　viewing, AC 308–309
Report Footer section, AC 313
Report Header section, AC 313
　reports, AC 308
Report tool, AC 306
Report view, AC 308, AC 309
Report Wizard, AC 306–307
research papers, formatting,
　WD 168–169
research tools, WD 116
resizing
　chart elements, EX 234, EX 235
　charts, EX 234, EX 235
　columns in datasheets, AC 266
　columns in reports, AC 310, AC 311
　graphics and images, PPT 338
　panes, PPT 328
　table columns, automatically, PPT 342
responsive design, PA 6
restoring files, WIN 74, WIN 75
Ribbon, OFF 86, WIN 38, WIN 62
　commands, OFF 88
　inserting page breaks, WD 160
　minimizing, OFF 88
Ribbon Display Options button, OFF 86
Rich Text Format, WIN 60
right angle bracket (>), AC 293
right indents, WD 138, WD 139
right-clicking, WIN 39
RM, ECC 8
ROM (read-only memory), ECC 8
routers, ECC 18
row headings, EX 184
row selectors, AC 264

rows, tables
    deleting, WD 154, WD 155
    inserting, WD 154, WD 155
    sorting, EX 218–219
rows, worksheets, EX 184, EX 185
    selecting, EX 181
royalty fees, PPT 336
ruler markers, setting indents, WD 139

S

sandbox, PA 15
Save As dialog box, AC 280, AC 281, OFF 92, OFF 93, WD 100,
    WD 101, WIN 60, WIN 61
Save button, OFF 96
Save command, Save As command compared, WIN 66
saving
    databases, to trusted locations, AC 280
    files, OFF 92–93, WIN 60, WIN 61, WIN 66, WIN 67
scanners, ECC 12
scatter charts, EX 231
screen, ECC 14, ECC 15
screen clip(s), copyright, INT 380
Screen Clipping feature, INT 380, INT 381
screen clippings, PA 2
screen recordings, PA 11
screen size, ECC 14
screenshots
    inserting screen clips into Word documents, INT 380–381
    sorted tables, capturing, AC 282
ScreenTips, OFF 94, OFF 95, WIN 38
scroll arrows, WIN 43
scroll bars, WIN 42, WIN 43
scroll wheels, ECC 12
SDRAM (synchronous dynamic random access memory), ECC 8
search criteria, WIN 72
search engines, ECC 2
Search Tools tab, WIN 72
security risk, ECC 20–21
    flash drives, ECC 10
    passwords, ECC 22
Select All command, WIN 46, WIN 47
Select pointer, WIN 38
select queries, AC 286
selecting
    cells in worksheets, EX 181
    chart elements, EX 240
    fields, AC 286
    file names, WD 100
    files, WIN 75
    icons, WIN 38
    items using touch-screen devices, WIN 39
    printers, PPT 364
    text, WD 104, WD 105

selection bar, WD 104
selection boxes, PPT 332
semipermanent memory, ECC 8
Send to command, WIN 68, WIN 69
sender, ECC 16
serial values, calculating dates using, EX 213
servers, ECC 18
shading, WD 164, WD 165
shadow effect, PPT 336, PPT 337
shadow type enhancement, WD 130
shapes, slides, PPT 338–339
Share button, OFF 86
sharing
    Office Mix presentations, PA 12
    saved documents, OFF 97
    Sways, PA 8
Short Text data type, AC 259
Show Table dialog box, AC 290, AC 291
Show/Hide ¶ button, WD 102, WD 128, WD 152
signing in, WIN 34
signing out, WIN 50–51
simple databases, AC 254
single-core processors, ECC 7
single-factor authentication, ECC 21
sizing handles, WD 158
slide(s), PPT 328. See also presentation(s); slide show(s)
    adding using keyboard, PPT 330
    animation effects, PPT 360–361
    footers, INT 378, PPT 343
    formatting text, PPT 332, PPT 333
    inserting Excel charts into PowerPoint slides, INT 376–377
    inserting tables, PPT 342–343
    moving in Slide Sorter view, PPT 328
    online images, PPT 336–337
    printing, PPT 365
    shapes, PPT 338–339
    Slide pane, moving to, PPT 332
    text entry, PPT 332, PPT 333
    timings, PPT 358, PPT 359
slide layouts, including placeholders, PPT 356
slide masters, PPT 359
Slide Notes feature, PA 11
Slide pane, PPT 328
    moving to slides in, PPT 332
slide recordings, PA 11
slide show(s), PPT 328. See also presentation(s); slide(s)
    adjusting sound playback, PPT 355
    Presenter view, PPT 363
    starting using keyboard, PPT 356
Slide Show view, PPT 328
Slide Sorter view, PPT 328
    moving slides, PPT 328
slide transitions, PPT 358, PPT 359
sliding, OFF 96
slots, ECC 16

Smart Lookup, OFF 94
SmartArt, PPT 340–341
SmartArt graphics
   color, PPT 340
   uses, PPT 341
smartphones, ECC 4, ECC 5
Snap Assist feature, WIN 44
Soc (System on a Chip), ECC 6
society, digital world, ECC 2–3
software, ECC 6. *See also* program(s); *specific programs*
   anti-spyware, ECC 20
   antivirus, ECC 20, ECC 21
   application, ECC 24–25
   network, ECC 18
   OCR, ECC 12
   system, ECC 22–23
   voice-recognition, ECC 12
solid-state devices, ECC 10
solid-state hybrid drives (SSHDs), ECC 10
solid-state storage, ECC 10, ECC 11
sorting
   files and folders, changing order, WIN 65
   on multiple fields, AC 283
   records in tables, AC 282–283
   rows in tables, EX 218–219
   undoing results, EX 218
sound clips, PPT 354–355
   adjusting playback, PPT 355
   formatting, PPT 357
   playback volume, PPT 354
source file, INT 384
sparklines, EX 244–245
   changing type, EX 244
   colors, EX 244
speaker(s), ECC 14
speaker notes, PPT 362–33
specifications, hardware, ECC 6
speed
   animation effects, PPT 360
   microprocessors, ECC 7
spell checking, WD 114, WD 115
Spelling pane, WD 114, WD 115
spin boxes, dialog boxes, WIN 47
split forms, AC 268
spreadsheet(s), EX 180
spreadsheet apps. *See* Microsoft Excel
spreadsheet software, ECC 24. *See also* Microsoft Excel
spyware, ECC 20
stacked column charts, EX 232, EX 233
standard colors, WD 130
Start button, WIN 36
Start Mail Merge button, INT 390
Start menu
   closing, WIN 36
   navigating, WIN 36, WIN 37
   opening, WIN 36

start screen, OFF 84, OFF 85
starting
   apps, OFF 84–85, WIN 40–41
   slide shows using keyboard, PPT 356
   Windows 10, WIN 34–35
statistical functions, EX 214–215
status bar, OFF 86
   viewing sum data, EX 188
stock images, PPT 336
storage media, types, ECC 10–11
Store button, WIN 37
Storylines, PA 6
stretching, OFF 96
strong passwords, ECC 22
style(s), WD 102, WD 142–143
   chart styles, EX 236, EX 237
   font, WD 112
   fonts, WD 130, WD 131
   table styles, WD 156–157
   worksheet cells, EX 192, EX 193
style sets, WD 142
Styles gallery, WD 142, WD 143
subfolders, WIN 58
subtitle placeholder, PPT 330
subtraction operator (-), EX 187
suites, OFF 82
sum(s), viewing sum data on status bar, EX 188
SUM calculations, reports, AC 317
SUM function, EX 188–189, EX 210, EX 211
summary information, reports, AC 316–317
Summary Information dialog box, AC 316, AC 317
supercomputers, ECC 4, ECC 5
Sway. *See* Microsoft Sway
Sway sites, PA 6
swiping, OFF 96
switching views, OFF 88
synchronous dynamic random access memory (SDRAM), ECC 8
syncing notebooks to cloud, PA 2–3
System on a Chip (Soc), ECC 6
system resources, ECC 22
system software, ECC 22
   components, ECC 22–23

T

tab(s), OFF 86, WD 136–137, WIN 38
   contextual, WD 152
tab selector, WD 136
tab stops, WD 136
table(s), AC 255, WD 152–157
   adding fields, AC 306
   calculated fields, AC 294–295
   cells, WD 152
   changing back to normal range, EX 220
   columns. *See* column(s), tables

creating, WD 152–153, WD 155
creating in Datasheet view, AC 258–259
creating in Design view, AC 260–261
data entry, AC 264–265
filtering data, EX 220–221
filtering records, AC 284–285
formatting, WD 156–157
inserting in slides, PPT 342–343
modifying, AC 262, AC 263
placing Access tables in Word documents, INT 382
relating, AC 290–291
rows. *See* rows, tables
setting properties, AC 262, AC 263
sorting records, AC 282–283
sorting rows, EX 218–219
two, creating queries using, AC 292–293
table styles, WD 156–157
tablets, ECC 4, ECC 5
tapping, OFF 96
Task View button, WIN 37, WIN 70
taskbar, WIN 36
adding buttons, WIN 36
buttons, WIN 37
displaying, WIN 36
using, WIN 45
TBs (terabytes), ECC 17
telecommunications, ECC 19
telecommuting, ECC 2, ECC 3
Tell Me box, OFF 94, OFF 95
templates, OFF 84, PA 2
creating Access apps, AC 256
creating databases, AC 256, AC 257
creating new documents, WD 100
creating presentations, PPT 330, PPT 335
themes, WD 166
temporary memory, ECC 8
terabytes (TBs), ECC 17
terms of use, PPT 336
text
adding to chart sheets, EX 242
converting handwriting to, PA 3–4
copying, WD 106–107
dragging, WD 108, WD 109
editing, WD 104, WD 105
entering in documents, WD 102–103
finding and replacing, WD 110–111
formatting. *See* formatting text
indenting, PPT 333
moving, WD 108–109
pasting, WD 106, WD 107
selecting, WD 104, WD 105
unindenting, PPT 333
text boxes, dialog boxes, WIN 47
text functions, EX 213
text pane, closing, PPT 340

themes, WD 130, WD 166–167
custom, creating, WD 166
forms, AC 268
presentations, PPT 330, PPT 334–335
variants, PPT 334
Themes button, AC 268
Themes gallery, PPT 334, PPT 335
3D printers, ECC 15
thumbnail(s), PPT 328
Thumbnail pane, PPT 328
tiles, WIN 36
time functions, EX 212, EX 213
adjusting, PPT 356
Times New Roman, WD 112
timings, slides, PPT 358, PPT 359
title(s), chart axes, EX 230
Title and Content slide master, PPT 359
title bar, OFF 86, WIN 42
title placeholder, PPT 330
Title slide layout, PPT 330
To Do Tags, PA 2
TODAY function, EX 212, EX 213
toner, ECC 14
toolbars, WIN 42, WIN 60
total rows, tables, EX 218
touch screens, WIN 34
selecting and moving items, WIN 39
using Office on touch screen devices, OFF 96
touchpads, ECC 12, ECC 13
touchscreens, ECC 4, ECC 12, ECC 13
trackballs, ECC 12, ECC 13
trackpads, ECC 12, ECC 13
transitions, slides, PPT 358, PPT 359
translating documents into other languages, WD 115
trendlines, charts, EX 238
Trim Video dialog box, PPT 356, PPT 357
Trojan horses, ECC 20
trusted locations, saving databases to, AC 280
two-factor authentication (2FA), ECC 21

U

UIs (user interfaces), OFF 86, WIN 36
ultraportable computers, ECC 4
underlined type, WD 130
Undo button, WD 104
undoing sorts, EX 218
unindenting text, PPT 333
universal apps, WIN 40–41
Universal Serial Bus (USB). *See* USB (Universal Serial Bus); USB flash drives (USB drives)
updates, firmware, ECC 8
updating linked Excel charts in Word docs, INT 386–387
upgrading RAM, ECC 9

URLs, ECC 20
USB (Universal Serial Bus), ECC 16
  connectors, ECC 16
  types, ECC 16
USB flash drives (USB drives), ECC 10, ECC 11, WIN 60
user interfaces (UIs), OFF 86, WIN 36

V

value(s), entering in worksheets, EX 182, EX 183
value axis, EX 230
variant, PPT 334
verifying page breaks, EX 194
vertical axis, EX 230
VGA (video graphics array), ECC 16
video, presentations, PPT 356–357
video cards, ECC 14
video clips, capturing, PA 11
video display adapters, ECC 14
video graphics array (VGA), ECC 16
video objects, formatting, PPT 357
videoconferencing, ECC 2, ECC 3
video-editing software, ECC 24
view(s), ee also specific views
  available in Word, WD 117
  files and folders, WIN 64–65
  reports, AC 309
  switching, OFF 88
View buttons, OFF 86
View tab, OFF 88
viewing. See also displaying
  footers, WD 162
  headers, WD 162
  presentations, PPT 328, PPT 329
  query results, AC 292, AC 293
  reports, AC 308–309
  sum data on status bar, EX 188
virtual assistant, Edge, PA 14–15
virtual memory, ECC 8
virtual private networks (VPNs), ECC 2
virus(es), ECC 20
virus protection software, ECC 20, ECC 21
voice-recognition software, ECC 12
volatile memory, ECC 8
volume, playback, sound clips, PPT 354
VPNs (virtual private networks), ECC 2

W

waterfall charts, EX 231
wearables, ECC 4
web, uses, ECC 2

web browser. See Microsoft Edge
web images. See online images
Web Layout view, WD 117
Web Note tools, PA 15
webpages
  annotating, PA 15
  live, inserting in slides, PA 12
website creation and management
  software, ECC 24
Wi-Fi (wireless fidelity), ECC 18
window(s), WIN 42–43
  active and inactive, WIN 44
  borders, WIN 44
  elements, WIN 42, WIN 43
  multiple, managing, WIN 44–45
  panes, WIN 58
Window control buttons, WIN 42
Windows accessories, WIN 40
Windows Action Center, WIN 64
Windows Clipboard, WD 106
  clearing, WD 106
Windows Defender, ECC 20, ECC 21
Windows Search, WIN 72–73
Windows Store, WIN 40
Windows 10
  exiting, WIN 50–51
  hardware requirements, ECC 23
  help, WIN 48–49
  starting, WIN 34–35
Windows 10 desktop, WIN 35,
  WIN 36–37
  navigating, WIN 36, WIN 37
Windows 10 UI, WIN 36
win/loss sparklines, EX 244, EX 245
wireless fidelity (Wi-Fi), ECC 18
wireless local area networks (WLANs), ECC 18
WLANs (wireless local area networks), ECC 18
word count indicator, WD 102
word processing programs. See Microsoft Word
word size, ECC 7
word wrap, WD 102
workbooks, ECC 24
  navigating, EX 180–181
worksheets, ECC 24, EX 179–195
  alignment, EX 190, EX 191
  cell styles, EX 192, EX 193
  cells, EX 180
  columns. See column(s), worksheets
  conditional formatting, EX 216–217
  custom formatting, EX 216
  footers, EX 192, EX 193
  formulas, EX 186–187
  headers, EX 192, EX 193
  labels, EX 182, EX 183

margin settings, EX 194
navigating, EX 180
number format, EX 190, EX 191
previewing, EX 194, EX 195
printing, EX 194, EX 195
rows. *See* rows, worksheets
selecting, EX 181
sparklines, EX 244–245
values, EX 182, EX 183
workstations, ECC 18
World Wide Web, ECC 18
worms, ECC 20
wrapping styles, WD 158
wrapping text, WD 102
writing tools, WD 116

X

x-axis, EX 230

Y

y-axis, EX 230
Yes/No data type, AC 259

Z

z-axis, EX 230
Zoom In pointer, AC 308
Zoom slider, OFF 86